R U N N I N G

MICROSOFT®
EXCEL

RUNNING

MICROSOFT® EXCEL

The Cobb Group

Douglas Cobb

Judy Mynhier

The Complete Reference to Microsoft® Excel on the IBM® PC, PS/2,™ and Compatibles

PUBLISHED BY
Microsoft Press
A Division of Microsoft Corporation
16011 NE 36th Way, Box 97017, Redmond, Washington 98073-9717

Library of Congress Cataloging in Publication Data
Cobb, Douglas Ford.
Running Microsoft Excel.
Includes index.
1. Microsoft Excel (Computer program)   2. IBM microcomputers—Programming.
3. Business—Data processing.   I. Mynhier, Judy.   II. Title.
HF5548.4.E93C637   1988   005.36'9   88-5163
ISBN 1-55615-108-X

Printed and bound in the United States of America.

1 2 3 4 5 6 7 8 9   FGFG   3 2 1 0 9 8

Distributed to the book trade in the
United States by Harper & Row.

Distributed to the book trade in
Canada by General Publishing Company, Ltd.

Distributed to the book trade outside the
United States and Canada by Penguin Books Ltd.

Penguin Books Ltd., Harmondsworth, Middlesex, England
Penguin Books Australia Ltd., Ringwood, Victoria, Australia
Penguin Books N.Z. Ltd., 182–190 Wairau Road, Auckland 10, New Zealand

British Cataloging in Publication Data available

This book is dedicated to my son David.

Douglas Cobb

Contents

Acknowledgments

Once again we offer our most sincere thanks to the many people whose hard work and support made this book possible. At Microsoft Press: Claudette Moore, for setting up the deal; Dorothy Shattuck, for the patient and thorough edit; Charles Brod and David Rygmyr, for the technical support. At Microsoft: Phil Welt and Dawn Trudeau, for making sure we had what we needed; Mike Slade, for getting us started with Microsoft Excel; and all of the members of the technical support team, for helping us unravel the mysteries. Here at home: Tom Cottingham, for creating the opportunity; Barbara Wells, Denise Rogers, Brenda Bankston, Shannon Portman, Grand Britt, Donald Fields, Franny Corrigan, Kevin Fuqua, Jo McGill, Sandy Jetter, Patty Flynn, Mark Crane, Joseph Pierce, Eric Schlene, Linda Baughman, Allan McGuffey, Linda Watkins, Toni Frank, Maureen Pawley, Elayne Noltemeyer, Chris Brown, Dennis Thomas, Luanne Flynn, Tracy Milliner, and Julie Tirpak, for sharing yet another memorable experience.

Preface

Bigger, better, faster, stronger—those are the buzz words for every new generation of personal computing software. With the latest generation, two new terms can be added to the list: intuitive and easy to learn.

Microsoft Excel meets all these qualifications, and more. This program, which has already enjoyed tremendous success in the Apple Macintosh market, is the star performer of the exciting new generation of personal computing software. The program's intuitive graphical interface, made possible by Microsoft Windows, features pull-down menus, dialog boxes, and icons that make it easy, even for computer novices, to get up and running. Now you don't have to think like a computer to get the most out of your software.

Don't mistake ease of use with lack of depth, however. Microsoft Excel is a versatile and powerful program with a tremendous number of sophisticated features. The program's 131 built-in worksheet and 224 macro-sheet functions (not to mention the ability to create an unlimited number of user-defined functions) are just the beginning. You'll also discover sophisticated business graphics, an excellent macro facility, fantastic formatting capabilities, customization features, and presentation-quality output. These features, combined with the ability to run Microsoft Excel concurrently with other Windows applications such as Write and Paint, set a new standard for integrated business software on the PC.

So even though you'll find it easy to come up to speed on Microsoft Excel, you'll also find that you have a lot of exploration ahead of you as you delve into this trendsetting program. We hope this book helps you realize the full potential of Microsoft Excel.

What is Microsoft Excel?

Microsoft Excel is an integrated spreadsheet and graphics software package. It features three work environments—a spreadsheet (which can also be used to design databases), graphics, and macros—all bundled into one easy-to-use package. This combination of features makes Microsoft Excel a powerful tool that allows you to perform a variety of tasks for business, science, and engineering.

Although Microsoft Excel's business graphics and macro capabilities are very powerful, at heart Microsoft Excel is a spreadsheet program. As you'll discover in a few pages, the first thing you see when you load Microsoft Excel is a worksheet.

Microsoft Excel's worksheet offers many features and capabilities, such as user-defined formats, that are not available in any other spreadsheet program.

Microsoft Excel's worksheet is an electronic replacement for traditional planning tools: the pencil (and eraser), the accountant's ledger sheet, and the calculator. In fact, the electronic spreadsheet is to these tools what a word processor is to a typewriter. In addition, the Microsoft Excel worksheet can be used as a database manager. Now you can store basic information within easy reach, only a worksheet away.

Because Microsoft Excel holds your reports, analyses, and projections in your computer's memory, making changes to them is as easy as typing a few characters and pressing a key or two. In fact, one of the most important reasons for building a projection in Microsoft Excel or any other spreadsheet program is that you can play "what-if games, varying assumptions and measuring their effects on "the bottom line."

In addition to this powerful spreadsheet, Microsoft Excel offers the best business graphics available in an integrated program. Microsoft Excel's chart capabilities allow you to create six basic types of charts—area, bar, column, line, pie, and scatter—and even combine two of these types. The program also offers tools that you can use to add titles, legends, arrows, and other enhancements to your charts.

Finally, Microsoft Excel offers macro programming capability, which enables you to create "scripts" that automate routine or tedious tasks. Microsoft Excel's macros could even be used by more experienced users to write sophisticated application programs in the Microsoft Excel worksheet. Probably the most exciting aspect of Microsoft Excel's macros is that they enable you to create user-defined functions—your own personal supplements to Microsoft Excel's extensive library of built-in functions—as well as your own menus and dialog boxes. With these powerful customization features, the possibilities are almost limitless.

About this book

This book is a user's guide and tutorial for Microsoft Excel. It is designed to help you, the Microsoft Excel user, gain the deepest possible understanding of Microsoft Excel in the shortest time.

This book has six sections. The first section, which includes only Chapter 1, is an introduction to Microsoft Excel. In this chapter, we cover the basics of using Microsoft Excel, give you a tour of the Microsoft Excel screen, and show you how to save and open files.

The second section, which includes Chapters 2 through 9, covers the Microsoft Excel worksheet. This section begins by showing you how to make entries in the worksheet, and then covers such topics as formatting entries, using functions, and editing the worksheet.

The next section, which includes Chapters 10 through 13, covers Microsoft Excel's business-graphics capabilities. Chapter 10 walks you through the process of creating and enhancing a simple chart. The next chapters show you how to add more data to your charts and then how to use each of Microsoft Excel's types of charts. The last part of this section shows you how to print charts.

The fourth section discusses Microsoft Excel's database capabilities. A brief discussion of the general principles of database management in Chapter 14 is followed by a discussion of sorting databases in Chapter 15, and by a detailed survey of how to create and use databases in Chapter 16.

The fifth section, which includes Chapters 17 through 20, explains macros. In this section, we tell you what macros are and how you can use them. We also explain each of Microsoft Excel's special macro functions. Then, in Chapter 19, we show you how to build user-defined functions. In Chapter 20, we show you how to customize your Microsoft Excel program with autoexec macros, user-defined dialog boxes and menus, and even screens.

Finally, Section Six is an appendix that covers the use of Microsoft Excel in conjunction with other programs. You can use Microsoft Excel with Windows to set up your own "integrated" software packages. Imagine being able to create a complicated chart from worksheet data, copy it, and paste it into a Microsoft Word or Write document in a matter of seconds. Microsoft Excel also has two-way file compatibility with Lotus 1-2-3. Methods for exchanging worksheets with these programs are presented.

INTRODUCTION

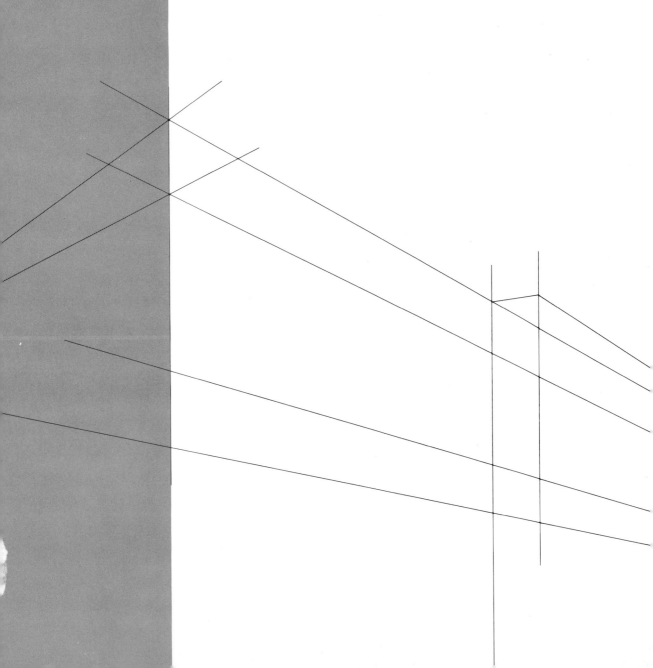

1

Introducing Microsoft Excel

*I*n this chapter, we'll show you how to get started with Microsoft Excel. We'll describe the program's hardware requirements; then we'll briefly walk you through the installation process. Next, we'll show you how to load the program and give you a tour of the working environment. We'll also look at file management and briefly show you how to use the Help facility.

If you're a first-time Microsoft Excel user, we suggest that you read this chapter carefully before you move on. In the next few pages, we'll introduce key terms and concepts that are used throughout the book. Even if you've used the program before, we suggest that you scan the section entitled *A brief tour* before you proceed, to ensure that you're familiar with the terminology we'll be using.

Hardware requirements

Microsoft Excel is designed to run on an IBM PS/2, an IBM PC/AT, or an IBM PC/AT-compatible computer that uses the 80286 or 80386 microprocessor. Your system must have a minimum of 640 KB of memory, one 5$1/4$-inch or 3$1/2$-inch floppy-disk drive, and a hard disk with at least 5 MB of free space. The system must operate under MS-DOS or PC-DOS version 3.0 or later.

Your computer must also have a graphics display adapter card. You can use the IBM VGA or EGA, the Hercules Graphics Card, or any other graphics card compatible with Microsoft Windows. (More on Microsoft Windows in a moment.)

Optional components

Several additional components may help speed your work in Microsoft Excel. All these components are optional—the choice depends on your personal requirements. Your hardware dealer can advise you which items are best suited to your needs.

Printers and plotters

If you plan to produce hard-copy output, you'll obviously need a printer. You have a number of printer choices, including the Hewlett-Packard LaserJet, the Apple LaserWriter (or any PostScript-compatible printer), the IBM ProPrinter or Graphics printer, the Epson FX 80, and a number of other printers compatible with Microsoft Windows version 2.0 or later.

You may also want to use a plotter to print high-quality color charts and graphs. Microsoft Excel supports the Hewlett-Packard 7470A plotter and compatibles and any other plotter compatible with Microsoft Windows version 2.0 or later.

The mouse

We recommend that you use a mouse with Microsoft Excel. As you'll see when we tour the working environment, Microsoft Excel uses a graphical interface, taking advantage of drop-down menus and icons to let you make selections quickly and easily. Although the mouse is in no way a required component—every function you perform with the mouse can also be performed from the keyboard—many operations can be carried out more efficiently with the mouse than with standard keyboard commands.

You can choose either a serial mouse or a bus mouse, depending primarily on which output ports you use for your printer, communications devices, and so forth. For example, if your computer's serial port is occupied by a printer, chances are you'll want to use a bus mouse.

Many mouse-driven applications require that you use a two-button mouse; Microsoft Excel requires only one button. If you do use a two-button mouse, the left button will initially be active. If you prefer to use the right button, you must run the Windows Control Panel program to make the change. (See your *Microsoft Windows Reference Guide* for more information on using the Control Panel program.)

Microsoft Windows

The Microsoft Windows program, which features a sophisticated graphical interface, is an extension of the MS-DOS operating environment. Using Microsoft Windows, you can run two or more applications concurrently and switch between them in seconds. You can even transfer data from one program to another with the Clipboard facility and establish "live" links between documents created in different programs. Microsoft Windows also offers an MS-DOS Executive facility that gives you easy access to many common MS-DOS functions, such as copying and deleting files, creating directories, and formatting disks.

The Microsoft Excel software includes a system called RunTime Windows, which takes advantage of the Microsoft Windows graphical interface to provide those services required by Microsoft Excel. In order to run Microsoft Excel within the full Windows environment, however, you must use Microsoft Windows version 2.0 or later. The program does not operate under previous versions of Microsoft Windows. If your computer uses an Intel 80386 microprocessor, you can use Windows/386, which takes advantage of the special features of the 80386, including use of your computer's extra memory.

We'll talk more about Microsoft Windows in the Appendix, Sharing Data with Other Programs.

Networks

You can install Microsoft Excel on a computer attached to a network so that two or more users can share data stored on a common network drive. Networking also allows two or more users to share printing resources.

You can choose from a variety of network packages, including the IBM PC Network, the IBM Token Ring Network, AT&T Starlan, and several other popular systems. Microsoft Excel supports any network compatible with Microsoft Windows version 2.0 or later. If you're part of a network, you may need a version of MS-DOS later than 3.0. Check with your dealer for details about your network system.

Expanded and extended memory

As we mentioned before, you need a minimum of 640 KB of memory to run Microsoft Excel. Depending on your speed requirements, the size of your worksheet models, and your plans to run other applications concurrently, you may need additional memory.

Again, you have several options here. One option is to install an expanded memory card. If you have extended memory, you can take advantage of Microsoft Excel's built-in extended memory driver. In addition, if you have enough extra memory, you can use the Smartdrive utility included with Microsoft Excel to speed up operations. Detailed information on expanded and extended memory and the Smartdrive utility can be found by running the Microsoft Excel Setup program and choosing the View the Special Information File option.

Math coprocessor
A math coprocessor can help speed your work by enabling Microsoft Excel to perform mathematical calculations faster. Microsoft Excel supports the Intel 8087, 80287, and 80387 math coprocessors.

Installing Microsoft Excel

When you have all your hardware components in place, the next step is to install Microsoft Excel on your hard disk. Although that stack of floppy disks you received in your Microsoft Excel package may look a bit intimidating, the installation process is actually simple.

Before you begin the installation procedure, you must be prepared to answer a few questions. As it configures the program for your hardware, the Setup program will prompt you to define the type of PC, mouse, monitor, display adapter, and printer you're using.

To install Microsoft Excel, simply insert the Setup disk in drive A, type *setup* at the MS-DOS prompt, and press the Enter key. The Setup program will take it from there, prompting you for information about your computer system, telling you when to change disks, and copying the appropriate files from each of the floppy disks to your hard disk.

Installing Microsoft Excel under Microsoft Windows

When you run the Setup program, you'll be asked for the name of the directory in which you want to store your Microsoft Excel program files. If you plan to run the program within the Microsoft Windows environment, it's a good idea to place Microsoft Excel and Microsoft Windows in the same directory. Because the two programs share common files, this technique lets you run the program more efficiently. (It doesn't matter which program you install first.)

Loading Microsoft Excel

After you've installed Microsoft Excel on your computer, you're ready to load the program and get to work. First, use the CHDIR command, if necessary, to access the directory in which Microsoft Excel is stored. Then type *excel* at the MS-DOS prompt and press the Enter key. Alternatively, you can create an AUTOEXEC file that loads the program automatically. See your *MS-DOS User's Guide* for instructions.

You can also load Microsoft Excel by first loading the Microsoft Windows program. When in Windows, simply choose the EXCEL.EXE file from the MS-DOS Executive window and then choose Run from the File menu or press the Enter key. (You can also choose Load from the File menu to load Microsoft Excel into memory without activating the program right away.) If you use a mouse, you can start the program by simply double-clicking on the filename EXCEL.EXE. See your *Microsoft Windows Reference Guide* for more information on running programs in the Microsoft Windows environment.

When you run Microsoft Excel, a copyright box will be displayed briefly, followed by a screen like the one shown in Figure 1-1. As you can see, Microsoft Excel creates a new, blank worksheet file, ready for your input. This document is called Sheet1. (Of course, you can save the document under any name you like. We'll show you how to do that later in this chapter.)

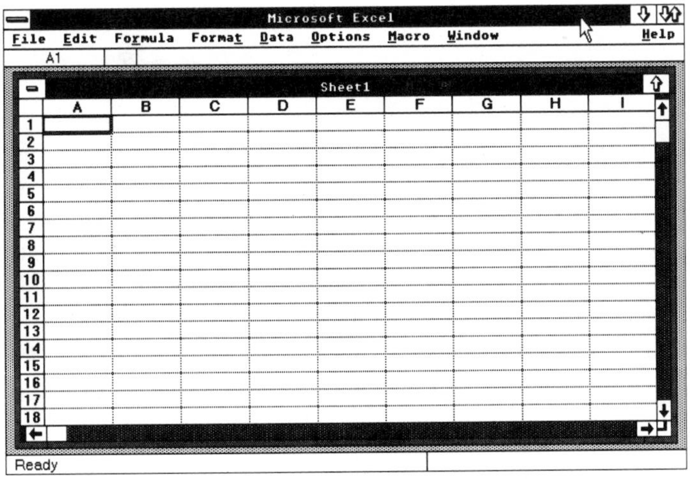

FIGURE 1-1. *When you load Microsoft Excel, your screen initially looks like this.*

If you're using Microsoft Windows, you can load the Microsoft Excel program and open a file at the same time by selecting the name of the file you want from the MS-DOS Executive window. If you use a mouse, simply double-click on the filename. From the keyboard, select the desired file and choose Run from the File menu or press the Enter key.

A brief tour

Windows are much like portholes through which you view information. All the work you do in Microsoft Excel is performed in a window. There are two basic types of windows available: application and document. Let's look first at application windows; then we'll look at the document windows you'll be using to hold your Microsoft Excel data.

The Microsoft Excel application window

If you temporarily close the worksheet window shown in Figure 1-1, your screen will look like the one in Figure 1-2. This is the Microsoft Excel application window. This window contains four main elements: the application window title bar, the menu bar, the formula bar, and the status bar.

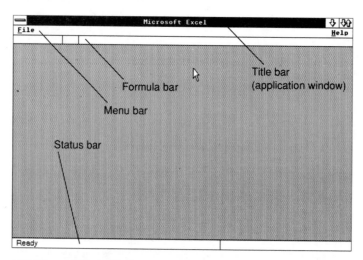

FIGURE 1-2. *The application window provides your working environment for Microsoft Excel.*

At the top of your screen is the application window's title bar, which identifies the program you're working in. Below the title bar is the menu bar, where you select from Microsoft Excel's bill of fare to manipulate the information you've entered in your worksheet. In Figure 1-2, this bar contains only one menu name, File, because no document is open. The contents of the menu bar change according to the application you're running and the type of document window open in the workspace. For example, if you look back at Figure 1-1, you'll see that nine menu names appear when a worksheet window is open: File, Edit, Formula, Format, Data, Options, Macro, Window, and Help. Different menu names appear when you open chart and macro-sheet files. We'll talk more about using menus in a moment.

Below the menu bar is the formula bar—your link to the document windows. As you'll see in Chapter 2, you enter and edit information in your documents using the formula bar. In addition, the formula bar displays the underlying formulas and values in your documents.

The formula bar is split into three portions. On the left is the cell-reference area. When a worksheet is open, this area displays the active cell reference. When you activate the formula bar (more on this in the next chapter), the middle area displays a set of Cancel and Enter boxes. You use these boxes to lock in worksheet entries or to cancel entries and revert to the previous contents of the cell. The majority of the formula bar is taken up by the data-entry and display areas, where you make your entries into the worksheet and view the contents of cells.

At the bottom of the application window is the status bar. The left portion of this bar, the message area, brings you information about current menu and command selections. The right side of the bar, the keyboard-indicator area, displays information about the current state of certain keys on the keyboard, such as Caps Lock or Microsoft Excel's Extend key (F8). For example, you might see the notation NUM in this area, indicating that the Num Lock keyboard setting is in effect. We'll describe the contents of the status bar as we discuss relevant topics throughout this book.

Other types of application windows

In addition to the Microsoft Excel application window, you'll use a number of other application windows in the course of your work, including the Help window, the Control Panel window, the Clipboard window, the Macro Translation Assistant window, and the Spooler window. One additional window, Info, gives you special information about the contents, formats, and notes attached to a cell.

The worksheet window

The bulk of the screen shown in Figure 1-1 is occupied by the worksheet window. This window contains a number of additional elements, labeled in Figure 1-3 on the following page, with which you should be familiar before we move on to worksheet basics in Chapter 2. Let's take a brief look at each.

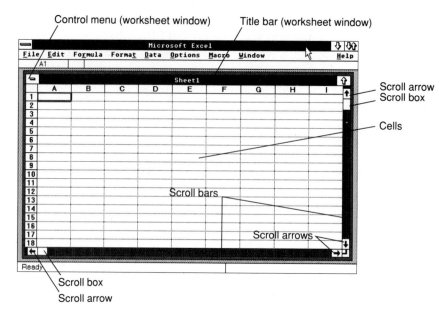

FIGURE 1-3. *The worksheet window also contains a number of special tools.*

The title bar

Immediately above the column headers on the worksheet is the window's title bar, which identifies the worksheet and window in which you're working. When you start Microsoft Excel without loading an existing worksheet, the title bar always displays the name *Sheet1*.

Cells

Like a paper accounting ledger, the Microsoft Excel worksheet is divided into a grid made up of columns and rows. Each column is assigned a letter, which appears in the column header below the title bar. The column letters range from A through IV. (After column Z comes column AA, after AZ comes BA, and so on to IV.) Each row is assigned a number, which appears in the row header to the left of the worksheet grid. The rows are sequentially numbered from 1 through 16384.

The intersection of each column and row is a cell. Cells are the basic building blocks of every worksheet. Each cell occupies a unique location on the worksheet where you can store and display information, and each cell is assigned a unique set of coordinates called a cell reference. For example, the intersection of column Z and row 100 has the cell reference Z100.

With 256 columns and 16384 rows, each worksheet contains a total of 4,194,304 individual cells! Before you try to unravel the mysteries of the universe on a single worksheet, however, keep in mind that the number of cells you can use at any one time is limited by the memory capacity of your computer. Even though the program uses a sophisticated sparse matrix system for efficient memory management, you probably won't be able to fill all the cells in one worksheet. Like most spreadsheet programs, Microsoft Excel was created in anticipation of the day when microcomputers will be able to access several megabytes of memory directly.

If you were to lay an entire default-sized worksheet out like a paper ledger, it would measure more than 21 feet wide by 341 feet long! Because the worksheet is so large, you can see only a small percentage of it on your screen at any given time. In the worksheet in Figure 1-1, only 162 cells are visible. Thus, the worksheet window is like a porthole that lets you look at a limited portion of the worksheet document.

With a large worksheet, you might soon find it tedious to move the window back and forth across the "page" every time you want to see a different set of cells. Fortunately, you can create multiple windows to get different views of the same worksheet. You can move the windows independently to compare different parts of the worksheet simultaneously. We'll show you how to do this in Chapter 5.

Other kinds of document windows

Microsoft Excel actually uses three different types of files: worksheets like the one shown in Figure 1-3, charts, and macro sheets. For the first several chapters of this book, you'll be working only with worksheet files. After you've learned how to build a worksheet, we'll show you how to plot your worksheet data in a chart window and how to use macros to automate your work in Microsoft Excel.

Issuing commands

Microsoft Excel uses drop-down menus. That is, under each menu name is a list of related command names from which you can choose. When you pull down a menu, you'll notice that some commands are darkened, whereas others are dimmed to indicate that they are not currently available. The program monitors the status of your workspace and allows you to select only those options applicable at any given time.

If you use a mouse, you can select a command from a menu by pointing to the menu name and pressing the mouse button. The menu will drop down to show a list of available commands. Without releasing the mouse button, drag the arrow-shaped mouse pointer through the list of available commands. As you drag the pointer, you'll see a brief description of each command on the left side of the status bar at the bottom of your screen. When the command you want is highlighted, release the mouse button to choose that command.

After you pull down a menu, that menu stays active until you choose a command, click elsewhere on your screen, or click on the menu name again. Therefore, after you've learned the available commands and don't need the descriptive messages to help guide you, you can click on a menu, release the mouse button, move the pointer to the command you want, and click again.

You can also use the keyboard to select commands. To access a menu from the keyboard, simply press the Alt key to activate the menu bar and then select the menu you want to use. (The F10 function key and the slash key [/] serve the same purpose as the Alt key. Although we'll refer to the Alt key in this book, keep in mind that F10 and / produce the same results.) Notice that one of the letters in each menu name in Figure 1-1 is underlined. After pressing Alt, you can select a menu by entering the letter that represents the menu name. For example, to access the Edit menu, press Alt and then press E.

Alternatively, after pressing Alt to activate the menu bar, you can use the Left and Right arrow keys to highlight the name of the menu you want to use. After highlighting the menu name, press the Down arrow key to pull down that menu. For example, to access the Format menu, press Alt, press the Right arrow key three times, and then press the Down arrow key.

When you use the mouse or the keyboard to pull down the File menu, you'll see a box like the one in Figure 1-4. Again, one letter in each of the command names on this menu is underlined. To select that command from the keyboard, simply type the appropriate letter. Alternatively, after you pull down a menu, you can use the Up and Down arrow keys to move through the list of available commands. Using the arrow keys is much like using the mouse to move through the list of commands in the active menu—as you highlight each command name in turn, you'll see a brief description of that item at the bottom of your screen. When the command you want is highlighted, press Enter to execute the command.

FIGURE 1-4. *When you pull down the File menu, you see a list of available file-management commands.*

If you want to access another menu after you've already pulled one down, you can type another Alt and character-key combination or you can use the Left and Right arrow keys to move to adjacent menus.

To deactivate the menu bar without issuing a command, press the Esc key.

In some cases, you can bypass the menu bar altogether and use keyboard shortcuts to issue commands. For example, to issue the Save As command on an enhanced keyboard you can press F12; to issue the Copy command, you can press the Ctrl and Ins keys simultaneously. We'll talk about these keyboard shortcuts as we discuss each command in turn.

Dialog boxes

Notice that some of the command names on the File menu in Figure 1-4 are followed by an ellipsis (...). This ellipsis indicates that the program needs additional information to carry out the command. You provide this information in a special window called a dialog box, which is displayed after you choose the command. For example, when you select the Font command from the Format menu, you'll see a dialog box like the one in Figure 1-5.

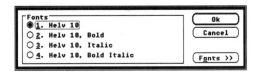

FIGURE 1-5. *Dialog boxes give additional command information.*

Certain dialog boxes allow you to give even more detailed information. For example, the dialog box in Figure 1-5 contains a command button labeled Fonts. The greater-than signs indicate that, by choosing this button, you can expand the dialog box to obtain additional choices. Selecting the Fonts button gives you the expanded dialog box shown in Figure 1-6.

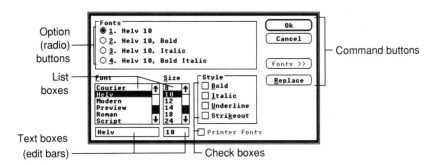

FIGURE 1-6. *Choosing a command button with a >> symbol offers you additional choices.*

You can select options in a dialog box in a number of different ways: with option (radio) buttons, command buttons, list boxes, check boxes, and text boxes (edit bars). Each of these option types works a little differently. Before we show you how to make dialog-box selections, however, you need to know how to move around in the dialog box.

Dialog boxes are split into option areas. For example, the dialog box shown in Figure 1-6 contains Fonts, Font, Size, and Style areas, plus two edit bars, four command buttons, and one independent check box. To select an option, you must first activate the appropriate area of the dialog box. A dotted border appears in the active area. For example, in the dialog box shown in Figure 1-6, the Font area is active. (The dotted border in this area is a bit difficult to see, because it appears around the Helv option, which is highlighted.)

If you use a mouse, you can simply point to the desired option to activate that area of the dialog box as well as the option. If you're selecting dialog-box options from the keyboard, however, you must first use the Tab key to move to the appropriate area. Then use the Up and Down arrow keys to select the desired option in that area. After the dotted border appears around your selection, simply press the Spacebar to activate the option. (In some cases you won't need to press the Spacebar—Microsoft Excel will activate the option when you point to it using the Up and Down arrow keys.)

You can also use option codes to make dialog-box selections. As with menu and command names, the appropriate code letter—or number, in the case of the Fonts dialog box—is underlined in the dialog box. Thus, by pressing the Alt key and a character code, you can move around the dialog box and make selections. For example, to activate the Style portion of the Font dialog box and choose a style option, you can press Alt-B, Alt-I, Alt-U, or Alt-K.

The dialog box in Figure 1-6 contains four Fonts options that you select with radio buttons. The Helv 10 radio button—the default selection for this dialog box—is already highlighted. To select another option, you can click on the button or the option name with the mouse. Alternatively, you can activate the Fonts portion of the dialog box and then type an option code number or use the arrow keys to move to the desired option and select it.

Notice the Style options in the bottom right portion of the dialog box. You select these options with check boxes. You select check-box options in exactly the same way you select radio-button options. When you choose a check-box option, an X appears to indicate your selection.

You may be wondering why some options are selected with radio buttons and others with check boxes. Radio buttons indicate that the options in that area of the dialog box are mutually exclusive; you can select only one option. As soon as you select another option, the original option will be deselected. Check boxes, on the other hand, indicate that you can choose more than one option in this area. To deselect a check-box option, you must choose that option a second time.

Sometimes you'll notice that a check box is shaded. This indicates that you've already applied that option to some (but not all) of the cells in the selected area of the worksheet. If you want to apply the setting to all the cells in the selection, select the option so that an X is displayed in the check box. To remove the option from all the cells in the current selection, choose the check box a second time to deselect it.

In the bottom left corner of the dialog box in Figure 1-6 are two list boxes that contain a number of additional font and size options. List boxes save space—instead of displaying dozens of options at once, Microsoft Excel lets you scroll through the lists to choose the desired setting. Generally, list-box options are mutually exclusive; you can select only one item at a time.

To make a selection in a list box with your mouse, simply point to the name of the option you want and click. If the desired option is not currently displayed, use the scroll bar at the right of the list box to bring additional options into view. You can click on the up and down scroll arrows to move through the list box one line at a time. Alternatively, you can drag the scroll box to move through the list more quickly. Or you can click in the shaded area of the scroll bar to bring a new group of options into view. Click below the scroll box to move down the list one boxful at a time; click above the scroll box to move up the list one boxful at a time. When the option you want is in view, click on the name of that option.

To make a list-box selection from the keyboard, you must first activate the list box; then you can use the Up and Down arrow keys to move through the list of options. To move quickly through a long list, type the first letter of the option name; the first option that begins with that letter will scroll into view. If more than one option name begins with the same character, use the Up and Down arrow keys to select the appropriate one. You can also use the PgUp and PgDn keys to move through the list one boxful at a time.

Many dialog boxes also contain text boxes, or edit bars, where you type instructions. When you activate an edit bar by clicking on it or by using the keyboard, a blinking insertion-point marker appears in the box. For example, in the Font dialog box shown in Figure 1-6, you can bypass the Size list box by activating the Size edit bar and typing your own size value, or you can edit the existing contents of the edit bar to alter the current setting. Editing entries in an edit bar is much like editing cell entries in the formula bar. We'll talk more about this topic in the next chapter.

Finally, notice the four large buttons labeled OK, Cancel, Fonts, and Replace. These rectangular buttons are called command buttons. The OK and Cancel command buttons appear in nearly every dialog box. The OK command button closes the dialog box and carries out the selected command; the Cancel command button closes the dialog box without carrying out the command. To select the OK command button, either use the mouse to click on OK or press the Enter key. (The heavy outline around the OK button indicates that this is the option that will be selected when you press Enter. In other dialog boxes, other buttons may be outlined.) To select the Cancel command button, use the mouse to click on Cancel or press the Esc key.

Alert boxes

In addition to dialog boxes, you'll sometimes see another kind of window called an alert box. Figure 1-7 shows the alert box that appears if you type an invalid option in the Font dialog box's Size text box. These alert boxes contain informational messages, warnings, and prompts for further information. They also contain command buttons that you use to acknowledge a warning or message, cancel an operation, or issue further instructions. You choose the command buttons in alert boxes just as you do in dialog boxes.

FIGURE 1-7. *Alert boxes carry informational messages and warnings.*

Full menus vs *short menus*

As you already know, the contents of the menu bar change according to the type of application or document currently active. You can also change the structure of the menus themselves by choosing the Full Menus command or the Short Menus command from the Options menu. With the Short Menus setting (the default), you see only those basic commands you use most often in your day-to-day work. When you choose Full Menus from the Options menu, you see an expanded set of Microsoft Excel's more sophisticated and less-often-used commands. (By the way, Full Menus and Short Menus are toggle commands. That is, when you choose Full Menus from the Options menu, the command changes to Short Menus. To change back to the Short Menus setting, simply choose the Short Menus command. The menu structure will again change and the command will become Full Menus.) Figure 1-8 shows the different commands available when the Short Menus and Full Menus settings are in effect. (We'll use Full Menus in this book.) The Help and Control menus are not affected by the Short Menus and Full Menus commands.

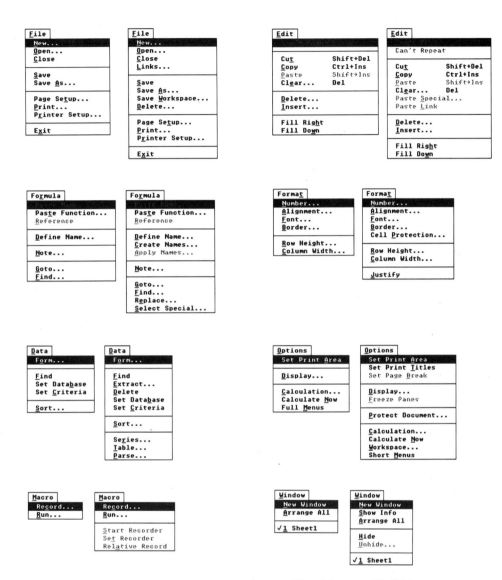

FIGURE 1-8. *Microsoft Excel offers two menu formats: Short Menus and Full Menus.*

The Control menus

In addition to the menus you access through the menu bar, every application and document window has a Control menu you can use to activate, resize, reposition, and close windows. (Some dialog boxes have Control menus too.) The application-window Control menu also offers a Run command you can use to access the Clipboard, Control Panel, and Macro Translator applications. The document-window Control menu offers similar commands, except that the Run command is replaced by the Split command. We'll talk more about the Control menus when we discuss window management in Chapter 5.

To access the application-window Control menu, point to the Control icon at the upper left corner of the application window or press Alt-Spacebar. To access a document-window Control menu, use the mouse to point to the Control icon at the upper left corner of the document window or press the Alt and hyphen keys.

File management

You use the File menu commands to create new files, save those files, open and close existing files, and exit from the program. We'll begin our discussion of file management with creating new files and then show you how to save the files you've created. Next, we'll show you how to retrieve files from disk. We'll also talk about deleting files and creating special workspace files that let you build document "collections." In this chapter, we use worksheet files as examples, but the techniques discussed here also apply to chart and macro files.

The File menu also contains commands that control printing tasks and let you access linked documents. We'll save the printing commands for Chapter 9 and file linking for Chapter 8.

Creating a new file

As you've already seen, when you load Microsoft Excel without loading a document, you see a new, blank worksheet window called Sheet1. To create a new document at any other time, simply choose New from the File menu. You'll see a dialog box like the one shown in Figure 1-9.

FIGURE 1-9. *Select the type of document you want to create from the*
New dialog box.

Notice that the Worksheet option is already selected in this dialog box. Whenever you issue the New command, Microsoft Excel looks at the type of document window currently active and suggests that file type for your new document as well. If you want to create another type of file, simply select another option before you choose OK or press Enter to execute the New command.

If you select the Worksheet option, Microsoft Excel will display a new, empty worksheet window on your screen. If another document is already open, the new window appears on top of the existing document. If Sheet1 was the previous worksheet, the new worksheet file will be named Sheet2. Subsequent worksheet files will be numbered sequentially—Sheet3, Sheet4, and so forth. As you'll learn in Chapter 5, you use the Window menu to switch from one worksheet to another.

Saving files

After you've invested time and energy in creating a worksheet, you'll probably want to save the file so you can retrieve it later. When you save a worksheet, you save the settings you've assigned to that worksheet—including the window configurations and display characteristics, formulas, functions, formats, fonts, and styles—in addition to its alphanumeric contents.

On the File menu, you'll find five commands—Save, Save As, Close, Save Workspace, and Exit—that allow you to save your Microsoft Excel files. Each of these commands works in a slightly different way. Generally, you'll use the Save As command to save a document for the first time and the Save command to save changes to existing documents. However, as you'll see in a moment, the program also asks if you want to save your changes when you choose the Close, Save Workspace, or Exit command, to ensure against accidentally losing your work.

When you save a document with one of the Save commands, that file remains open in your workspace. When you save a file with the Close or Exit command, however, the file is removed from the screen as soon as it is saved.

Saving a file for the first time

Before you can save a document for the first time, you must assign a name to the file and indicate where you want to store it. To name your document, first choose Save As from the File menu. You'll see a dialog box like that in Figure 1-10.

FIGURE 1-10. *Use the Save As dialog box to name your file when you save it for the first time.*

The current filename—Sheet1 in this example, because we haven't yet as-signed a new name to the document—appears in the Save Worksheet as edit bar. This filename is already highlighted; to change the filename, simply type a new name. The original contents of the edit bar will disappear as soon as you begin typ-ing. After the file has been saved, the worksheet's new name will appear in the document-window title bar.

Filename rules

File naming in Microsoft Excel follows the same basic rules you use under MS-DOS. Filenames can be as many as eight characters and can include any combina-tion of alphanumeric characters, as well as the special characters &, $, %, ', (,), -, @, {,], ~, !, and _. Blank spaces are not allowed. Although you can use any combination of uppercase and lowercase letters, keep in mind that Microsoft Excel does not distinguish case in your filenames. For example, the names *MYFILE*, *MyFile*, and *myfile* are identical as far as Microsoft Excel is concerned.

In addition to the eight-character filename, you can append a three-character file extension to help identify your document. Usually, you'll want to use the default extensions:

Document type	Extension
Worksheet	XLS
Chart	XLC
Macro sheet	XLM
Workspace	XLW

Occasionally, however, you may want to create your own file extensions to flag special files. To do so, simply type the filename, a period character, and then the extension. For example, you might create a file called MYFILE.EXT.

If you want to accept the program's default file extension, simply type the file-name with no trailing period character or extension name. If you don't want any file extension at all attached to the filename, type a single period character after the filename.

At the bottom left corner of the Save As dialog box is the name of the current directory. Unless you specify another path, this directory is where the file will be stored. If you want to store a document in a different directory, you must type the full pathname in the edit bar, including the name of the root directory and the names of any subdirectories, followed by the filename and the file extension, if any. Each of these elements must be preceded by a backslash character (\). The pathname can be preceded by a drive letter if you want to store the file on a disk in another drive.

For example, suppose you want to store the file MYFILE.EXT in a subdirectory called MYDIR. MYDIR is located in MAINDIR, which is a subdirectory of the root directory on drive C. To name this file and store it in the desired location, simply type

C:\MAINDIR\MYDIR\MYFILE.EXT.

File formats and options

In addition to providing the filename and location, you can specify a number of additional options in the Save As dialog box. To access these options, choose the Options button. The dialog box will expand to look like the one in Figure 1-11.

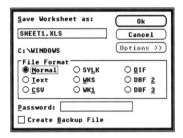

FIGURE 1-11. *Choosing the Options button allows you to access additional file-management options.*

You can save your files in nine formats. The default format is Normal, and you'll almost always use this option. If you want to export your Microsoft Excel file to another program, however, you may need to use one of the other options to convert the file into a format that is readable by that program. We'll talk more about these file-format options in the Appendix.

You can also protect your documents by typing a password in the Password edit bar. Your password can be as many as 16 characters. When you assign a password to a document, Microsoft Excel will prompt you to supply that word before it allows you to reopen the file. Case *does* count in passwords. Thus, if you've assigned the password *Secret* to a file, you can't reopen that file by typing *SECRET* or *secret*.

Finally, you can use the Create Backup File option to create a duplicate copy of your file on disk. This duplicate file carries the same filename as your original, but the file extension changes to .BAK. If this is the first time you've saved the file, the backup file and the worksheet file will be identical. If you've saved the file previously with the Create Backup File option selected, Microsoft Excel will rename the last saved version of your file, giving it a .BAK extension, and will overwrite the existing .BAK file.

Keep in mind that Microsoft Excel always uses a .BAK extension when creating backup files, regardless of the file type. Suppose you save a worksheet named MYFILE.XLS and a chart named MYFILE.XLC, both assigned the Create Backup File option. Because there can be only one MYFILE.BAK, the most recently saved file will create the .BAK file and the other file's backup, if one exists, will be overwritten.

Resaving a file

After you save a file for the first time, you need not use the Save As command again unless you want to save that file under a new name or choose one of the file options discussed above. To save your changes to a file that has already been saved, simply select Save from the File menu. Microsoft Excel will overwrite the last saved version of the file with the current contents of the worksheet and leave the window open in the workspace.

By choosing the Save As command again, you can save a file under a new name. When you choose Save As to store a previously saved file, you'll see the same Save As dialog box shown in Figure 1-10, except that the name under which you last saved the file will be displayed. If you type a new name before pressing Enter or clicking OK, Microsoft Excel will save the current worksheet under that new name and leave the previous version of the file intact under the old name. If you don't change the name before choosing OK, Microsoft Excel will ask you whether you want to overwrite the existing file. If you choose to overwrite the old version and the Create Backup File option is active, a .BAK file will be created or updated with the previously saved version of the file.

Saving your workspace

In addition to saving individual files, you can save a collection of files with the Save Workspace command. Save Workspace stores a list of the open document windows so that you can reopen all these windows at one time by issuing a single Open command and selecting the appropriate workspace file. This technique makes it easy to pick up where you left off the last time you worked with this group of documents.

Save Workspace works like Save As, except that the default filename extension for workspace files is .XLW. For example, suppose you're working on a budget proposal and you've collected data from several departments on different worksheets. You need to consolidate the data into a summary worksheet. You've also developed a chart to show budget trends and designed a macro to help speed up your calculations. Instead of reopening each of these files individually when you're ready to resume work on your budget, use the Save Workspace command to simultaneously save all the files to disk and save a list of those files in a special workspace file.

When you issue the Save Workspace command, you'll see a dialog box like the one in Figure 1-12. This dialog box works like the Save As dialog box in Figure 1-10, except that no additional file options are available.

FIGURE 1-12. *Use the Save Workspace dialog box to save a list of all open worksheets and windows.*

Remember, the workspace file contains only instructions for reopening all the documents and windows currently open in the workspace; it does not contain the files themselves. Do not delete the original files from disk after creating a workspace file. (Of course, you can still open individual files that are saved as part of a workspace.)

Retrieving files

To retrieve a file from disk, choose the Open command from the File menu. Microsoft Excel will display a dialog box, like the one shown in Figure 1-13, that contains a list of the Microsoft Excel files stored in the current directory.

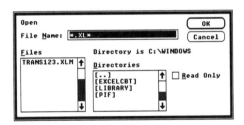

FIGURE 1-13. *Use the Open dialog box to retrieve files.*

As with saving a file, you must provide two pieces of information: the name of the file you want to open and its location. The name of the current directory appears near the center of the dialog box. In the Files list box on the left you'll see a list of the files available in that directory. To change directories, select the directory you want from the Directories list box. The selected directory will remain open until you make a new selection.

The File Name edit bar near the top of the dialog box determines which files are available for selection. The default entry is *.XL*, which tells the program to display only Microsoft Excel files in the Files list box—that is, only those files whose extensions begin with the characters *XL*. (As in MS-DOS, the * characters in this entry serve as wildcards.) If you want to view all the files in the current directory, simply type *.* in the File Name edit bar and press Enter. Alternatively, you can zero in on a particular file type by entering *. followed by the full extension, such as XLS, XLC, XLM, XLW, or BAK.

Instead of selecting a name from the Files list box, you can type the full filename in the File Name edit bar. If that file is located in the current directory, Microsoft Excel will open it when you choose OK.

If you want to retrieve a file in another directory without changing the current directory, you can type the full pathname for the file you want. For example, earlier we used C:\MAINDIR\MYDIR\MYFILE.EXT to save a file called MYFILE.EXT. To retrieve this file from disk, you can type that pathname in the File Name edit bar.

Finally, you can use the Read Only option on the right side of the dialog box to prevent changes to the saved version of the file on disk. If this check box is turned on, you can view and even edit the file, but you can't save it under its current name. Instead, you'll need to use the Save As command to save the edited file under a new filename.

The Read Only option is most useful when you're working on a network. If you open a file without selecting the Read Only option, others on the network can still view the file if they choose the Read Only option, but only you can save any changes. If anyone else tries to open the same file *without* using the Read Only option, they'll get an error message.

Deleting files

You can also delete files from a disk while you're working in Microsoft Excel. To delete a file, choose Delete from the File menu. The program will display a dialog box like the one in Figure 1-14. Choose the directory and the name of the file you want to delete, just as you would choose a file to open.

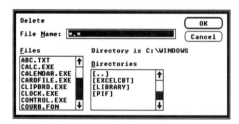

FIGURE 1-14. *Use the Delete dialog box to erase a file from a disk.*

Remember, you cannot recover a file after it has been deleted. Therefore, when you select a file for deletion, Microsoft Excel asks you to confirm your choice. If you're sure you want to delete the specified file, choose Yes; if you're not sure, choose No or Cancel. If you choose No, the Delete dialog box will reappear and you can select another file for deletion. Choose Cancel to return to the worksheet without deleting any files.

Closing files and exiting Microsoft Excel

When you finish your work on a document, you'll probably want to remove that document from your screen and then either exit from Microsoft Excel or work on another file. To close all open windows for a single document, choose Close from the File menu. To simultaneously close all the windows for all documents currently open in the workspace, hold down the Shift key as you access the File menu. This changes the Close command to Close All. Close All lets you clear the entire workspace without leaving the program. Then you can open another file or create a new document to work with.

To close all files and exit from the program, choose Exit from the File menu. After all the active files are closed, Microsoft Excel returns you to the MS-DOS level or to the Microsoft Windows MS-DOS Executive window, depending on which method you used to load the program.

No matter which command you choose, if you've changed any of the files in the workspace since you last saved them, you'll see an alert box that asks whether you want to save your changes for each altered file. Choose Yes to save the new version of the file before closing it. If you choose No to close the document without updating the file on disk, any changes you've made since you last used the Save or Save As command are lost. Choose the Cancel button to cancel the Close or Exit command and return to Microsoft Excel.

In addition to the File menu commands, you can use the Control menus to close individual document windows and to exit from the program. We'll talk about these menus in Chapter 5.

Getting help

If you forget the procedure for performing a task or need a reminder of the arguments for a particular function, help is only a few keystrokes or mouse clicks away. Microsoft Excel provides a complete on-line reference facility to help you learn the program and get quick reminders on specific topics.

Because the program gives you step-by-step instructions on how to use this facility when you issue a Help command—there is even a "help" topic to teach you how to use the Help facility—we won't cover the Help window in great detail here; we'll simply show you how to access the Help application window and give you an overview of the available options.

You can access the Help facility in two ways: by choosing a command from the Help menu or by pressing the F1 function key. The Help menu offers seven commands: Index, Keyboard, Lotus 1-2-3, Multiplan, Tutorial, Feature Guide, and About. When you issue the Index command, you'll see a listing of available Help topics. Similarly, the Keyboard command offers a listing of keyboard shortcuts and special keys you can use to speed your work in Microsoft Excel. The Lotus 1-2-3 and Multiplan commands let you type the command sequence for a 1-2-3 or Multiplan command and see the equivalent command sequence for the Microsoft Excel program. If you're new to Microsoft Excel or want to learn about a feature you've never used before, you may want to use Tutorial or Feature Guide to get a quick overview of that topic. The About command tells you which version of Microsoft Excel you're using and displays the copyright notice; it also tells you the status of the computer's conventional and expanded memory and whether or not you have a math coprocessor installed.

You can also get information about a specific command or action by using the program's context-sensitive help capabilities. To get context-sensitive help, choose a command or a dialog-box option and then press the F1 key to get more information about that topic. Alternatively, press Shift-F1 to access the Help facility and then choose the command you want to learn about. When you press Shift-F1, a question-mark shape appears next to your pointer. Use the mouse or the standard keyboard techniques described earlier in this chapter to select the command you want to learn about. If you use a mouse, you can also press Shift-F1 and then point to an object on the screen, such as the scroll bar or split bar, to get information about that object.

You can also get help on techniques for using the Help application by pressing F1 to access the Help window if it is not already open and then typing Alt-H, or you can choose the Help command from the Help window menu.

WORKSHEETS

2

Worksheet Basics

*I*n this chapter, we'll show you how to select cells and move around in the worksheet, make cell entries, and perform some basic editing tasks. We'll also discuss how Microsoft Excel makes calculations and explain the concept of memory management.

If you're a new user, we suggest that you follow along with the examples in this chapter, experimenting as you read. When you feel comfortable with the basic techniques described here, you'll be ready to move on to the more advanced worksheet topics in Chapters 3 through 8.

Cell selection and navigation

Before you can enter information into (or perform just about any other operation on) the cells in your worksheet, you must indicate the cell or range of cells with which you want to work. After you've made your selection, you can enter data or formulas; copy, move, erase, and format entries; or otherwise manipulate the contents of your worksheet.

When you select a single cell, that cell becomes the active cell in the worksheet. Only one cell can be active at a time. You can identify the active cell in two ways: First, the cell reference box at the left end of the formula bar always displays the reference of the active cell; second, a heavy border appears in the worksheet around the active cell.

Although only one cell can be active at a time, you can often speed up data entry, formatting, and editing by selecting groups of cells called ranges. As you'll see in a moment, when you select a range of cells, you can move through the individual cells in that range (and not those outside the range) without changing your range selection. You can make entries in a range one cell at a time or all at once.

As you know, only a small portion of the worksheet is visible in the document window at any given time. In order to select and view different cells and ranges, you must be able to move the document window. This process is called navigation. Often, the processes of selection and navigation overlap. For example, if cell A1 is the active cell and you want to make an entry in cell G100, you'll want to bring cell G100 into view and select that cell. However, if you simply want to view another area of the worksheet, you can also use a technique called scrolling to change your view without changing your selection.

In this chapter, we include selection and navigation instructions for both mouse users and those who feel more at home at the keyboard. In subsequent chapters, we won't give directions for both the mouse and the keyboard; instead, we'll simply tell you to, for example, select a cell.

Using the mouse

To select a single cell with the mouse, simply point to the cell and click. When you do this, the active cell border appears around the cell and the cell's reference appears in the reference box on the left side of the formula bar.

To select a range of cells with the mouse, point to one corner of the range, press the mouse button, drag to the opposite corner of the range, and then release the mouse button. When you select a range, the first cell you select always becomes the active cell when you release the mouse button.

For example, to select the range from A1 through B6 of your worksheet, point to cell A1, press the mouse button, and drag to cell B6. As you drag the pointer down and to the right, the cells in your selection are highlighted. In the cell reference box on the left side of the formula bar, the size of the selected range appears as you drag; when cells A1:B6 are highlighted, you'll see the notation 6Rx2C (6 rows by 2 columns) in the cell reference box. When you release the mouse button, cells A1 through B6 will be selected and A1 will be the active cell, as shown in Figure 2-1.

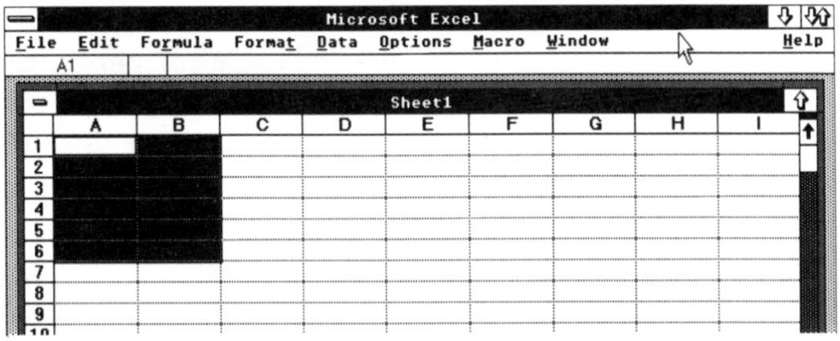

FIGURE 2-1. *The selected cells are highlighted as you drag through a range.*

Microsoft Excel always uses references to the cells at the upper left and lower right corners of a range to describe the range. For example, the range we just selected would be identified as A1:B6.

The active cell—the first cell you select—is the pivot point for your selection. That is, this cell always occupies one corner of the selected range. To test this for yourself, click on a cell near the center of your worksheet and then drag your mouse pointer in a circular pattern around the active cell. As you drag, notice that the active cell always anchors one corner of the highlighted range.

Extending a selection

Instead of dragging through all the cells you want to work with, you can indicate any two diagonal corners of the range. This technique is known as extending a selection. To begin, select a cell in any corner of the range you want to select. Now you can either hold down the Shift key or press the F8 function key to enter the Extend mode. (When you press F8, you see the notation EXT in the status bar at the lower right edge of your screen.) Finally, click on the cell at the opposite corner of the range.

For example, to select the range A1:C12, click on C12, press and hold the Shift key, then click on cell A1. Cell C12, which you clicked to begin defining the range, becomes the active cell in this range. Alternatively, you could select the range A1:C12 by clicking on one corner of the range, pressing the F8 key to enter Extend mode, and then clicking on the opposite corner. To leave Extend mode, press F8 again or make a cell entry.

Keep in mind that it doesn't matter which diagonal corners of the range you use to make your selection. In the example above, you could just as easily have used cells A12 and C1 as your range markers. However, this selection would still be defined by the upper left and lower right corners—A1 and C12—even though you did not actually click on those cells.

Selecting beyond the window borders

Often, when you need to select a large range of cells, some of those cells are hidden from view. When this occurs, you can drag the mouse pointer past the window border to bring additional cells into view as you highlight them. Alternatively, you can scroll the cells you need into view (more on this in a few pages) and then use the range extension technique described above to make your selection.

If your selection is relatively small, you may prefer to move beyond the borders of the current window by dragging to the edge of the window. For example, suppose you want to select the range A14:A25. Click on cell A14 and then drag the pointer to the bottom of the screen. When the pointer reaches the horizontal scroll bar at the bottom of the window, the window will begin scrolling down one row at a time. When cell A25 comes into view, release the mouse button at that cell. Figure 2-2 shows the screen at this point.

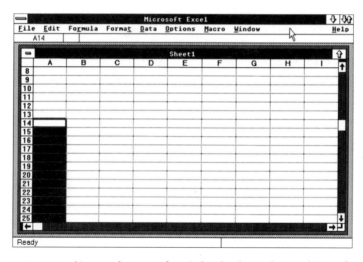

FIGURE 2-2. *You can drag past the window borders to bring additional cells into view as you make your selection.*

Now suppose you want to select the range A3:A11, beginning from the screen shown in Figure 2-2. To do this, click on cell A11 and then drag the pointer up to the title bar. This time, the window will scroll up one row at a time. When cell A3 comes into view, release the mouse button. Cells A3:A11 will be selected and cell A11 will be the active cell.

You can also drag past the left and right borders of the screen to bring additional columns into view as you make your selection.

When you need to select large ranges, this dragging technique may be too time-consuming. For example, suppose you want to select the range A1:M38.

Because M38 is out of view, you can click on cell A1 and then use the scroll bars to move the window until cell M38 is in view (A1 will be out of sight). You can then hold down the Shift key or press F8 and click on cell M38. As soon as you click on M38, Microsoft Excel will highlight the range A1:M38; A1 will be the active cell. (We'll talk more about the scroll bars in a few pages.)

Selecting multiple ranges

Microsoft Excel allows you to include several separate ranges in a single selection. Multiple-area ranges are also called discontinuous ranges, because they are not extensions of a single rectangle. To select a discontinuous range with the mouse, use the Ctrl key. For example, suppose you've already selected the range A1:B6 and you want to add cells C7:E10 to this range without eliminating cells A1:B6 from the selection. Simply hold down the Ctrl key and drag through cells C7:E10. Microsoft Excel will add the new area to your selection without deselecting the original range. As you can see in Figure 2-3, when you press the Ctrl key and drag through a new area, the first cell you click on in the new area becomes the active cell.

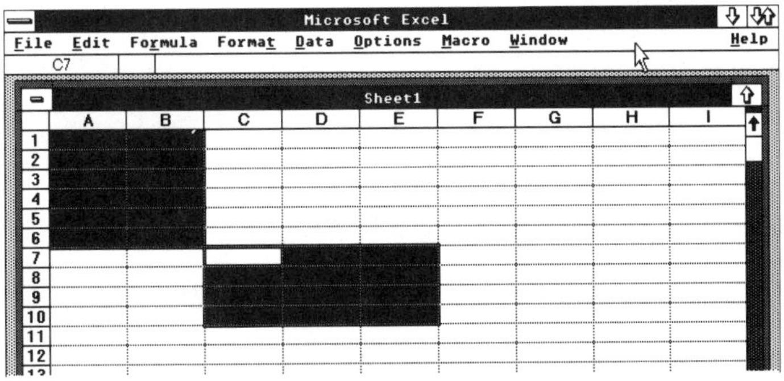

FIGURE 2-3. *Use the Ctrl key to select a discontinuous range with the mouse.*

You can also select a discontinuous range by using Add mode. For example, if cells A1:B6 are selected, you can add cells C7:E10 to your selection by first pressing Shift-F8 to enter Add mode. When you see the notation ADD in the status bar at the bottom of your screen, drag through cells C7:E10 to add that range to your discontinuous selection. Press Shift-F8 again to leave Add mode.

Selecting rows and columns

When you want to insert, delete, format, or move an entire row or column of data, select the entire row or column of cells by clicking on the row or column header. When you click on a row or column header, the first cell in that row or column that is visible in the window becomes the active cell. For example, if you click on row header 6 when columns A through I are visible on the screen, Microsoft Excel selects cells A6 through IV6 and cell A6 becomes the active cell.

Similarly, you can select an entire column of cells by clicking on the header for that column. If you click on the header for column B, Microsoft Excel selects cells B1 through B16384 and cell B1 becomes the active cell. If cell B1 is not in view when you select the header, Microsoft Excel makes the first visible cell in the column the active cell.

You can select more than one entire adjacent row or column at a time by dragging through several row or column headers. Alternatively, you can click on the row or column header that will form one edge of the range, press the F8 or Shift key, and click on the header for the opposite side of the range. For example, to select columns B, C, and D, begin by clicking on the column B header. Then press F8 to enter Extend mode and click on the column D header.

To select entire nonadjacent rows or columns, use the Ctrl key or Shift-F8 as already described.

You can even select entire rows *and* columns at the same time. For example, suppose you've entered a series of identifying labels in column A and rows 1 through 3 of your worksheet and you want all these entries to appear in bold type for emphasis. To select all these cells at once, click on row header 1 and drag down to row header 3; then press Ctrl and click on column header A. As you can see in Figure 2-4, all of column A and rows 1, 2, and 3 are highlighted.

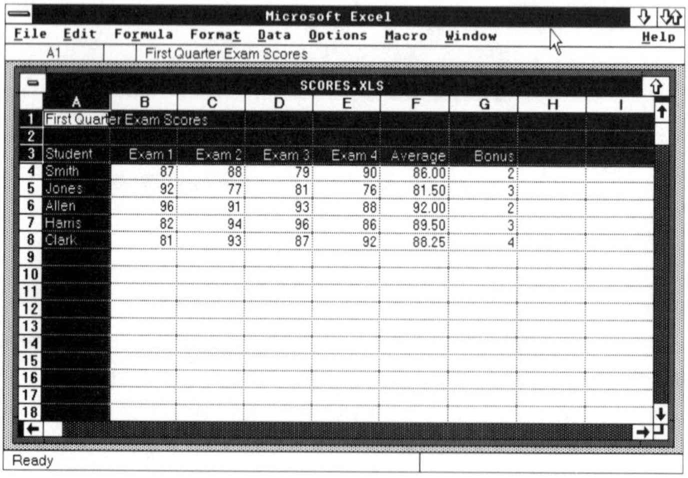

FIGURE 2-4. *You can select an entire row and an entire column at the same time.*

Often, you'll want to select all the cells in the worksheet to change a default format or to copy the entire contents of one document to another. Fortunately, you can do this easily, without a lot of clicking and scrolling. Simply click in the box that appears near the top left corner of your document window, where the row and column headers intersect.

Using the keyboard

You can also use the keyboard to navigate and make selections in your worksheet. The simplest way to select a single cell with the keyboard is to use the arrow keys to activate the desired cell. For example, if cell A1 is currently active, you can select cell A2 by pressing the Right arrow key once. When you do this, the active-cell border appears around cell A2 and the cell reference A2 appears in the cell reference box. Similarly, to move from cell A1 to cell C5, press the Right arrow key twice and the Down arrow key four times.

You can also use the Tab and Shift-Tab keys to move the active cell. Tab activates the cell immediately to the right of the currently active cell. For example, if cell B2 is active, pressing Tab activates cell C2. Pressing Shift-Tab activates the cell immediately to the left of the currently active cell.

Of course, if you need to move through several rows or columns of a worksheet, these arrow-key and Tab-key techniques could soon become quite tedious. Fortunately, you can use keyboard shortcuts to move around more rapidly in your worksheet. We'll discuss some of these shortcuts next.

Moving between blocks of cells
You can use the Ctrl key in conjunction with the arrow keys to move through blocks of cells in your worksheet.

A cell block is a range of cell entries bounded by blank cells. For example, in the worksheet in Figure 2-5, the range A3:E7 is a block of cells, as are the ranges G3:H7, A9:E10, and G9:H10. Suppose cell A3 is the active cell. If you press the Ctrl and Right arrow keys from this position, cell E3 becomes active. Press Ctrl-Right while E3 is selected and cell G3 becomes active. Press Ctrl-Right once more and H3 becomes active. Similarly, if you press Ctrl-Down while cell A3 is selected, cell A7 becomes active.

If a blank cell is active when you use a Ctrl-arrow key combination, Microsoft Excel moves to the first cell in the direction of the arrow that contains a cell entry. For example, if cell D18 in our example is active when you press the Ctrl and Up arrow keys, cell D10 becomes active.

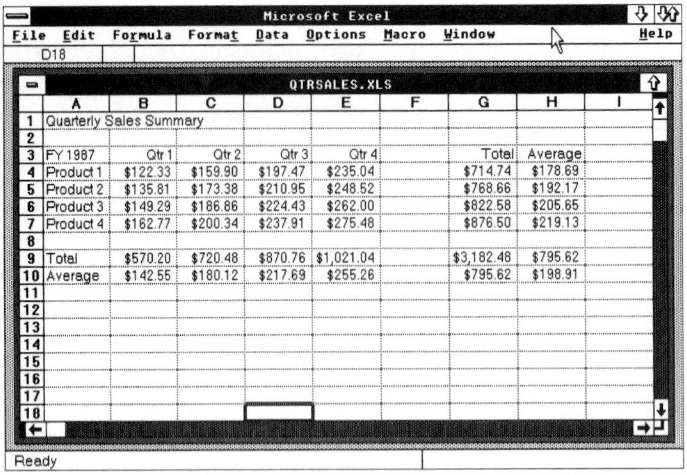

FIGURE 2-5. *You can use the Ctrl and arrow keys to move between blocks of cells.*

Using the Home and End keys

The Home and End keys are also valuable navigational and selection tools. The Home key lets you move to column A of the current row; the End key lets you move to the last column of the current row. By last column, we mean the last column in the active area of the worksheet, not necessarily the last column that contains an entry. For example, in Figure 2-5, if you press End while cell A8 is active, Microsoft Excel moves to cell H8. Even though row 8 does not contain any entries, column H is the end of the active area of our sample worksheet.

To move to the first cell in the worksheet, cell A1, press Ctrl-Home. To move to the last cell in the active area (cell H10 in our sample), press Ctrl-End. Finally, to activate the first cell in the current window, press the Scroll Lock key and then press Home. We'll talk more about the Scroll Lock key in a moment.

Extending a selection

As with the mouse, you can extend a keyboard selection by using the Shift or F8 key. To select a range with the keyboard, hold down Shift and use the arrow keys to draw the rectangular range. (You can't extend a selection with the Tab key.) To select the range of cells from A1 through B6 of your worksheet, begin by selecting cell A1; then, while holding down Shift, press the Right arrow key once and the Down arrow key five times. When you release Shift, your screen will look like Figure 2-1.

Or suppose you want to select the range A1:C12. To do this, select C12, hold down the Shift key, and press the Left arrow key twice and the Up arrow key 11 times. Cell C12, the first cell you selected to begin defining the range, will be the active cell in this range.

You can also use the F8 function key to extend a selection. To select the range A1:C12, first select cell A1. Next, press the F8 key to put Microsoft Excel in Extend mode. (Watch for the EXT indicator in the status bar at the bottom of your screen.) Now press the Right arrow key twice and the Down arrow key 11 times to select cells A1:C12.

You can also use the keyboard to extend a selection beyond the window border. Suppose you want to select the range A1:C38. Select cell A1, hold down Shift, and then press the Right arrow key twice to select cells A1:C1. Then (assuming your worksheet window is sized to display 18 rows at a time, like the ones in our examples), to extend the selection through row 38, continue to hold down the Shift key and press the PgDn key twice. Cells A1:C37 will now be highlighted. Complete your selection by pressing the Down arrow key once as you continue to hold down the Shift key. Microsoft Excel selects the range A1:C38, with A1 as the active cell.

Selecting multiple ranges

To select multiple ranges with the keyboard, you use Add mode. Suppose, for example, you've already selected the range A1:B6 and want to add cells C7:E10 to this range without eliminating cells A1:B6 from the selection. First, enter Add mode by pressing Shift-F8. (You'll see the notation ADD in the status bar at the bottom of your screen.) Then use the arrow keys to select cell C7. Now you can add this second group of cells by selecting the same way you selected the range A1:B6—hold down Shift and use the arrow keys to extend the selection, or press F8 and use the arrow keys.

Selecting rows and columns

You can select an entire row or column from the keyboard simply by selecting a cell in the desired row or column and then pressing Shift-Spacebar to select the row or Ctrl-Spacebar to select the column.

To select several entire adjacent rows or columns from the keyboard, first highlight a range that includes the rows or columns you want to work with and then use Ctrl-Spacebar or Shift-Spacebar. For example, to select columns B, C, and D, you can select any range that includes cells in these three columns; then press Ctrl-Spacebar.

Finally, to select the entire worksheet from the keyboard, press Ctrl-Shift-Spacebar.

Navigating within a selection

When you're making cell entries, it's often more convenient to select the entire range in which you want to work than to select each cell individually. Microsoft

Excel offers some special keyboard techniques to help you move around within a range or discontinuous selection.

As you know, you can lock in a cell entry either by clicking on the check box in the formula bar or by pressing the Enter key. When you're making entries in a range, Microsoft Excel simultaneously locks in your entry and moves down one row to the next cell in the selection. If you're working in a single-row range or if the current active cell is in the last row of the range selection, Microsoft moves to the top of the next column in the selection. To move up row by row through a selection, press Shift-Enter to lock in your entries.

If the active cell is the last cell in the selection, pressing Enter takes you back to the first cell in the selection. Conversely, if the first cell in the selection is the active cell, pressing Shift-Enter moves you to the last cell in the selection.

If you prefer to move through the selection by columns rather than by rows, you can use Tab and Shift-Tab to lock in your entries and activate the next cell in the selection. Tab moves the active cell one column to the right; Shift-Tab moves it one column to the left. If you're working in a single-column range or if the active cell is at the edge of the range, Tab and Shift-Tab move the active cell to the next row in the selection. To move from one corner of a selection to the next, press the Ctrl and period keys.

If you're working in a discontinuous range, you can press Ctrl-Tab to move to the first cell in the next area of the range or press Ctrl-Shift-Tab to move to the first cell in the previous area.

By the way, don't use the arrow keys when you're making entries in a range. If you do, Microsoft Excel deselects the current range and activates the cell in the direction you specify.

Scrolling the window

All the selection and navigation techniques we've described so far have been geared toward selecting cells and ranges. Often, however, you'll want to view different areas of your worksheet without necessarily changing your selection. For example, you might want to compare the results of a formula you just entered with the results of a similar formula in a remote area of the worksheet. To change your view of the worksheet without changing your current selection, you must use a technique called scrolling. As with cell selection, you can scroll through the worksheet with either the mouse or the keyboard.

To scroll through the worksheet with your mouse, you use the scroll bars that appear on the right side and at the bottom of your document window. By clicking on the scroll arrows that appear at either end of the scroll bars, you can move up, down, left, or right one row or column at a time. By clicking in the shaded area of the scroll bar, you can move a new screenful of information into view.

The distance you cover when you click in the shaded area of the scroll bar depends on the size of the document window. If you've resized the document window so that only 5 rows are visible, clicking in the gray area of the vertical scroll bar brings the next five rows into view; if 20 rows are visible, the next 20 rows scroll into view.

To move long distances in the worksheet rather than a line or a screenful at a time, you can drag the scroll boxes to the desired positions. The position of the scroll box in the scroll bar gives you an idea of your relative position in the active area of your worksheet. As you'll learn a little later in this chapter, the active area of the worksheet is a rectangle that encompasses all the row and column entries in the document. Thus, in a worksheet whose active area is only 30 rows deep, dragging the scroll box to the middle of the vertical scroll bar brings row 15 into view. If the active area is 200 rows deep, however, dragging the scroll box to the middle of the vertical scroll bar brings row 100 into view. In a large worksheet, dragging the scroll boxes to the bottom and right side of the scroll bars brings the end of the active rectangle into view at the upper left corner of the window.

To scroll the worksheet window with the keyboard, press the Scroll Lock key and then use the arrow keys or the PgUp or PgDn key. The notation SCRL appears in the status bar at the bottom of your screen when Scroll Lock is in effect. As you might guess, the arrow keys let you scroll up, down, left, and right one row or column at a time; the PgUp and PgDn keys let you move a new screenful of data into view. For example, to scroll down through your worksheet a screen at a time without changing your selection, press Scroll Lock and then press PgDn. To scroll left and right a screen at a time, press Scroll Lock and then press Ctrl-PgDn to move right or Ctrl-PgUp to move left.

When you scroll through the worksheet, you'll often lose sight of the active cell. To quickly bring the active cell back into view, press Ctrl-Backspace or begin typing the cell entry.

Making cell entries

Microsoft Excel accepts two basic types of cell entries: constant values and formulas. Constants fall into three main categories: text, numeric values, and date and time values (which are represented as a special type of number). We'll discuss text and numeric values first; then we'll look at techniques for building formulas. We'll deal with date and time values in Chapter 7.

Microsoft Excel also recognizes two special categories of constants: logical values and error values. We'll address error values a little later in this chapter and save logical values for our discussion of functions in Chapter 6.

Simple text and numeric values

In general, any entry that includes only the numerals 0 through 9 or one of a select group of special characters is a numeric value. For example, 123, 345678, 999999, and 1 are all numeric values. An entry that includes almost any other character—that is, any cell entry that can't be interpreted as a number—is treated as a text value. The entries *Sales, Hello, A Label,* and *123 Main Street* are all text values. (We'll sometimes refer to text values as labels or strings.)

The distinction between numbers and text is important. Although you can create formulas that link number cells to number cells and text cells to text cells, you can't create a formula that links a number cell directly to a text cell. Any formula that attempts to do this produces a #VALUE! error. However, the distinction between text and numeric values is less important in Microsoft Excel than in some other spreadsheet programs because you can perform the same mathematical operations on numeric text entries that you can on numbers.

If you aren't sure whether a value will be treated as text or as a number, check the way the value appears in the cell after you press Enter. Unless you use a formatting command (described in Chapter 3) to change the cell display, numbers are always aligned to the right side of the cell and text entries to the left side of the cell.

Making numeric entries

You can enter a number in your worksheet simply by selecting a cell and typing the number. For example, suppose you want to enter the number 100 in cell C5 in your worksheet. First select cell C5 and then type 100. As you type, the number 100 appears in the formula bar and also in cell C5.

Notice the flashing vertical bar that appears in the formula bar when you begin typing. This bar is called the insertion point. The insertion point moves in front of the characters as you type, to show your current position. Later in this chapter, you'll see how to move this insertion point to edit cell entries.

Locking in the entry

When you've finished typing, you must "lock in" the entry to store it permanently in the selected cell.

You can lock in an entry in several ways. The simplest way is to press the Enter key. When you press Enter, the insertion point disappears from the formula bar and the entry you typed is stored in the active cell. When a single cell is selected, pressing Enter does not deselect the cell as clicking on another cell with the mouse does.

If you press Tab, Shift-Tab, or one of the arrow keys after you've finished typing the entry, Microsoft Excel locks in the entry and simultaneously activates an adjacent cell. For example, pressing Tab to lock in the entry activates the cell immediately to the right of the cell into which the entry was made; pressing Shift-Tab locks in the entry and activates the cell to the left.

When you begin typing an entry, two new icons appear on the screen: the Enter box and the Cancel box. (We mentioned these briefly in Chapter 1.) The Enter box, which contains a check mark, is another way to lock in your entry when you're finished typing. For example, to lock in the entry in cell C5 and keep cell C5 active, you could click the Enter box with the mouse instead of pressing Enter.

The Cancel box, which contains an X, allows you to cancel an entry before you lock it in. If you make a mistake while typing in the formula bar, you can click the Cancel box with the mouse to delete the information you typed. If the cell originally contained another entry, that entry is restored. To use the keyboard to cancel an entry, press Esc.

Other numeric characters

In addition to the numerals 0 through 9, numeric values can sometimes include the following characters:

> + – E e $, . % ( )

You can begin any numeric entry with a plus sign (+) or a minus sign (–). If you begin a numeric entry with a minus sign, Microsoft Excel interprets that entry as a negative number and retains the minus sign. If you begin a numeric entry with a plus sign, Microsoft Excel simply drops the plus sign.

The characters E and e can be used to enter a number in scientific notation. For example, if you select a cell and enter 1E6, Microsoft Excel interprets that entry as the number 1,000,000 (or 1 times 10 to the sixth power).

Microsoft Excel interprets numbers enclosed in left and right parentheses as negative numbers. This notation is common in accounting, to ensure that negative cash amounts are not overlooked. For example, if you make the entry (100) in a cell, Microsoft Excel interprets that entry as –100.

The decimal point can be used as you normally use it. You can also use commas to separate the hundreds from the thousands, the thousands from the millions, and so on, as you normally would in numeric entries. However, the program simply ignores the commas. For example, if you enter 1,234,567.89, Microsoft Excel interprets that entry as the number 1234567.89. To display this number with commas, you must specifically format the cell to include them.

If you begin a numeric entry with a dollar sign, Microsoft Excel assigns one of its currency formats to the cell. (We'll learn more about formats in the next chapter.) For example, if you select a cell and enter the number $123456, Microsoft Excel assigns a special dollar format to that cell and displays the number as $123,456. Note that, in this case, commas are added by Microsoft Excel.

Similarly, if you end a numeric entry with a percent sign (%), Microsoft Excel interprets the entry as a percentage and assigns one of its percentage formats to the cell that contains the entry. For example, if you type the number 23%, Microsoft Excel interprets and displays that number in the formula bar as 0.23 and assigns a percentage format to the cell.

Displayed values vs *underlying values*

A cell entry in Microsoft Excel can be as many as 255 characters. Because the standard column width in Microsoft Excel is only 8.43 characters, the program clearly needs some rules for displaying long entries. If you enter a number that is too wide to be displayed in the cell, Microsoft Excel converts the number into scientific notation so that it can be displayed in a single cell. For example, if you select cell A1 and enter the numeric value 1234567890123, Microsoft Excel will display this number as 1.23E+12, as shown in Figure 2-6, rather than let the number overlap into the next cell. If you look at the formula bar, you'll see that Microsoft Excel has stored the number the way you entered it. Although Microsoft Excel has changed the appearance of the entry in cell A1, the actual contents of cell A1 have stayed the same.

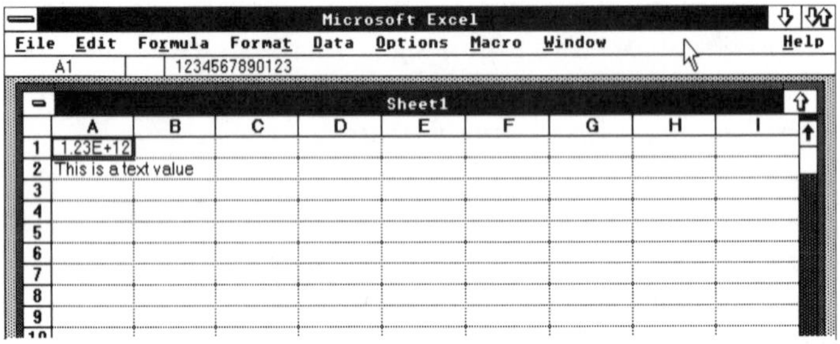

FIGURE 2-6. *The number 1234567890123 is too long to be displayed in cell A1, so Microsoft Excel displays it in scientific notation.*

This is the first example we've shown of an important Microsoft Excel concept: What you see in a cell and what is actually in the cell may be entirely different things. The values that you see when you look at the worksheet are called displayed values; the values that appear in the formula bar are called underlying values. Keep in mind that, unless you tell it otherwise, Microsoft Excel always remembers the underlying values in your cells, no matter how those values are displayed. When you build formulas, Microsoft Excel uses the underlying values rather than the displayed values, so that your calculations will always be correct.

The number of digits that appear in a cell depends on the width of the column that contains the long number. If you change the width of a column that contains a long entry, Microsoft Excel changes the displayed value according to the width of the cell. Keep in mind, however, that the column width affects only the displayed values of numbers on your worksheet; it has no effect on the actual numbers stored in the cells.

We'll come back to this concept again in Chapters 3 and 4, where you'll learn to control the way cell entries are displayed by changing the formats and column widths assigned to cells.

Making text entries

The process of making a text entry is nearly identical to that of making a numeric entry: All you need do to enter a text value into a cell is select that cell and type. When you've finished typing, you can use any of the techniques discussed above to lock in the entry. If you make an error, you can cancel the entry by clicking the Cancel box with the mouse or by pressing Esc.

Long text entries

We've seen that Microsoft Excel converts long numbers into scientific notation for display purposes. Microsoft Excel treats long text values somewhat differently. If you create a label too long to be displayed in a single cell, Microsoft Excel allows that label to overlap into adjacent cells. For example, we entered the label *This is a text value* in cell A2 of the worksheet in Figure 2-6. Notice that this text entry spills into cell B2.

Don't let this ability to overlap mislead you, however. The entire label is still stored in cell A2. If you select cell B2 and look at the formula bar, you'll see that it is still empty. The characters that seem to be contained in cell B2 are really in cell A2 and overlap B2 only for display purposes.

Now, let's select cell B2 and type *This is another text value*. As you can see in Figure 2-7, this new entry makes it impossible for Microsoft Excel to display all of the long text value in cell A2. Again, this change affects only the way the label is

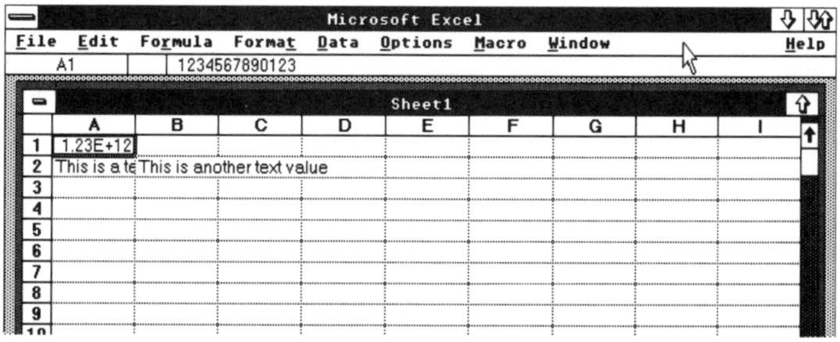

FIGURE 2-7. *When the cell to the right contains an entry, long text values cannot spill over and therefore appear to be truncated.*

displayed and has no effect on the contents of either cell. If you move back to cell A2 and look at the formula bar, you'll see that the entire label is still stored intact.

Numeric text entries

At times, you'll want to create text entries that are made up partly or entirely of numbers. If you want to enter a text value like *1234 Main Street* into the worksheet, you need only select a cell, type the entry, and press Enter. Because this entry includes nonnumeric characters, Microsoft Excel assumes it is a text value.

Sometimes you may want to create text entries made up entirely of numbers, however. For example, suppose you're developing a price list like the one shown in Figure 2-8. Column A contains a series of part numbers. If you want Microsoft Excel to treat these part numbers as text rather than as numbers, you must enter them into the worksheet as "literal strings." For example, part number 1234 in cell A4 was entered as

    ="1234"

Unless you treat all the part numbers this way, Microsoft Excel left-aligns those that include text (1237B, for example) and right-aligns those that are purely numbers.

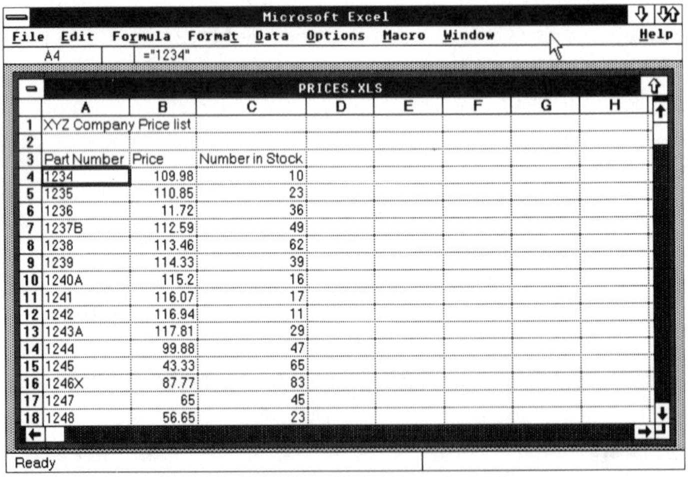

	A	B	C	D	E	F	G	H
1	XYZ Company	Price list						
2								
3	Part Number	Price	Number in Stock					
4	1234	109.98	10					
5	1235	110.85	23					
6	1236	11.72	36					
7	1237B	112.59	49					
8	1238	113.46	62					
9	1239	114.33	39					
10	1240A	115.2	16					
11	1241	116.07	17					
12	1242	116.94	11					
13	1243A	117.81	29					
14	1244	99.88	47					
15	1245	43.33	65					
16	1246X	87.77	83					
17	1247	65	45					
18	1248	56.65	23					

FIGURE 2-8. *These part numbers have been entered as literal strings rather than numeric values.*

When you enter a number as a literal string, it appears *exactly* as you've typed it and is not formatted by any future calculations.

Making entries in ranges

If you want to make a number of entries in a range of adjacent cells, select those cells before you begin making entries. Then you can use Enter, Tab, Shift-Enter, and Shift-Tab to move the active cell within the range. When you're working in a selected range, Microsoft Excel restricts movement to that range. When you reach the end of a column or row, you automatically move to the next column or row in the range. Because Microsoft Excel does not allow the active cell to move out of the range of selected cells, you can devote your attention to making entries, without worrying about the location of the active cell.

For example, suppose you want to make some entries in the range B2:D4. To begin, select the range. (Select from B2 to D4, so that cell B2 is the active cell.) Then type the number 100 in cell B2 and press Enter. When you press Enter, cell B3 becomes the active cell. If you type the number 200 and press Enter again, cell B4 becomes the active cell. If you now type the number 300 and press Enter yet again, cell C2, the first cell in the next column of the range, becomes the active cell, as shown in Figure 2-9. You can continue like this until the entire range is filled.

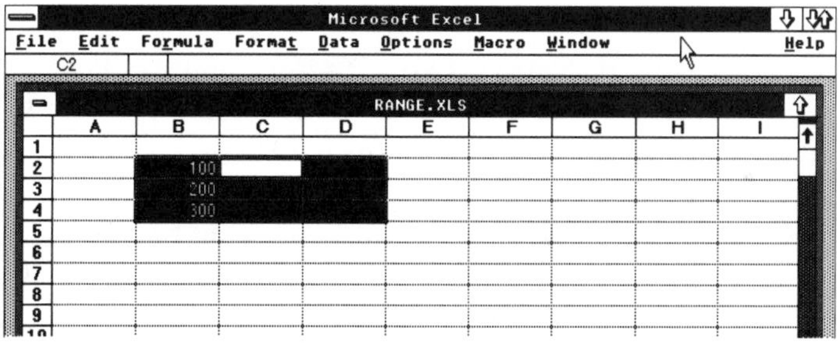

FIGURE 2-9. *When making entries in a range, you can lock in your entry and move to the next cell in the range automatically.*

Pressing Enter activates the cell below the currently active cell. As you might expect, pressing Shift-Enter activates the cell above the currently active cell. For example, if cell B3 is active and you press Shift-Enter, B2 becomes the active cell.

The Tab key activates the cell one column to the right of the current active cell. If cell C2 is the active cell and you press Tab, cell D2 becomes active. If you press Tab again, however, the active-cell border moves to cell B3; Microsoft Excel has restricted the movement of the active cell to the range of selected cells. If you press Shift-Tab, the cell one column to the left becomes the active cell.

When you're working with a discontinuous range, you can move between selected areas in two ways: You can use the Tab, Shift-Tab, Enter, and Shift-Enter keys as described above to move from the last cell in one area to the first cell in the next, or you can press Ctrl-Tab or Ctrl-Shift-Tab to jump directly to the first cell in another area.

Correcting errors in entries

No matter how good a typist you are, you'll sometimes make errors in cell entries. Fortunately, however, Microsoft Excel makes it easy to edit your cell entries in the formula bar.

Correcting errors before you lock in the entry

If you make simple typing errors as you're making an entry, you can correct them by pressing the Backspace key. For example, suppose you've selected cell A1 and are entering the text *This is a label*. As you make the entry, however, you type *This is ala*. To correct this error, press Backspace twice to erase the *a* and the *l* and then type the space you forgot the first time and complete the entry. Each time you press Backspace, Microsoft Excel erases the character to the left of the insertion point. When you've finished making the entry, press Enter to lock it in.

The Backspace method is good for correcting errors if you catch them quickly. However, if you don't catch the error until you've done quite a bit more typing, you're better off not using Backspace. If you discover an error before you lock in an entry but too late to use Backspace, you can simply reposition the insertion point in the entry and erase, insert, or replace characters.

For example, suppose you enter the text *This is a label* in cell A1 of your worksheet. Before you lock in the entry, you realize you want to add the words *rather long* before the word *label*. To add characters to an entry, use the mouse to point to the position in the formula bar where you want the characters to appear. (The pointer will assume an I-beam shape.) Then simply click at this insertion point and begin typing. Microsoft Excel pushes the insertion point—and any characters after it—to the right as you type. To add the words *rather long* to the entry in cell A1, point in front of the first letter *l* in the word *label* in the formula bar. When you click the mouse button, the insertion point will move to the indicated spot in the entry—in this case, in front of the letter *l*. Now type *rather long*, followed by a space. If the entry is now correct, press Enter to lock it in.

If you want to delete several adjacent characters, you can drag across all the characters you want to delete and press Del. (Backspace erases one letter at a time; Del erases the highlighted portion of the entry.) For instance, to erase the word *rather*, position the pointer before the first *r* in *rather*, press the mouse button, drag to the right until the entire word plus one space is highlighted, and press Del once.

If you prefer to use the keyboard, you can activate the formula bar by pressing the F2 function key. When you press F2, two things happen: The status bar at the bottom left of the screen changes from Enter to Edit, telling you that Microsoft Excel is ready for editing, and the insertion point appears at the end of the cell entry. Use the arrow keys to position the insertion point to the right of the letter or letters you want to remove, use Backspace to erase the letters, and then type the correction. To move quickly from one end of the formula bar to the other, press Home or End. You also can hold down the Ctrl key and press the Left or Right arrow key to move through an entry one word at a time. When you've finished, lock in your changes by pressing Enter or selecting another cell with the Tab or Shift-Tab keys.

To use keyboard techniques to replace several characters, position the insertion point in front of or behind the block of characters you want to work with and use the Shift key in conjunction with the Left and Right arrow keys to extend your selection in the formula bar. Then erase the characters by pressing the Del key or overwrite them by typing the new characters. Microsoft Excel deletes the selected characters as you begin typing the replacement characters. When you finish making the change, press Enter.

You can also replace characters in the formula bar by entering the Overwrite mode. Generally, when you activate the formula bar and type new characters, they are inserted to the left of the insertion point marker. If you want to replace the characters to the right of the insertion point, press the Ins key before you begin typing. The notation OVR appears in the status bar at the bottom of the screen. To cancel Overwrite mode and reenter the default Insert mode, simply press Ins again or deactivate the formula bar by pressing Enter or selecting another cell.

Correcting errors after you lock in the entry

If you've locked in an entry but haven't left the cell, you can erase the entire contents of the cell by pressing the Backspace key once. You don't have to create an insertion point to do this. If you press Backspace accidentally, simply click on the Cancel box with the mouse or press Esc to restore the contents of the cell.

If you've already locked in the entry and left the cell, you must select the cell again before you can correct any errors. When you select a cell that already contains a value or formula, the formula bar is not active; that is, no blinking insertion point appears in the bar. To activate the formula bar, click on it or press F2.

If you want to replace the entire contents of a cell with another entry, simply select the cell and type. Microsoft Excel will erase the previous entry as soon as you begin typing. For example, suppose you want to enter the word *Sales* in cell A1, which currently contains the word *Purchases*. To make this change, simply select cell A1, type *Sales*, and press Enter. If you decide you want to retain the original contents of the cell, click on the Cancel box with the mouse or press Esc to revert to the original entry.

Building formulas

Microsoft Excel's strength lies in its ability to calculate new values from existing ones. Armed with a few mathematical operators and rules for cell entry, you can turn your worksheet into a powerful calculator.

Let's walk through a series of simple formulas to see how they work. Begin by selecting a blank cell, A20, and typing the simple formula

    =10+5

As soon as you press Enter or click on the Enter box with the mouse, you'll see the value 15 in the active cell. If you look at the formula bar, however, you'll see that Microsoft Excel also remembers the underlying formula you typed. Similarly, if you type

    =10–5

you'll see the displayed value 5 in the active cell. Now enter the formulas

    =10*5

and

    =10/5

Microsoft Excel displays the values 50 and 2, respectively.

Notice that each of these formulas begins with an equal sign (=). The equal sign serves as a flag to tell Microsoft Excel that a formula follows. If you forget to begin the formula with an equal sign, Microsoft Excel interprets the entry as text, unless it's a simple numeric value.

Each of the above formulas uses one of Microsoft Excel's mathematical operators: the plus sign (+), the minus sign (–), the asterisk multiplication sign (*), and the slash division sign (/).

Precedence of operators

As you begin complex formulas that use more than one operator, you'll need to consider the precedence that Microsoft Excel assigns to each operator. You may remember warnings about the precedence of operators from high-school math classes. The term *precedence* simply refers to the order in which Microsoft Excel performs calculations in complex formulas.

Microsoft Excel multiplies and divides before it adds and subtracts. If two operations are of the same level, the program processes them from left to right. For example, the formula

    =4+12/6

returns the value 6. When Microsoft Excel evaluates this formula, it calculates the value 12/6 first and then adds 4. The formula

    =4*12/6

returns the value 8. In this case, Microsoft Excel calculates the value 4*12 first and then divides by 6.

When you're building long, complex formulas, it can be difficult to predict exactly how Microsoft Excel will calculate your formula. To avoid this problem, you can use parentheses to override Microsoft Excel's built-in operator precedence and specify the order in which you want the elements of your formula to be evaluated. For example, each of the following formulas uses the same values and operators; only the parentheses differ:

Formula	Result
=3*6+12/4–2	19
=(3*6)+12/(4–2)	24
=3*(6+12)/4–2	11.5
=(3*6+12)/4–2	5.5
=3*(6+12/(4–2))	36

When you use parentheses in your formulas, be sure you include a closing parenthesis for each opening parenthesis. Otherwise, Microsoft Excel will display the message *Error in formula*.

Using cell references in formulas

Although simple formulas like the ones you've built so far are convenient for quickly calculating values, Microsoft Excel's real magic lies in its ability to use references to other cells in formulas. When you create a formula that contains cell references, you link the formula to other cells in your worksheet. As a result, the value of the formula always reflects the values in the source cells. You'll find this capability enormously valuable when you begin using your worksheet for financial planning or similar calculations.

For example, suppose you've entered the formula

    =10*2

in cell A1 of your worksheet. If you later select A2 and type the formula

    =A1

cell A2 will also display the value 20. So why not simply type the value 20 in cell A2? To see why, select cell A1 and change the entry to 100. Now look at the displayed value in cell A2. When you changed the value of cell A1, Microsoft Excel updated cell A2 as well. The formula in cell A2 links cell A2 to cell A1 so that the value in cell A2 will always equal the value in cell A1.

Now select cell A3 in your worksheet and type the formula

=A1+A2

Microsoft Excel returns the value 200. Of course, you can create much more complex formulas in Microsoft Excel using references to cells or ranges. When we discuss worksheet functions in Chapter 6, you'll discover a number of applications for cell references.

Pasting cell references. You can save time and avoid typographical errors by clicking on the cells you want Microsoft Excel to include in your formulas rather than typing their references. This technique is called pasting a cell reference into a formula. (We recommend pasting cell references with the mouse. Although it's possible to paste cell references with the keyboard, the technique is cumbersome and time-consuming.)

Suppose you want to create a formula in cell A26 that totals the values you've entered in cells A20:A24. To do this, select cell A26 and type an equal sign (=). Next, click on cell A20; then type a plus sign and click on cell A21; then type another plus sign and click on cell A22; and so on. (Notice that Microsoft Excel surrounds each cell with a flashing border as you select it. This border is called a marquee.) Your finished formula will be

=A20+A21+A22+A23+A24

Of course, you can use operators other than the plus sign.

When you finish entering a formula, be sure to lock in your entry by clicking the Enter box or by pressing Enter or Tab before you attempt to select another cell. Whenever you click on a cell while the formula bar is active, Microsoft Excel assumes you want to paste in a cell reference.

A cell does not have to be visible in the current window for you to make an entry in that cell. As we mentioned earlier, you can scroll through the worksheet with the mouse and scroll bars without changing the currently selected cell. (If you use the keyboard, you will deselect the cell.) You can use this capability to point to cells in remote areas of your worksheet as you build formulas. Suppose you want to enter a formula in cell M50 that calculates the sum of your first-quarter and second-quarter sales. You know that the totals for first-quarter sales are located somewhere in column G of your worksheet, but you don't remember the exact cell reference. After you select cell M50 and enter an equal sign, you can simply scroll through your worksheet, find the correct cell, and select it. Microsoft Excel will include this cell reference in the formula in cell M50.

Absolute and relative references. The cell references used in the sample formulas you've seen so far are called relative references. Microsoft Excel also allows you to create absolute references to other cells in your worksheet.

Basically, relative references refer to cells by their position in relation to the cell that contains the formula. Absolute references refer to cells by their absolute, or fixed, position in the worksheet.

You specify absolute references in your formulas by typing a dollar sign ($) before the column and row coordinates. For example, to enter an absolute reference to cell A1 in your worksheet, you would type

=$A$1

You can also use the Reference command on the Formula menu to quickly define absolute and relative references. To enter an absolute reference to cell A1 in your worksheet, type

=A1

and then choose the Reference command from the Formula menu. Microsoft Excel will change the reference nearest the insertion point to an absolute reference and the formula will appear as

=$A$1

If you choose the Reference command again, Microsoft Excel will change your entry to a mixed reference, with a relative column coordinate and an absolute row coordinate:

=A$1

If you choose Reference a third time, the reference will be changed to

=$A1

Here, the column coordinate is absolute and the row coordinate is relative.

Absolute and mixed references become very important when you begin moving cells around and copying them in your worksheet. We'll cover this concept again in Chapter 4.

Editing formulas

You edit formulas just as you do text entries, using either the mouse or the keyboard.

To delete a cell reference or other character from a formula with the mouse, simply click to the right of the reference and backspace over it or drag through the reference and then press Del. Alternatively, you can select the portion of the entry you want to replace, point to the replacement cell, and click. As soon as you click on the new cell, Microsoft Excel replaces the old reference with the new one.

If you want to undo your changes and you haven't yet locked in the new formula, you can select the Cancel box or press Esc. If you've locked in the entry but haven't issued another command, you can use the Undo command on the Edit menu.

You can also insert additional cell references in a formula. Simply click on the desired insertion point and then select the cell you want to add to the formula. (Of course, you can also type the cell reference.) For example, suppose you want to change the formula

    =A1+A3

to

    =A1+B1+A3

To do this, place the insertion point after the reference A1, type *+*, and then either type *B1* or point to cell B1 and click.

To delete a cell reference or other character from a formula with the keyboard, press the F2 function key to enter Edit mode. The insertion point will appear at the end of the formula. Use the arrow keys to position the insertion point, press Backspace to erase the incorrect reference, and then type the correction. If you want to undo your changes and you've locked in the entry but haven't issued another command or typed in another cell, you can use the Undo command on the Edit menu.

To insert additional cell references with the keyboard, select the cell containing the formula and press F2 to enter Edit mode, use the arrow keys to position the insertion point, and then type the cell reference.

Using numeric text in formulas

Unlike most other spreadsheet programs, Microsoft Excel allows you to use numeric text values to perform any mathematical operation, as long as the numeric string contains only the characters

    0 1 2 3 4 5 6 7 8 9 . + − E e

You can also use the five number-formatting characters

    $, % ( )

with numeric text, but if you do, you must enclose the numeric string in quotation marks. For example, the formula

    =$1234+$123

causes Microsoft Excel to display an alert box stating *Error in formula.* However, the formula

="$1234"+"$123"

produces the result 1357. In effect, Microsoft Excel translates the numeric text entry into a numeric value when it performs the addition.

Text values

Throughout this section, we've referred to text entries as text "values." The concept of using alphabetic characters as values may seem a bit confusing until you begin using formulas to manipulate text entries.

Microsoft Excel allows you to perform many of the same manipulations on text values that you perform on numeric values. For example, suppose cell A1 in your worksheet contains the text *abcde*. If you enter the formula

=A1

in cell A10 of your worksheet, that cell also displays *abcde*. Because this type of formula treats a string of text as a value, it is often called a string value.

You can use a special operator, &, to concatenate, or string together, several text values. For example, suppose cell A2 in the same worksheet contains the text *fghij*. You can use the formula

=A1&A2

to produce the text *abcdefghij*. You can also include a space between the two strings by changing the formula to

=A1&" "&A2

to create the string *abcde fghij*. Notice that this last formula uses two concatenation operators. The formula also includes a literal string, or string constant—a space enclosed in quotes—to separate the two halves of the string value. When you use literal strings in a worksheet formula, you must include double quotation marks before and after the string.

You can also use the & operator to concatenate a string of numeric values. For example, suppose cell A3 in your worksheet contains the numeric value 123 and cell A4 contains the numeric value 456. The formula

=A3&A4

produces the string *123456*. This string appears left-aligned in the worksheet cell, indicating that Microsoft Excel considers it a text value. (Keep in mind that you can use numeric text values to perform any mathematical operation, as long as the numeric string contains only the numeric characters listed on page 52.)

You can also use the & operator to concatenate a combination of numeric and text values. For example, if cell A1 contains the text *abcde* and cell A3 contains the numeric value 123, the formula

=A1&A3

produces the string *abcde123*.

Of course, the string values we've created so far are meaningless, but you'll find several practical applications for the concatenation operator. For example, suppose cell A1 in your worksheet contains the first name of a client, Gena, and cell B1 contains her last name, Woods. You can use the formula

=A1&" "&B1

to produce the string *Gena Woods*. Alternatively, you might use a formula like

=B1&", "&A1

to produce the string *Woods, Gena*.

Using functions: A preview

The formulas we've built thus far perform relatively simple mathematical calculations. In Chapter 6, you'll see a special set of operators, called functions, that help you build more sophisticated formulas.

Many of Microsoft Excel's functions are shorthand versions of tedious formulas that are used often in worksheets. For example, earlier in this chapter we showed you how to calculate the sum of a range of cells by pasting each cell reference individually into a formula. This is fine when you're adding the values in only two or three cells, but imagine pasting 20 or 30 cells into a formula! Microsoft Excel's SUM function lets you add a series of cell values by simply selecting a range. For example, compare the formula

=A1+A2+A3+A4+A5+A6+A7+A8+A9+A10

with the formula

=SUM(A1:A10)

Obviously, the SUM function makes the formula a lot shorter and easier to create.

Other Microsoft Excel functions let you perform extremely complex calculations that would be difficult, if not impossible, to perform with standard mathematical operators. For example, Microsoft Excel's NPV function lets you calculate the net present value of investments.

Using functions and references to cell ranges rather than building formulas with references to individual cells offers other advantages, too, as you'll see in Chapter 6.

Naming cells in your worksheet

So far, we've shown you how to build formulas using references to cells in the worksheet. However, Microsoft Excel also allows you to assign English-language names to cells and use those names in your formulas.

To name a cell, first select it; then choose the Define Name command on the Formula menu. Microsoft Excel looks at the selected cell, the cell immediately to the left, and then the cell immediately above the selection to see if one of them contains a label that might serve as a cell name. If a label is found, Microsoft Excel displays it in the Define Name dialog box. For example, suppose you want to assign a name to cell B4 in Figure 2-5. First, select cell B4 and choose Define Name from the Formula menu. The Define Name dialog box will look like the one in Figure 2-10.

FIGURE 2-10. *Microsoft Excel looks at surrounding cells to suggest a name for a cell or range.*

Notice that, in this example, Microsoft Excel is displaying the name *Product_1* in the Name edit bar and that the name is highlighted. Notice also that Microsoft Excel has added the underline character (_) to indicate a blank space in the name, because spaces are not allowed in reference names.

The coordinates of the selected cell appear in the Refers To edit bar, in the form of an absolute reference. (Microsoft Excel assumes you want to use absolute references when you name cells in your worksheet.)

If you want to accept Microsoft Excel's suggested name, simply select the OK button or press Enter. After you define a name, it is added to the Names in Sheet box, which contains a listing of all the defined names for that worksheet. Of course, you can also type your own cell name or edit Microsoft Excel's suggested name. To enter your own cell name, simply type the name you want; when you begin typing, Microsoft Excel will delete the existing contents of the Name edit bar. For example, you might want to use the name *Qtr_1* instead of *Product_1*. To do this, you would simply type over Microsoft Excel's suggested name with your own and then press Enter or select the OK button.

You can also edit the cell reference in the Define Name dialog box as you would edit the contents of the formula bar. Begin by selecting the Refers to edit bar. When you change the reference in the Refers to edit bar, be sure your entry begins with an equal sign (=). You can then use the techniques described earlier to add, delete, and replace characters.

In addition to naming individual cells, you can assign names to continuous and discontinuous ranges of cells in your worksheet. For example, to name the range B4:B7 in Figure 2-5, select cells B4:B7 and then choose Define Name from the Formula menu. The Define Name dialog box will look like Figure 2-11.

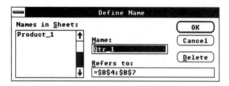

FIGURE 2-11. *If you select cells B4:B7, the Define Name dialog box looks like this.*

Notice that the Refers to edit bar contains the reference of the range you selected, not just the reference of the active cell, and that Microsoft Excel suggests the name *Qtr_1* for the range. To accept Microsoft Excel's suggested name, choose OK or press Enter.

Range name rules

Range names must comply with a few rules. First, the name must begin with a letter. You can use numbers and some special symbols in the name, but Microsoft Excel won't accept a name that *begins* with a number, period, dollar sign, and so on. Microsoft Excel also returns an error message if you enter blank spaces in the name. For example, it will not accept the names *1st Quarter* or *Region A*. If you want to indicate a blank space in your range name, use the underline character (_).

Microsoft Excel displays an alert box if you specify a name that looks like a cell reference. For example, the program does not accept names like A1 or R2C1. In addition, although you can use single-letter names such as A, B, and Z, Microsoft Excel does not allow you to use the single letters *R* and *C*.

Using range names

You can use range names in formulas just as you use cell references. For example, if you've assigned the name *Region_1* to cell A10, you can create the formula

=Region_1–21

This formula is evaluated identically to

=A10–21

Editing range names

You can use any of the editing techniques already described to edit the contents of the Refers to edit bar in the Define Name dialog box. To change the cells associated with a range name, choose the Define Name command, select the name of the range whose reference you want to edit from the Names in Sheet list box, and select the Refers to edit bar. Then either select the characters you want to change and type over them or select the entire contents of the Refers to edit bar and drag through the cells you want to use. Microsoft Excel will paste the new cell or range reference into the Refers to edit bar, much as it pastes references into the formula bar. If the cells you want to select are hidden behind the dialog box, you can use the mouse to drag the dialog box by clicking anywhere in the title bar. (For more on dragging windows, see Chapter 5.) You can also use the keyboard to move the dialog box by pressing Alt-Spacebar-M and then using the arrow keys to reposition the box. After typing your changes or selecting the desired cells, press Enter or select OK to lock in the new range reference.

To delete a range name, simply select the name from the list in the Names in Sheet box and select Delete. Microsoft Excel will delete only the name you select from the Names in Sheet list box; if another name is displayed in the Name edit bar, Microsoft Excel will replace it with the one to be deleted. You can use this fact to your advantage: When you want to delete a range name, you can select the Define Name command on the Formula menu from any cell in the worksheet and delete a range name without actually being in the range.

Be careful! When you delete a range name, every formula in the worksheet that refers to that name will be unable to complete its calculations and will return the error message #NAME!.

The Create Names command

Microsoft Excel's Create Names command lets you name several individual cells or continuous cell ranges at once. The command uses the labels in the top or bottom row or the left or right column of the range (or some combination of these) to name the other cells in the range.

For example, the sample worksheet in Figure 2-5 contains a series of labels in column A and row 3. To assign to each of the values in columns B through E names that correspond to the labels in column A, select cells A4:E7 and choose the Create Names command on the Formula menu. You'll see the dialog box shown in Figure 2-12. Select the Left Column option and choose OK or press Enter. Microsoft Excel will assign the name *Product_1* to the range B4:E4, the name *Product_2* to the range B5:E5, and so on. (If another name has previously been used for these cells, Microsoft Excel will ask whether the existing definition should be replaced.)

FIGURE 2-12. *The Create Names dialog box lets you quickly name several ranges.*

Similarly, you can use the labels in cells B3:E3 to name cells B4:E7. Simply select cells B3:E7 and then choose Create Names from the Formula menu. When you select Top Row in the Create Names dialog box, Microsoft Excel will assign the name *Qtr_1* to cells B4:B7, *Qtr_2* to cells C4:C7, and so forth.

If you select both Top Row and Left Column in the Create Names dialog box, Microsoft Excel uses the label in the top left corner of the range to name the entire group of cells. The range begins with the cell one row down and one column over from the top left cell. In our example, if you select cells A3:E7 and then select the Top and Left Column options, Microsoft Excel assigns the name *FY_1987* to cells B4:E7 and applies the labels in row 3 and column A to the columns and rows as well.

You can't use the Create Names command to name discontinuous ranges of cells. For example, if you attempt to use the Left Column option in the Create Names dialog box to name cells B4:E4 and G4:H4 in Figure 2-5, Microsoft Excel returns the alert message *Selection is invalid*. To name a discontinuous range of cells, you must use the Define Name command.

The names you create with the Create Names command appear in the Names in Sheet box when you use the Define Name command. You can delete or edit these names just as you would a name you created with the Define Name command.

Using Define Name to name constants and formulas

You can assign names as long as 255 characters to formulas and constants, independent of the cells in your worksheet. For example, suppose you use the value 5% often in your worksheet to calculate sales tax on products sold by your company. Instead of typing 5% or *.05*, you want to use the name *Tax* in your calculations. If you choose the Define Name command, type *Tax* into the Name edit bar, and type *.05* or 5% directly in the Refers to edit bar, Microsoft Excel assigns the name *Tax* to the constant value 5%. Afer you've created this name, you can use the formula

=Price+(Price*Tax)

to calculate the cost of items with sales tax.

If you enter a formula in the Refers to edit bar that refers to a cell in your worksheet, Microsoft Excel updates that formula whenever the value in the cell changes. In other words, Microsoft Excel treats named formulas just as it does formulas entered directly into the worksheet. For example, you can enter the formula

=C5−($B$2*C5)+D5

in the Refers to edit bar and the name *Amount_Billed* in the Name edit bar in the Define Name dialog box. This formula, when used in the worksheet in Figure 2-13, calculates the purchase amount, subtracts the 10-percent preferred-customer discount, and adds shipping charges to calculate the total invoice amount. Notice that the reference to cell B2 is absolute so that Microsoft Excel will always refer to cell B2 for the correct discount rate. The remaining references are relative, however, telling Microsoft Excel to draw the billing information from the appropriate row each time the formula

=Amount_Billed

is entered in column E of the worksheet. Thus, when you enter this formula name in cell E8, Microsoft Excel uses the formula

=C8−($B$2*C8)+D8

to calculate a total billing amount of $429.34.

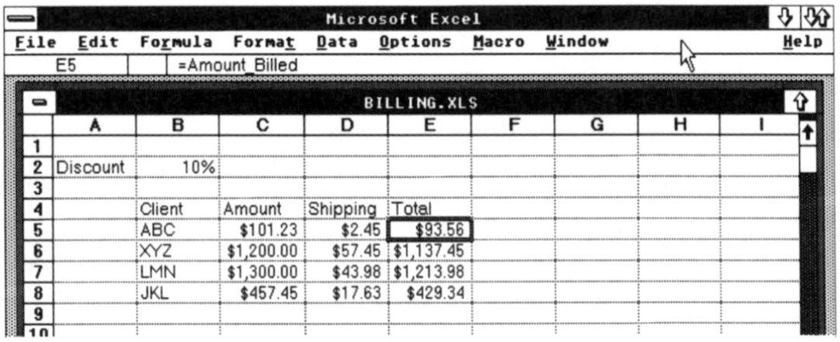

FIGURE 2-13. *You can increase your efficiency by defining names for often-used values and formulas.*

Whenever you create a named formula that contains relative references, keep in mind that Microsoft Excel interprets the position of the cells being referenced relative to the cell that is active when you issue the Define Name command. Thus, when you create the named formula Amount_Billed, you should ensure that cell E5 is the active cell, so that when you enter

=Amount_Billed

in cells E6 through E8, Microsoft Excel will adjust the relative references in your named formulas to refer to the corresponding cells in columns C and D.

The Paste Name command

After defining one or more names in your worksheet, you can use the Paste Name command on the Formula menu to paste those names into your worksheet formulas. For example, suppose you've assigned the name *Discount* to cell B2 and the name *Amount* to the cells in C5:C8 of the worksheet shown in Figure 2-13. You want to use these values in a formula like this:

=Discount*Amount

To create this formula, you can type *Discount* and *Amount* directly into the formula bar. Alternatively, you can use the Paste Name command to paste the names into the formula. Paste Name not only saves time when you need to enter several names, it also helps reduce typographical errors and serves as a memory aid when your worksheet contains many name definitions.

To use the Paste Name command, first select the cell in which you want to enter the name. If the name is to appear at the beginning of the formula, simply issue the Paste Name command to access the dialog box shown in Figure 2-14; then choose the name you want to paste and choose OK or press Enter. Microsoft Excel will enter an equal sign in the formula bar, followed by the selected name. The formula bar will remain active so that you can type the remainder of the formula. If you want the name to appear in the middle of a formula, select the cell that is to contain the formula, type an equal sign and the first portion of the formula, and then, at the spot where you want the name to appear, issue the Paste Name command and choose the desired name. The name you select will appear at the current insertion point and the insertion-point marker will move to the right of the name so that you can continue typing the formula. You can also paste names into an existing formula by placing the insertion point at the spot where you want the name to appear and issuing the Paste Name command as usual.

FIGURE 2-14. *Use the Paste Name dialog box to enter names into your formulas.*

The Paste List option

To help you keep track of the names you've created in your worksheet, Microsoft Excel provides a Paste List option in the Paste Name dialog box. When you choose Paste List, the program creates a list of the names in your worksheet, similar to the one shown in Figure 2-15. The list occupies two columns. The first column contains the names and the second column contains the definitions. The cell that is active when you choose the Paste List option becomes the first cell in the list.

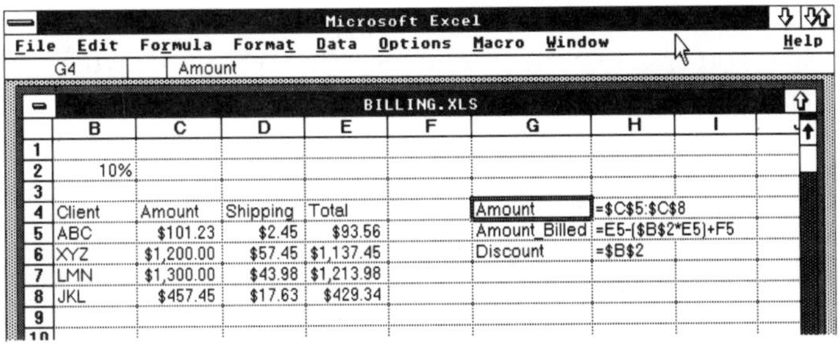

FIGURE 2-15. *Use the Paste List option to create a list of the names and definitions in your worksheet.*

(In a macro sheet, you must allow four columns to hold the results of the Paste List option. Here, Microsoft Excel pastes not only the names and their definitions, but also the macro types and the Ctrl-key shortcuts you can use to run the command macros. We'll talk more about macros in Chapter 17.)

The Apply Names command

When you create names in your worksheet, Microsoft Excel does not automatically apply those names in your worksheet formulas. Continuing with the sample worksheet in Figure 2-13, suppose you enter a series of formulas like

    =$B$2*C5

and

    =$B$2*C6

in cells F5:F8 and then use the Define Name command to assign the name *Discount* to cell B2. The formulas in cells F5:F8 will not automatically change to read

    =Discount*C5

and so forth. To use the named reference *Discount* in your formulas, you must either edit the formulas and type over the current reference to cell B2 with the name *Discount*, select the characters $B$2 in the formula bar and use the Paste Name command to paste the name *Discount* over the cell reference, or use the Apply Names command on the Formula menu to instruct Microsoft Excel to replace the reference with the appropriate name. You are already familiar with the first two techniques; let's look now at the Apply Names command.

The Apply Names command searches through the formulas in your worksheet and locates cell and range references for which you've defined names. If you've selected a range on your worksheet, Microsoft Excel applies those names to the selected cells only. However, if only one cell is selected when you issue the command, Microsoft Excel applies the names throughout the worksheet.

When you issue the Apply Names command, you see a dialog box like the one in Figure 2-16. (The last three options appear only if you choose the Options button to expand the dialog box.)

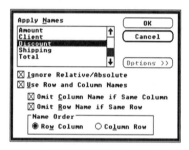

FIGURE 2-16. *Use the Apply Names command to substitute names for cell and range references in your formulas.*

In the Apply Names list box are all the cell and range names you've defined in the worksheet. (Named values and formulas do not appear in this list.) To select more than one name with the keyboard, press the Ctrl key and use the arrow keys to move through the list; as each name you want is outlined, press the Spacebar to select it. To select more than one name with the mouse, press the Shift key as you click on the names you want.

The Ignore Relative/Absolute option indicates whether you want to replace references with names regardless of the type of reference—relative or absolute— you've used in your name definitions or in your worksheet formulas. Generally, you'll want to leave this checkbox selected, because most of your name definitions will use absolute references (the default when you use the Define Name and Create Names commands) and most of your formulas will use relative references (the default when you paste cell and range references into the formula bar). If you deselect this option, however, Microsoft Excel will replace absolute, relative, and mixed references in your worksheet only if your name definitions use the corresponding reference style.

The Use Row and Column Names option determines whether Microsoft Excel uses only range names that exactly match the references in your formulas. If this option is deselected, Microsoft Excel applies the range names in your formulas only if the name definition refers to the exact range referenced in your formulas. If this option is selected, however, Microsoft Excel attempts to build a substitute from existing name definitions.

For example, in Figure 2-5 we assigned the name *Qtr_1* to cells B4:B7. Suppose we enter the formula

    =B4*4

in cell I4 of the worksheet. If we then select the Use Row and Column Names option, Microsoft Excel changes the formula in cell I4 to

    =Qtr_1*4

This formula tells Microsoft Excel to look to the cell in the range named Qtr_1 that lies in the same row as the cell containing our formula.

If a formula refers to a cell in a different row and column than the cell containing the formula, the reference is replaced with the two row-oriented and column-oriented names that contain the reference. These names are separated by a blank space, indicating that we want to locate the cell at the intersection of the two ranges. (If Microsoft Excel can't locate both a row-oriented and a column-oriented range, it doesn't replace the reference with a name.) If we enter our formula in a row other than row 4, Microsoft Excel changes the reference to cell A4 to

    =Product_1 Qtr_1*4

This formula tells Microsoft Excel to look to the cell that lies at the intersection of the range named Product_1 and the range named Qtr_1.

If a formula refers to a cell in the same row as the cell containing the formula but in a different column, the reference is replaced with the column-oriented name (if any). If a row-oriented range also contains the referenced cell, Microsoft Excel adds that name to the reference as well, creating a reference to the intersection of the two named ranges. Similarly, if a formula refers to a cell in the same column as the cell containing the formula but in a different row, the reference is replaced with the row-oriented name (if any). If a column-oriented range also contains the referenced cell, Microsoft Excel adds that name to the reference as well.

If you choose the Options button in the Apply Names dialog box, the Omit Column Name if Same Column and Omit Row Name if Same Row options appear. These options, which are available only if you have selected Use Row and Column Names, tell Microsoft Excel not to use the intersection referencing technique described above. In other words, if the referenced cell is in the same column as the cell that contains the formula but in a different row, Microsoft Excel uses the name of the row-oriented range only, ignoring any column-oriented ranges that may intersect the row-oriented range. By the same token, if the referenced cell is in the same row as the cell that contains the formula but in a different column, Microsoft Excel uses the name of the column-oriented range only, ignoring any row-oriented ranges that may intersect the column-oriented range.

The last set of options in the Apply Names dialog box is Name Order. These options appear when you choose the Options button and are available only if you have selected Use Row and Column Names. The Name Order option lets you determine which range is listed first when a reference is being replaced by a combination of row-oriented and column-oriented range names. The Row Column option lists rows first (Product_1 Qtr_1, for example); the Column Row option lists columns first (Qtr_1 Product_1).

The Goto command

Microsoft Excel's Goto command on the Formula menu lets you move around your worksheet and select cells quickly. For example, suppose cell A1 is currently selected and you want to select cell M50. Instead of scrolling over and down to cell M50, choose Goto from the Formula menu. When you choose this command, Microsoft Excel displays a dialog box like the one shown in Figure 2-17. In the Reference edit bar, type *M50* and then select OK or press Enter. Immediately, Microsoft Excel will move the window so that cell M50 appears in the lower right corner and is the active cell.

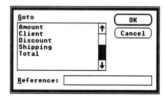

FIGURE 2-17. *Use the Goto dialog box to quickly select a cell or range.*

As you can see in Figure 2-17, if you've created range names in your worksheets, those names appear in the list at the left side of the Goto dialog box. To go to one of these ranges, simply select the range name in the dialog box. For example, suppose you've assigned the name *Subtotals* to cells C5:F5 in your worksheet. When you choose Subtotals from the list of your worksheet's named ranges, Microsoft Excel highlights cells C5:F5 and makes the first cell in the range, C5, the active cell.

You can also use the Goto command to move to another worksheet. To do this, select Goto and type the name of the worksheet, followed by an exclamation point and the name or reference. For example, to go to cell D5 in a worksheet called *Sales*, type *Sales!D5*.

Although Microsoft Excel moves you to a new location with the Goto command, it also remembers the last place you were. That is, the next time you issue the Goto command, you'll see a reference to the cell or range that was selected before you issued the last Goto command. Thus, you can toggle between two points in your worksheet simply by repeating the Goto command.

Error values

On occasion, a set of rather unfriendly-looking codes will pop up in your worksheet. These flags, which are called error values, indicate that Microsoft Excel is unable to resolve one of your formulas. In this section, we'll look briefly at these seven error values—#DIV/0!, #NAME?, #VALUE!, #REF!, #NULL!, #N/A, and #NUM!. We'll refer to these values again throughout the book as we explain potential error conditions you may experience as you use Microsoft Excel.

One of the most common error values is #DIV/0!. As you might have guessed, #DIV/0! indicates that you've attempted to divide a number by zero. This error usually shows up when you create a division formula with a divisor that refers to a blank cell. For example, suppose cell A1 contains the formula

=32/A2

As long as a numeric value other than zero appears in cell A2, Microsoft Excel can resolve the formula correctly. If A2 is blank or contains a label, however, Microsoft Excel can't resolve the formula. To correct the problem, you must either edit the formula or enter a value in cell A2.

The #NAME? error value indicates that you've entered in a formula a name that Microsoft Excel can't find in the Define Name dialog-box listing. If you see this error, check to see if you've mistyped the name reference or included a reference to a deleted name. You may also see this error value if you've neglected to place quotation marks around a text string. For example, suppose you've created the string formula

=My name is &A1

This formula is intended to combine the string *My name is* with the contents of cell A1. However, unless you enclose the literal string in quotation marks, Microsoft

Excel will treat it as a name and return the #NAME? error value. To correct the problem, enter the formula like this:

=″My name is ″&A1

You may also see the #NAME? error if you leave out the colon in a range reference. For example, when Microsoft Excel runs into such formulas as

=SUM(A1C4)

or

=SUM(A1.C4)

it tries to interpret the range reference as a name.

The #VALUE! error value usually means you've entered a mathematical formula that refers to a text entry. For example, if you enter the formula

=A1*A2

in your worksheet and cell A1 contains a text string, the formula returns the error value #VALUE!.

You'll see a #REF! error value if you use the Delete command to eliminate a range of cells whose references are included in a formula. For example, suppose you enter the formula

=A1+A2+A3

in cell A5 of your worksheet. If you then delete row 3 from the worksheet, the formula changes to

=A1+A2+#REF!

and cell A5 displays the value #REF!.

The #N/A error value indicates that no information is available for the calculation you want to perform. For example, you may see this value if you omit a required argument from a worksheet function. (More on functions in Chapter 6.)

Like #N/A, the #NUM! error value often indicates that you've provided an invalid argument to a worksheet function. For example, if you use a negative argument in a SQRT function, you'll receive a #NUM! error value. The #NUM! value may also appear if you create a formula that results in a number too large or too small to be represented in the worksheet.

The last, and least common, error value is #NULL!. This value often appears when you enter a formula in the form

=SUM(A1:C1 A6:F6)

The blank space between the two sets of references tells Microsoft Excel to find the value of the cell at the intersection of the range A1:C1 and A6:F6. Because these two ranges have no common cells, Microsoft Excel returns the #NULL! error value.

Calculating the worksheet

As you've already seen, you can enter formulas into your worksheet that refer to other cells in the worksheet. When you change the values in the cells that these formulas refer to, Microsoft Excel updates the values of the formulas as well. This process of updating is called calculation or recalculation. (Because Microsoft Excel uses the underlying values in cells, not their displayed values, when it performs calculations, you can format a cell without affecting the calculation.)

In many spreadsheet programs, the entire worksheet is recalculated every time you make a cell entry. This can be quite time-consuming and frustrating, particularly when you're making minor editing changes in a large spreadsheet. Microsoft Excel, on the other hand, performs "smart recalculation." That is, when you add or edit a cell in Microsoft Excel, only those cells affected by the entry are recalculated. For example, if you enter the formula

    =A1*B2

in cell C1 of your worksheet and then make a change to cell A1, Microsoft Excel automatically recalculates cell C1, but not the remaining cells in your worksheet. However, if other formulas in the worksheet refer to cell A1 or to cell C1, then those cells—and only those cells—are also recalculated.

Manual recalculation

When you're working with a large worksheet containing many interdependent formulas, or with charts, Microsoft Excel may need several seconds to recalculate your worksheet and redraw any open charts. To save time, you may prefer to change the method of recalculation to Manual while you enter data. With calculation set to Manual, you can enter values and formulas in your worksheet or work on charts without waiting for Microsoft Excel to recalculate dependent cells after each entry.

To set calculation to Manual, choose Calculation from the Options menu. Microsoft Excel will display a dialog box like the one in Figure 2-18. Next, select the Manual option in the dialog box; then select OK or press Enter.

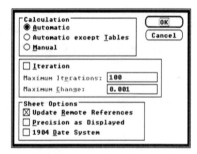

FIGURE 2-18. *The Calculation dialog box controls worksheet calculation and iteration.*

When you're ready to see the effects of your cell entries, simply choose Calculate Now from the Options menu or press Ctrl-=. When you choose this command, Microsoft Excel calculates all the cells in the worksheet that are affected by the changes you've made since you last recalculated and then updates all open charts. If you want Microsoft Excel to calculate only the active worksheet, hold down Shift while you select the Options menu. The Calculate Now command will then appear as Calculate Document.

While Microsoft Excel is calculating the worksheet, you can continue to choose commands or enter numbers or formulas. The program will halt the calculation long enough to do what you ask and will then resume.

You can also tell Microsoft Excel to automatically recalculate all the cells in your worksheet except for your data tables by selecting Automatic except Tables in the Calculation dialog box. We'll talk more about data tables in Chapter 8.

The order of recalculation

When Microsoft Excel recalculates a group of cells, it starts with the most basic cell in the group—the cell that must be calculated first if the others are to be recalculated properly—and then moves to the next most basic cell, and so on until all the cells in the group have been recalculated. The order of recalculation resembles an inverted pyramid, with the most fundamental cells on the bottom and a hierarchy of dependent cells above.

Unlike some spreadsheet programs, Microsoft Excel does not allow you to change the order of recalculation. However, because natural recalculation is by far the preferred order, you probably won't miss this capability.

Changing formulas to values

You can also use the Calculate Now command to change one or more of the cell references in your formulas into values. For example, suppose A6 in your worksheet contains the formula

=A1+A2+A3

Cell A1 contains the value 100, cell A2 contains the value 200, and cell A3 contains the value 300. If you drag across the cell reference A1 in this formula with the mouse and choose Calculate Now from the Options menu (or press Ctrl-=), Microsoft Excel converts the formula to

=100+A2+A3

If you select the entire formula or activate the formula bar without making any selection and then choose the Calculate Now command, Microsoft Excel computes the sum of the values and displays 600, with no equal sign, in the formula bar.

You can then select the Enter box or press Enter to lock in the change. Keep in mind, however, that unless you immediately choose Undo Entry from the Edit menu, you can't retrieve the original cell references after you lock in the entry. This means, in this example, that after you change the cell references to values with Calculate Now, the formula in cell A6 is no longer linked to the values in the range A1:A3.

Circular references

Circular references occur when a formula depends, either directly or indirectly, on its own cell. When this happens, Microsoft Excel cannot resolve the formula in either cell correctly. The most obvious type of circular reference occurs when you create a formula in a cell that contains a reference to that same cell.

For example, if you enter a formula like

=C1–A1

in cell A1 of your worksheet, Microsoft Excel displays an alert box with the message *Can't resolve circular references*. When you select OK or press Enter to acknowledge the error, the formula returns the value 0.

Why can't Microsoft Excel solve this formula? Because each time it arrives at a value for the formula in cell A1, the value of cell A1 changes. When it evaluates the formula in A1 using the new value in A1, the value in cell A1 changes again. Obviously, the program could continue to go around this circle forever.

Unlike the previous example, many circular references can be resolved. For example, look at the simple series of formulas in the worksheet in Figure 2-19. This worksheet has been formatted to display the underlying formulas in each cell. As you can see, cell A1 contains the formula

=A2+A3

cell A2 contains the value 1000, and cell A3 contains the formula

=0.5*A1

This set of formulas is circular because the formula in A1 depends on the value in A3, and the formula in A3 depends on the value in A1. In fact, Microsoft Excel identifies the first circular reference it finds in the status bar at the bottom of the screen: Circular: A3. (The program won't identify subsequent circular references until you fix the first one.)

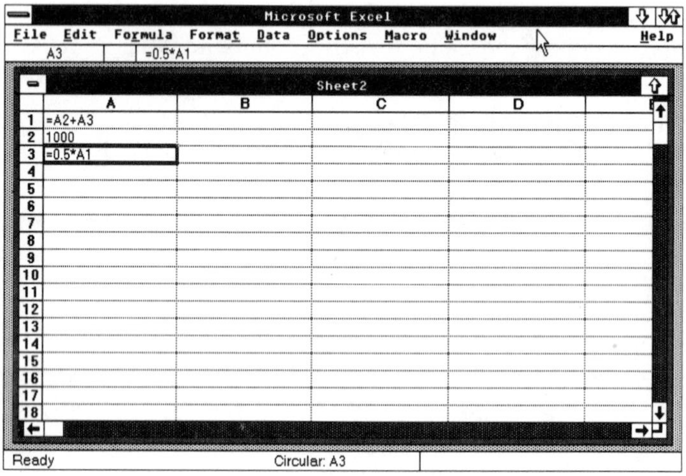

FIGURE 2-19. *This worksheet contains a circular reference.*

You can use the Iteration option in the Calculation dialog box to resolve this kind of circular reference. When Iteration is selected, Microsoft Excel recalculates the cells in all open worksheets that contain a circular reference a specified number of times. Each time the formulas are recalculated, the results in each cell get closer and closer to the correct values.

To resolve the circular reference in our example, select OK in the *Can't resolve circular references* alert box or press Enter; then choose Calculation from the Options menu. Next, select the Manual and Iteration boxes in the Calculation dialog box and select OK or press Enter.

When you select the Iteration option in the Calculation dialog box, Microsoft Excel sets the Maximum Iterations option to 100 and the Maximum Change option to 0.001. These settings tell Microsoft Excel to recalculate the cells involved in the circular reference up to 100 times or until the values in these cells change less than 0.001 between iterations, whichever comes first. Microsoft Excel lets you set Maximum Iterations as high as 32,765! You'll probably find that the default 100 iterations is enough to resolve most intentional circular references in your worksheet, however. Similarly, you can set Maximum Change to any number greater than zero, although the 0.001 default is adequate in most cases.

Begin the calculation by selecting Calculate Now from the Options menu. Table 2-1 shows how the values in cells A1 and A3 in our example from Figure 2-19 change as Microsoft Excel recalculates the circular reference. Notice that the values change less with each iteration as Microsoft Excel closes in on the correct answer. The final results in cells A1 and A3 are very close to correct—999.999 is almost exactly half of 1999.999. The recalculation stops after 21 iterations because the change in the values in cells A1 and A3 in that iteration is less than 0.001.

Table 2-1. Resolution of the circular references in cells A1 and A3 by convergence.

Iteration number	A1	A3
0	(=A2+A3)	(=0.5*A1)
1	1000	0
2	1500	500
3	1750	750
4	1875	875
5	1937.5	937.5
6	1968.75	968.75
7	1984.375	984.375
8	1992.188	992.188
9	1996.094	996.094
10	1998.047	998.047
11	1999.023	999.023
12	1999.512	999.512
13	1999.756	999.756
14	1999.878	999.878
15	1999.939	999.939
16	1999.969	999.969
17	1999.985	999.985
18	1999.992	999.992
19	1999.996	999.996
20	1999.998	999.998
21	1999.999	999.999

Unfortunately, Microsoft Excel does not repeat the *Cannot resolve circular reference* message if it fails to resolve the circular reference within the specified number of iterations. Instead, it displays the values of the formulas as of the last iteration. You must rely on your common sense to determine whether the value produced by Microsoft Excel is really the answer you're looking for.

The process we just described is called convergence, meaning that the difference between results becomes smaller with each iterative calculation. Sometimes circular references are resolved through a process called divergence, meaning that the difference between results becomes larger, rather than smaller, with each iterative calculation. In this case, Microsoft Excel ignores your Maximum Change setting and continues its calculations until it completes the maximum number of calculations you specify in the Calculation dialog box.

Microsoft Excel's ability to perform smart recalculation is a real timesaver when it comes to using the Iteration option. Because only those cells needed to resolve the circular reference are recalculated, Microsoft Excel can perform 100 iterations in a matter of seconds. However, when you're using iterative calculation, be sure the Calculation option is set to Manual or Microsoft Excel will attempt to recalculate the circular references every time you press the Enter key.

Although you occasionally will build circular references into your worksheet intentionally, Microsoft Excel's circular-reference warning usually indicates that you've made an error in one of your formulas. Sometimes it takes a little detective work to track down these errors.

To correct the problem, first select OK in the alert box or press Enter; then look back at the formula you just entered. Did you inadvertently include the formula cell in your calculation? When you're calculating the sum of a series of values, it's easy to select one cell too many and inadvertently include the total cell itself in the formula. This kind of error is easy to correct: You simply edit the formula to remove the formula cell reference.

If the circular reference is not immediately obvious, check the cells referenced in the formula. Do those cells contain references to the formula cell itself? As you've already seen, this type of circular reference is impossible to resolve, no matter how many iterations you specify.

Precision of numeric values

Microsoft Excel stores numbers with as much as 15-digit accuracy. If you enter an integer longer than 15 digits, Microsoft Excel converts any digits after the fifteenth to zeros. If you enter a decimal fraction longer than 15 digits, Microsoft Excel drops any digits after the fifteenth. In addition, as you saw earlier in this chapter, Microsoft Excel displays numbers that are too long for their cells in scientific notation.

Thus, if you enter a number like 123456789123456789 in a cell, Microsoft Excel displays that number as 1.23E+17 but retains only the first 15 digits of the number in the cell. The remaining digits are converted to zeros without rounding, like this: 123456789123456000.

Here are several other examples of how Microsoft Excel treats integers and decimal fractions longer than 15 digits when they are entered into cells with the default column width of 8.43 characters:

Entry	Displayed value	Underlying value
123456789012345678	1.23E+17	123456789012345000
1.23456789012345678	1.2345678	1.23456789012345
1234567890.12345678	1.23E+09	1234567890.12345
123456789012345.678	1.23E+14	123456789012345

Notice that each of the displayed values in the table is 8 characters wide, to fit the standard column width in your Microsoft Excel worksheet. If you change the column width (using the Column Width command, described in Chapter 4), Microsoft Excel will change the displayed value to fill the width of the cell. Keep in mind that the column width affects only the displayed value of numbers on your worksheet; it has no effect on precision. In other words, Microsoft Excel still stores and calculates numbers with as much as 15-digit accuracy, no matter what the displayed value.

Microsoft Excel is able to calculate positive values as large as 1.798E+305 and as small as 2.225E–307. If you create a formula that results in a value outside this range, Microsoft Excel stores the number as text and assigns a #NUM! error value to the formula cell. We doubt you'll ever have to worry about these limitations in a typical Microsoft Excel worksheet, however.

With 15-digit accuracy and the ability to use numbers in the zillions, you should be able to perform almost any kind of calculation in your Microsoft Excel worksheets. In fact, you'll generally want to use numbers less precisely than Microsoft Excel's standards. For example, when you're performing financial calculations, you'll probably want to round numbers to two decimal places. In Chapter 3, we'll show you how to format the cells in your worksheet to display currency, percentages, fixed decimal places, and other numeric formats.

Memory management

Microsoft Excel uses a highly variable amount of RAM, depending on such factors as the size of your computer's memory and the number and content of all the worksheets open during the session. "Desk accessories" also affect memory use. When you add to the equation the memory devoted to the resident portion of your system software, you have only about 100 KB left to work with. If memory becomes tight during a session with Microsoft Excel, the program can run without having all of itself loaded into memory, exchanging sections of the program on disk with those in memory as needed. This is called dynamic memory management.

You can determine the amount of memory free at any time by choosing the About command from the Help menu. The percentage of memory that is free appears at the bottom of the Help box, below the copyright information.

When free space becomes scarce, certain signs warn you to take steps to conserve memory: The amount of free memory shown in the About dialog box gets low, the speed of recalculation seems to slow considerably (signifying that Microsoft Excel is frequently swapping program sections in cramped space), or you get an alert box warning you that Microsoft Excel is out of memory.

Although the amount of available memory is adequate for most of the worksheets you're likely to create, you should know a few things about how Microsoft Excel uses memory, so that you can get the most out of the space available to you.

Every entry you make in your Microsoft Excel worksheet uses memory; however, all entries are not created equal—some require more memory than others. For example, integer values use less memory than floating-point values. Text values require 1 byte per character. For example, the entry *This is a text string* would require 21 bytes (blank spaces count). Formulas require more memory than simple numeric values. Although the number of bytes used depends on the length and complexity of the formula, you can roughly estimate about 20 bytes for every formula in your worksheet.

The windows you use to view different areas of the worksheet use memory. If you find yourself running out of memory, you might close a few windows and use the scroll bars to move around the worksheet.

When you're working with a large worksheet, you should make it a point to keep track of the amount of memory available. If it gets low, you should start looking for ways to trim down the file before you make any more additions. (After checking the amount of free memory, simply select the OK button to get back to your worksheet.)

The active rectangle

If your worksheet is consuming more memory than you expected, press Ctrl-End. This instructs Microsoft Excel to go to the lower right cell in the active portion of your worksheet so that you can determine the size of the worksheet.

The active portion of the worksheet is a rectangle that includes every cell that contains an entry, has been assigned a format, or is referred to by a cell reference. The active rectangle always begins at cell A1 and ends with the last cell in your worksheet. For example, suppose you make a simple numeric entry in cell C12 of an otherwise empty, unformatted worksheet. The active rectangle in this worksheet is now A1:C12; when you press Ctrl-End, Microsoft Excel jumps to cell C12.

Here's the problem: Microsoft Excel always allocates at least 6 bytes of memory to each of the cells in the active rectangle, even if some of those cells do not contain entries. Thus, your single entry in cell C12 consumes over 200 bytes of memory: 20 or so bytes for the entry in cell C12 and 6 bytes each for all the cells in the active worksheet, even when these cells are empty. Although it may seem a waste to allocate memory to empty cells, that's the way it works. In effect, these empty cells become "holding cells" in your worksheet.

To complicate matters, the last cell in the active rectangle won't necessarily contain a cell entry or format. For example, suppose you make entries in cells B20 and Z1 of your worksheet. The active rectangle would extend from cell A1 to cell Z20 (the intersection of row 20, which contains the bottom entry in the worksheet, and column Z, which contains the rightmost entry). Although you have only two cell entries in your worksheet, Microsoft Excel allocates 6 bytes to each cell in the 20-row by 26-column active rectangle. Rather than 12 bytes, these two entries take more than 3000 bytes!

One more warning: When you refer to a cell in a formula, Microsoft Excel expands the active rectangle to include that cell. This should not be a problem, because you don't typically refer to cells that don't contain entries. However, a simple typographical error can boost your memory consumption considerably.

Recovering memory

Because every cell in the active rectangle consumes memory, you can generally save memory by keeping the active rectangle as small as possible—that is, by keeping your entries to the upper left corner of the worksheet. If you find that your cell entries are unnecessarily spread out, you can delete a few rows or columns or cut and paste some entries to reduce the size of the active rectangle.

You can also reduce the amount of memory Microsoft Excel uses by keeping a minimum number of documents open, using fewer fonts, and breaking your worksheet into smaller worksheets and linking them together. Changing several repetitive formulas into array formulas (explained in Chapter 8) also conserves memory.

Another waste of memory is formatting cells that lie below or to the right of the last real entry in the worksheet. Microsoft Excel always expands the active rectangle to include such formatted cells. Because these cells usually don't serve any purpose, you can save memory by selecting them, choosing the Clear command from the Edit menu, and selecting the Format or All option in the Clear dialog box.

Empty formatted cells can be difficult to track down. Unless you've placed a border around the cells, there is no visible indication that they've been formatted. Your best bet is to simply select all the empty cells in the rows and columns outside the area you're really working with and choose the Clear command. If the selected cells weren't formatted, the command will have no effect; if they were, you may recover some memory.

Unfortunately, you may not realize any immediate memory savings by clearing or deleting cells. Here's why: As you build a worksheet, Microsoft Excel builds a dependency list that keeps track of all the cells in the active rectangle. This dependency list grows with every addition to your worksheet. It tells Microsoft Excel which cells are affected when you make a new entry, edit an existing one, or move and copy cells. Microsoft Excel does not eliminate erased or deleted cells from the dependency list until you save the worksheet. For this reason, you won't realize any memory savings from deleting cells until you save your changes to disk, close the document, and then reopen it.

If you're a new Microsoft Excel user, the techniques we've just discussed may seem more complex than they really are, but they'll become second nature as we work our way through the book.

3

Formatting the Worksheet

*I*n Chapter 2, you learned to make entries in the worksheet. You may have noticed that all the entries you've made so far have the same format: All numbers (and the numeric results of formulas) are right-aligned and carry what is called the General format; all labels are left-aligned. In this chapter, you'll learn to use the Format menu commands to change the formats, alignments, and fonts of text and numeric cell entries. You'll also learn to use borders and to change column widths and row heights. (We'll save the Format menu's Justify and Cell Protection commands for Chapters 4 and 8.) Finally, you'll learn how to change the overall appearance of the worksheet window and workspace with the Display and Workspace commands on the Options menu.

Why use formats?

Formatting your worksheets gives them a professional appearance and makes them easier to read and use. Look at the unformatted worksheet in Figure 3-1. Although this worksheet provides much valuable information, the data is difficult to interpret. The reader has few visual clues about what is being presented. Important totals and key headings blend into the background, many columns appear to be misaligned, and some entries are truncated.

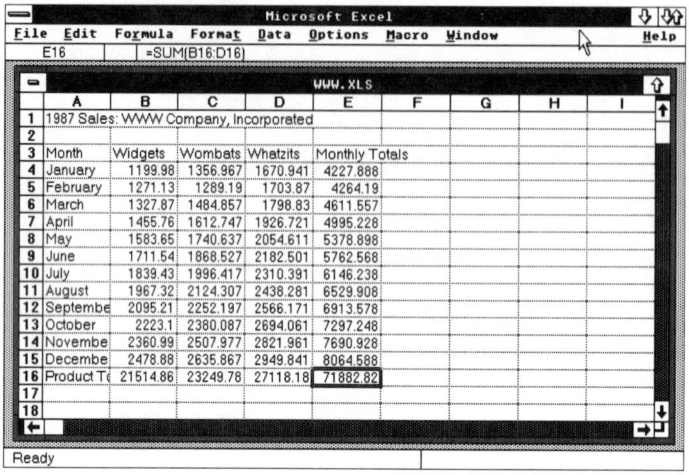

	A	B	C	D	E
1	1987 Sales: WWW Company, Incorporated				
2					
3	Month	Widgets	Wombats	Whatzits	Monthly Totals
4	January	1199.98	1356.967	1670.941	4227.888
5	February	1271.13	1289.19	1703.87	4264.19
6	March	1327.87	1484.857	1798.83	4611.557
7	April	1455.76	1612.747	1926.721	4995.228
8	May	1583.65	1740.637	2054.611	5378.898
9	June	1711.54	1868.527	2182.501	5762.568
10	July	1839.43	1996.417	2310.391	6146.238
11	August	1967.32	2124.307	2438.281	6529.908
12	Septembe	2095.21	2252.197	2566.171	6913.578
13	October	2223.1	2380.087	2694.061	7297.248
14	Novembe	2360.99	2507.977	2821.961	7690.928
15	Decembe	2478.88	2635.867	2949.841	8064.588
16	Product T	21514.86	23249.78	27118.18	71882.82
17					
18					

FIGURE 3-1. *All entries in this worksheet carry Microsoft Excel's default formats.*

Now look at the formatted worksheet in Figure 3-2. The contents of this worksheet are identical to those of the worksheet in Figure 3-1, but the newer worksheet looks better and is easier to read.

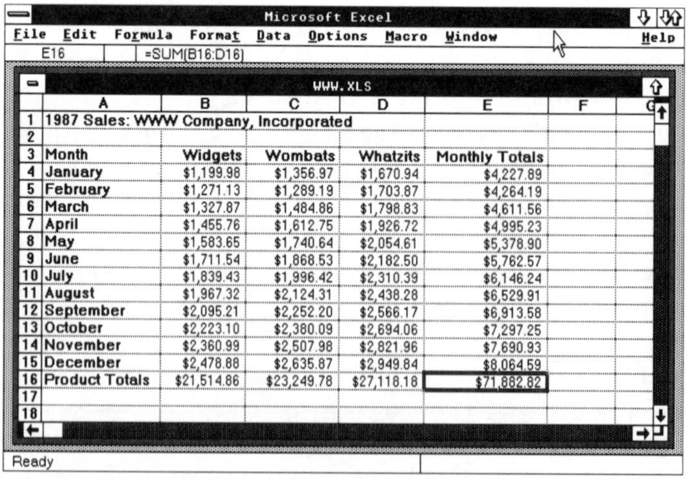

	A	B	C	D	E
1	**1987 Sales: WWW Company, Incorporated**				
2					
3	**Month**	**Widgets**	**Wombats**	**Whatzits**	**Monthly Totals**
4	**January**	$1,199.98	$1,356.97	$1,670.94	$4,227.89
5	**February**	$1,271.13	$1,289.19	$1,703.87	$4,264.19
6	**March**	$1,327.87	$1,484.86	$1,798.83	$4,611.56
7	**April**	$1,455.76	$1,612.75	$1,926.72	$4,995.23
8	**May**	$1,583.65	$1,740.64	$2,054.61	$5,378.90
9	**June**	$1,711.54	$1,868.53	$2,182.50	$5,762.57
10	**July**	$1,839.43	$1,996.42	$2,310.39	$6,146.24
11	**August**	$1,967.32	$2,124.31	$2,438.28	$6,529.91
12	**September**	$2,095.21	$2,252.20	$2,566.17	$6,913.58
13	**October**	$2,223.10	$2,380.09	$2,694.06	$7,297.25
14	**November**	$2,360.99	$2,507.98	$2,821.96	$7,690.93
15	**December**	$2,478.88	$2,635.87	$2,949.84	$8,064.59
16	**Product Totals**	$21,514.86	$23,249.78	$27,118.18	$71,882.82
17					
18					

FIGURE 3-2. *The worksheet is much easier to read after formatting.*

Assigning and removing formats

Formatting is easy: Simply select the cell or range you want to format and choose the appropriate Format menu commands. You can select a single cell, a block range of cells, a discontinuous range of cells, a named range of cells, an entire column or row, or the entire worksheet. You can even assign a format to cells that do not yet contain entries, although your actions may not have any visible effect until you make entries in those cells.

For example, to add a dollar sign and commas to the values in cells B4:E16 in Figure 3-1 and round each value to two decimal places, simply select cells B4:E16, choose Number from the Format menu, and choose the $#,##0.00 ;($#,##0.00) option from the Format Number dialog box. As you can see in Figure 3-2, Microsoft Excel changes the numbers in those cells to display currency values. (Notice that values with more than two numbers to the right of the decimal point are rounded to two places. We'll discuss this in a few pages.)

After you format a cell, that cell remains formatted until you apply a new format or issue the Clear command to remove its formats. When you overwrite or edit an entry, you need not reformat that cell.

To remove all assigned formats, select the cell or range of cells whose formats you want to delete and then press the Del key or choose Clear from the Edit menu. When the Clear dialog box appears, select the Formats option to return the selected cells to their default formats. The *values* in the cells will not change unless

E X C E L

Format before you paste!

When you copy a cell entry, you copy both the contents and the formats assigned to that cell. If the cell you're pasting into is already formatted, the formatting of the cell you're copying replaces the old formatting. You can take advantage of this fact by formatting your source cell before you choose the Copy and Paste commands, the Fill command, or the Series command. For example, suppose you've entered 123 in cell A1 of your worksheet. You want to format this cell to display currency with no decimal place, and you also need to copy this value to several other cells. Be sure you assign the special format before you use the Copy and Paste commands. Then, when you copy cell A1, the pasted cells will assume identical formats. (We'll talk more about the Cut, Copy, Paste, Fill, and Series commands in Chapter 4.)

you select All from the Clear dialog box to erase both the contents of the cells and the assigned formats. (If you choose Formulas, all values and formulas are removed but the formatting remains unchanged. We'll look more closely at the Clear command in Chapter 4.)

The Number command

The Number command on the Format menu controls the display of numeric values. When you select this command, you'll see a dialog box like the one in Figure 3-3. This box contains a list of 21 built-in numeric formats. You can use these formats to display numbers and formula results as integers, currency, percentages, dates, times, or exponents.

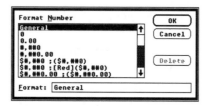

FIGURE 3-3. *Microsoft Excel offers 21 built-in numeric formats.*

We'll look at 10 built-in numeric formats in this chapter: General, 0, 0.00, #,##0, #,##0.00, $#,##0;($#,##0), $#,##0.00;($#,##0.00), 0%, 0.00%, and 0.00E+00. (Two additional numeric formats, $#,##0;[Red]($#,##0) and $#,##0.00;[Red]($#,##0.00), are identical to the formats that precede them in the list, except that negative values are displayed on the screen in red. The remaining built-in formats apply only to date and time values, which we'll cover in Chapter 7.) We'll also show you how to design your own numeric and text formats and how to change the color of cell entries with the Number command.

Before we proceed, it is important that you understand the difference between underlying and displayed worksheet values. Numeric formats do not affect the underlying values in your cells. For example, when we assigned the currency format to cells B4:E16 in Figure 3-2, we did not change the underlying values in those cells. Even though cell C4, which contains the number 1356.967, appears as $1,356.97, Microsoft Excel still uses the underlying value, 1356.967, in its calculations.

Also, remember that the Number command's built-in numeric formats do not affect labels. If you're working with a range that contains both text and numbers, you can assign a numeric format to that range without affecting your text entries. But if you overwrite a text entry with a number or with a formula that results in a numeric value, the number will take on the format you originally assigned.

(As you'll see in a few pages, you can work with text when you create your own custom formats.)

The General format

Until you specifically change the format of a cell, any numbers you enter in that cell appear in the General numeric format. Think of the General format as the "what you see is what is really there" format. In other words, the General format usually shows you exactly what you've entered in a cell. If you enter the number 123.45 in a cell with the General format, that cell displays the number 123.45; if you enter the number –654.3, the cell displays the number –654.3.

This rule has one exception: If a number is too long to be displayed in its entirety, the General format displays the number in scientific notation or displays only a portion of the number, depending on the type of number and the cell width. In a standard-width cell, integers (numbers with no decimals) with nine or more digits appear in scientific notation. For example, if you enter 12345678901234, the General format displays it as 1.23E+13. Long decimal values, however, are either rounded or displayed in scientific notation, depending on cell width. For example, if you enter 123456.7812345 in a standard-width cell, the General format displays the number as 123456.8.

The integer, fixed, and punctuated formats

The next four options in the Number dialog box are 0, 0.00, #,##0, and #,##0.00. These options let you display numbers in integer, fixed-decimal, and punctuated format.

The 0 format displays numbers as integers. For example, if you enter the number 1234.567 in a cell and then assign the 0 format to that cell, Microsoft Excel rounds the displayed value to 1235.

The 0.00 format displays numbers with two decimal places. If you enter 1234.567 in a cell that has the 0.00 format, the value appears as 1234.57. Notice that the number is rounded to two decimal places. If the number being formatted has only one decimal place, Microsoft Excel adds a zero to the number for display purposes. For example, 1234.5 appears as 1234.50. If the number is an integer, Microsoft Excel adds a decimal point and two trailing zeros.

The #,##0 and #,##0.00 formats are similar to the 0 and 0.00 formats except that they display numbers with commas between the hundreds and thousands, thousands and millions, and so on. For example, 1234.567 appears as 1,235 under the #,##0 format and as 1,234.57 under the #,##0.00 format. Like the 0.00 format, the #,##0.00 format adds zeros to the number, if necessary, to achieve the requested appearance. This ensures that all decimal points align properly in the columns of your worksheet.

The currency formats

Two built-in currency formats are available in Microsoft Excel: $#,##0 ;($#,##0) and $#,##0.00 ;($#,##0.00). These formats are identical except that the first displays the number with no decimal places and the second displays the number with two decimal places. Both formats cause Microsoft Excel to place a dollar sign in front of the formatted number and to use commas to separate hundreds from thousands, thousands from millions, and so on.

The currency formats have two parts, separated by a semicolon. The first part of each format applies to positive numbers, the second to negative numbers. Both currency formats tell Microsoft Excel to enclose negative numbers in parentheses. For example, if you enter 1245.22 in a cell that carries the $#,##0.00 ;($#,##0.00) format, Microsoft Excel displays the value $1,245.22; if you enter –1245.22, Microsoft Excel displays ($1,245.22).

Notice that one blank space appears after the positive-value portion of the currency format. This blank space ensures that the positive and negative values in your worksheet columns align evenly. Without this extra blank space, the closing parenthesis that marks the end of a negative value would throw your columns out of alignment.

The percentage formats

The next two choices in the Format Number dialog box, 0% and 0.00%, display numbers as percentages. When you select one of the percentage formats, the decimal point of the formatted number shifts two places to the right and a percent sign (%) appears at the end of the number. For example, 0.1234 appears as 12% under the 0% format and as 12.34% under the 0.00% format.

The scientific (exponential) format

The next option in the Format Number dialog box, 0.00E+00, displays numbers in scientific, or exponential, notation with two decimal places. For example, the exponential format displays the number 987654321 as 9.88E+08.

If you're not familiar with exponential notation, this number may be confusing. However, it's quite simple. The number 9.88E+08 can be read *9.88 times 10 to the eighth power*. The symbol *E* stands for the word *exponent*, a synonym here for the words *10 to the nth power*. The expression *10 to the eighth power* means eight 10s multiplied together ($10 \times 10 \times 10 \times 10 \times 10 \times 10 \times 10 \times 10$), or 100,000,000. Multiplying this value by 9.88 gives 988000000, an approximation of our original number.

You can also use exponential format to display very small numbers. For example, 0.000000009 can be displayed as 9.00E–09, which can be read *9 times 10 to the negative ninth power*. This time, the expression *10 to the negative ninth power* means 1 divided by 10 to the ninth power, or 1 divided by 10 nine times, or 0.000000001. Multiplying this number by 9 gives our original number, 0.000000009.

Typing cell entries in a numeric format

Often, you can kill two birds with one stone by entering numbers exactly as you want them to appear. If you include special formatting characters such as dollar signs, percent signs, or commas when you enter a number in a cell, Microsoft Excel assigns the appropriate numeric format to that cell. For example, if you type *$45.00*, Microsoft Excel interprets your entry as the value 45 formatted as currency with two decimal places—$#,##0.00 ;($#,##0.00). Only the value 45 appears in the formula bar, but the formatted value is displayed in the cell.

Because you format the cell when you type a "preformatted" number, any new entry you make in that cell will be formatted in the same way. This can lead to some confusion. For example, suppose you enter the preformatted value $20.00 in an unformatted cell of your worksheet. Later, you select the same cell and type over your original entry with the new preformatted value 10%. Microsoft Excel immediately changes your display to $0.10. Although the correct value (0.1) appears in the formula bar, your entry appears as currency. To change the format to percentage, you must choose the Number command. (In other words, you can enter preformatted numbers only in cells that have not previously been formatted.)

Sometimes Microsoft Excel has to guess which format you want. If, for example, you enter the number $4444 in a cell, the program assigns the $#,##0 ;(#,##0) format to that cell, even though the number you typed lacks a comma. If you enter the number 4,444.4 in a cell, however, Microsoft Excel assigns the General format to that cell, because no additional characters (such as $ or %) tell it otherwise.

When you're working with only a few cells, it may be more efficient to type your entries "in format" than to enter the numbers and then choose the Number command. If you're working with more than two or three cells, however, you save keystrokes and avoid typing errors by using the Number command. In general, it's better to let Microsoft Excel do the work for you so that you don't have to edit individual cells for omitted or misplaced formatting characters.

Creating your own numeric formats

Microsoft Excel lets you create custom display formats and save them along with your worksheets. The formats you design can be variations on the built-in formats or they can be radically different. You're free to create almost any format you wish. You can even format worksheet entries to appear in different colors! To create your own formats to add to the list in the Format Number dialog box, select from the symbols in Table 3-1.

Table 3-1. Symbols for creating custom display formats.

Symbol	Meaning
0	Digit placeholder. Adds extra zeros if the number has fewer digits on either side of the decimal point than there are zeros on that side of the decimal point in the format. Rounds the number to as many decimal places as there are zeros to the right if the number has more digits to the right of the decimal point than in the format. Displays the extra digits if the number has more digits to the left of the decimal point than in the format.
#	Digit placeholder. Follows the same rules as for 0 except extra zeros do not appear if the number has fewer digits on either side of the decimal point than there are #s on that side in the format.
.	Decimal point. Determines how many digits (0s or #s) to display to the right and left of the decimal point. If the format contains only #s to the left of this symbol, Microsoft Excel begins numbers smaller than 1 with a decimal point; to avoid this, use 0 as the first digit placeholder to the left of the decimal point instead of #.
%	Percentage indicator. Multiplies by 100 and inserts the % character.
,	Thousands separator. Uses commas to separate hundreds from thousands, thousands from millions, and so forth, if the format contains a comma surrounded by #s or 0s.
E– E+ e– e+	Scientific format characters. Display the number in scientific format and insert E or e in the displayed value if a format contains one 0 or # to the right of an E–, E+, e–, or e+. The number of 0s or #s to the right of the E or e determines the number of digits in the exponent. Use E– or e– to place a negative sign by negative exponents; use E+ or e+ to place a negative sign by negative exponents and a positive sign by positive exponents.
: $ – + ( ) space	Standard formatting characters. Enter these characters directly into your format. To display a character other than :, $, –, +, (,), or space, use a backslash (\) before the character or enclose the character in double quotation marks (".").
\	Literal character demarcator. Each character you want to include in the format (except for :, $, –, +, (,), and space) must be preceded by a backslash. The backslash is not displayed. To insert several characters, use the quotation-mark technique described below.
"Text"	Literal character string. Works like the backslash technique except that all text can be included within one set of quotation marks without separate demarcators for each literal character.
*	Repetition initiator. Repeats the next character in the format enough times to fill the column width. Only one asterisk can be used in a format.
@	Text placeholder. If the cell being formatted contains a label, includes that label at the spot where the @ appears in the format.

Editing existing formats

Often, you can use built-in formats as a starting point for creating your own formats. To build on an existing format, select the cells you want to format and choose the Number command. Select the format you want to change from the Format Number list box and then edit the contents of the Format edit bar just as you would edit a cell entry in the formula bar. The original format will not be affected by your changes. The new format is appended to the list of numeric formats in the Format Number dialog box.

For example, to create a format to display percentages with three decimal places, select the 0.00% format, place the insertion point between the last 0 and the % sign in the Format edit bar, and add another 0. Then choose OK or press Enter. Microsoft Excel will apply your new format to the selected range in your worksheet. When you choose the Number command again, your new format will appear at the end of the listing in the Format Number dialog box so that you can assign this custom format to other cells in the worksheet without having to re-create the format each time.

Building new formats from scratch

To create a new numeric format from scratch, select the cells you want to format and choose the Number command. Next, instead of selecting an option in the Format Number dialog box, select the contents of the Format edit bar at the bottom of the dialog box and type the format. As soon as you begin typing, the highlighted characters in the edit bar will disappear and the characters you type will appear. When you're done, choose OK or press Enter. The contents of the selected range will appear in the new format and your custom format will be appended to the list in the dialog box.

For example, suppose you're creating an inventory worksheet and you want all the entries in the range A5:A100 in the worksheet to appear in the format *Part XXX-XXXX*. To create this format, first select the range A5:A100 and choose the Number command. Next, instead of selecting one of the standard options, select the contents of the Format edit bar, type *"Part" 000-0000*, and choose OK or press Enter. Now begin making entries in column A. (You may have to widen the column.) Simply type the numbers for each part; Microsoft Excel will add the word *Part* and the hyphen. For example, if you select cell A10 and enter *1234567*, you'll see the entry displayed as Part 123-4567.

Similarly, to create a telephone number format for your worksheet, you might use the format *(000) 000-0000*. Then, when you enter *1234567890* into a cell having that format, Microsoft Excel will display the entry as (123) 456-7890.

Formatting positive, negative, zero, and text entries

When we discussed currency formats, we mentioned that Microsoft Excel assigns different formats to positive and negative currency values in your worksheet. You can also specify different formats for positive and negative values when you create custom formats, and you can specify how you want zero and text values to appear.

To do this, you need to create a four-part custom format with the portions separated by semicolons, like this:

Positive format;Negative format;Zero format;Label format

If your custom format includes only one part, Microsoft Excel applies that format to positive, negative, and zero values. If your custom format includes two parts, the first format applies to positive and zero values; the second format applies only to negative values. Unless you explicitly include label formatting in your custom format, your instructions will have no effect on the labels in cells that use your custom format. Label formatting instructions must always be the last format in your list.

For example, suppose you're creating a billing statement worksheet and you want to format the entries in the Amount Due column to display different text, depending on the value in each cell. You might create a format like this:

"Amount Due: "$#,##0.00 ;"Credit: "($#,##0.00);"Let's call it even.";"Please Note: "@

The table below shows the effects of this format on various worksheet entries:

Entry	Display
12.98	Amount due: $12.98
-12.98	Credit: ($12.98)
0	Let's call it even.
This is not a bill.	Please Note: This is not a bill.

If you want to specify a custom label format without changing the formats for your positive, negative, and zero values, simply enter the label argument portion of the custom format alone. The @ symbol alerts Microsoft Excel that the format applies only to labels.

Adding color to your formats

In addition to controlling the display of numeric values, the Number command can change the color of selected cell entries. Microsoft Excel gives you eight color options: red, green, blue, yellow, magenta, cyan, black, and white. This color capability gives you tremendous flexibility for emphasizing selected areas of your worksheet. For example, you might use different colors to help distinguish the categories of information in a worksheet model, or you might apply a color to the Total cells to make them stand out from the rest of your worksheet data.

To change the color of an entry, simply type the name of the color you want, in brackets, in front of the definition of the format. For example, suppose you want the totals in row 16 of the worksheet shown in Figure 3-2 to appear in blue. Because you also want these values to appear in currency format with two decimal places, you can simply edit Microsoft Excel's built-in $#,##0.00 ;($#,##0.00) format to create a custom format, like this:

[Blue]$#,##0.00 ;($#,##0.00)

This format tells Microsoft Excel to display positive and zero values in blue. Text and negative values still appear in the program's default color, black.

Even if you want to use Microsoft Excel's default General format to display your worksheet entries, you can specify color options for different types of entries by typing the colors you want to use in the Format edit bar. For example, the custom format

[Blue];[Red];[Yellow];[Green]

tells Microsoft Excel to display positive values in blue, negative values in red, zero values in yellow, and labels in green. Of course, you can add color to your custom formats as well.

E X C E L

Using formatting templates

Although your custom formats are saved along with your worksheet, they do not carry over from one file to another unless you explicitly copy or cut and paste them between worksheets. One way around this problem is to create a blank worksheet template that contains all the special formats you want to use. Each time you want to create a worksheet that uses these formats, open the template file and use the Save As command to save the template under a different name. By saving the template under a different name before making worksheet entries, you preserve the original template for later use.

You can also use this technique to create template worksheets with different "default" Font, Alignment, Column Width, and Display settings. Simply apply the formats you want to use and save them in the empty worksheet template file.

Deleting custom formats

To delete a format from the Number dialog box, simply select the format you want to erase and then select the Delete button. You can delete only those formats you have created; you cannot delete any of the 21 built-in selections.

The Alignment command

The Alignment command controls the positioning of cell entries. You can also use this command to repeat a series of characters within one or more cells. As you can see in Figure 3-4, Microsoft Excel offers five cell-alignment options: General, Left, Center, Right, and Fill.

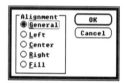

FIGURE 3-4. *Microsoft Excel offers five alignment options.*

General is the default alignment option. When you use the General format, cells that contain numeric values are always right-aligned and cells that contain labels are always left-aligned.

The Left, Right, and Center options

The Left, Right, and Center options do exactly what they say: They cause the contents of the selected cells to be aligned to the left side, the right side, or the center of the cell. For example, look at the entries in the worksheet in Figure 3-5. The entries in cells B3 and C3 have the General alignment. Therefore, the number in cell B3 is right-aligned and the label in cell C3 is left-aligned. The entries in cells B4:C4 are left-aligned, those in B5:C5 are right-aligned, and those in B6:C6 are centered.

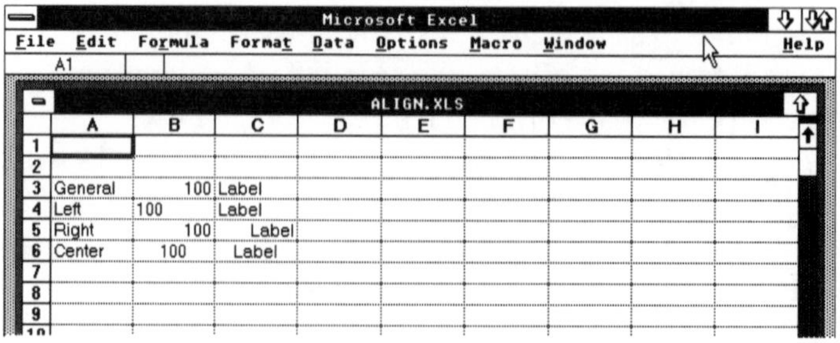

▬				Microsoft Excel					⇩ ⟪⟫
File	Edit	Formula	Format	Data	Options	Macro	Window		Help
A1									

▭				ALIGN.XLS					⇧
	A	B	C	D	E	F	G	H	I
1									
2									
3	General	100	Label						
4	Left	100	Label						
5	Right	100	Label						
6	Center	100	Label						
7									
8									
9									

FIGURE 3-5. *Use the Alignment command to change the alignment of cell entries.*

The Alignment command has some interesting effects on labels that extend beyond the cell borders. As you know, unless an adjacent cell contains an entry that causes your long label to be truncated, Microsoft Excel will allow that label to extend past the cell border and flow into adjacent columns. Thus, when you use the Left and Right alignment options, your long labels may extend past the right and left edges of the cell border, respectively. Similarly, when you use the Center option, your entry may extend past both edges of the cell border.

The Fill option

The Fill option repeats your cell entry to fill the width of the column. For example, suppose cell A8 of your worksheet contains a formula that totals the entries in cells A1 through A6. You want to enter a row of hyphens in cell A7 to separate the values in cells A1:A6 from the total in cell A8. To do this, enter a single hyphen in cell A7 and then choose the Alignment command. When you select the Fill option in the Alignment dialog box and choose OK, Microsoft Excel will repeat the hyphen across cell A7, as shown in Figure 3-6.

E X C E L *Tip*

The "hidden" format

If you want to ensure that certain sets of values do not appear in your worksheet, you can "hide" these values by assigning them a null format. To create a null format, enter only the semicolon separator for that portion of the format, with no other formatting symbols. For example, if you want positive and text values to appear in your worksheet but you want to hide negative and zero values, you might use a format like this:

$#,##0.00;;

This format tells Microsoft Excel to display positive numbers in the currency format. The two semicolons instruct the program to hide negative and zero values. Because we did not include a third semicolon separator for text entries, Microsoft Excel will display those entries.

To hide all the entries in a cell, create a custom format that consists only of three semicolons, like this:

;;;

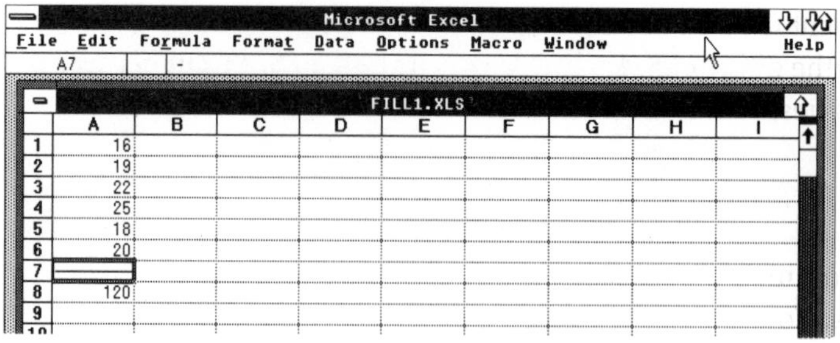

FIGURE 3-6. *Use the Fill option to repeat a character across a cell.*

Although cell A7 seems to contain a series of 12 hyphens, the formula bar at the top of the screen reveals that the actual entry in the cell is a single hyphen. Like the other Format menu commands, the Alignment command's Fill option affects only the appearance, not the actual contents, of the cell.

Although the entries you repeat with the Fill alignment option will usually be single characters such as a hyphen (–), an asterisk (∗), or an equal sign (=), you can use this command to repeat multicharacter entries as well.

You may think it would be as easy to type the repeating characters as it is to use Fill. However, the Fill option offers two important advantages. First, if you adjust the column width, Microsoft Excel increases or decreases the number of characters in the cell to accommodate the new column width; you don't have to edit filled cells to correspond to their column width. In addition, the Fill option lets you repeat a single character across several adjacent cells in your worksheet. For example, in the sample worksheet shown in Figure 3-7, we created a series of hyphens across cells A6:D6 of the worksheet. To create this line, we simply entered a single hyphen character in cell A6; then we selected cells A6:D6 and assigned the

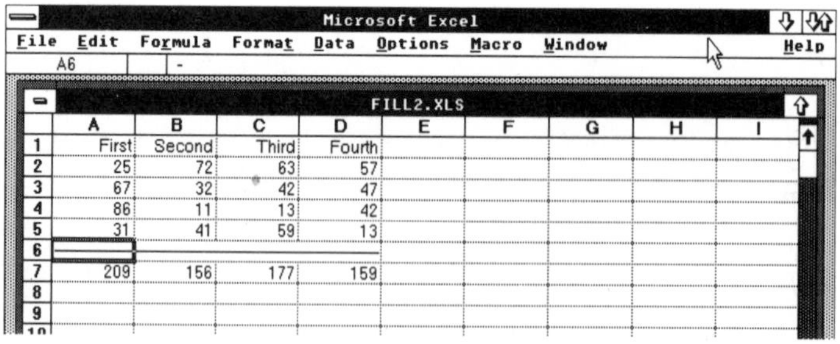

FIGURE 3-7. *You can also use the Fill option to repeat a character across several adjacent cells.*

Fill alignment format to that range. Microsoft Excel extended our hyphen characters across the entire range, with no breaks between cells. Although they appear to contain entries, cells B6:D6 are empty.

The Font command

The Font command lets you choose the typeface, character style, and size of your cell entries. You can use as many as four fonts in a single worksheet. You might select different typefaces and sizes to emphasize major headings, or you might use bold, italic, and regular type styles to distinguish different kinds of information.

Before we show you how to select fonts for your worksheet, let's define that term more explicitly. In some programs, the term *font* refers only to the typeface you have selected (such as Helvetica or Times Roman); different type sizes and styles are considered variations of the same font. In Microsoft Excel, the term *font* encompasses not only the typeface, but the character size and style as well. Thus, 10-point Helv regular type and 10-point Helv italic type are considered different fonts. By the same token, 10-point Helv regular type and 18-point Helv regular type are considered different fonts.

Applying a font

To see how the Font command works, let's revisit the worksheet shown in Figure 3-7. Suppose you want to display the entries in row 1 in bold type for emphasis. First, select cells A1:D1; then select Font from the Format menu. You'll see a dialog box like the one in Figure 3-8. The box contains a list of the four fonts currently available in the worksheet. This is your default font set. (The fonts available depend on the system configuration you've selected, so your Fonts list may contain font options other than those listed here.)

FIGURE 3-8. *Use the Font dialog box to change the typeface, size, and style of cell entries.*

To change the current font to Helv 10-point bold type, simply select the second option from the Fonts list by clicking on it or by typing 2. It's as easy as that! When you choose OK, Microsoft Excel applies the chosen font to the selected cells, as shown in Figure 3-9.

	A	B	C	D	E	F	G	H	I
1	First	Second	Third	Fourth					
2	25	72	63	57					
3	67	32	42	47					
4	86	11	13	42					
5	31	41	59	13					
6									
7	209	156	177	159					
8									
9									

Microsoft Excel — FILL2.XLS

FIGURE 3-9. *We used the Font command to display cells A1:D1 in bold type.*

Changing the font set

Now, suppose you want cells A1:D1 of the same worksheet to appear in 18-point Helv bold type. Because that option is not listed in your current font set, you'll need to replace one of the existing font options with your new selection.

To change your worksheet's font set, issue the Font command and select the option you want to replace—we'll replace the fourth option, Helv 10-point bold italic. Next, select the Fonts button in the lower right corner of the dialog box. You'll see an expanded dialog box, like the one in Figure 3-10, that tells you which typefaces are available, with recommended type sizes and available style options.

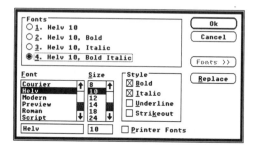

FIGURE 3-10. *To change your font set, choose the Fonts button to expand the dialog box.*

The current selections for the font you're changing are already chosen in the bottom portion of the dialog box. In addition, several other typefaces, sizes, and styles are listed. Because you don't want to use the italic format, deselect that option in the Style portion of the dialog box. Now select the 18 option in the Size list box. Next, select the OK or Replace button. If you choose OK, Microsoft Excel will add the new font specifications to your Fonts list, apply that font to the selected cell or range in your worksheet, and close the dialog box. If you choose Replace, the new font will replace the one you selected in the Fonts list, but the dialog box will remain open so that you can make further changes to the Fonts list.

Notice that the four options in the Fonts list are numbered. When you apply a font to the cells of your worksheet, you're actually assigning a font number to those cells. The definition of that font number changes when you replace the corresponding entry in the Fonts list. Thus, when you choose the Replace button in the dialog box, any cells that were assigned that font number receive the new font specifications. When you choose the OK button, Microsoft Excel also applies the selected font to the selected cells in your worksheet, if they didn't already carry that font number. Figure 3-11 shows our worksheet after we applied our new font option. (In addition, we made columns A through D wider, to accommodate the new font size.)

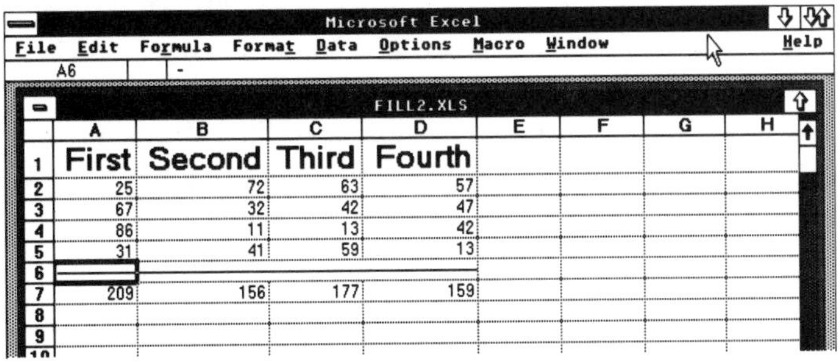

FIGURE 3-11. *We applied the new font option, 18-point Helv bold, to cells A1:D1.*

Now, suppose you want to change the default font for a new worksheet to 12-point Tms Rmn regular. Because the first option in the Fonts list applies to any cells you haven't specifically reformatted—that is, the first option is the default for the entire worksheet—you need to replace that option. To do so, issue the Font command, select option 1 from the current font set, and then choose the Fonts button. Next, choose the Tms Rmn option from the Font list box and the 12 option from the Size list box. Be sure that no special Style options are selected. That's it! Choose OK to lock in your changes and return to the worksheet. Now all the entries in your worksheet, including the column headings and row numbers, will appear in the new default font. Figure 3-12 shows a worksheet that uses 12-point Tms Rmn regular as its default font.

	Microsoft Excel						⇩ 卧
File **Edit** **For_mula** **Forma_t** **_Data** **_Options** **Macro** **Window** ⟋							**Help**
E8		=SUM(E4:E7)					

	TMSRMN.XLS						⇧
	A	**B**	**C**	**D**	**E**	**F**	**G**	**H**
1	Projected Sales							
2								
3		1988	1989	1990	1991			
4	Product 1	$14,252	$15,251	$18,271	$18,281			
5	Product 2	$18,282	$19,292	$16,029	$14,232			
6	Product 3	$16,272	$17,253	$18,281	$18,282			
7	Product 4	$15,034	$14,092	$10,827	$18,283			
8	Total	$63,840	$65,888	$63,408	$69,078			
9								

FIGURE 3-12. *We changed the default font for this worksheet to 12-point Tms Rmn regular.*

Notice that the height and width of the worksheet cells changed when you altered the first item in the font set. As long as you're using standard row height settings, Microsoft Excel adjusts your row heights and column widths for you when you select a new default font specification. If you manually change the height of a row or the width of a column, however, you must readjust the height or width manually when you subsequently change font sizes. When you change the type size or style of the second, third, or fourth option in your font set, you always must adjust the column width manually.

Suggested sizes

When you select options from the Font list box, the number of options in the Size list box changes. The Size list box contains only those sizes explicitly defined for each font—some fonts have several recommended size options; others offer only one size.

You can bypass the Size list box and assign any size for the selected font. To use a nonstandard font size, simply type the size you want in the Size edit bar. The minimum number and the maximum number you can enter depend on the selected font and your machine configuration. If you use a nonstandard size, you may find that the screen display and printed output are not legible. Your degree of flexibility depends, in large part, on the type of printer you use.

Screen fonts vs printer fonts

Although Microsoft Excel offers a range of fonts, not all printers can reproduce these character styles. The Printer Fonts check box at the bottom of the Font dialog box lets you see which fonts are available for the currently installed printer. This check box is turned off in Figure 3-10, which means that the fonts shown are for the screen. If you want to know which typefaces, sizes, and styles are available for your printer, select the Printer Fonts box. If you haven't yet installed a printer to use with Microsoft Excel, the Printer Fonts check box on your screen will be dimmed. (We'll discuss printer fonts fully in Chapter 9.)

The Border command

The Border command lets you add solid-line borders and shading to cells in your worksheet. These can be effective tools for dividing your worksheet into defined areas or for drawing attention to important cells.

When you choose Border from the Format menu, a dialog box like the one in Figure 3-13 comes into view. The Border dialog box offers six choices—Outline, Left, Right, Top, Bottom, and Shade—which you can combine to create any combination of borders. The effect of each of these options is what you would expect: The Outline option places a solid line on all four sides of the selected cell or range; the Left, Right, Top, and Bottom options place solid lines across their respective edges; the Shade option adds shading to a cell or range of cells.

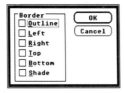

FIGURE 3-13. *Use the Border dialog box to add solid lines and shading to your worksheet.*

To illustrate, let's add a set of double dividing lines beneath a row of cells, to set a group of worksheet totals apart from the data above. First, select the row you want to set apart and then choose the Insert command from the Edit menu, if necessary, to add a blank row between that row and the rows above it. Next, select the appropriate cells in the blank row, choose the Border command from the Format menu, select the Top and Bottom options, and then choose OK. (You may also want to decrease the height of the row to bring the border lines closer together.)

Similarly, to create a double dividing line between columns in your worksheet, use the Insert command to add an extra column, if necessary; then apply the Left and Right border options to the appropriate cells in that column and decrease the width of the column to bring the border lines closer together. (We'll talk more about the Row Height and Column Width commands in a few pages.) Figure 3-14 shows a sample Budget worksheet that uses double borders to set apart the Total row and column.

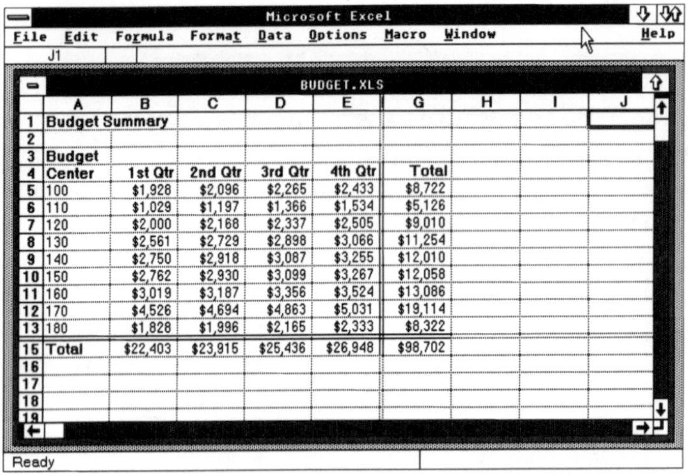

	A	B	C	D	E	G
1	Budget Summary					
2						
3	Budget					
4	Center	1st Qtr	2nd Qtr	3rd Qtr	4th Qtr	Total
5	100	$1,928	$2,096	$2,265	$2,433	$8,722
6	110	$1,029	$1,197	$1,366	$1,534	$5,126
7	120	$2,000	$2,168	$2,337	$2,505	$9,010
8	130	$2,561	$2,729	$2,898	$3,066	$11,254
9	140	$2,750	$2,918	$3,087	$3,255	$12,010
10	150	$2,762	$2,930	$3,099	$3,267	$12,058
11	160	$3,019	$3,187	$3,356	$3,524	$13,086
12	170	$4,526	$4,694	$4,863	$5,031	$19,114
13	180	$1,828	$1,996	$2,165	$2,333	$8,322
15	Total	$22,403	$23,915	$25,436	$26,948	$98,702

FIGURE 3-14. *We used the Border command to set our totals apart from the rest of the data in the worksheet.*

Now, suppose you want to place a solid border around the column heading in cell D2 of a worksheet. To do this, select cell D2, choose the Border command, select the Outline option, and choose OK or press Enter. Figure 3-15 shows the result—a solid-line border around cell D2.

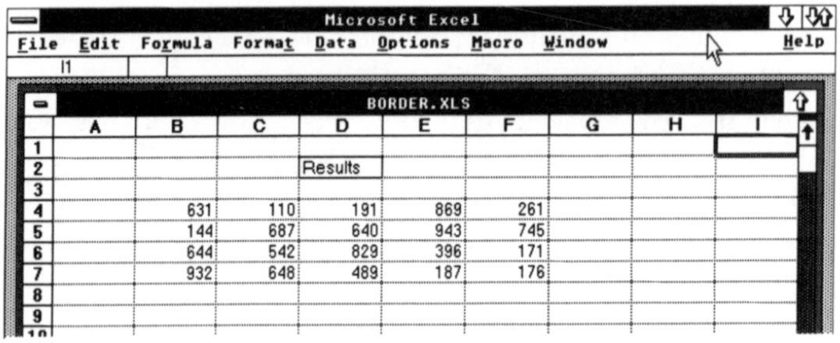

	A	B	C	D	E	F
1						
2				Results		
3						
4		631	110	191	869	261
5		144	687	640	943	745
6		644	542	829	396	171
7		932	648	489	187	176

FIGURE 3-15. *We used the Outline option in the Border dialog box to put a solid-line border around cell D2.*

If you reissue the Border command while cell D2 is still active, you'll see that Microsoft Excel has deselected the Outline option and has instead selected the

Left, Right, Top, and Bottom options. The Outline option simply serves as a shortcut for outlining a cell or range without having to select each side of the border manually. This feature is particularly important when you want to place borders around a range.

For example, if you select cells B4:F7 in Figure 3-15 and select the Outline option from the Border dialog box, a solid line appears around the entire range, as shown in Figure 3-16. No solid lines appear within the range—you'd have to select the Top, Bottom, Left, and Right options to do that. Instead, Microsoft Excel assigns the appropriate Border formats to each of the cells along the perimeter of the selected range: Cell B4 in Figure 3-16 carries the Top and Left options, cell C4 carries the Top option, cell F4 carries the Top and Right options, and so on.

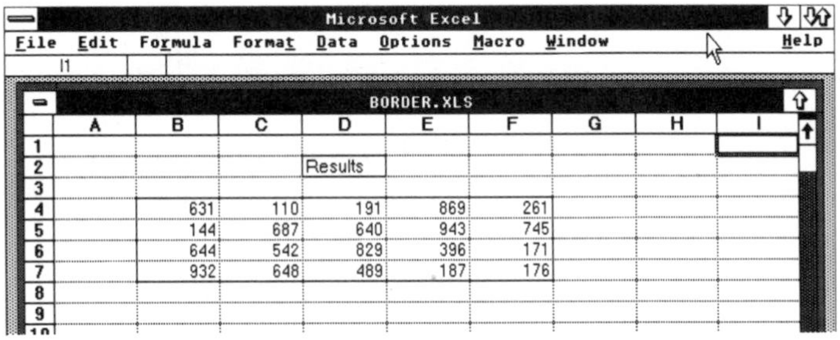

FIGURE 3-16. *We used the Outline option to place a border around cells B4:F7.*

The Shade option in the Border dialog box can also be used to add emphasis to selected cells in your worksheet. For example, you might use shading to set apart worksheet totals or to draw attention to cells in which you want the user to make an entry in a worksheet template. Figure 3-17 shows the effects of the Shade option on cells B4:F7 of Figure 3-16.

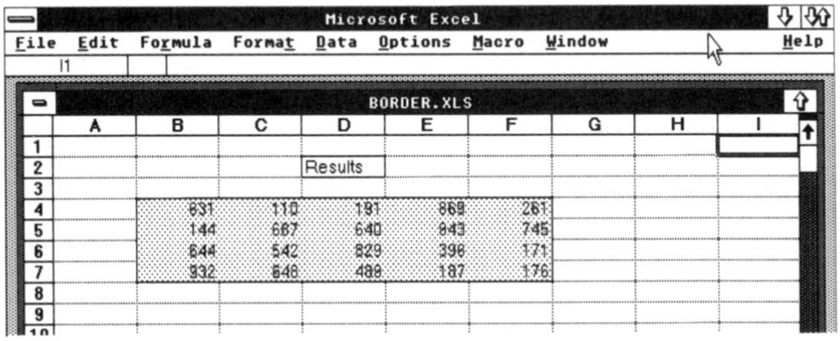

FIGURE 3-17. *We added shading to cells B4:F7.*

You can remove borders as easily as you can create them. Simply select the range, choose the Border command, and select the appropriate option to deactivate it. When you choose OK or press Enter, Microsoft Excel will remove the borders from the selected cells. To remove an Outline border, select the entire outlined cell or range and then reissue the Border command, choosing the Left, Right, Top, and Bottom options to deselect all those border formats.

Notice that the borders in our examples are barely visible. As you'll see in a few pages, you can increase the effectiveness of cell borders by using the Display command from the Options menu to turn off the dotted-line worksheet grid.

Controlling column width

Microsoft Excel's default column width is 8.43 characters. This does not necessarily mean that each cell in your worksheet can display only 8.43 characters, however. Because Microsoft Excel uses proportional fonts rather than fixed-pitch fonts, each character takes up a different amount of space in the worksheet. For example, an *i* takes up less room than an *M* or a *W*; similarly, bold characters take up more space than plain characters. The 8.43-character standard width is simply an indication of the number of numeric characters that fit in each standard-width column. (For any given font, all numeric characters are the same width in Microsoft Excel.)

Often, you'll find that the standard column width is not wide enough to display the complete contents of a cell. When a label is too long, it simply runs over into adjacent cells; if the adjacent cell contains an entry, the label is truncated. When you enter a long number into a narrow column that has the General numeric format, that number appears in scientific notation. If, when you assign a numeric format to a cell, its entry is too long to be completely displayed in that format, a series of pound signs (#) appears.

To overcome these problems, simply change the width of the column or columns that contain the long entries. Microsoft Excel offers two ways to control the width of cells in a worksheet: You can use the mouse to change the width of one column at a time, or you can use the Column Width command on the Format menu to change the widths of several columns or to set a new column width for the entire worksheet.

For example, to use the mouse to change the width of column A in Figure 3-1, place your mouse pointer on the vertical line in the column header between columns A and B. The pointer will change to a double-arrow shape when it nears the vertical line. To widen the column, hold the mouse button down and drag the pointer to the right until the divider line between columns A and B falls to the right of the longest entry in column A, as shown in Figure 3-2. Unfortunately, you can't see the effect of the new column width until you've released the mouse button, so it may take a few tries to get the desired result.

To change the widths of several columns at once, you'll probably want to use the Column Width command rather than drag each column's divider line. Simply select any cells in the columns whose widths you want to change (you can choose

E X C E L *tip*

Hiding a column or row

You may, on occasion, want to hide certain information in your worksheet. For example, suppose you're developing a departmental budget and need to list employee salaries and benefits in your worksheet in order to forecast next year's personnel expenditures. You may want to display overall salary information without revealing sensitive information about individual employees.

Unfortunately, Microsoft Excel doesn't offer any built-in way to completely hide selected cells in your worksheet. (The Hide option in the Cell Protection dialog box hides only formulas, not the displayed values of the cells, and the null Number format hides the cell display but not the formulas.) In order to hide information on your worksheet, you must set the width of the column or row that contains the sensitive information to 0. When you do this, the column or row is almost completely ignored by Microsoft Excel. If you select a range that includes the hidden column or row and then press Enter to move the active cell marker from cell to cell, the marker will skip over the hidden column or row. In addition, the column or row letter will disappear. For example, if you hide column C in your worksheet, the column header line will read *A, B, D,* and so on.

Opening up a column or row that you've hidden can be a bit tricky. Because the column or row no longer appears on the screen, you can't select it with the mouse. If you try to use one of the direction keys to select a cell in a hidden column or row, Microsoft Excel simply jumps past that cell to the next column or row. The easiest solution to this problem is to use the Goto command on the Formula menu to activate a cell in the column or row you want to open and then use the Column Width or Row Height command again to "reopen" the column or row.

nonadjacent columns by holding down the Ctrl key as you select the columns) and
issue the Column Width command. To change the widths of all columns in the
worksheet, simply click on one of the row headers at the left edge of the worksheet
(or select any cell and press Shift-Spacebar) before you issue the Column Width
command.

When you select the Column Width command, you'll see a dialog box like the
one shown in Figure 3-18. If all the columns you select have the same width, that
width will appear in the dialog-box edit bar; if the columns you select have different widths, the edit bar will be blank. Either way, type a number from 0 through
225 in integer or decimal-fraction form. (The old width setting will be erased as
soon as you begin typing.) When you choose OK, Microsoft Excel will redraw your
worksheet and adjust the selected columns.

FIGURE 3-18. *Use the Column Width dialog box to change the width of
columns.*

If you want to restore the width of one or more columns to the default, select
any cells in those columns, choose the Column Width command, and select the
Standard Width box. As soon as you select Standard Width, the standard column
width (8.43 for Helv 10-point text) will appear in the Column Width box. Then simply choose OK or press Enter.

Controlling row height

Microsoft Excel's default row height varies according to the default font you select
for your worksheet. In addition, the size of the largest letter in a row determines
the standard height for that row. For example, when a worksheet uses the default
font, Helv 10-point, the default row height is 13. If you apply the Tms Rmn 12-point
font to a cell, however, the height of that entire row will change to 16.

Like font size, row height is measured in points. One point equals 1/72 of an
inch. Thus, to make a row one inch high, use a row height setting of 72; to make a
row one-half inch high, use a row height setting of 36.

Adjusting the height of a row is similar to adjusting the width of a column.
With the mouse, go to the row header and point to the line under the number of the
row you want to change. When the pointer takes on the double-arrow shape, hold
the mouse button down and drag the line dividing the rows to the desired position;
then release the mouse button.

As with the Column Width command, you can use the Row Height command to change the heights of several adjacent or nonadjacent rows at once. Simply select at least one cell in each of the rows you want to change and issue the Row Height command to access the dialog box shown in Figure 3-19. If you want to change the height of all the rows in the worksheet, click on one of the column headers (or select any cell and press Ctrl-Spacebar) before you issue the Row Height command. If all the rows you select are the same height, that height will appear in the dialog-box edit bar; if the rows are of different heights, the edit bar will be blank. Either way, you can change the height of all the selected rows by entering a new row height and then choosing OK or pressing Enter.

FIGURE 3-19. *Use the Row Height dialog box to change the height of selected rows in your worksheet.*

To restore the height of a row to its default, select any cell in that row, choose the Row Height command, and select the Standard Height box. As soon as you select Standard Height, Microsoft Excel will display the standard row height for the font you're using in the Row Height edit bar. Then simply choose OK or press Enter.

The Display and Workspace commands

In addition to the formatting commands available on the Format menu, the Options menu offers two other important formatting elements: the Display command and the Workspace command.

You may find the relationship between the Format and Options commands a bit confusing at first. After all, why should Microsoft Excel's formatting commands be divided between two menus? The distinction is really very simple: Format commands control the appearance of only selected cells; Options commands control the overall appearance of your worksheet. In other words, Format commands are cell-specific and Options commands are global.

The Display command

The Options menu's Display command controls the display of formulas, gridlines, column and row headings, and zero values in your worksheet. When you issue the Display command, you'll see the dialog box shown in Figure 3-20.

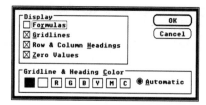

FIGURE 3-20. *Use the Display dialog box to control the appearance of your worksheet.*

The options you select in the Display dialog box affect only the currently active worksheet window; they do not change the display of other windows in the workspace. Thus, if you've used the New Window command on the Window menu to create two or more windows to view the same worksheet, you can use different display options in each. For example, you may want to view formulas in one window and see the results of those formulas in another window. (If you use the split bar to view different areas of the same document window, both areas are affected by the Display options selected—more on this in Chapter 5.)

The Formulas option
Normally when you enter a formula in a cell, you see the results of that formula, not the formula itself. Similarly, when you format a number, you no longer see the underlying (unformatted) value. You can see the underlying values and formulas only by selecting individual cells and looking at the formula bar.

The Formulas option lets you see all the underlying values and formulas in your worksheet at once. For example, to see all the underlying numbers and formulas in the worksheet shown in Figure 3-2, choose the Display command, select the Formulas option, and choose OK. As you can see in Figure 3-21, the underlying contents of each cell appear and all cells are now left-aligned. (Any alignment formatting is ignored when you choose the Formulas option.)

In addition, notice that the width of each column in the worksheet increases from 8.43 to 17.86 characters so that the underlying formulas can be better displayed. When you select the Formulas option, all columns in the worksheet expand to twice their actual width setting, plus one character. Thus, a column 3 characters wide becomes 7 characters wide when you select the Formulas option. When you deselect the Formulas option, Microsoft Excel restores all the columns to their former widths.

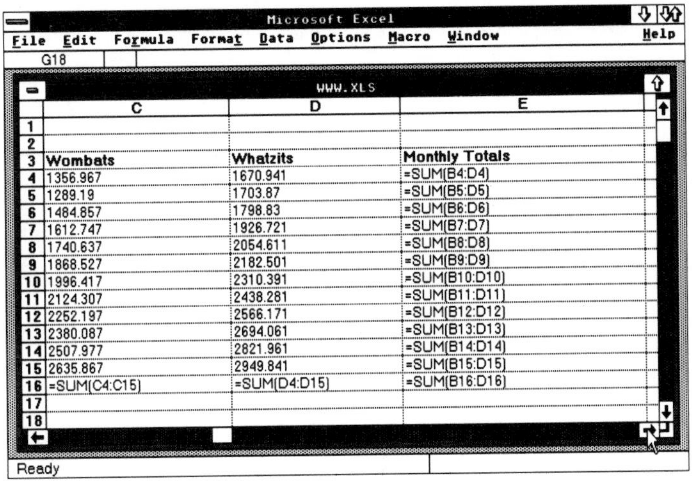

FIGURE 3-21. *Use the Formulas option to view underlying values and formulas.*

The Formulas option is particularly helpful when you need to edit a large worksheet. You can see all your formulas at a glance without having to activate each cell and see its contents in the formula bar. You can also use the Formulas option to document your work: After you select Formulas, you can print your worksheet for historical purposes. (See Chapter 9 for information on printing.)

The Gridlines option

Typically, Microsoft Excel uses a dotted-line grid to mark the boundaries of each cell in the worksheet. Although this grid is usually helpful for selection and navigation, sometimes you would rather not have it in view. To suppress the display of these gridlines on your screen, issue the Display command and deselect the Gridlines option.

You can increase the effectiveness of your border formats dramatically by eliminating the gridlines in your worksheet. Figure 3-22 shows a worksheet with borders but without gridlines. The borders are much more prominent in this worksheet than they were in Figure 3-14.

Turning off the Gridlines option in the Display dialog box removes the gridlines only from your screen display, however. If you want to print a document without gridlines, you must choose the Page Setup command from the File menu. We'll talk more about this in Chapter 9.

Budget Summary					
Budget Center	1st Qtr	2nd Qtr	3rd Qtr	4th Qtr	Total
100	$1,928	$2,096	$2,265	$2,433	$8,722
110	$1,029	$1,197	$1,366	$1,534	$5,126
120	$2,000	$2,168	$2,337	$2,505	$9,010
130	$2,561	$2,729	$2,898	$3,066	$11,254
140	$2,750	$2,918	$3,087	$3,255	$12,010
150	$2,762	$2,930	$3,099	$3,267	$12,058
160	$3,019	$3,187	$3,356	$3,524	$13,086
170	$4,526	$4,694	$4,863	$5,031	$19,114
180	$1,828	$1,996	$2,165	$2,333	$8,322
Total	$22,403	$23,915	$25,436	$26,948	$98,702

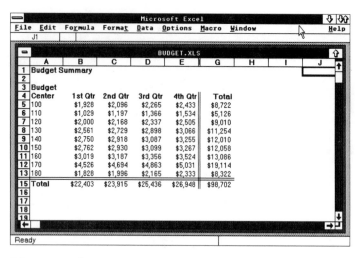

FIGURE 3-22. *Suppressing gridlines increases the effectiveness of borders.*

The Row & Column Headings option

The third option in the Display dialog box is Row & Column Headings. If you select this option, the column letters and row numbers you usually see at the top and left edges of the worksheet disappear. Like the Gridlines option, this option lets you polish your finished worksheets for display purposes. Figure 3-23 shows the worksheet from Figure 3-22 without column and row headers.

Budget Summary					
Budget Center	1st Qtr	2nd Qtr	3rd Qtr	4th Qtr	Total
100	$1,928	$2,096	$2,265	$2,433	$8,722
110	$1,029	$1,197	$1,366	$1,534	$5,126
120	$2,000	$2,168	$2,337	$2,505	$9,010
130	$2,561	$2,729	$2,898	$3,066	$11,254
140	$2,750	$2,918	$3,087	$3,255	$12,010
150	$2,762	$2,930	$3,099	$3,267	$12,058
160	$3,019	$3,187	$3,356	$3,524	$13,086
170	$4,526	$4,694	$4,863	$5,031	$19,114
180	$1,828	$1,996	$2,165	$2,333	$8,322
Total	$22,403	$23,915	$25,436	$26,948	$98,702

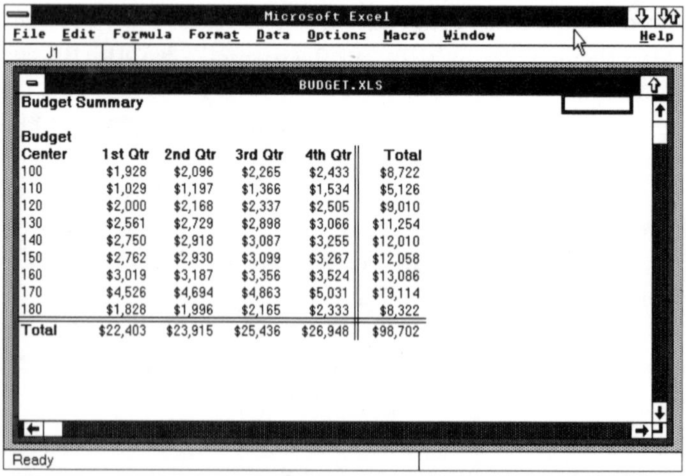

FIGURE 3-23. *You can also suppress the display of row and column headers.*

The Zero Values option

Normally, zero values are displayed in your worksheet, but you can deselect the Zero Values option to hide all those values. With Zero Values deselected, any cells that contain zeros or formulas that result in zero values appear to be blank. The underlying entries are unaffected, however. If you edit an entry or if the result of a formula changes so that the cell no longer contains a zero value, the value immediately becomes visible again.

The sample worksheet shown in Figure 3-24 contains several zero values. If you find these zeros distracting, you can suppress their display by deselecting the Zero Values option. Figure 3-25 shows the results.

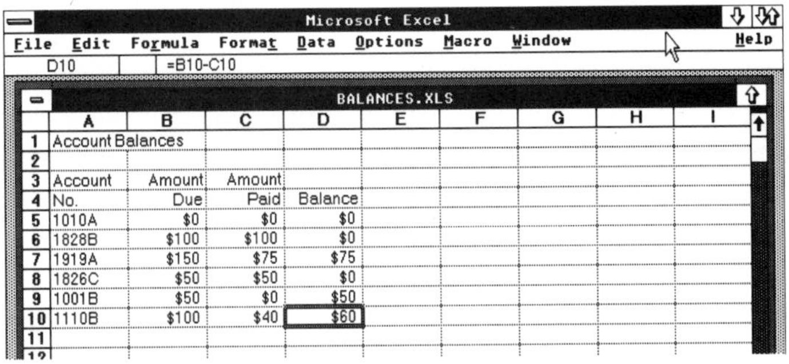

FIGURE 3-24. *This worksheet contains several zero values.*

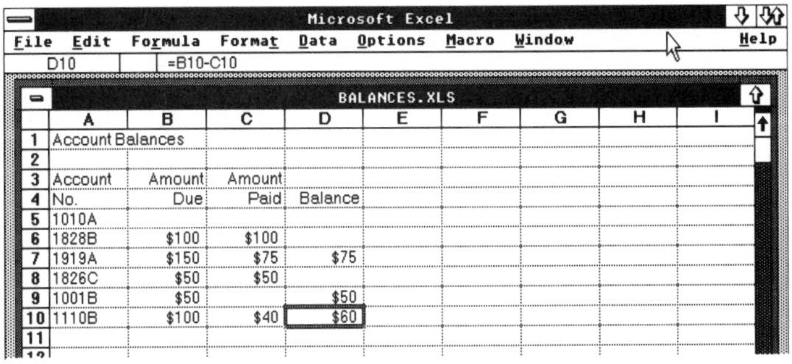

FIGURE 3-25. *Deselect the Zero Values option to suppress the display of zeros.*

Changing the color of your gridlines and headers

You can also change the color of the gridlines and the row and column headers in your worksheet windows. Simply select the color option you want from the

Gridline & Heading Color portion of the Display dialog box and choose OK. Select the Automatic option to change back to the default screen colors (the text color currently defined in the Control Panel).

The Gridline & Heading Color option you select also affects the color of any shaded cells you've formatted in your worksheet. The shading is always the same color as the gridlines and the row and column headers. Thus, if you've used the Number command on the Format menu to change the color of some of your cell entries, you may also want to change the color of the gridlines and shading to create a better contrast in your worksheet display.

The Workspace command

The Options menu's Workspace command is similar to the Display command in that it affects the overall appearance of your worksheet window, not just a selected cell or range. Unlike the Display command, however, the Workspace command applies to *all* open windows. When you issue the Workspace command, you'll see a dialog box like the one in Figure 3-26. In this chapter, we'll take a look

E X C E L

Displaying selected zero values

When you deselect the Zero Values option, Microsoft Excel suppresses the display of every zero value in your worksheet unless you explicitly instruct otherwise. If you want some zero values to remain in view in your worksheet, you can use the Number command on the Format menu to build a three-part custom format to display those cell entries.

As we explained earlier, the third set of instructions you enter into the Format edit bar applies to zero values. Thus, if you want to create a currency format that displays zero values as $0.00, you would enter the following instructions in the Format edit bar of the Number dialog box:

$#,##0.00 ;($#,##0.00);$0.00

Remember to enter an extra blank space after the zero-value portion of this format so that your $0.00 display aligns properly with any negative values in the same column of your worksheet.

at the Fixed Decimal, Display, and Alternate Menu Key options. Because the Ignore Remote Requests option applies only if you're working in the Windows environment to share data with another program, we'll save that option for the Appendix.

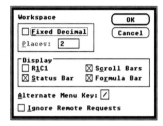

FIGURE 3-26. *The Workspace dialog-box options apply to all open windows.*

The Fixed Decimal option

The Fixed Decimal option is handy when you need to enter long lists of numeric values. For example, suppose you're entering data into an accounting journal. All your entries must contain two decimal places. Instead of typing the decimal point for each entry, select the Fixed Decimal option and, in the Places edit bar, indicate the number of decimal places you want to use. After you type each numeric value into your worksheet, Microsoft Excel will add a decimal point at the specified position. For example, if you select Fixed Decimal and use the default Places option of 2 and then enter the number 12345 into a cell of your worksheet, your entry will be converted to 123.45; if you enter a single-digit value, such as 9, it will be converted to 0.09.

The Fixed Decimal option does not affect existing entries in your worksheet; it applies only to entries you make after you select the option. Thus, you can select or deselect the option at any time or change the number of decimal places without altering existing data. When you choose the Fixed Decimal option, the FIX indicator appears at the right side of the status bar at the bottom of the screen.

The R1C1 option

Worksheet formulas usually refer to cells by a combination of column letter and row number, such as A1 or Z100. However, the R1C1 option causes Microsoft Excel to refer to cells by row and column *numbers* instead. The cell reference R1C1 means row 1, column 1, so cell R1C1 is the same as cell A1. When you choose this option, all the cell references in your formulas change to R1C1 format. For example, cell M10 becomes R10C13, and cell IV16384, the last cell in your worksheet, becomes R16384C256. Figure 3-27 shows a worksheet in R1C1 format.

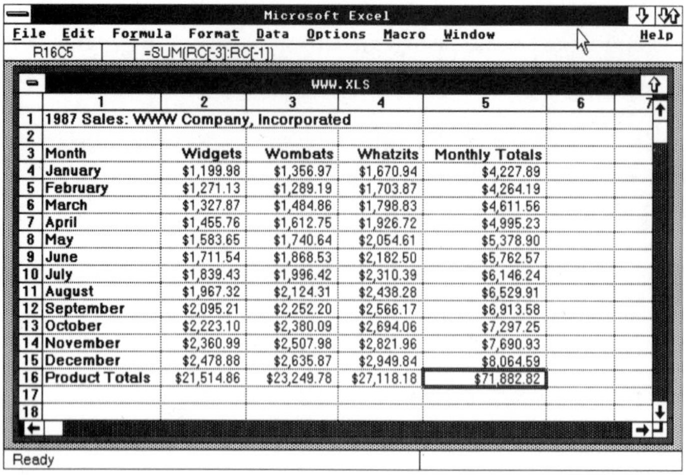

	1	2	3	4	5	6
1	1987 Sales: WWW Company, Incorporated					
2						
3	Month	Widgets	Wombats	Whatzits	Monthly Totals	
4	January	$1,199.98	$1,356.97	$1,670.94	$4,227.89	
5	February	$1,271.13	$1,289.19	$1,703.87	$4,264.19	
6	March	$1,327.87	$1,484.86	$1,798.83	$4,611.56	
7	April	$1,455.76	$1,612.75	$1,926.72	$4,995.23	
8	May	$1,583.65	$1,740.64	$2,054.61	$5,378.90	
9	June	$1,711.54	$1,868.53	$2,182.50	$5,762.57	
10	July	$1,839.43	$1,996.42	$2,310.39	$6,146.24	
11	August	$1,967.32	$2,124.31	$2,438.28	$6,529.91	
12	September	$2,095.21	$2,252.20	$2,566.17	$6,913.58	
13	October	$2,223.10	$2,380.09	$2,694.06	$7,297.25	
14	November	$2,360.99	$2,507.98	$2,821.96	$7,690.93	
15	December	$2,478.88	$2,635.87	$2,949.84	$8,064.59	
16	Product Totals	$21,514.86	$23,249.78	$27,118.18	$71,882.82	
17						
18						

FIGURE 3-27. *Use the R1C1 option to refer to cells by row and column numbers.*

When you use R1C1 notation, relative cell references are displayed in terms of their relationship to the cell that contains the formula rather than by their actual coordinates. For example, suppose you want to enter a formula in cell R10C2 (B10) that adds cells R1C1 and R1C2. After selecting cell R10C2, type an equal sign, then select cell R1C1, type a + sign, select R1C2, and press Enter. Microsoft Excel will display

=R[–9]C[–1]+R[–9]C

This formula can be read *Add the cell nine rows up and one column to the left to the cell nine rows up in the same column.* Negative row and column numbers indicate that the referenced cell is above and to the left of the formula cell; positive numbers indicate that the referenced cell is below and to the right of the formula cell.

To type a relative reference to another cell, you must include square brackets around the reference. If you don't include the brackets, Microsoft Excel assumes you're using absolute references. For example, the formula

=R9C1+R8C1

uses absolute references to the cells in rows 8 and 9 of column 1.

The Status Bar, Scroll Bars, and Formula Bar options

The remaining three options in the Display portion of the Workspace dialog box let you suppress the display of the status bar, scroll bars, and formula bar. Figure 3-28 shows how your worksheet looks if you select these three options. Because you need the status bar, scroll bars, and formula bar to navigate and edit your worksheet, you'll use these three options only when you complete a worksheet and want to hide these objects for display purposes.

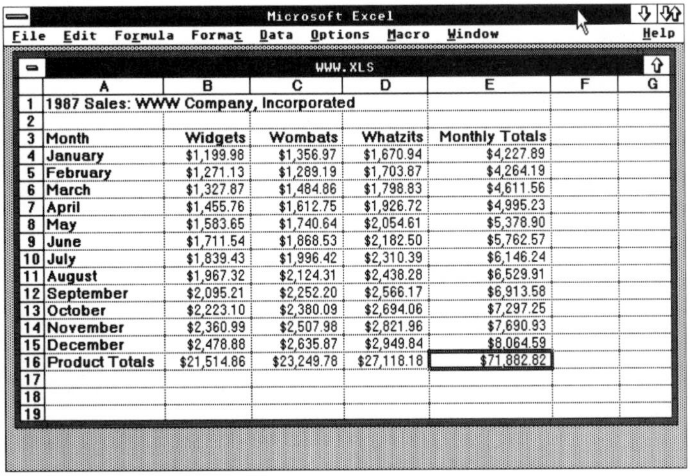

	A	B	C	D	E	F	G
1	1987 Sales: WWW Company, Incorporated						
2							
3	Month	Widgets	Wombats	Whatzits	Monthly Totals		
4	January	$1,199.98	$1,356.97	$1,670.94	$4,227.89		
5	February	$1,271.13	$1,289.19	$1,703.87	$4,264.19		
6	March	$1,327.87	$1,484.86	$1,798.83	$4,611.56		
7	April	$1,455.76	$1,612.75	$1,926.72	$4,995.23		
8	May	$1,583.65	$1,740.64	$2,054.61	$5,378.90		
9	June	$1,711.54	$1,868.53	$2,182.50	$5,762.57		
10	July	$1,839.43	$1,996.42	$2,310.39	$6,146.24		
11	August	$1,967.32	$2,124.31	$2,438.28	$6,529.91		
12	September	$2,095.21	$2,252.20	$2,566.17	$6,913.58		
13	October	$2,223.10	$2,380.09	$2,694.06	$7,297.25		
14	November	$2,360.99	$2,507.98	$2,821.96	$7,690.93		
15	December	$2,478.88	$2,635.87	$2,949.84	$8,064.59		
16	Product Totals	$21,514.86	$23,249.78	$27,118.18	$71,882.82		
17							
18							
19							

FIGURE 3-28. *You can suppress the display of the status bar, scroll bars, and formula bar.*

The Alternate Menu Key option

As we explained in Chapter 1, in addition to the Alt key on your keyboard, you can use the slash (/) key as an alternate function key. If you like, you can assign the alternate function to any other key on your keyboard. Simply select the Alternate Menu Key edit bar and type the key you want to use.

4

Editing the Worksheet

*T*he Edit menu commands take the place of old-fashioned erasers, scissors, and paste. Among other things, they let you erase, copy, and move cells and ranges. In this chapter, we'll discuss these commands and then explain the importance of relative, absolute, and mixed references, introduced in Chapter 2. We'll also look at the Series, Justify, and Parse commands, which are not on the Edit menu.

The Undo command

The Undo command lets you recover from editing mistakes without having to reenter data or patch information back in place. If you catch your mistake before you use another command or make another cell entry, you can simply choose Undo to reverse the previous command.

You can use Undo to reverse the effect of any command on the Edit menu and to restore any entry in the formula bar. For example, if you accidentally delete an important range of data, you can choose Undo to paste the entries back in place. If you edit the contents of a cell and subsequently discover that your changes are incorrect, you can use Undo to restore the original cell entry. In addition, Undo reverses the effects of the Replace and Apply Names commands from the Formula menu, the Justify command from the Format menu, the Parse command from the Data menu, and the Paste List option in the Paste Name dialog box.

The Undo command changes to reflect your last Edit command or cell entry. For example, suppose you've just chosen the Clear command to erase the contents of a range of cells. When you pull down the Edit menu, the Undo command appears as Undo Clear. If you've just entered a formula in a cell, the Edit menu displays Undo Entry.

With the exceptions listed above, you can't choose Undo to reverse commands from menus other than Edit. After you choose any other command, you'll see the dimmed command Can't Undo on the Edit menu. The loss of the Undo capability is usually not a problem in these cases, however, because these commands generally don't change the contents of your cells. You can usually undo their effects by choosing the command again and changing your selection. For example, if you format a range incorrectly, you can always select the cells again and choose another format.

If you're working with a large range, you may find that Microsoft Excel can't undo your mistakes for you. For example, suppose you try to use the Cut and Paste commands to move all the cells in column A (cells A1:A16384) into column C (cells C1:C16384). You'll see the alert message *Not enough memory. Continue without Undo?* If you choose OK, Microsoft Excel will disable the Undo command and attempt to carry out the requested operation (although sufficient memory still isn't guaranteed). A better choice is to select Cancel and then perform the editing task in smaller chunks—by using two or more sets of Cut and Paste commands, for example. By breaking the command into more digestible portions, you can achieve the desired effect without losing the capabilities of the Undo command.

E X C E L

An extra precaution

A few commands have irreversible effects. For example, the Delete command on the File menu can't be reversed. If you're not sure whether a file is needed, open the file and take a look before you delete it. Similarly, you can't reverse the Delete, Extract, and Sort commands on the Data menu. It is a good idea to save your worksheet before you enter these commands. Then, if you later find that you've deleted or rearranged cells incorrectly, you can always retrieve your original worksheet.

Actions that don't affect Undo

As we've mentioned, you can undo an action only if you haven't used another command or made another cell entry. However, you can take several actions in the worksheet without affecting the Undo command. For instance, you can use the cell pointer and scroll bars to move through your worksheet and activate other cells without affecting Undo. (After you activate a cell's formula bar, however, the Undo command becomes Can't Undo and is dimmed.) The cursor-movement commands that move the cell pointer, discussed in Chapter 2, are also safe. You can use the Goto and Find commands on the Formula menu without affecting Undo, and you can move to other windows by selecting window names from the Window menu or by clicking on the window itself.

The Redo command

After you use the Undo command, the command name changes to Redo. This option undoes the Undo, restoring the worksheet to its condition before you used the Undo command. For example, when you pull down the Edit menu after you've issued the Undo Clear command, the command appears as Redo Clear. If you choose this option, Microsoft Excel again clears the contents of the selected range and then changes the command name back to Undo Clear.

You can take advantage of the Undo/Redo combination to see the effects of an editing change in your worksheet. Suppose you edit a cell that is referenced in several formulas throughout your worksheet. To see the effects of your change, you can scroll around the worksheet and view the other cells. If you don't remember what a cell looked like before the change, you can use the Undo and Redo commands to get a "before and after" view.

The Repeat command

The Repeat command lets you repeat an action—a great time-saver when you need to perform the same action in several areas of your worksheet. Repeat is particularly handy with commands like Insert and Delete, which can't be performed on discontinuous selections.

In many ways, the Repeat command is similar to Undo. Like Undo, the text of the Repeat command changes to reflect your last action in the worksheet. For example, suppose you issue the Clear command and select the Formats option in the Clear dialog box. When you access the Edit menu, you'll see that this command appears as Repeat Clear. If you select another cell or range and select the Repeat Clear command, Microsoft Excel assumes that you want to apply the same set of dialog-box options—the Formats option in this case—to the new selection.

Also like Undo, the Repeat command applies only to the last command you issued. As soon as you choose another command, the Repeat command updates its memory of your most recent action.

Unlike Undo, Repeat works with almost any command on any menu. The only exceptions are those commands that can't logically be repeated. For example, if you use the Workspace command on the Options menu to change the appearance of your workspace, that command applies to all open documents and windows; you need not repeat it. In this case, the Repeat command is dimmed.

The Clear command

The Clear command lets you erase the contents of a cell or range, the format assigned to that cell or range, or both. You can also use the Clear command with cell notes and charts. (We'll discuss notes in Chapter 8 and charts in Chapter 13.)

To clear the contents or format of a cell or range, simply select that cell or range and choose the Clear command from the Edit menu. Alternatively, you can bypass the Edit menu and press the Del key. Either way, you'll see the dialog box shown in Figure 4-1. (Note: If you're working in the formula bar, pressing the Del key erases only the characters you've selected. The Clear dialog box does not appear.)

FIGURE 4-1. *Use the Clear dialog box to erase cell formats, formulas, and notes.*

This dialog box offers four options: All, Formats, Formulas, and Notes. The All option erases the contents of the selected cells and any formats (other than column width and row height) and notes attached to those cells. The Formats option removes the formats from the selected cells but leaves their contents and notes in place; the selected cells then revert to the default General format. The Formulas option erases the contents of the selected cells but leaves their formats and notes alone. Finally, Notes removes any notes from the selected cells but leaves their contents and formats in place.

If you clear a cell to which other cells refer, the cleared cell takes on a 0 value.

The Delete command

The Delete command lets you remove cells from your worksheet. Unlike Clear, which erases the contents, formats, or notes in a cell but leaves the cell in place, Delete removes the selected cell or range from the worksheet. In other words, Clear works like an eraser and Delete works like a pair of scissors.

Deleting entire rows and columns

You can use the Delete command to remove entire rows and columns from your worksheet and eliminate wasted space. For example, consider the worksheet in Figure 4-2. Three blank rows appear between the last items in the lists in columns A through G and the totals in row 13. To delete one of these blank rows from the worksheet (we'll use row 10), select the row either by clicking the row number (10) at the left side of the screen or by selecting any cell in the row and pressing Shift-Spacebar. Then choose the Delete command from the Edit menu. As you can see in Figure 4-3, row 10 is removed from the worksheet and every entry in the rows below the deleted row is shifted up so that the totals that were in row 13 now appear in row 12.

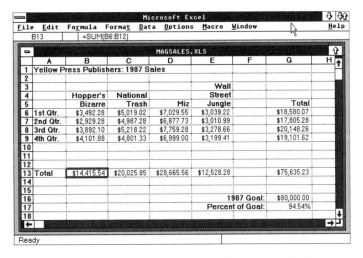

FIGURE 4-2. *Three extra rows appear above the totals row in this worksheet.*

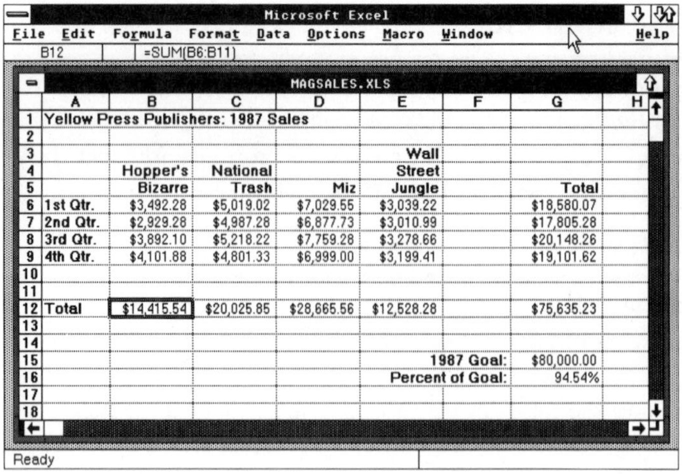

FIGURE 4-3. *When we deleted row 10, the remaining rows in the work-sheet moved up to fill the gap.*

In addition to deleting a row from the worksheet, Microsoft Excel adjusted the formula in row 12 to account for the deleted row. Before we deleted the extra row, the formula in cell B13 (now in cell B12) was

=SUM(B6:B12)

However, cell B12 now contains the formula

=SUM(B6:B11)

You can also use Delete to remove columns from the worksheet. Simply select the column you want to delete and choose the Delete command. That column disappears from your worksheet and all subsequent columns shift one cell to the left. Again, Microsoft Excel updates any formulas affected by the deletion.

To delete more than one row or column, you need only select all the rows or columns you want to delete and then choose the Delete command. For example, to delete rows 10 and 11 from the worksheet in Figure 4-3, select those rows and choose Delete. Microsoft Excel will then remove the selection from the worksheet and shift all the entries below those rows up two more cells. Figure 4-4 shows the adjusted formula in what is now cell B10:

=SUM(B6:B9)

You can't delete discontinuous rows or columns in one operation. For example, if you select columns A and F in your worksheet and issue the Delete command, you'll see the alert message *Can't do that to a multiple selection.*

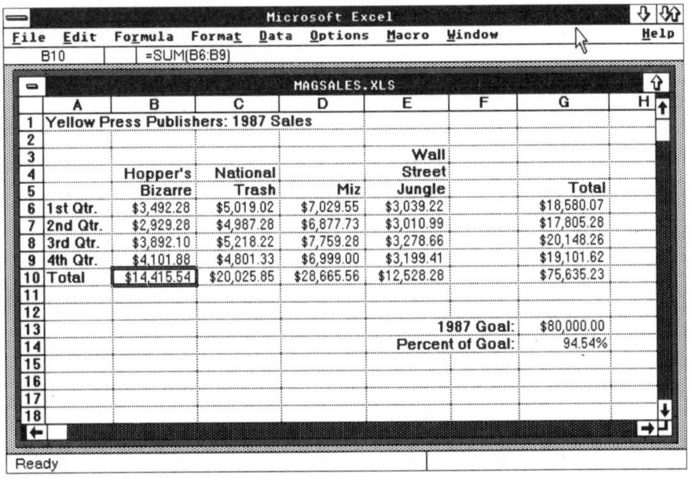

FIGURE 4-4. *We deleted rows 10 and 11 from the worksheet.*

Deleting partial rows and columns

Microsoft Excel lets you delete partial rows and columns—in fact, you can delete a range as small as a single cell. Simply select the cells you want to delete and choose the Delete command. Only the selected portion of the column or row will be affected.

For example, to delete cells F6:F10 from the worksheet in Figure 4-4 without changing the remaining cells in column F, select cells F6:F10; then choose Delete from the Edit menu. You'll see a dialog box like the one in Figure 4-5.

FIGURE 4-5. *Use the Delete dialog box to remove partial rows or columns from the worksheet.*

This dialog box offers two choices: Shift Cells Left and Shift Cells Up. Use these options to specify how you want to adjust the spreadsheet after the selected range is deleted. If you select the Shift Cells Left option, all cells to the right of the selected cells will move to the left; if you select the Shift Cells Up option, all cells below the selected range will move up.

When you select a partial row or column to delete, Microsoft Excel tries to guess how you want to arrange the remaining cells in your worksheet. If you select a horizontal range (wider than it is deep), the program assumes you want to close up the range by moving up any cells below the selected range; if you select a vertical range (longer than it is wide), the program assumes you want to close up the range by moving to the left any cells to the right of the selected range.

Because the selected range in our example is taller than it is wide, Microsoft Excel selects the Shift Cells Left option in the Delete dialog box. We do want to shift the cells on the right of the deleted cells to the left, so we can simply select the OK button. As you can see in Figure 4-6, cells F6 through F10 are deleted and all the cells to the right of the range are shifted one cell to the left. Notice, however, that cells F13 and F14, just below the deleted range, are unchanged by the Delete command.

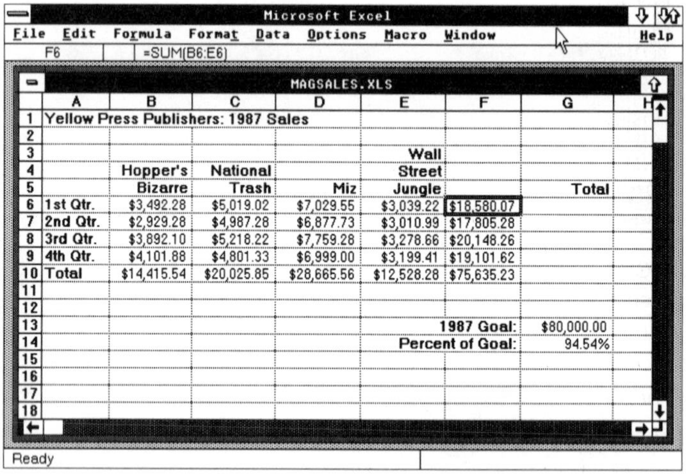

	Microsoft Excel						⇩ ⇪⇩
File Edit Formula Format Data Options Macro Window							Help
F6		=SUM(B6:E6)					

	MAGSALES.XLS						⇧
	A	B	C	D	E	F	G	H
1	Yellow Press Publishers: 1987 Sales						
2							
3					Wall		
4		Hopper's	National		Street		
5		Bizarre	Trash	Miz	Jungle		Total
6	1st Qtr.	$3,492.28	$5,019.02	$7,029.55	$3,039.22	$18,580.07	
7	2nd Qtr.	$2,929.28	$4,987.28	$6,877.73	$3,010.99	$17,805.28	
8	3rd Qtr.	$3,892.10	$5,218.22	$7,759.28	$3,278.66	$20,148.26	
9	4th Qtr.	$4,101.88	$4,801.33	$6,999.00	$3,199.41	$19,101.62	
10	Total	$14,415.54	$20,025.85	$28,665.56	$12,528.28	$75,635.23	
11							
12							
13						1987 Goal:	$80,000.00
14						Percent of Goal:	94.54%
15							
16							
17							
18							

Ready

FIGURE 4-6. *We used the Shift Cells Left option to delete cells F6:F10.*

When you delete a partial row or column, it is easy to misalign data. For example, in Figure 4-6, the label *Total* in column G did not move left with the other data in that column. As a result, the heading for column F now appears in the wrong column. This problem could have been avoided by selecting cells F5:F10 before choosing the Delete command.

The Insert command

The Insert command lets you add cells to your worksheet. For example, suppose you've created the worksheet in Figure 4-7. As you're putting on the finishing touches, your boss tells you that your company has added a new product line. If you were working with a paper spreadsheet, you might throw away the entire plan and start on a new set of calculations. Fortunately, with the Insert command, you can add a new row or column to your electronic worksheet without a lot of shuffling and recalculation.

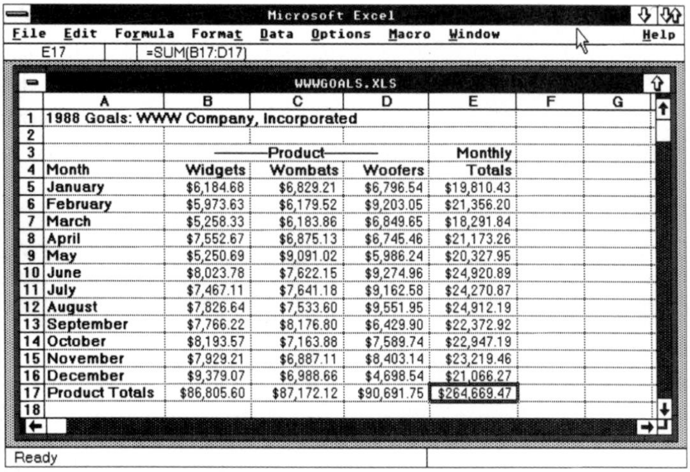

FIGURE 4-7. *This worksheet sets annual sales goals by product and by month.*

Microsoft Excel always inserts the same size and shape range as the one selected. When you insert a column, it is inserted to the left of the selected column; when you insert a row, it is inserted above the selected row. As a bonus, the inserted range carries the same formats as the selected column or row.

To insert a column for a new product line in the sample worksheet, simply select column B, C, or D (we'll use D) and choose Insert from the Edit menu. The contents of columns D and E will move into columns E and F, leaving column D blank and ready for new information. In addition to inserting a new column, the Insert command will adjust the formulas in cells F5:F17 to account for the expanded range.

You're now ready to enter the new product line's sales goals and add these goals to the totals in column F. Figure 4-8 shows the finished worksheet with the data for Whatzits in column D.

Similarly, suppose you want to insert an extra row to the worksheet in Figure 4-8 so that you can add a series of dashed lines to separate the monthly sales data in rows 5 through 16 from the totals appearing in row 17. Simply select row 17 and choose Insert from the Edit menu. Cells A17:F17 will move down one row, as shown in Figure 4-9.

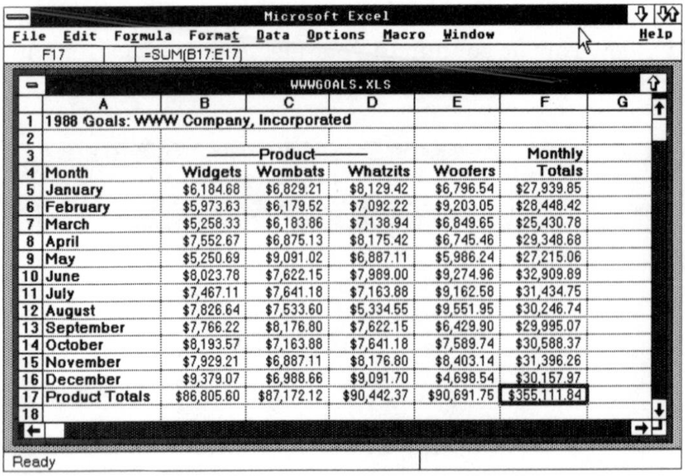

FIGURE 4-8. *We used the Insert command to add a column for a new product line.*

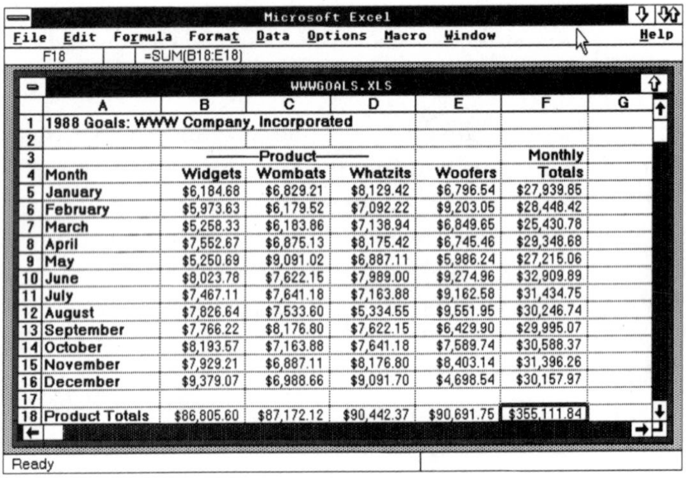

FIGURE 4-9. *We used the Insert command to create a new row to set off the totals.*

Often, you'll need to insert only a partial row or column into the spreadsheet. For example, suppose rows 22 through 35 in the sample worksheet in Figure 4-7 include information that would be damaged if you inserted a column all the way down the spreadsheet. You therefore need to insert cells in column D only between rows 4 and 18. Simply select cells D4:D18 and choose Insert from the Edit menu. You'll see an Insert dialog box like the one in Figure 4-10.

FIGURE 4-10. *Use the Insert dialog box to add partial rows or columns to your worksheet.*

As with the Delete command, Microsoft Excel tries to guess how you want to arrange the remaining cells in your worksheet. If you select a horizontal range, the program assumes you want to use the Shift Cells Down option; if you select a vertical range, it assumes you want to use the Shift Cells Right option.

In the example, you would accept the guess to move cells D4:E18 into cells E4:F18, leaving D4:D18 blank and ready to receive your new product-line information. None of the other cells in the worksheet would be disturbed.

Again, be careful not to misalign data when you're adding partial rows and columns. All cells to the right of the selected range move when you select Shift Cells Right in the Insert dialog box; similarly, the Shift Cells Down option affects all cells below the range you select. You can quickly misalign many entries with the Insert command. For example, if you select only cells D4:D16 in Figure 4-7 and then choose Insert, your worksheet will look like Figure 4-11, where the word *Monthly* in cell E3 is not aligned with the Totals data in column F and the product totals for the last two columns are no longer aligned with their associated columns of values.

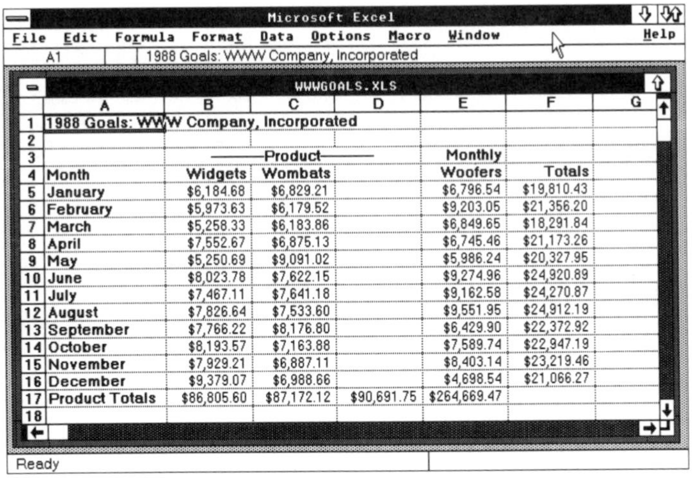

	A	B	C	D	E	F	G
1	1988 Goals: WWW Company, Incorporated						
2							
3			——Product——		Monthly		
4	Month	Widgets	Wombats		Woofers	Totals	
5	January	$6,184.68	$6,829.21		$6,796.54	$19,810.43	
6	February	$5,973.63	$6,179.52		$9,203.05	$21,356.20	
7	March	$5,258.33	$6,183.86		$6,849.65	$18,291.84	
8	April	$7,552.67	$6,875.13		$6,745.46	$21,173.26	
9	May	$5,250.69	$9,091.02		$5,986.24	$20,327.95	
10	June	$8,023.78	$7,622.15		$9,274.96	$24,920.89	
11	July	$7,467.11	$7,641.18		$9,162.58	$24,270.87	
12	August	$7,826.64	$7,533.60		$9,551.95	$24,912.19	
13	September	$7,766.22	$8,176.80		$6,429.90	$22,372.92	
14	October	$8,193.57	$7,163.88		$7,589.74	$22,947.19	
15	November	$7,929.21	$6,887.11		$8,403.14	$23,219.46	
16	December	$9,379.07	$6,988.66		$4,698.54	$21,066.27	
17	Product Totals	$86,805.60	$87,172.12	$90,691.75	$264,669.47		
18							

FIGURE 4-11. *Misalignment can result if you're not careful when inserting partial rows or columns.*

Finally, as with Delete, you can't choose a discontinuous range when you issue the Insert command. If you attempt to do so, you'll see the alert message *Can't do that to a multiple selection.*

The Cut and Paste commands

The Cut and Paste commands on the Edit menu let you move entries from one place to another on your worksheet. Unlike the Delete and Clear commands, which simply remove cells and cell entries from your worksheet, the Cut command places your selection on the Clipboard, where it is stored until you paste it in another location.

E X C E L *tip*

Deletion pitfalls

Although you can generally use the Undo command to cancel a deletion, there are still a few pitfalls you'll want to avoid.

First, before you select an entire row or column for deletion, scroll through your worksheet to be sure you're not erasing important information that is not visible in the current window.

Second, if you delete a cell upon which formulas in other cells depend, you'll see a *#REF!* error message in those formula cells. For example, in this worksheet

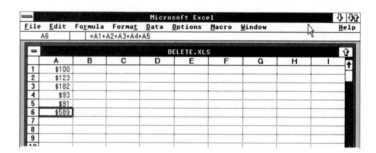

cell A6 contains the formula

    =A1+A2+A3+A4+A5

If you delete row 5 (by selecting row 5 and choosing the Delete command), this formula will be shifted to cell A5 and become

    =A1+A2+A3+A4+#REF!

The Cut command puts a dotted-line marquee around any entries you select and places a record of the number of rows and columns within the marquee on the Clipboard. When you select the range to which you want to move the cut cells, the Paste command pastes them into their new location and then clears the contents of the cells within the marquee and erases the marquee.

Microsoft Excel offers keyboard shortcuts for the Cut and Paste commands. Instead of opening the Edit menu, you can press Shift-Del for the Cut command and Shift-Ins or Enter for the Paste command.

When you use the Cut and Paste commands to move a range of cells, Microsoft Excel clears both the contents and the formats of the cut range and transfers them

---

The result of the formula is also #REF!:

Clearly, the results of deleting a row that contains cells referred to by formulas can be disastrous!

Interestingly, functions behave differently than pure formulas in this regard. When you delete a row or column referred to by an argument of a function, Microsoft Excel modifies the argument, if at all possible, to account for the deletion. For example, if cell A6 contained the formula

    =SUM(A1:A5)

and you deleted row 5, the formula (now in cell A5) would be changed to

    =SUM(A1:A4)

This adaptability is a compelling reason for using functions instead of formulas where possible.

to the cells in the paste range. For example, to move the contents of the range A1:A5 in Figure 4-12 to cells C1:C5, select cells A1:A5 and then choose Cut from the Edit menu. When you choose Cut, a marquee will appear around the cells you've selected. Next, select cell C1 and choose Paste from the Edit menu. Figure 4-13 shows the results: Both the contents and the formats assigned to cells A1:A5 have been transferred to cells C1:C5; cells A1:A5 are blank. If you now make an entry in cells A1:A5, you'll see that those cells have reverted to their default formats.

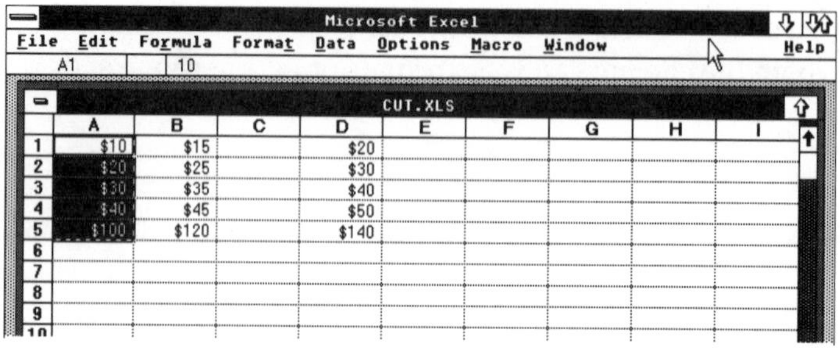

FIGURE 4-12. *We want to use Cut and Paste to move the contents of the range A1:A5 to cells C1:C5.*

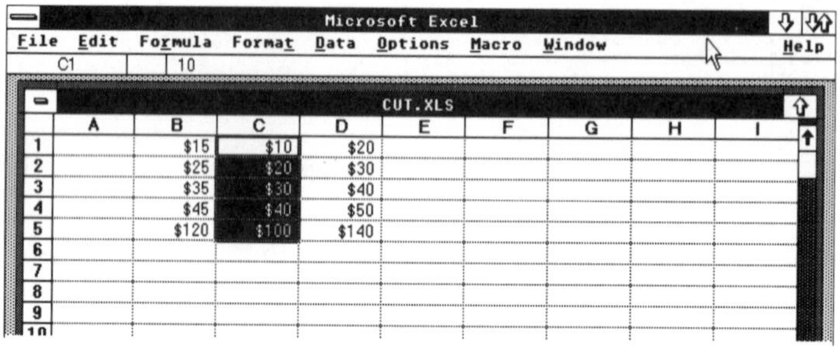

FIGURE 4-13. *The contents and formats of cells A1:A5 now appear in cells C1:C5.*

Cut and Paste rules

You must remember a few rules as you use the Cut and Paste commands. First, the cut area you select must be a single rectangular block of cells. If you try to select a discontinuous range, you'll see the message *Can't do that to a multiple selection.*

Next, cutting and pasting operations can be carried out only once for each range of selected cells. In other words, you can specify only one paste area after you use the Cut command. The contents of the cells, when moved, disappear from their original locations and cannot be referred to for further pasting. If you want to paste the selected data into two or more locations, use the Copy command and then use Clear to erase the contents of the original cell or range.

You don't have to select the entire paste range before you issue the Paste command. When you select a single cell as your paste range, Microsoft Excel extends the paste area to match the size and shape of the cut area. The cell you select becomes the upper left corner of the paste area. However, if you do select the entire paste area, be sure the range you select is the same size and shape as the cut area. If the cut and paste areas are not identical in size and shape, you'll see the alert message *Cut and Paste areas are different shapes*. To correct the problem, select OK in the alert box and select a new paste area.

Finally, remember that Microsoft Excel overwrites the contents and formats of any existing cells in the paste range when you use the Paste command. If you don't want to lose existing cell entries, be sure your worksheet has enough blank cells below and to the right of the cell you select as the upper left corner of the paste area to hold the entire cut area.

Using overlapping cut and paste ranges

Suppose you want to move cells A1:B5 in Figure 4-12 into cells B1:C5 to fill the empty column, C. You could simply select cells A1:A5 and choose the Insert command, but this would cause all the cells in rows 1 through 5 across the worksheet to be shifted one column to the right.

Fortunately, there's a way around this problem. We mentioned earlier that Microsoft Excel overwrites any existing contents of the cells in the paste range when you use the Paste command. But, because the program transfers the contents of your cut area to your paste area before it erases them from the cut area, you can specify overlapping cut and paste areas without losing information in the overlapping cells.

In the sample worksheet, select cells A1:B5 as your cut area and cells B1:C5 as your paste area. As you can see in Figure 4-14, the entries that were in cells A1:B5 in Figure 4-12 are now in cells B1:C5, but the entries to the right of column C in rows 1 to 5 have not moved.

FIGURE 4-14. *You can use overlapping cut and paste areas when moving information.*

E X C E L *tip*

The Clipboard application

The Clipboard serves as a temporary holding area for data when you use the Cut or Copy command. To access the Clipboard application window, choose the Run command from the Control menu or press Alt-Spacebar-U to get the Run Application dialog box. Be sure the Clipboard option is selected and then choose OK.

If you open the Clipboard application window after cutting cells A1:B5 in Figure 4-12, you'll see a window like this:

In Microsoft Excel, the Clipboard does not display the contents of the cells you've selected to cut or copy. Instead, the proportions of the cut area or copy area appear in the Clipboard window. If you can't remember the size or shape of the cut or copy area when you're selecting a paste area, you can open the Clipboard to display the number of rows and columns in the area.

Moving formulas

When you move a cell, Microsoft Excel adjusts any formulas outside the cut area that refer to that cell. For example, in Figure 4-12, cell A5 contains the formula

=SUM(A1:A4)

When we moved cells A1:A5 into cells C1:C5 (Figure 4-13), the move had no apparent effect on the cell contents. However, the formula in cell C5 now reads

=SUM(C1:C4)

The Copy and Paste commands

You can use the Copy and Paste commands to duplicate the contents and formats of selected cells in another area of your worksheet without disturbing the contents of the original cells. You use the Copy command to indicate the range of cells you want to copy and the Paste command to indicate where you want the copies to be placed.

Microsoft Excel offers a keyboard shortcut for the Copy command. After selecting the copy range, instead of opening the Edit menu and choosing Copy, you can press Ctrl-Ins. After selecting the paste range, you can press Shift-Ins to paste the copy. (You can also press Enter instead of choosing the Paste command, but only if you want to paste a single copy. Pressing Enter after you choose the Copy command pastes one copy and then cancels the Copy command.)

The Paste command copies everything in the cell—entries, formats, and notes. If you want to paste only certain properties, use the Paste Special command, explained later in this chapter.

Copying a single cell

Suppose cell A1 of your worksheet contains the value 100 formatted to display currency with no decimal places. To copy the contents of cell A1 into cell C1, which is in General format, select cell A1 and then choose Copy from the Edit menu. A marquee will appear around the selected cell to show your copy selection. Now select cell C1 and choose Paste from the Edit menu. Figure 4-15 shows the result.

The marquee around cell A1 does not disappear after you use the Paste command. This marquee indicates that your copy area is still active. As long as the marquee appears, you can continue to use the Paste command to create additional duplicates of the cell. You can even use the commands on the Window menu and the Open and New commands on the File menu to access other worksheets and

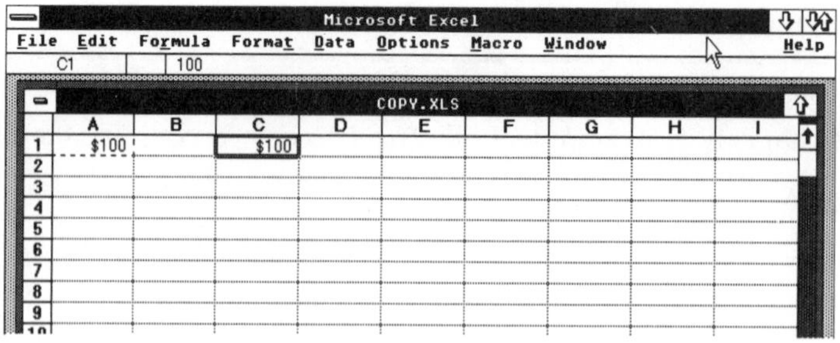

FIGURE 4-15. *A duplicate of cell A1, including its format, appears in cell C1.*

windows without losing your copy area. For example, you might copy a cell into another area of your worksheet and then use the File menu's Open command to access a second worksheet and paste the cell into that new worksheet as well.

By specifying paste areas of different sizes and shapes, you can create multiple copies of the contents of the copy area. For example, if you specify the range C1:D1 as the paste range, Microsoft Excel will copy the contents of cell A1 into both cells C1 and D1, as shown in Figure 4-16.

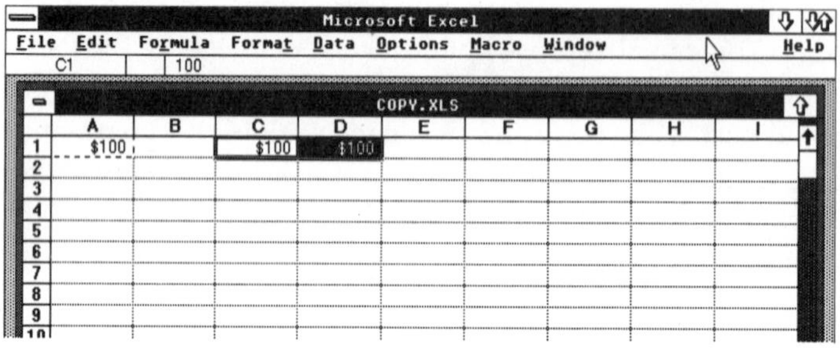

FIGURE 4-16. *You can create multiple copies of a single cell.*

You can also specify multiple discontinuous paste areas. For example, to copy the contents of cell A1 into cells C1, C3, and D2, select cell A1 and choose the Copy command. Next, select C1 and press Shift-F8 to enter Add mode, select cell C3, press Shift-F8 twice, select cell D2, and press Enter. (Alternatively, select cell C1 with the mouse and, holding down the Ctrl key, click on cells C3 and D2.) When you choose the Paste command, your worksheet will look like the one shown in Figure 4-17.

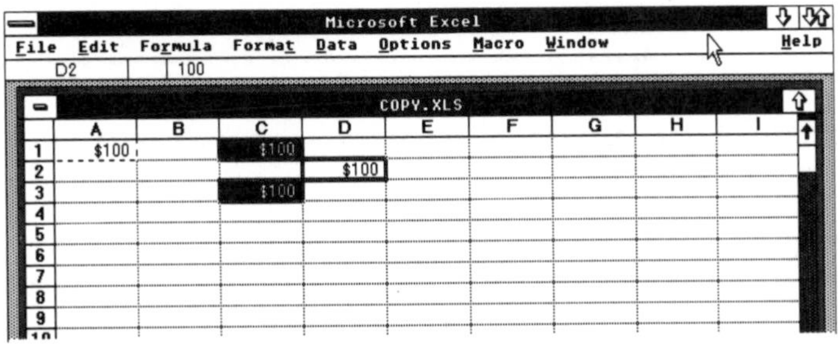

FIGURE 4-17. *You can select multiple discontinuous paste areas.*

Copying ranges

You can use the Copy command to copy ranges as well as single cells. For example, to copy the contents of cells A1:A3 into cells C1:C3, select cells A1:A3 and then choose Copy from the Edit menu. A marquee will appear around the range of cells to be copied. Now select cell C1 and choose Paste from the Edit menu to copy A1:A3 into C1:C3.

As with the Cut and Paste commands, you don't have to select the entire paste area when you copy cells. You need only indicate the upper left corner of the range by selecting a single cell.

You can also create multiple copies of the copy range. For example, you can select C1:D1 as the paste range to create two copies of A1:A3, side by side, in columns C and D. The same result could be achieved by selecting the range C1:D3. Not every paste range works when you're copying ranges, however. For example, if you copy cells A1:A3 and then designate the range C1:C2, C1:D2, C1:C4, or C1:E5, the alert message *Copy and Paste areas are different shapes* will appear. In other words, you must either select only the first cell in each paste area or select one or more paste ranges of exactly the same size and shape as the cut area.

Using overlapping copy and paste ranges

With one exception, you cannot specify overlapping copy and paste ranges. For example, if you select the range A1:A3, choose the Copy command, select cell A2, and then choose the Paste command, you'll see the message *Selection is not valid*.

The exception to this rule is that you can specify a paste range that contains the entire copy range. Generally, it serves no purpose to specify a paste range that exactly overlaps the copy range, because the contents of the selected cells don't change. When you're using the Paste Special command, however, this technique can be quite useful. You'll see why in just a moment.

Copying relative, absolute, and mixed references

As you learned in Chapter 2, Microsoft Excel uses two types of cell references: relative and absolute. These two types of references behave very differently when you use the Copy command.

Relative references

When you copy a cell that contains relative cell references, the formula in the paste area doesn't refer to the same cells as the formula in the copy area. Instead, Microsoft Excel changes the formula references in relation to the position of the pasted cell.

Returning to the sample worksheet in Figure 4-6, suppose you enter the formula

=AVERAGE(B6:E6)

in cell G6. This formula averages the values in the four-cell range that begins five columns to the left of cell G6. Of course, you want to repeat this calculation for the remaining categories as well. Instead of typing a new formula in each cell in column G, select cell G6 and choose Copy from the Edit menu; then select cells G7:G10 and choose Paste from the Edit menu. The results appear in Figure 4-18.

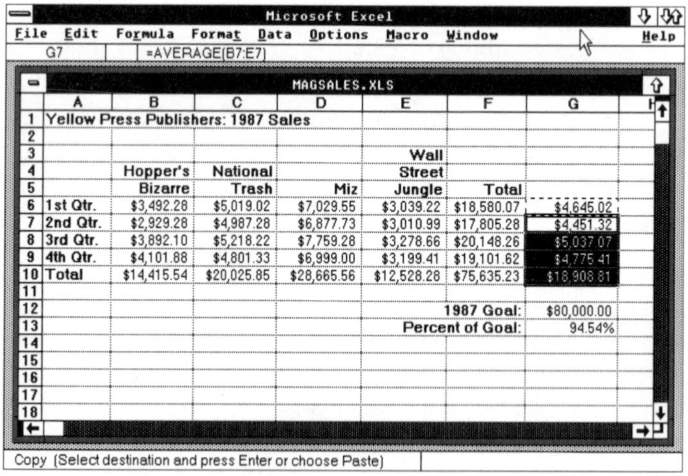

FIGURE 4-18. *We copied the relative references from cell G6 into cells G7:G10.*

Because the formula in cell G6 contains a relative reference, the references in each copy of the formula are adjusted. As a result, each copy of the formula calculates the average of the cells in the corresponding row. For example, cell G7 contains the formula

=AVERAGE(B7:E7)

Absolute references

When you want to ensure that cell references do not change when you copy them, use absolute references instead of relative references.

For example, in the worksheet in Figure 4-19, cell C5 contains the formula

=B2*B5

Cell B2 contains the wage rate at which employees are to be paid.

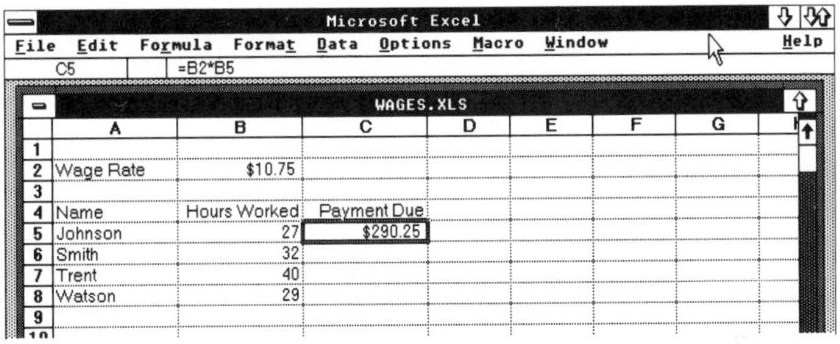

FIGURE 4-19. *The entry in cell C5 is a formula containing relative references.*

Suppose you want to copy this formula into the range C6:C8. Figure 4-20 shows what happens if you copy the existing formula into this range. The formula in cell C6 returns the value 0 and cell C7 contains the error value #VALUE!. If you look at the formulas in cells C6:C8, you'll see that none of them refer to cell B2. The formula in cell C6 is

=B3*B6

Because cell B3 is empty, the formula returns a zero value. Similarly, cell C7 contains the formula

=B4*B7

Because cell B4 contains a label rather than a value, the formula in cell C7 returns an error value.

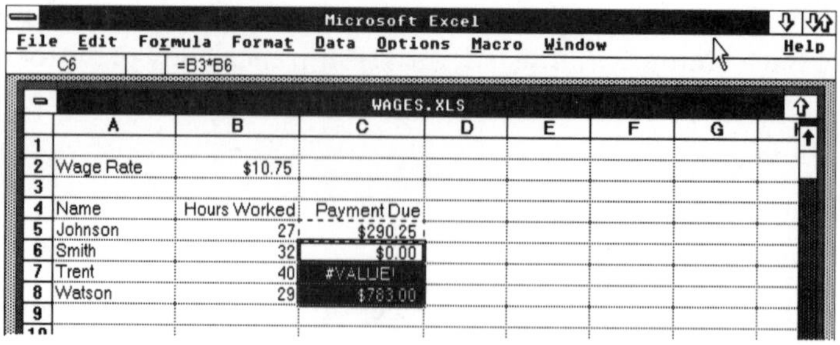

FIGURE 4-20. *We copied the relative formula in cell C5 into cells C6:C8.*

Because the reference to cell B2 in the original formula is relative, it changes as you copy the formula through the worksheet. To apply the wage rate in cell B2 to all the calculations, you must change the reference to cell B2 to an absolute reference before you copy the formula.

You can change the reference style in two ways: by typing a dollar sign ($) in front of the row and column references or by using the Reference command from the Formula menu to insert dollar signs for you. The $ symbol tells Microsoft Excel to "lock in" the reference. For example, on the worksheet in Figure 4-19, you could select cell C5 and insert the $ symbol before the B and the 2 in the formula bar so that the formula becomes

=$B$2*B5

Alternatively, you could select the cell reference B2 in the formula bar and then choose Reference from the Formula menu to have Microsoft Excel change the relative reference to an absolute reference. The reference to cell B5 will not be affected.

When you copy the modified formula into cells C6:C8, the second cell reference, but not the first, is adjusted within each formula. In Figure 4-21, cell C6 now contains the formula

=$B$2*B6

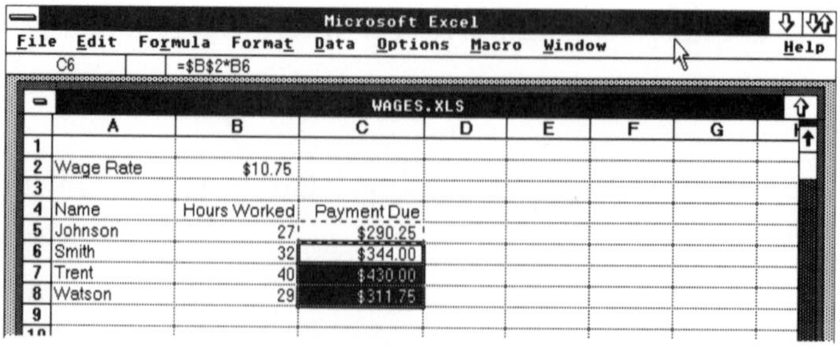

FIGURE 4-21. *We created an absolute reference to cell B2.*

Mixed references

You can also use mixed references in your formulas, to anchor only a portion of a cell reference. In a mixed reference, one portion of the reference is absolute and the other is relative. When you copy mixed references, Microsoft Excel anchors the absolute portion and adjusts the relative portion in relation to the location of the copy cell.

In a mixed reference, a dollar sign appears in front of the absolute portion of the reference but not in front of the relative portion. For example, the references $B2 and B$2 are mixed references. $B2 uses an absolute column reference and a relative row reference; B$2 uses a relative column reference and an absolute row reference.

To create a mixed reference, you can type the $ symbol in front of the row or column reference or you can use the Reference command to cycle through the four combinations of absolute and relative references—from B2 to $B$2 to B$2 to $B2. (You must repeat the entire command to see the next selections.)

The loan-payment table in Figure 4-22 shows one situation in which mixed references are convenient. Cell B5 uses the formula

=PMT($A5,10,B$4)

to calculate the annual payments on a $10,000 loan over a period of 10 years at an interest rate of 10 percent. We have copied this formula into cells B5:D8 to calculate payments on three different loan amounts using several different interest rates.

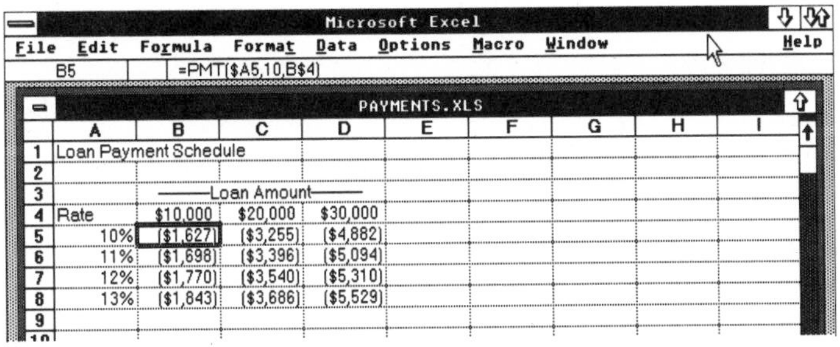

FIGURE 4-22. *This loan-payment table uses formulas containing mixed references.*

The first cell reference, $A5, indicates that we always want to refer to the values in column A. The row reference remains relative, however, so that the copied formulas in rows 6 through 8 refer to the appropriate interest rates in cells A6 through A8. Similarly, the second cell reference, B$4, indicates that we always want to refer to the loan amounts displayed in row 4. In this case, the column reference remains relative so that the copied formulas in columns B through D refer to the appropriate loan amounts in cells B4 through D4. For example, cell D8 contains the formula

=PMT($A8,10,D$4)

Without mixed references, we would have to manually edit the formula for each column or row of the calculations in cells B5 through D8.

Using Cut, Copy, Paste, and Clear in the formula bar

You can also use the Cut, Copy, Paste, and Clear commands to edit entries in the formula bar. Often, it is easier to simply reenter a value or formula, but the Edit menu commands can be convenient when you're working with a long, complex formula or label. For example, to add another *very* to the label

This is a very, very long label.

you can place the insertion point to the left of the space before the word *long*, type a comma, and then type the word *very*. Alternatively, you can select the first instance of the word *very*, the comma, and the space after the comma in the formula bar and issue the Copy command. Then you can place the insertion point in front of the *v* in the second *very* and choose Paste from the Edit menu. Your label now reads

This is a very, very, very long label.

You can also use this capability to copy all or part of a formula from one cell to another. For example, suppose cell A10 contains the formula

=IF(NPV(.15,A1:A9)>0,A11,A12)

and you want to enter

=NPV(.15,A1:A9)

in cell B10. Select cell A10 and select the characters you want to copy—in this case, NPV(.15,A1:A9). Then choose Copy from the Edit menu and click on the Enter box or press Enter. Now select cell B10, type =, and choose the Paste command to insert the contents of the copy range in that cell's formula bar. The formula's cell references are not adjusted when you cut, copy, and paste in the formula bar.

The Paste Special command

At times, you may want to copy the value in a cell without carrying over the underlying formula on which the value is based. Or you may want to copy the formula but not the format of a cell. The Paste Special command on the Edit menu offers a convenient way to copy only a selected aspect of a cell.

For example, cell F4 in Figure 4-23 contains the formula

=AVERAGE(B4:E4)

To use the value from cell F4 in cell G4 of your worksheet without copying the formula from cell F4 to the new location—that is, to make the pasted entry an absolute value—select cell F4 and choose Copy. (You must choose Copy in order to use the Paste Special command. When you choose Cut, Paste Special is dimmed.) Then select cell G4 and choose Paste Special. You'll see the dialog box shown in Figure 4-24.

			Microsoft Excel				⇩ ⇩⇩	Help
File	Edit	Formula	Format	Data	Options	Macro	Window	

F4	=AVERAGE(B4:E4)

SCORES.XLS

	A	B	C	D	E	F	G	H	I
1	First Quarter Exam Scores								
2									
3	Student	Exam 1	Exam 2	Exam 3	Exam 4	Average			
4	Smith	87	88	79	90	86.00			
5	Jones	92	77	81	76	81.50			
6	Allen	96	91	93	88	92.00			
7	Harris	82	94	96	86	89.50			
8	Clark	81	93	87	92	88.25			
9									

FIGURE 4-23. *We want to use the value from cell F4 in cell G4.*

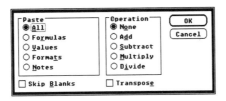

FIGURE 4-24. *The Paste Special dialog box lets you paste formulas, values, formats, or notes.*

The dialog box lets you selectively paste the formulas, values, formats, or notes from the copy range into the paste range. (We'll cover cell notes in detail in Chapter 8.) If you select Values in the Paste Special dialog box, Microsoft Excel will copy only the displayed value of the formula in cell F4 into cell G4. After the copy operation is complete, cell G4 will contain the number 86. As you can see in Figure 4-25, the formula and numeric format of the original cell were not copied, so if you later change any of the values in cells B4:E8, the value in cell G4 will remain unchanged.

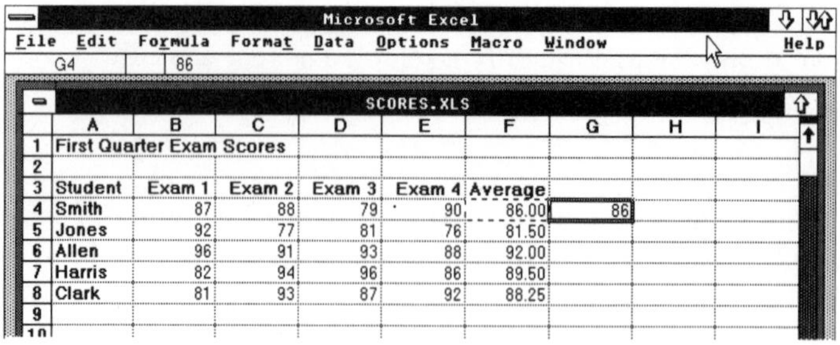

FIGURE 4-25. *We used Paste Special to copy the value of the formula in F4 into G4.*

The Formats option transfers only the formats from the cells in the copy range to the cells in the paste range. This command has the same effect as selecting a range of cells and choosing the appropriate options from the Format menu. Copying formats does not change the values of the cells in the paste area.

You can select Formulas from the Paste Special dialog box to copy the formulas in the cells in the copy range to the paste range without copying the formats assigned to those cells. For example, in Figure 4-26, cells A1:A5 are formatted to display currency with two decimal places (the $#,##0.00 format) and cells B1:B5 are formatted to display integers (the 0 format). If you copy cells A1:A5 into cells B1:B5 using the Paste Special Formulas option, the worksheet will look like Figure 4-27. The values in cells B1:B5 have changed, but the formats have not.

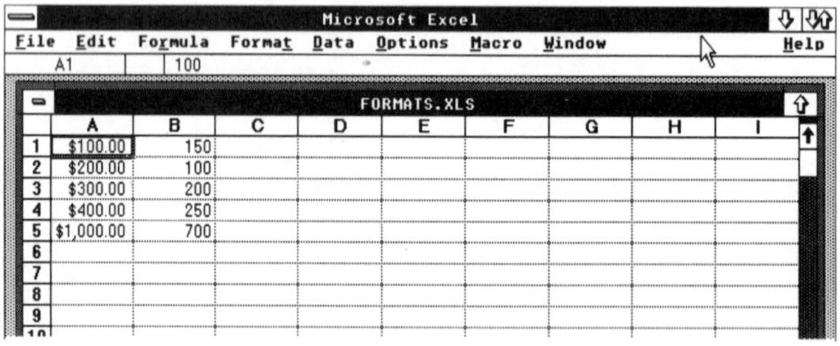

FIGURE 4-26. *The range A1:A5 is formatted to display currency with two decimal places; the range B1:B5 is formatted to display integers.*

If you select All in the Paste Special dialog box, the values, formulas, formats, and cell notes from the copy range are all copied to the paste range. Because selecting All has the same effect as selecting the regular Paste command, you may wonder why Microsoft Excel offers this option. That question brings us to our next topic—the Operation options.

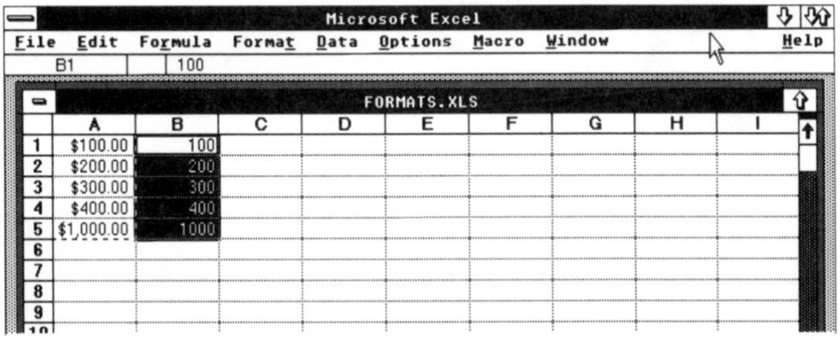

FIGURE 4-27. *We've used the Formulas option to paste the formulas from A1:A5 into B1:B5 without changing the latter's format.*

The Operation options

The options in the Operation box let you mathematically combine the contents of the copy area with the contents of the paste area. When you select any option in this box other than None, Microsoft Excel does not overwrite the paste range. Instead, it uses the specified operator to combine the copy and paste ranges.

For example, suppose you want to add the average exam scores and bonus points in columns F and G of Figure 4-28 to calculate each student's final score. First, select cells F4:F8 and choose Copy. Then select cell H4 and choose Paste Special. Click the Values option in the Paste Special dialog box to copy only the values in cells F4:F8 into cells H4:H8. (Because the pasted cells are still selected, you can now choose Number to give them the 0.00 format.) Next, select the range G4:G8 and choose Copy again. Then select cell H4 and choose Paste Special. Select the Values and Add options in the Paste Special dialog box and then select OK or press Enter. As you can see in Figure 4-29, Microsoft Excel adds the values in cells F4:F8 to the values in cells G4:G8.

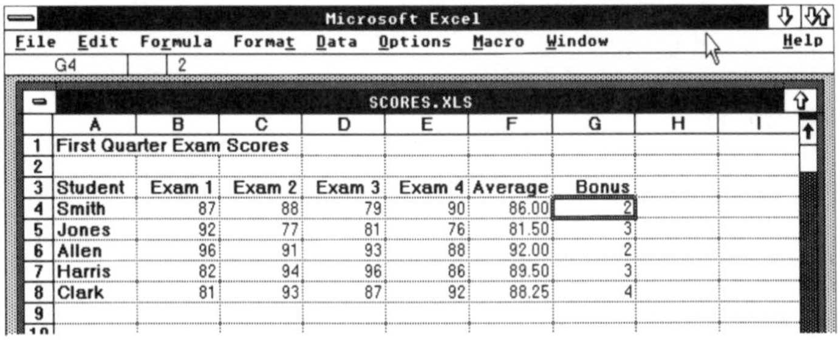

FIGURE 4-28. *The exam-scores worksheet contains average scores and bonus points.*

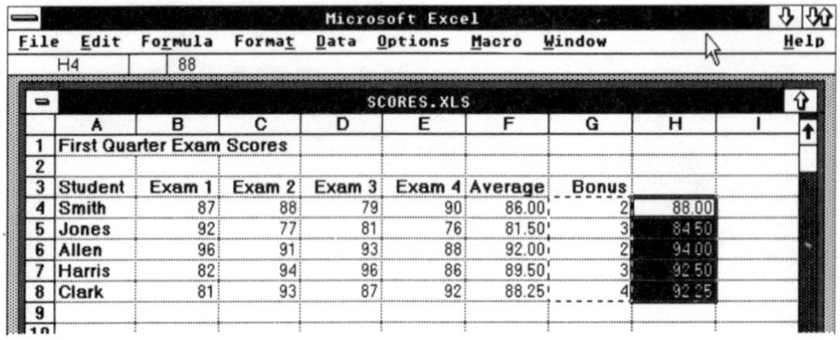

	Microsoft Excel								⇩ 🕮
File	Edit	Formula	Format	Data	Options	Macro	Window		Help

| H4 | | 88 | | | | | | |

				SCORES.XLS					⇧
	A	B	C	D	E	F	G	H	I
1	First Quarter Exam Scores								
2									
3	Student	Exam 1	Exam 2	Exam 3	Exam 4	Average	Bonus		
4	Smith	87	88	79	90	86.00	2	88.00	
5	Jones	92	77	81	76	81.50	3	84.50	
6	Allen	96	91	93	88	92.00	2	94.00	
7	Harris	82	94	96	86	89.50	3	92.50	
8	Clark	81	93	87	92	88.25	4	92.25	
9									

FIGURE 4-29. *We used the Values and Add options to combine the average scores and bonus points into a total score.*

The other options in the Operation box combine the contents of the copy and paste ranges using different operators. The Subtract option subtracts the contents of the copy range from the contents of the paste range, the Multiply option multiplies the contents of the ranges, and the Divide option divides the contents of the paste range by the contents of the copy range.

You'll usually choose the Values option from the Paste portion of the Paste Special dialog box when you take advantage of the Operation options. As long as the entries in the copy range are numbers, you can use the All option, instead of Values, to copy the numbers and the formats from the copy range to the paste range. If the copy range contains formulas, however, the result of using All may be a bit surprising.

For example, suppose cell A1 contains the value 10, cell A2 contains the formula

    =A1

which returns the value 10, and cell B2 contains the value 2. If you select cell A2, choose the Copy command, and then select cell B2, choose the Paste Special command, and select All and Add, Microsoft Excel combines the formula from cell A2—adjusted, because it is a relative reference—with the entry in cell B2. The result is the formula

    =2+B1

The same occurs if the cells in the paste range include formulas, even if you select the Values options.

As a rule, you should avoid using the All option with any of the Paste Special Operation options when the copy range includes formulas. In fact, you'll probably want to avoid the Operation options altogether if the paste range contains formulas.

If the copy range contains text entries and you use Paste Special with an Operation option, Microsoft Excel does not copy those text entries into the paste range. Blank spaces in the copy range are assigned the value 0, regardless of which Operation option you select. For example, suppose you use the Multiply option to copy the values in cells B1:B7 into cells A1:A7 in Figure 4-30. As you can see in Figure 4-31, cells A2, A4, and A6 contain zeros, because Microsoft Excel assigns the value 0 to blank cells and the result of multiplying any number by zero is zero.

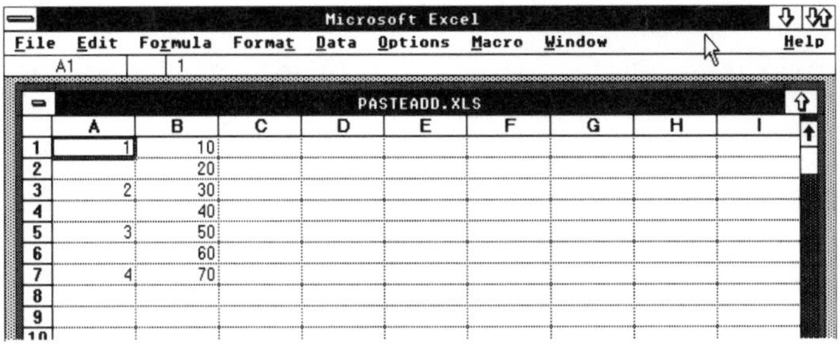

FIGURE 4-30. *The range A1:A7 contains some blank cells.*

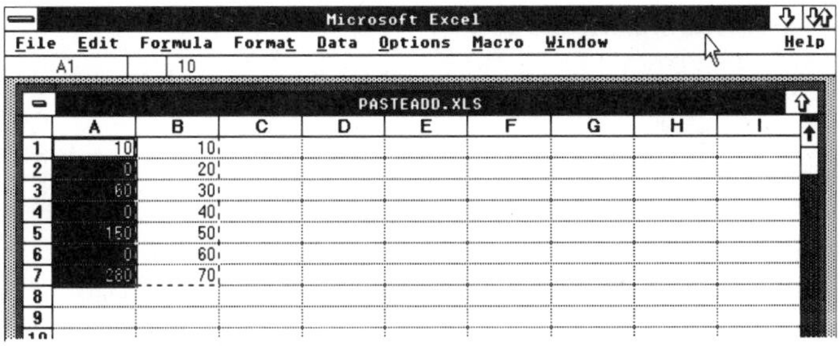

FIGURE 4-31. *Multiplying B1:B7 into A1:A7 causes a zero to be displayed in A2, A4, and A6, because Microsoft Excel assigns the value 0 to blank cells when performing mathematical operations with the Paste Special command.*

Skipping blank cells

At the lower left of the Paste Special dialog box is a Skip Blanks check box. Use this option when you want Microsoft Excel to ignore any blank cells in the copy range. Generally, if your copy range contains blank cells, Microsoft Excel pastes those blank cells over the corresponding cells in the paste area. As a result, the contents, formats, and notes in the paste area are overwritten by the empty cell. When you use the Skip Blanks option, however, the corresponding cells in the paste area are unaffected.

For example, let's use the Skip Blanks option to copy cells A1:A7 into the range B1:B7 in Figure 4-32. As you can see in Figure 4-33, the blank cells A2, A4, and A6 don't affect the entries in cells B2, B4, and B6. Instead, the entries from the two ranges are interwoven.

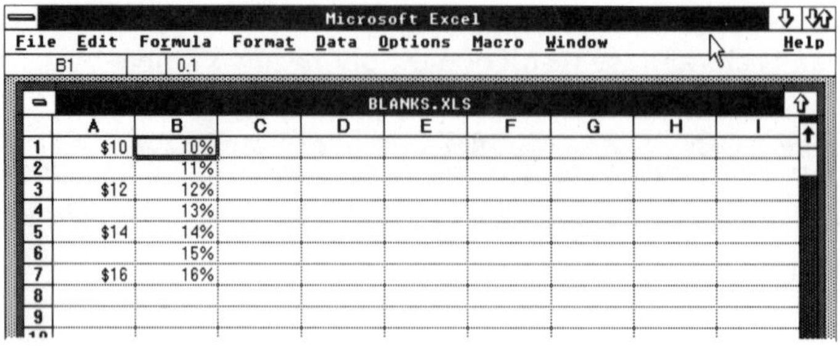

FIGURE 4-32. *Cells A2, A4, and A6 contain blank cells.*

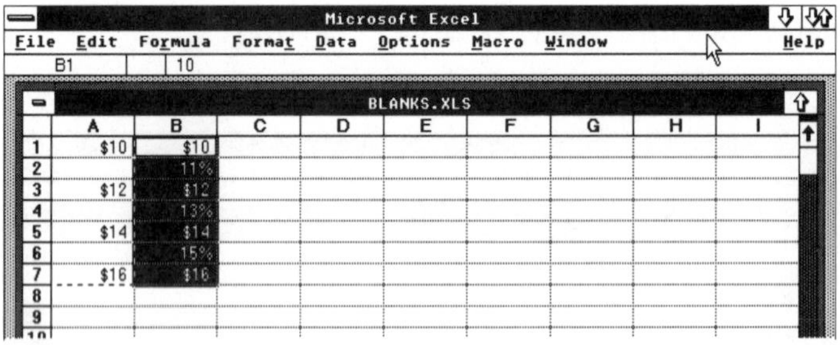

FIGURE 4-33. *When we use the Skip Blanks option, the empty cells in the copy range don't affect corresponding cells in the paste range.*

Transposing entries

The last option in the Paste Special dialog box is Transpose, which lets you reorient the contents of the copy range in the selected paste range. When you use the Transpose option, entries in the top row of the copy area appear in the left column of the paste range; entries in the left column appear in the top row. To illustrate, let's use the Transpose option to paste the contents of cells A4:C8 in Figure 4-21. If we specify cell E4 as the top left corner of our Paste Special range, our worksheet will look like the one in Figure 4-34.

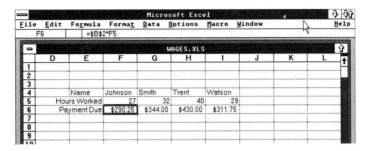

FIGURE 4-34. *The Transpose check box reorients a pasted selection.*

Microsoft Excel not only transposes the absolute values from the Hours Worked column, it also transposes the formulas in the Payment Due cells. For example, cell F6 now contains the formula

=$B$2*F5

Similarly, the copied and transposed formula in cell G6 contains the formula

=$B$2*G5

The Fill commands

The Fill Right, Fill Left, Fill Down, and Fill Up commands are handy shortcuts when you want to copy one or more cells into an adjacent set of cells. Fill Right copies the entries in the leftmost column of a range into the rest of the cells in the range; Fill Down copies the entries in the top row of a range down into the rest of the cells in the range. If you press the Shift key before accessing the Edit menu, Microsoft Excel changes the Fill Right and Fill Down commands to read Fill Left and Fill Up. As you might have guessed, Fill Left copies the entries in the rightmost column of a range into the rest of the cells in the range and Fill Up copies the entries in the bottom row of a range up into the rest of the cells in the range.

For example, in Figure 4-18, we used the Copy and Paste commands to copy the formula in cell G6 into cells G7:G10. We could also have used the Fill Down command to copy this formula. To use Fill Down, simply type the desired formula in cell G6, select cells G6:G10, and choose Fill Down from the Edit menu. The resulting worksheet will look exactly like the one in Figure 4-18. As with the Copy and Paste commands, any relative cell references in the filled cells will be adjusted.

Similarly, you can use the Fill Right command to copy a series of cells across your worksheet. Let's use the simple worksheet in Figure 4-35 as an example. To copy the contents of cells A1:A4 into cells B1:E4 of the worksheet, simply select cells A1:E4 and choose Fill Right from the Edit menu. The results appear in Figure 4-36.

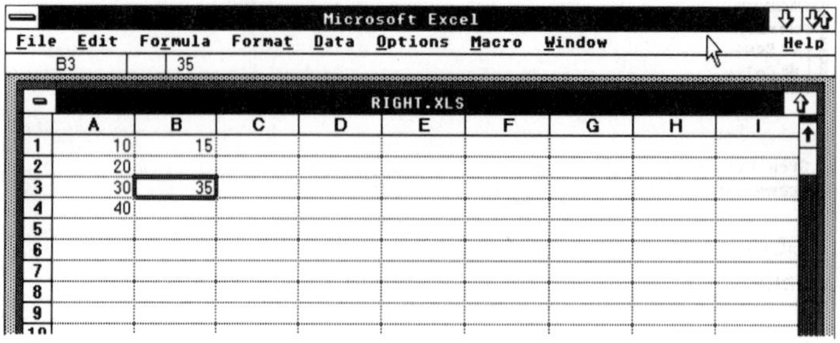

FIGURE 4-35. *This simple worksheet contains entries in cells A1:A4, B1, and B3.*

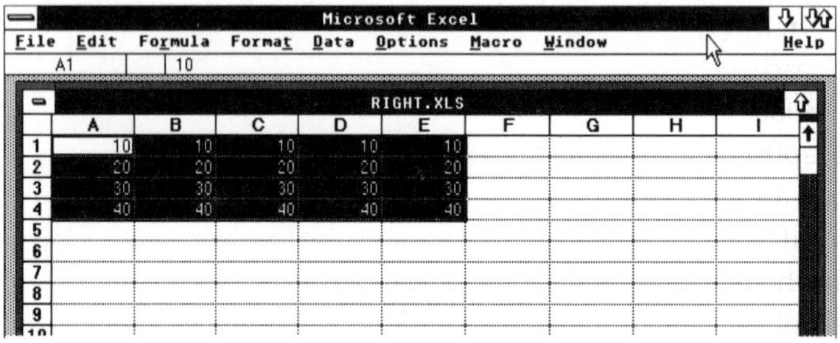

FIGURE 4-36. *We used the Fill Right command to copy the entries in cells A1:A4 into B1:E4.*

Notice that the contents of cells B1 and B3 were overwritten as a result of the Fill Right command. Whenever you use a Fill command, any existing cell entries in the fill range are replaced with the values that reside in the leftmost or top cells of the range.

The Series command

The Series command on the Data menu is similar to the Fill commands. It lets you quickly create a regular series of numbers in your worksheet. You supply a starting value, the range to be filled, an interval, and, if you wish, a maximum value for the range.

Let's look at the Series command in action. Suppose cells A1 and B1 contain the values 10 and 100, respectively, and cell C1 contains the formula

    =A1*B1

If you select cells A1:C10 and choose Series from the Data menu, Microsoft Excel displays a dialog box like the one in Figure 4-37.

Series in
Rows
Columns
Type
Linear
Growth
Date
Date Unit
Day
Weekday
Month
Year
OK
Cancel
Step Value: 1
Stop Value:

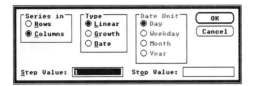

FIGURE 4-37. *Use the Series dialog box to create a regular series of numbers.*

To create a data series, first tell Microsoft Excel whether you want to create the series in rows or in columns. Like Fill Right, the Rows option tells Microsoft Excel to use the first value in each row to fill the cells to the right; like Fill Down, the Columns option tells Microsoft Excel to use the first value in each column to fill the cells below. In this case, because our selection is taller than it is wide, the Columns option is already selected.

Next, choose the type of data series you want to create: Linear, Growth, or Date. Microsoft Excel will use the Type option in conjunction with the start values in cells A1:C1 and will use the value in the Step Value edit bar at the lower left corner of the dialog box to create your data series. The Linear option adds the value specified in the Step Value edit bar to the values in your worksheet. The Growth option multiplies the start values in the worksheet by the step value. If you select the Date option, Microsoft Excel also makes the options in the Date Unit box available to let you specify the type of date series you want to create.

We'll cover the Series command in more detail in Chapters 7 and 16. For now, we'll enter a 2 in the Step Value edit bar, select the Growth option, and click OK. The resulting series is shown in Figure 4-38.

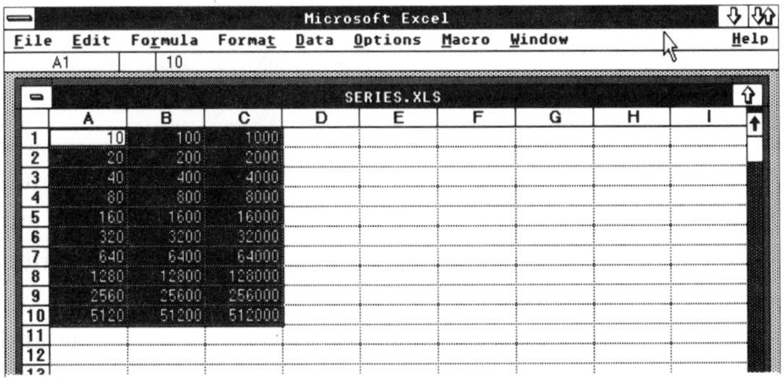
Microsoft Excel
File Edit Formula Format Data Options Macro Window Help
A1
10
SERIES.XLS
A B C D E F G H I
1 10 100 1000
2 20 200 2000
3 40 400 4000
4 80 800 8000
5 160 1600 16000
6 320 3200 32000
7 640 6400 64000
8 1280 12800 128000
9 2560 25600 256000
10 5120 51200 512000
11
12

FIGURE 4-38. *Choosing the Growth option in the Series dialog box causes subsequent selected cells to be multiplied by the value in the Step Value edit bar—in this case, 2.*

The Justify and Parse commands

The Justify command on the Format menu lets you split a cell entry and distribute it into two or more adjacent rows of your worksheet. Unlike other formatting commands, Justify affects the contents of your cells, not just the way in which entries are displayed.

For example, cell A2 in Figure 4-39 contains a long label. Suppose we want to extend this label into cells A3 through A7 to make it more readable. If we select the range A2:A7 and choose Justify from the Format menu, our worksheet will look like the one in Figure 4-40.

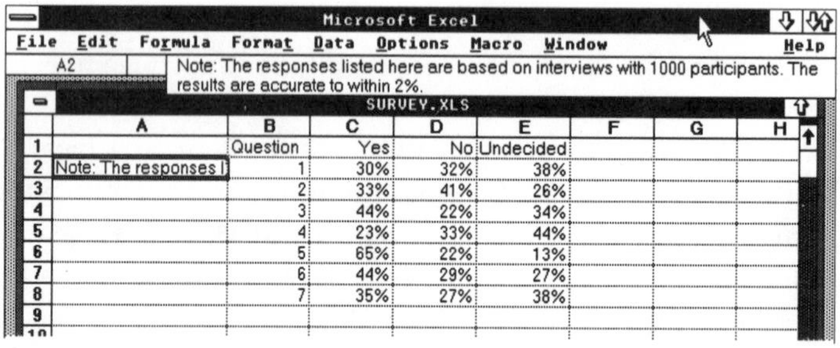

FIGURE 4-39. *Cell A2 contains a long label.*

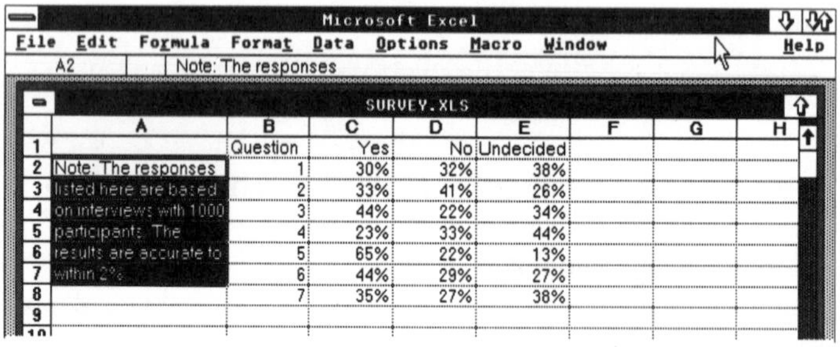

FIGURE 4-40. *We used the Justify command to distribute the label from cell A2 into cells A2:A7.*

If the selected Justify range isn't large enough to accommodate the long cell entry, Microsoft Excel displays the message *Text will extend below range.* Clicking OK in the alert box (or pressing Enter) causes the program to extend the length of the selected range to the length required for justification, overwriting the contents of any cells within the extended range. To avoid this, choose Cancel in the alert box, widen the column containing the range, and repeat the Justify command.

If we later decide to edit the entries in cells A2:A7 or to change the width of the column that contains those labels, we can use the Justify command to redistribute the text. For example, suppose we decide to widen column A in Figure 4-40. We can rejustify the text in cells A2:A7 by selecting the range and again choosing Justify from the Format menu. Figure 4-41 shows the result.

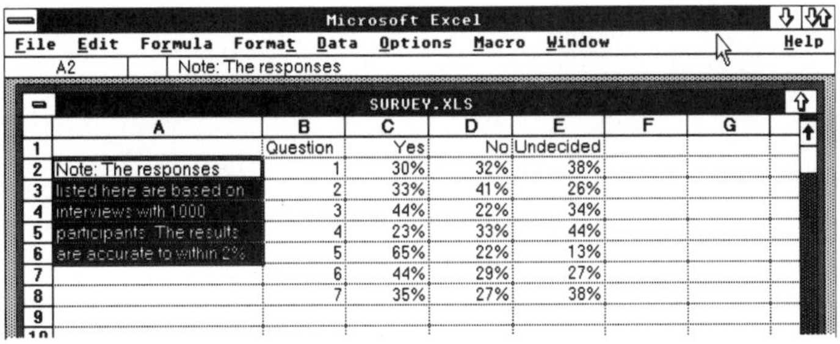

FIGURE 4-41. *After editing, we used Justify to redistribute the labels.*

If you select a multicolumn range when you issue the Justify command, Microsoft Excel justifies the entries in the leftmost column of the range, using the total width of the range you select as its guideline for determining the length of the justified labels. The cells in adjacent columns are not affected by the command. As a result, you may find that some of your label displays are truncated by the entries in subsequent columns.

Any blank cells in the leftmost column of the justify range serve as "paragraph" separators. That is, Microsoft Excel groups the labels above and below the blank cells when it justifies text entries.

The Parse command is similar to Justify, except that it distributes cell entries horizontally rather than vertically. For example, if cell A1 contains a long label that you want to distribute into cells A1:E1, you can use Parse to break that label into appropriate portions. Parse is located on the Data menu because you'll use it most often when you import database information from other programs into Microsoft Excel. For that reason, we'll save our main discussion of Parse for the Appendix.

5

One Worksheet,
Many Windows

*A*s we explained in Chapter 1, document windows are like portholes through which you view a small portion of your total worksheet. With Microsoft Excel, you can open two or more documents in the workspace at the same time. For example, you can have two or more related worksheets and macro sheets open simultaneously.

In this chapter, we'll show you how to open several windows that view the same worksheet and how to use them to make your work easier and faster. Then we'll show you how to move between windows with the mouse, the keyboard, and the Window menu. We'll also show you how to move, size, and reposition document windows with the mouse, the keyboard, and the Control menu. (The Control menu appears at the top left corner of the document window. To access this menu, point to the bar icon at the top left corner of the document window or press Alt-Hyphen.)

All the window techniques we will describe here apply to macro sheets as well as to worksheets. All the selection, sizing, and positioning techniques apply to chart windows as well; however, because the entire chart is visible in the document window, you can open only one window into a chart document at a time.

Many techniques we'll show you in the following pages can be applied to application windows as well as to document windows. (To access the application-window Control menu, simply click on the bar icon at the top left corner of the application window or press Alt-Spacebar.) Because you'll generally need to manipulate the application window only when you're running Microsoft Excel concurrently with other programs, we'll save our main discussion of the application window for the Appendix.

Opening and selecting multiple windows

Suppose you've created a worksheet called BUDGET.XLS, like the one shown in Figure 5-1. (For your reference, we've labeled the icons you'll be using to manipulate the document window. We'll be discussing each of these icons in the next several pages.) Currently, only cells A1:H18 are visible. To open a new window for this document, simply choose the New Window command from the Window menu. Your screen will then look like Figure 5-2.

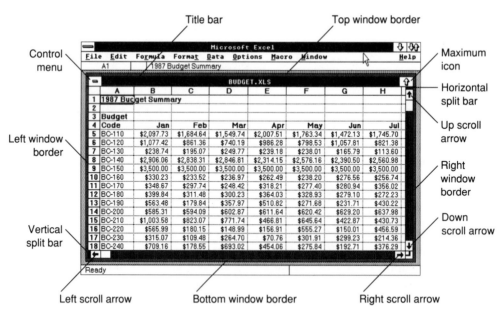

FIGURE 5-1. *Cells A1:H18 are currently visible in this document window.*

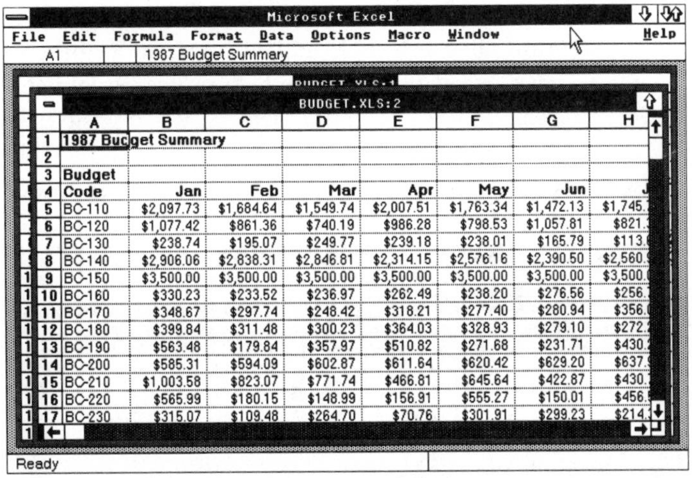

	A	B	C	D	E	F	G	H
1	1987 Budget Summary							
2								
3	Budget							
4	Code	Jan	Feb	Mar	Apr	May	Jun	J
5	BC-110	$2,097.73	$1,684.64	$1,549.74	$2,007.51	$1,763.34	$1,472.13	$1,745.
6	BC-120	$1,077.42	$861.36	$740.19	$986.28	$798.53	$1,057.81	$821.
7	BC-130	$238.74	$195.07	$249.77	$239.18	$238.01	$165.79	$113.
8	BC-140	$2,906.06	$2,838.31	$2,846.81	$2,314.15	$2,576.16	$2,390.50	$2,560.
9	BC-150	$3,500.00	$3,500.00	$3,500.00	$3,500.00	$3,500.00	$3,500.00	$3,500.
10	BC-160	$330.23	$233.52	$236.97	$262.49	$238.20	$276.56	$256.
11	BC-170	$348.67	$297.74	$248.42	$318.21	$277.40	$280.94	$356.
12	BC-180	$399.84	$311.48	$300.23	$364.03	$328.93	$279.10	$272.
13	BC-190	$563.48	$179.84	$357.97	$510.82	$271.68	$231.71	$430.
14	BC-200	$585.31	$594.09	$602.87	$611.64	$620.42	$629.20	$637.
15	BC-210	$1,003.58	$823.07	$771.74	$466.81	$645.64	$422.87	$430.
16	BC-220	$565.99	$180.15	$148.99	$156.91	$555.27	$150.01	$456.
17	BC-230	$315.07	$109.48	$264.70	$70.76	$301.91	$299.23	$214.

FIGURE 5-2. *Use the New Window command to open a second window.*

Notice that Microsoft Excel assigns the name BUDGET.XLS:2 to the new worksheet window and renames the original worksheet window BUDGET.XLS:1. In addition, BUDGET.XLS:2 becomes the active window, as indicated by its highlighted title bar. Because the top of the new window appears slightly lower on the screen, BUDGET.XLS:2 is one row smaller than BUDGET.XLS:1.

It's important to understand the difference between the File menu's New command and the Window menu's New Window command. The New command creates a new worksheet (or chart or macro sheet), which is displayed in a new window. The worksheet that results from the New command is completely separate from any worksheets that existed before you issued the New command. The New Window command, on the other hand, does not create a new worksheet. Instead, this command simply offers a new porthole through which you can view an existing worksheet. If more than one document is open when you issue the New Window command, Microsoft Excel creates a new window only for the active document.

Any work you do through a window affects the entire document, not just the worksheet as viewed through that window. For instance, when you make an entry into the worksheet through one window, you can view that entry through any of the windows associated with that worksheet. By the same token, if you edit or erase the contents of a cell through one window, you'll see the change when you look at the same cell through another window.

Notice that the new window in Figure 5-2, BUDGET.XLS:2, offers the same view of BUDGET.XLS as the first window. Whenever you choose the New Window command, cell A1 appears in the upper left corner of the screen.

Of course, you can scroll through this new window to look at another portion of the worksheet. For example, if you click on the Down and Right scroll arrows in BUDGET.XLS:2 a few times, or use the scrolling techniques explained in Chapter 2 or the selection commands from the Formula menu, you can position that window over cells H17:N33, as shown in Figure 5-3. You can also use the Goto command from the Formula menu to move the new window to a different location.

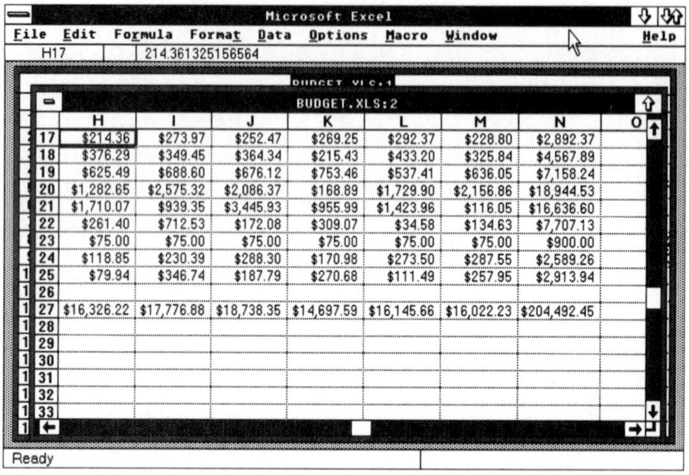

FIGURE 5-3. *Cells H17:N33 now appear in the second window.*

Shuffling the stack

Whenever you open a new document or create a new window to view an existing document, the new window appears on top of the "stack" of windows and becomes the active window. Microsoft Excel provides a number of ways to move between open windows to view different data or to make entries.

If you use a mouse, the easiest way to move between windows is to click on the window you want. If you can see part of the window you want under the top document, you can use the mouse to shuffle between windows as you would shuffle a deck of cards.

For example, to reactivate BUDGET.XLS:1 in Figure 5-3, simply point to the exposed portion of that window and click. BUDGET.XLS:1 will appear on top of BUDGET.XLS:2. Cells A1:H18 will still be visible in BUDGET.XLS:1, even though you were just looking at cells H17:N33 in BUDGET.XLS:2. When you scroll through one window that views a worksheet, the contents of the other windows that view that worksheet do not move. In fact, the cell or range you last selected in each window is automatically reselected when you return to that window. For example, in Figure 5-3, cell H17 is active; when you reactivate BUDGET.XLS:1, however, cell A1 in that window is active. Thus, if you create more than one window on a worksheet, you can position those windows on different parts of the worksheet and move from one location to another simply by jumping from window to window.

If you can't point to a window or if you prefer to use the keyboard, you can press Ctrl-F6 to activate the next window in the stack. For example, if BUDGET.XLS:2 is active, pressing Ctrl-F6 makes BUDGET.XLS:1 active. If more than two windows are open, Ctrl-F6 lets you move through the windows in turn. Shift-Ctrl-F6 lets you move through the windows in reverse order.

Alternatively, you can select the window name from the Window menu to quickly bring the window you want directly to the top of the stack. If you use a mouse, click on the name of the window you want; from the keyboard, use the Up and Down arrow keys to highlight the name of the window, or type the number of the window you want. If you have more than nine windows open at once, the names of the first nine appear at the bottom of the Window menu and the More Windows command appears at the bottom of the list. When you select More Windows, Microsoft Excel displays the Activate dialog box (Figure 5-4), which lists all the open windows. To activate a window that doesn't appear on the Windows menu, simply select it from the Activate dialog box and choose OK or press Enter.

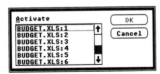

FIGURE 5-4. *The Activate dialog box allows you to bring another window to the top of the stack.*

Sizing windows

Initially, all the windows you open will overlap. Generally, the active window blocks your view of the other open windows. To see the contents of two or more windows at the same time, you can resize and reposition those windows so that they are more easily accessible.

To change the size of a window with the mouse, simply point to one of the window borders and drag it to the desired position. When the pointer is on the border, it will take on a double-arrow shape. Point to the top or bottom window border to change the height of the window; point to the left or right border to change the width of the window. To change both the height and the width of the window, point to one of the corners of the border and drag diagonally. As you drag, a shadow border will appear to show you the proposed window size. When you release the mouse button, Microsoft Excel will redraw the window to the size you've indicated.

For example, to see both windows in Figure 5-3, use the mouse to click in BUDGET.XLS:1, point to the bottom border, and drag up until the window is about eight rows deep. Your screen should look like Figure 5-5. (The bottom scroll bar will cover the eighth row.) Now click in the BUDGET.XLS:2 window. Microsoft Excel will bring BUDGET.XLS:2 to the top, covering BUDGET.XLS:1. Point to the top border of BUDGET.XLS:2 and drag down until that window is about seven rows deep. As you drag BUDGET.XLS:2 down, BUDGET.XLS:1 will be uncovered. In Figure 5-6, both windows are now visible.

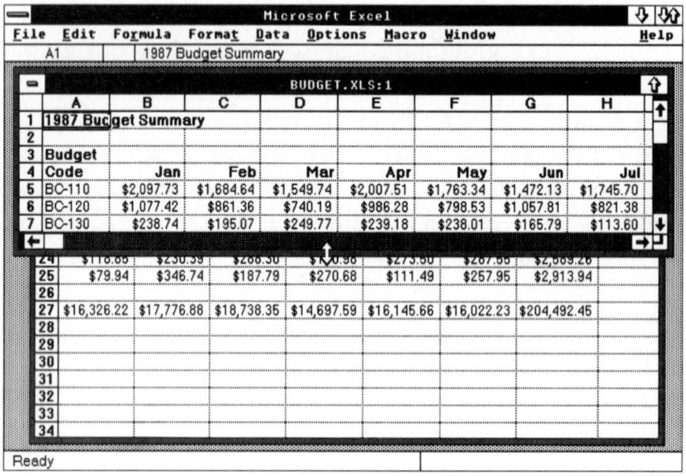

	Microsoft Excel							⇩ ⇧⇩
File **Edit** **Formula** **Format** **Data** **Options** **Macro** **Window**							**Help**
A1	1987 Budget Summary						

BUDGET.XLS:1

	A	B	C	D	E	F	G	H
1	1987 Budget Summary							
2								
3	Budget							
4	Code	Jan	Feb	Mar	Apr	May	Jun	Jul
5	BC-110	$2,097.73	$1,684.64	$1,549.74	$2,007.51	$1,763.34	$1,472.13	$1,745.70
6	BC-120	$1,077.42	$861.36	$740.19	$986.28	$798.53	$1,057.81	$821.38
7	BC-130	$238.74	$195.07	$249.77	$239.18	$238.01	$165.79	$113.60
24	$118.85	$230.39	$266.50	$180.96	$273.50	$267.55	$2,563.26	
25	$79.94	$346.74	$187.79	$270.68	$111.49	$257.95	$2,913.94	
26								
27	$16,326.22	$17,776.88	$18,738.35	$14,697.59	$16,145.66	$16,022.23	$204,492.45	
28								
29								
30								
31								
32								
33								
34								

Ready

FIGURE 5-5. *We resized the first window.*

If you prefer to use the keyboard, you can resize the active window by first either choosing the Size command from the Control menu (Alt-Hyphen-S) or pressing Ctrl-F8. Whichever method you use, you can then move the window's borders by using the arrow keys. Initially, you'll see a four-way arrow. To indicate which border you want to change, press the Left, Right, Up, or Down arrow key to move the pointer to a window border. Then use the arrow keys to move the border to the desired position. A shadow border will appear, indicating the proposed size of the window. When the shadow border is at the desired position, press the Enter key to redraw the window.

For example, to see both windows in Figure 5-3, first press Ctrl-F6 to activate BUDGET.XLS:1. Then press Ctrl-F8, press the Down arrow key once to position

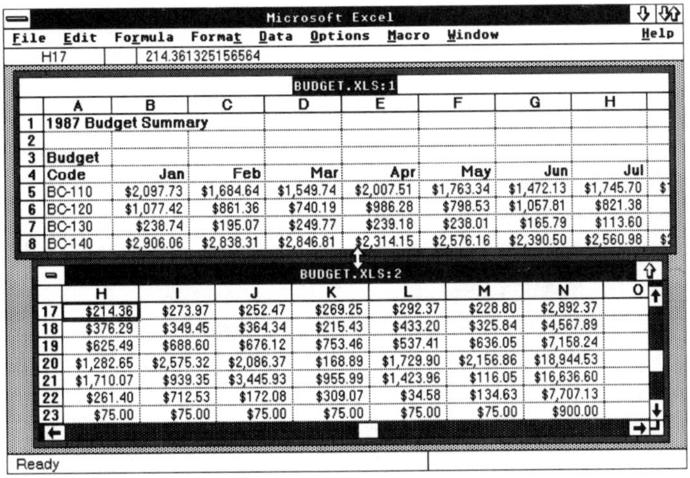

FIGURE 5-6. *We resized the second window so that it no longer overlaps the first.*

the pointer on the bottom border, and use the Up arrow key to move the bottom border of the top window up so that both windows are exposed. After you press Enter, Microsoft Excel redraws the window. To size BUDGET.XLS:2, press Ctrl-F6 to activate it, press Ctrl-F8, and then press the Up arrow key once to position the pointer on the top border. Next, use the Down arrow key to move the top border of BUDGET.XLS:2 down so that both windows are exposed. After you press Enter, your screen will look like Figure 5-6.

If you've used the Left or Right arrow key to change the width of the active window and haven't yet pressed Enter, you can then press the Up or Down arrow key to move to the corner of the window border. Your pointer will take on a diagonal double-arrow shape, indicating that you can now change the height of the active window. By the same token, if you've used the Up or Down arrow key to change the height of the active window, you can then press the Left or Right arrow key to move to the corner of the window border.

Maximizing and restoring windows

Instead of manually resizing a window, you can use the Maximize icon or the Maximize command on the Control menu to quickly enlarge the window to fill the entire workspace. This technique is particularly helpful when you have several partial-screen windows open at once and you want to zoom in on a particular window.

To maximize a window with the mouse, simply click on the Maximize icon to the right of the document window's menu bar. You can also use the keyboard to maximize a window, either by choosing the Maximize command from the Control menu (Alt-Hyphen-X) or by pressing Ctrl-F10.

As we've explained, when you use the maximize feature, the window expands to fill the entire screen. For example, if your worksheet shows cells A1:I16, when you use the maximize feature the document expands to display cells A1:J20. As you can see in Figure 5-7, when you maximize a window, the document's title bar becomes part of the application window title bar. To select another window, you must select the window name from the Window menu; you can't click in another window unless you resize or reposition the enlarged window first. The window's borders also disappear when it is maximized. Before you can resize a maximized window, you must restore it to its previous size.

1987 Budget Summary								
	A	B	C	D	E	F	G	H
1	1987 Budget Summary							
2								
3	Budget							
4	Code	Jan	Feb	Mar	Apr	May	Jun	Jul
5	BC-110	$2,097.73	$1,684.64	$1,549.74	$2,007.51	$1,763.34	$1,472.13	$1,745.70
6	BC-120	$1,077.42	$861.36	$740.19	$986.28	$798.53	$1,057.81	$821.38
7	BC-130	$238.74	$195.07	$249.77	$239.18	$238.01	$165.79	$113.60
8	BC-140	$2,906.06	$2,838.31	$2,846.81	$2,314.15	$2,576.16	$2,390.50	$2,560.98
9	BC-150	$3,500.00	$3,500.00	$3,500.00	$3,500.00	$3,500.00	$3,500.00	$3,500.00
10	BC-160	$330.23	$233.52	$236.97	$262.49	$238.20	$276.56	$256.74
11	BC-170	$348.67	$297.74	$248.42	$318.21	$277.40	$280.94	$356.02
12	BC-180	$399.84	$311.48	$300.23	$364.03	$328.93	$279.10	$272.23
13	BC-190	$563.48	$179.84	$357.97	$510.82	$271.68	$231.71	$430.22
14	BC-200	$585.31	$594.09	$602.87	$611.64	$620.42	$629.20	$637.98
15	BC-210	$1,003.58	$823.07	$771.74	$466.81	$645.64	$422.87	$430.73
16	BC-220	$565.99	$180.15	$148.99	$156.91	$555.27	$150.01	$456.59
17	BC-230	$315.07	$109.48	$264.70	$70.76	$301.91	$299.23	$214.36
18	BC-240	$709.16	$178.55	$693.02	$454.06	$275.84	$192.71	$376.29
19	BC-250	$822.61	$573.59	$108.24	$403.79	$776.08	$556.80	$625.49
20	BC-260	$822.61	$1,219.36	$977.55	$3,231.77	$2,090.95	$602.30	$1,282.65

FIGURE 5-7. *We maximized the first document window.*

To return expanded windows to their original sizes, either choose the Restore command from the Control menu (Alt-Hyphen-R) or press Ctrl-F5.

Moving windows

In addition to resizing windows, you can move the windows around to arrange your workspace more efficiently. To reposition a window with the mouse, simply drag the window's title bar to the desired position. To reposition a window with the keyboard, either choose the Move command from the Control menu (Alt-Hyphen-M) or press Ctrl-F7 and then use the arrow keys to drag the window to the desired position.

For example, suppose you want BUDGET.XLS:2 in Figure 5-6 to appear above window BUDGET.XLS:1. With the mouse, begin by dragging BUDGET.XLS:1 to the bottom of the screen. Next, activate BUDGET.XLS:2 and drag it to the top of the screen. Figure 5-8 shows the results.

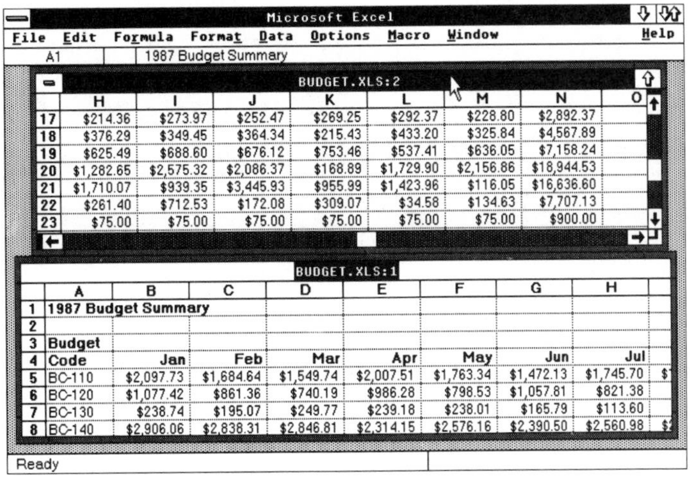

FIGURE 5-8. *We changed the position of the document windows.*

You can achieve the same effect from the keyboard by activating BUDGET.XLS:1, choosing the Move command or pressing Ctrl-F7, and then using the Down arrow key to drag the window to the bottom of the screen. Then activate BUDGET.XLS:2, choose the Move command or press Ctrl-F7, and use the Up arrow key to drag the window to the top of the screen.

A shortcut: The Arrange All command

When you have several windows open and you need to see all of them at the same time, you can choose the Arrange All command from the Window menu to position the open windows more efficiently on your screen. The Arrange All command causes Microsoft Excel to resize and reposition all open windows so that they do not overlap on your screen. For example, if you have four windows open, Arrange All displays them with two on the top and two on the bottom, as shown in Figure 5-9.

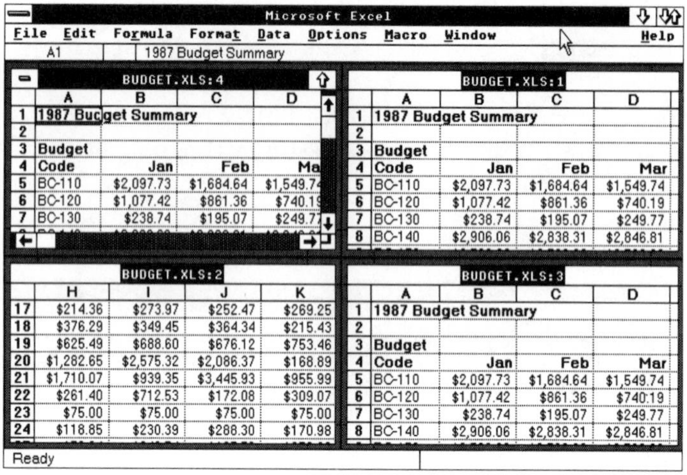

FIGURE 5-9. *The Arrange All command positions open documents more efficiently.*

Hiding windows

At times, you may need to keep a worksheet or macro sheet open so that you can use the information in that document, but you don't need to see it often. For example, you may want to have a supporting worksheet open so that you can access information in that file for your dependent documents. Or you may want to keep a macro sheet open so that you can run macros from that sheet, but you don't want the macro window to take up room on your screen. When several open documents clutter your workspace, you can use the Hide command to conceal some of them. Microsoft Excel can still work with the information in the hidden documents, but the documents themselves won't clutter your workspace.

To hide an active window, simply activate the window and choose the Hide command from the Window menu. Microsoft Excel will remove the window display from your workspace, but the document will remain open. If you want to bring the hidden window into view, choose the Unhide command from the Window menu. Microsoft Excel will display an Unhide dialog box, like the one shown in Figure 5-10, that lists all hidden windows. Select the window you want to see, then click OK or press Enter, and the hidden window will appear and become the active window.

If you've protected the hidden window by choosing the Protect Document command (discussed in Chapter 8), you must enter your password before you can hide or unhide the document window.

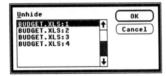

FIGURE 5-10. *Select the name of the window you want to display from the Unhide dialog box.*

If you've hidden all the windows in your workspace, Microsoft Excel displays an Unhide Windows command on the File menu rather than on the Window menu. When you choose the Unhide Windows command from the File menu, you'll see a dialog box from which you can select the windows you want to view.

Splitting windows into panes

Windowpanes offer another way to view different areas of your worksheet at the same time. Microsoft Excel's windowpane feature lets you split any window on the screen vertically, horizontally, or both vertically and horizontally to create panes of any size.

The principal advantage of the pane feature is its synchronized scrolling capability. Let's use the worksheet in Figure 5-1 as an example. Columns B through M and rows 5 through 25 in this worksheet contain monthly budget data. Column N and row 27 contain budget totals for the entire company. Suppose you want to keep an eye on the totals in column N as you work with the monthly budget figures in columns B through M. You could do this by splitting the window into two panes, one five columns wide and the other one column wide.

To create a vertical pane using the mouse, point to the black bar on the left side of the horizontal scroll bar. This is the vertical split bar. When your pointer touches the vertical split bar, it will change to a pair of vertical lines with small horizontal arrows. Now drag the split bar to the right so that it falls on the border between columns F and G. Your worksheet will look like Figure 5-11. Notice that you now have two horizontal scroll bars. Next, move your pointer to the horizontal scroll bar beneath the right pane and scroll column N into view. Your worksheet will look like Figure 5-12.

Now you can use the scroll bars in the large pane, the scrolling techniques we discussed in Chapter 2, or the selection commands on the Formula menu to scroll between columns A and M without losing sight of the totals in column N. In addition, when you scroll between rows 1 and 27, you'll always see the corresponding totals in column N. For example, if you scroll down until rows 20 through 27 are in view in the large pane, those same rows will be visible in the smaller pane.

A	B	C	D	E	F	F	G
1 1987 Budget Summary							
2							
3 Budget							
4 Code	Jan	Feb	Mar	Apr	May	May	Jun
5 BC-110	$2,097.73	$1,684.64	$1,549.74	$2,007.51	$1,763.34	$1,763.34	$1,472.13
6 BC-120	$1,077.42	$861.36	$740.19	$986.28	$798.53	$798.53	$1,057.81
7 BC-130	$238.74	$195.07	$249.77	$239.18	$238.01	$238.01	$165.79
8 BC-140	$2,906.06	$2,838.31	$2,846.81	$2,314.15	$2,576.16	$2,576.16	$2,390.50
9 BC-150	$3,500.00	$3,500.00	$3,500.00	$3,500.00	$3,500.00	$3,500.00	$3,500.00
10 BC-160	$330.23	$233.52	$236.97	$262.49	$238.20	$238.20	$276.56
11 BC-170	$348.67	$297.74	$248.42	$318.21	$277.40	$277.40	$280.94
12 BC-180	$399.84	$311.48	$300.23	$364.03	$328.93	$328.93	$279.10
13 BC-190	$563.48	$179.84	$357.97	$510.82	$271.68	$271.68	$231.71
14 BC-200	$585.31	$594.09	$602.87	$611.64	$620.42	$620.42	$629.20
15 BC-210	$1,003.58	$823.07	$771.74	$466.81	$645.64	$645.64	$422.87
16 BC-220	$565.99	$180.15	$148.99	$156.91	$555.27	$555.27	$150.01
17 BC-230	$315.07	$109.48	$264.70	$70.76	$301.91	$301.91	$299.23
18 BC-240	$709.16	$178.55	$693.02	$454.06	$275.84	$275.84	$192.71

FIGURE 5-11. *We split the window into two vertical panes.*

A	B	C	D	E	F	N	O
1 1987 Budget Summary							
2							
3 Budget						Total by	
4 Code	Jan	Feb	Mar	Apr	May	Month	
5 BC-110	$2,097.73	$1,684.64	$1,549.74	$2,007.51	$1,763.34	$21,615.78	
6 BC-120	$1,077.42	$861.36	$740.19	$986.28	$798.53	$10,469.31	
7 BC-130	$238.74	$195.07	$249.77	$239.18	$238.01	$2,401.78	
8 BC-140	$2,906.06	$2,838.31	$2,846.81	$2,314.15	$2,576.16	$29,984.87	
9 BC-150	$3,500.00	$3,500.00	$3,500.00	$3,500.00	$3,500.00	$42,000.00	
10 BC-160	$330.23	$233.52	$236.97	$262.49	$238.20	$3,027.45	
11 BC-170	$348.67	$297.74	$248.42	$318.21	$277.40	$3,608.81	
12 BC-180	$399.84	$311.48	$300.23	$364.03	$328.93	$3,714.63	
13 BC-190	$563.48	$179.84	$357.97	$510.82	$271.68	$4,407.90	
14 BC-200	$585.31	$594.09	$602.87	$611.64	$620.42	$7,370.59	
15 BC-210	$1,003.58	$823.07	$771.74	$466.81	$645.64	$7,378.88	
16 BC-220	$565.99	$180.15	$148.99	$156.91	$555.27	$4,202.49	
17 BC-230	$315.07	$109.48	$264.70	$70.76	$301.91	$2,892.37	
18 BC-240	$709.16	$178.55	$693.02	$454.06	$275.84	$4,567.89	

FIGURE 5-12. *We scrolled column N into view in the right pane.*

If you also want to keep an eye on the monthly totals in row 27, you can create a horizontal pane. Before you split the window, scroll the worksheet so that row 28 appears at the bottom of the window. (The new window will scroll up one row— that's why you have to include row 28.) Next, drag the horizontal split bar (the black bar at the top of the vertical scroll bar) toward the bottom of the window so that only two rows appear in the bottom two panes. Figure 5-13 shows the result.

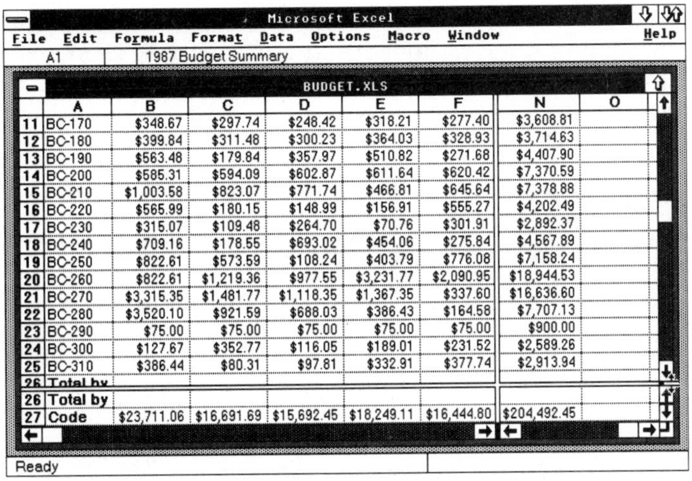

▭			, Microsoft Excel				⬇⬆	
File	**Edit**	**Formula**	**Format**	**Data**	**Options**	**Macro**	**Window**	**Help**

| A1 | | 1987 Budget Summary | | | | | | |

▭				BUDGET.XLS				⇧
	A	**B**	**C**	**D**	**E**	**F**	**N**	**O**
11	BC-170	$348.67	$297.74	$248.42	$318.21	$277.40	$3,608.81	
12	BC-180	$399.84	$311.48	$300.23	$364.03	$328.93	$3,714.63	
13	BC-190	$563.48	$179.84	$357.97	$510.82	$271.68	$4,407.90	
14	BC-200	$585.31	$594.09	$602.87	$611.64	$620.42	$7,370.59	
15	BC-210	$1,003.58	$823.07	$771.74	$466.81	$645.64	$7,378.88	
16	BC-220	$565.99	$180.15	$148.99	$156.91	$555.27	$4,202.49	
17	BC-230	$315.07	$109.48	$264.70	$70.76	$301.91	$2,892.37	
18	BC-240	$709.16	$178.55	$693.02	$454.06	$275.84	$4,567.89	
19	BC-250	$822.61	$573.59	$108.24	$403.79	$776.08	$7,158.24	
20	BC-260	$822.61	$1,219.36	$977.55	$3,231.77	$2,090.95	$18,944.53	
21	BC-270	$3,315.35	$1,481.77	$1,118.35	$1,367.35	$337.60	$16,636.60	
22	BC-280	$3,520.10	$921.59	$688.03	$386.43	$164.58	$7,707.13	
23	BC-290	$75.00	$75.00	$75.00	$75.00	$75.00	$900.00	
24	BC-300	$127.67	$352.77	$116.05	$189.01	$231.52	$2,589.26	
25	BC-310	$386.44	$80.31	$97.81	$332.91	$377.74	$2,913.94	
26	Total by							
27	**Code**	$23,711.06	$16,691.69	$15,692.45	$18,249.11	$16,444.80	$204,492.45	

Ready

FIGURE 5-13. *We created a horizontal split so that we can keep an eye on our totals in row 27.*

You can also split your screen using the keyboard. Choose the Split command from the Control menu and then use the arrow keys to split the window into two or four panes. The Up and Down arrow keys let you split the window horizontally; the Left and Right arrow keys let you split the window vertically. Press the Enter key to lock in your window panes.

To activate a pane, click in that pane with the mouse or press F6 to move from one pane to the next. Use Shift-F6 to move backward through the panes.

You can change the size of your windowpanes at any time by dragging the split bars or choosing the Split command from the Control menu and pressing the arrow keys. To get rid of a pane, simply use the mouse or keyboard techniques described above to move the split bar to the window border.

Freezing panes

After you've split a window into panes, you can freeze the top panes, the left panes, or both by choosing the Freeze Panes command from the Options menu. If you've split a window vertically, Freeze Panes "locks in" the columns that are in view in the left pane so that you can scroll through the worksheet without losing sight of these columns. Similarly, if you've split a window horizontally, Freeze Panes locks in the rows that are in view in the top pane. If you've split the window both vertically and horizontally, both the rows in the top pane and the columns in the left pane are frozen.

In Figure 5-14, we split the window vertically and horizontally to display the code entries in column A and the month entries in row 4. To keep this information in view as we enter and edit data in the worksheet, we can issue the Freeze Panes command. Figure 5-15 shows the result.

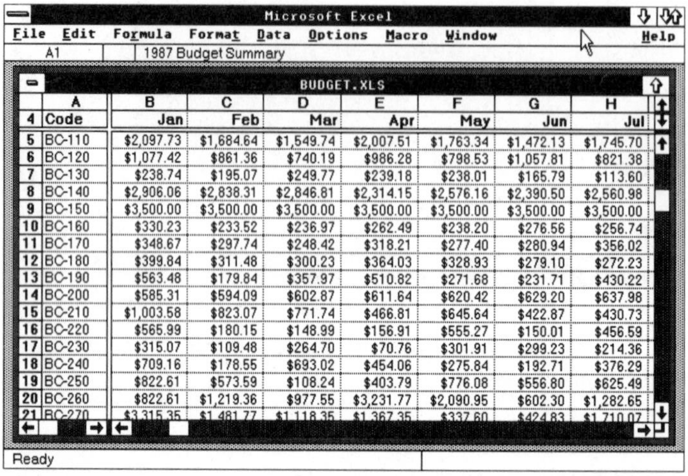

FIGURE 5-14. *Column A and row 4 are displayed in separate windowpanes.*

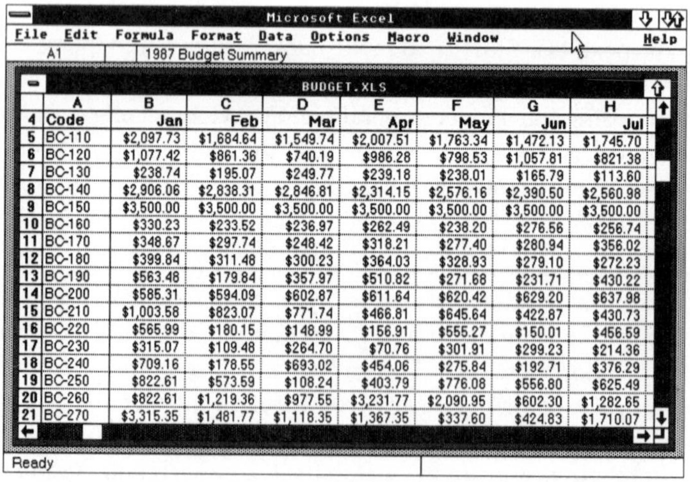

FIGURE 5-15. *We used the Freeze Panes command to lock in the data in the top and left panes.*

Notice that the double-line pane dividers have changed to single-line pane dividers. Now we can scroll through the remainder of the worksheet without losing sight of the entries in column A and row 4.

If you've created two or more windows to view the same document, you can split each window into panes and use the Freeze Panes command to freeze different areas in each window.

Saving and closing windows

You already know how to save your current workspace with the Save Workspace command on the File menu. You don't have to save each window individually when you save your workspace—Microsoft Excel will remember all your window settings. When you open the workspace file again, your windows will reappear exactly as you last saved them.

To completely close a worksheet, including any secondary windows, select the Close command from the File menu. To close only a secondary window without closing the worksheet itself, either double-click on the Control menu icon for the secondary window, choose the Close command from the window's Control menu (Alt-Hyphen-C), or press Ctrl-F4. When you close a secondary window, Microsoft Excel deletes that window permanently. The window name is deleted from the Window menu and the remaining windows in your worksheet are renumbered. For example, suppose you created three windows, named Sheet1:1, Sheet1:2, and Sheet1:3. If you close Sheet1:2, Microsoft Excel will delete Sheet1:2 and assign the name Sheet1:2 to Sheet1:3.

If you delete one of these secondary windows accidentally, don't panic: You haven't lost any worksheet data. There is still only one underlying worksheet, no matter how many windows you're working with. To recover from your error, simply choose the New Window command to recreate the closed window.

If you have only one window open for your worksheet and you try to close it, Microsoft Excel assumes you want to close the entire file. If you've made changes to the worksheet, a dialog box will appear, asking whether you want to save the contents of the worksheet before you close it. If you did not mean to close the worksheet, simply select the Cancel option.

EXCEL

Editing between windows

Microsoft Excel allows you to paste references to cells visible in one window into a formula you're creating in another window. For example, suppose you have two open windows: Sheet1:1 is positioned over cells A1:I16 and Sheet1:2 over cells S20:AA35. You want to enter the formula

=SUM(A4:A15)

in cell S25. You can easily paste a reference to cells A4:A15 in cell S25 without scrolling those cells into view in the currently active window.

Begin by selecting cell S25 in Sheet1:2; then type *=SUM(* to start the formula. Now select Sheet1:1 by clicking in that window, by choosing the window name from the Window menu, or by pressing Ctrl-F6. Microsoft Excel will bring the selected window into view, but Sheet1:2 will remain the active window. A glance at the formula bar and cell address block at the top of the screen tells you that you haven't changed the status of S25, the active cell.

When you select Sheet1:1, Microsoft Excel partially activates that window. You can tell that a window is partially active when the scroll bars appear to let you move through the window but the title bar is not highlighted. When the window is partially activated, you can paste cell references into the formula bar by selecting cells A4:A15, exactly as you would in a single-window worksheet. After you've pasted the cell references, typed) to complete the formula, and pressed Enter, Sheet1:2 will be displayed again.

If the cells you need are not immediately visible, you can scroll through the cells in Sheet1:1 or change the dimensions of the window. You can also use the Find and Goto commands on the Formula menu to move around in the partially active window.

As you'll see in Chapter 8 when we talk about linking documents, you can use the same techniques to paste references to other documents into the formula bar.

Microsoft Excel's windowing capabilities can also be a real timesaver when you need to copy or move cells across a large worksheet. For example, suppose you're looking at cells A1:I16 through the Sheet1:1 window and Sheet1:2 is positioned over cells Q1:Y16. You want to copy the contents of cells A1:A5 into cells Q1:Q5. To do this, you can select cells A1:A5, choose Copy from the Edit menu, and then activate Sheet1:2. The last cell you selected when you last used Sheet1:2 will be the active cell. Simply use the scroll bars, the scrolling techniques discussed in Chapter 2, or the cell selection commands on the Formula menu to bring cells Q1:Q5 into view in the active window. When you select cell Q1 and choose the Paste command, Microsoft Excel will copy the contents of the range A1:A5 into cells Q1:Q5.

Again, you can use the same technique to copy or move data from one document to another.

6

Built-in Functions

Worksheet functions are special tools that let you perform complex calculations quickly and easily. You can use some functions, such as SUM, AVERAGE, and NPV, instead of mathematical formulas. Other functions, such as IF and VLOOKUP, cannot be duplicated by formulas.

In a way, worksheet functions are like the special function keys on sophisticated calculators. Just as many complex calculators have buttons that compute square roots, logarithms, and present values, Microsoft Excel has built-in functions that perform these calculations—and many more. After you begin using functions, you'll find that creating a budget or investment analysis without them is like using an abacus to calculate the national debt!

The power of functions

Let's look at an example that demonstrates the power of Microsoft Excel's functions. The worksheet in Figure 6-1 shows monthly apple sales for a 12-month period. To find the total Winesap sales for the year, you could enter the formula

=B4+B5+B6+B7+B8+B9+B10+B11+B12+B13+B14+B15

in cell B16, but this formula is bulky and takes too long to enter. Now consider the shorthand formula

=SUM(B4:B15)

which also tells Microsoft Excel to add the numbers stored in the range B4 through B15. The results of this formula and the longer version are identical: $8,094.

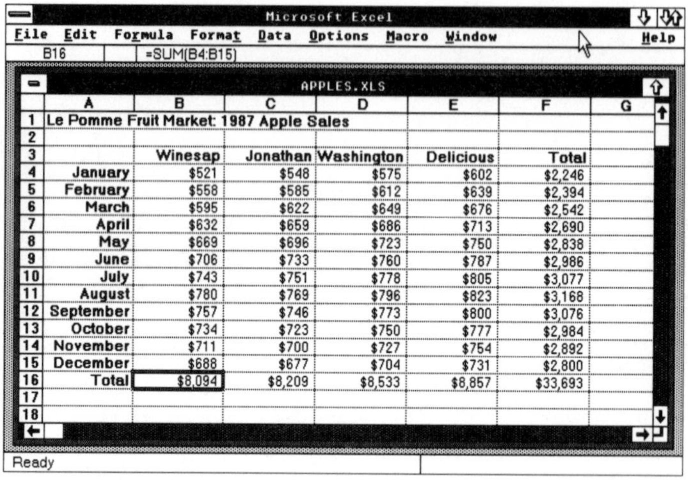

	A	B	C	D	E	F	G
1	Le Pomme Fruit Market: 1987 Apple Sales						
2							
3		Winesap	Jonathan	Washington	Delicious	Total	
4	January	$521	$548	$575	$602	$2,246	
5	February	$558	$585	$612	$639	$2,394	
6	March	$595	$622	$649	$676	$2,542	
7	April	$632	$659	$686	$713	$2,690	
8	May	$669	$696	$723	$750	$2,838	
9	June	$706	$733	$760	$787	$2,986	
10	July	$743	$751	$778	$805	$3,077	
11	August	$780	$769	$796	$823	$3,168	
12	September	$757	$746	$773	$800	$3,076	
13	October	$734	$723	$750	$777	$2,984	
14	November	$711	$700	$727	$754	$2,892	
15	December	$688	$677	$704	$731	$2,800	
16	Total	$8,094	$8,209	$8,533	$8,857	$33,693	
17							
18							

FIGURE 6-1. *We used the SUM function to calculate apple sales for a 12-month period.*

The more complex the formula you need to build, the more time you're likely to save by using functions. For example, suppose you're considering a real-estate purchase and you want to calculate the net present value of the purchase price to determine whether the investment is worthwhile. To do this calculation without functions, you would have to build a formula similar to this:

=(A1/(1+.15))+(B1/(1+.15)^2)+(C1/(1+.15)^3)+(D1/(1+.15)^4)

Fortunately, Microsoft Excel's NPV function lets you perform the same calculation with only 15 keystrokes:

=NPV(.15,A1:D1)

(We'll cover the SUM and NPV functions in more detail later in this chapter.)

The form of functions

Spreadsheet functions have two elements: the function name and the argument. Function names are descriptive terms, such as SUM and AVERAGE, that identify the operation you want to perform. Arguments tell Microsoft Excel which values or cells you want the function to act on. For example, in the function

=SUM(C3:C5)

SUM is the function name and C3:C5 is the argument. This function sums, or totals, the numbers in cells C3, C4, and C5.

The equal sign at the beginning of this statement indicates that the entry is a formula, not a text entry. If you were to leave out the equal sign, Microsoft Excel would interpret this entry as the text *SUM(C3:C5)*.

Notice that the argument in the sample function above is surrounded by parentheses. The left parenthesis marks the beginning of the function's argument. This delimiter must appear immediately after the function name, with no spaces. If you enter a space or some other character between the function name and the left parenthesis, you'll see the error value #NAME?. This error value indicates that Microsoft Excel does not recognize the function name. You must also use a right parenthesis to designate the end of the argument. Otherwise, you'll see the alert message *Error in formula*.

Using arguments

In many cases, you can use more than one argument in a function. The individual arguments are separated from each other by commas. For example, the function

=SUM(C1,C2,C5)

tells Microsoft Excel to total the numbers in cells C1, C2, and C5.

You can include as many as 14 arguments in a function (as long as you don't exceed the 255-character limit for cell entries). However, a single argument can refer to any number of cells in your worksheet. For example, the function

=SUM(A1:A5,C2:C10,D3:D17)

has three arguments but totals the numbers in 29 cells. These cells, in turn, could contain numbers or formulas that refer to more ranges or cells. With practice, you can create a powerful hierarchy of calculations to perform complex worksheet operations.

Different types of arguments

In the examples we've presented so far, all the arguments have been cell references. You can, however, also use literal numbers, arrays, text, range names, logical values, error values, other functions, and other types of entries as the arguments in functions.

Numbers

The arguments in a function can be literal numbers. For example, the function

=SUM(327,209,176)

totals the numbers 327, 209, and 176. Most of the time, however, you'll enter the numbers you want to use in cells of the worksheet and then use references to those cells as the arguments in your functions. By using cell references, you make your functions easier to understand and easier to modify.

Range names

You can also use range names as the arguments of functions. For example, if you used the Define Name command from the Formula menu to assign the name *Test* to the range C3:C5, you could use the formula

=SUM(Test)

to tell Microsoft Excel to compute the sum of the numbers in cells C3, C4, and C5.

Other functions

You can even use other functions as arguments, using a technique called nesting. For example, in the function

=SUM(ROUND(A1,0),ROUND(A2,0))

the ROUND(A1,0) and ROUND(A2,0) functions are arguments of the SUM function.

Arrays

You can use arrays as arguments in functions. Some functions, such as TREND, GROWTH, and TRANSPOSE, require the use of array arguments; other functions can accept array arguments even though they do not require them. (For more information on arrays and array functions, see Chapter 8.)

Mixed argument types

You can also mix argument types within a function. For example, the formula

=AVERAGE(Group1,A3,5*3)

uses a named range, a single cell reference, and an embedded formula to arrive at a single value. All three arguments are perfectly acceptable to Microsoft Excel.

Functions without arguments

A few of Microsoft Excel's functions, such as PI and TRUE, have no arguments. These functions are generally embedded, or nested, in other formulas or functions. You can nest as many as 14 functions within a formula.

Other types of arguments

Microsoft Excel accepts two other types of arguments: conditional tests and text strings. The uses of conditional tests and text strings will become clear to you as you learn more about Microsoft Excel's functions.

Entering functions

You can enter functions in your worksheet in two different ways: You can type the function from the keyboard, or you can choose the Paste Function command from the Formula menu. If you prefer the keyboard approach, here's a tip: Type the function name in lowercase letters. Microsoft Excel won't change the function to capital letters if you've made a spelling mistake.

Using the Paste Function command

When you select a cell and choose the Paste Function command, Microsoft Excel provides you with a list of function names. Figure 6-2 shows part of this list. To select a function, you can scroll through this alphabetic list and choose the function you want to use, or you can type the first letter of the function until the name appears in the box. When you click OK or press Enter, Microsoft Excel will enter the equal sign (if you're inserting the function at the beginning of a formula), the function name, and a set of parentheses in the formula bar. The insertion point appears between the parentheses. All you have to do is enter the arguments and separators.

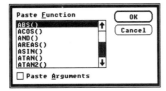

FIGURE 6-2. *Use Paste Function to enter functions into the formula bar.*

Pasting arguments

The Paste Arguments option in the Paste Function dialog box offers a quick reminder when you forget the proper form of the function. When you choose this option, Microsoft Excel pastes both the function name and the names of its arguments into the formula bar. Then you can select each argument name in turn and replace it with the appropriate argument.

For example, suppose you want to use the PMT function in your worksheet but you can't remember the proper order of the function's arguments. If you choose the Paste Arguments option, you'll see this entry in the formula bar:

=PMT(rate,nper,pv,fv,type)

Now, to put the function to work, you can select the argument name *rate* (if it isn't already selected) and type the appropriate value or indicate the cell that contains the value you want to use. Repeat this procedure for the remaining four arguments.

Some functions, such as INDEX, can take more than one form. If this is the case, Microsoft Excel presents you with a Select Arguments dialog box, like the one in Figure 6-3, from which you can select the form you want to use.

FIGURE 6-3. *If a function has more than one form, you'll see another dialog box when you choose the Paste Arguments option.*

Pasting cell references and range names

As with any other formula, you can also paste cell references and range names into your functions. For example, suppose you want to enter in cell C11 a function that totals the cells in the range C2:C10. Select cell C11 and either type *=SUM(* or use the Paste Function command to select the function. Then select the range C2:C10. A marquee will appear around the selected cells to show your selection. (If you typed the formula name, don't forget to add the closing right parenthesis.) When you press Enter or click the Enter box to lock in the formula, the marquee will disappear and a reference to your selected range will appear in the formula bar.

If you've defined range names in your worksheets, you can also paste them into your formulas. To paste a range name, choose Paste Name from the Formula menu and select the desired range name from the list in the Paste Name dialog box. When you choose OK or press Enter, the range name will appear in the formula bar at the insertion point. You can also select the desired range name from the dialog box by pointing to the appropriate name and double-clicking.

Now that you're familiar with the basic structure of functions, we're ready to put Microsoft Excel's functions through their paces. We'll start with the number crunchers: the statistical, mathematical, trigonometric, and financial functions.

Statistical functions

Microsoft Excel's statistical functions let you calculate the sum (SUM) or average (AVERAGE) of the numbers in a range of cells, identify the high (MAX) and low (MIN) numbers in a range, compute how many cells in a range contain numbers (COUNT) and how many contain either text or numeric entries (COUNTA), and compute standard deviation (STDEV) and variance (VAR) for a sample population and for a total population (STDEVP and VARP). The program also offers the advanced statistical functions LINEST, LOGEST, TREND, and GROWTH. Because these advanced functions operate on arrays, we'll save our discussion of them for Chapter 8.

The SUM function

You already know that SUM computes the total of a series of numbers. The SUM function has the form

    =SUM(*numbers*)

The *numbers* argument can contain as many as 14 entries consisting of any number, formula, range name, or cell reference that results in a number. SUM ignores any arguments that refer to text strings, logical values, and blank cells.

Several advantages of the SUM function become obvious when you need to edit your worksheet. For one thing, expanding a SUM range to include a new value is much easier than changing a regular formula. For example, suppose cell F4 in Figure 6-1 contained the formula

    =B4+C4+D4+E4

Now, suppose you discover, after entering this formula, that you left out a category—Granny Smith. To include this new category, you can select cells C3:C16 and then choose the Insert command from the Edit menu to add a column of cells. Microsoft Excel will adjust the totals formulas, which now appear in column G, to account for your insertion, but it won't add the new category to those totals. For example, in Figure 6-4, the formula in cell G4 now reads

    =B4+D4+E4+F4

The SUM function, on the other hand, is much more adaptable to changes in your worksheet. If you had used the SUM function to enter the formula

    =SUM(B4:E4)

in cell F4 of Figure 6-1, Microsoft Excel would have expanded the range referred to in the *numbers* argument to include your addition. Because Microsoft Excel always

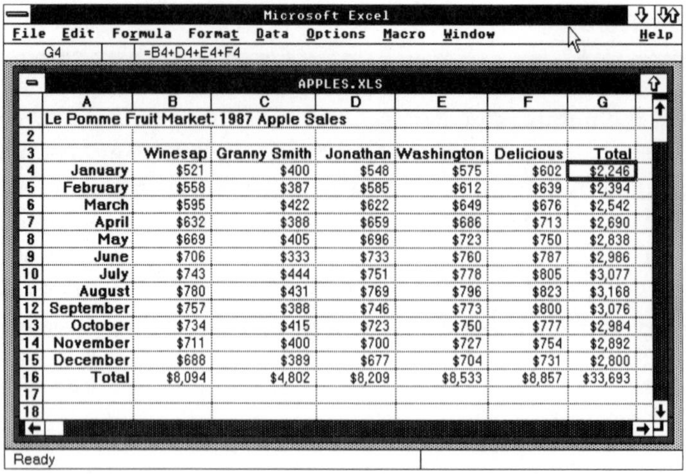

	A	B	C	D	E	F	G
1	Le Pomme Fruit Market: 1987 Apple Sales						
2							
3		Winesap	Granny Smith	Jonathan	Washington	Delicious	Total
4	January	$521	$400	$548	$575	$602	$2,246
5	February	$558	$387	$585	$612	$639	$2,394
6	March	$595	$422	$622	$649	$676	$2,542
7	April	$632	$388	$659	$686	$713	$2,690
8	May	$669	$405	$696	$723	$750	$2,838
9	June	$706	$333	$733	$760	$787	$2,986
10	July	$743	$444	$751	$778	$805	$3,077
11	August	$780	$431	$769	$796	$823	$3,168
12	September	$757	$388	$746	$773	$800	$3,076
13	October	$734	$415	$723	$750	$777	$2,984
14	November	$711	$400	$700	$727	$754	$2,892
15	December	$688	$389	$677	$704	$731	$2,800
16	Total	$8,094	$4,802	$8,209	$8,533	$8,857	$33,693
17							
18							

FIGURE 6-4. *The totals do not change, even though a new category has been added.*

adjusts cell ranges when you insert or delete rows and columns within the range, the formula would have automatically been updated to read

=SUM(B4:F4)

Keep in mind that the *numbers* argument of a SUM function does not have to refer to a continuous range. Suppose you wanted to add a set of numbers located in cells A3, B12, and G13 through H15 of your worksheet. You could enter each of these cell references as a separate argument:

=SUM(A3,B12,G13:H15)

You could also assign a range name to this set of cells and use that name as the *numbers* argument. To assign a name to the cells in the above formula, simply click in cell A3, hold down the Ctrl key, and click in cell B12. Then, without releasing the Ctrl key, select cells G13 through H15. (From the keyboard, use the Add mode.) After selecting the eight cells in this range, use the Define Name command to assign a range name, such as Group1, to this collection of cells, and enter the formula

=SUM(Group1)

The AVERAGE function

The AVERAGE function computes the arithmetic mean, or average, of the numbers in a range. The form of this function is

=AVERAGE(*numbers*)

AVERAGE computes the average in the same way you would: It sums a series of numeric values and then divides the result by the number of values in the argument. AVERAGE can include as many as 14 arguments. Like SUM, AVERAGE ignores blank, logical, and text cells.

Also like SUM, the AVERAGE function can be used instead of long formulas. For example, to calculate the average sales in cells B4 through B15 of Figure 6-4, you might use the formula

=(B4+B5+B6+B7+B8+B9+B10+B11+B12+B13+B14+B15)/12

to arrive at the number $675. This method has the same drawbacks as using the + operator instead of the SUM function: You have to edit the cell references and the divisor each time you change the range to be averaged.

The AVERAGE function makes life easier by calculating the sum and number of values for you. For example, you could use the formula

=AVERAGE(B4:B15)

to arrive at the arithmetic mean: $675.

The MAX function

Microsoft Excel's MAX function returns the largest value in a range. The form of this function is

=MAX(*numbers*)

As with SUM and AVERAGE, the argument of MAX is usually a range. For example, you could use the formula

=MAX(B4:B15)

in the worksheet in Figure 6-4 to determine the amount of the largest monthly sales of Winesaps: $780.

MAX can include as many as 14 arguments. If you've assigned a name to the range you want to analyze, you can use that name as the argument of this function. Like SUM, MAX ignores cells in the argument range that are blank or that contain text or logical values. If there are no numbers in the arguments, MAX returns 0.

The MIN function

The MIN function returns the smallest value in a range. The form of the MIN function is

=MIN(*numbers*)

As with MAX, the argument of MIN is usually a range. For example, in the worksheet in Figure 6-4, you could use the formula

=MIN(B4:B15)

to determine the smallest monthly Winesap sales: $521.

MIN can include as many as 14 arguments. If you've assigned a name to the range you want to analyze, you can use that name as the argument of this function. Also like MAX, MIN ignores cells in the argument range that are blank or that contain text or logical values. If there are no numbers in the arguments, MIN returns 0.

The COUNT and COUNTA functions

The COUNT function tells you how many cells in a given range contain numbers, including dates and formulas that evaluate to numbers. The form of the COUNT function is

=COUNT(*range*)

For example, in the worksheet in Figure 6-5, you could use the formula

=COUNT(B4:B15)

to determine the number of cells in the range B4:B15 that contain numbers: 8.

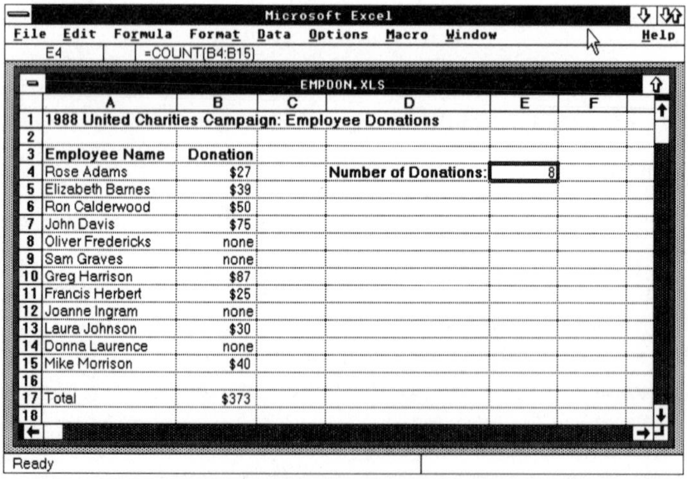
Microsoft Excel
File Edit Formula Format Data Options Macro Window Help
E4
=COUNT(B4:B15)
EMPDON.XLS
A B C D E F
1 1988 United Charities Campaign: Employee Donations
2
3 Employee Name Donation
4 Rose Adams $27 Number of Donations: 8
5 Elizabeth Barnes $39
6 Ron Calderwood $50
7 John Davis $75
8 Oliver Fredericks none
9 Sam Graves none
10 Greg Harrison $87
11 Francis Herbert $25
12 Joanne Ingram none
13 Laura Johnson $30
14 Donna Laurence none
15 Mike Morrison $40
16
17 Total $373
18
Ready

FIGURE 6-5. *The COUNT function ignores cells that don't contain numbers.*

COUNT can contain as many as 14 arguments, and it ignores blank cells and cells that contain text, logical, and error values.

Whereas the COUNT function counts only the numbers in a range, the COUNTA function tells you how many cells in a given range contain *any* type of entry. The form of the COUNTA function is

=COUNTA(*range*)

Continuing with the sample worksheet shown in Figure 6-5, the formula

=COUNTA(B4:B15)

returns the value 12, because the range B4:B15 contains 12 numbers and labels.

You can include as many as 14 arguments in the COUNTA function. Microsoft Excel ignores blank cells.

Calculating variance and standard deviation

The next four statistical functions—VAR, VARP, STDEV, and STDEVP—compute the variance and standard deviation of the numbers in a range. (Because the standard deviation is the square root of the variance, we have grouped the discussions of these functions together.)

Variance and standard deviation are both statistics that measure the dispersion of a group of numbers. As a rule, about 68 percent of a normally distributed population falls within one standard deviation of the mean and about 95 percent of the population falls within two standard deviations. A large standard deviation indicates that the population is widely dispersed; a small standard deviation indicates that the population is tightly packed.

Before you calculate the variance and standard deviation of a group of values, you must determine whether those values represent the total population or only a representative sample of that population. The VAR and STDEV functions assume that the values you are working with represent only a sample of your total test population; the VARP and STDEVP functions let you treat the set of values you're analyzing as a total population.

You can use as many as 14 arguments in each of the four functions. Microsoft Excel ignores all blanks, logical values, and text.

Calculating sample statistics: VAR and STDEV
The VAR and STDEV functions take the forms

=VAR(*numbers*)

and

=STDEV(*numbers*)

Let's look at an example. The worksheet in Figure 6-6 shows aptitude-test scores for 60 students and assumes that the test scores in cells A4 through D18 represent only a part of the total population.

Cell G5 contains the formula

=AVERAGE(A4:D18)

which returns the average of the test scores: 82.82%. Cells G6 and G7 use the VAR and STDEV functions to calculate the variance and the standard deviation for this sample group of test scores with the formulas

=VAR(A4:D18)

and

=STDEV(A4:D18)

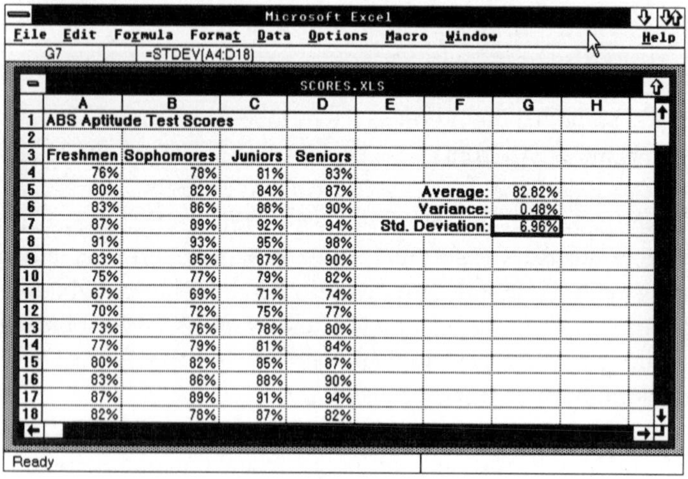

	Microsoft Excel							↓ ↓↓
File **Edit** **Formula** **Format** **Data** **Options** **Macro** **Window**							↳	**Help**
G7		=STDEV(A4:D18)						

	A	B	C	D	E	F	G	H
1	ABS Aptitude Test Scores							
2								
3	Freshmen	Sophomores	Juniors	Seniors				
4	76%	78%	81%	83%				
5	80%	82%	84%	87%		Average:	82.82%	
6	83%	86%	88%	90%		Variance:	0.48%	
7	87%	89%	92%	94%		Std. Deviation:	6.96%	
8	91%	93%	95%	98%				
9	83%	85%	87%	90%				
10	75%	77%	79%	82%				
11	67%	69%	71%	74%				
12	70%	72%	75%	77%				
13	73%	76%	78%	80%				
14	77%	79%	81%	84%				
15	80%	82%	85%	87%				
16	83%	86%	88%	90%				
17	87%	89%	91%	94%				
18	82%	78%	87%	82%				

Ready

FIGURE 6-6. *We used the VAR and STDEV functions to measure the dispersion of sample aptitude-test scores.*

These functions return the numbers 0.48% and 6.96%, respectively. Assuming that the test scores in our example are normally distributed, we can deduce that about 68 percent of the students scored between 75.87 percent (82.80 − 6.93) and 89.73 percent (82.80 + 6.93).

Calculating total population statistics: VARP and STDEVP
If the numbers you're analyzing represent the entire population rather than only a sample, the VARP and STDEVP functions should be used to calculate variance and standard deviation. Use the formula

=VARP(*numbers*)

to compute the population variance. To find the standard deviation for the total population, use the formula

=STDEVP(*numbers*)

For example, if we assume that cells A4 through D18 in the worksheet in Figure 6-6 represent the total population, we can calculate the variance and standard deviation with the formulas

=VARP(A4:D18)

and

=STDEVP(A4:D18)

These functions return the numbers 0.48% and 6.90%, respectively.

Mathematical functions

Microsoft Excel's mathematical functions—ABS, SIGN, ROUND, INT, TRUNC, RAND, FACT, PRODUCT, SQRT, MOD, and PI—allow you to perform specialized mathematical calculations quickly and easily. (We've put the logarithmic functions LOG10, LOG, LN, and EXP in a separate section, which we'll come to in a moment.)

The ABS function

The ABS function simply returns the absolute value of a number or formula. The form of this function is

=ABS(*number*)

where *number* is a number or a reference to a cell that contains a value. For example, if cell A1 contains the number –75, the formula

=ABS(A1)

returns 75. If the number referred to by the argument is positive, ABS returns that number unchanged. For example, if cell A1 contains the number 75, the formula above returns the value 75.

The SIGN function

You can use the SIGN function to determine whether an argument results in a negative, positive, or zero value. The form of this function is

=SIGN(*number*)

The *number* argument can be a number, a reference to a cell that contains a number, or an embedded formula that results in a number. If *number* is positive, the SIGN function returns the value 1; if *number* is negative, it returns the value –1; if *number* is 0, it returns 0.

For example, suppose cells A1 through A3 contain the numbers 10, –20, and –5. The formula

=SIGN(SUM(A1:A3))

adds the numbers 10, –20, and –5 (resulting in the value –15) and determines whether the resulting value is positive or negative. Because the embedded SUM formula results in a negative value, the SIGN function returns the value –1.

The ROUND function

The ROUND function lets you eliminate unwanted decimal places from numbers. ROUND rounds the number referred to by its argument to the number of decimal places you specify. The form of the ROUND function is

=ROUND(*number,decimal places*)

E X C E L *Tip*

Rounding vs formatting

Don't confuse the ROUND function with fixed formats like 0 and 0.00, which are available when you choose Number from the Format menu. When you use the Number command to round the contents of a cell to a specified number of decimal places, you change only the way the number in that cell is displayed; you don't actually change the value in that cell. In performing calculations, Microsoft Excel always uses the underlying value, not the displayed value.

For example, suppose cell A1 contains the number 123.456. If you use the 0.00 format to round this number to two decimal places, the value 123.46 appears in cell A1. However, Microsoft Excel still uses the underlying value, 123.456, in its calculations. If you use the formula

=A1+.001

to add .001 to the value in cell A1, the result is 123.457.

When you use the ROUND function, however, you are actually changing the value itself. For example, if cell A1 contains the value 123.456, the function

=ROUND(A1,2)

returns the value 123.46. Adding .001 to this value will return 123.461. ROUND has changed the value itself, not only the display of the value.

The *decimal places* argument can be any positive or negative integer. Specifying a negative *decimal places* argument causes rounding to the left of the decimal. Microsoft Excel rounds as you would expect it to: Digits less than 5 are rounded down and digits greater than or equal to 5 are rounded up. The following table shows several examples of the ROUND function at work:

Entry	Display
=ROUND (123.4567,–1)	120
=ROUND (123.4567,–2)	100
=ROUND (123.4567,0)	123
=ROUND(123.4567,1)	123.5
=ROUND(123.4567,2)	123.46
=ROUND(123.4567,3)	123.457

The INT function

Whereas ROUND rounds a number up or down to a specified number of digits, the INT function rounds numbers *down* to the nearest whole number. The form of this function is

=INT(*number*)

For example, the formula

=INT(100.01)

returns the value 100, as does the formula

=INT(100.99999999)

even though the number 100.99999999 is essentially equal to 101.

When *number* is negative, INT still rounds that number down to the nearest integer. For example, the formula

=INT(–100.99999999)

results in the value –101.

The TRUNC function

Although ROUND, INT, and TRUNC can all be used to get rid of unwanted decimals, the three functions work differently. ROUND rounds up or down to the number of decimal places you specify and INT rounds down to the nearest whole number. TRUNC, however, simply truncates everything to the right of the decimal, resulting in an integer with no decimal places. The form of the TRUNC function is

=TRUNC(*number*)

For example, the function

=TRUNC(13.978)

returns the number 13.

The primary difference between INT and TRUNC is in the treatment of negative values. As we mentioned above, if you use the value –100.99999999 as your *number* argument in an INT function, you get the result –101. However, the TRUNC function

=TRUNC(–100.99999999)

simply eliminates the decimal portion of the *number* argument and returns the number –100.

The RAND function

The RAND function generates a random number between 0 and 1. The form of the function is

=RAND()

RAND is one of the few Microsoft Excel functions that doesn't take an argument. Even though RAND has no arguments, you must still enter the parentheses after the function name.

E X C E L *tip*

Using Paste Special with RAND

The Paste Special command lets you lock in a series of random numbers so that you can recreate a set of calculations later. To lock in the results of your RAND function, select the cell or range that contains the function and choose the Copy command from the Edit menu. Next, choose Paste Special from the Edit menu. Select the Values option from the Paste Special dialog box and check to be sure the Operation option is set to None. Choose OK to overwrite the RAND formulas with the displayed values. Because the entries are now numbers, not formulas, their values will not change when the worksheet is recalculated.

If you prefer using the keyboard, you can also lock in a series of random numbers by typing *=RAND()* in the formula bar, choosing the Options Calculate Now command to resolve the formula, and then locking in the resulting value.

The result of a RAND function changes each time you recalculate your worksheet. If you're using automatic recalculation, this means that the value of the RAND function changes each time you make a worksheet entry.

The FACT function

The FACT function calculates the factorial value of any number. (The factorial of a number is the product of all the positive integers from 1 to the specified number. For example, 3 factorial, or 3!, is the product $1 \times 2 \times 3 = 6$.)

The FACT function takes the form

=FACT(*number*)

The *number* argument must be a positive integer. For example, FACT(1) equals 1, but FACT(–1) equals #NUM!. If *number* is not an integer, FACT truncates it.

To solve for 10!, use the formula

=FACT(10)

This formula returns the factorial value 3628800.

The PRODUCT function

The PRODUCT function multiplies all the numbers included as arguments. The function takes the form

=PRODUCT(*numbers*)

The PRODUCT function can multiply as many as 14 arguments. If you include text, logical values, or blank cells in an argument, Microsoft Excel ignores them.

Suppose you want to multiply 225 times 860. The formula

=PRODUCT(225,860)

returns 193500.

The SQRT function

The SQRT function computes the square root of a number. The form is

=SQRT(*number*)

The *number* argument must be a positive value or a reference to a cell that contains a positive value. The result of the function is the square root of the *number* argument. For example, the function

=SQRT(4)

returns the value 2.

If you enter a negative number, SQRT returns a #NUM! error value.

The MOD function

The MOD function computes the remainder from a division operation. The form of the function is

=MOD(*dividend,divisor*)

The result of the function is the remainder that results from dividing *dividend* by *divisor*. For example, the function

=MOD(9,4)

returns 1, the remainder that results from dividing 9 by 4. Similarly, the function

=MOD(11,3)

returns 2.

If the dividend is smaller than the divisor, the result of the function equals the dividend. For example, the function

=MOD(5,11)

returns 5. If the dividend is exactly divisible by the divisor, the result of the function is 0. If the divisor is 0, MOD returns a #DIV/0! error value.

The PI function

The PI function returns the value of the constant π, accurate to 14 decimal places: 3.14159265358979. The form of the function is

=PI()

As with RAND, even though PI has no arguments, you must still enter the empty parentheses after the function name.

You'll probably use PI in conjunction with another formula or function. For example, to calculate the area of a circle, you would multiply PI by the square of the circle's radius. The formula

=PI()*(5^2)

computes the area of a circle with a radius of 5. The result of this formula is 78.54.

Logarithmic functions

Microsoft Excel offers four logarithmic functions: LOG10, LOG, LN, and EXP. If you're an engineer or a scientist, you may find these functions valuable. If you're in business, you probably won't use them often.

The LOG10 function

The LOG10 function returns the base 10 logarithm for the number or cell reference in the argument. The form of this function is

=LOG10(*number*)

The *number* argument must be a positive value or a reference to a cell that contains a positive value. If the *number* argument is negative, the function returns the error value #NUM!.

For example, the formula

=LOG10(100)

returns the value 2.

The LOG function

The LOG function returns the logarithm of a positive number using a base you specify. The form of the function is

=LOG(*number,base*)

For example, the formula

=LOG(5,2)

returns the value 2.321928.

If you don't include *base* in the argument, Microsoft Excel will assume the base to be 10.

The LN function

The LN function returns the natural (base e) logarithm of the positive number referred to by its argument. The form of the function is

=LN(*number*)

For example, the formula

=LN(2)

returns the value 0.693147.

The EXP function

EXP computes the value of the constant e (which equals 2.71828182845904) raised to the power specified by the function's argument. The form of the function is

=EXP(*number*)

For example,

    =EXP(2)

equals 7.3890561, or 2.7182818 times 2.7182818.

    EXP is the inverse of the LN function. For example, if cell A1 contains the formula

    =LN(8)

then, because EXP is the inverse of the LN function, the formula

    =EXP(A1)

returns 8.

Trigonometric functions

Microsoft Excel includes several functions that compute common trigonometric values such as sine, cosine, tangent, arcsine, arccosine, and arctangent.

    Microsoft Excel measures angles in radians rather than degrees. Radians measure the size of an angle based on the constant π (approximately 3.14). You can convert radians to degrees with the formula

    angle in degrees=angle in radians*(180/π)

For example,

    1.57 radians*(180/π)=90 degrees

The SIN function

The SIN function returns the sine of an angle. This function takes the form

    =SIN(*angle in radians*)

For example, the formula

    =SIN(1.5)

returns the value 0.997495.

The COS function

COS, the complement of SIN, calculates the cosine of an angle. This function takes the form

    =COS(*angle in radians*)

For example, the formula

=COS(1.5)

returns the value 0.070737.

The TAN function

The TAN function computes the tangent of an angle. TAN has the form

=TAN(*angle in radians*)

For example, the formula

=TAN(1.5)

returns the tangent of an angle of 1.5 radians: 14.10142.

The ASIN and ACOS functions

The ASIN and ACOS functions compute the arcsine and arccosine of a value. These functions return a value that represents the radian measure of an angle. The forms of these functions are

=ASIN(*sine of angle*)

and

=ACOS(*cosine of angle*)

You can remember the purpose of these functions with the phrase "the angle whose." For example, the function

=ASIN(0)

returns the value 0, or the radian measure of "the angle whose" sine is 0. The function

=ACOS(0)

returns the value 1.570796, or the radian measure of "the angle whose" cosine is 0.

The argument for the ACOS and ASIN functions must be in the range –1 through 1. Any value outside this range results in a #NUM! error value. ASIN always returns a value between –1.57 and 1.57 radians. ACOS always returns a value between 0 and 3.14 radians.

The ATAN and ATAN2 functions

The ATAN function computes the arctangent of a tangent value. Its form is

=ATAN(*tangent of angle*)

For example, the function

=ATAN(2)

returns the measure, in radians, of the angle whose tangent is 2: 1.107149.

ATAN always returns a value between –1.57 and 1.57 radians.

ATAN2 returns the four-quadrant arctangent of the tangent described in the argument. ATAN2 requires two arguments and has the form

=ATAN2(*x-number,y-number*)

where *x-number* and *y-number* are the x-axis and y-axis coordinates of a point. The result of the function is the measure of the angle from the x-axis to the specified point. The result of ATAN2 always falls in the range –3.1416 through 3.1416. Either *x-number* or *y-number* can be 0; if both values are 0, however, the function returns the error value #DIV/0!

Financial functions

Microsoft Excel offers 13 functions that let you perform common business calculations such as net present value and future value without building long and complex formulas: PV, NPV, FV, PMT, IMPT, PPMT, NPER, RATE, IRR, MIRR, DDB, SLN, and SYD. If you plan to use Microsoft Excel in your business, you will almost certainly use these financial functions.

The PV function

Present value is one of the most common methods for measuring the attractiveness of an investment. Simply put, the present value of an investment is the amount of money you are willing to pay to buy the investment. The present value is determined by discounting the inflows of the investment back to the present time. If the present value of the inflows is greater than the cost of the investment, the investment is a good one.

Microsoft Excel's PV function computes the present value (the value today) of a series of equal periodic payments or of a lump-sum payment. (A stream of constant payments is often called an ordinary annuity.) The PV function has the form

=PV(*rate,number of periods,payment,future value,type*)

where *rate* is the discount rate, *number of periods* is the term of the investment, and *payment* is the periodic payment. The *future value* and *type* arguments are optional. You use the *future value* argument in place of *payment* to compute the present value of a lump-sum payment. The *type* argument indicates whether the payments are received at the beginning or at the end of each period.

Suppose you are presented with an investment opportunity that returns $1,000 a year over the next five years. To receive this annuity, you would have to invest $3,000. Are you willing to pay $3,000 today to earn $5,000 over the next five years? To decide whether this investment is acceptable, you need to determine the present value of the stream of $1,000 payments you will receive.

We'll assume you can also invest your money in a money-market account at 10 percent, so we'll use 10 percent as the discount rate of the investment. (Because this discount rate is a sort of "hurdle" over which an investment must leap before it becomes attractive to you, it is often called the hurdle rate.)

To determine the present value of this investment, you can use the formula

=PV(10%,5,1000)

This formula returns the value –3790.79, meaning that you should be willing to spend $3,790.79 now to receive $5,000 over the next five years. Because your investment is only $3,000, you decide that this is an acceptable investment.

The future value *argument*

Now, suppose that you're offered $5,000 at the end of five years, rather than $1,000 for each of the next five years. Is the investment still as attractive? To find out, you could use the formula

=PV(10%,5,,5000)

This formula returns the present value –3104.61, which means that, at a hurdle rate of 10 percent, you should be willing to spend $3,104.61 to receive $5,000 in five years. Although the proposal is not as attractive under these terms, it is still acceptable because your investment is only $3,000.

Don't forget your argument delimiters when you use the optional *future value* argument. If you skip an argument in the middle of a formula, you must enter an extra comma as a place marker for that argument. For example, in the formula

=PV(10%,5,,5000)

we did not include an argument for *payment*. If we had not included the extra comma between the *number of periods* (5) and *future value* (5000) arguments, however, Microsoft Excel would have assumed that the number 5000 was a payment. As a result, the formula would have returned the present value of five $5,000 payments: $18,953.96!

The type *argument*

The *type* argument lets you determine whether payments are to be made at the beginning or at the end of each period. A *type* argument of 1 means the payments are to be made at the beginning of each period; a *type* argument of 0 means the payments occur at the end of each period. If you don't enter a value for *type*, Microsoft Excel uses the default value 0.

The NPV function

Net present value is another common formula used to determine the profitability of an investment. In general, any investment that yields a net present value greater than zero is considered profitable.

Although NPV is similar to PV, the two functions have a couple of important differences. First, whereas PV calculates the present value of a constant stream of inflows, NPV allows the stream of inflows to be uneven. In addition, NPV considers the cost of the investment, not just the inflows. The form of this function is

=NPV(*rate,investment,inflow 1,inflow 2,…,inflow* n)

where *rate* is the discount rate, *investment* is the cost of the investment, and *inflow 1*, *inflow 2*, and so on are the cash inflows.

Suppose you're considering a $15,000 investment that will return $5,000 the first year, $7,500 the second year, and $8,200 the third year. Assuming a hurdle rate of 10

E X C E L

The timing of payments

As we've noted, the NPV function assumes all payments occur at the end of each period. In many cases, however, your investment is likely to occur at the beginning of the first period. In other words, your initial investment probably will occur today; the return on your investment probably will begin one period from now. To account for this difference, you could pull your initial investment out of the NPV function and put it at the end of the formula:

=NPV(*rate,inflow 1,inflow 2,…,inflow* n)–*investment*

For example, again suppose you're considering a $15,000 investment that will return $5,000 one year from today, $7,500 two years from today, and $8,200 three years from today. Assuming a hurdle rate of 10 percent, you can use the formula

=NPV(10%,5000,7500,8200)–15000

to calculate the net present value: $1,904.58.

percent, you can use the formula

=NPV(10%,–15000,5000,7500,8200)

to calculate the net present value of this investment: $1,731.44. Because the result of this formula is greater than zero, the investment is acceptable.

The *inflow* arguments in NPV can be either positive or negative. Microsoft Excel assumes that a negative value is a payment made (an investment or production cost, for example) and a positive value is a payment received (such as rental income or sales revenues).

Notice that there is no *type* argument for NPV. Microsoft Excel assumes that payments are evenly distributed and occur at the end of each period. Thus, the program assumes that the first cash flow—the initial investment—actually occurs one time period from today.

The FV function

The FV function computes the future value of an investment. The investment can occur as a lump sum or as a stream of payments. Future value is essentially the opposite of present value. This function calculates the value at some future date of a constant stream of payments made over a period of time.

FV takes the form

=FV(*rate,number of periods,payment,present value,type*)

where *rate* is the interest rate, *number of periods* is the term of the investment, and *payment* is the periodic investment. The *present value* and *type* arguments are optional. You use *present value* instead of *payment* to compute the future value of a lump-sum investment. The *type* argument tells Microsoft Excel whether the payments are received at the beginning or at the end of each period.

Suppose you're thinking about starting an IRA account. You plan to deposit $2,000 at the beginning of each year and you expect the average rate of return on the IRA to be 11 percent per year for the entire term. Assuming you're now 30 years old, how much money will your account have accumulated by the time you're 65? You can use the formula

=FV(11%,35,–2000,,1)

to learn that your IRA will have accumulated $758,328.81 at the end of 35 years.

Now assume that you started an IRA account three years ago and have already accumulated $7,500 in your account. You can use the formula

=FV(11%,35,–2000,–7500,1)

to learn that your IRA will have accumulated $1,047,640.19 at the end of 35 years.

The *type* argument—1 if payments occur at the beginning of the period or 0 if they occur at the end—is particularly important in financial calculations that span many years. For example, if you had used the default value 0 for the *type* argument in the formula above, Microsoft Excel would have returned the value $972,490.49—a difference of more than $75,000!

The PMT function

The PMT function computes the periodic payment required to amortize a loan across a specified number of periods. The form of this function is

=PMT(*rate,number of periods,present value,future value,type*)

where *rate* is the interest rate, *number of periods* is the term of the loan, and *present value* is the principal amount you plan to borrow. The *future value* and *type* arguments are optional; if you omit them, Microsoft Excel uses 0.

Suppose you want to take out a 25-year mortgage for $100,000. Assuming an interest rate of 11 percent, what will your monthly payments be?

First, divide the 11-percent interest rate by 12 to arrive at a monthly rate (approximately 0.92 percent). Next, convert the number of periods into months by multiplying 25 by 12 (300). Now plug the monthly rate, number of periods, and loan amount into the PMT formula

=PMT(0.92%,300,100000)

to compute the monthly mortgage payment: –$983. (Remember, when you pay out cash, the amount is a negative number; when you receive cash, the amount is a positive number.)

EXCEL *tip*

Consistency counts

Keep in mind that the *rate* and *number of periods* arguments in financial functions must be consistent. For example, if you're using an annual interest rate and want to calculate monthly payments, you must convert the annual rate into a monthly rate before you use the PMT function. To do this, simply divide the annual interest rate by 12 to arrive at a monthly interest rate. For example, a 10-percent annual interest rate divided by 12 months gives an approximate 0.83-percent monthly interest rate.

Because 0.92 percent is an approximation, you could use the formula

=PMT((11/12)%,300,100000)

for a more accurate result. This formula returns –$980.11.

The IPMT function

The IPMT function computes the interest component of the payment required to repay an amount over a specified time period with constant periodic payments and a constant interest rate. The IPMT function has the form

=IPMT(*rate,period,number of periods,present value,future value,type*)

where *rate* is the interest rate, *period* is the period for which you want to compute the interest payment and must be an integer between 1 and *number of periods, number of periods* is the term of the loan, and *present value* is the value today or the amount borrowed. The *future value* argument is the amount you want to reach in the future; when computing loans, it is assumed to be 0. The *type* argument indicates whether the payments are made at the beginning or at the end of each period. The *future value* and *type* arguments are optional; if you omit them, Microsoft Excel assumes they are 0.

Going back to our previous example, suppose you've borrowed $100,000 for 25 years at 11-percent interest. The formula

=IPMT((11/12)%,1,300,100000)

tells you that the interest component of the payment due for the first month is –$916.67. The formula

=IPMT((11/12)%,300,300,100000)

tells you that the interest component of the final payment of the same loan is –$8.90.

The PPMT function

The PPMT function computes the principal component of the payment that is required to repay an amount over a specified time period with constant periodic payments and a constant interest rate. If you compute both IPMT and PPMT for the same period, you can add the results to obtain the total payment.

The PPMT function has the form

=PPMT(*rate,period,number of periods,present value,future value,type*)

where *rate* is the interest rate, *period* is the period whose payment you want to compute and must be an integer between 1 and *number of periods, number of periods* is the term of the loan, and *present value* is the value today or the amount borrowed. The *future value* argument is the amount you want to reach in the future. The *type* argument tells Microsoft Excel whether the payments are made at the beginning or at the end of each period. The *future value* and *type* arguments are optional; if you omit them, Microsoft Excel assumes they are 0.

Again using our previous example, suppose you borrow $100,000 for 25 years at 11-percent interest. The formula

    =PPMT((11/12)%,1,300,1000000)

tells you that the principal component of the payment for the first month of the loan would be –$63.45. The formula

    =PPMT((11/12)%,300,300,100000)

tells you that the principal component of the final payment of the same loan is –$971.21.

The NPER function

NPER computes the number of periods required to amortize a loan, given a specified periodic payment. The form of this function is

    =NPER(*rate,payment,present value,future value,type*)

where *rate* is the interest rate, *payment* is the periodic payment, and *present value* is the principal amount you plan to borrow. The *future value* and *type* arguments are optional; if you omit them, Microsoft Excel assumes they are 0.

Let's turn our example around a bit to see how the NPER function works. Suppose you can afford mortgage payments of $1200 per month and you want to know how long it will take you to pay off the $100,000 loan at 11% interest. The formula

    =NPER((11/12)%,–1200,100000)

tells you that your mortgage payments will extend over 158.18 months.

If the *payment* argument is too small to amortize the loan at the indicated rate of interest, the function returns an error message. The monthly payment must always at least equal the period interest rate times the principal amount; otherwise the loan will never be amortized. For example, the formula

    =NPER((11/12)%,–750,100000)

returns the error value #NUM!. In this case, the monthly payment must be at least $916.66, or $100,000 times (11/12)%.

Functions for calculating the rate of return

The RATE, IRR, and MIRR functions compute the continuously paid rates of return on investments. RATE computes the rate of return on an investment that generates constant periodic payments, IRR computes the internal rate of return on investments that have fluctuating payments, and MIRR computes the modified internal rate of return.

The RATE function

RATE lets you determine the rate of return of an investment that generates a series of equal periodic payments or a single lump-sum payment. The RATE function has the form

=RATE(*number of periods,payment,present value,future value,type,guess*)

where *number of periods* is the term of the loan or investment, *payment* is the periodic payment, and *present value* is the principal amount you plan to borrow or invest.

The *future value* and *type* arguments are optional. You can use *future value* in place of *payment* to compute the rate of a lump-sum payment. The *type* argument tells Microsoft Excel whether the payment occurs at the beginning or at the end of each period. The *guess* argument, which is also optional, simply gives Microsoft Excel a starting place for calculating the rate. If you omit the *future value* and *type* arguments, Microsoft Excel assumes they are zero.

Suppose you're considering an investment that will pay you five annual $1,000 payments. The investment costs $3,000. To determine the actual annual rate of return on your investment, you can use the formula

=RATE(5,1000,–3000)

This formula returns 0.1986 (19.86%), the rate of return on this investment.

The RATE function uses an iterative process to compute the rate of return. The function begins by computing the net present value of the investment at the *guess* rate. If that first net present value is greater than zero, the function selects a higher rate and repeats the net present value calculation; if the first net present value is less than zero, a lower rate is selected for the second iteration. RATE continues this process until it arrives at the correct rate of return or until it has gone through 20 iterations.

If you omit the *guess* argument, Microsoft Excel begins with a guess of 0.1 (10%). If you receive the error value #NUM! when you enter the RATE function, the program is probably trying to tell you that it could not calculate the rate within 20 iterations. If this occurs, try entering a different *guess* rate to give the function a running start. A rate between 10 percent and 100 percent usually does the trick.

The IRR function

The internal rate of return of an investment is the rate that causes the net present value of the investment to equal zero. To put it another way, the internal rate of return is the rate that causes the present value of the inflows from an investment to exactly equal the cost of the investment.

Internal rate of return, like net present value, is used to compare one investment opportunity with another. Remember, we said that an attractive investment is one whose net present value, discounted at the appropriate hurdle rate, is greater than zero. Turn that equation around and you can see that the discount rate required to generate a net present value of zero must be greater than the hurdle rate. In other words, an attractive investment is one where the discount rate required to yield a net present value of zero—that is, the internal rate of return—is greater than the hurdle rate.

Microsoft Excel's IRR function is closely related to the RATE function. The difference between RATE and IRR is similar to the difference between the PV and NPV functions: Like NPV, IRR accounts for investment costs and irregular payments.

The form of the IRR function is

=IRR(*values,guess*)

where *values* is an array or a reference to a range of cells containing numbers. You must include at least one positive and one negative value in the *values* array or range. IRR ignores blanks, logical values, and text. IRR assumes that transactions occur at the end of a period and returns the equivalent interest rate for that period's length.

Notice that the IRR function allows only one argument for *values*. To use the function, you must set up a simple worksheet containing your investment and income information. For example, suppose you agree to pay $120,000 to buy a condominium. Over the next five years, you expect to receive $25,000, $27,000, $35,000, $38,000, and $40,000 in net rental income. If you enter these six values into cells A1:A6 of a worksheet, you can then use the formula

=IRR(A1:A6)

to compute the internal rate of return of 10.63 percent. If the hurdle rate you've selected is 10 percent, this condominium purchase would be considered a good investment.

As with RATE, the *guess* argument is optional. If you receive a #NUM! error value when you enter an IRR function, you can include a *guess* argument in the function to help nudge Microsoft Excel toward the answer.

The MIRR function

The MIRR function is similar to IRR in that it also calculates the rate of return of an investment. The difference is that MIRR takes into account the cost of the money you borrow to finance the investment and the fact that you will almost certainly reinvest the cash generated by it. MIRR assumes that transactions occur at the end of a period and returns the equivalent interest rate for that period's length.

MIRR takes the form

=MIRR(*values,safe,risky*)

The *values* argument must be either an array or a reference to a range of cells containing numbers. You must include at least one positive and one negative value in the *values* array or range. The *safe* argument is the rate at which you borrow the money you need to make the investment. The *risky* argument is the rate at which you invest the cash flow.

To continue with the previous example, you can use the formula

=MIRR(A1:A6,10%,12%)

to calculate a modified internal rate of return of 11.17 percent, assuming a *safe* rate of 10 percent and a *risky* rate of 12 percent.

E X C E L

A word of caution

If you switch from one depreciation method to another during the life of the asset, be sure to adjust your *cost* and *life* arguments to compensate for this change. For example, suppose you're calculating the annual depreciation for a $10,000 asset with a 10-year useful life. During the first 5 years, you use the declining-balance depreciation method; then you decide to switch to the straight-line method to depreciate the asset for the remaining 5 years. You must subtract any prior years' depreciation from the *cost* argument before you calculate the remaining years' depreciation, and you must reduce the life of the asset from 10 to 5 years.

Functions for calculating depreciation

The SLN, DDB, and SYD functions determine the depreciation of an asset for a specific period. SLN computes the straight-line depreciation, DDB computes the depreciation using the double-declining balance method, and SYD computes the sum-of-years'-digits depreciation.

The SLN function

SLN lets you determine the straight-line depreciation for an asset for a single period. The straight-line depreciation method assumes that depreciation is uniform throughout the useful life of the asset. The cost or basis of the asset, less its estimated salvage value, is deductible in equal amounts over the life of the asset. The SLN function has the form

=SLN(*cost,salvage,life*)

where *cost* is the initial cost of the asset, *salvage* is the asset's value when it has been fully depreciated, and *life* is the length of time the asset will be in service.

Suppose you want to depreciate a machine that costs $8,000 new and has a lifetime of 10 years and a salvage value of $500. The formula

=SLN(8000,500,10)

tells you that the straight-line depreciation would be $750 each year.

The DDB function

DDB computes an asset's depreciation with the double-declining balance method, which returns depreciation at an accelerated rate—more in the early periods and less later. Under this method, depreciation is computed as a percentage of the net book value of the asset (the cost of the asset less any prior years' depreciation).

The first three arguments for the DDB function are the same as the arguments for SLN. However, because the double-declining depreciation method produces a different depreciation expense for each period during the life of the asset, DDB requires an extra argument. The function has the form

=DDB(*cost,salvage,life,period*)

where *cost* is the initial cost of the asset, *salvage* is the asset's value when it has been fully depreciated, *life* is the length of time the asset will be in service, and *period* is the period in the asset's life for which you want to compute the depreciation expense. All DDB arguments must be positive numbers and you must use the same time units for *life* and *period*—that is, if you express *life* in months, *period* must also be in months.

Suppose you want to depreciate a machine that costs $5,000 new and has a lifetime of five years (60 months) and a salvage value of $100. The formula

=DDB(5000,100,60,1)

tells you that the double-declining balance depreciation for the first month would be $166.67. The formula

=DDB(5000,100,5,1)

tells you that the double-declining balance depreciation for the first year would be $2,000.00. The formula

=DDB(5000,100,5,5)

tells you that the double-declining balance depreciation for the last year would be $259.20.

The SYD function

SYD computes an asset's depreciation for a specific time period with the sum-of-years'-digits method. Under the sum-of-years'-digits method, depreciation is calculated on the cost of the item less its salvage value. Like the double-declining balance method, sum-of-years'-digits is an accelerated depreciation method. The SYD function has the form

=SYD(*cost,salvage,life,period*)

where *cost* is the initial cost of the asset, *salvage* is the asset's value when it has been fully depreciated, *life* is the length of time the asset will be in service, and *period* is the period in the asset's life for which you want to compute the depreciation expense. As with DDB, you must use the same time units for *life* and *period*.

Suppose you want to depreciate a machine that costs $15,000 and has a lifetime of three years and a salvage value of $1,250. The formula

=SYD(15000,1250,3,1)

tells you that the sum-of-years'-digits depreciation for the first year would be $6,875. The formula

=SYD(15000,1250,3,3)

tells you that the sum-of-years'-digits depreciation for the third year would be $2,291.67.

Text functions

Four of Microsoft Excel's text functions—VALUE, TEXT, DOLLAR, and FIXED—convert numeric text entries into numbers and number entries into text strings.

The VALUE function converts a string into a number; TEXT, DOLLAR, and FIXED convert numbers into formatted text strings. Seventeen other functions—REPT, LEN, MID, CHAR, CODE, TRIM, CLEAN, REPLACE, SUBSTITUTE, EXACT, FIND, SEARCH, RIGHT, LEFT, UPPER, LOWER, and PROPER—let you manipulate the text strings themselves.

The VALUE function

If you've entered numbers in your worksheet in text format (enclosed in quotation marks), you can use the VALUE function to convert that text into a numeric value. The VALUE function has the form

=VALUE("*text*")

The *text* argument can be a literal string enclosed in quotation marks or it can be a reference to a cell that contains text. The text string to be converted can be in any recognized format, including user-created custom formats. (See Chapter 3 for more information on Microsoft Excel's formats.)

For example, the formula

=VALUE("40205")

returns the numeric value 40205. If cell A10 contained the text entry ="*40205*", the formula

=VALUE(A10)

would also return the number 40205.

VALUE can also be used to convert text entries in the form of dates into numeric date values. For example, the formula

=VALUE("1/1/87")

returns the serial date value 31778. (We'll discuss Microsoft Excel's handling of dates in Chapter 7.)

Keep in mind that Microsoft Excel converts numeric text into numbers as necessary when you perform calculations, so you generally don't have to use VALUE before using a number entered as text in a formula.

The TEXT function

The TEXT function converts a number into a text string with a specified format. TEXT has the form

=TEXT(*number,format*)

The *number* argument can be a number, a formula, or a cell reference. The *format* argument tells Microsoft Excel how you want the resulting string to be displayed. You can use any of Microsoft Excel's formatting symbols ($, #, 0, and so on) except the asterisk to specify the format you desire; you cannot use the General format. For example, the formula

=TEXT(98/4,"0.00")

returns the text string 24.50.

The DOLLAR function

The DOLLAR function is similar to the TEXT function in that it converts a number into a string. The difference is that DOLLAR formats the resulting string as currency with the number of decimal places you specify. The DOLLAR function has the form

=DOLLAR(*number,number of decimals*)

For example, the formula

=DOLLAR(45.899,2)

returns the text string $45.90, and the formula

=DOLLAR(45.899,0)

returns the text string $46. Notice that Microsoft Excel rounds the number when necessary, just as it does when you choose Number from the Format menu and select the $#,##0.00 or $#,##0 format.

If you omit a *number of decimals* argument for the DOLLAR function, Microsoft Excel uses two decimal places. If you use a negative number for the *number of decimals* argument, Microsoft Excel rounds to the left of the decimal point.

The FIXED function

The FIXED function rounds a number to the specified number of decimal places and displays the result as text. The form of this function is

=FIXED(*number,number of decimals*)

For example, the formula

=FIXED(98.786,2)

returns the text string 98.79.

If you don't include a *number of decimals* argument for the FIXED function, Microsoft Excel uses two decimal places. If you use a negative number for *number of decimals*, Microsoft Excel rounds to the left of the decimal point. For example, the formula

=FIXED(98.786,–1)

returns the text string 100.

The REPT function

The REPT function lets you create a string made up of one or more characters repeated a specified number of times. The form of REPT is

=REPT("*text*",*repeat number*)

The *text* argument specifies the text string to be repeated. This argument must be enclosed in quotation marks. The *repeat number* argument tells Microsoft Excel how many times to repeat the text string and can be any integer from 0 through 255. If you enter 0 for the *repeat number* argument, REPT leaves the cell blank; if *repeat number* is not an integer, REPT ignores the decimal portion of the number.

Suppose you want to create a row of asterisks across 10 columns of a worksheet and each column is 15 characters wide. Assuming the cells to the right of the one you want to format are blank, you could select a cell in the first column that is to display the asterisks and then enter the formula

=REPT("*",150)

The result is a string of 150 asterisks overlapping the ten 15-character-wide columns.

The *text* argument can be more than one character. For example, the formula

=REPT("*–",75)

E X C E L *Tip*

Functions vs *formats*

Be careful. Formatting a value with the TEXT, DOLLAR, and FIXED functions is not the same as formatting a value with the Number command. These functions convert values to text and can change a number's precision. When you use the Number command, a number remains a number and its underlying precision is not affected.

results in a row of asterisks and dashes 150 characters long. Keep in mind that the *repeat number* argument specifies the number of times you want the text argument to be repeated, not the total number of characters you want to create. If the text string is two characters long, the length of the resulting label is twice the *repeat number* argument.

The LEN function

The LEN function returns the number of characters in an entry. The form of the function is

    =LEN(*text*)

The *text* argument can be a literal number, a literal string in quotes, or a reference to a cell. For example, the formula

    =LEN("Test")

returns 4. If cell A1 contains the label *Test*, then the formula

    =LEN(A1)

also returns 4.

The LEN function returns the length of the displayed text or value, not the length of the underlying cell contents. For example, suppose cell A10 contains the formula

    =A1+A2+A3+A4+A5+A6+A7+A8

and the result of this formula is the value 25. The formula

    =LEN(A10)

returns the value 2, the length of the *result* of the formula.

The cell referred to by the argument of the LEN function can also be a cell that contains another string function. For example, if cell A1 contains the REPT function

    =REPT("*-",75)

the formula

    =LEN(A1)

returns the value 150.

The MID function

You can use the MID function to extract a series of characters (a substring) from a text string. The form of the function is

=MID(*text,starting position,number of characters*)

where *text* is the string from which you want to extract the substring, *starting position* is the place in the string where the substring begins (relative to the left end of the string), and *number of characters* is the number of characters you want to extract. The *text* argument can be a literal string enclosed in quotes, but it is usually a reference to a cell that contains text.

For example, suppose cell A1 contains the label *This is a long label entry.* You could use the formula

=MID(A1,11,10)

to extract the characters *long label* from the entry in cell A1.

The ASCII functions: CHAR and CODE

Every computer uses numeric codes to represent characters. The most prevalent system of numeric codes is called ASCII, or American Standard Code for Information Interchange. ASCII uses a three-digit code to represent each number, letter, and symbol.

The CHAR and CODE functions deal with these ASCII codes. The CHAR function returns the ASCII character that corresponds to a code number; the CODE function returns the ASCII code number for the first character specified. The forms of these two functions are

=CHAR(*number*)

and

=CODE(*text*)

For example, the formula

=CHAR(83)

returns the letter *S* (you need not type the leading zero), and the formula

=CODE("S")

returns the ASCII code 83. Similarly, if cell A1 contains the letter *S*, the formula

=CODE(A1)

also results in the code value 83.

The argument for CODE can be a number. For example, the formula

=CODE(8)

results in 56, the ASCII code for the number 8.

If you type a literal character as your *text* argument, don't forget to place the text character in quotation marks. Otherwise, you'll get a #NAME? error value.

The removal functions: TRIM and CLEAN

Microsoft Excel offers two removal functions: the TRIM function, which eliminates leading, trailing, and extra blank characters from a string, leaving only a single space between words; and the CLEAN function, which eliminates all nonprintable characters from a string.

Often leading and trailing blank characters can prevent you from correctly sorting entries in your worksheet or database. In addition, if you use string functions to manipulate labels in your worksheet, these extra spaces can prevent your formulas from working correctly. The TRIM function, which has the form

=TRIM(*text*)

removes all spaces in *text* except for one space between words. For example, if cell A1 of your worksheet contains the string *Fuzzy Wuzzy was a bear*, the formula

=TRIM(A1)

returns *Fuzzy Wuzzy was a bear.*

The CLEAN function is similar to TRIM, except that it operates only on nonprintable characters. CLEAN is especially useful if you've imported data from another program and some entries contain nonprintable characters such as tab markers and other program-specific codes. (These characters are displayed in your worksheet as bold vertical bars.) You can use CLEAN to remove these characters from your text. The CLEAN function has the form

=CLEAN(*text*)

The REPLACE function

The REPLACE function replaces one string of characters in a label with another string of characters. The REPLACE function takes the form

=REPLACE(*old text,start num,num chars,new text*)

The *old text* argument is the text string in which you want to replace some characters. The next two arguments, *start num* and *num chars*, indicate which characters you want to replace (relative to the left end of the string). The *new text* argument is the text string you want to insert. The *old text* and *new text* arguments must be literal strings surrounded by quotation marks, or formulas or references that result in strings. If the new text would make the label longer than 255 characters, REPLACE returns a #N/A! error value.

Suppose cell A3 in your worksheet contains the label *Millie Potter, Psychic.* You want to replace the first through sixth characters of this label with the string *Mildred.* To do this, you can use the formula

=REPLACE(A3,1,6,"Mildred")

The new label is *Mildred Potter, Psychic.* Note that the label in A3 remains unchanged—the new label is displayed only in the cell in which you entered the formula.

The SUBSTITUTE function

The SUBSTITUTE function substitutes new text for old text, just as REPLACE does. However, with SUBSTITUTE you don't tell Microsoft Excel the start number and the number of characters to replace; instead, you simply include the exact text you want replaced.

The SUBSTITUTE function takes the form

=SUBSTITUTE(*text,old text,new text,instance number*)

For example, suppose cell A4 in your worksheet contains the label *candy* and you want to change it to *dandy.* To do this, you can use the formula

=SUBSTITUTE(A4,"c","d")

When you enter this formula, the label in cell A4 doesn't change—the new label is displayed only in the cell containing the formula.

The *instance number* argument is optional. It tells Microsoft Excel to replace only the specified occurrence of *old text.* For example, suppose cell A1 contains the label *through the hoop* and you want to create a similar label that substitutes the word *loop* for *hoop.* You could do this with the formula

=SUBSTITUTE (A1,"h","l",4)

In this formula, the 4 tells Microsoft Excel to substitute an *l* for the fourth *h* in the label in cell A1. If you don't include *instance number,* Microsoft Excel changes all occurrences of *old text* to *new text.*

The EXACT function

The EXACT function lets you determine whether two strings match exactly, including uppercase and lowercase letters. The EXACT function takes the form

=EXACT(*text1,text2*)

If *text1* and *text2* are identical, including capitalization, EXACT returns TRUE; if *text1* and *text2* are not identical, EXACT returns FALSE. In other words, EXACT is a conditional-testing function that operates on strings. The *text1* and *text2* arguments must be either literal strings enclosed in quotes or references to cells that contain text.

For example, if cell A5 and cell A6 of your worksheet both contain the label *Totals*, the formula

=EXACT(A5,A6)

returns a TRUE value.

If you want to compare two strings where differences in capitalization don't matter, use the equal sign (=) instead of EXACT. We'll discuss this technique under *Conditional Tests*.

The substring functions

Microsoft Excel provides four functions to locate and report portions of a text string: FIND, SEARCH, RIGHT, and LEFT.

The FIND and SEARCH functions

The FIND and SEARCH functions let you locate the position of a substring within a string. Both functions return the number of the character where Microsoft Excel first finds the text. (In counting characters, Microsoft Excel includes blank spaces and punctuation marks.)

These two functions work the same way, except that FIND is case-sensitive and SEARCH lets you use wildcards. The functions follow the form

=FIND(*find text,within text,start at num*)

and

=SEARCH(*find text,within text,start at num*)

The *find text* argument identifies the text sought and the *within text* argument indicates where to look for it. You can use either literal text enclosed in double quotation marks or a cell reference for either of these arguments. The optional *start at num* argument specifies the character position in *within text* where you want to begin your search. This argument can be helpful when there is more than one occurrence of *find text* in *within text*. If you omit *start at num*, Microsoft Excel reports the first match located.

You get a #VALUE! error if *find text* isn't contained in *within text*, if *start at num* isn't greater than zero, or if *start at num* is greater than the number of characters in *within text* or greater than the position of the last occurrence of *find text*.

To locate the *p* in the string *A Night at the Opera,* use the formula

=FIND("p","A Night at the Opera")

This formula returns 17, because the *p* is the seventeenth character in the string.

If you're not sure of the character sequence you're searching for, you can use the SEARCH function and include wildcards in your *find text* string. To search for a single character occupying a specific position, use a question mark character (?); to search for any sequence of characters occupying a specific position, use an asterisk (∗). (We'll talk more about wildcards when we discuss database criteria in Chapter 15.)

Suppose you've used the names *Smith* and *Smyth* in your worksheet. To ensure that either name is found when cell A1 is checked, use the formula

=SEARCH("Sm?th",A1)

Then, if cell A1 contains the name *John Smith* or the name *John Smyth*, the SEARCH function will return the value 5—the starting point for the string *Sm?th*. If you're not sure of the number of characters, use the ∗ wildcard. For example, to find the position of the name *Allan* or *Alan* in cell A1, use the formula

=SEARCH("A∗an",A1)

The RIGHT and LEFT functions

The RIGHT function returns the rightmost series of characters from a string argument; the LEFT function returns the leftmost series of characters from a string argument. These functions take the forms

=RIGHT(*text,number of characters*)

and

=LEFT(*text,number of characters*)

The *number of characters* argument indicates the number of characters to extract from the *text* argument. Keep in mind that these functions count blank spaces in the *text* argument as characters. If you don't want the blank characters to be included in the extracted label, use RIGHT or LEFT within a TRIM function to remove unwanted blanks from the *text* argument.

The *number of characters* argument must be greater than zero. If you omit *number of characters*, Microsoft Excel assumes it is 1. If *number of characters* is greater than the number of characters in *text*, RIGHT and LEFT return the entire *text* argument.

Suppose you've entered the label *This is a test* in cell A1 of your worksheet. The formula

=RIGHT(A1,4)

returns the label *test*.

The case functions: UPPER, LOWER, and PROPER

Microsoft Excel provides three functions for manipulating case in text strings. The UPPER and LOWER functions convert a text string to all uppercase and all lowercase letters, respectively. The PROPER function lets you capitalize the first letter in each word of a text string and any other letters in the text that do not follow another letter; all other letters are converted to lowercase. These functions take the form

=UPPER(*text*)

and

=LOWER(*text*)

and

=PROPER(*text*)

For example, suppose you've entered a series of names in your worksheet and you want to ensure that all these entries appear in capital letters. Cell A1 might contain the label *john Johnson*. You could use the formula

=UPPER(A1)

to return *JOHN JOHNSON*. Similarly, the formulas

=LOWER(A1)

and

=PROPER(A1)

return the labels *john johnson* and *John Johnson*.

Logical functions

Microsoft Excel's logical functions include IF, TRUE, and FALSE; the special operators AND, OR, and NOT; and the specialized functions ISBLANK, ISERR, ISERROR, ISNA, ISREF, ISNUMBER, ISTEXT, ISNONTEXT, and ISLOGICAL.

Conditional tests

A conditional test is an equation that compares two numbers, functions, formulas, or labels. For example, each of these formulas is a conditional test:

```
=A1>A2
=5–3>5*2
=AVERAGE(B1:B6)=SUM(6,7,8)
=C2="Female"
=COUNT(A1:A10)=COUNT(B1:B10)
=LEN(A1)<10
```

Every conditional test must include at least one logical operator. Logical operators define the test relationship between elements of the conditional test. For example, in the conditional test A1>A2, the greater-than symbol (>) is the logical operator used to compare the test values stored in cells A1 and A2. Microsoft Excel offers these six logical operators:

Operator	Definition
=	Equal to
>	Greater than
<	Less than
>=	Greater than or equal to
<=	Less than or equal to
<>	Not equal to

Every conditional test must be either true or false. For example, the conditional test

```
=Z1=10
```

is true if the value in Z1 is equal to 10 and false if Z1 contains any other value.

The IF function

Of course, Microsoft Excel's conditional tests would be of little value if you could use them only to check your math. This is where the IF function comes in. The form of the IF function is

```
=IF(conditional test,true value,false value)
```

This function can be read *If the conditional test is true, then return the true value; otherwise, return the false value.*

For example, the formula

```
=IF(Z100<22,5,10)
```

returns 5 if the value in cell Z100 is less than 22; otherwise, it returns 10.

You can use other functions as the arguments within an IF function. For example, the formula

=IF(SUM(A1:A10)>0,SUM(A1:A10),0)

returns the result of SUM(A1:A10) if SUM(A1:A10) is greater than 0; otherwise, the function returns the value 0.

Using text in IF

Text can also be used as the arguments in IF functions. For example, the worksheet in Figure 6-7 lists semester exam scores for a group of students. The formula

=IF(AVERAGE(B4:D4)>80,"Pass","Fail")

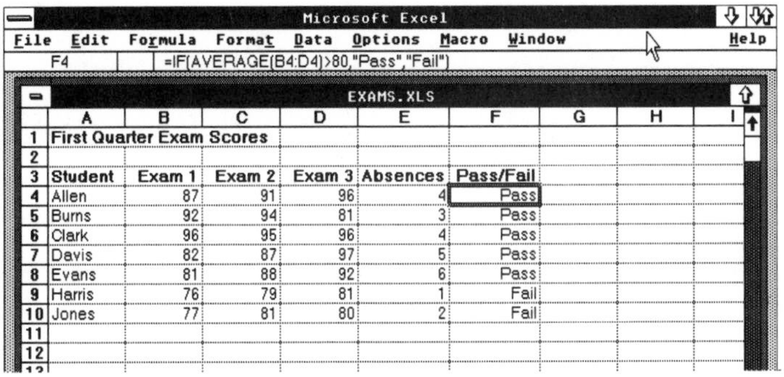

	A	B	C	D	E	F
1	First Quarter Exam Scores					
2						
3	Student	Exam 1	Exam 2	Exam 3	Absences	Pass/Fail
4	Allen	87	91	96	4	Pass
5	Burns	92	94	81	3	Pass
6	Clark	96	95	96	4	Pass
7	Davis	82	87	97	5	Pass
8	Evans	81	88	92	6	Pass
9	Harris	76	79	81	1	Fail
10	Jones	77	81	80	2	Fail

FIGURE 6-7. *You can use the IF function to return a text string.*

entered in cell F4 tells Microsoft Excel to average the test scores contained in the range B4:D4. If AVERAGE(B4:D4) is greater than 80, the function returns the true value *Pass;* if AVERAGE(B4:D4) is less than or equal to 80, the function returns the false value *Fail.*

You can take advantage of Microsoft Excel's ability to use text in IF to return nothing, instead of a 0, as the result of a false IF function. For example, the formula

=IF(SUM(A1:A10)>0,SUM(A1:A10)," ")

returns nothing if the conditional test is false.

The *conditional test* argument of an IF function can also consist of text. For example, the formula

=IF(A1="Test",100,200)

returns the value 100 if cell A1 contains the text *Test* and 200 if it contains any other entry. The match between the two text entries must be exact in all respects except capitalization.

You must always enclose text strings in quotes when you use them in the IF function (or in any other function, for that matter). If you don't enclose the strings in quotes, Microsoft Excel assumes they are range names.

The TRUE and FALSE functions

The TRUE and FALSE functions offer alternative ways to represent the logical conditions TRUE and FALSE. Neither of these accepts arguments; they take the form

=TRUE()

and

=FALSE()

For example, suppose cell B5 contains a logical test formula. If you enter the formula

=(B5=FALSE(),"Warning!","OK")

in another cell, the new formula returns *Warning!* if the result of the logical formula in B5 is FALSE or *OK* if the result of B5 is TRUE.

Complex operators

Microsoft Excel offers three additional functions that let you develop more sophisticated conditional tests: AND, OR, and NOT. These functions work in conjunction with the simple logical operators =, >, <, >=, <=, and <>. Basically, AND, OR, and NOT let you develop compound conditional tests. AND and OR can take up to 14 logical arguments each, in the form

=AND(*logical 1,logical 2,...,logical 14*)

and

=OR(*logical 1,logical 2,...,logical 14*)

NOT takes only one argument, in the form

=NOT(*logical*)

Arguments for AND, OR, and NOT can be conditional tests or they can be arrays or references to cells that contain logical values.

To illustrate the power of these operators, let's expand on the formula we developed in Figure 6-7. Suppose you want Microsoft Excel to return the text string *PASS* only if the student has an average test score above 80 and fewer than 5 unexcused absences. You can accomplish this with the formula

=IF(AND(AVERAGE(B4:D4)>80,E4<5),"PASS","FAIL")

Although the OR function takes the same arguments as AND, the results are radically different. For example, if you enter the formula

=IF(OR(AVERAGE(B4:D4)>80,E4<5),"PASS","FAIL")

you're instructing Microsoft Excel to return the value PASS if the student's average test score is greater than 80 *or* if the student has fewer than 5 absences. In other words, OR returns the true value if any *one* of the conditional tests is true, but AND returns the true value only if *all* the conditional tests are true.

The NOT function is used to negate a condition. This concept is a little confusing at first, because NOT instructs Microsoft Excel to return *true value* if the argument is false and *false value* if the argument is true. NOT might be better described as the UNLESS function. For example, the formula

=IF(NOT(A1=2),"Go","NoGo")

tells Microsoft Excel to return the text string *Go* UNLESS the value of cell A1 is 2.

The ISBLANK function

You can use the ISBLANK function to determine whether a referenced cell is blank. ISBLANK follows the form

=ISBLANK(*value*)

where *value* is a reference to a cell or range. If *value* refers to a blank cell or range, the function returns the value TRUE; otherwise, it returns FALSE.

Trapping errors: ISERR, ISERROR, and ISNA

If a formula in your worksheet refers to a cell that returns an error, that formula also returns an error. For example, if cell A1 returns an error, the formula

=A1/10

also returns an error. The same thing happens if the formula refers to a cell that returns a #N/A message.

Three specialized logical functions—ISERR, ISERROR, and ISNA—let you test the value of an argument or cell to determine whether it contains either an error value or the value #N/A. ISERR tests for all error values except #N/A; ISERROR tests for all error values, including #N/A; and ISNA tests for #N/A values only. These functions let you selectively "trap" errors and #N/A values, preventing them from filtering through the worksheet. These functions take the form

ISERR(*value*)

and

    =ISERROR(*value*)

and

    =ISNA(*value*)

Although *value* can be a number, a formula, or literal text, it is usually a reference to a cell or range. Only one cell within a range need contain an applicable error for the function to return a TRUE value.

    Typically, ISERR, ISERROR, and ISNA are used as conditional tests in IF functions. For example, the formula

    =IF(ISERROR(A1/A2),0,A1/A2)

tests the formula A1/A2. If A1/A2 returns an error (as it will if A2 is blank or contains the value 0), then the ISERROR function is true and the IF function returns the value 0. If A1/A2 does not return an error, the function returns the result of A1/A2. Similarly, the formula

    =IF(ISNA(A1),0,A1*10)

tests the value in cell A1. If that value is #N/A, the IF function returns a 0; otherwise, it returns the product of A1 times 10.

The ISREF function

The ISREF function works much like ISERROR and ISNA. Instead of testing the contents of a cell for an error or #N/A value, however, ISREF tests to see what kind of entry the cell contains.

    ISREF takes the form

    =ISREF(*value*)

It returns the logical value TRUE if the *value* argument is a cell reference; if the argument is any other kind of entry, it returns the value FALSE.

    You probably won't use ISREF at all unless you become heavily involved in macro programming.

The ISNUMBER function

You can use the ISNUMBER function to determine whether an entry is a number. ISNUMBER takes the form

    =ISNUMBER(*value*)

Suppose you want to know if the entry in cell A5 is a number. The formula

    =ISNUMBER(A5)

returns TRUE if cell A5 contains a number or a formula that results in a number; otherwise, it returns FALSE.

The ISTEXT and ISNONTEXT functions

The ISTEXT and ISNONTEXT functions let you test whether an entry is text. These functions take the form

=ISTEXT(*value*)

and

=ISNONTEXT(*value*)

Suppose you want to determine whether or not the entry in cell C35 is text. If you use the formula

=ISTEXT(C35)

and the entry in C35 is text or a formula that returns text, Microsoft Excel returns TRUE. If you test the same cell using the formula

=ISNONTEXT(C35)

Microsoft Excel returns FALSE.

The ISLOGICAL function

You can use the ISLOGICAL function to determine whether a cell contains a logical value. ISLOGICAL follows the form

=ISLOGICAL(*value*)

If the cell contains a logical value, Microsoft Excel returns TRUE; otherwise, it returns FALSE.

Nested IF functions

At times, a logical problem cannot be resolved even with complex operators like AND, OR, and NOT. Fortunately, with Microsoft Excel you can build even more sophisticated conditional tests by nesting IF functions to create a hierarchy of tests for complex logical problems. For example, the formula

```
=IF(A1=100,"Always",IF(AND(A1<100,A1>=80),"Usually",
    IF(AND(A1<80,A1>60),"Sometimes","Who cares?")))
```

uses three separate IF functions. The formula can be read *If the value in cell A1 equals 100, return the text string* Always; *otherwise, if the value in cell A1 falls between 80 and 100 (that is, 81 through 99), return the text string* Usually; *otherwise, if the value in cell A1 falls between 60 and 80 (61 through 79), return the text string* Sometimes; *and, finally, if none of these conditions is true, return the text string* Who cares?.

You can string together as many as seven nested IF arguments, as long as you don't exceed the 255-character limit on single-cell entries.

Other uses for conditional functions

Keep in mind that any of the conditional functions we've described can be used as stand-alone formulas in your worksheet. Although you'll usually use functions like AND, OR, NOT, ISERROR, ISNA, and ISREF within an IF function, you can also use formulas like

    =AND(A1>A2,A2<A3)

to perform simple conditional tests. This formula returns the value TRUE if the value in A1 is greater than the value in A2 and the value in A2 is less than the value in A3. You might use a simple formula like this one to assign TRUE and FALSE values to a range of numeric database cells and then use the TRUE and FALSE conditions as selection criteria for printing a specialized report. We'll talk more about this in Chapter 14, "Database Management."

Lookup functions

Microsoft Excel offers several functions that make it possible to "look up" information that has been stored in a list or a table. These functions are CHOOSE, MATCH, HLOOKUP, VLOOKUP, LOOKUP, and INDEX.

The CHOOSE function

The CHOOSE function lets you retrieve items from a list of values, labels, or cell references in a cell by using an index number. CHOOSE has the form

    =CHOOSE(*index,value 1,value 2,...value n*)

where *index* is the number of the item that you want to look up and *value 1, value 2,* and so on are the elements of the list. The *index* value must always be positive and cannot exceed the number of elements in the list. If you use an *index* value less than 1 or greater than the number of values in the list, Microsoft Excel returns a #VALUE! error.

The CHOOSE function returns the value of the element of the list that occupies the position indicated by *index*. For example, the function

    =CHOOSE(2,6,1,8,9,3)

returns the value 1, because 1 is the second item in the list (the *index* value itself is not part of the list).

The arguments of CHOOSE can be cell references. If you use a cell reference for *index*, Microsoft Excel selects an item from the list according to the value stored in that cell. For example, suppose cell A11 contains the formula

=CHOOSE(A10,0.15,0.22,0.21,0.21,0.26)

If cell A10 contains the value 5, the CHOOSE function returns the value 0.26; if cell A10 contains the value 1, the function returns the value 0.15. Similarly, if cell C1 contains the value 0.15, C2 the value 0.22, and C3, C4, and C5 the value 0.21, then the formula

=CHOOSE(A10,C1,C2,C3,C4,C5)

returns 0.15 if cell A10 contains the value 1 and it returns 0.21 if cell A10 contains the value 3, 4, or 5.

The list of values cannot be a range. You might be tempted to create a function like

=CHOOSE(A10,C1:C5)

to take the place of the longer function in the previous example. If you did, however, all you would get back would be a #VALUE! error.

The elements in the list can be text strings. For example, the function

=CHOOSE(3,"First","Second","Third")

selects the third item from the list and returns the text string *Third*.

The MATCH function

The MATCH function is closely related to the CHOOSE function. However, where CHOOSE returns the item that occupies the position in a list specified by the *index* argument, MATCH returns the position of the item in the list that most closely matches a lookup value. The form of this function is

=MATCH(*lookup value,lookup range,type*)

where *lookup value* is the value or string to look up and *lookup range* is the range that contains the values with which to compare the lookup value. The *lookup value* argument can be a value, a cell reference, or text enclosed in quotation marks; the *lookup range* must be a reference to a range or a range name.

Consider the worksheet in Figure 6-8. If you enter the formula

=MATCH(10,A1:D1)

in cell E1, the result will be 1, because the cell in the first position of the *lookup range* argument contains a value that matches *lookup value*.

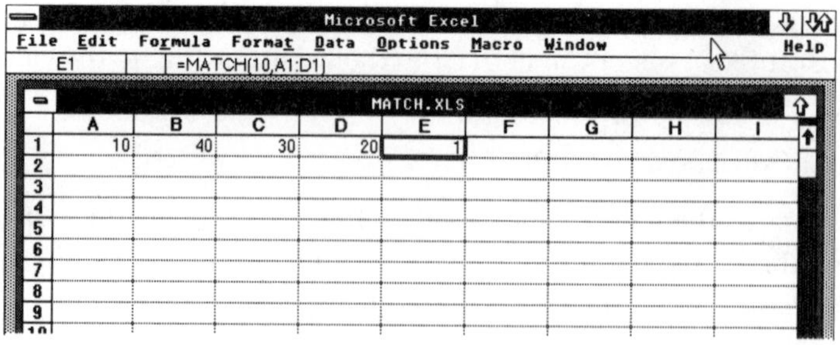

FIGURE 6-8. *You can use the MATCH function to locate the position of a value in a list.*

The *type* argument defines the rules for the search. This argument, which is optional, must be 1, 0, or –1; it cannot be a cell reference. If the *type* argument is 1 or is omitted altogether, the MATCH function looks for the largest value in the range that is less than or equal to the lookup value. For example, going back to the worksheet in Figure 6-8, the formula

=MATCH(19,A1:D1,1)

returns the value 1, because 10, the first item in the range, is the largest value in the range that doesn't exceed the lookup value, 19. If no items in the range are less than or equal to *lookup value*, the function returns the error value #N/A.

If *type* is 0, the MATCH function looks for an exact match between the lookup value and the values in the range. If no items in the range exactly match *lookup value*, the function returns the error value #N/A.

If *type* is 0 and *lookup value* is text, you can use the wildcards * and ? in the *lookup value* argument.

If type is 1 or 0, the elements in the lookup range must be in ascending order for the function to work properly. For example, if you rearrange the items in the range A1:D1 to look like Figure 6-9, the formula

=MATCH(20,A1:D1,1)

returns the value 1, instead of the value you probably expected: 4.

If *type* is –1, MATCH looks for the smallest value in the range that is greater than or equal to the lookup value. When *type* is –1, the items in the list must be in descending order. If no items in the range are greater than or equal to *lookup value*, the function returns the error value #N/A.

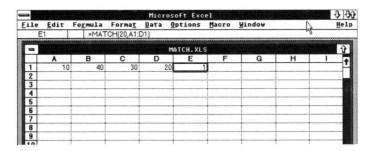

FIGURE 6-9. *The MATCH function does not work properly with a type argument of 1 or 0 if the lookup range is not in ascending order.*

The lookup value and the items in the range can also be text strings. For example, if cells A1:D1 contain the text entries shown in Figure 6-10, the formula

=MATCH("Twenty",A1:D1,0)

returns the value 2. When you use MATCH to locate text strings, you probably will want to specify a *type* argument of 0 (an exact match).

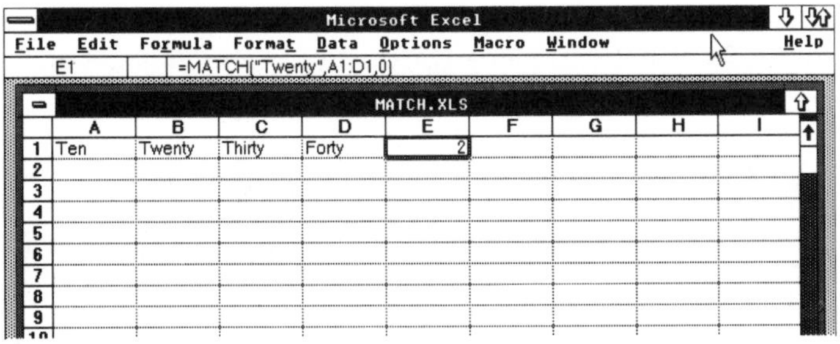

FIGURE 6-10. *You can use MATCH to locate the position of a text string.*

The HLOOKUP and VLOOKUP functions

HLOOKUP and VLOOKUP are nearly identical functions that let you look up information stored in a table that you've constructed. The forms of these lookup functions are

=VLOOKUP(*lookup value,lookup range,index number*)

and

=HLOOKUP(*lookup value,lookup range,index number*)

where *lookup value* is the value to look up in the table, *lookup range* is the range that contains the lookup table, and *index number* designates the column or row of the table from which to select the result.

The HLOOKUP and VLOOKUP functions work by comparing the lookup value to a list of comparison values in a lookup table. This table is defined by the *lookup range* argument. The only difference between HLOOKUP and VLOOKUP is the type of table each function uses: HLOOKUP works with horizontal tables (tables arranged in rows); VLOOKUP works with vertical tables (tables arranged in columns).

When we say that a table is horizontal or vertical, we're really telling Microsoft Excel where the comparison values are located. If the values are in the leftmost column of the table, the table is vertical; if the values are in the first row of the table, the table is horizontal. (We'll occasionally use the term *comparison range* to denote the row or column that contains the comparison values.)

The comparison values in a lookup table can be numbers or text. In either case, they must be arranged in ascending order if the table is to function properly. In addition, no comparison value should be used more than once in a table.

Figure 6-11 shows a simple vertical lookup table. In this table, column A contains the comparison values, arranged in ascending numeric order. Columns B and C contain the information to look up; this information is not arranged in any special order.

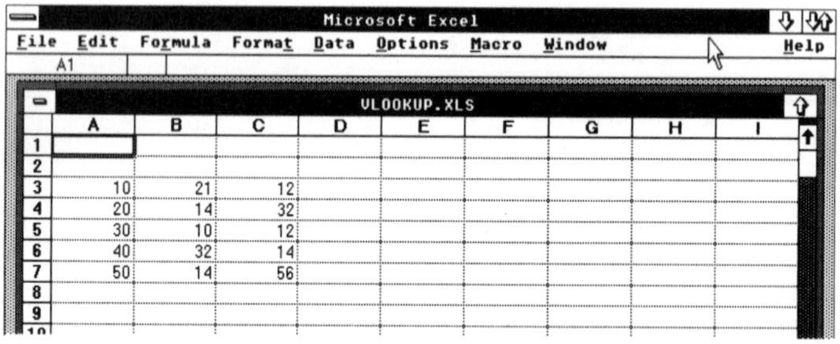

FIGURE 6-11. *We'll use this simple vertical lookup table to demonstrate the VLOOKUP function.*

The *index number* argument (sometimes called the offset) tells the lookup function which column or row of the table to look in for the function's result. The first row or column in the table has an index number of 1, so if the index number in a lookup function is 1, the result of the function will be one of the comparison values. In our example, column B has an index number of 2 and column C has an index number of 3.

The *index number* argument must be greater than or equal to 1 and must never be greater than the number of rows or columns in the table; that is, if a vertical table is three columns wide, the offset cannot be greater than 3. Any offset value that does not meet these rules causes the function to return an error value. Index numbers larger than the number of columns or rows in the table range are one of the most frequent errors in working with lookup tables. Always be sure your index number and your table range agree.

The VLOOKUP function

Let's look at how these functions work. To access the table in Figure 6-12, you would use the VLOOKUP function. In this example, the formula

    =VLOOKUP(8,B2:E6,3)

returns the value 21.

The function locates first the table range and then the column containing the comparison values—in this case, column B. Next, it scans the comparison values in column B to find the largest value less than or equal to the lookup value in the formula. In the example, because the third comparison value, 8, is equal to the lookup value and the fourth comparison value, 11, is greater than the lookup value, the function knows that its result is somewhere in row 4.

FIGURE 6-12. *You can use the VLOOKUP function to retrieve information from a table like this one.*

Next, the function uses the index number to determine which column in the lookup table should be probed for the data. In this case, the index number is 3, so column D contains the desired data. (Remember, the column containing the comparison values has an index number of 1.) The function therefore returns the number from row 4, column D:21.

The *lookup value* argument in a lookup function can be a value, a cell reference, or text enclosed in quotes; the table range can be indicated by cell references or a range name. If we assign the name *Table* to the range B2:E6 in Figure 6-12 and enter the number 8 in cell A1, the formula

=VLOOKUP(A1,Table,3)

returns the same result as the previous example.

Remember that these lookup functions look for the greatest comparison value that is less than or equal to the lookup value, not for an exact match between the comparison value and the lookup value. If all the comparison values in the first row or column of the table range are greater than the lookup value, the function returns the value #N/A. If, on the other hand, all the comparison values are less than the lookup value, the function returns the data value that corresponds to the last (largest) comparison value in the table.

You can also use the lookup functions to look up text. For example, the formula

=VLOOKUP(8,B2:E6,4)

returns the text string *Barb* from the table in Figure 6-12.

Not only can the data items in a table be text strings, the comparison values can be strings as well. Figure 6-13 shows a vertical lookup table that uses text comparison values. For example, the formula

=VLOOKUP("Doug",B2:C6,2)

returns the value 46000. (As with most other functions, if you use a text string as the lookup value in your lookup table, the string must be enclosed in double quotation marks.)

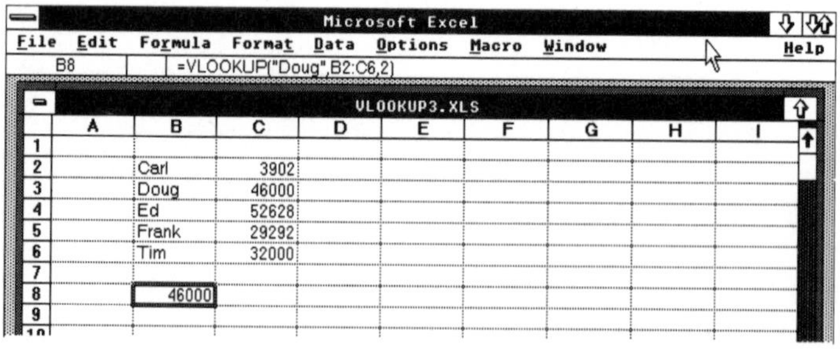

FIGURE 6-13. *You can use VLOOKUP with text comparison values.*

Unfortunately, the usefulness of text comparison values is limited in Microsoft Excel. For one thing, the program requires that the comparison values be arranged in alphabetic order if the table is to work properly. In addition, Microsoft Excel uses the same "greatest value that is not greater than the lookup value" method it uses with numeric values, rather than an absolute match method, for selecting the correct comparison value. Thus, the formula

=VLOOKUP("Steve",B2:C6,2)

returns the value 29292, the number that corresponds to the comparison value *Frank*, which is the "greatest" comparison value that is "less than" the lookup value *Steve*. Although this method is consistent, it does not yield the result you might expect.

You can even combine numbers, text entries, and logical entries in the comparison range, although it's unlikely you'll find an application that requires such a mixture. If you do this, however, the elements in the range still must be arranged in ascending order according to Microsoft Excel's sorting rules: numbers first, then text, then logical values.

Do you recall our saying that the comparison values in a lookup table must be in ascending order for the table to work properly? Let's look at a table that fails. The vertical lookup table in Figure 6-14 doesn't work properly because the comparison values in column B are not in ascending order. The formula

=VLOOKUP(4,B2:C6,2)

returns the value 100 instead of 500, the number you might expect. This occurs because the VLOOKUP function searches the comparison value list only until it comes to a number greater than the lookup value. When it finds such a value—in this case, when it comes to 5—it stops the search, backs up to the previous comparison value, and uses that row to obtain the result. Any comparison values below the first value that are greater than the lookup value are ignored.

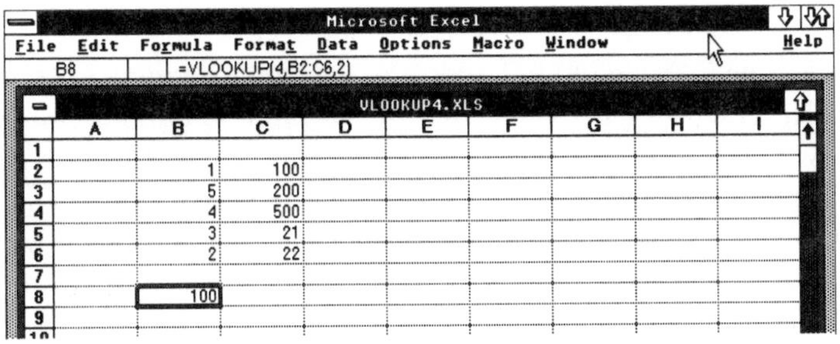

FIGURE 6-14. *The VLOOKUP function does not work properly unless the comparison values are in ascending order.*

The HLOOKUP function

The horizontal lookup function, HLOOKUP, is similar to the vertical lookup function, except that it reads information from horizontal tables. All the rules that apply to VLOOKUP also apply to HLOOKUP.

The worksheet in Figure 6-15 shows an example of a horizontal lookup table. The formula

=HLOOKUP(6,B2:E7,3)

returns the value 101 from this table because the lookup value, 6, equals the comparison value in column C and the index number, 3, tells the function to look in the third row of the table for the correct item.

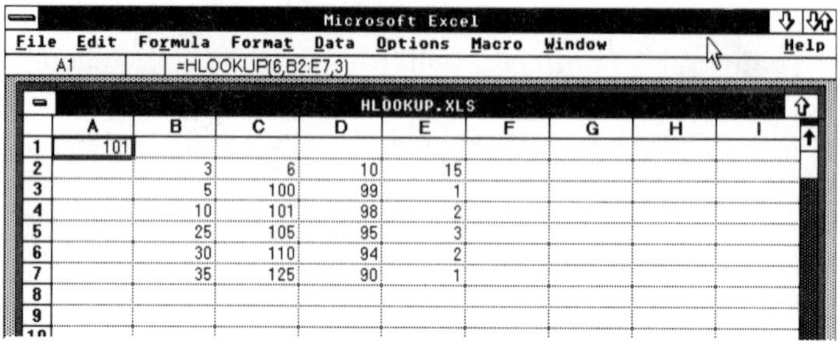

FIGURE 6-15. *You can use the HLOOKUP function to retrieve information from a horizontal table.*

The LOOKUP function

The LOOKUP function has two forms. In both forms, it is similar to VLOOKUP and HLOOKUP.

The first form
The first form of LOOKUP is

=LOOKUP(*lookup value,lookup range,result range*)

where *lookup value* is the value to look up in the lookup range, *lookup range* is the range that contains the comparison values, and *result range* is the range that contains the possible results. (The Microsoft Excel manual uses the terms *lookup vector* and *result vector* to describe the lookup range and the result range.)

Like HLOOKUP and VLOOKUP, LOOKUP searches *lookup range* for the largest comparison value that is not greater than *lookup value*. It then selects the matching result from *result range*. For example, consider the worksheet in Figure 6-16. The formula

=LOOKUP(3,B3:B7,E3:E7)

compares the lookup value, 3, with the values in the lookup range, B3:B7. After determining that the entry in cell B5, the third cell of the lookup range, is the largest entry in the range that is not greater than the lookup value, the function then looks to the third cell of the result range, E5, for the result of the formula: 300.

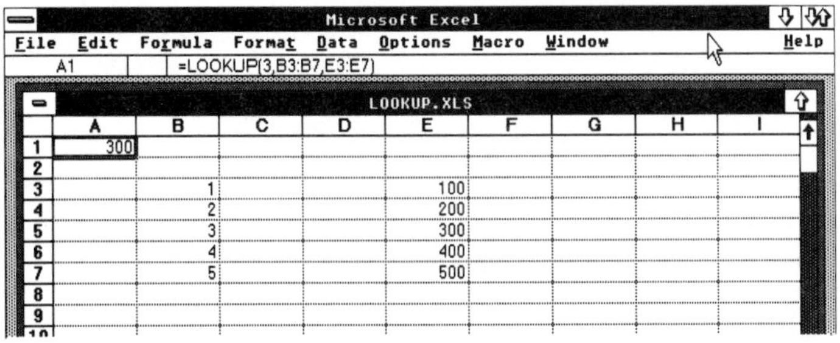

FIGURE 6-16. *You can also use the LOOKUP function to retrieve information from a range.*

Although the lookup range and the result range often are parallel in the worksheet, they don't have to be. In fact, one range can be horizontal and the other vertical. All that is required is that the result range have exactly the same number of elements as the lookup range. For example, in Figure 6-17, the formula

=LOOKUP(3,A1:A5,D6:H6)

returns 300. Both the lookup range, A1:A5, and the result range, D6:H6, have five elements. The lookup value, 3, matches the entry in the third cell of the lookup range. The result of the formula is therefore the entry in the third cell of the result range: 300.

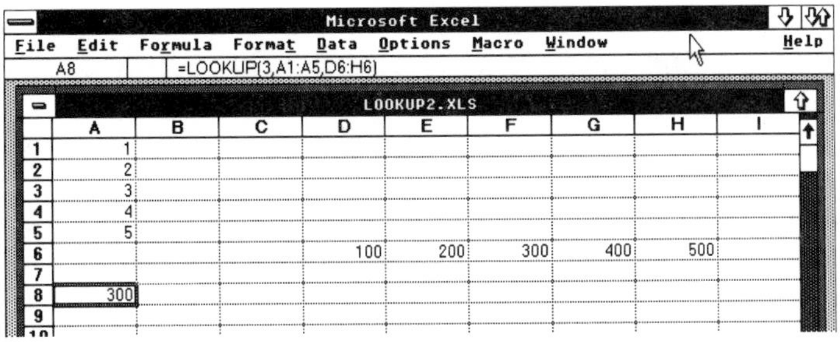

FIGURE 6-17. *You can use the LOOKUP function to retrieve information from a nonparallel cell range.*

In every other way, the first form of LOOKUP is identical to HLOOKUP and VLOOKUP. All the rules that apply to VLOOKUP and HLOOKUP also apply to LOOKUP.

The second form

The second form of LOOKUP is

=LOOKUP(*lookup value,lookup range*)

where *lookup value* is the value to look up in the table and *lookup range* is the range that contains the lookup table. This form of the LOOKUP function doesn't have an index number argument or result range. The result is always taken from the last row or the last column of the lookup range.

This form of LOOKUP can be used to read from either a horizontal or a vertical table. LOOKUP uses the dimensions of the table to figure out where the comparison values are. If the table is taller than it is wide or if the table is square, the function assumes that the comparison values are in the leftmost column of the table; if the table is wider than it is tall, the function views the table as horizontal and assumes the comparison values are in the first row of the table.

In every other way, the second form of the LOOKUP function is identical to HLOOKUP and VLOOKUP. All the rules that apply to VLOOKUP and HLOOKUP also apply to LOOKUP.

For the most part, you'll find HLOOKUP and VLOOKUP preferable to LOOKUP because they are more predictable and controllable. LOOKUP will probably be important to you only if you import Multiplan models into Microsoft Excel.

The INDEX function

Like CHOOSE and LOOKUP, INDEX is a lookup function. Its form is

=INDEX(*index range,row,column,area*)

where *index range* is the range or ranges that contain the index table and *row* and *column* describe the row and column coordinates of the particular cell being referenced. The *area* argument comes into play only when *index range* contains more than one range. (More on this in a few paragraphs.)

The INDEX function requires that you create an index table—a rectangular range that includes at least four cells. The cells in the table can contain numbers, text, or formulas. Figure 6-18 shows an example of an index table. The formula in cell A1

=INDEX(C3:E6,A2,A3)

uses the row coordinate in cell A2 and the column coordinate in cell A3 to extract a value from the table. Because cell A2 contains the number 3 and cell A3 contains the number 2, the function returns the address of the cell in the third row and the second column of the table: D5.

The INDEX function returns the address of the cell at the indicated position in the table, not the entry stored in that cell. However, Microsoft Excel *displays* the contents of the cell, not the cell address. In other words, even though the actual

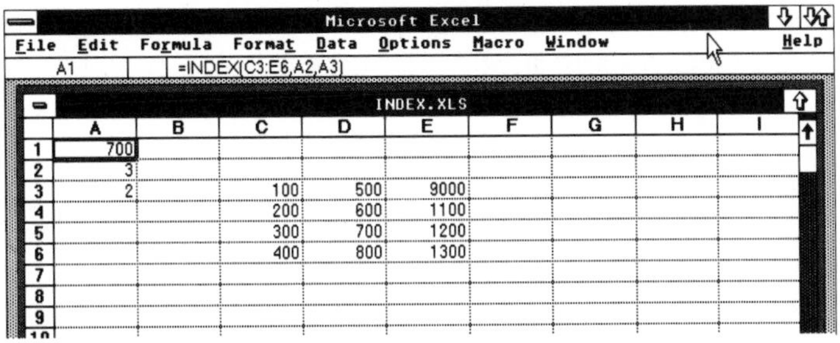

FIGURE 6-18. *Use the INDEX function to retrieve the address of the cell where information is located.*

result of the previous INDEX function is D5, the apparent result is the number 700—the contents of that cell.

The *row* and *column* arguments must be positive. If *row* or *column* is less than or equal to 0, the function displays the error value #VALUE!. However, because the INDEX function returns the cell address of the indicated position in the table, a *row* or *column* argument of 0 actually returns a reference to the entire column or row indicated. For example, using the worksheet shown in Figure 6-18, the formula

=INDEX(C3:E6,0,2)

would return the result #VALUE!. However, the formula

=SUM(INDEX(C3:E6,0,2))

would sum the values in the second column, D, and return the result 2600.

If the *row* argument is greater than the number of rows in the table or if the *column* argument is greater than the number of columns, the function returns the error value #REF!.

If the index table is only one row deep or one column wide, you can use only one index to select a value. For example, the formula

=INDEX(C3:C6,2)

returns the value 200 from the table in Figure 6-18. Similarly, the formula

=INDEX(C3:E3,2)

returns the value 500. The INDEX function is similar to the CHOOSE function when used with a one-dimensional table.

The *area* argument is important only when *index range* contains several areas. Then, you must include the *area* argument to tell the INDEX function which area to use. For example, in the formula

=INDEX((A1:C5,D6:F10),1,1,2)

the index range is made up of two areas: A1:C5 and D6:F10. The *area* argument, 2, tells INDEX to work on the second of these areas.

The *area* argument must always be a positive integer. If *area* is less than 1, the function returns the error value #REF!.

We'll discuss the array form of INDEX in Chapter 8.

Miscellaneous functions

In addition to all the functions you've learned about so far, Microsoft Excel offers a handful of functions that don't fit into any particular group. We'll cover those functions—CELL, N, T, INDIRECT, TYPE, AREAS, ROW, COLUMN, and NA—in this section.

The CELL function

You can use the CELL function to obtain information about the formatting, location, or contents of a cell. Usually, you'll use the CELL function to learn about a single cell, but you can use it for a range as well. When you do this, Microsoft Excel furnishes information about the upper left cell in the selection.

CELL takes the form

=CELL(*type of info,reference*)

The result of the function depends on the type of entry in the referenced cell. Table 6-1 shows the nine available *type of info* arguments and the information that each returns. These arguments must be inside quotation marks. Table 6-2 shows the codes for Microsoft Excel's formats. (If you've formatted *reference* with a customized format, Microsoft Excel returns the format closest to the custom format.)

Table 6-1. The *type of info* arguments used with the CELL function.

Argument	Returns
"width"	Width of specified cell, rounded to nearest whole number
"row"	Row number of specified cell; same as ROW(*reference*)
"col"	Column number of specified cell; same as COLUMN(*reference*)

(continued)

Table 6-1. continued

Argument	Returns
"protect"	Protection status of specified cell:
	0 if cell not locked
	1 if cell locked
"address"	Absolute address of specified cell
"contents"	Contents of specified cell
"format"	Format of specified cell, represented as a code (see Table 6-2)
"prefix"	Label prefix of specified label-containing cell:
	' if left alignment
	" if right alignment
	^ if centered alignment
	\ if fill alignment
	' if General alignment
"type"	Type of entry in specified cell:
	b if cell is blank
	l (lowercase L) if cell contains a text constant
	v if cell contains anything else

Table 6-2. Codes used by the CELL function to describe cell formats.

Format	Code
General	G
0 or #,##0	F0
0.00 or #,##0.00	F2
$#,##0; ($#,##0)	C0
$#,##0.00; ($#,##0.00)	C2
0%	P0
0.00%	P2
0.00E+00	S2
d-mmm-yy	D1
d-mmm	D2
mmm-yy	D3
m/d/yy or m/d/yy h:mm	D4
h:mm:ss AM/PM	D6
h:mm AM/PM	D7
h:mm:ss	D8
h:mm	D9

The translation functions: N and T

The N function translates values into numbers; the T function translates values into text. With most Microsoft Excel functions, when you enter an argument that doesn't generate the correct type of data, the program automatically translates it, so you don't generally need to use N or T in formulas. Microsoft Excel has included them for compatibility with other worksheet programs.

The translation functions have the forms

=N(*value*)

and

=T(*value*)

With the N function, if you enter a number or a reference to a cell containing a number, N returns that number. If you enter the logical value TRUE or a reference to a cell that evaluates to TRUE, N returns 1. If you enter a date with one of Microsoft Excel's date formats, N returns that date's serial number. If you enter anything else, it returns 0.

If the *value* argument of a T function is text, the function returns that text. If the argument is anything else, the T function returns a null text string (" ").

The INDIRECT function

You can use the INDIRECT function to find out the contents of a cell from its reference. INDIRECT takes the form

=INDIRECT(*reference,type of ref*)

where *reference* is an A1 reference, an R1C1 reference, or a cell name, and *type of ref* is a logical value that indicates which of these types of reference you're using. If *type of ref* is FALSE, Microsoft Excel interprets *reference* as the R1C1 format; if *type of ref* is TRUE or is omitted, Microsoft Excel interprets *reference* as the A1 format. If your entry for *reference* isn't valid, INDIRECT returns #REF!.

For example, if cell C6 contains the text value B3 and cell B3 contains the value 2.888, the formula

=INDIRECT(C6)

returns the value 2.888. If cell C6 contains the text value R3C2, you would use the formula

=INDIRECT(R6C3,FALSE)

to obtain this value.

You must select the R1C1 option with the Workspace command on the Options menu before you can use the R1C1 form of INDIRECT.

The TYPE function

You can use the TYPE function to determine whether a cell contains text, a number, a logical value, or an error value. TYPE takes the form

=TYPE (*cell reference*)

The result of the TYPE function is a code for the type of entry in the referenced cell: 1 for a number, 2 for text, 4 for a logical value (TRUE or FALSE), 16 for an error value, and 64 for an array.

If cell A1 contains the number 100, the formula

=TYPE(A1)

returns 1. If A1 contains the text entry *Microsoft Excel*, the formula returns 2.

The AREAS function

An area is a single cell or a rectangular block of cells. Use the AREAS function to determine the number of areas in a range. The function has the form

=AREAS(*range reference,range reference,...,range reference*)

The result of the function is the number of areas referred to by the argument. For example, the formula

=AREAS(A1,B1:C5,A1:D10,Z100:Z101)

returns the number 4, because the argument refers to four areas.

Although this function has limited applications, one clever use is with a named range. Suppose you've assigned the name *Test* to the range A1:C5,D6,E7:G10. The function

=AREAS(Test)

returns the number 3, the number of areas in the range Test.

The ROW and COLUMN functions

Although the names of the ROW and COLUMN functions are nearly the same as the names of two array functions, ROWS and COLUMNS, which we discuss in Chapter 8, the functions are quite different.

The forms of the ROW and COLUMN functions are

=ROW(*cell reference*)

and

=COLUMN(*cell reference*)

The result of these functions is the row number or column number of the cell referred to by the function's argument. For example, the formula

=ROW(H5)

returns the result 5.

If the argument is omitted, the result is the row or column number of the cell that contains the function.

If the argument of the ROW or COLUMN function is a range or a range name, the result of the function is an array consisting of the row or column numbers of each of the rows or columns in the range. For example, the formula

=ROW(A1:A10)

returns the array {1,2,3,4,5,6,7,8,9,10}.

The NA function

NA is a placeholder function. Unlike most functions, NA takes no arguments. The form of the function is simply

=NA()

When you enter the NA function in a cell, that cell and all formulas that refer to that cell return the result #N/A. Some functions return the NA function as a type of error value.

Suppose several formulas in your worksheet depend on the value in a cell, but you aren't yet certain of the value the cell should contain. Instead of entering a guess, you can enter the NA function in the cell as a placeholder. Until you replace the NA function with the correct value, any formula in the worksheet that refers to that cell will display the result #N/A.

You'll use #N/A primarily for marking blank cells to help you avoid including those cells in calculations.

Other functions

Microsoft Excel offers three other groups of functions that we haven't discussed here: date and time functions, array functions, and database statistical functions.

Because each of these types of functions requires more knowledge about how Microsoft Excel works, we'll discuss them separately.

We'll cover date functions in Chapter 7, arrays in Chapter 8, and database statistical functions in Chapter 15.

In addition to all these built-in functions, Microsoft Excel lets you create your own functions. You'll learn to do this in the section on building macro functions in Chapter 19.

7

Date and Time

*M*icrosoft Excel allows you to enter date values and time values in your worksheet. You can use these values to "date stamp" documents or to perform date and time arithmetic. In this chapter, we'll show how you can work with dates and times in your Microsoft Excel worksheets.

If you've ever tried to create a production schedule or a monthly billing system by counting the days on your desk calendar, you'll be thrilled by Microsoft Excel's date and time capabilities. For example, the Series command on the Data menu lets you enter a long series of row or column headers in your worksheet in date format; instead of spending your time entering dozens of individual dates, you can enter a month or even a year of dates in seconds. Or you can go beyond simply entering dates in the spreadsheet and take advantage of Microsoft Excel's convenient date and time functions to perform calculations quickly and accurately. For example, if you're using your worksheet to calculate your company's monthly payroll, you might use the HOURS function to determine the number of hours worked each day and the WEEKDAY function to determine whether employees should be paid at the standard rate (for Monday through Friday) or at the overtime rate (for Saturdays and Sundays). We'll look at each of these topics in the following pages, but first let's see how Microsoft Excel defines date and time values.

How Microsoft Excel remembers dates and times

The basic unit of time in Microsoft Excel is the day. Each day is represented by an integer from 1 through 65380. The program's base date, represented by the integer 1, is January 1, 1900. The maximum day value, 65380, represents December 31, 2078. Each day value you enter in your worksheet represents the number of days that have elapsed between the base date and the specified date. Thus, the date January 1, 1988, is represented by the integer 32143, because 32143 days elapsed between the base date and January 1, 1988.

The time of day is a decimal value representing the portion of a day that has elapsed between the beginning of the day—12:00 midnight—and the specified time. The time 12:00 noon is represented by the value 0.5, because the difference between midnight and noon is exactly half a day. Thus, the time/date combination 9:50 AM, July 20, 1988, is represented in Microsoft Excel by the number 32344.41.

You may find it confusing at first to think of dates and times in terms of serial values, but this technique makes sense if you think about it for a moment. By assigning serial values to days, hours, minutes, and even seconds, Microsoft Excel lets you perform sophisticated date and time arithmetic. You can manipulate dates and times in your worksheet formulas just as you do other types of values.

Functions and formats

Because the serial values that represent dates and times don't look anything like dates and times, they're nearly impossible to understand. Fortunately, Microsoft Excel offers two sets of tools that make it easy to work with these serial values: functions, which allow you to enter dates and times in cells, and formats, which convert serial values into an understandable form.

Entering a date or a time in the Microsoft Excel worksheet is usually a two-step process. First you use a date or time function to enter the date or time in a cell; the result of this function is the serial value of the specified date or time. Then you use a date or time format to display the result in recognizable form. (You can often combine these two steps by entering your date and time values "in format." More about this in a few pages.)

The DATE function

The basic date function in Microsoft Excel is DATE, which lets you enter a date in a cell of the worksheet. The form of this function is

=DATE(*yy,mm,dd*)

where *yy* is the year, *mm* is the month, and *dd* is the day. The easiest way to remember the form of the DATE function is to remember that the arguments must appear in descending order of magnitude: years first, then months, then days.

The result of DATE is a serial value that represents the number of days that have elapsed between the base date and the indicated date. For example, if you use the formula

=DATE(88,12,25)

to enter the date December 25, 1988, in the worksheet, the result is the serial value 32502.

Microsoft Excel is quite liberal in interpreting DATE function arguments. When you enter a DATE function, your day argument can be much higher than the last day of the month; the program will simply count forward into the next month. For example, if you enter the formula

=DATE(86,7,50)

the program stores the serial date value for August 19, 1986.

Your day argument can be as high as you want, as long as it doesn't cause the serial date value to go beyond Microsoft Excel's maximum of 65380 (December 31, 2078). Similarly, your month argument can be higher than 12. As you might expect, Microsoft Excel simply counts forward into subsequent years to interpret a DATE function whose month argument is 13 or higher.

If you use 0 as the day argument in a DATE function, Microsoft Excel interprets the value as the last day of the previous month. Thus, if you enter

=DATE(86,6,0)

the program stores the serial date value for May 31, 1986. Similarly, if you enter 0 for the month, December of the previous year is displayed. When you enter =DATE(88,0,0), Microsoft Excel moves back both the month and the day, to store the serial value for November 30, 1987.

Finally, you can use a negative number in the day argument to "count backwards" into the previous month. If you enter the formula

=DATE(88,4,-6)

Microsoft Excel stores the serial value for the date March 25, 1988.

The year 2000 and beyond

Most of the date values you enter will fall in the 1900s. As you saw in the example above, when you're entering a date value that falls within this range, you need enter only the last two digits of the year value. If you want to enter a year value from 2000 through 2078, however, you must use the values 100 through 178 or you must enter the full year value.

For example, to enter the date January 1, 2010, you could use either

=DATE(110,1,1)

or

=DATE(2010,1,1)

Alternatively, you could type the date value 1/1/2010 directly in the worksheet.

Formatting dates

After you've used the DATE function to enter a date in the worksheet, you can use the Number command on the Format menu to present that date in recognizable form. Microsoft Excel offers four date formats: m/d/yy, d-mmm-yy, d-mmm, and mmm-yy. The results of the function DATE(88,12,25)—serial value 32502—under each of these formats are

Format	Display
m/d/yy	12/25/88
d-mmm-yy	25-Dec-88
d-mmm	25-Dec
mmm-yy	Dec-88

To assign a date format to a cell, simply select that cell, choose Number from the Format menu, select the date format you want to use, and choose OK.

A word of warning: When you enter a date in a previously formatted cell, Microsoft Excel interprets the date as a serial number but displays it in the format you previously applied to the cell. Therefore, if you format a cell with the 0.00% format and then enter the date 1/1/88 into the cell, Microsoft Excel stores the serial number for the date, 32143, and displays it as 3214300.00%. If you want to see the number as a date, you must select the Number command from the Format menu and then select a date format.

An easier way

Now that you understand how dates are stored and are familiar with the two-step method for entering dates in the worksheet, let's look at a simpler way to create date entries. Recall from Chapter 3 that you can enter a number in a cell and format that number in one step by simply typing the number "in format." You can use this same technique to enter dates in the worksheet. For example, to enter the date December 25, 1988, in a cell, you can choose that cell and type *12/25/88* or *12-25-88*. (Either slashes or hyphens can be used as separators.) When you use this technique, Microsoft Excel does not display the date's serial value in the formula bar; instead, it assigns the m/d/yy format to the cell (if the cell hasn't been previously formatted) and displays 12/25/1988 in the formula bar. (For the years 2000 through 2078, you must type the complete year value; the program doesn't accept a year value of 100 or above for "in format" date entries.)

You can use any built-in format to enter dates in this way. If your entry doesn't exactly match a built-in format, Microsoft Excel will attempt to apply the closest matching format to your entry. For example, when you type *1 Dec* in a cell, you'll see the formatted entry 1-Dec. The entry in the formula bar still appears in mm/dd/yyyy format (12/1/1988), however, so that you can edit the date value more easily. You can also create your own date formats, as we'll explain shortly.

E X C E L *Tip*

Use the VALUE function to determine a date's serial value

When you type a date value in your worksheet instead of using the DATE function, you won't see the underlying serial date value for that date. Using Microsoft Excel's VALUE function, however, you can easily determine the serial value. For example, if cell A1 of your worksheet contains the date entry 5/1/88, you can use the formula

=VALUE(A1)

to determine that the serial date value for this entry is 32264.

Using date arithmetic

After you've entered a date in a worksheet, you can use it in formulas and functions much as you would any other value. Suppose you want to figure the date 200 days after December 25, 1988. If cell A1 contains the formula

    =DATE(88,12,25)

you can use the formula

    =A1+200

to compute the serial value of the date 200 days later: 32702. After the formula is in place, you can use one of Microsoft Excel's date formats to display the result in an understandable form.

Now suppose you want to know how many weeks will elapse between December 25, 1988 and May 13, 1989. You can use the formula

    =(DATE(89,5,13)−DATE(88,12,25))/7

to find the answer: 19.85714 weeks.

If you enter a date value "in format," you can still perform mathematical calculations on that date, even though the serial date value doesn't appear in the cell or formula bar.

Creating date series

Although you can create an evenly spaced series of dates in a row or column of a spreadsheet in several ways, Microsoft Excel offers a special tool that makes the job easy: the Series command on the Data menu. This command lets you build a series of dates that are days, weeks, months, or years apart.

Let's look at an example of the Series command. Suppose you want to create a series of dates in cells A1 through A16 in a worksheet. The series is to begin with March 1, 1988, and the dates in the series must be exactly one month apart. First, enter the formula

    =DATE(88,3,1)

in cell A1. Next, select the range A1:A16 and choose Series from the Data menu. Figure 7-1 shows the Series dialog box. From this box, choose Columns to create a columnar series and then choose Date to create a date series. Finally, choose Month to specify the interval, be sure Step Value is 1, and then choose OK.

Series in
Rows
Columns
Type
Linear
Growth
Date
Date Unit
Day
Weekday
Month
Year
OK
Cancel
Step Value: 1
Stop Value:

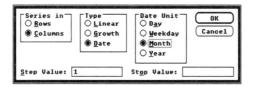

FIGURE 7-1. *You can use the Series dialog box to create date series.*

Figure 7-2 shows the result of this command. Each of the cells in the range A1:A16 contains a serial date value. If you now select this range, choose the Number command from the Format menu, and apply the m/d/yy format, you'll see that these date values are exactly one month apart. Figure 7-3 shows the worksheet after these cells have been formatted.

EXCEL *tip*

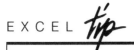

Creating an end-of-month series

To create a series using the last day of each month, begin with a month that has 31 days. For example, suppose you begin with March 31, 1988. Here are the results of entering this date in cell A1 and then creating the series.

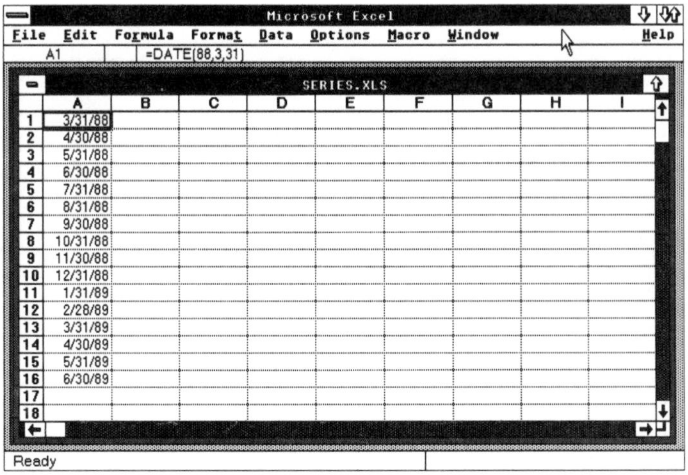

Microsoft Excel
File Edit Formula Format Data Options Macro Window Help
A1 =DATE(88,3,31)
SERIES.XLS
A B C D E F G H I
1 3/31/88
2 4/30/88
3 5/31/88
4 6/30/88
5 7/31/88
6 8/31/88
7 9/30/88
8 10/31/88
9 11/30/88
10 12/31/88
11 1/31/89
12 2/28/89
13 3/31/89
14 4/30/89
15 5/31/89
16 6/30/89
17
18
Ready

The dates no longer have the same day; instead, they all fall on the last day of the month.

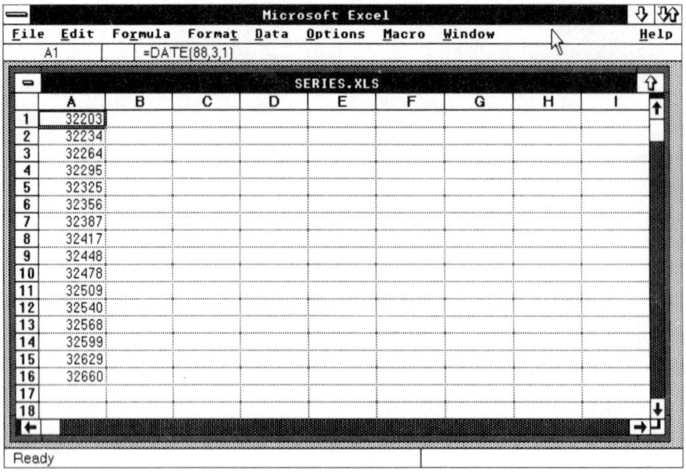

FIGURE 7-2. *We used the DATE function and the Series command to create a series of dates one month apart.*

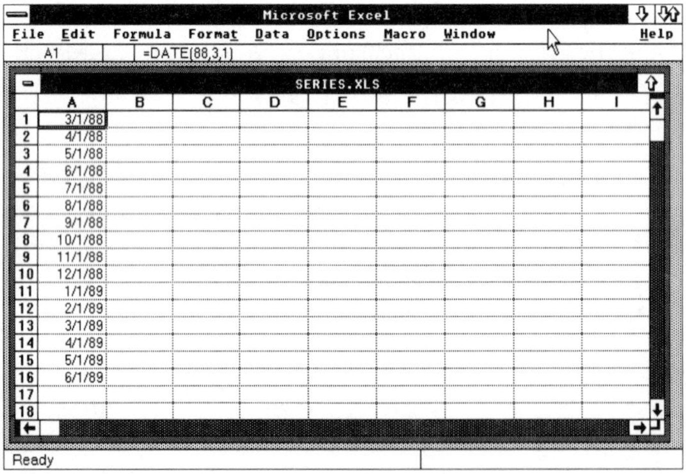

FIGURE 7-3. *We used the Number command to format the date series in an understandable form.*

The other choices in the Date Unit box of the Series dialog box allow you to specify different intervals for your date series. The Day option builds a series of dates one or more days apart (depending on the step value); the Weekday option creates a series of dates using only the five working days of the week. (The ability to specify weekdays in your date series and functions is a unique luxury. If you've used other spreadsheet programs, you know that most programs have to perform a tedious series of calculations to distinguish between weekday and weekend dates.) The Year option builds an annual date series.

Microsoft Excel provides further flexibility with the Step Value and Stop Value options. The Step Value option allows you to specify the amount by which each successive cell in the series increases. For example, by typing 2 in the Step Value edit bar and selecting Date in the Type bar and Month in the Date Unit bar, you can create a series of dates for every other month. By typing a negative number in the Step Value box, you can create a descending (decreasing) series.

You can even enter a formatted date value in the Stop Value edit bar. For example, suppose you want to enter a series of dates extending from 1/1/86 through 12/31/90 in your worksheet. Chances are you don't know the serial date value for December 31, 1990. Fortunately, you can simply type the formatted date value 12/31/90 in the Stop Value edit bar; the program will interpret the entry as 33238.

The TIME function

Making time entries is similar to making date entries: First you use a function to enter the appropriate time into a cell and then you use one of Microsoft Excel's four time formats to make the result understandable.

The primary time function is TIME. The form of this function is

=TIME(*hh,mm,ss*)

where *hh* is the hours, *mm* is the minutes, and *ss* is the seconds. The *ss* argument is optional. If you do omit it, however, you still must include a comma after the *mm* argument:

=TIME(*hh,mm,*)

As with the DATE function, the easiest way to remember the arguments for this function is to keep in mind that the terms occur in descending order of magnitude—first hours, then minutes, then seconds.

The result of the TIME function is a decimal value that represents how much of the day has elapsed between midnight and the specified time.

The TIME function uses the 24-hour, or military, time convention. On the 24-hour clock, 3:00 AM is 3 o'clock, 2:00 PM is 14 o'clock, and 11:00 PM is 23 o'clock. Thus, 2:15 PM is represented by the formula

=TIME(14,15,)

which returns the decimal value 0.59375. For times between 12:00 midnight and 1:00 AM, the *hh* argument is always 0.

As with the DATE function, Microsoft Excel lets you use large numbers and negative numbers as arguments in TIME. For example, if you want to know the time 35 seconds before 5:00:14, you can use the formula

=TIME(5,0,14-35)

Microsoft Excel returns 0.2080902777778, or 4:59.39 AM. Similarly, the formula

=TIME(12,60,)

refers to the time 1:00 PM. Normally, the maximum value for the *mm* argument is 59, so when Microsoft Excel encounters the minute value 60, it simply carries the extra minute over into the next hour.

Formatting times

Microsoft Excel offers four built-in time formats: h:mm AM/PM, h:mm:ss AM/PM, h:mm, and h:mm:ss. Here is the result of the function *TIME(13,52,32)*—serial value 0.578148—under each of these formats:

Format	Display
h:mm AM/PM	1:52 PM
h:mm:ss AM/PM	1:52:32 PM
h:mm	13:52
h:mm:ss	13:52:32

Notice that the first two formats display the time in traditional 12-hour clock form and the last two formats use the 24-hour convention.

To assign a time format to a cell, simply choose that cell, choose Number from the Format menu, select the time format you want to use, and choose OK.

You may run into trouble when you enter a time into a previously formatted cell. Microsoft Excel interprets the time as a decimal value but displays it in the format that already applies to the cell. For example, if you assign the 0.00% format to a cell and then enter

=TIME(15,16,)

in that cell, Microsoft Excel stores the decimal value for the time, 0.636111, and displays it as 63.61%. If you want to see the number as a time, you must select the Number command from the Format menu and select a time format.

An easier way

You can bypass the standard two-step method of entering times by entering the time "in format." Simply choose the cell in which you want to make the entry and type the time in one of the following forms:

hh:mm:ss
hh:mm
hh:mm:ss AM/PM
hh:mm AM/PM

The parts of time entries must be separated by colons.

To enter the time 2:15 PM in a cell, choose the cell and type *2:15 PM* or *14:15*. Either way, Microsoft Excel will enter the serial time value 0.59375 in the cell and assign a time format to that value. (Remember, if you don't include the AM/PM or am/pm notation in the time, Microsoft Excel interprets the time using the 24-hour clock convention.)

Using time arithmetic

Like date values, time values can be used in formulas and functions. However, the results of time arithmetic are not as easy to understand as the results of date arithmetic.

For example, suppose you want to know how much time elapsed between 2:45 PM and 10:22 AM. You could determine this with the formula

=TIME(14,45,)−TIME(10,22,)

Unfortunately, the result of the formula, 0.18263888, is not at all easy to interpret. If you want to get a more meaningful answer, you can change the formula to

=(TIME(14,45,)−TIME(10,22,))*24

The result of this formula, 4.38333, is the number of hours that have elapsed between the two times. Although this number is still not in the form you're used to using, it is at least understandable.

Now suppose you want to determine the time that is 2 hours, 23 minutes, and 17 seconds after 12:35:23 PM. The formula

=TIME(12,35,23)+TIME(2,23,17)

returns the correct answer: 0.624074074. In this formula, the arguments 2, 23, and 17 represent not an absolute time (2:23:17 AM) but an interval of time (2 hours, 23 minutes, 17 seconds). This is perfectly acceptable to Microsoft Excel.

Combining date and time formats

In addition to the built-in formats that let you display dates and times, Microsoft Excel offers a combined format—m/d/yy h:mm—that lets you display the date and time in one cell. For example, if a cell in your worksheet contains the serial value 32261.125 and you apply the m/d/yy h:mm format to that entry, you'll see the date and time displayed as 4/28/88 3:00. When you're entering both date and time "in format," you can type either *6/21/87 16:30* or *4:30 PM 6-21-87*.

The NOW function

The NOW function can be used to enter the current date and time in a cell. The form of this function is simply

=NOW()

NOW does not take an argument. The result of the function is a date/time value that includes both an integer (the date) and a decimal value (the time). For example, if today is July 21, 1988, and the time is 11:45 AM, the NOW function returns the value 32345.49.

Microsoft Excel doesn't update the value of NOW continuously. Instead, the function is updated each time you calculate the spreadsheet (by making an entry, by choosing Calculate Now from the Options menu, or by pressing Ctrl-=). If you should notice that the value of a cell that contains the NOW function is not up to date, you can correct the problem by recalculating the worksheet.

Creating your own date and time formats

To supplement the four standard date and time formats, Microsoft Excel lets you create your own custom formats. The general technique is the same as the technique for creating custom numeric formats.

Table 7-1 shows the formatting symbols you can use to create special date and time formats. There are a couple of things to keep in mind about these symbols. First, when you use the symbol *m* immediately after an *h* or the symbol *mm* immediately after an *hh*, Microsoft Excel displays minutes instead of months; otherwise, the program assumes that *m* means months. Second, if you include one of the symbols AM/PM, am/pm, A/P, or a/p in a time format, Microsoft Excel displays the time in conventional 12-hour clock form; if you omit these symbols, the time appears in 24-hour form.

TABLE 7-1. Formatting symbols for custom date and time formats.

Symbol	Display
General	Number in General format
d	Day number without leading 0 (1–31)
dd	Day number with leading 0 (01–31)
ddd	Day-of-week abbreviation (Sun–Sat)
dddd	Day-of-week name (Sunday–Saturday)
m	Month number without leading 0 (1–12)
mm	Month number with leading 0 (01–12)
mmm	Month name abbreviation (Jan–Dec)
mmmm	Complete month name (January–December)
yy	Last two digits of year number (00–99)
yyyy	Entire year number (1900–2078)
h	Hour without leading 0 (0–23)
hh	Hour with leading 0 (00–23)
m	Minute without leading 0 (0–59)
mm	Minute with leading 0 (00–59)
s	Second without leading 0 (0–59)
ss	Second with leading 0 (00–59)
AM/PM	Time in AM/PM notation
am/pm	Time in am/pm notation
A/P	Time in A/P notation
a/p	Time in a/p notation

Suppose you want to create a format that displays a date in the fullest possible form—that is, the date entry 12/25/88 would be displayed as December 25, 1988. Simply choose the cell containing the entry you want to format, choose Number from the Format menu, and type

mmmm d, yyyy

in the Format edit bar. When you choose OK, the new format will be stored in the list of formats and the date in the selected cell will be displayed in full.

Similarly, to create a format that displays the day of the week for a date in addition to the date itself, use the format

dddd, mmmm d, yyyy

This format causes the result of the formula

=DATE(88,12,25)

to be displayed as Friday, December 25, 1988.

These techniques can also be used to display only a portion of a date or time. For example, the format mmmm displays the date December 25, 1986, as the word *December.*

After a custom format has been added to the Number dialog box, all you have to do to use it is select the cells you want to format, choose the Number command from the Format menu, select the custom format from the dialog box, and choose OK or press Enter.

Secondary date and time functions

In addition to the primary date and time functions, DATE, TIME, and NOW, Microsoft Excel offers a convenient set of secondary functions—WEEKDAY, YEAR, MONTH, DAY, HOUR, MINUTE, and SECOND—that let you extract information about the date and time values in your worksheet. Two other secondary functions—DATEVALUE and TIMEVALUE—are helpful when you need to perform date and time calculations.

The WEEKDAY function

The WEEKDAY function returns the day of the week that a date falls on. The form of this function is

=WEEKDAY(*date*)

The *date* argument can be a serial value, a reference to a cell that contains either a date function or a serial date value, or text, such as 1/27/87 or January 27, 1987. If you use text, be sure to enclose it in quotation marks.

The result of the WEEKDAY function is a number from 1 through 7 that matches the day of the week that the date falls on. For example, if the date falls on a Sunday, the function returns the number 1.

The YEAR, MONTH, and DAY functions

The YEAR, MONTH, and DAY functions return the value of the year, month, and day terms of a serial date/time number. The forms of these functions are nearly identical:

=YEAR(*date*)

and

=MONTH(*date*)

and

=DAY(*date*)

The *date* argument can be a serial date value, a reference to a cell that contains either a date function or a serial date value, or a text date enclosed in quotes.

The result of these functions is the value of the specified term of the *date* argument. For example, if cell A1 contains the formula

=DATE(88,12,25)

the formula

=YEAR(A1)

returns the value 1988, the formula

=MONTH(A1)

returns the value 12, and the formula

=DAY(A1)

returns the value 25.

The HOUR, MINUTE, and SECOND functions

Just as the YEAR, MONTH, and DAY functions let you extract the year, month, and day terms of a serial date/time number, the HOUR, MINUTE, and SECOND functions extract the hour, minute, and second portions of a serial date/time number. The forms of these functions are similar:

=HOUR(*time*)

and

=MINUTE(*time*)

and

=SECOND(*time*)

The result of these functions is the value of the specified term of the *time* argument. For example, if cell B1 contains the formula

=TIME(12,15,35)

then the formula

=HOUR(B1)

returns the value 12, the formula

=MINUTE(B1)

returns the value 15, and the formula

=SECOND(B1)

returns the value 35.

The DATEVALUE and TIMEVALUE functions

DATEVALUE translates a date into a serial number. It is similar to the DATE function, except that you must enter a text argument. The form of this function is

=DATEVALUE("*date text*")

where *date text* represents any date between January 1, 1900, and December 31, 2078, in any of Microsoft Excel's built-in date formats. (Remember to enclose the text in quotation marks.) For example, the formula

=DATEVALUE("1/1/88")

returns the serial number 32143. If you enter *date text* without a year, Microsoft Excel uses the current year from your computer's internal clock.

Similarly, TIMEVALUE translates a time into a decimal value. It is similar to the TIME function, except that you must enter a text argument. The form of this function is

=TIMEVALUE("*time text*")

where *time text* represents a time in any of Microsoft Excel's built-in time formats. (Remember to enclose the text in quotation marks.) For example, if you enter

=TIMEVALUE("3:32 PM")

the function returns the decimal value 0.6472.

8

Other Worksheet Topics

*I*n earlier chapters, we covered many of Microsoft Excel's major features and capabilities. A few advanced topics remain, however, such as arrays, data tables, linking worksheets, finding and replacing cell entries, auditing and documenting worksheets, and worksheet security. We'll cover those topics in this chapter.

Arrays

Arrays are special calculating tools you can use to build formulas that produce multiple results or to operate on groups of values rather than on single arguments. If that definition doesn't offer much help, bear with us for a moment. When you see arrays in action, their function will become clearer.

Before we proceed, we need to briefly define a few terms. An *array formula* takes much the same form as a standard worksheet formula, except that it acts on two or more sets of values, called *array arguments*, to return either a single result or multiple results. An *array range* is a block of cells that share a common array formula. An *array constant* is a specially organized list of constant values that you can use as arguments in your array formulas.

Using arrays

Perhaps the easiest way to learn about arrays is to look at a few examples. Typically, the formulas you enter in your worksheet produce a single result. For example, suppose cells A1 and A2 of your worksheet contain the values 10 and 15. To determine the sum of these two values, you could enter the simple formula

=A1+A2

which results in a single value, 25, that occupies a single cell in the worksheet.

Now suppose you've entered several groups of values in rows 1 and 2 of your worksheet, as shown in Figure 8-1. Typically, to total the values in each of these columns, you would create five separate formulas, as we've done in cells A3:E3. The formula in cell A3 calculates the total of the values in cells A1 and A2, the formula in cell B3 calculates the total of the values in cells B1 and B2, and so forth.

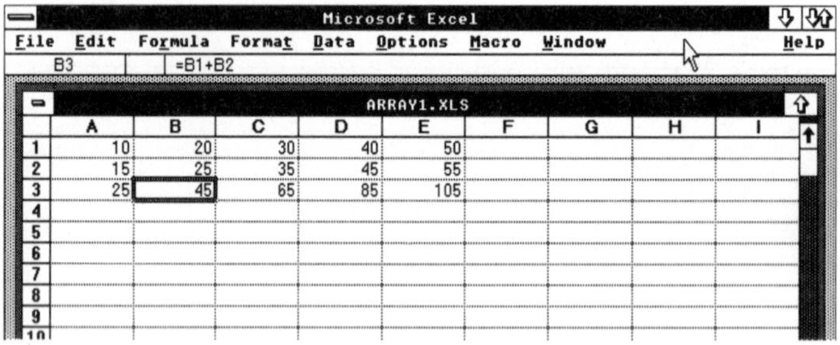

FIGURE 8-1. *We used five formulas to calculate the totals of the values in columns A through E.*

But here's an alternative. Using arrays, you could calculate the sum of each column of values in Figure 8-1 with a single formula. Begin by selecting cells A3:E3 and typing

=A1:E1+A2:E2

To lock in this formula, press Shift-Ctrl-Enter. Figure 8-2 shows the results.

As you can see, a single array formula computes the sum of each group of values: A1:A2, B1:B2, C1:C2, D1:D2, and E1:E2. Cells A3:E3 serve as our array range in this simple example, and the array formula

{=A1:E1+A2:E2}

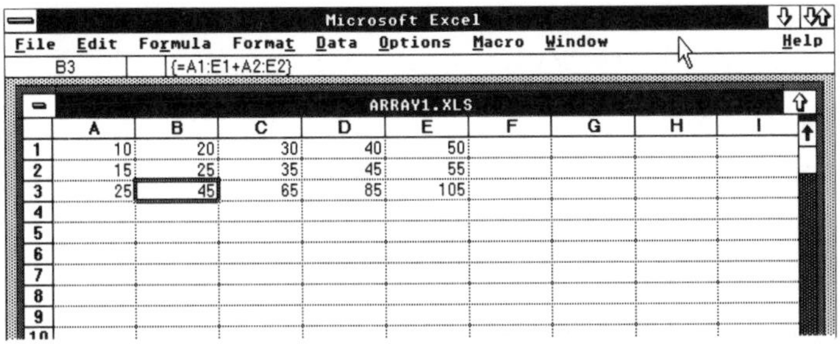

FIGURE 8-2. *We used a single array formula to total the values in each column.*

is stored in each cell of the array range. (Microsoft Excel adds the braces automatically as it distributes the array formula throughout the cells of the array range.) In this example, our array arguments are the range references A1:E1 and A2:E2.

The array formula in Figure 8-2 occupies a horizontal array range. Let's look at a similar example that uses a vertical array range. Suppose you want to calculate the product of each pair of values in columns A and B of Figure 8-3. Simply select the range C1:C7 and type

=A1:A7*B1:B7

Figure 8-3 shows what happens when you press Shift-Ctrl-Enter to lock in this formula as an array.

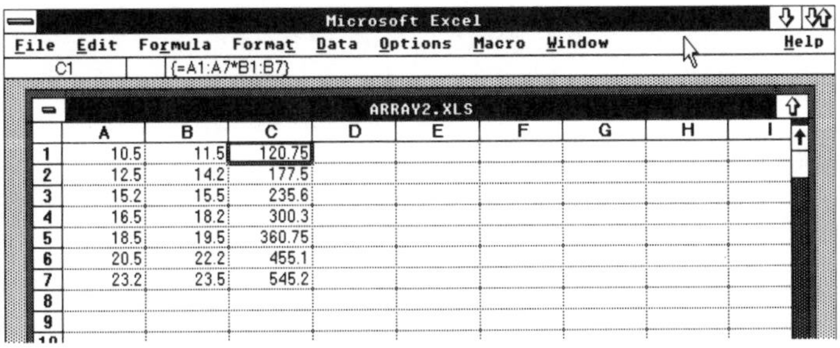

FIGURE 8-3. *In this worksheet, a vertical array formula calculates the products of the values in each row.*

Now suppose you want to compute the sum of the products of each pair of values in this worksheet—that is, the sum of A1*B1 plus A2*B2 plus A3*B3, and so on. With an array formula, you can reduce this calculation to one step. All you need do is select cell D1 (or any blank cell), type

=SUM(A1:A7*B1:B7)

and press Shift-Ctrl-Enter. Figure 8-4 shows the result. Notice that, instead of producing multiple results, this array formula operates on multiple arguments to produce a single result.

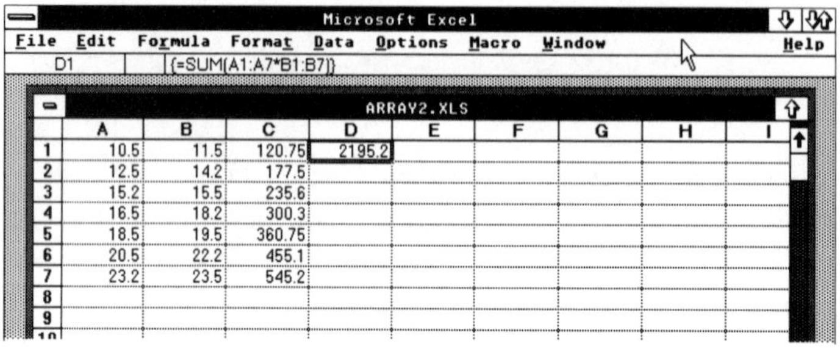

FIGURE 8-4. *We used an array formula in cell D1 to compute the sum of the products of the pairs of values in columns A and B.*

Two-dimensional arrays

In the examples above, we saw array formulas that resulted in a vertical, a horizontal, and a single-cell array range. You can also create two-dimensional array ranges.

For example, suppose you want to calculate the integer values of each of the entries in cells A1:C7 of Figure 8-4. First, select a range the same size and shape as the range you want to work with. In this case, you would select a seven-row-by-three-column range, such as E1:G7. Next, enter the formula

=INT(A1:C7)

and press Shift-Ctrl-Enter. As you can see in Figure 8-5, each cell in the range E1:G7 displays the integer value of the corresponding cell in the range A1:C7. In fact, Microsoft Excel has entered the array formula

{=INT(A1:C7)}

in each cell in the range E1:G7.

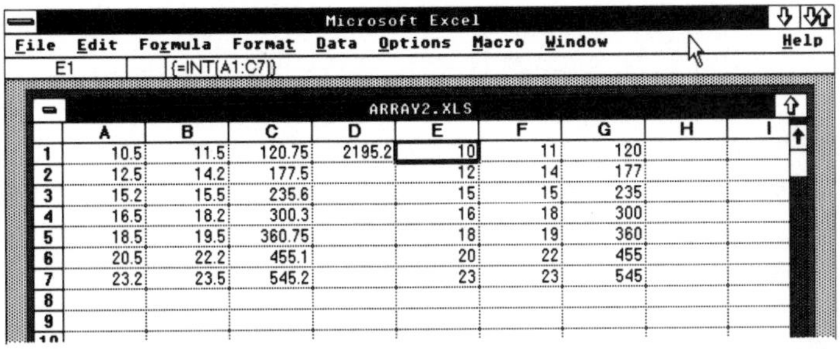

FIGURE 8-5. *We used an array formula to compute the integer value of each of the entries in cells A1:C7.*

Array formula rules

As you saw in the examples above, array formulas can return either single or multiple values. Either way, you enter array formulas by first selecting the cell or range that will contain your result(s). If the formula will produce multiple results, you would typically select a range the same size and shape as the range(s) on which you're performing your calculations. In the preceding example, we selected a seven-row-by-three-column array range to hold our array-formula results.

You must press Shift-Ctrl-Enter to lock in an array formula. When you do this, Microsoft Excel places a set of braces around the formula to indicate that it is an array formula. Don't try to type the braces yourself. If you do, Microsoft Excel will interpret your entry as a label.

Because array formulas are specially structured, the rules for editing array ranges differ slightly from the rules you learned in Chapters 2 and 4. You cannot edit, clear, or move individual cells in an array range, nor can you insert or delete cells. You must treat the cells in the array range as a single unit and edit them all at once. For example, if you try to clear cell E1 in Figure 8-5, Microsoft Excel will display the message *Can't change part of array* and prevent you from clearing the cell.

To edit either a single-cell or multiple-cell array formula, first select any cell in the array and then activate the formula bar. When the formula bar is active, the braces around the formula will disappear. Now edit the formula as needed and press Shift-Ctrl-Enter to lock in your changes. Microsoft Excel will reinsert the braces and distribute your change to all the cells in the array range.

To move or clear the contents of an array range, you must first select all the cells in the range. If the array range is large or if you're not sure of the dimensions of the range, you can select any cell in the range and then press the Ctrl and slash (/) keys to select the entire array. (Or you can use the Select Special command to select the entire array range. We'll talk more about Select Special in a few pages.) Then you can use the Cut or Clear command to move or clear the selection.

Although you can't cut, clear, or edit part of an array, you can assign different formats to individual cells. You can also copy a single cell from an array range and paste it in another area of your worksheet; Microsoft Excel adjusts any relative references in the pasted array formula just as it does when you copy and paste any standard worksheet formula.

As with any other formula, you can convert the results of an array formula into a series of constant values by selecting the array range, issuing the Copy command, and, without changing your selection, issuing the Paste Special command. When you use the Values option in the Paste Special dialog box, Microsoft Excel overwrites the array formulas with constant values. Because the range now contains constant values rather than a formula, Microsoft Excel will no longer treat the selection as an array.

Using array constants

Array constants are to arrays what literal values are to cell references. Array constants can be made up of numbers, text, or logical values. You must enclose an array constant in braces ({ }) and separate its elements with commas and semicolons.

As with array formulas, the best way to understand array constants is to look at an example. Suppose you want to compute the integer values of the three numbers 123.456, 1.234, and 12345.678. You can perform these three computations with a single array formula by selecting any horizontal three-cell range, typing the formula

    =INT({123.456,1.234,12345.678})

and pressing Shift-Ctrl-Enter. Notice that the argument of the INT function is made up of the three numbers enclosed in braces. The braces indicate that the enclosed values make up an array constant.

Figure 8-6 shows the results of this formula. Each cell in the range B2:D2 contains the array formula

    {=INT({123.456,1.234,12345.678})}

However, the value displayed in each cell is the result of the INT function for the element of the array constant that corresponds to the position of that cell in the range. For example, cell C2, the second cell in the range, displays the result of INT for the value 1.234, the second element in the array constant.

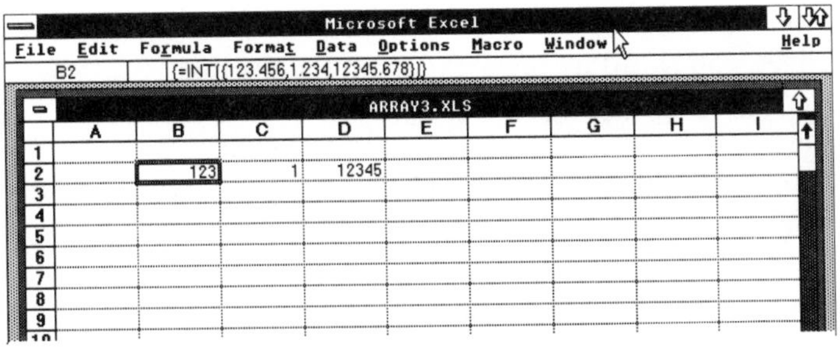

FIGURE 8-6. *We used an array constant as the argument for this array formula.*

Microsoft Excel also allows you to create vertical array constants. In a vertical array constant, the elements in the array are separated by semicolons instead of commas. For example, the array constant

{123.456;1.234;12345.678}

is a three-row vertical array. As you might expect, you must enter formulas that refer to vertical array constants in vertical ranges. For example, if you want to compute the integer values of the three numbers in this vertical array constant, you can select the range A1:A3, type the formula

=INT({123.456;1.234;12345.678})

and press Shift-Ctrl-Enter. Figure 8-7 shows the result.

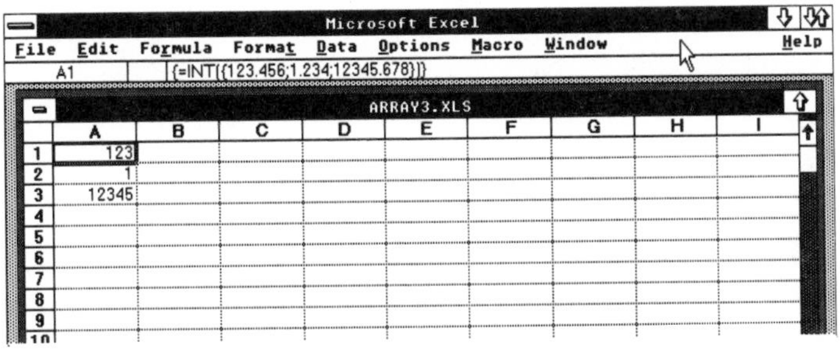

FIGURE 8-7. *In a vertical array constant, the elements in the array are separated by semicolons.*

Just as you can create two-dimensional variable arrays, you can also create two-dimensional array constants. In a two-dimensional array constant, commas are used to separate the elements in each row of the constant, and semicolons are used to separate the rows that make up the constant. For example, suppose you want to calculate the square roots of a series of 12 values and display them as a block rather than as a list. Instead of entering each of the values in individual cells of the worksheet, you could use an array formula like this:

=SQRT({4,9,16,25;36,49,64,81;100,121,144,169})

To enter this formula into your worksheet, you must first select a four-column-by-three-row range of cells—we used A1:D3—and type the formula with the array constant in braces. When you press Shift-Ctrl-Enter to lock in the formula, Microsoft Excel will supply the outer set of braces for you. Figure 8-8 shows the resulting array of square-root calculations.

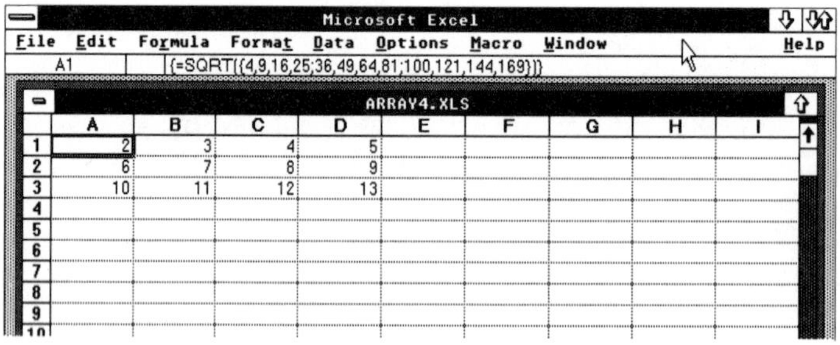

FIGURE 8-8. *This array formula uses a four-column-by-three-row array constant.*

Notice that the commas and semicolons in our array argument correspond to the row and column positions of the resulting square-root calculations. That is, the argument {4,9,16,25;36,49,64,81;100,121,144,169} represents an array constant shaped like this:

4	9	16	25
36	49	64	81
100	121	144	169

You can also mix array-constant arguments with cell references, much as you mix constant values and references in a standard worksheet formula. But before we show you this technique, we need to introduce one more topic: array expansion.

Array expansion

When you use arrays as arguments in a formula, all your arrays should be the same dimension. If the dimensions of your array arguments or array ranges don't match, Microsoft Excel often expands the arguments as required to complete its calculations. For example, suppose you want to multiply all the values in cells A1:B5 of your worksheet by 10. You could accomplish this with a simple array formula like

   =A1:B5*10

or, if you're using array constants, you could use a formula like

   ={1,2;3,4;5,6;7,8;9,10}*10

Notice that these two formulas are not balanced—we have 10 values on the left side of the multiplication operator and only one value on the right. Fortunately, Microsoft Excel can expand the second argument to match the size and shape of the first. In the preceding examples, the first formula is equivalent to

   =A1:B5*{10,10;10,10;10,10;10,10;10,10}

and the second is equivalent to

   ={1,2;3,4;5,6;7,8;9,10}*{10,10;10,10;10,10;10,10;10,10}

When you're working with two or more sets of multivalue arrays, each set of arguments must have the same number of rows as the argument with the greatest number of rows and the same number of columns as the argument with the greatest number of columns. As you've already seen, single-value arguments are repeated as needed to match the dimensions of the other arguments in your array formula. If you use a one-row or one-column array argument, Microsoft Excel repeats that row or column of values as needed to match the dimensions of the other arguments. For example, the formula

   ={1,2,3;4,5,6}*{7,8,9}

is equivalent to

   ={1,2,3;4,5,6}*{7,8,9;7,8,9}

and results in an array range like this:

   7   16   27
   28   40   54

Microsoft Excel doesn't expand an array when you use cell references as your array arguments. For example, in the formula

{=A1:A6*B1:B3}

you might expect Microsoft Excel to repeat the argument B1:B3 to match the size and shape of the argument A1:A6, like this:

={A1;A2;A3;A4;A5;A6}*{B1;B2;B3;B1;B2;B3}

Instead, the formula above results in an array like this:

={A1;A2;A3;A4;A5;A6}*{B1;B2;B3;#N/A;#N/A;#N/A}

However, whether you're using array constants or cell references, if you select a result range that is larger than the array argument, Microsoft Excel will attempt to expand the array formula to fill the selection. For example, in the worksheet shown in Figure 8-2, we used two one-row-by-five-column array arguments and a corresponding one-row-by-five-column result range. If we had selected cells A3:E7 rather than A3:E3 when we entered our array formula, our worksheet would look like the one in Figure 8-9. In effect, the formula in the range A3:E7 produces a five-by-five array by repeating the one row, A3:E3, five times.

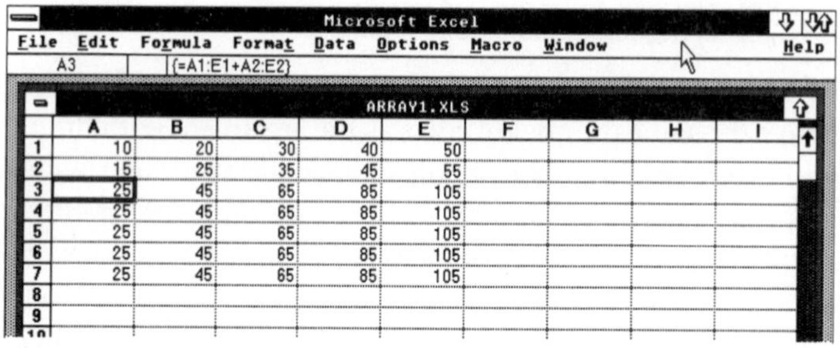

FIGURE 8-9. *When you select a result range larger than the array arguments, Microsoft Excel repeats the array formula to fill the selection.*

If the array range is not a multiple of the same dimensions as the array arguments, however, Microsoft Excel returns #N/A error values. For example, in the worksheet shown in Figure 8-5, if we had selected the range E1:H8 rather than E1:G7 to enter our INT function, our worksheet would look like the one in Figure 8-10. Notice that #N/A error values appear in row 8 and column H because the array argument, A1:C7, is only three columns wide and seven rows deep.

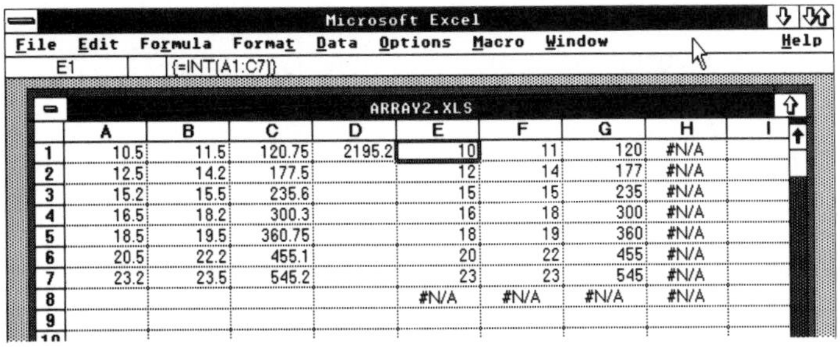

FIGURE 8-10. *If the array range is not a multiple of the same dimension as the array arguments, Microsoft Excel returns #N/A error values.*

Finally, when you select a result range smaller than the argument range, Microsoft Excel simply fills the available rows and columns, beginning with the upper left corner of the result range. For example, continuing with the sample worksheet in Figure 8-5, if we had selected the range E1:F3 rather than E1:G7 to enter our INT function, our worksheet would look like the one in Figure 8-11.

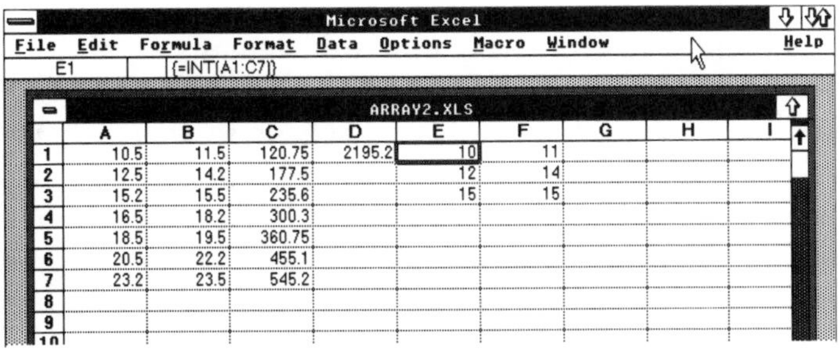

FIGURE 8-11. *If you select a result range smaller than the argument range, Microsoft Excel fills only the available rows and columns.*

Array functions

As you've already seen, you can use arrays as arguments in almost any type of formula. Although most Microsoft Excel functions can accept array arguments, a few, such as ROWS, COLUMNS, TRANSPOSE, and INDEX (form two), *require* arrays as arguments. Microsoft Excel also offers four advanced statistical functions—LINEST, TREND, LOGEST, and GROWTH—that require arrays as arguments. We'll cover these eight functions in the following pages.

The ROWS and COLUMNS functions

The ROWS function returns the number of rows in an array. The form of the ROWS function is

=ROWS(*array*)

The *array* argument can be an array constant, a range reference, or a range name. The result of the function is the number of rows in the array. For example, the result of the formula

=ROWS({100,200,300;1000,2000,3000})

is 2, because the array-constant argument contains two "rows." Similarly, the formula

=ROWS(A1:A10)

returns 10, because the range A1:A10 contains 10 rows.

The COLUMNS function is identical to the ROWS function, except that it returns the number of columns in the *array* argument. For example, the formula

=COLUMNS(A1:C10)

return 3, because the range A1:C10 contains three columns.

The ROWS and COLUMNS functions are analogous to the COUNT and COUNTA functions. However, unlike these functions, which return the number of cells in a range that contain numbers (or the number of cells that contain any type of entry, in the case of COUNTA), ROWS and COLUMNS return the absolute number of rows or columns in the range. Because of this difference, these functions can be used in combination with COUNT or COUNTA to determine the ratio between the cells in a range that contain values and the total number of cells in the range.

For example, in Chapter 6 we used the COUNT function to determine the number of employees who had contributed to the United Charities Fund. We could combine the COUNT and ROWS functions to determine the percentage of employees who made a contribution, using a formula in the form

=COUNT(##:##)/ROWS(##:##)

where ##:## is the range of cells containing the donations.

The TRANSPOSE function

The TRANSPOSE function can be used to exchange the rows and columns of a range or an array. The form of this function is

=TRANSPOSE(*array*)

If the array is vertical, the resulting array will be horizontal. If the array is horizontal, the resulting array will be vertical. For example, the result of the formula

=TRANSPOSE({5,4,3,2,1})

is the array {5;4;3;2;1}, and the result of the formula

=TRANSPOSE({1;2;3;4;5})

is the array {1,2,3,4,5}.

Suppose you want to transpose the entries in cells A1:C7 in the worksheet shown in Figure 8-5 so that they fill cells A9:G11. Simply select the range A9:G11, type the function

=TRANSPOSE(A1:C7)

and press Shift-Ctrl-Enter. The result is shown in Figure 8-12. Each cell in this range contains the array formula

{=TRANSPOSE(A1:C7)}

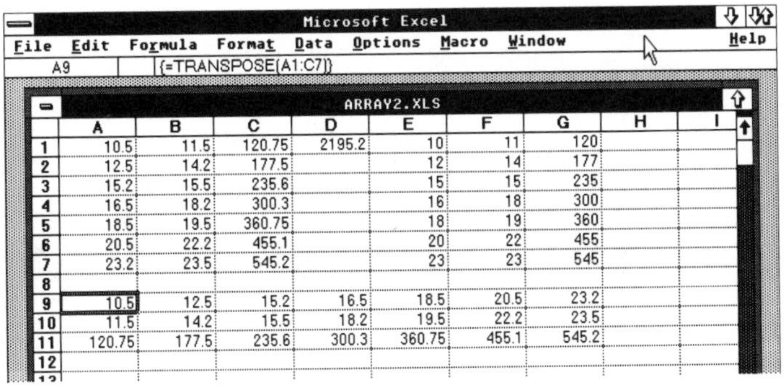

FIGURE 8-12. *We used the TRANSPOSE function to transpose the entries from cells A1:C7 into cells A9:G11.*

The INDEX function (form two)

We introduced form one of the INDEX function in Chapter 6. Form two is used only with arrays. It has the general form

=INDEX(*array,row,column*)

The result is the value at the position in the *array* argument indicated by the *row* and *column* arguments.

For example, the formula

=INDEX({10,20,30;40,50,60},1,2)

returns the value 20, because 20 is the item in the second column of the first row of the array.

As with the first form of INDEX, you need supply only the *column* argument if the array is only one row deep or only the *row* argument if the array is only one column wide. Also like form one, the *row* and *column* arguments must be positive integers. In addition, if the *row* or *column* argument exceeds the number of rows or columns in the array, the function will return the error message #REF!.

The LINEST function

The LINEST function computes the slope and y-axis intercept of the regression line that describes a set of numbers. The form of this function is

=LINEST(*Y-array*,*X-array*)

The easiest way to understand LINEST is to consider an example. Look at the worksheet shown in Figure 8-13. The entries in column B of this worksheet represent a year's monthly sales figures for a small business. The numbers in column A represent the months of the year. Suppose you want to compute the slope and y-axis intercept of the regression line that best describes the relationship between the sales figures and the months of the year. In other words, you want to describe the trend of the data. To do this, select the range F5:G5, type the formula

=LINEST(B3:B14,A3:A14)

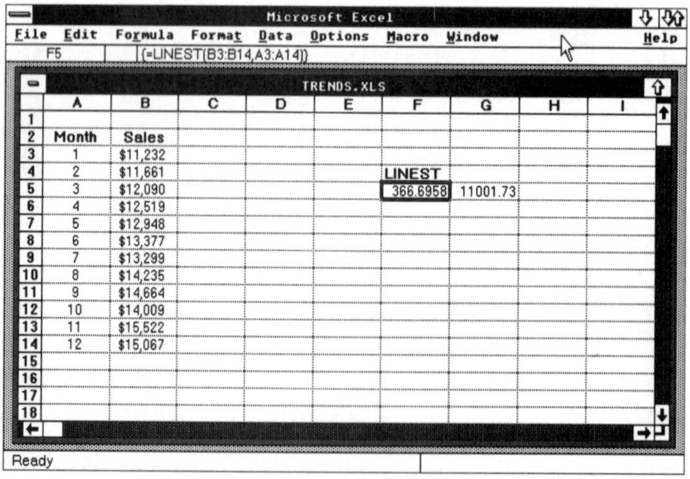

FIGURE 8-13. *We used the LINEST function to compute the slope and y-axis intercept of a regression line.*

and press Shift-Ctrl-Enter. The resulting number in cell F5, 366.6958, is the slope of the regression line; the number in cell G5, 11001.73, is the y-axis intercept of the line.

If you omit the *X-array* argument from the LINEST function, Microsoft Excel assumes that the *X-array* values are 1, 2, 3, 4, and so on. If, as in the example, the values in this array are in fact 1, 2, 3, 4, and so on, you can omit this argument without affecting the result of the function. In other words, you could reduce the function in cell F5 to

=LINEST(B3:B14)

Let's look at a practical example for this function. Suppose the sales figures in Figure 8-13 are for 1988 and you now want to know the sales you can expect for March 1989, which would be the fifteenth month in the series. Because the position of any point on a line is determined by the equation

$y = mx + b$

where m is the slope of the line and b is the y-axis intercept, you can use the formula

=(F5*15)+G5

to compute the predicted sales for March: 16502.16. This same result could be computed using the complex array formula

=SUM(LINEST(B3:B14)*{15,1})

The TREND function

The TREND function is closely related to the LINEST function. The difference is that LINEST computes the value of the y-axis intercept and the slope of the regression line, whereas TREND returns the actual predicted values for the points on the line. TREND can therefore be used to create a data series that can be plotted as a line on a graph. The form of the TREND function is

=TREND(*Y-array*,*X-array*,*x-array*)

where *Y-array* and *X-array* are the y and x values of the items in the data set. The *x-array* argument is optional; we'll discuss it in a moment.

Let's look at an example of the TREND function at work. Suppose you want to know the value of each point on the regression line that describes the data set from the previous example. To create these values, select the range C3:C14, type the formula

=TREND(B3:B14,A3:A14)

and press Shift-Ctrl-Enter. The result is shown in Figure 8-14. The numbers in the range C3:C14 are the y values for the points on the regression line.

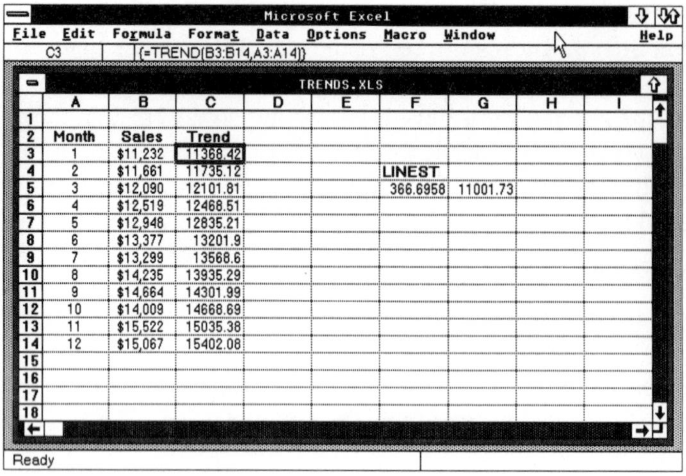

	A	B	C	D	E	F	G
1							
2	Month	Sales	Trend				
3	1	$11,232	11368.42				
4	2	$11,661	11735.12			LINEST	
5	3	$12,090	12101.81			366.6958	11001.73
6	4	$12,519	12468.51				
7	5	$12,948	12835.21				
8	6	$13,377	13201.9				
9	7	$13,299	13568.6				
10	8	$14,235	13935.29				
11	9	$14,664	14301.99				
12	10	$14,009	14668.69				
13	11	$15,522	15035.38				
14	12	$15,067	15402.08				

FIGURE 8-14. *We used the TREND function to create a data series that can be plotted as a line on a chart.*

As with LINEST, if you omit the *X-array* argument from the TREND function, Microsoft Excel assumes the *X-array* values are 1, 2, 3, 4, and so on.

Like LINEST, TREND can be used to predict the future. In this example, we could use the TREND function to predict the sales figures for months 13, 14, and 15. To do this, enter the values 13, 14, and 15 in cells A16:A18. Then select the range C16:C18. Next, enter the formula

=TREND(B3:B14,A3:A14,A16:A18)

and press Shift-Ctrl-Enter. The result is shown in Figure 8-15. The numbers in cells C16, C17, and C18 are the predicted sales values for the thirteenth, fourteenth, and fifteenth months in the series.

Notice that this last example included an *x-array* argument. If you include this argument in the function, the result of the function is an array the same size and shape as *x-array*. Because *x-array* in our example was a vertical array with three elements, the result of the function was a vertical array with three elements (in cells C16, C17, and C18). If it helps, you can think of *x-array* as being a "prediction array." If you include this argument in the function, Microsoft Excel returns the predicted y value for each of the values in *x-array*. If you don't include this argument, Microsoft Excel doesn't make any predictions; instead, it returns the y values of the points in the "known" portion of the regression line. (This is what occurred in the first example.)

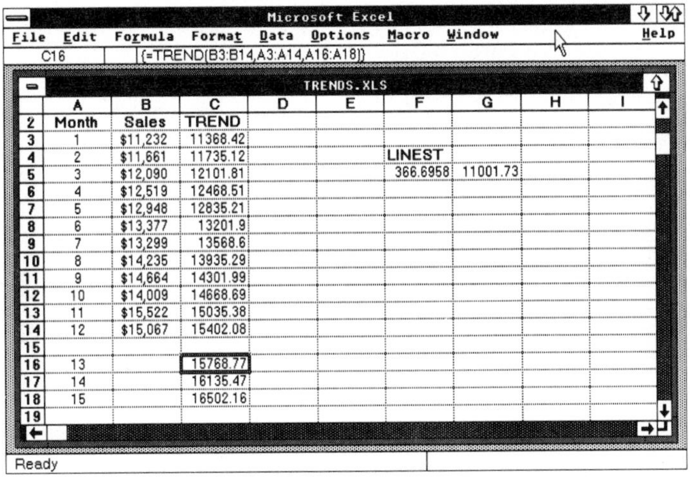

	A	B	C	D	E	F	G	H	I
2	Month	Sales	TREND						
3	1	$11,232	11368.42						
4	2	$11,661	11735.12			LINEST			
5	3	$12,090	12101.81			366.6958	11001.73		
6	4	$12,519	12468.51						
7	5	$12,948	12835.21						
8	6	$13,377	13201.9						
9	7	$13,299	13568.6						
10	8	$14,235	13935.29						
11	9	$14,664	14301.99						
12	10	$14,009	14668.69						
13	11	$15,522	15036.38						
14	12	$15,067	15402.08						
15									
16	13		15768.77						
17	14		16135.47						
18	15		16502.16						
19									

FIGURE 8-15. *We used TREND to predict the sales figures for months 13, 14, and 15.*

The LOGEST function

LOGEST is similar to LINEST. However, unlike LINEST, which returns the slope and y-axis intercept of the regression line that describes a data series, LOGEST returns the constants m (slope) and b (y-axis intercept) of the exponential regression *curve* that describes the data.

The form of LOGEST is

=LOGEST(*Y-array*,*X-array*)

The result of the function is a horizontal array consisting of the slope and y-axis intercept of the exponential regression curve that best fits the values in *Y-array*.

Let's apply LOGEST to our sample data set. Select the range F8:G8, enter the formula

=LOGEST(B3:B14,A3:A14)

and press Shift-Ctrl-Enter. Figure 8-16 shows the result.

To understand these results, you need to know that the position of any point on the curve is determined by the equation

$y=b*m^x$

The value in cell F8, 1.028028, is the constant m for the regression curve that describes the data. The value in cell G8, 11130.52, is the constant b.

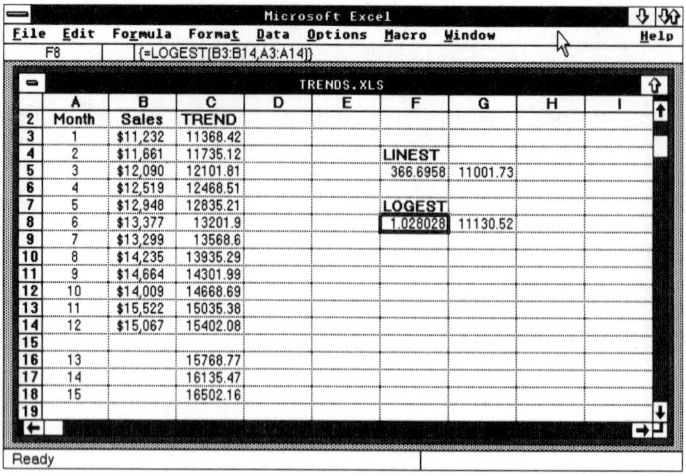

FIGURE 8-16. *We used the LOGEST function to define an exponential regression curve.*

As with LINEST, you can use the results of the LOGEST function to predict the future. For example, suppose you want to predict the sales volume for the fifteenth month in the series. Because the value in G8 is the b constant and the value in F8 is the m constant, the formula

=G8*(F8^15)

will return the predicted sales for the fifteenth month: 16849.53. Notice that this value is similar to, but slightly different from, the prediction offered by LINEST: 16052.16.

As with LINEST, if you omit the *X-array* argument from the LOGEST function, Microsoft Excel assumes the *X-array* values are 1, 2, 3, 4, and so on.

The GROWTH function

As you might expect, GROWTH is to LOGEST what TREND is to LINEST. As TREND returns the y values of the points on the regression *line* that describes a data series, so GROWTH returns the y values of the points on the regression *curve* that describes the data. The form of this function is

=GROWTH(*Y-array*,*X-array*,*x-array*)

As you can see, the form of GROWTH is identical to that of TREND. In fact, all the rules that apply to TREND also apply to GROWTH.

Let's work through an example with GROWTH, using the same sales-trend worksheet. To begin, select the range D3:D14. In cell D3, type the formula

=GROWTH(B3:B14,A3:A14)

and press Shift-Ctrl-Enter. The result is shown in Figure 8-17. The numbers in the range D3:D14 are the y values for each of the points on the regression curve that describes the data in column B.

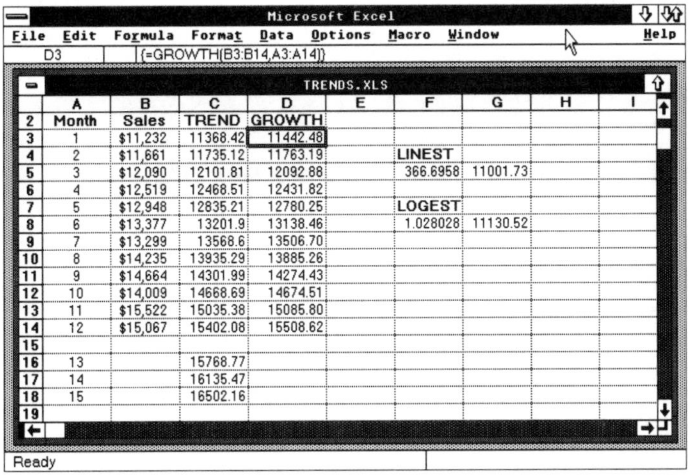

	Microsoft Excel									
File	**Edit**	**Formula**	**Format**	**Data**	**Options**	**Macro**	**Window**			**Help**
D3		{=GROWTH(B3:B14,A3:A14)}								

	A	B	C	D	E	F	G	H	I
2	Month	Sales	TREND	GROWTH					
3	1	$11,232	11368.42	11442.48					
4	2	$11,661	11735.12	11763.19		LINEST			
5	3	$12,090	12101.81	12092.88		366.6958	11001.73		
6	4	$12,519	12468.51	12431.82					
7	5	$12,948	12835.21	12780.25		LOGEST			
8	6	$13,377	13201.9	13138.46		1.028028	11130.52		
9	7	$13,299	13568.6	13506.70					
10	8	$14,235	13935.29	13885.26					
11	9	$14,664	14301.99	14274.43					
12	10	$14,009	14668.69	14674.51					
13	11	$15,522	15035.38	15085.80					
14	12	$15,067	15402.08	15508.62					
15									
16	13		15768.77						
17	14		16135.47						
18	15		16502.16						
19									

Ready

FIGURE 8-17. *We used the GROWTH function to create a data series that can be plotted as a curve on a chart.*

If you omit the *X-array* argument from the GROWTH function, Microsoft Excel assumes that the *X-array* values are 1, 2, 3, 4, and so on.

Like TREND, GROWTH can be used to predict the future. For example, let's use GROWTH to predict the sales figures for months 13, 14, and 15. First select the range D16:D18; then enter the formula

=GROWTH(B3:B14,A3:A14,A16:A18)

and press Shift-Ctrl-Enter. The result is shown in Figure 8-18. The numbers in cells D16, D17, and D18 are the predicted sales values for the thirteenth, fourteenth, and fifteenth months in the series.

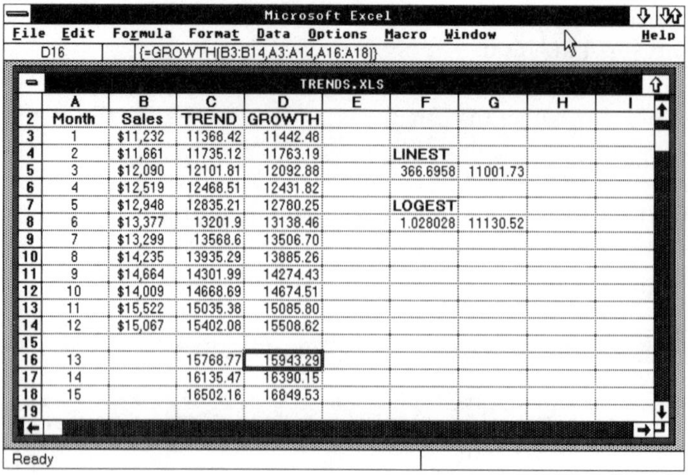

FIGURE 8-18. *We used GROWTH to predict the sales figures for months 13, 14, and 15.*

Data tables

One of the most important benefits of spreadsheet software is that it allows you to perform "what-if" analysis quickly and easily. When you perform what-if analysis, you change certain key variables and measure the effect of the change on the "bottom line."

Suppose you're considering buying a house that will require you to take out a 30-year, $100,000 mortgage. You need to calculate your monthly payments on that loan. Obviously, the size of the monthly payment is affected directly by the rate of interest the bank charges on the mortgage. You would like to see the outcome for several interest rates.

The Table command on the Data menu makes this type of what-if analysis easy. The command is very powerful—it automatically performs a series of calculations for you, given a formula and a set of variables.

You can build two kinds of data tables: one-variable and two-variable (also called one-input and two-input tables). We'll look at one-variable tables first.

One-variable tables

Let's build a data table that computes the monthly payment on the sample mortgage at six different interest rates: 10, 11, 12, 13, 14, and 15 percent. First, enter the various interest rates you want to test in cells B3:B8 of your worksheet. We'll call this range the input range, because it contains the inputs we want to test. Next, enter the formula

=PMT(A2/12,360,100000)

in cell C2. We'll call this formula the table formula. In this formula, A2/12 is the monthly interest rate, 360 is the term of the loan in months, and 100000 is the loan principal. Notice that this formula refers to cell A2, which is currently blank. As you can see in Figure 8-19, because A2 is blank (Microsoft Excel assigns a value of 0 to blank cells), the function returns a spurious result: the payment required to amortize the loan at an interest rate of 0 percent. Actually, cell A2 is merely a placeholder through which Microsoft Excel feeds the individual variables in the input range. This placeholder can be any cell in the worksheet outside the table range. You'll see in a moment why this formula refers to cell A2.

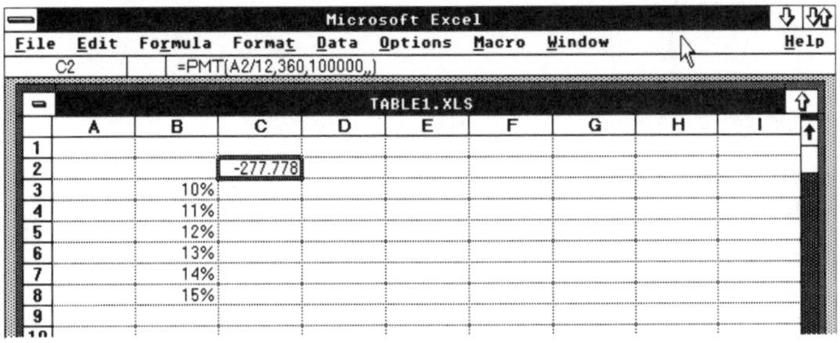

FIGURE 8-19. *The first step in building our data table is to enter the interest rates and the PMT function into the worksheet.*

Next, define the data-table range by selecting it. In Microsoft Excel, the data-table range is always the smallest rectangular range that includes the table formula and all the values in the input range. In this case, you need to select the range B2:C8.

Now choose Table from the Data menu. When you do this, you'll see the dialog box shown in Figure 8-20. The Row Input Cell and Column Input Cell options are used to define the location of what we will call the input cell. The input cell is the placeholder cell referred to, at least indirectly, by the table formula. In this example, A2 is the input cell. For the table to work properly, you have to enter the input-cell reference in the correct edit bar in the dialog box. If the values in the input range are arranged in a column, the input-cell reference should be entered in the Column Input Cell edit bar. If the input values are arranged in a row, the input-cell reference should be entered in the Row Input Cell edit bar. Because the input values in this example are arranged in a column, enter the input-cell reference in

the Column Input Cell edit bar by selecting the bar and either typing the absolute
reference of the input cell, $A$2, or pointing to that cell and clicking.

FIGURE 8-20. *Use the Table dialog box to specify your input cell.*

Notice that this dialog box contains a highlighted title bar and a Control menu
icon, much like a document or application window. In fact, you can manipulate
this dialog box like a window. For example, if the dialog box blocks your view of
the input cell you want to select, you can drag the box out of the way.

When you lock in your dialog-box settings, Microsoft Excel enters the six
results of the table formula (one result for each input value) into the range C3:C8,
as shown in Figure 8-21.

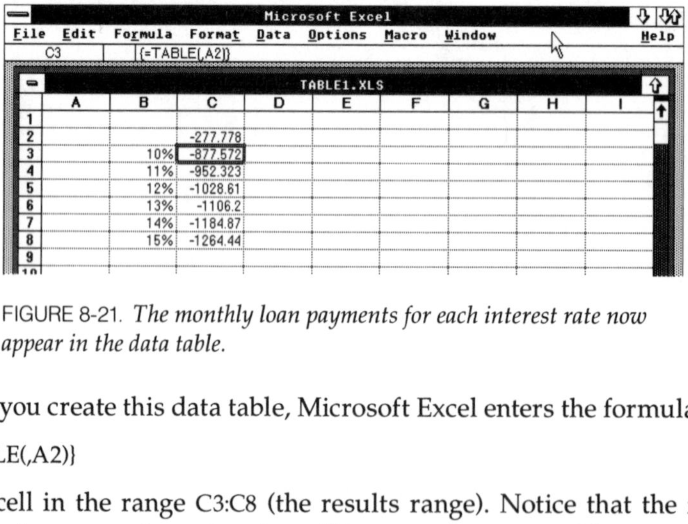

		Microsoft Excel						
File	Edit	Formula	Format	Data	Options	Macro	Window	Help

| C3 | | {=TABLE(,A2)} |

TABLE1.XLS

	A	B	C	D	E	F	G	H	I
1									
2			-277.778						
3		10%	-877.572						
4		11%	-952.323						
5		12%	-1028.61						
6		13%	-1106.2						
7		14%	-1184.87						
8		15%	-1264.44						
9									

FIGURE 8-21. *The monthly loan payments for each interest rate now
appear in the data table.*

When you create this data table, Microsoft Excel enters the formula

{=TABLE(,A2)}

into each cell in the range C3:C8 (the results range). Notice that the formula is
enclosed in braces to show that the cell is part of an array. The TABLE formula
takes the form

=TABLE(*row input cell,column input cell*)

Because the one-input table in our example is arranged in a columnar format,
Microsoft Excel places the column input reference, A2, as the second argument in
the formula. We're not using a row-input cell in this table, so that argument is left
blank. Notice, however, that the comma is used to tell Microsoft Excel that an
argument is being omitted.

In our sample table, the TABLE formula computes the results of the PMT function using each of the interest rates in column B. For example, the formula in cell C5 computes the payment at a rate of 12 percent per year.

After the table has been built, you can change the table formula or any of the variables in the list to create a different set of results. For example, suppose you decide to borrow only $85,000 to buy your house. If you change the formula in cell C2 to

=PMT(A2/12,360,85000)

the values in the table also change, as shown in Figure 8-22.

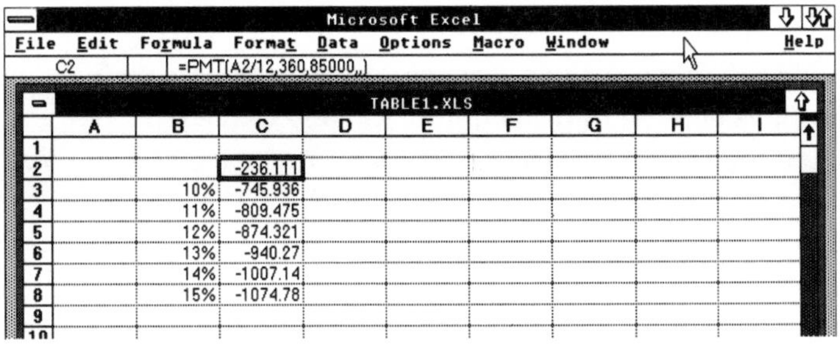

FIGURE 8-22. *When we changed the loan amount, Microsoft Excel recalculated the table.*

Horizontal tables

You can also create horizontal data tables. For example, Figure 8-23 shows a horizontal version of the simple one-variable vertical data table for the $100,000 loan. In the new table, the input values are in cells B3:G3. The formula

=PMT(A2/12,360,100000)

is in cell A4. Notice that this table formula also refers to cell A2, which is the input cell for the table.

To construct this table, first select the range A3:G4 (the smallest rectangular range that includes all the input values and the table formula); then choose the Table command. Because in this table the input values are stored in a row, enter the input-cell reference, $A$2, in the Row Input Cell edit bar of the Table dialog box.

As before, Microsoft Excel enters a series of TABLE formulas in the results range of the table. This time, however, the formulas are

{=TABLE(A2,)}

Notice that in this formula the reference to the input cell appears *before* the comma, indicating a horizontal table.

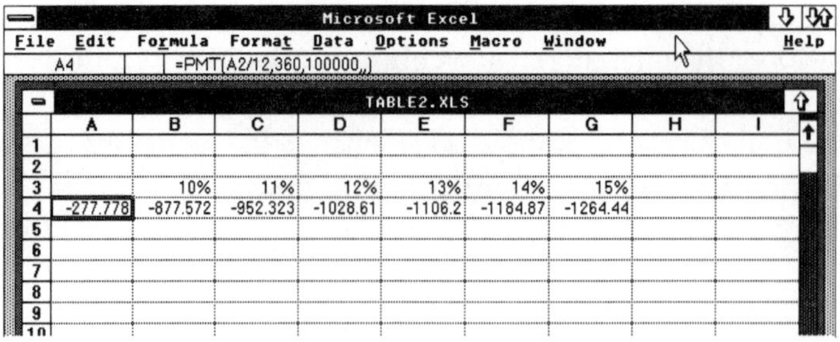

FIGURE 8-23. *We created a horizontal version of the table in Figure 8-21.*

Tables with two formulas

You can include as many formulas as you want in a one-variable data table. The second formula is entered in the cell immediately to the right of the cell that contains the first ("main") formula when the input range is a column. Additional formulas are entered in the same row to the right of the second formula, and so on.

For example, let's expand our first table in Figure 8-21 to include two formulas. Suppose you're also thinking about buying a house that would require you to take out a $90,000 mortgage. You want to know what your monthly payments would be on that mortgage at each of the interest rates in the input range and you want to be able to compare these payments with those for the $100,000 mortgage.

The first step in creating this new table is to enter the formula

=PMT(A2/12,360,90000)

in cell D2. Notice that, like the first formula, this table formula refers to cell A2, the input cell. Next, select the table range B2:D8, issue the Table command, and enter

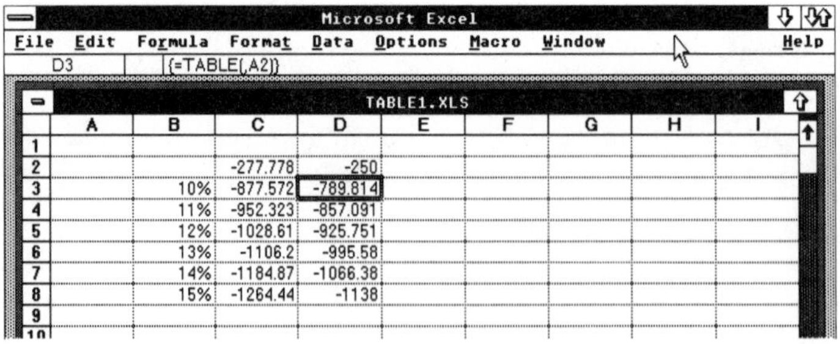

FIGURE 8-24. *This table computes the monthly payments on two loan amounts at various interest rates.*

the input-cell reference in the Column Input Cell edit bar. Figure 8-24 shows the results. As before, each cell in the range C3:D8 contains the formula

{=TABLE(,A2)}

These formulas compute the results of the formulas in cells C2 and D2 at each interest rate in the input range. For example, the formula in cell D4 computes the result of the formula in cell D2 at the rate in cell B4, 11 percent.

Indirect references to the input cell

In the three examples presented so far, the data-table formulas have referred directly to the input cell. However, you can also create data tables with formulas that refer indirectly to the input cell.

Consider the worksheet in Figure 8-25. The formula for the data table in this worksheet

=B4

is in cell E2. This formula is a simple reference to cell B4, which contains the formula

=PMT(B2/12,B3,B1)

This latter formula computes the monthly payments on the mortgage described by the entries in cells B1, B2, and B3.

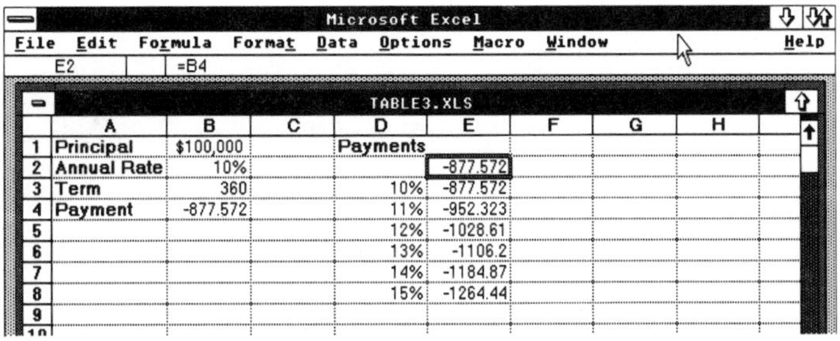

FIGURE 8-25. *The formula in cell E2 refers to cell B4, which contains a formula that refers to the input cell, B2.*

To compute this table, first select the table range, D2:E8; then choose the Table command. Next, specify the input cell. In this example, the input cell is B2. Because the input values in this table are stored in a column, enter the input-cell reference into the Column Input Cell edit bar. When you press Enter or choose OK to lock in the input-cell reference, Microsoft Excel will compute the table.

Notice that, although the table formula in E2 does not refer directly to the input cell, cell B2, the cells are linked indirectly: The formula in cell E2 refers to cell B4, and the formula in cell B4 in turn refers to cell B2. As long as at least this kind of indirect link exists between the table formula and the input cell, the table will work properly.

Also notice that the input cell in this table contains an entry. This is no problem for Microsoft Excel. The input cell of a data table can contain any value without affecting the final results of the table.

Two-variable tables

All the data tables we've considered so far have been alike in one important way: In each case, we computed the results of a formula (or formulas) as we changed a single variable, the interest rate. However, Microsoft Excel also allows you to create data tables that compute the results of a formula as two variables change.

Continuing with our previous scenario, suppose you want to build a data table that will compute the monthly payment on a $100,000 mortgage, but this time you want to vary not only the interest rate but also the term of the mortgage. You want to know what effect a term of 30, 25, 20, or 15 years (360, 300, 240, or 180 months) will have on your monthly payment.

The first step in creating this table is to enter the six interest rates you want to test—we'll use the range B3:B8 to enter the rates 10%, 11%, 12%, 13%, 14%, and 15%. Next, enter the different monthly terms you want to test—we'll enter these values in cells C2:F2.

Now you're ready to create the table formula. Because this is a two-variable table, the formula must be entered in the cell at the intersection of the row and column that contain the two sets of input values—cell B2 in this example. (Although you can include as many formulas as you want in a one-variable table, you can include only one formula in a two-variable table.) The formula for this table is

=PMT(A1/12,B1,100000)

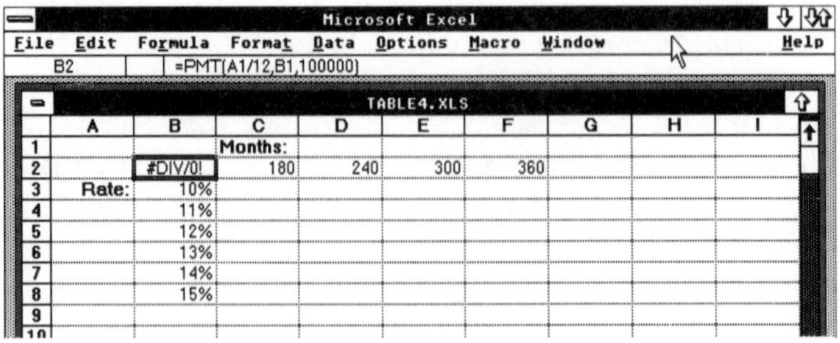

FIGURE 8-26. *We entered the formula for our two-variable table in cell B2.*

Notice that this formula, shown in Figure 8-26, refers to two blank cells: A1 and B1. Because both of these cells are blank, the table formula returns the error message #DIV/0!. This is a spurious result that does not affect the performance of the table.

Next, select the table range. As with the one-variable table, the table range for a two-variable table is the smallest rectangular block that includes all the input values and the table formula. In this example, the table range is therefore B2:F8.

After you've selected this range, you're ready to use the Table command and define the input cells. Because this is a two-variable data table, you must define two input cells: one for the input values stored in column B and one for the input values stored in row 2. The reference for the first input cell, $A$1, should be entered in the Column Input Cell edit bar, and the reference for the second input cell, $B$1, should be entered in the Row Input Cell edit bar. After the input cells have been entered, press Enter or choose OK to compute the table. The result is shown in Figure 8-27.

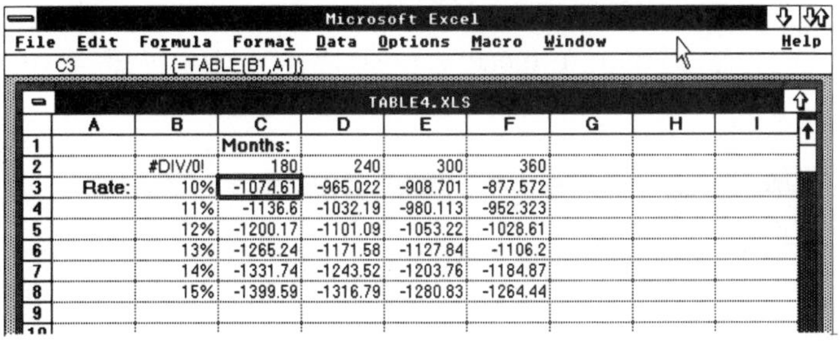

FIGURE 8-27. *This table calculates the monthly payments using various interest rates and terms.*

As in the previous examples, Microsoft Excel has entered a TABLE formula in each of the cells in the results range, C3:F8. Because this table has two sets of variables, the TABLE formulas include two references:

{=TABLE(B1,A1)}

The values in the results range are the monthly payments required to amortize the mortgage at each combination of interest rates and terms. For example, the number in cell D6, –1171.58, is the payment required to amortize a $100,000 mortgage over 240 months at an annual interest rate of 13 percent.

Be careful not to reverse the input cells in a two-variable table. If you do, Microsoft Excel will use the input values in the wrong place in the table formula, creating a set of meaningless results. For example, if you had reversed the input cells in this example, Microsoft Excel would have used the numbers in the range C2:F2 as interest rates and the numbers in the range B3:B8 as terms.

Editing tables

Although you can edit the input values or formulas in the left column or top row of a table, you can't edit the results in the individual cells. For example, if you try to edit cell D7 in Figure 8-27, Microsoft Excel will display the alert message *Can't change part of table*. In other words, if you make a mistake in setting up a data table, such as entering an incorrect reference as the input cell, you can't clear an individual cell. Instead, you must select all the results, choose the Clear command from the Edit menu, and then recompute the table.

You can copy the table results to a different part of the worksheet. You might want to do this to save the table's current results before you make a change to the table formula or to the variables. To copy the results of the sample table in Figure 8-27 from the range C3:F8 to the range C10:F15, select cells C3:F8, choose the Copy command from the Edit menu, select cell C10, and choose the Paste command. As you can see in Figure 8-28, the numbers in cells C10:F15 are constant numeric values, not array formulas. Microsoft Excel changes the results of the table from a set of array formulas to their numeric values when you copy the results out of the table range.

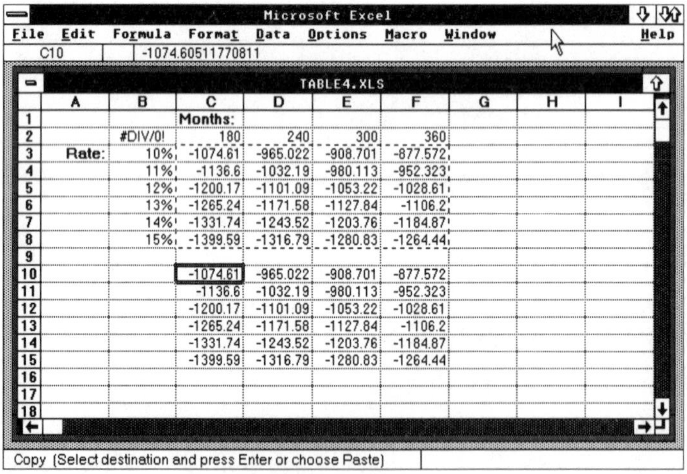

☰	Microsoft Excel							⇩ ⇩⇧
File	**Edit**	**Formula**	**Format**	**Data**	**Options**	**Macro**	**Window**	**Help**
C10		-1074.60511770811						

⊟					TABLE4.XLS				⇧
	A	**B**	**C**	**D**	**E**	**F**	**G**	**H**	**I**
1			Months:						
2		#DIV/0!	180	240	300	360			
3	Rate:	10%	-1074.61	-965.022	-908.701	-877.572			
4		11%	-1136.6	-1032.19	-980.113	-952.323			
5		12%	-1200.17	-1101.09	-1053.22	-1028.61			
6		13%	-1265.24	-1171.58	-1127.84	-1106.2			
7		14%	-1331.74	-1243.52	-1203.76	-1184.87			
8		15%	-1399.59	-1316.79	-1280.83	-1264.44			
9									
10			-1074.61	-965.022	-908.701	-877.572			
11			-1136.6	-1032.19	-980.113	-952.323			
12			-1200.17	-1101.09	-1053.22	-1028.61			
13			-1265.24	-1171.58	-1127.84	-1106.2			
14			-1331.74	-1243.52	-1203.76	-1184.87			
15			-1399.59	-1316.79	-1280.83	-1264.44			
16									
17									
18									

Copy (Select destination and press Enter or choose Paste)

FIGURE 8-28. *Copying the results range to another part of the worksheet transfers the numeric values, not the formulas.*

If you have no more need for a table, or have botched one so badly that the best remedy is to begin again, you can delete it. Simply select all cells that contain the table—input values, formulas, and results—and choose the Clear command from the Edit menu.

Linking worksheets

One of Microsoft Excel's most exciting features is its ability to create dynamic links between worksheets. You'll find a number of advantages to linking worksheets. First, you can break large, complex worksheet models into more manageable portions. For example, instead of placing all your company's budget data in one model, you might create several departmental budgets. Then you can create a master budget worksheet to draw relevant data from the individual departmental models. Linked worksheets also give you the flexibility to extract any number of reports and analyses from a group of supporting worksheets.

In addition to creating more manageable and flexible models, linked worksheets can save recalculation time and memory. You can keep only the data you need open in your workspace at any given time. As long as you use simple dependent formulas (more on this in a moment), Microsoft Excel can read the relevant data from disk to ensure that your linked references are always up to date.

Creating links

Creating a formula that links two worksheets is much like building any other formula. The only difference between a linked formula and a regular formula is that you must include the name of the remote worksheet, followed by an exclamation mark, in a linked formula.

For example, consider the two worksheets shown in Figure 8-29. We linked cell A1 in the worksheet named LINK2 to cell A8 in the worksheet named LINK1. To do this, we selected cell A1 in LINK2 and entered the dependent formula

=LINK1.XLS!$A$8

Notice that cell A1 in LINK2 has assumed the value of cell A8 in LINK1. In this example, LINK2 is the dependent worksheet and LINK1 is the supporting worksheet.

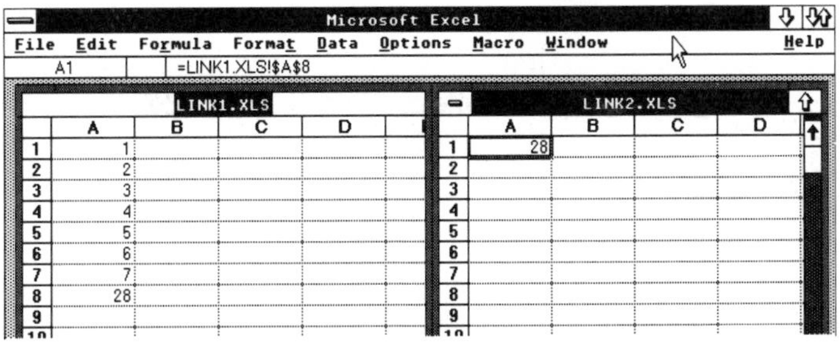

FIGURE 8-29. *Cell A1 in the dependent worksheet, LINK2, is linked to cell A8 in the supporting worksheet, LINK1.*

Pasting linked references into a formula is much like pasting standard cell references. For example, to enter the formula in cell A1 of LINK2, we selected the cell, typed an equal sign, and then activated the LINK1 worksheet and selected cell A8. Alternatively, we could have pasted the linked reference by first activating the worksheet and cell we wanted to refer to—cell A8 of LINK1, in our example— issuing the Copy command, and then activating the dependent worksheet and choosing the Paste Link command on the Edit menu. (We'll talk more about Paste Link in a moment.)

As you might expect, you can use names instead of cell references in dependent formulas. For example, if cell A8 in LINK1 is named Test, then the formula

   =LINK1.XLS!Test

is identical to

   =LINK1.XLS!$A$8

You can also create formulas that refer to entire ranges in the supporting worksheet. For example, suppose you want to enter a formula in cell A2 of LINK2 that averages the values in cells A1:A7 of LINK1. To do this, select cell 2 of LINK2, type

   =AVERAGE(

then activate LINK1, drag through cells A1:A7 to paste your linked range reference into the formula bar, and type a closing parenthesis to complete the formula. The result should look like this

   =AVERAGE(LINK1.XLS!$A$1:$A$7)

You can't use the Paste Link command to create the reference to the range A1:A7 in this formula. Paste Link allows you to create only simple dependent formulas. (We'll talk more about simple and complex links in a moment.) However, you can use Paste Link to create linked array references. For example, you could use Paste Link to create a linked array formula that refers to cells A1:A7 of LINKS1. To do this, select cells A1:A7 in LINKS1, issue the Copy command, activate LINKS2, select the cell you want to use as the first cell in your linked array formula, and choose Paste Link. Microsoft Excel will automatically select an array range the same size and shape as the copy range and enter the dependent array formula

   {=LINK1.XLS!$A$1:$A$7}

in each cell of that range.

Linking multiple worksheets

Microsoft Excel also lets you build formulas that link several worksheets at once. For example, suppose you've created three worksheets—Sheet1, Sheet2, and

Sheet3. You want to build a formula in cell A1 of Sheet1 that totals the values in cell A1 of Sheet2 and cell A1 of Sheet3. You can do this by entering the dependent formula

=Sheet2!A1+Sheet3!A1

into cell A1 of Sheet1. In this example, Sheet1 is directly dependent on both Sheet2 and Sheet3.

You can also create indirect links to other worksheets. Suppose you create a worksheet called LINK3 that contains the formula

=LINK2!$A$1

Suppose also that cell A1 in the supporting worksheet, LINK2, contains the formula

=LINK1!$A$8

In this case, LINK3 is indirectly linked to LINK1.

Saving linked worksheets

You probably remember from Chapter 1 that you use the Save As command from the File menu to give your worksheets descriptive names when you save them. For example, suppose you're modeling your company's 1988 budget in a worksheet called Sheet1. When you're ready to save the worksheet, you'll probably use the Save As command to give the spreadsheet a name such as Budget88.

Now suppose that another active worksheet, called Actual, contains links to your budget worksheet and is therefore dependent on the budget worksheet for some of its information. These links identify the budget worksheet as Sheet1. If you use Save As to save Sheet1 as Budget88 *while Actual is still open*, all the references to Sheet1 in the Actual worksheet will change to Budget88. Thus, if Actual contains the reference

=Sheet1!A1

it will change to

=Budget88!A1

If, on the other hand, you decide to close the dependent worksheet, Actual, before you save the supporting worksheet, Sheet1, you'll see the warning *Save with references to unsaved documents?*. If you choose OK or press Enter, Microsoft Excel will save Actual. However, if you then use the Save As command to save Sheet1 as Budget88, the references to Sheet1 in Actual will not be updated. The dependent formulas in Actual will continue to assume that the budget worksheet is named

Sheet1. Thus, when you reopen Actual, Microsoft Excel will be unable to find the worksheet Sheet1 and will display the dialog box shown in Figure 8-30. Normally when you see this dialog box, you simply select the name of the file or directory that contains the file Microsoft Excel is searching for. However, because Sheet1 doesn't exist anymore (it's now called Budget88), Microsoft Excel will never be able to update references to that worksheet. For this reason, when you create a set of linked worksheets, you should always save the supporting worksheets before you save the dependent worksheets.

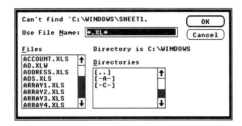

FIGURE 8-30. *The Can't Find dialog box appears if the supporting worksheet can't be located.*

Calculating dependent formulas

When you open a worksheet that depends on other worksheets or create a formula that refers to another worksheet, Microsoft Excel attempts to evaluate the dependent formulas in the opened worksheet. The program first checks to see whether the worksheets that the dependent formulas refer to are open. If the supporting worksheets are open, Microsoft Excel reads the values from those worksheets and calculates the dependent formulas. If the supporting worksheets are closed, however, things get a bit trickier.

Two kinds of dependent formulas

Microsoft Excel recognizes two kinds of dependent formulas: simple and complex. Simple dependent formulas include only absolute references to cells or ranges in another worksheet or references to named ranges or named constant values. For example, the formulas

=Sheet2!$A$1

and

{=Sheet2!$A$1:$A$10}

are simple dependent formulas. The formula

=Sheet2!Test

is a simple dependent formula if the name *Test* describes a single cell, a range, or a constant (such as 100).

All other dependent formulas are complex formulas. For example, the formulas

```
=Sheet2!A1
=Sheet2!A1+1
=SUM(Sheet2!A1:A10)
```

and

```
=Sheet2!A1+Sheet3!A1
```

are all complex dependent formulas. If the name *Test* describes a formula such as A1–A2, then

```
=Sheet2!Test
```

is also a complex dependent formula.

The distinction between simple and complex dependent formulas becomes important when you open a dependent worksheet without opening its supporting worksheets. Microsoft Excel can evaluate only simple dependent formulas that refer to closed worksheets. It cannot evaluate complex formulas that refer to closed worksheets, because those formulas would have to be recalculated to return a meaningful value and the worksheet must be open in order for a recalculation to occur. Instead, the program returns a #REF! error.

If you create a formula that includes a simple reference to a closed worksheet, Microsoft Excel attempts to evaluate the formula by reading the appropriate value from that worksheet on disk. If the program can't locate the supporting worksheet, it prompts you for the information needed to locate the file.

Microsoft Excel can access documents stored in different directories. As long as you use the Save As command to save all supporting worksheets before you close the dependent worksheet, Microsoft Excel will remember the location of all supporting files. However, if you rename a supporting worksheet or move it to another directory, you may have to redirect your worksheet links before Microsoft Excel can update your external references. For example, suppose you enter the formula

```
=Sheet2!$A$1
```

in cell A1 of Sheet1. If Microsoft Excel is able to locate Sheet2, it will immediately read the value from cell A1 of that file and display that value in cell A1 of Sheet1. If it can't locate Sheet2, you'll see a dialog box like the one already shown in Figure 8-30. From this box, you can tell Microsoft Excel to look in a different directory for the file Sheet2. If you've made an error, you can use the Cancel button to cancel the search for Sheet2. When you choose Cancel, the message *#REF!* appears in the cell that contains the formula with the external reference. (More about redirecting links in a few pages.)

Opening a dependent worksheet

When you save a worksheet that contains dependent formulas, Microsoft Excel remembers the most recent results of those formulas. When you open that worksheet, Microsoft Excel at first assigns the external references in the dependent formulas their old values. This is true for both simple and complex dependent formulas.

Remember, however, that if you've opened and used the supporting worksheet since you last used the dependent worksheet, the values of some of the cells in the supporting worksheet are likely to have changed. Fortunately, as soon as a worksheet that contains dependent formulas is opened, Microsoft Excel displays an alert box with the message *Update references to unopened documents?*. This alert box enables you to instruct Microsoft Excel whether to read the current values of the cells to which the formulas refer from the closed worksheets on the disk.

If you select No, Microsoft Excel opens the dependent worksheet without updating any references to the supporting worksheets. All the simple dependent formulas in the worksheet retain their last saved values; the values of all the complex formulas in the worksheet change from the last saved value to #REF!.

If you select Yes, Microsoft Excel attempts to find the supporting worksheets. If successful, it reads the values from the supporting files and updates the simple dependent formulas in the dependent worksheet. The program does not open the supporting worksheets; it merely reads the appropriate values from those worksheets. Again, the values of all complex dependent formulas become #REF!.

As already mentioned, if Microsoft Excel can't find one or more of the supporting files, it displays a dialog box like the one shown in Figure 8-30. From this box, you can choose to cancel the update process, change the current directory, or identify the file.

Updating complex formulas

As you've seen, Microsoft Excel can't evaluate complex dependent formulas that refer to closed worksheets. If you create a complex formula with a reference to a closed worksheet or open a worksheet that contains a complex formula with a reference to a closed worksheet, that formula returns the error #REF!. Until you actually open the worksheet to which the complex formula refers, Microsoft Excel is not able to evaluate the dependent formula. When you open the supporting worksheet and calculate the dependent worksheet, Microsoft Excel will then read the values it needs from the supporting worksheet and properly evaluate the complex formula.

The Links command

The Links command on the File menu is a convenient way to open in one step all the worksheets on which another worksheet depends. In many ways, this command is like the Open command. The main difference is that Open presents a list of *all* the files in the current directory, whereas Links limits the list to those files that support the active worksheet. (This is a handy way to look up the names of all the supporting worksheets of a dependent worksheet.)

For example, suppose you're building a spreadsheet, Sheet3, that depends on two other spreadsheets, Sheet1 and Sheet2. Sheet1 and Sheet2 are currently closed, but you want to open them so that the complex dependent formulas in Sheet3 can be calculated. To open both worksheets at once, simply choose the Links command. You'll see a dialog box like the one shown in Figure 8-31. Notice that the file list includes only the two files that support Sheet3. Now select both names, Sheet1 and Sheet2. You can select several names at one time with the mouse by holding down Shift and dragging through or clicking on the desired names. To select several names at one time with the keyboard, hold down Ctrl and use the arrow keys to select each worksheet; then press Spacebar to add the worksheet to the list you want to open. Finally, select Open. Microsoft Excel will open both of the worksheets on which Sheet3 depends.

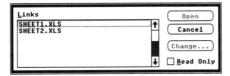

FIGURE 8-31. *Use the Links dialog box to quickly locate all your supporting worksheets.*

Although you'll usually open all the supporting worksheets at once, you can use Links to open them one at a time. To do this, you must issue a separate Links command for every worksheet you want to open. Be careful, though—the order in which you open the files is important. For example, suppose you choose the name Sheet1 in the Links dialog box and then choose Open. Sheet1 appears as the active document. However, when you try to use the Links command to open Sheet2, you'll get surprising results. Because Sheet1 is now the active worksheet, when you choose the Links command again Microsoft Excel displays a list of any worksheets that support Sheet1 instead of those that support Sheet3. To see a list of the worksheets that support Sheet3, you'll need to activate that worksheet after you open Sheet1 and before you repeat the Links command.

Of course, you don't have to use the Links command at all. Supporting worksheets can be opened with the Open command, and their links to the dependent worksheet will still be maintained.

If you want to prevent the user from saving changes to the supporting files, you can choose the Read Only option in the Links dialog box. This option works like its equivalent in the Open dialog box, described in Chapter 1.

Redirecting Links

If you've changed the name of a supporting worksheet or moved it to another directory, you may need to redirect your linked references to let Microsoft Excel know where to find the supporting data for your dependent formulas. To redirect your worksheet links, select the original name of the supporting file or files in the Links list box and then choose Change. You'll see a dialog box like the one in Figure 8-32. In this dialog box, select the name of the new file or renamed file you want to use for your dependent formulas. If necessary, you can choose a new directory from the list box on the right. Alternatively, you can type a new pathname in the Use File Name edit bar. When you choose OK or press Enter, Microsoft Excel will change all references to the supporting worksheet to use the new filename.

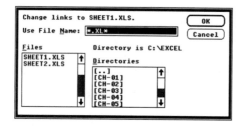

FIGURE 8-32. *When you use the Change button to redirect your worksheet links, you see a dialog box like this one.*

Copying, cutting, and pasting in linked worksheets

Just as you can use absolute or relative references to cells within a single worksheet, you can use absolute or relative references to cells in other worksheets. Absolute and relative references to cells in supporting worksheets respond to the Copy, Cut, and Paste commands in much the same way as do references to cells in the same worksheet.

For example, suppose you've created the formula

=Sheet2!Z1

in cell A1 of Sheet1 and used the Copy and Paste commands to copy this formula into cell B1. The formula in cell B1 will be

=Sheet2!AA1

The original formula changed when it was copied to cell B1 because the reference to cell Z1 in Sheet2 is relative. If, on the other hand, the formula in cell A1 of Sheet1 had contained an absolute reference to cell Z1 in Sheet2, as in

=Sheet2!$Z$1

the result of copying and pasting the formula in cell B1 would have remained

=Sheet2!$Z$1

Copying and pasting between worksheets

As you learned in Chapter 4, Microsoft Excel allows you to copy entries from one worksheet to another. As you might expect, this includes dependent formulas.

When you copy from one worksheet to another a dependent formula that includes a relative reference to yet another worksheet, that reference is adjusted to reflect the new position of the formula. For example, suppose cell A1 in Sheet1 contains the formula

=Sheet2!A1

If you copy and paste that formula from cell A1 in Sheet1 into cell B5 in Sheet3, the result is the formula

=Sheet2!B5

The formula is adjusted to take into account its new relative position.

If, on the other hand, you copy a formula that contains an absolute reference to another worksheet, that formula is not adjusted. For example, suppose cell A1 in Sheet1 contains the formula

=Sheet2!$A$1

If you copy and paste that formula into cell B5 in Sheet3, the resulting formula remains

=Sheet2!$A$1

Even if you copy a dependent formula into the worksheet to which the formula refers, it continues to be a dependent formula. For example, if you copy the formula

=Sheet2!A3

from cell A1 of Sheet1 into cell A1 of Sheet2, the result is still

=Sheet2!A3

The reference to the worksheet named Sheet2 remains, even though it now exists in the same worksheet.

Cutting and pasting between worksheets

You can also cut a dependent formula and paste it into another worksheet. Cutting and pasting dependent formulas is no different than cutting and pasting regular formulas.

Keep in mind that, unlike the case with copying, Microsoft Excel does not adjust the relative references in a formula when you cut it from one worksheet and paste it into another. For example, suppose cell A1 in Sheet1 contains the formula

=Sheet2!A1

If you cut that formula and paste it in cell B5 of Sheet3, the result is still the formula

=Sheet2!A1

Cutting and pasting cells referred to by dependent formulas

In Chapter 4, you learned that when you cut and paste cells, Microsoft Excel adjusts any references to those cells in the formulas of the worksheet. Unfortunately, this isn't true for formulas in other worksheets that refer to the cut and pasted cells with explicit cell references. When you cut and paste a cell referred to by a dependent formula in another worksheet, that formula is not adjusted to reflect the change unless the cell is a named cell.

For example, suppose you've created the formula

=Sheet2!A10

in cell A1 in Sheet1. If you use the Cut and Paste commands to move the entry in cell A10 of Sheet2 to cell B10 of Sheet2, the formula in cell A1 of Sheet1 remains

=Sheet2!A10

Because cell A10 in Sheet2 is blank after the cut and paste, the formula in cell A1 of Sheet1 now returns the result 0.

You can overcome this problem by using a name in the dependent formula. For example, suppose you name cell A10 in Sheet2 Test and then enter the formula

=Sheet2!Test

in cell A1 of Sheet1. Now, if you use Cut and Paste to move the entry in cell A10 of Sheet2 to cell B10 of Sheet2, Microsoft Excel will move the name *Test* to cell B10 as well, and the link will be preserved.

Severing links between worksheets

If you want to cut the links between worksheets, you can use the Paste Special command from the Edit menu to change all the external references in your dependent formula to constant values. Of course, you won't be able to update the references, because all ties to the supporting worksheets will be removed.

Begin by selecting the linked cell or cells and choosing the Copy and Paste Special commands from the Edit menu. When the Paste Special dialog box appears, select the Values option and choose OK or press Enter. (As a precaution, use the Find command from the Formula menu to look for any dependent formulas you may have missed.) Simply enter the exclamation point required in all dependent formulas in the Find What edit bar and then select the Formulas option. When you choose OK or press Enter, Microsoft Excel will search your worksheet for any references to supporting worksheets.

When a cell contains both an external reference and a formula, you can preserve the formula while eliminating the external reference. To do this, select the cell and then, in the formula bar, select the portion of the cell that contains the external reference. Now choose the Calculate Now command from the Options menu and press Enter. Microsoft Excel will change the external reference to a value without changing the rest of the formula.

Locating and replacing strings

Imagine that you've built a large worksheet and that you now need to find every formula in that worksheet that contains a particular character string or value. The Find command on the Formula menu lets you locate any string of characters, including cell references and range names, in the formulas or values in a worksheet. This command is particularly useful when you want to find linked formulas or error values such as #NAME? or #REF!. What's more, you can use the Replace command to overwrite the strings you locate with new entries.

The Find command

To locate a character string, begin by selecting the range you want to search. If you want to look through the entire worksheet, select a single cell. Microsoft Excel will begin its search from that cell, travel through the worksheet, and end back in the selected cell. If you want to search only a portion of the worksheet, select the appropriate range.

When you issue the Find command, you'll see a dialog box like the one in Figure 8-33. The first step in using this command is to specify the Find What string—that is, the group of characters you want to search for. The string can include any letter, number, punctuation mark, or special character.

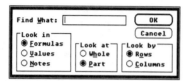

FIGURE 8-33. *Use the Find dialog box to locate a character string.*

The Look by options

The Look by options let you search by row or by column. When you select the Rows option, Microsoft Excel begins looking through the worksheet horizontally row by row, starting with the currently selected cell. If it finds an occurrence of the Find What string, the program highlights the cell that contains that occurrence and stops searching. If the program doesn't find an occurrence before it reaches the last cell in the active portion of the worksheet, it loops back to cell A1 and continues to search through the worksheet until it either finds an occurrence or returns to the cell that was selected when the search began. Select the Rows option if you think the string you're looking for is located to the right or left of the selected cell.

The Columns option works in almost the same way, except that it searches through the worksheet column by column, beginning with the selected cell. If you think the string you want to search for is located above or below the selected cell, choose the Columns option.

The Look in options

The Look in options tell Microsoft Excel whether you want to search the formulas or the values in the worksheet for the Find What string. When you select Formulas, Microsoft Excel searches for the string in the formulas contained in the worksheet cells. When you select Values, the program searches for the string in the displayed results of the entries in the worksheet. When you select Notes, Microsoft Excel examines any text you've attached as a note to a cell. (We'll discuss cell notes later in this chapter.)

The nuances of the Formulas and Values options can be confusing. To understand the difference between these options, you must remember that the underlying contents of a cell and the displayed value of that cell are often two different things. For example, if a cell contains a formula, the displayed value of the cell is usually the result of that formula—a number like 100 or a character string, if the formula involves text. If a cell contains a pure number, the displayed value of the cell may or may not agree with the cell's underlying contents. If the cell has been assigned the General format, the displayed value of the cell and the cell's contents usually agree; if the cell contains a number that has been assigned another format, however, the contents of the cell and its displayed value will be different. The underlying and displayed values of a cell that contains a text entry are almost always the same.

Consider the simple worksheet in Figure 8-34. Cells B2 and B3 in this worksheet contain the number 1000. The entry in cell B2 has the General format and the entry in cell B3 has the $#,##0 format. Cell C2, which contains the value 600, has been assigned the name *Test*. Cell C4 contains the formula

=Test+C3

which returns the value 1000. Cell E5 contains the label *Test*.

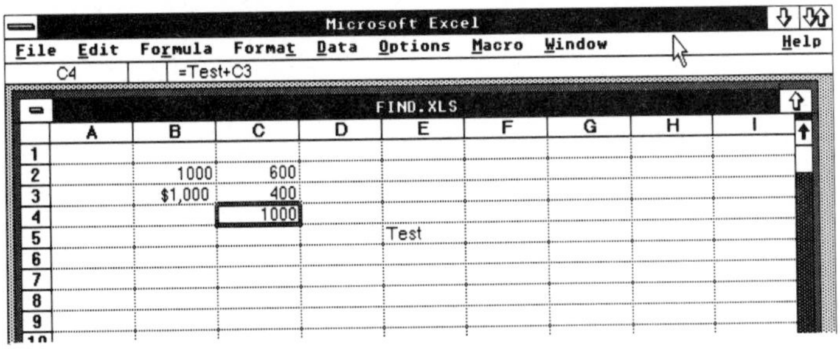

FIGURE 8-34. *We'll use this sample worksheet to demonstrate how you can search for a string in a value or in a formula.*

Now suppose you select cell A1, choose the Find command, and type *1000* to specify the Find What string. If you select Values as the Look in option, Microsoft Excel will look at what is displayed in each cell. It will first find the occurrence of the string *1000* in cell B2. If you press F7, it will next find the occurrence of the string in the displayed value of cell C4. Notice that Microsoft Excel ignores the entry in cell B3 when it searches for 1000 using the Look in Values option. This cell is skipped because its displayed value, $1,000, does not precisely match the Find What string, 1000. Because we're searching values and not formulas, Microsoft Excel ignores the fact that the underlying content of the cell is the number 1000.

Now suppose you once again select cell A1 and repeat the search, this time with the Formulas option selected. As before, Microsoft Excel will first find the occurrence of the Find What string in cell B2. If you press F7, Microsoft Excel will next highlight cell B3, which contains the number 1000. Because you're now searching the formulas and not the displayed values, the program ignores the format assigned to this cell. Instead, it matches the Find What string to the underlying contents of the cell.

If you press F7 again, Microsoft Excel will once again highlight cell B2. Because this time you're searching the formulas and not the displayed values of the cells, the value in cell C4 is ignored by the search. Even though this cell displays the value 1000, it actually contains the formula =*Test+C3*, which does not match the Find What string.

Let's look at one more example. If you specify *test* as the Find What string and select the Look in Formulas option, Microsoft Excel will first find the string *test* in the formula =*Test+C3* and highlight the cell that contains that formula, C4. (Note that this search is not case-sensitive.) If you press F7, Microsoft Excel will next highlight cell E5, which contains the label *Test*. If you repeat the search but this time select the Look in Values option, Microsoft Excel will find only the occurrence in the text entry *Test* in cell E5. If you want to find the defined name *Test* in C2, you must use the Goto command on the Formula menu.

The Look at options

The Look at options in the Find dialog box tell Microsoft Excel whether you want it to find only whole-word occurrences of the string or any occurrence of the string, even when it is a part of another string. For example, suppose a worksheet contains only two entries: the number 998, and the number 99. If you specify 99 as the Find What string and select Whole as the Look at option, Microsoft Excel will find only the entry 99. But if you select the Part option, Microsoft Excel will find both the entry 99, which matches the Find What string exactly, and the entry 998, which *contains* a string that matches the Find What string.

The Part option will find more occurrences of the string than the Whole option. The Whole option should be used when you want to narrow the search to precise matches.

Wildcard characters

You can use the wildcard characters * and ? to widen the scope of your searches. Wildcards are helpful when you're searching for a group of similar but not identical entries or when you're searching for an entry you don't quite remember.

The ? character takes the place of any single character in the Find What string. For example, the Find What string *100?* will match the values 1000, 1001, 1002, 1003, and so on up to 1009. (It will also match entries like 100A, 100B, and so on.)

The * character takes the place of one or more characters in a Find What string. For example, the string *1** will match the entries 10, 15, 100, 1111, 10001, 123456789, 123 Maple Street, and 1-800-223-8720.

The wildcard characters need not be used only at the end of a Find What string. For example, you could use the string *s to find all entries in the worksheet that end with *s*. Or you could use the string *es* to find each cell that contains the string sequence *es* anywhere in its formula or value.

If you want to look for a string that *contains* ? or *, enter a tilde (~) before the character. For example, to tell Microsoft Excel to search for the string *What?*, enter *What~?* as your Find What text.

Repeating the search

As you've already seen, after you've found the first occurrence of the Find What string, you can press the F7 function key to instruct Microsoft Excel to search for the next occurrence. If another occurrence is found, Microsoft Excel highlights that cell; if not, the highlight remains on the cell that contains the first occurrence of the string.

You can jump from occurrence to occurrence by repeatedly pressing F7. If you press F7 while the highlight is on the last occurrence of the string, the highlight jumps back to the first occurrence. To search backward through the worksheet, press Shift-F7.

The Replace command

Microsoft Excel allows you not only to locate characters in your worksheet but also to replace the specified character string with a new string. The Replace command works much like the Find command. When you select Replace from the Formula menu, you'll see a dialog box like the one in Figure 8-35. Simply type the character string you want to search for in the Replace edit bar and the string you want to substitute in the With edit bar.

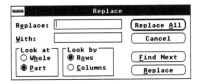

FIGURE 8-35. *Use the Replace command to replace a specified string with a new string.*

For example, suppose you want to replace each occurrence of the name *Joan Smith* with *John Smith*. Type *Joan* in the Replace edit bar and *John* in the With edit bar. Use the Find Next button to move from one occurrence of the Replace string to the next without changing the contents of the current cell. When you locate an occurrence you want to change, use the Replace button to substitute the Replace string with the contents of the With edit bar. After replacing the character string in the current cell, Microsoft Excel automatically moves to the next occurrence.

If you want to replace every occurrence of the Replace string with the contents of the With edit bar, choose the Replace All button. Instead of pausing at each occurrence to allow you to change or skip the current cell, Microsoft Excel will seek out all the cells that contain the Replace string and change them automatically.

You can change the contents of the With edit bar for each occurrence of the Replace string that Microsoft Excel locates. Simply use the Find Next button to perform a selective search. Each time you locate an occurrence of the Replace string, enter the appropriate replacement characters in the With edit bar and choose the Replace button.

For example, suppose you want to change the names *Joan Smith* and *John Smith* to *Joan Smythe* and *John Smythe*. Begin by typing Jo∗n Smith in the Replace edit bar; then choose the Find Next button. When you locate an occurrence of the Replace string, you can type either *Joan Smythe* or *John Smythe* in the With edit bar and choose the Replace button. When you locate the next occurrence, edit the contents of the With edit bar as needed to provide the correct replacement characters.

One note of warning: Although you can use wildcards in the Replace edit bar to aid in your search, don't enter wildcard characters in the With edit bar. If you do, Microsoft Excel will use a literal ∗ or ? symbol as it replaces each occurrence of your Replace text.

Worksheet auditing and documentation

Microsoft Excel offers a number of powerful and flexible commands that help you audit and debug your worksheets and document your work. In this section, we'll look at cell notes, the Info window, and the Select Special command.

Cell notes

Microsoft Excel's notes facility lets you attach notes to cells to document your work, explain calculations and assumptions, or provide reminders. Simply select the cell you want to work with and then select Note from the Formula menu or press Shift-F2. You'll see a window like the one in Figure 8-36. Notice that the reference to the active cell appears in the Cell edit bar at the top of the window. Type your entry in the Note edit box and choose Add or OK to attach the note to the active cell. When you choose OK, Microsoft Excel closes the window and returns to the worksheet. When you choose Add, the window remains open so that you can edit or add additional notes.

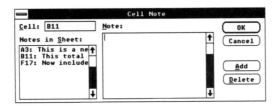

FIGURE 8-36. *Use the Cell Note window to attach a note to a cell.*

Although you can attach only one note to a cell, you can make your note text as long as you like. As you make entries in the Note edit box, Microsoft Excel automatically wraps text from one line to the next—don't use the Enter key to insert line breaks or you'll lock in the note and close the dialog box. If you want to begin a new paragraph of Notes text, press Ctrl-Enter.

After you add a note to a cell, the cell reference and the first few characters of that note appear in the Notes in Sheet list box on the left side of the window. To edit a note, select it from the list box, activate the Note edit box, and make your changes. Use the Delete button to delete the selected note. (You can also use the Notes option in the Clear dialog box to remove notes from a cell or range of cells.)

While the Cell Note window is active, you can also select other cells, to edit their notes or add new notes. First, activate the Cell edit bar and type a cell reference or use the mouse or arrow keys to select a cell. (If the window blocks your view of the cell you want to select, you can move it around on the screen by dragging the title bar or by using the Move command on the Cell Note window Control menu.) After selecting the cell you want, reactivate the Note edit box by pressing Alt-N, or clicking on the box with the mouse. Then edit the contents of this edit box just as you would edit an entry in the formula bar.

While working in the worksheet window, you can review, edit, or delete your notes by double-clicking on the cell you want to work with. The Cell Note window will reappear and the note for the active cell will be displayed.

In addition to using the OK button, you can close the Cell Note window by choosing the Cancel button or by choosing Close from the Control menu. Cancel and Close don't undo any additions or deletions you've already locked in; they simply cancel any new entries in the Note edit box and remove the Cell Note window from your screen.

You can print your notes by choosing the Notes option in the Print dialog box, described in Chapter 9, or by printing the contents of the Info Window, which is discussed on the following page.

The Info window

The Info window offers a great way to monitor the status of the cells in your worksheet. Using this special application window, you can quickly see all the "vital statistics" on the active cell. To open an Info window, select a cell and choose Show Info from the Window menu. Figure 8-37 shows a sample Info window. At the top of the window is the window name, Info, and the name of the currently active worksheet window.

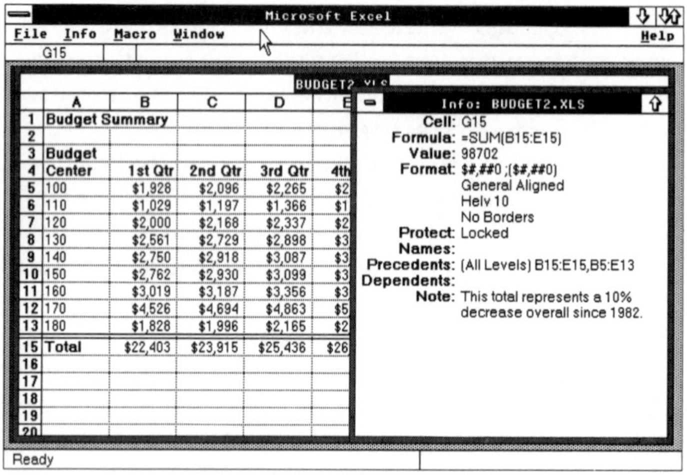

FIGURE 8-37. *The Info window lets you monitor the status of your cells.*

Notice that the contents of the application menu bar change when the Info window is active. The Edit, Formula, Format, Data, and Options menus disappear and a new menu called Info takes their place. Initially, you'll see only three pieces of information in the Info window: the cell reference, the underlying formula in the cell, and any note attached to the cell. However, you can use the commands on the Info menu to display more information. The Info menu offers nine display options: Cell, Formula, Value, Format, Protection, Names, Precedents (a list of cells the active cell refers to), Dependents (a list of cells that refer to the active cell), and Note. All the commands on the Info menu are toggle commands. A check mark appears beside those currently selected. (We selected all nine display options in Figure 8-37.) To deselect a display option, simply choose that option again.

To toggle between the active worksheet and the Info window, use the Show Document and Show Info commands on the Window menu. Alternatively, if you want to keep the Info window in view as you work in your document, resize and reposition the worksheet and Info windows so that they don't overlap. To quickly arrange the windows on your screen, choose Arrange All from the Window menu.

To print the contents of the Info window, select the cell or range for which you want to print information (the entire worksheet, if you like); then activate the Info window and issue the Print command. (For more information about printing, see Chapter 9.)

The Select Special command

Select Special is a powerful debugging and auditing tool that lets you quickly find cells that meet certain specifications. For example, suppose you find an error in a formula and want to trace all the cells that support that formula, to locate your mistake. You can use the Precedents option in the Select Special dialog box to locate all the direct and indirect precedents.

When you choose Select Special from the Formula menu, you'll see a dialog box like the one in Figure 8-38. The options in the Select Special dialog box allow you to specify certain selection criteria. When you choose one of these options and then choose OK or press Enter, Microsoft Excel highlights the cell or cells that match the criteria you chose. If you select a range of cells before opening the Select Special dialog box, Microsoft Excel searches only the selected range; if a single cell is active, Microsoft Excel searches the entire worksheet.

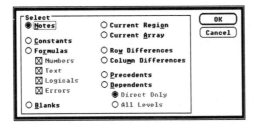

FIGURE 8-38. *The Select Special dialog box is a handy auditing and debugging tool.*

Several of the Select Special options, such as Notes, Precedents, and Dependents, may result in multiple discontinuous ranges. To navigate through these selections, you can use the Enter and Tab keys to move down or to the right one cell at a time. Shift-Enter and Shift-Tab let you move up or to the left one cell at a time. Ctrl-Tab and Shift-Ctrl-Tab let you jump forward and backward between ranges.

The Constants, Formulas, and Blanks options locate cells that contain the specified type of entries. When you choose the Constants or Formulas option,

Microsoft Excel activates the Numbers, Text, Logicals, and Errors options as well. Use these options to narrow your selection criteria.

The Current Region option is handy when you're working in a large, complex worksheet and need to select blocks of cells. (Recall that a region is defined as a continuous rectangular block of cells bounded by blank rows, blank columns, or worksheet borders.) When you choose Current Region, your search is limited to that area of the worksheet.

If the selected cell is part of an array range, you can use the Current Array option to select all the cells in that array. As we mentioned in our discussion of arrays, you can also choose this option by pressing Ctrl-/.

The Row Differences and Column Differences options let you compare the entries in a range of cells to spot potential inconsistencies. To use these debugging tools, first select the range of cells you want to compare. The position of the active cell in your selection determines which cell or cells Microsoft Excel uses to make its comparisons. When searching for row differences, Microsoft Excel compares the cells in the selection to the cells in the same column as the active cell; when searching for column differences, Microsoft Excel compares the cells in the selection to the cells in the same row as the active cell.

For example, suppose you've selected the range B10:G20 and cell B10 is the active cell. If you use the Row Differences option, Microsoft Excel will compare the entries in cells C10:G10 to the entry in cell B10; the entries in cells C11:G11 will be compared to cell B11, and so forth. If you choose the Column Differences option, Microsoft Excel will compare the entries in cells B11:B20 to the entry in cell B10; the entries in cells C11:C20 will be compared to cell C10, and so forth.

Among other things, Microsoft Excel looks for differences in your cell and range references and selects those cells that don't conform to the comparison cell. Suppose cell B10 is your comparison cell and contains the formula

    =SUM(B1:B9)

This comparison formula refers to the range of cells that begins nine rows above and ends one row above the formula cell. If you select cells B10:G10 and choose the Row Differences option, Microsoft Excel will scan through cells C10:G10 to check for any formulas that don't fit this pattern. For example, cells C10 and D10 should, presumably, contain the formulas

    =SUM(C1:C9)

and

    =SUM(D1:D9)

If any of the formulas in row 10 don't match this pattern, the Select Special command will flag those cells.

Of course, Row Differences and Column Differences also check to ensure that all the cells in the selected range contain the same type of entries. For example, if your comparison cell contains a SUM function, Microsoft Excel flags any cells that contain a function, formula, or value other than SUM. If the comparison cell contains a constant text or numeric value, Microsoft Excel flags any cells in the selected range that don't exactly match the comparison value.

(To quickly search for row differences from the keyboard, you can simply highlight the range you want to search and press Ctrl-\. To search for column differences, highlight the range you want to search and press Ctrl-¦. These keyboard shortcuts let you bypass the Select Special dialog box.)

The Precedents and Dependents options are perhaps the most powerful options in the Select Special dialog box. They let you trace calculations by locating all the cells that feed into a formula or that depend on the formula in the selected cell. To use these options, begin by selecting the cell whose dependents or precedents you want to trace; then issue the Select Special command and choose the Precedents or Dependents option. When you choose either of these options, Microsoft Excel activates the Direct Only and All Levels options. Use these options to set the parameters of your search: Direct Only finds only those cells that are directly dependent on or which directly refer to the active cell; All Levels locates direct precedents and dependents plus those cells that are indirectly linked to the active cell.

E X C E L

Using Select Special with Show Info

You can also use Select Special in conjunction with the Info window to select a range of cells and then move through the range to review the relevant data on each cell in the selection. For example, suppose you want to quickly scan all the notes you've entered in a specific range of your worksheet. First, select the range you're interested in (or a single cell, for the entire worksheet); then issue the Show Info command and select the Notes command from the Info menu, if necessary. Arrange the worksheet and Info windows so that they don't overlap—that way, you can see the selected cells and the Info window at the same time. Next, issue the Select Special command, select the Notes option, and choose OK or press Enter. Microsoft Excel will highlight all the cells in the selected range that have notes attached to them. Now you can use the Enter and Tab key combinations previously described to browse through the annotated cells and view their notes in the Info window.

Worksheet security

Microsoft Excel lets you protect the contents of your worksheets from accidental or unauthorized changes. Worksheet protection is controlled by three commands: Save As, Cell Protection, and Protect Document. As you learned in Chapter 1, you can use the Password option in the Save As dialog box to prevent unauthorized users from opening a protected document. In addition, the Cell Protection command on the Format menu controls the protection of individual cells and the Protect Document command on the Options menu controls the protection of the worksheet as a whole. Protect Document also lets you protect the position, size, and format of your worksheet windows. We'll look at the Cell Protection and Protect Document commands in this section.

The Cell Protection command

Microsoft Excel has two different protection attributes—Locked and Hidden—that you can assign to any cell in the worksheet. Both of these attributes are controlled by the Cell Protection command on the Format menu.

When a cell is locked and the worksheet protected, you won't be able to edit the contents of the cell or replace them with a different entry. If the locked cell is blank, you won't be able to make an entry into that cell. If you try to edit or make any other change to a locked cell, Microsoft Excel will return the error message *Locked cells can't be changed.*

When you assign the Hidden attribute to a cell that contains a formula, you won't see the formula in the formula bar when you select that cell. Unless you've also used the ;;;; format described in Chapter 3 to hide the formula display, however, you will see the result of the formula in the spreadsheet.

Use the Cell Protection command to assign the Locked attribute, the Hidden attribute, or both, to any cell or range in the worksheet or to remove those attributes from any cell. When you choose this command, you'll see the dialog box shown in Figure 8-39. To lock or hide a cell or range, select that cell or range, choose the Cell Protection command, and select the check box next to the attribute you want to assign. To remove an attribute, simply deselect the appropriate box.

FIGURE 8-39. *Use the Cell Protection dialog box to turn protection on or off for individual cells.*

Unless you use the Cell Protection command to change their attributes, every cell in the worksheet is locked but not hidden. Even though every cell in a newly created worksheet is assigned the Locked attribute, the worksheet as a whole is unprotected. In order for cell protection to take effect, you must choose the Protect Document command from the Options menu to protect the entire worksheet. Protecting the worksheet activates the Locked and Hidden attributes that have been assigned to the cells of the worksheet. You can think of the Protect Document command as a master switch that controls the protection status of all the cells in a worksheet.

The Protect Document command

Because every cell in a new worksheet is automatically assigned the Locked attribute, all you have to do to protect the worksheet from accidental changes is use the Protect Document command on the Options menu. When you choose this command, Microsoft Excel displays the dialog box shown in Figure 8-40. This dialog box lets you protect the worksheet and gives you the option of specifying a password that will prevent someone else from unprotecting what you've protected.

FIGURE 8-40. *Use the Protect Document dialog box to activate the Locked and Hidden cell-protection attributes.*

If you type a password before you select OK, you can make it almost impossible for anyone who doesn't know the password to unprotect the worksheet. The password can be as many as 255 characters and can contain any character. However, you'll usually want the password to be short and to contain characters that are easy to remember.

A word of caution: Entering a password in the Protect Document dialog box protects your document from being altered, not from being opened. A password entered in the Protect Document dialog box is not the same as a password entered in the Save Worksheet as dialog box, which prevents any unauthorized opening of the document.

You can protect the worksheet window itself by choosing the Windows option from the Protect Document dialog box. This option prevents moving, resizing, or hiding the document's windows. If you want Microsoft Excel to protect the worksheet but not the windows, select only the Contents check box.

Most of the time, you won't want every cell in a worksheet to be locked. Although you may want to protect every cell that contains an important formula, you'll want to leave a few cells unlocked so that you can change variables or enter new information. For this reason, you'll usually use the Cell Protection command to unlock a few cells before you use the Protect Document command.

In addition to activating the protection attributes of all the cells in the worksheet, protecting the worksheet disables many of Microsoft Excel's commands, including all commands on the Format menu, all commands on the Edit menu except Copy, and the Paste Name, Reference, Define Name, Create Names, Apply Names, Replace, and Select Special commands on the Formula menu. This is because the Protect Document command makes it impossible to clear any cell in the worksheet, to delete rows or columns, to assign or remove range names, or to change the format or protection attribute of any cell.

Unless you use the Info window to monitor the status of the cells in your worksheet, Microsoft Excel does not give you any kind of constant on-screen indication of the protection status of a cell. However, if you use the Display command from the Options menu to deactivate gridlines in the worksheet, Microsoft Excel will continue to display a horizontal gridline below every unlocked cell in the worksheet. In Figure 8-41, for example, only cells B5:E13 are unlocked. Because we've used Display to turn off gridlines, Microsoft Excel has removed the grid from the screen. However, gridlines still appear beneath the unlocked cells.

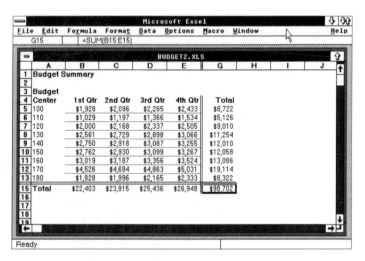

FIGURE 8-41. *Even though we deactivated the Gridlines setting, gridline displays remain below unlocked cells.*

Unprotecting the worksheet

If you pull down the Options menu when a worksheet is protected, you'll see that the Protect Document command has changed to Unprotect Document. When you choose this command, Microsoft Excel deactivates the protection attributes of all the cells in the worksheet and reactivates all the menu commands.

If you supplied a password when you protected the worksheet, Microsoft Excel will not unprotect the worksheet until you type that password. If you type the wrong password, you'll see the message *Incorrect password*. The password you type must match the worksheet's protection password in every detail, including case. For example, if the worksheet's password is aaaa, you must type aaaa; AAAA or Aaaa won't work.

9

Printing the Worksheet

Microsoft Excel makes it easy to produce polished, professional-looking reports from a worksheet. In this chapter, we'll show you how to select a printer using the Printer Setup command and how to use the Page Setup command to define the layout of your printed pages. Then we'll show you how to restrict your print range, define print titles, and control awkward page breaks with the printing commands from the Options menu. We'll talk about Microsoft Excel's Print command and preview capabilities, and then we'll look at two print-related utility applications: Spooler and Control Panel.

In this chapter, we'll concentrate on printing worksheet reports. However, all the techniques described here also apply to macro sheets. When we discuss charting in Chapter 13, we'll show you a few more tricks and techniques that will enable you to produce high-quality printed charts and graphs as well.

Selecting a printer

Microsoft Excel allows you to install a variety of printers and plotters. If you installed more than one printer when you ran the Setup program, you must identify which printer you want to use the first time you print (or whenever you want to change printers). If you installed only one printer, you won't have to select a printer, but you may still need to use the Printer Setup command to give Microsoft Excel information about a particular printing job.

The Printer Setup command

To tell Microsoft Excel the kind of printer or plotter you're using, choose the Printer Setup command from the File menu. Microsoft Excel will present you with a dialog box like the one in Figure 9-1, with a list of the printers you installed when you ran the Setup program. Highlight the name of the printer or plotter you plan to use. Then use the Setup option to define how you want the report to be oriented on the paper, the quality of the print job, and what type of paper you're using. When you choose the Setup button, another dialog box will appear on the screen. The contents of this dialog box depend on which printer name you highlighted in the Printer Setup dialog box. If you selected an ink-jet printer or a dot-matrix printer, such as the Epson FX-80, you'll see a dialog box like the one in Figure 9-2. If you selected a laser printer, such as the Apple LaserWriter or the HP LaserJet, you'll see a dialog box like the one in Figure 9-3.

FIGURE 9-1. *Use the Printer Setup dialog box to choose a printer.*

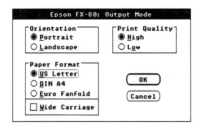

FIGURE 9-2. *When you select a dot-matrix printer in the Printer Setup dialog box and then choose the Setup button, you see a dialog box similar to this one.*

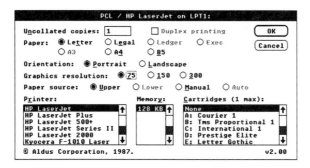

FIGURE 9-3. *You see a dialog box similar to this one when you select a laser printer and then choose the Setup button.*

The dialog box Microsoft Excel displays may not look exactly like either of those shown in Figures 9-2 and 9-3. You may see more or fewer options, and the options may not appear in the same order or location in the dialog box. We'll explain all the options that can appear in these dialog boxes, beginning with those in the smaller box—the one you see when you select a non-laser printer.

Setup options for non-laser printers

As we just mentioned, when you choose to use a non-laser printer such as a dot-matrix printer or an ink-jet printer, your Setup dialog box looks like the one in Figure 9-2. Let's take a closer look at each of the options in this dialog box.

The Orientation options. The Orientation setting tells Microsoft Excel whether you want your report printed vertically or horizontally. The term *Portrait* describes normal, horizontal printing; the term *Landscape* describes vertical printing. Figure 9-4 shows a sample page printed in Portrait mode. Portrait is the default setting, and you'll probably use it most of the time.

When you select Landscape orientation, Microsoft Excel prints the worksheet so that each line runs lengthwise on the page. Figure 9-5 shows a page printed in Landscape mode. The Landscape option is useful for printing worksheets that are wider than they are high on 8½-by-11-inch paper. For example, to print a worksheet 15 columns wide but only 8 rows deep, you could use the Landscape option to print the whole model on one sheet of paper.

The Print Quality options. The Print Quality setting determines how "crisply" your printer prints a document. Print quality is generally measured by resolution, or the number of dots per inch (dpi). The High option produces well-defined print, with high resolution; the Low option produces lower-quality print, with lower resolution. The speed at which your printer prints varies inversely with the quality of the print: When you select High, Microsoft Excel prints slowly; when you select Low, Microsoft Excel prints more quickly.

BUDGET88.XLS

	A	B	C	D	E
1				Budget 1988	
2					
3		Code	Description	January	February
4	ACTUAL EXPENSES				
5		Employees	(E)		
6		E 101		$1,300	$1,234
7		E 102		$850	$390
8		E 103		$2,105	$565
9		E 104		$970	$1,300
10		E 105		$550	$2,100
11		E 106		$650	$870
12		Subtotal		$6,425	$6,459
13					
14		Facilities			
15		F 201	Rent	$1,200	$1,200
16		F 202	Utilities	$250	$250
17		F 203	Phone	$205	$350
18		F 204	Maintenance	$150	$105
19		Subtotal		$1,805	$1,905
20					
21		Transportation			
22		T 101		$1,300	$1,234
23		T 102		$850	$390
24		T 103		$2,105	$565
25		T 104		$970	$1,300
26		T 105		$550	$2,100
27		T 106		$650	$870
28		T 107		$970	$1,300
29		Subtotal		$7,395	$7,759
30					
31		Shipping			
32		S 201	Materials	$125	$125
33		S 202	Freight In	$250	$250
34		S 203	Freight Out	$205	$350
35		Subtotal		$580	$725
36					
37		Miscellaneous			
38		M 301	Office	$1,200	$1,200
39		M 302	Paper	$250	$250
40		M 303	Petty Cash	$205	$350
41		M 304	Taxes	$150	$105
42		Subtotal		$1,805	$1,905
43					
44		Commissions			
45		Rep 01		$1,300	$1,234
46		Rep 02		$850	$390
47		Rep 03		$2,105	$565

Page 1

FIGURE 9-4. *This page was printed in Portrait mode.*

The Paper Format options. The Paper Format options define the size of the sheets of paper on which you'll be printing. Simply select the option that matches the paper you'll be using.

Option	Size
US Letter	8 1/2 by 11 inches
DIN A4	210 by 297 millimeters
Euro Fanfold	8 1/4 by 12 inches

The Printing options. For some printers, the Setup dialog box displays two Printing options: Bidirectional and Unidirectional. If your printer normally prints in a bidirectional fashion—that is, both while the print head is moving from left to right and while it is moving from right to left—select the Bidirectional option,

BUDGET88.XLS

	A	B	C	D	E	F	G
1				Budget 1988			
2							
3		Code	Description	January	February	March	April
4	ACTUAL EXPENSES						
5		Employees	(E)				
6		E 101		$1,300	$1,234	$955	$895
7		E 102		$850	$390	$455	$566
8		E 103		$2,105	$565	$670	$705
9		E 104		$970	$1,300	$1,050	$1,145
10		E 105		$550	$2,100	$1,680	$1,400
11		E 106		$650	$870	$967	$1,000
12		Subtotal		$6,425	$6,459	$5,777	$5,711
13							
14		Facilities					
15		F 201	Rent	$1,200	$1,200	$1,200	$1,200
16		F 202	Utilities	$250	$250	$250	$250
17		F 203	Phone	$205	$350	$175	$255
18		F 204	Maintenance	$150	$105	$75	$85
19		Subtotal		$1,805	$1,905	$1,700	$1,790
20							
21		Transportation					
22		T 101		$1,300	$1,234	$955	$895
23		T 102		$850	$390	$455	$566
24		T 103		$2,105	$565	$670	$705
25		T 104		$970	$1,300	$1,050	$1,145
26		T 105		$550	$2,100	$1,680	$1,400
27		T 106		$650	$870	$967	$1,000
28		T 107		$970	$1,300	$1,050	$1,145
29		Subtotal		$7,395	$7,759	$6,827	$6,856
30							
31		Shipping					
32		S 201	Materials	$125	$125	$125	$125
33		S 202	Freight In	$250	$250	$250	$250

Page 1

FIGURE 9-5. *This page was printed in Landscape mode.*

which allows for much faster printing. If your printer can print only while the print head is moving from left to right, select Unidirectional.

Setup options for laser printers

Now let's take a look at the options available in the Setup dialog box for laser printers. Some of these options are identical to the ones in the dialog box for non-laser printers, although the option names are somewhat different.

The Uncollated copies option. Use the Uncollated copies option to tell Microsoft Excel how many copies of each worksheet page to print. As the name implies, this option does not collate document pages during the print operation. Instead, it prints the specified number of copies of the first page before moving on to the second page. Thus, if you ask for five uncollated copies of a multipage document, you'll get five copies of page 1, then five copies of page 2, and so forth.

The Duplex printing option. If your printer is capable of duplex printing—that is, printing on both sides of the page—you can select the Duplex printing option to invoke that feature.

The Paper options. The Paper options in Figure 9-3 work much like the Paper Format options we described for non-laser printers. Depending on the type of printer you've selected, you can choose from the following paper sizes:

Option	Size
Letter	8 $1/2$ by 11 inches
Legal	8 $1/2$ by 14 inches
Ledger	11 by 17 inches
Half Letter	4 $1/4$ by 5 $1/2$ inches
Exec	7 $1/4$ by 10 $1/2$ inches
A3	285 by 375 millimeters
A4	210 by 297 millimeters
B5	182 by 257 millimeters

The Orientation options. Similarly, the Orientation options in the dialog box shown in Figure 9-3 work like the Orientation options for non-laser printers: Use Landscape to print lengthwise on the page and Portrait for normal, horizontal printing.

The Graphics resolution options. The Graphics resolution options let you control the quality of your printed output. These values represent the number of dots per inch your printer will produce. The higher the dpi value, the crisper the quality of your printed output. However, higher quality settings may mean that your document will take longer to print. Thus, you may want to use a lower Graphics resolution setting for drafts of your documents and switch to a higher setting to produce the final printed output.

The Paper source options. If your printer uses paper trays, you can use the Paper source options to specify which tray contains the paper you want to use. Alternatively, you can choose the Manual option to hand-feed the paper into your printer. Some printers offer only Manual and Auto feed options, which allow you to determine whether the paper is to be loaded automatically or hand-fed into the printer.

The Printer, Memory, and Cartridges options. If you've installed a laser printer, you'll see a list of available printers in the Printer list box. The contents of this list vary according to the printer types you selected when you installed Microsoft Excel. Depending on the type of printer you select from this list, you may also see Memory and Cartridges list boxes. Use these list boxes to tell Microsoft Excel the amount of memory available in your printer and which font cartridges you've installed.

The Page Setup command

The Page Setup command on the File menu lets you control the layout of your printed reports. When you choose this command, you'll see a dialog box like the one in Figure 9-6. This box lists all your page-layout options. You can create a header across the top of the page and a footer across the bottom, change the page margins, and indicate whether row and column headers and gridlines should appear on your printed report. Let's consider each of these options in more detail.

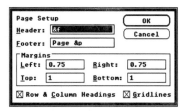

FIGURE 9-6. *Use the Page Setup dialog box to define your page layout.*

The Header and Footer options

The Page Setup command allows you to insert headers and footers in your printed reports. A header is a single line of text printed one-half inch from the top of each page of a report; a footer is a single line of text printed one-half inch from the bottom of each page.

Microsoft Excel automatically creates both a header and a footer for your reports. The default header, &f, instructs Microsoft Excel to print the name of the document file at the top of each page. The default footer, Page &p, tells Microsoft Excel to print the word *Page*, followed by the page number, at the bottom of each page. Microsoft Excel centers headers and footers unless you tell it to do otherwise.

The symbols &f and &p are among 12 special codes you can use in headers and footers. These codes are summarized in Table 9-1.

Table 9-1. Header and footer codes for the Page Setup command.

Code	Action
&l	Left-aligns subsequent characters
&c	Centers subsequent characters (the default)
&r	Right-aligns subsequent characters
&p	Includes page number
&p+*number*	Includes page number and adds *number* to it (allows you to change starting page numbers)
&p–*number*	Includes page number and subtracts *number* from it (allows you to change starting page numbers)
&d	Includes current date in mm/dd/yy format
&t	Includes current time in hh:mm AM/PM format
&f	Includes document name
&&	Includes single ampersand (&)
&b	Prints subsequent characters in bold type
&i	Prints subsequent characters in italic type

You can use these header and footer symbols alone, or you can mix and match them with regular text and with other symbols. For example, you can change the default header to

&l&f

to print the document name aligned at the left margin of the printed page, or you can change this header to

&b&l&f

to print the document name in bold type starting at the left margin.

The typeface and alignment options apply to each individual portion of the header. Thus, you can format each portion of the header and footer separately, to emphasize key information. For example, the header

&l&i&d&c&b&f&r&i&t

prints the date, left-aligned and in italic, followed by the filename, centered and in bold, and the time, right-aligned and in italic:

7/10/86   **Sheet1**   *9:08 AM*

As you can see in Figure 9-6, when you choose Page Setup from the File menu, Microsoft Excel highlights the Header edit bar. To print your document without a header, press the Del key. To enter a new header, simply begin typing in the edit bar. To use the existing header as the basis for your new one, edit the header just as you would edit a formula in the formula bar. For example, if you want to change &f, Microsoft Excel's standard header, to &l&f, position the insertion point in the space before the & in the existing header and type &l.

You create a new footer in exactly the same way you create a header. The only difference is that you begin creating a footer by selecting the Footer edit bar instead of the Header edit bar.

The Margins options

The Page Setup dialog box also gives you control over the left, right, top, and bottom margins of your printed reports. In Microsoft Excel, margins are expressed in inches. As shown in Figure 9-6, the default left and right margins are 0.75 inch, and the default top and bottom margins are 1 inch.

The Row & Column Headings and Gridlines options

The Page Setup dialog box includes options that determine whether row numbers, column letters, and gridlines appear in your printed report. As you learned in

Chapter 3, you can suppress the display of gridlines and of row and column headers on your screen by deselecting those options in the Display dialog box. The printing of these elements, however, is completely independent of their display on the screen. Therefore, you must use the Gridlines and Row & Column Headings options in the Page Setup dialog box to control the appearance of these items in your printed report.

Typically, you'll want to print your rough drafts with the Row & Column Headings and Gridline options active. These elements make it easy to identify the location of any entry in the worksheet. When you print the final version, however, you'll probably want to turn these options off so that the row and column headings don't clutter the report.

Figure 9-7 shows a sample worksheet printed without gridlines or row and column headers.

```
                              BUDGET88.XLS


                          Budget 1988

           Code        Description   January   February    March    April      May
ACTUAL EXPENSES
        Employees (E)
        E 101                        $1,300    $1,234      $955     $895     $1,045
        E 102                        $850      $390        $455     $566     $700
        E 103                        $2,105    $565        $670     $705     $805
        E 104                        $970      $1,300      $1,050   $1,145   $1,123
        E 105                        $550      $2,100      $1,680   $1,400   $1,350
        E 106                        $650      $870        $967     $1,000   $1,200
        Subtotal                     $6,425    $6,459      $5,777   $5,711   $6,223

        Facilities
        F 201       Rent             $1,200    $1,200      $1,200   $1,200   $1,200
        F 202       Utilities        $250      $250        $250     $250     $250
        F 203       Phone            $205      $350        $175     $255     $305
        F 204       Maintenance      $150      $105        $75      $85      $200
        Subtotal                     $1,805    $1,905      $1,700   $1,790   $1,955

        Transportation
        T 101                        $1,300    $1,234      $955     $895     $1,045
        T 102                        $850      $390        $455     $566     $700
        T 103                        $2,105    $565        $670     $705     $805
        T 104                        $970      $1,300      $1,050   $1,145   $1,123
        T 105                        $550      $2,100      $1,680   $1,400   $1,350
        T 106                        $650      $870        $967     $1,000   $1,200
        T 107                        $970      $1,300      $1,050   $1,145   $1,123
        Subtotal                     $7,395    $7,759      $6,827   $6,856   $7,346

        Shipping
        S 201       Materials        $125      $125        $125     $125     $125
        S 202       Freight In       $250      $250        $250     $250     $250
        S 203       Freight Out      $205      $350        $175     $255     $305



                          Page 1
```

FIGURE 9-7. *We printed this report with the Row & Column Headings and Gridlines options turned off.*

If you select Draft Quality in the Print dialog box, Microsoft Excel won't print gridlines, regardless of whether the Gridlines option is active in the Page Setup dialog box. (We'll talk more about the Print command later in this chapter.)

The Options menu printing commands

In addition to the File menu's Page Setup and Printer Setup commands, three commands on the Options menu affect the way your worksheet is printed: Set Print Area, Set Print Titles, and Set Page Break.

The Set Print Area command

Normally, when you choose the Print command, Microsoft Excel prints the entire area of your worksheet that contains entries. The Set Print Area command lets you print only selected sections of your worksheet. To define a print area, simply select the cells you want to print and choose Set Print Area from the Options menu. If you select multiple discontinuous ranges to be printed, Microsoft Excel will print the ranges in the order you selected them, each area on a separate page.

Microsoft Excel defines the print area you select as a range named Print_Area. You can edit or delete the range name by using the Define Name command from the Formula menu. If you delete the range Print_Area, Microsoft Excel will again print your entire worksheet when you use the Print command.

The Set Print Titles command

When you print a large report, Microsoft Excel breaks that report into page-sized sections based on the current Page Setup settings. The width of your columns, the height of your rows, and the size of the type you select also affect the number of rows and columns that can fit on each page.

Although Microsoft Excel's automatic page-break capability is a big help, it can lead to a problem. Most of the time, the column and row labels that identify the contents of your worksheet are located in only the top few rows and leftmost columns of your worksheet. For example, in the worksheet shown in Figure 9-8, the row labels (division and product names) are in column A and the column labels (1/1/87, 2/1/87, and so on) are in rows 3 and 4. When Microsoft Excel breaks this large report into pages, these labels are not printed on every page. For example, in Figure 9-8 only the first page, which includes the upper left corner of the worksheet, has both row labels and column labels. Page 2 has row labels but no column labels, and page 3 has column labels but no row labels. Page 4 has no labels at all, which makes it next to impossible to figure out what the numbers on that page mean.

SALES.XLS

	A	B	C	D	E	F	G	H
1	Monthly Sales: 1/1/87 through 1/1/88							
2								
3	Division/							
4	Product	1/1/87	2/1/87	3/1/87	4/1/87	5/1/87	6/1/87	7/1/87
5								
6	Division 1							
7	Wombats	$1,129	$1,177	$1,225	$1,273	$1,321	$1,369	$1,417
8	Woofers	$2,001	$2,035	$2,069	$2,103	$2,137	$2,171	$2,205
9	Whatzits	$438	$451	$464	$477	$490	$503	$516
10	Widgets	$923	$915	$907	$899	$891	$883	$875
11	Total	$4,491	$4,578	$4,665	$4,752	$4,839	$4,926	$5,013
12								
13								
14	Division 2							
15	Wombats	$1,369	$1,400	$1,431	$1,462	$1,493	$1,524	$1,555
16	Woofers	$2,171	$2,202	$2,233	$2,264	$2,295	$2,326	$2,357
17	Whatzits	$503	$534	$565	$596	$627	$658	$689
18	Widgets	$883	$914	$945	$976	$1,007	$1,038	$1,069
19	Total	$4,926	$5,050	$5,174	$5,298	$5,422	$5,546	$5,670
20								
21								
22	Division 3							
23	Wombats	$1,273	$1,281	$1,289	$1,297	$1,305	$1,313	$1,321
24	Woofers	$2,103	$2,111	$2,119	$2,127	$2,135	$2,143	$2,151
25	Whatzits	$477	$485	$493	$501	$509	$517	$525
26	Widgets	$899	$907	$915	$923	$931	$939	$947
27	Total	$4,752	$4,784	$4,816	$4,848	$4,880	$4,912	$4,944
28								
29								
30	Division 4							
31	Wombats	$1,177	$1,170	$1,163	$1,156	$1,149	$1,142	$1,135
32	Woofers	$2,035	$2,028	$2,021	$2,014	$2,007	$2,000	$1,993
33	Whatzits	$451	$444	$437	$430	$423	$416	$409

Page 1

SALES.XLS

	A	B	C	D	E	F	G	H
34	Widgets	$915	$908	$901	$894	$887	$880	$873
35	Total	$4,578	$4,550	$4,522	$4,494	$4,466	$4,438	$4,410
36								
37								
38	Division 5							
39	Wombats	$1,465	$1,469	$1,473	$1,477	$1,481	$1,485	$1,489
40	Woofers	$2,239	$2,243	$2,247	$2,251	$2,255	$2,259	$2,263
41	Whatzits	$529	$533	$537	$541	$545	$549	$553
42	Widgets	$867	$871	$875	$879	$883	$887	$891
43	Total	$5,100	$5,116	$5,132	$5,148	$5,164	$5,180	$5,196
44								
45								
46	Division 6							
47	Wombats	$1,225	$1,237	$1,249	$1,261	$1,273	$1,285	$1,297
48	Woofers	$2,069	$2,081	$2,093	$2,105	$2,117	$2,129	$2,141
49	Whatzits	$464	$476	$488	$500	$512	$524	$536
50	Widgets	$907	$919	$931	$943	$955	$967	$979
51	Total	$4,665	$4,713	$4,761	$4,809	$4,857	$4,905	$4,953
52								
53								
54	Division 7							
55	Wombats	$1,465	$1,476	$1,487	$1,498	$1,509	$1,520	$1,531
56	Woofers	$2,239	$2,250	$2,261	$2,272	$2,283	$2,294	$2,305
57	Whatzits	$529	$540	$551	$562	$573	$584	$595
58	Widgets	$867	$878	$889	$900	$911	$922	$933
59	Total	$5,100	$5,144	$5,188	$5,232	$5,276	$5,320	$5,364
60								
61	Combined Sales: All Divisions							
62	Wombats	$9,103	$9,210	$9,317	$9,424	$9,531	$9,638	$9,745
63	Woofers	$14,857	$14,950	$15,043	$15,136	$15,229	$15,322	$15,415
64	Whatzits	$3,391	$3,463	$3,535	$3,607	$3,679	$3,751	$3,823
65	Widgets	$6,261	$6,312	$6,363	$6,414	$6,465	$6,516	$6,567
66	Total	$33,612	$33,935	$34,258	$34,581	$34,904	$35,227	$35,550

Page 2

FIGURE 9-8. *This sample printout shows Microsoft Excel's default placement of row and column labels.* (continued)

FIGURE 9.8. *continued*

SALES.XLS

	I	J	K	L	M	N	O
1							
2							
3							
4	8/1/87	9/1/87	10/1/87	11/1/87	12/1/87	1/1/88	Total
5							
6							
7	$1,465	$1,513	$1,561	$1,609	$1,657	$1,705	$18,421
8	$2,239	$2,273	$2,307	$2,341	$2,375	$2,409	$28,665
9	$529	$542	$555	$568	$581	$594	$6,708
10	$867	$859	$851	$843	$835	$827	$11,375
11	$5,100	$5,187	$5,274	$5,361	$5,448	$5,535	$65,169
12							
13							
14							
15	$1,586	$1,617	$1,648	$1,679	$1,710	$1,741	$20,215
16	$2,388	$2,419	$2,450	$2,481	$2,512	$2,543	$30,641
17	$720	$751	$782	$813	$844	$875	$8,957
18	$1,100	$1,131	$1,162	$1,193	$1,224	$1,255	$13,897
19	$5,794	$5,918	$6,042	$6,166	$6,290	$6,414	$73,710
20							
21							
22							
23	$1,329	$1,337	$1,345	$1,353	$1,361	$1,369	$17,173
24	$2,159	$2,167	$2,175	$2,183	$2,191	$2,199	$27,963
25	$533	$541	$549	$557	$565	$573	$6,825
26	$955	$963	$971	$979	$987	$995	$12,311
27	$4,976	$5,008	$5,040	$5,072	$5,104	$5,136	$64,272
28							
29							
30							
31	$1,128	$1,121	$1,114	$1,107	$1,100	$1,093	$14,755
32	$1,986	$1,979	$1,972	$1,965	$1,958	$1,951	$25,909
33	$402	$395	$388	$381	$374	$367	$5,317

Page 3

SALES.XLS

	I	J	K	L	M	N	O
34	$866	$859	$852	$845	$838	$831	$11,349
35	$4,382	$4,354	$4,326	$4,298	$4,270	$4,242	$57,330
36							
37							
38							
39	$1,493	$1,497	$1,501	$1,505	$1,509	$1,513	$19,357
40	$2,267	$2,271	$2,275	$2,279	$2,283	$2,287	$29,419
41	$557	$561	$565	$569	$573	$577	$7,189
42	$895	$899	$903	$907	$911	$915	$11,583
43	$5,212	$5,228	$5,244	$5,260	$5,276	$5,292	$67,548
44							
45							
46							
47	$1,309	$1,321	$1,333	$1,345	$1,357	$1,369	$16,861
48	$2,153	$2,165	$2,177	$2,189	$2,201	$2,213	$27,833
49	$548	$560	$572	$584	$596	$608	$6,968
50	$991	$1,003	$1,015	$1,027	$1,039	$1,051	$12,727
51	$5,001	$5,049	$5,097	$5,145	$5,193	$5,241	$64,389
52							
53							
54							
55	$1,542	$1,553	$1,564	$1,575	$1,586	$1,597	$19,903
56	$2,316	$2,327	$2,338	$2,349	$2,360	$2,371	$29,965
57	$606	$617	$628	$639	$650	$661	$7,735
58	$944	$955	$966	$977	$988	$999	$12,129
59	$5,408	$5,452	$5,496	$5,540	$5,584	$5,628	$69,732
60							
61							
62	$9,852	$9,959	$10,066	$10,173	$10,280	$10,387	$126,685
63	$15,508	$15,601	$15,694	$15,787	$15,880	$15,973	$200,395
64	$3,895	$3,967	$4,039	$4,111	$4,183	$4,255	$49,699
65	$6,618	$6,669	$6,720	$6,771	$6,822	$6,873	$85,371
66	$35,873	$36,196	$36,519	$36,842	$37,165	$37,488	$462,150

Page 4

Fortunately, the Set Print Titles command on the Options menu lets you print the contents of one or more rows, one or more columns, or a combination of rows and columns on every page of a report. Suppose you want to print the contents of rows 3 and 4 and column A on all four pages of the sample worksheet report in Figure 9-8. To do this, first select rows 3 and 4 and column A. To make your selection with a mouse, select rows 3 and 4 and hold down the Ctrl key while you click the header for column A. To select with the keyboard, select cell A3 and press Ctrl-Spacebar to select all of column A; then press Shift-F8 to enter Add mode and press Shift-Spacebar to select all of row 3; finally, press Shift and the Down arrow key to select all of row 4. After selecting rows 3 and 4 and column A, choose the Set Print Titles command from the Options menu.

You must select entire rows and columns for your print-titles range; Microsoft Excel does not accept partial rows or columns. Although you can select multiple columns and rows for your print-titles area, the rows and columns you select must be adjacent. In other words, you can include rows 1 and 2 and columns C and D in your print-titles range, but you can't use rows 1 and 3 or columns A and C. If you attempt to select nonadjacent rows or columns, Microsoft Excel presents an alert box with the message *Print title is not valid*.

Like the print area, the rows and columns you select for print titles are stored as a named range, this time with the name *Print_Titles*. You can edit or delete the print-titles range through the Define Name dialog box.

When you use the Set Print Titles command, you must be sure your print area doesn't overlap the print-titles range; otherwise, you'll have two sets of row and column titles on the first page of your printed report. The effects can be quite confusing, as you can see in Figure 9-9. In this sample report, we specified rows 3 and 4 and column A as the print-titles range. However, we also included these cells in our print area. As you can see, Microsoft Excel has printed the contents of rows 3 and 4 and column A once in response to the Set Print Titles command and a second time in response to our print-area specification.

Remember, the default print area includes the entire active worksheet. Unless you use the Set Print Area command to exclude the print-title cells from the print area, Microsoft Excel will assume these cells are to be printed twice. The printed report in Figure 9-10 shows the same worksheet with a print area of B5:O66. This print area includes all the cells below and to the right of the print-titles range, so the cells in rows 1 and 2 are not included in the printed report. Fortunately, these rows contain only the title used to identify the document, and we can easily place this information in the page header in the Page Setup dialog box. As you develop a worksheet, however, you should keep this restriction in mind. If you plan to use print titles, be sure you don't place important information above or to the left of the rows and columns in your print-titles range.

SALES.XLS

	A	A	B	C	D	E	F
3	Division/	Division/					
4	Product	Product	1/1/87	2/1/87	3/1/87	4/1/87	5/1/87
1	Monthly Sales	Monthly Sales: 1/1/87 through 1/1/88					
2							
3	Division/	Division/					
4	Product	Product	1/1/87	2/1/87	3/1/87	4/1/87	5/1/87
5							
6	Division 1	Division 1					
7	Wombats	Wombats	$1,129	$1,177	$1,225	$1,273	$1,321
8	Woofers	Woofers	$2,001	$2,035	$2,069	$2,103	$2,137
9	Whatzits	Whatzits	$438	$451	$464	$477	$490
10	Widgets	Widgets	$923	$915	$907	$899	$891
11	Total	Total	$4,491	$4,578	$4,665	$4,752	$4,839
12							
13							
14	Division 2	Division 2					
15	Wombats	Wombats	$1,369	$1,400	$1,431	$1,462	$1,493
16	Woofers	Woofers	$2,171	$2,202	$2,233	$2,264	$2,295
17	Whatzits	Whatzits	$503	$534	$565	$596	$627
18	Widgets	Widgets	$883	$914	$945	$976	$1,007
19	Total	Total	$4,926	$5,050	$5,174	$5,298	$5,422
20							
21							
22	Division 3	Division 3					
23	Wombats	Wombats	$1,273	$1,281	$1,289	$1,297	$1,305
24	Woofers	Woofers	$2,103	$2,111	$2,119	$2,127	$2,135
25	Whatzits	Whatzits	$477	$485	$493	$501	$509
26	Widgets	Widgets	$899	$907	$915	$923	$931
27	Total	Total	$4,752	$4,784	$4,816	$4,848	$4,880
28							
29							
30	Division 4	Division 4					
31	Wombats	Wombats	$1,177	$1,170	$1,163	$1,156	$1,149

Page 1

FIGURE 9-9. *If your print titles and print area overlap, the results can be confusing.*

In the example in Figure 9-10, the print-titles range and the print area occupy adjacent rows and columns, but this need not be the case. Microsoft Excel allows you to select any rows or columns as your print-titles range and any range of cells as your print area. Thus, you can include widely separated areas of the worksheet in the same printed report. For example, suppose you want to print only cells K61:O66 of the Sales worksheet. Because the labels in rows 3 and 4 and column A are not included in the print area, they will not appear on the printed report. To include the labels in the print area, simply select rows 3 and 4 and column A, choose the Set Print Titles command, then select cells K61:O66, and choose the Set Print Area command. The resulting printed report will look like Figure 9-11.

SALES.XLS

	A	B	C	D	E	F	G	H
3	Division/							
4	Product	1/1/87	2/1/87	3/1/87	4/1/87	5/1/87	6/1/87	7/1/87
5								
6	Division 1							
7	Wombats	$1,129	$1,177	$1,225	$1,273	$1,321	$1,369	$1,417
8	Woofers	$2,001	$2,035	$2,069	$2,103	$2,137	$2,171	$2,205
9	Whatzits	$438	$451	$464	$477	$490	$503	$516
10	Widgets	$923	$915	$907	$899	$891	$883	$875
11	Total	$4,491	$4,578	$4,665	$4,752	$4,839	$4,926	$5,013
12								
13								
14	Division 2							
15	Wombats	$1,369	$1,400	$1,431	$1,462	$1,493	$1,524	$1,555
16	Woofers	$2,171	$2,202	$2,233	$2,264	$2,295	$2,326	$2,357
17	Whatzits	$503	$534	$565	$596	$627	$658	$689
18	Widgets	$883	$914	$945	$976	$1,007	$1,038	$1,069
19	Total	$4,926	$5,050	$5,174	$5,298	$5,422	$5,546	$5,670
20								
21								
22	Division 3							
23	Wombats	$1,273	$1,281	$1,289	$1,297	$1,305	$1,313	$1,321
24	Woofers	$2,103	$2,111	$2,119	$2,127	$2,135	$2,143	$2,151
25	Whatzits	$477	$485	$493	$501	$509	$517	$525
26	Widgets	$899	$907	$915	$923	$931	$939	$947
27	Total	$4,752	$4,784	$4,816	$4,848	$4,880	$4,912	$4,944
28								
29								
30	Division 4							
31	Wombats	$1,177	$1,170	$1,163	$1,156	$1,149	$1,142	$1,135
32	Woofers	$2,035	$2,028	$2,021	$2,014	$2,007	$2,000	$1,993
33	Whatzits	$451	$444	$437	$430	$423	$416	$409
34	Widgets	$915	$908	$901	$894	$887	$880	$873
35	Total	$4,578	$4,550	$4,522	$4,494	$4,466	$4,438	$4,410

Page 1

SALES.XLS

	A	B	C	D	E	F	G	H
3	Division/							
4	Product	1/1/87	2/1/87	3/1/87	4/1/87	5/1/87	6/1/87	7/1/87
36								
37								
38	Division 5							
39	Wombats	$1,465	$1,469	$1,473	$1,477	$1,481	$1,485	$1,489
40	Woofers	$2,239	$2,243	$2,247	$2,251	$2,255	$2,259	$2,263
41	Whatzits	$529	$533	$537	$541	$545	$549	$553
42	Widgets	$867	$871	$875	$879	$883	$887	$891
43	Total	$5,100	$5,116	$5,132	$5,148	$5,164	$5,180	$5,196
44								
45								
46	Division 6							
47	Wombats	$1,225	$1,237	$1,249	$1,261	$1,273	$1,285	$1,297
48	Woofers	$2,069	$2,081	$2,093	$2,105	$2,117	$2,129	$2,141
49	Whatzits	$464	$476	$488	$500	$512	$524	$536
50	Widgets	$907	$919	$931	$943	$955	$967	$979
51	Total	$4,665	$4,713	$4,761	$4,809	$4,857	$4,905	$4,953
52								
53								
54	Division 7							
55	Wombats	$1,465	$1,476	$1,487	$1,498	$1,509	$1,520	$1,531
56	Woofers	$2,239	$2,250	$2,261	$2,272	$2,283	$2,294	$2,305
57	Whatzits	$529	$540	$551	$562	$573	$584	$595
58	Widgets	$867	$878	$889	$900	$911	$922	$933
59	Total	$5,100	$5,144	$5,188	$5,232	$5,276	$5,320	$5,364
60								
61	Combined Sales : All Divisions							
62	Wombats	$9,103	$9,210	$9,317	$9,424	$9,531	$9,638	$9,745
63	Woofers	$14,857	$14,950	$15,043	$15,136	$15,229	$15,322	$15,415
64	Whatzits	$3,391	$3,463	$3,535	$3,607	$3,679	$3,751	$3,823
65	Widgets	$6,261	$6,312	$6,363	$6,414	$6,465	$6,516	$6,567
66	Total	$33,612	$33,935	$34,258	$34,581	$34,904	$35,227	$35,550

Page 2

FIGURE 9-10. *This sample report contains row and column labels on each page.*

(continued)

FIGURE 9-10. *continued*

SALES.XLS

	A	I	J	K	L	M	N	O
3	Division/							
4	Product	8/1/87	9/1/87	10/1/87	11/1/87	12/1/87	1/1/88	Total
5								
6	Division 1							
7	Wombats	$1,465	$1,513	$1,561	$1,609	$1,657	$1,705	$18,421
8	Woofers	$2,239	$2,273	$2,307	$2,341	$2,375	$2,409	$28,665
9	Whatzits	$529	$542	$555	$568	$581	$594	$6,708
10	Widgets	$867	$859	$851	$843	$835	$827	$11,375
11	Total	$5,100	$5,187	$5,274	$5,361	$5,448	$5,535	$65,169
12								
13								
14	Division 2							
15	Wombats	$1,586	$1,617	$1,648	$1,679	$1,710	$1,741	$20,215
16	Woofers	$2,388	$2,419	$2,450	$2,481	$2,512	$2,543	$30,641
17	Whatzits	$720	$751	$782	$813	$844	$875	$8,957
18	Widgets	$1,100	$1,131	$1,162	$1,193	$1,224	$1,255	$13,897
19	Total	$5,794	$5,918	$6,042	$6,166	$6,290	$6,414	$73,710
20								
21								
22	Division 3							
23	Wombats	$1,329	$1,337	$1,345	$1,353	$1,361	$1,369	$17,173
24	Woofers	$2,159	$2,167	$2,175	$2,183	$2,191	$2,199	$27,963
25	Whatzits	$533	$541	$549	$557	$565	$573	$6,825
26	Widgets	$955	$963	$971	$979	$987	$995	$12,311
27	Total	$4,976	$5,008	$5,040	$5,072	$5,104	$5,136	$64,272
28								
29								
30	Division 4							
31	Wombats	$1,128	$1,121	$1,114	$1,107	$1,100	$1,093	$14,755
32	Woofers	$1,986	$1,979	$1,972	$1,965	$1,958	$1,951	$25,909
33	Whatzits	$402	$395	$388	$381	$374	$367	$5,317
34	Widgets	$866	$859	$852	$845	$838	$831	$11,349
35	Total	$4,382	$4,354	$4,326	$4,298	$4,270	$4,242	$57,330

Page 3

SALES.XLS

	A	I	J	K	L	M	N	O
3	Division/							
4	Product	8/1/87	9/1/87	10/1/87	11/1/87	12/1/87	1/1/88	Total
36								
37								
38	Division 5							
39	Wombats	$1,493	$1,497	$1,501	$1,505	$1,509	$1,513	$19,357
40	Woofers	$2,267	$2,271	$2,275	$2,279	$2,283	$2,287	$29,419
41	Whatzits	$557	$561	$565	$569	$573	$577	$7,189
42	Widgets	$895	$899	$903	$907	$911	$915	$11,583
43	Total	$5,212	$5,228	$5,244	$5,260	$5,276	$5,292	$67,548
44								
45								
46	Division 6							
47	Wombats	$1,309	$1,321	$1,333	$1,345	$1,357	$1,369	$16,861
48	Woofers	$2,153	$2,165	$2,177	$2,189	$2,201	$2,213	$27,833
49	Whatzits	$548	$560	$572	$584	$596	$608	$6,968
50	Widgets	$991	$1,003	$1,015	$1,027	$1,039	$1,051	$12,727
51	Total	$5,001	$5,049	$5,097	$5,145	$5,193	$5,241	$64,389
52								
53								
54	Division 7							
55	Wombats	$1,542	$1,553	$1,564	$1,575	$1,586	$1,597	$19,903
56	Woofers	$2,316	$2,327	$2,338	$2,349	$2,360	$2,371	$29,965
57	Whatzits	$606	$617	$628	$639	$650	$661	$7,735
58	Widgets	$944	$955	$966	$977	$988	$999	$12,129
59	Total	$5,408	$5,452	$5,496	$5,540	$5,584	$5,628	$69,732
60								
61	Combined Sales							
62	Wombats	$9,852	$9,959	$10,066	$10,173	$10,280	$10,387	$126,685
63	Woofers	$15,508	$15,601	$15,694	$15,787	$15,880	$15,973	$200,395
64	Whatzits	$3,895	$3,967	$4,039	$4,111	$4,183	$4,255	$49,699
65	Widgets	$6,618	$6,669	$6,720	$6,771	$6,822	$6,873	$85,371
66	Total	$35,873	$36,196	$36,519	$36,842	$37,165	$37,488	$462,150

Page 4

FIGURE 9-11. *We specified nonadjacent print-area and print-titles ranges and printed only a selected part of the worksheet.*

Notice that only the row labels in columns K through O appear in the printed report, even though the print-titles range includes all of rows 3 and 4. Similarly, only the labels in cells A61:A66 appear, even though all of column A was included in the print-titles range. Microsoft Excel matches the labels in the print-titles range with the corresponding columns and rows in the print area so that the titles and data are correctly aligned.

To cancel print titles, select the Define Name command from the Formula menu. When the dialog box appears, select Print_Titles and then select Delete. After you choose OK or press Enter, the print titles will be gone.

The Set Page Break command

As you know, when you print a report that is too large to fit on a single sheet of paper, Microsoft Excel breaks that report into page-sized sections based on the current settings in the Page Setup dialog box. As you can see in Figure 9-12, Microsoft Excel's automatic page breaks are indicated on the screen by dashed gridlines.

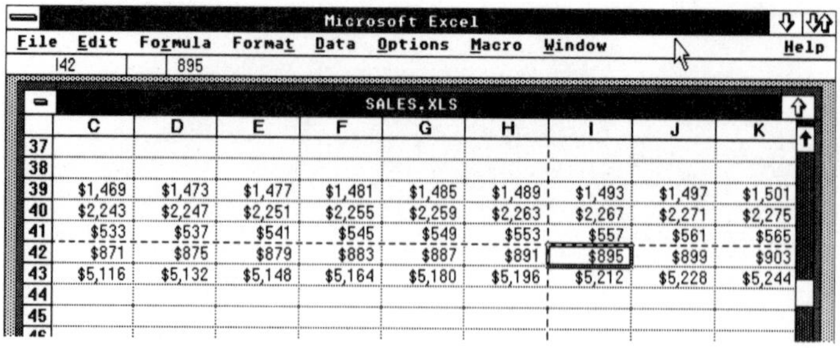

FIGURE 9-12. *Automatic page breaks are indicated on the screen with dashed lines.*

Frequently, you'll want to divide a report into pages yourself, rather than leave the decision to Microsoft Excel. You can use the Set Page Break command on the Options menu to place vertical and horizontal page breaks in your printed report.

For example, the report in Figure 9-13 spans cells A1:N56. As you can see, Microsoft Excel's automatic page breaks make this report a little awkward to read. The last five columns of data (plus the print-titles range) appear on pages 3 and 4 of the report. In addition, the first few rows of data for the 1989 summary portion of the budget are separated from the rest of the 1989 summary. To distribute the data in this four-page report more evenly, select cell H29 of the worksheet and choose Set Page Break from the Options menu. The Set Page Break command tells Microsoft Excel to insert forced page breaks above and to the left of the selected cell. As you can see in Figure 9-14, a forced page break is indicated on the screen by a darker dashed line in the worksheet. When you add a manual page break, Microsoft Excel adjusts the automatic page breaks in your document as well. Your worksheet will now be printed like Figure 9-15.

To remove a forced page break, select the cell below or to the right of the bold dashed line and choose Remove Page Break, which will have replaced the Set Page Break command on the Options menu. You can't remove Microsoft Excel's automatic page breaks.

If you want to add a horizontal page break without affecting the vertical breaks in your document, select the row with which you want to begin a new page, place the active cell in column A of that row, and choose the Set Page Break command. Microsoft Excel will insert the horizontal page break just above the row you selected. If you want to insert a vertical page break without affecting the horizontal pagination, select the column with which you want to begin the new page, place the active cell in row 1 of that column, and choose the Set Page Break command. The page break will occur to the left of the column you select.

	A	B	C	D	E	F	G	H	I
1	1988 BUDGET SUMMARY								
2									
3	Budget								
4	Code	1/1/88	2/1/88	3/1/88	4/1/88	5/1/88	6/1/88	7/1/88	8/1/88
5	100	$2,098	$1,685	$1,550	$2,008	$1,763	$1,472	$1,746	$1,804
6	150	$1,077	$861	$740	$986	$799	$1,058	$821	$909
7	200	$239	$195	$250	$239	$238	$166	$114	$175
8	250	$2,906	$2,838	$2,847	$2,314	$2,576	$2,391	$2,561	$2,495
9	300	$3,500	$3,500	$3,500	$3,500	$3,500	$3,500	$3,500	$3,500
10	350	$330	$234	$237	$262	$238	$277	$257	$248
11	400	$349	$298	$248	$318	$277	$281	$356	$290
12	450	$400	$311	$300	$364	$329	$279	$272	$292
13	500	$563	$180	$358	$511	$272	$232	$430	$345
14	550	$585	$594	$603	$612	$620	$629	$638	$626
15	600	$1,004	$823	$772	$467	$646	$423	$431	$525
16	650	$566	$180	$149	$157	$555	$150	$457	$375
17	700	$315	$109	$265	$71	$302	$299	$214	$274
18	750	$709	$179	$693	$454	$276	$193	$376	$349
19	800	$823	$574	$108	$404	$776	$557	$625	$689
20	850	$823	$1,219	$978	$3,232	$2,091	$602	$1,283	$2,575
21	900	$3,315	$1,482	$1,118	$1,367	$338	$425	$1,710	$939
22	950	$3,520	$922	$688	$386	$165	$402	$261	$713
23	1000	$75	$75	$75	$75	$75	$75	$75	$75
24	1050	$128	$353	$116	$189	$232	$203	$119	$230
25	1100	$386	$80	$98	$333	$378	$384	$80	$347
26	Total								
27	by Month	$23,711	$16,692	$15,692	$18,249	$16,445	$13,996	$16,326	$17,777
28									
29									
30	1989 BUDGET SUMMARY								
31									
32	Budget								
33	Code	1/1/89	2/1/89	3/1/89	4/1/89	5/1/89	6/1/89	7/1/89	8/1/89
34	100	$2,098	$1,685	$1,550	$2,008	$1,763	$1,472	$1,746	$1,804
35	150	$1,077	$861	$740	$986	$799	$1,058	$821	$909
36	200	$239	$195	$250	$239	$238	$166	$114	$175
37	250	$2,906	$2,838	$2,847	$2,314	$2,576	$2,391	$2,561	$2,495

Page 1

	A	B	C	D	E	F	G	H	I
38	300	$3,500	$3,500	$3,500	$3,500	$3,500	$3,500	$3,500	$3,500
39	350	$330	$234	$237	$262	$238	$277	$257	$248
40	400	$349	$298	$248	$318	$277	$281	$356	$290
41	450	$400	$311	$300	$364	$329	$279	$272	$292
42	500	$563	$180	$778	$511	$272	$232	$430	$345
43	550	$585	$594	$603	$612	$620	$629	$638	$626
44	600	$1,004	$823	$772	$467	$646	$423	$431	$525
45	650	$566	$180	$149	$157	$555	$150	$457	$375
46	700	$315	$109	$265	$71	$302	$299	$214	$274
47	750	$613	$179	$693	$454	$276	$193	$376	$349
48	800	$823	$235	$108	$404	$776	$557	$625	$689
49	850	$823	$1,219	$978	$3,232	$2,091	$602	$1,283	$2,575
50	900	$3,315	$1,482	$1,118	$1,367	$338	$425	$1,710	$939
51	950	$3,520	$922	$688	$386	$165	$402	$261	$713
52	1000	$75	$75	$75	$75	$75	$75	$75	$75
53	1050	$128	$353	$116	$189	$232	$203	$119	$230
54	1100	$386	$80	$98	$333	$378	$384	$80	$347
55	Total								
56	by Month	$55,738	$48,812	$48,583	$50,515	$48,696	$45,968	$48,936	$50,151

Page 2

FIGURE 9-13. *This sample report shows Microsoft Excel's default page breaks.*

(continued)

FIGURE 9-13. *continued*

	A	J	K	L	M	N
1	1988 BUDGET					
2						
3	Budget					Total
4	Code	9/1/88	10/1/88	11/1/88	12/1/88	by Code
5	100	$1,649	$1,906	$1,888	$2,048	$21,616
6	150	$792	$704	$818	$904	$10,469
7	200	$203	$198	$173	$213	$2,402
8	250	$2,288	$2,404	$2,105	$2,259	$29,985
9	300	$3,500	$3,500	$3,500	$3,500	$42,000
10	350	$262	$209	$251	$223	$3,027
11	400	$302	$285	$289	$314	$3,609
12	450	$284	$300	$306	$277	$3,715
13	500	$312	$377	$404	$424	$4,408
14	550	$605	$626	$612	$620	$7,371
15	600	$578	$498	$602	$610	$7,379
16	650	$414	$502	$285	$411	$4,202
17	700	$252	$269	$292	$229	$2,892
18	750	$364	$215	$433	$326	$4,568
19	800	$676	$753	$537	$636	$7,158
20	850	$2,086	$169	$1,730	$2,157	$18,945
21	900	$3,446	$956	$1,424	$116	$16,637
22	950	$172	$309	$35	$135	$7,707
23	1000	$75	$75	$75	$75	$900
24	1050	$288	$171	$274	$288	$2,589
25	1100	$188	$271	$111	$258	$2,914
26	Total					
27	by Month	$18,738	$14,698	$16,146	$16,022	$204,492
28						
29						
30	1989 BUDGET					
31						
32	Budget					Total
33	Code	9/1/89	10/1/89	11/1/89	12/1/89	by Code
34	100	$1,649	$1,906	$1,888	$2,048	$21,616
35	150	$792	$704	$818	$904	$10,469
36	200	$203	$198	$173	$213	$2,402
37	250	$2,288	$2,404	$2,105	$2,259	$29,985

Page 3

	A	J	K	L	M	N
38	300	$3,500	$3,500	$3,500	$3,500	$42,000
39	350	$262	$209	$251	$223	$3,027
40	400	$302	$285	$289	$314	$3,609
41	450	$284	$300	$306	$277	$3,715
42	500	$312	$377	$404	$424	$4,828
43	550	$605	$626	$612	$620	$7,066
44	600	$578	$498	$602	$610	$7,379
45	650	$414	$502	$285	$411	$4,202
46	700	$252	$269	$292	$229	$2,892
47	750	$364	$215	$433	$326	$4,472
48	800	$676	$753	$537	$636	$6,819
49	850	$2,086	$169	$1,730	$2,157	$18,945
50	900	$3,446	$956	$1,424	$116	$16,637
51	950	$172	$309	$35	$135	$7,707
52	1000	$75	$75	$75	$75	$900
53	1050	$288	$171	$274	$288	$2,589
54	1100	$188	$271	$111	$258	$2,914
55	Total					
56	by Month	$51,303	$47,209	$48,847	$48,607	$201,259

Page 4

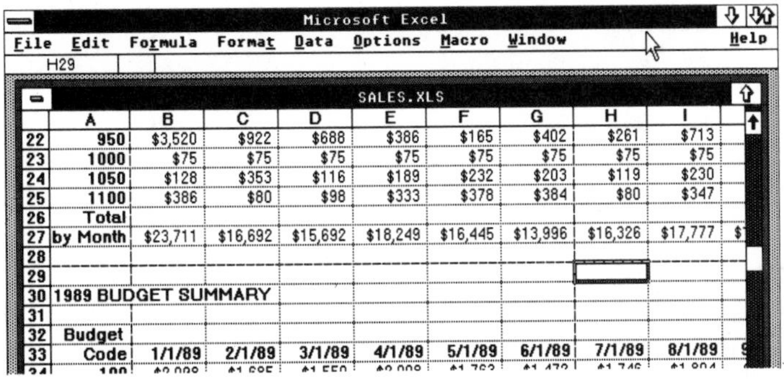

FIGURE 9-14. *Forced page breaks are indicated on the screen with darker dashed lines.*

FIGURE 9-15. *We forced new page breaks, to create a better-balanced report.*

(continued)

FIGURE 9-15. *continued*

	A	B	C	D	E	F	G
29							
30	1989 BUDGET SUMMARY						
31							
32	Budget						
33	Code	1/1/89	2/1/89	3/1/89	4/1/89	5/1/89	6/1/89
34	100	$2,098	$1,685	$1,550	$2,008	$1,763	$1,472
35	150	$1,077	$861	$740	$986	$799	$1,058
36	200	$239	$195	$250	$239	$238	$166
37	250	$2,906	$2,838	$2,847	$2,314	$2,576	$2,391
38	300	$3,500	$3,500	$3,500	$3,500	$3,500	$3,500
39	350	$330	$234	$237	$262	$238	$277
40	400	$349	$298	$248	$318	$277	$281
41	450	$400	$311	$300	$364	$329	$279
42	500	$563	$180	$778	$511	$272	$232
43	550	$585	$594	$603	$612	$620	$325
44	600	$1,004	$823	$772	$467	$646	$423
45	650	$566	$180	$149	$157	$555	$150
46	700	$315	$109	$265	$71	$302	$299
47	750	$613	$179	$693	$454	$276	$193
48	800	$823	$235	$108	$404	$776	$557
49	850	$823	$1,219	$978	$3,232	$2,091	$602
50	900	$3,315	$1,482	$1,118	$1,367	$338	$425
51	950	$3,520	$922	$688	$386	$165	$402
52	1000	$75	$75	$75	$75	$75	$75
53	1050	$128	$353	$116	$189	$232	$203
54	1100	$386	$80	$98	$333	$378	$384
55	Total						
56	by Month	$55,738	$48,812	$48,583	$50,515	$48,696	$45,968

Page 2

	A	H	I	J	K	L	M	N
1	1988 BUDGET							
2								
3	Budget							Total
4	Code	7/1/88	8/1/88	9/1/88	10/1/88	11/1/88	12/1/88	by Code
5	100	$1,746	$1,804	$1,649	$1,906	$1,888	$2,048	$21,616
6	150	$821	$909	$792	$704	$818	$904	$10,469
7	200	$114	$175	$203	$198	$173	$213	$2,402
8	250	$2,561	$2,495	$2,288	$2,404	$2,105	$2,259	$29,985
9	300	$3,500	$3,500	$3,500	$3,500	$3,500	$3,500	$42,000
10	350	$257	$248	$262	$209	$251	$223	$3,027
11	400	$356	$290	$302	$285	$289	$314	$3,609
12	450	$272	$292	$284	$300	$306	$277	$3,715
13	500	$430	$345	$312	$377	$404	$424	$4,408
14	550	$638	$626	$605	$626	$612	$620	$7,371
15	600	$431	$525	$578	$498	$602	$610	$7,379
16	650	$457	$375	$414	$502	$285	$411	$4,202
17	700	$214	$274	$252	$269	$292	$229	$2,892
18	750	$376	$349	$364	$215	$433	$326	$4,568
19	800	$625	$689	$676	$753	$537	$636	$7,158
20	850	$1,283	$2,575	$2,086	$169	$1,730	$2,157	$18,945
21	900	$1,710	$939	$3,446	$956	$1,424	$116	$16,637
22	950	$261	$713	$172	$309	$35	$135	$7,707
23	1000	$75	$75	$75	$75	$75	$75	$900
24	1050	$119	$230	$288	$171	$274	$288	$2,589
25	1100	$80	$347	$188	$271	$111	$258	$2,914
26	Total							
27	by Month	$16,326	$17,777	$18,738	$14,698	$16,146	$16,022	$204,492
28								

Page 3

(continued)

FIGURE 9-15. *continued*

	A	H	I	J	K	L	M	N
29								
30	1989 BUDGET							
31								
32	Budget							Total
33	Code	7/1/89	8/1/89	9/1/89	10/1/89	11/1/89	12/1/89	by Code
34	100	$1,746	$1,804	$1,649	$1,906	$1,888	$2,048	$21,616
35	150	$821	$909	$792	$704	$818	$904	$10,469
36	200	$114	$175	$203	$198	$173	$213	$2,402
37	250	$2,561	$2,495	$2,288	$2,404	$2,105	$2,259	$29,985
38	300	$3,500	$3,500	$3,500	$3,500	$3,500	$3,500	$42,000
39	350	$257	$248	$262	$209	$251	$223	$3,027
40	400	$356	$290	$302	$285	$289	$314	$3,609
41	450	$272	$292	$284	$300	$306	$277	$3,715
42	500	$430	$345	$312	$377	$404	$424	$4,828
43	550	$638	$626	$605	$626	$612	$620	$7,066
44	600	$431	$525	$578	$498	$602	$610	$7,379
45	650	$457	$375	$414	$502	$285	$411	$4,202
46	700	$214	$274	$252	$269	$292	$229	$2,892
47	750	$376	$349	$364	$215	$433	$326	$4,472
48	800	$625	$689	$676	$753	$537	$636	$6,819
49	850	$1,283	$2,575	$2,086	$169	$1,730	$2,157	$18,945
50	900	$1,710	$939	$3,446	$956	$1,424	$116	$16,637
51	950	$261	$713	$172	$309	$35	$135	$7,707
52	1000	$75	$75	$75	$75	$75	$75	$900
53	1050	$119	$230	$288	$171	$274	$288	$2,589
54	1100	$80	$347	$188	$271	$111	$258	$2,914
55	Total							
56	by Month	$48,936	$50,151	$51,303	$47,209	$48,847	$48,607	$201,259

Page 4

The Print command

After you've selected a printer, defined your page layout, specified the print area, and adjusted any other relevant settings, you're ready to select the Print command from the File menu. When you do, you'll see the dialog box shown in Figure 9-16. This dialog box contains five settings that control the printing of a Microsoft Excel document: Copies, Pages, Draft Quality, Preview, and Print.

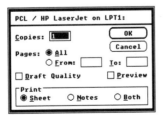

FIGURE 9-16. *Use the Print dialog box to print your reports.*

The Print options

The bottom portion of the Print dialog box is where you tell Microsoft Excel what you want to print. You can print the worksheet, any notes attached to the worksheet, or both the worksheet and the notes.

If you select Sheet, Microsoft Excel will print the entire worksheet (or the part you've defined with the Set Print Area command) but will ignore the notes. If you select Notes, Microsoft Excel will print all notes attached to the cells in the print area you've defined. The notes are printed by rows—row 1, then row 2, and so on. Microsoft Excel ignores the worksheet when printing notes, but you can tell it to include the cell references to make it easier to identify the location of each note. To do this, activate the Row & Column Headings check box in the lower left corner of the Page Setup dialog box.

Of course, you can also use the Both option to print the contents of the worksheet as well as your cell notes.

The Pages options

The Pages setting allows you to specify which pages of a document you want Microsoft Excel to print. The default setting, All, instructs Microsoft Excel to print every page of the defined print area. If you want to print only part of a document, type the number of the first page you want to print in the From edit bar. Then select the To edit bar and type the number of the last page you want to print.

If you leave the From edit bar blank and enter a number in the To edit bar, Microsoft Excel prints from page 1 to the end of the page specified in To. If you enter a number in the From edit bar and leave the To edit bar blank, Microsoft Excel begins printing with the specified From page and prints to the end of the document (or the end of the selected print area).

The Copies setting

Use the Copies setting to specify how many copies of the document you want to print. The default setting is 1. If you want Microsoft Excel to print the document more than once, type the number of copies you want to print into the Copies edit bar. When Microsoft Excel prints multiple copies of a document, it prints the first copy in its entirety, then the second copy, and so forth.

By the way, as we mentioned earlier, if you're using a laser printer, you have the option of specifying a number of uncollated copies in the Printer Setup dialog box. Using the Uncollated copies option instead of the Copies option will speed up the time required to print a multi-page document, at the cost of some hand collating on your part. For example, assume you have a five-page document and you want to print three copies. If you enter a 3 in the Copies edit bar, Microsoft Excel

will print page 1 through page 5 three times, formatting each of the 15 pages individually. This repetitive formatting takes considerable time. If you enter a 3 in the
Uncollated copies edit bar instead, Microsoft Excel will print page 1 three times,
page 2 three times, and so on. Because each page is formatted only once, this
method is much faster, although you'll have to collate the documents manually.

The Draft Quality option

The Draft Quality option tells Microsoft Excel to use your printer's default font to
print your document. Although this usually results in lower-quality type than if
you used Microsoft Excel's fonts, your report will print faster. For non-laser
printers, if you choose the Landscape orientation in the Printer Setup dialog box,
Microsoft Excel dims the Draft Quality option in the Print dialog box, indicating
that it is not available.

The Preview option

If you want to take a look at the page breaks and format of your report before you
begin printing, select the Preview option inside the Print dialog box and choose
OK. Microsoft Excel will show you a picture of the printed page on the screen,
reflecting all the Page Setup and Print options you've selected. For example,
Figure 9-17 shows a preview of the first page of the printed report in Figure 9-8.

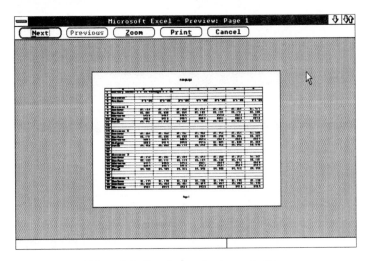

FIGURE 9-17. *We used the Preview option to create this on-screen*
preview of the first page of the sales report.

If you want to see the next page as you're previewing a report, select the Next
button at the top of the screen. (If you select Next on the last preview page,

Microsoft Excel returns you to the worksheet.) Similarly, to see the previous page, select Previous. To return to your worksheet, select Cancel.

Zooming in on selected areas

Although you can get a general idea of the page layout from this preview, the image is too small to read clearly. Fortunately, Microsoft Excel provides two methods for getting a closer look.

If you're using a mouse, Microsoft Excel turns your pointer into a magnifying glass while the Preview option is in effect, so that you can zoom in on the selected portion of the page to take a closer look. For example, to be sure your page header is formatted correctly, place the magnifying-glass pointer at the top of the page and click. Your screen will then look like Figure 9-18. If you want to see another area of the worksheet, use the scroll bars at the edge of the window. Or you might first return to the full-page preview by clicking again, and then use the mouse to move the magnifier to a new location.

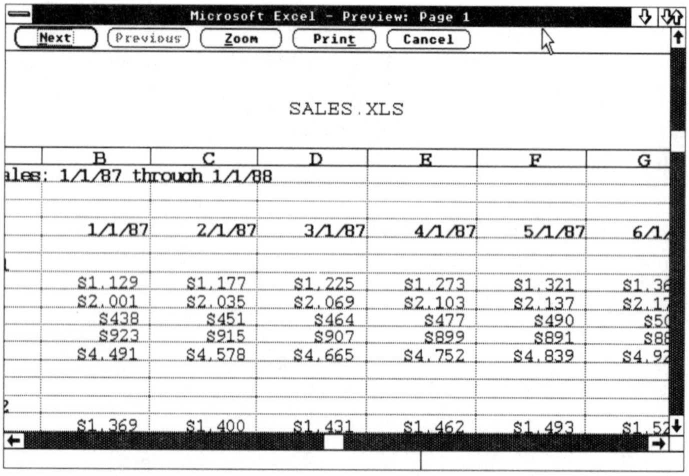

FIGURE 9-18. *You can magnify an area of the preview screen to verify the contents and formatting of a report.*

If you prefer to use the keyboard, select the Zoom button from the top of the Preview screen by pressing Alt-Z. Microsoft Excel will enlarge the preview image and you'll be able to use the arrow keys to navigate around the page. You can also use PgUp, PgDn, Home, and End to move around the page. PgUp and PgDn work like the Up and Down arrow keys, except that they allow you to move about half a screenful of data at a time, rather than only about an inch. Ctrl-PgUp and Ctrl-PgDn work like the Left and Right arrow keys, except that they move the image about 2 inches across the screen at a time instead of less than an inch. The Home key takes you to the left side of the page and End moves you to the right border. Ctrl-Home takes you to the top left corner of the page and Ctrl-End takes you to the bottom right corner. You can also use the scroll bars to change your view of the page, just as in a worksheet window.

When you've finished viewing the enlarged page image, select Zoom again or click on the Preview screen; the page will return to preview size.

Printing the document

When you're satisfied with your print settings, you can begin printing from the Print dialog box by simply selecting OK. (Remember to turn Preview off first.) Microsoft Excel will display a status box, letting you know its progress, until the entire document (or the specified number of pages) has been printed.

To cancel the printing process at any time, select Cancel. Microsoft Excel will stop sending information to the printer and close the dialog box. If the printer is in the middle of a page, it may take a moment to stop—it will continue printing until it has printed all the information already transmitted to it by Microsoft Excel.

Printing from the Preview window
After you've previewed a document and decided to print it, you don't need to leave the Preview window to select the Print command. You can tell Microsoft Excel to print a document by selecting Print from the top of the Preview window. If you need to make some changes or don't want to print, select Cancel.

The Spooler

The Spooler lets you queue printing jobs so that you can continue working while your documents print. Because this background utility program is invoked automatically when you print a document, you need not concern yourself with the Spooler program unless you want to monitor the status of your print jobs.

When the Spooler is running, the Spooler icon appears at the bottom left corner of your screen. To access the Spooler as a document is printing, double-click on this icon or press Alt-Esc to select the icon and then press Alt-Spacebar-R to access the Spooler window. (You may need to reduce the size of the application window first so that the Spooler icon is visible.) When you open the Spooler application, you'll see a window like the one in Figure 9-19.

In the status bar near the top of the Spooler window, you'll see the name of the current printer port, the status of the printer, and the printer name. Below this status line is a list of the documents currently in the print queue and the application from which each document originated. Spooler sends the documents to the printer in the order in which they're listed.

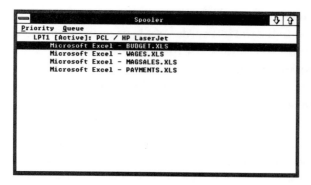

FIGURE 9-19. *Use the Spooler window to monitor the status of your print jobs.*

When the Spooler window is active, two names appear in the menu bar at the top of that window: Priority and Queue. The Priority menu lets you specify how quickly you want your documents to print. The High command on the Priority menu lets you print your documents more quickly, but it requires more of your computer's processing time and thus causes other applications, such as Microsoft Excel, to run more slowly. If you want to continue working in Microsoft Excel while you print, you'll probably want to choose the Low command from the Priority menu. Although it will take a little longer to print your documents, you'll be able to continue your other work with little slowdown in processing time.

The Pause and Terminate commands on the Queue menu let you interrupt or cancel the printing of a document. Simply select the name of the job you want to interrupt or cancel from the queue list and then select the appropriate command from the Queue menu. If you choose to terminate the print job, Spooler will present a dialog box asking you to confirm the cancellation. If you interrupt a job, you can use the Resume command on the Queue menu to start printing again.

Adding, deleting, and configuring printers

Before you can use a printer or plotter, you must install a driver file for that printer on your hard disk. You probably installed the appropriate driver files when you ran the Setup program, as described in Chapter 1. If at any time you need to add a new printer or plotter to your current set of driver files, however, you can use the Control Panel application instead of running the Setup program again.

To use Control Panel, choose Run from the application-window Control menu (press Alt-Spacebar-U). Then select the Control Panel option in the Run dialog box. When the Control Panel window appears, select the Add New Printer command from the Installation menu. You'll be prompted to insert the disk that contains your printer driver files. (The printer drivers supplied with Microsoft Excel are located on the Utilities disk.) Next, you'll see a dialog box like the one shown in Figure 9-20. Simply select the printer you want to add and choose the Add button. You'll then be asked where you want to store the driver file. The default directory is the directory in which your Microsoft Excel program file is stored; however, you can specify a different directory if you like.

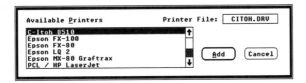

FIGURE 9-20. *Use the Add New Printer command to see a list of available printers.*

If you no longer need a particular driver file, you can delete that file from disk by choosing Delete Printer from the Control Panel Installation menu. Then select the name of the printer you want to remove and choose the Delete button. You'll be asked to verify the deletion.

Printer connections

Whenever you add a printer or change your printer connections, you must use the Connections command from the Control Panel Setup menu to specify your new configuration. When you issue the Connections command, you'll see the dialog box shown in Figure 9-21. Choose the name of the printer you want to change from the Printer list box; then choose the desired port from the Connection list box and choose OK or press Enter.

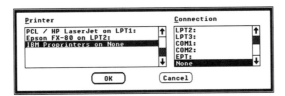

FIGURE 9-21. *Use the Connections command to specify your printer connections.*

Printer setup

As we explained at the beginning of this chapter, you can use the Printer Setup command on Microsoft Excel's File menu to choose the printer you want to use.

You can also use the Printer command on the Control Panel Setup menu to choose a printer. When you issue the Setup Printer command, you'll see a dialog box like the one in Figure 9-22.

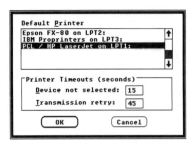

FIGURE 9-22. *You can also use the Printer command on the Control Panel Setup menu to select a printer.*

In addition to choosing a printer, you can use the Device not selected option to specify the amount of time Microsoft Excel should wait to send you messages about printing problems. Use the Transmission retry option to specify how long the program should wait to attempt to send the document to the printer again.

When you choose OK in the Setup Printer dialog box, Microsoft Excel will expand the dialog box to display a Printer Setup dialog box like the ones we showed you in Figures 9-2 and 9-3. Here, you can choose your paper size, orientation, and other output-mode options.

Changing the font set

The Setup program automatically installs fonts based on the printing devices you've installed and the type of graphics adapter you're using. You can add new font sets by choosing the Add New Font command from the Control Panel Installation menu. You'll be asked to insert the disk that contains your font files. (The font files supplied with Microsoft Excel are located on the Fonts disk.)

When you insert the Fonts disk, you'll see a dialog box like the one in Figure 9-23. Choose the name of the font you want and then choose the Add button. You'll be asked to select the directory in which you want to store the font file. You can accept the default directory, which is the directory in which your Microsoft Excel program file is stored, or you can enter a new pathname.

As we mentioned in Chapter 3, the fonts you use to display data on your screen are not necessarily the fonts you'll use to print your documents. The font that appears in your printed documents depends on your printer's font capabilities. When the screen font you've chosen doesn't match one of the available printer fonts, Microsoft Excel substitutes the closest matching font.

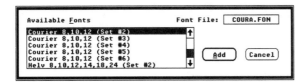

FIGURE 9-23. *Use the Add New Font command on the Control Panel Installation menu to see a list of available fonts.*

You can select from two types of fonts: raster and stroke. Raster fonts are generally used for dot-matrix printers and screen displays; stroke fonts are generally used for plotters. Table 9-2 describes each of the available fonts.

Table 9-2. Microsoft Excel font names and characteristics.

Font	Type	Description
Helv	Raster	Proportional, sans serif
Courier	Raster	Fixed-width, serif
Tms Rmn	Raster	Proportional, serif
Roman	Stroke	Proportional, serif
Modern	Stroke	Proportional, sans serif
Script	Stroke	Proportional, slanted characters

A font-set number appears in parentheses next to each font name in the Available Fonts list box. The fonts that come with your Microsoft Excel disk are designed for specific types of graphics adapters and printers. Depending on your configuration, you can choose from the sets in the following list:

Font set	Designed for
1	Stroke fonts for screen, printer, or plotter of any resolution
2	Raster fonts for 640 by 200 resolution screen
3	Raster fonts for 640 by 350 resolution screen
4	Raster fonts for 60 dpi printers
5	Raster fonts for 120 dpi printers
6	Raster fonts for 640 by 480 resolution screen

You may also be able to select from a series of device fonts provided by your printer. For example, if you use a print-wheel printer, you can select a device font that corresponds to one of the print wheels available for your printer.

In addition to the fonts listed above, two other fonts are installed when you install Microsoft Excel: Terminal and System. System is the font used for menu and dialog-box displays; Terminal is the font your computer displays in MS-DOS. You cannot add or delete these fonts.

CHARTS

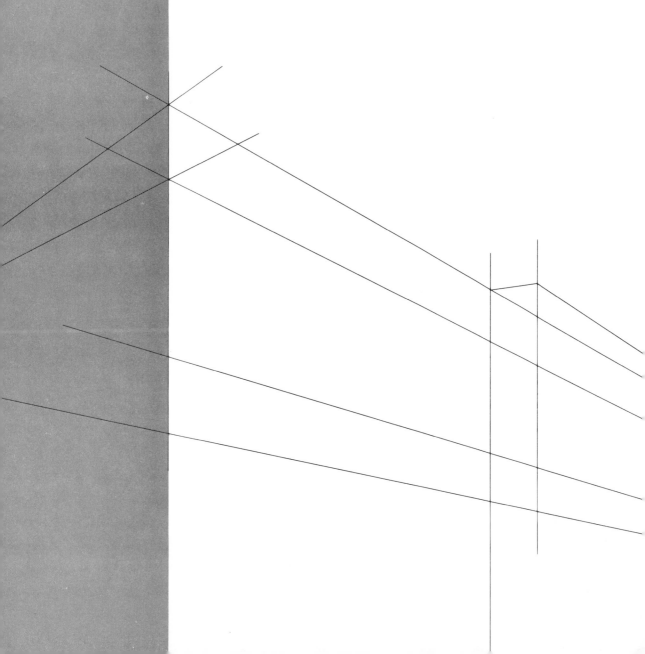

10

Basic Charting Techniques

*T*he well-worn phrase *A picture is worth a thousand words* holds true for numbers as well. Often, you can summarize pages of complex data in one or two easily understandable charts. Microsoft Excel offers a powerful and flexible charting facility that makes it easy to create sophisticated graphics from your worksheets.

You can choose from six main types of charts: column, area, bar, line, pie, and scatter. Each of these major chart types has several formats. For example, if you're creating a column chart, you can choose stacked, overlapped, or clustered columns. Five combination formats allow you to display two charts at once. You can also create your own formats and combine different chart types by creating overlay charts. All these chart types, combined with a number of powerful custom formatting options, let you tailor a virtually endless variety of graphic presentations.

Creating a chart

The easiest way to learn about charting is to experiment with the many options available. We'll use the simple worksheet in Figure 10-1 to create a basic column chart and then we'll build on this basic chart throughout the remainder of this section.

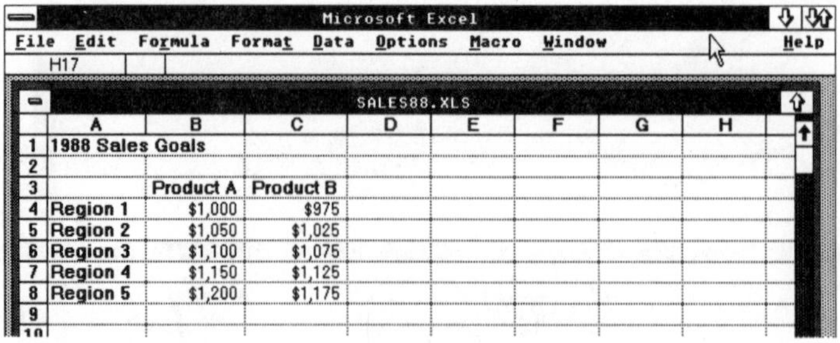

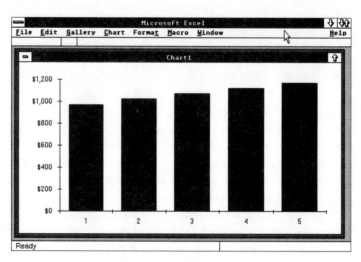

FIGURE 10-1. *We'll use this worksheet as the basis for our examples throughout the chapter.*

To chart the sales values in column B of the worksheet, begin by selecting the range B4:B8. Next select New from the File menu and then select the Chart option in the New dialog box. It's that easy! Your new chart will look like the one shown in Figure 10-2.

FIGURE 10-2. *We used the New command with the Chart option to graph the sales from column B.*

As you can see, Microsoft Excel has built a simple column chart from the data in the Sales worksheet. Each of the five columns (also called markers) in the chart represents a data point. Each data point corresponds to one of the values in cells B4:B8 in Figure 10-1: The first column corresponds to cell B4, the second column corresponds to cell B5, and so on. All the data points are collectively called a data series. In Chapter 11, we'll show you how to add additional data series to a chart.

Every chart you create initially appears as a column chart unless you've assigned another default format. As you'll learn in Chapter 12, you can use the Gallery menu commands and the Main Chart command from the Format menu to change the chart type.

The area defined by the two chart axes is called the plot area. The bottom axis is called the category axis; the axis on the left is called the value axis. You probably know these as the x and y axes. In mathematics, the x axis is always horizontal and the y axis is always vertical, as shown in our sample column chart. In Microsoft Excel, however, the orientation of the axes may be reversed, so the names have been changed to avoid confusion.

Notice that the values along the value axis range from 0 to 1200. Microsoft Excel sets the upper and lower limits of the value axis according to the chart type and the range of values being plotted. (You can also use the Scale command on the Format menu to manually create your own limits.) Notice also that the numbers along the value axis appear in the $#,##0 ;($#,##0) currency format. Any formats you apply to the data in your worksheet are carried over to the chart documents as well.

The points on the category axis are currently numbered 1 through 5. Because we haven't specified any labels for these points, Microsoft Excel has simply numbered them consecutively. In a few pages, we'll show you how to replace these numbers with descriptive labels.

A tour of the chart window

Before we jump into any major enhancements of this basic chart, we'll take a brief tour of the chart window and introduce a few new terms. Then we'll look at how chart data is organized.

Initially, your new charts will be displayed in a partial-screen chart window. We've expanded the window in our figures to make it easier to view our sample charts. As with other document windows, you can size, move, shrink, and enlarge the chart window. Microsoft Excel will change the size and proportions of a chart in order to display it in its entirety, no matter what size you choose for the window. You can also have more than one chart and worksheet window open at the same time.

As you can see in Figure 10-2, at the top of the chart window is the title bar. As with worksheet windows, you can move the chart window around the screen either by dragging the title bar with the mouse or by pressing Alt-Hyphen-M and then using the arrow keys.

As you can see, Microsoft Excel has named this first chart Chart1. Subsequent charts will be named Chart2, Chart3, and so on. Of course, you can assign the chart any name you like when you save the file.

Notice that no scroll bars or split bars appear in the chart window. Because the entire chart is visible within the window no matter what the window's size, scrolling is unnecessary. Similarly, if you take a look at the Window menu, you'll see that no New Window command appears in the Chart environment. Again, this is because the entire chart appears within the borders of the chart window.

The menu bar

Because you're now working with a chart (the chart window is active and in front of all other windows), Microsoft Excel displays the Chart environment's menu bar at the top of the screen. Some of the choices on this menu—File, Edit, Format, Macro, and Window—should look familiar to you. You'll discover, though, that many of the chart commands work differently than the worksheet commands we've discussed so far.

The other menus on the menu bar—Gallery and Chart—appear only in the Chart window. You select the chart type and format you want to use from the Gallery menu. If you want to tailor your own chart instead of using one of Microsoft Excel's standard formats, you can use the Chart menu commands to control the use of axes and gridlines, legends, text, and arrows.

Chart objects

Microsoft Excel divides a chart into classes. A class is a major component of the chart, such as chart area, plot area, attached and unattached text, legend, data series, or axes. Within each class, items may be divided into individual objects, such as data-point markers and labels, individual text blocks, and so forth.

Before you can perform many editing and formatting actions in a chart window, you must select the chart object you want to work with. To select a chart object with the mouse, simply point and click. To select the entire chart or plot area, use the Select Chart and Select Plot Area commands from the Chart menu.

If you prefer the keyboard, you can use the direction keys to move around in the chart window. To move between classes of objects, use the Up and Down arrow keys. As you press the Up arrow key, Microsoft Excel moves through the various chart classes in this order:

Chart area
Plot area
Legend
Value axis
Category axis
Text
Arrows
Gridlines
Data-point labels

First data series
Second and subsequent data series
Drop lines
Hi-lo lines

When you've selected the correct class, you can use the Left and Right arrow keys to move between objects. For example, to select the second column marker in our sample chart, you would need to press the Up arrow key four times to move to the desired class (data series) and then press the Right arrow key once to move to the second data marker.

Whichever selection method you use, Microsoft Excel places a set of squares on the object or class that is currently selected. An item marked with white squares can't be moved or sized with the mouse or the keyboard, but you may be able to format or realign it using commands. Black squares mark objects or text that can be moved or sized with the mouse or keyboard and formatted or realigned with commands.

As you move between classes and between objects, the reference area at the left side of the formula bar tells you what type of item is selected. For example, if you select the value axis, you see the notation *Axis 1*. If you select the first column in the sample chart, as shown in Figure 10-3, you see the notation S1P1, which indicates that you've selected the first data point in the first (and only, in this case) data series (series 1, point 1).

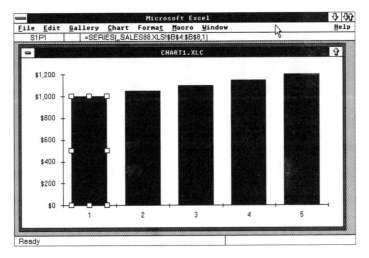

FIGURE 10-3. *When you select the first data marker, you see a set of white boxes to indicate your selection and the notation S1P1 in the reference area of the formula bar.*

Adding chart text

Now that you know how easy it is to create a chart, let's look at how the basic chart we've just created can be enhanced. In this part of the chapter, we'll show you how to create and format chart titles, axis titles, and data-point labels. We'll also show you how to add unattached text to your charts.

Automatic chart text

In creating our first sample chart, we selected only the worksheet cells that contained the values we wanted to graph. By including a few adjacent cells in the chart range, however, we can add category-axis labels and a title to the chart.

To see how this works, go back to the Sales worksheet window and select the range A3:B8. Now choose New from the File menu and select the Chart option. Figure 10-4 shows the resulting chart.

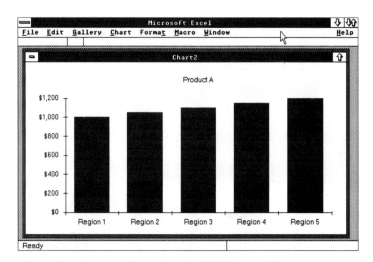

FIGURE 10-4. *To produce the category labels and title, we included labels in the range selected in the worksheet.*

In most ways, this new chart is identical to the first one we created. However, notice that Microsoft Excel has used the text *Product A* from cell B3 as a chart title. In addition, Microsoft Excel uses this name as a series name, to identify the data series in cells B4:B8. The importance of the series name will become evident as you learn more about how Microsoft Excel builds charts.

Also notice that Microsoft Excel has used the text entries in cells A4:A8 as labels for the data points along the category axis. These labels are called tick-mark or category labels, because they identify the categories of information in the chart.

When you create a chart, Microsoft Excel looks for a series name and category labels in the top row and left column of the worksheet range you select. If the first row and first column in the range you select don't contain labels, as in our first example, Microsoft Excel assumes you don't want to use a series name or category labels in your chart.

Notice also that the new chart is slightly smaller than the first one. As you add titles, legends, and other objects to a chart, Microsoft Excel adjusts the size of the plot area to make room for your additions. The more enhancements you add to the chart area, the less room remains for the plot area, which contains the chart itself.

Adding your own text

In addition to the tick-mark labels along the category and value axes, two types of text can appear in a chart window: attached and unattached. Attached text is linked to a specific chart object—a data point, data series, or axis, for example. You can also attach a title to the chart itself, if Microsoft Excel doesn't provide a title for you. If you move a chart object, the attached text moves with it. Unattached text, on the other hand, is freestanding text that you can position anywhere on the chart. For example, you may use unattached text to create a subtitle for your chart or to add a comment line.

Let's start with attached text. To add attached text to a chart, you must first select the Attach Text command from the Chart menu. When you choose this command, you'll see a dialog box like the one in Figure 10-5. If no chart object was selected when you issued the Attach Text command, the Title option will be your default selection. However, you can speed up the process by selecting the object to which you want to attach text before issuing the command. When you do this, Microsoft Excel chooses the appropriate dialog-box settings for you. For example, if you want to attach a label to the second column in the chart, select that data marker and then select the Attach Text command. Microsoft Excel will select the Series or Data Point option in the dialog box and will enter the values 1 and 2 in the Series Number and Point Number edit bars. Simply press Enter or choose OK to accept these settings.

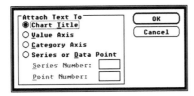

FIGURE 10-5. *Use the Attach Text dialog box to add text to a chart.*

Adding a new title

For the chart in Figure 10-2, Microsoft Excel did not provide a chart title, because we didn't include the label *Product A* in cell B3 in our selection. If you want to add a title to a chart, choose the Attach Text command from the Chart menu and select the Chart Title option; then choose OK to lock in your selection and return to the chart window. You'll see a group of white squares above the chart, which indicate the position of the title. The formula bar will display the generic text *Title*, because no default chart title exists.

Now all you need do is edit the chart title to change the default to something more descriptive. You edit the contents of the chart formula bar as you edit the contents of the worksheet formula bar—with one important difference: By pressing Ctrl-Enter, you can insert a line break while you're entering text in the chart formula bar. If you press only Enter, Microsoft Excel considers your entry finished and locks it in. (Of course, you can also lock in your entry by selecting the Enter box to the left of the formula bar.)

For example, to create a title for our sample chart, we simply type *1988 Sales Goals:*, press Ctrl-Enter to start a new line, and type *By Region*. When we press Enter to lock in our new title, our chart looks like the one in Figure 10-6. Notice that Microsoft Excel centers both lines of the title over the plot area.

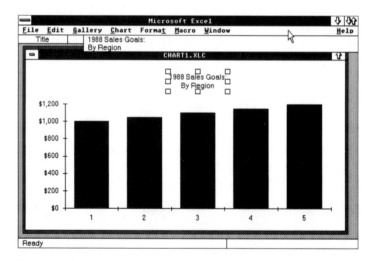

FIGURE 10-6. *We added a title to our first sample chart.*

If you want to edit an existing title instead of creating a new one, select the title by clicking on it or by pressing the arrow keys. Then click on the formula bar to activate it (or press F2) and use the standard editing techniques you learned in Chapter 2 to make your changes. (You can even cut, copy, and paste entries in the chart formula bar, just as you would in a worksheet window.) If you want to completely overwrite the existing title, select all the title text in the formula bar and begin typing. The original entry will be replaced with your new entry.

To delete a title altogether, select the text in the formula bar and press the Del key. Microsoft Excel will immediately erase the contents of the formula bar. Select the Enter box or press Enter to lock in your deletion. (To restore the contents of the formula bar before they are locked in, select the Cancel box.)

Adding axis titles

Now that our chart title is in place, let's assign titles to the category and value axes. Begin by issuing the Attach Text command and selecting the Category Axis option in the Attach Text dialog box. (To preselect this option in the dialog box, select the category axis before you issue the Attach Text command.) When you lock in your dialog-box selection and return to the chart window, you'll see an X, surrounded by a set of white squares, below the category axis. These squares indicate the position of your axis title in the chart area. You'll also see an X in the formula bar, indicating that you're assigning a title to this chart's x, or category, axis. Type the category-axis label *Regions* in the formula bar and then press Enter or choose the Enter box to lock in your title.

To add a title to the value axis, choose the Attach Text command again and select the Value Axis option. Microsoft Excel places a Y, surrounded by white squares, near the chart's value axis and displays a Y in the formula bar to indicate that you're assigning text to this chart's y, or value, axis. Replace this generic title with the label *Goals*. Figure 10-7 shows our revised sample chart.

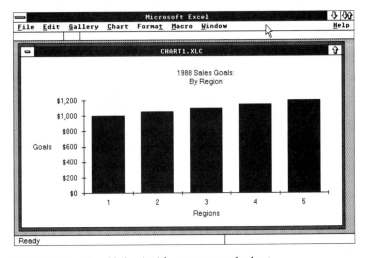

FIGURE 10-7. *We added axis titles to our sample chart.*

Adding series or data-point labels

Now let's attach descriptive labels to the data points in our chart. Suppose you want to include at the top of each column the actual projected sales goal for each region. To do this, first choose Attach Text from the Chart menu. Then select the Series or Data Point option in the Attach Text dialog box. When you do this, Microsoft Excel changes the display of the Series Number and Point Number options to black type, to indicate that they are now active.

Now select the Series Number edit bar and type *1*; then move to the Point Number edit bar and type *1* again. (Because our chart has only one series so far, you could leave the Series Number edit bar blank. We'll show you how to label multiseries charts in the next chapter.) Alternatively, you can select the first column marker before issuing the Attach Text command, so that Microsoft Excel will enter the appropriate series number and data-point number for you. When you've entered the desired numbers, press the Enter key or choose OK to return to the chart window.

Microsoft Excel enters $1,000 in the formula bar and above the first column in the chart. If you look back at the worksheet in Figure 10-1, you'll see that $1,000 is the value in cell B4—the cell on which the first column of the chart is based. For every data point in the chart, Microsoft Excel sets up a link between the value in the appropriate cell in the worksheet and the chart. If the value in cell B4 changes, Microsoft Excel will change the label to reflect the new value.

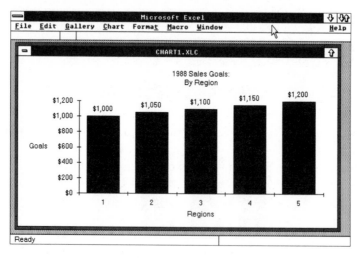

FIGURE 10-8. *Our chart now includes data-point labels.*

Now that you've defined the data-point label for the first column, you can repeat the same procedure to define data-point labels for data points 2, 3, 4, and 5. To define these other labels, select each marker in turn before you issue the Attach Text command, or type the appropriate data-point number (2 for the second column, 3 for the third, and so on) for each marker in the Point Number edit bar. Figure 10-8 shows the chart with these data-point labels in place. As you can see, Microsoft Excel uses the values from cells B5, B6, B7, and B8 as the labels for the second, third, fourth, and fifth columns in the chart.

Of course, instead of accepting the default data-point labels, you can overwrite or edit Microsoft Excel's entries with your own labels for each data point.

Adding unattached text

To add unattached, or floating, text to your chart, simply type the text in the formula bar. Use Ctrl-Enter to begin a new line of text and the Enter key or Enter box to lock in your entry.

Before you begin typing, be sure you haven't selected any chart objects. If no chart object is selected, no white squares or black squares appear in the chart window and no text appears in the formula bar. If a chart object is selected, particularly a data point or a text block, you may inadvertently destroy information in your chart when you create the unattached text. If you're using a mouse, you can ensure that no chart object is selected by clicking on a blank area of the chart window.

Let's add a comment line to the chart in Figure 10-8. First, be sure no chart object is selected; then type *Product A sales goals reflect an average 10% increase over last year's sales*. Unless you want to control how the text is broken in this long entry, you need not press Ctrl-Enter at the end of each line; the text you enter will wrap to fit the allotted space. As you'll see in a few moments, this automatic wrapping feature can be handy when you need to resize a text block.

When you lock in your entry, the text will initially appear in the middle of the plot area, making it difficult to read on the screen. You'll probably want to move the unattached text to an empty area of the chart window so that it is more legible. To reposition the text with the mouse, point to the text block and drag it to the desired position. As you point and drag, the black boxes around the text block will be replaced by a rectangular border called a positioning box, to show the new placement. To move the unattached text block with the keyboard, select the text and choose Move from the Format menu. Then use the arrow keys to move the selection around on the screen. Again, a rectangular positioning box will appear to show the new placement. To fine-tune your positioning, press the Ctrl key as you press the arrow keys. Press Enter when the positioning block reaches the desired location.

For the moment, we'll place the text block near the bottom of the chart window, as shown in Figure 10-9.

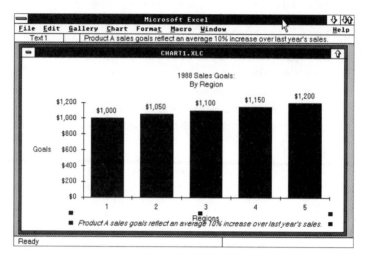

FIGURE 10-9. *We entered a comment line and placed it near the bottom of the chart window.*

You can also change the proportions of the text block by dragging the black squares that appear around the block or by using the Size command on the Chart menu. To change the height or width of the text block with the mouse, drag one of the black squares at the sides of the text block; to change the height and width simultaneously, drag one of the corner squares.

For example, suppose we want our text block to appear in a narrower, multiline format rather than as a long, single line. We can achieve this effect by selecting the text block, clicking on the square marker at the top right corner of the selection, and dragging up and to the left. Figure 10-10 shows the results. (For readability, we also repositioned the text block in a blank area of the window.)

To resize the unattached text block with the keyboard, first select the text block and then choose Size from the Format menu. Now use the arrow keys to make your changes. The Up and Down arrow keys let you increase and decrease the height of the box; to increase and decrease the width of the box, use the Left and Right arrow keys. When the text box reaches the desired proportions, press Enter to lock in your changes.

When the position box is larger than the text block, the text is centered in the box area. When the position box is smaller than the text block, Microsoft Excel displays as much text as it has room for. The effects of resizing a text block become particularly important when you're using the Patterns command to place borders around your text. We'll look at chart patterns a little later in this chapter.

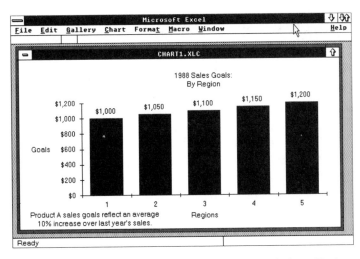

FIGURE 10-10. *We resized and repositioned the unattached text block.*

Linking text to the worksheet

In Chapter 8, you learned how to link worksheets. When you're creating a chart from values in a worksheet, changing the worksheet automatically changes the values in the chart. You can also link any text—attached or unattached—to a cell in a worksheet so that changes you make to the text in the worksheet will automatically be made in the chart as well.

To link text to the worksheet, first be sure the worksheet is open. Then build a formula that contains an external reference to either a name or a single cell in the worksheet. For example, suppose that you want to use the contents of cell A1 in the worksheet in Figure 10-1 as attached text for the title of the chart we've been creating. To link the title of the chart to cell A1 of the worksheet, select the Attach Text command from the Chart menu, select the Chart Title option, and click OK or press Enter. Next, type an equal sign (=) in the formula bar. Now activate the worksheet and select cell A1 to paste the external reference in the formula bar. When you choose the Enter box or press Enter, your chart title will read *1988 Sales Goals* and the formula bar will contain the linked reference

=SALES88.XLS!$A$1

You can also link unattached text to a worksheet. To do this, first be sure no text is selected on your screen. Then type an equal sign in the formula bar, activate the source worksheet, and select the cell that contains the label you want to use. Finally, choose the Enter box or press Enter to lock in your linked text formula.

Of course, you can type a cell reference instead of clicking on the cell. You also can type a cell name or value name. For more on linking documents, see Chapter 8.

Formatting chart text

To format the text in your chart, first select the attached or unattached text block you want to work with. Then use the Font and Text commands on the Format menu to specify your formats. The Font command controls typeface, size, style, background, and color of the text; the Text command primarily controls the alignment of the text. You can also use the Patterns command on the Format menu to place borders around your text blocks and to place area patterns behind the text. We'll talk more about Patterns later in this chapter.

In addition to formatting attached and unattached text, you can control the format of your chart's axis labels and legend text. We'll show you how to format category and values axis labels later in this chapter. We'll take a look at legends when we discuss multiseries charts in the next chapter.

The Font command

The default font in a new chart is Helv 10-point regular. To assign a new font for the entire chart (including all attached and unattached text, as well as the axis labels and the legend, if one exists), issue the Select Chart command or use the arrow keys to select the entire chart area before you issue the Font command.

When you choose Font from the Format menu, you'll see a dialog box like the one in Figure 10-11. Many of the options in this dialog box should look familiar to you by now—you used them in Chapter 3 to format your worksheet text.

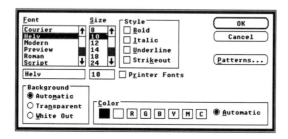

FIGURE 10-11. *Use the Font dialog box to change the typeface, style, size, color, and background of your chart text.*

As you might expect, you use the Font, Size, and Style options to specify the typeface and format you want to use for the selected text. To be sure that the font you're using on your screen is also available for your printer, activate the Printer Fonts option before you make your selections.

The Background options let you control the appearance of the area behind the text. If you use the default setting, Automatic, Microsoft Excel selects a pattern for you. If you choose Transparent, the area behind the text is "see-through," so that any objects behind the text are visible—that is, the text appears as if it were simply typed on top of the chart. If you choose White Out, on the other hand, Microsoft Excel blocks out an area behind your text. The blocked-out area obscures any chart objects behind it, making your text stand out more from the chart. (By the way, when you choose White Out, the area that's blocked out around your text doesn't necessarily appear in white; it appears in the color or pattern you've selected for your background.) The effects of the Background options become more evident when you use the Patterns options to format the text block and the rest of the chart. We'll return to these options later in this chapter when we talk about the Patterns command.

You can use the Color options in the Font dialog box to change the color of selected chart text for emphasis. Be sure to choose a color for your text that contrasts sufficiently with any background colors you may choose. (To change the background color of the text area or underlying areas of the chart, you'll need to use the Patterns command, which we'll discuss later in this chapter.)

Now let's look at the effects of using some of the Font dialog-box options. As we hinted earlier, all you need do to change the default font for your chart is select the entire chart and then choose a new typeface, size, and style. For example, Figure 10-12 shows the results of selecting the chart area and choosing the Tms Rmn and 10 options.

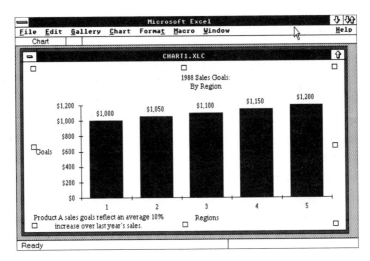

FIGURE 10-12. *We changed the default font for the entire chart to 10-point Tms Rmn regular.*

Let's go back to the chart appearing in Figure 10-10 and change the format of the chart title and the axis titles. Start by selecting the chart title, issuing the Font command, and choosing the 14 and Bold options. Next, select the value-axis label, issue the Font command, and select the 12 and Bold options. Now, select the category-axis label and choose Repeat Font from the Edit menu to apply the same Font specifications to that title. Finally, choose the comment line at the bottom of the screen, issue the Font command again, and choose the Italic option. Figure 10-13 shows the results.

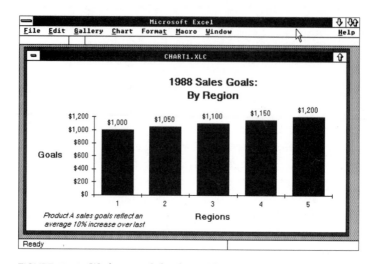

FIGURE 10-13. *We formatted the chart title, axis titles, and comment line to add emphasis.*

When you select a data-point label before issuing the Font command, one additional option appears in the dialog box: Apply to All. Choose this option if you want your font selections to apply to all the data-point labels in the chart. If you don't activate Apply to All, only the selected data-point label will be formatted with the options you select.

The Font dialog box contains two more options: Patterns and Text. You can use these buttons to access the Patterns and Text dialog boxes without leaving the current dialog box. You also can access the Patterns and Text dialog boxes by choosing the Patterns and Text commands from the Format menu.

The Text command

The Text command lets you control the alignment of your chart text and the use of Microsoft Excel's automatic labeling and sizing features. When you choose this command, you'll see the dialog box shown in Figure 10-14.

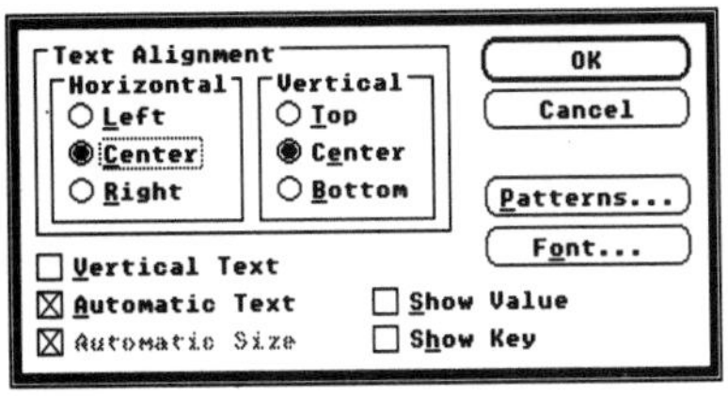

FIGURE 10-14. *Use the Text dialog box to change the alignment of your text and to select automatic labeling and sizing.*

Unless you specify otherwise, Microsoft Excel assumes you want all the text in your chart window displayed horizontally. However, you can use the Vertical Text option in the lower portion of the dialog box to indicate that you want the text to run vertically instead. About the only time you'll use the Vertical Text setting is to change the display of your value-axis title so that it occupies less room in the chart area. For example, Figure 10-15 shows the results of the Vertical Text option on the value-axis title in our sample chart. As you can see, the characters in the word *Goals* now appear one above the other, rather than side by side. As a result, the value-axis title is only one character wide, rather than five characters wide. Although this format is less attractive that the standard horizontal format, it does leave more room to display the chart's plot area.

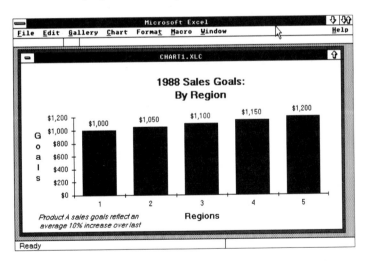

FIGURE 10-15. *We used the Vertical Text option to display the value-axis title vertically.*

The Horizontal and Vertical options at the top of the Text dialog box let you specify how you want your chart text to be aligned. The Vertical options go into effect only if you've selected the Vertical Text option in the lower portion of the dialog box. Figure 10-16 shows the effects of the various Text Alignment options on your vertical and horizontal text.

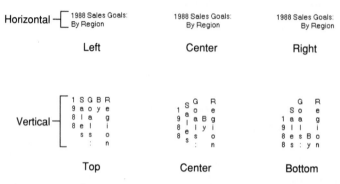

FIGURE 10-16. *The Text Alignment options let you display chart text six ways.*

The Automatic Text option

As we mentioned earlier, when you select label entries in your worksheet as you're creating a chart, Microsft Excel uses those labels as chart text. Similarly, the values you use to plot data are used as data-point labels when you attach text to your data-point markers. The Automatic Text option allows you to return to Microsoft Excel's default text after you've edited some attatched text on a chart.

For example, going back to the sample chart that we created in Figure 10-4, Microsoft Excel automatically created the chart title *Product A* because we included the label in cell B3 in our worksheet selection. Suppose we edited this title to read *Sales Goals: Product A*. If we later decided to revert to the original title, we could simply select the title text on the chart and then activate the Automatic Text option in the Text dialog box. Microsoft Excel would change the edited title back to *Product A*. (After you use Automatic Text to revert to the original title, you can't reverse the process and return to the text you entered manually. You'll have to reedit the title.)

The Automatic Size option

The Automatic Size option applies only to unattached text. Although this is the default setting, Microsoft Excel deselects Automatic Size whenever you manually resize a text block, as we did in Figure 10-10. After you've manually resized an unattached text block, you can use this option to revert to automatic sizing. When the Automatic Size option is in effect, the text block fits exactly around the text. The advantage of the Automatic Size option is that Microsoft Excel will adjust the size of the text block as needed whenever you edit the text or use the Font or Text commands to change the display characteristics of that text.

Sizing text blocks in the chart window becomes particularly important when you're using borders, because the size of the block determines the size of the border that appears around the text. (We'll show you how to create borders when we discuss the Patterns command.)

The Show Value and Show Key options

The last two options in the Text dialog box, Show Value and Show Key, appear only when you select a data-point label before issuing the Text command. The Show Value option works in conjunction with the Automatic Text option to determine the default text for your data-point labels. When Show Value is in effect, Microsoft Excel labels your data markers by extracting the corresponding values from the worksheet. If you deselect this option, Microsoft Excel uses the series name instead. If your chart contains only one data series, Microsoft Excel labels the data marker with the category name when you deselect show value, and if your data series doesn't contain a series name at all, Microsoft Excel places the numbers 1, 2, 3, and so forth over each data-point marker.

The Show Key option tells Microsoft Excel to display next to the data-point label a small square that reflects the pattern or color you've applied to the corresponding data marker. This option can be a handy alternative to a chart legend when you're short on space.

The Main Chart command

The Main Chart command on the Format menu lets you change your chart type and format. If you choose Main Chart while your window displays a column chart, you'll see a dialog box like the one in Figure 10-17. This dialog box contains two major sections: Type and Format. Initially, the option that's selected in the Type section will reflect the kind of chart with which you're working. For instance, when you choose Main Chart from within our sample chart window, you'll see the Column option selected. We'll look at the other Type options in Chapter 12.

As you can see, some of the options in the Format section of this dialog box appear dimmed, indicating that they are not available. The type of chart you're working with determines which of the Format options are available at any given time. For now, we'll cover two of the Format options that apply to column charts: Vary by Categories and % Cluster Spacing. In Chapter 11, we'll look at additional

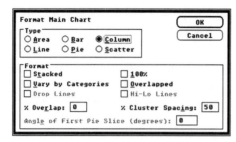

FIGURE 10-17. *Use the Main Chart dialog box to change the chart type and format.*

Format options as we discuss multiseries column charts. When we cover other chart types in Chapter 12, we'll examine the Format options that are available for each chart type.

The % Cluster Spacing setting

The % Cluster Spacing setting lets you control the spacing between the columns (or clusters of columns, if you have more than one data series) in a chart. The default cluster spacing, 50 percent, means that the distance between each column in the chart will be half the width of one column. Remember, the width of the column depends on the number of columns in the chart. Microsoft Excel adjusts the size of the columns to create an equal distribution across the chart. By expressing cluster spacing as a percentage of the column width, Microsoft Excel can also adjust the distance between columns as you add or remove data points. If you're working with a chart that contains only a few data points, you may want to increase the cluster spacing so that the columns aren't so wide and bulky.

The Vary by Categories option

When you create a chart with only one data series, Microsoft Excel makes all the columns red for color monitors and solid black otherwise. If you want to use a different color or pattern for each data point, select the Vary by Categories option in the Main Chart dialog box. Your chart will be redrawn to display the different colors or patterns. For example, Figure 10-18 shows our sample chart after we used the Vary by Categories option to display a different pattern on each column.

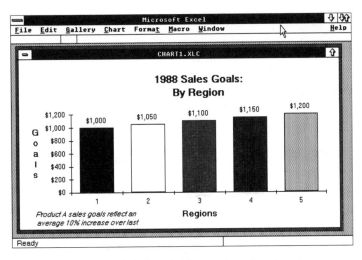

FIGURE 10-18. *We used the Vary by Categories option to assign a different pattern to each column.*

Formatting the axes

Microsoft Excel gives you a great deal of control over the format and contents of your chart's category and value axes. You can use the Axes command on the Chart menu to determine which axes appear—value, category, or neither. When you choose to display one or both axes, you can use the Scale command on the Format menu to maintain precise control over the axis content and format. Let's look at the Axes and Scale commands in detail.

The Axes command

The Axes command on the Chart menu lets you control the display of the category and value axes. When you choose the Axes command, Microsoft Excel displays the dialog box shown in Figure 10-19.

FIGURE 10-19. *Use the Axes dialog box to control the display of your chart axes.*

As you can see, Microsoft Excel allows you to control the display of each axis independently. Notice that the Axes options are already checked for both the category and the value axis. If you deselect both of these options, Microsoft Excel removes not only both sets of axis lines but also the tick-mark labels for each axis, so that your chart looks like Figure 10-20.

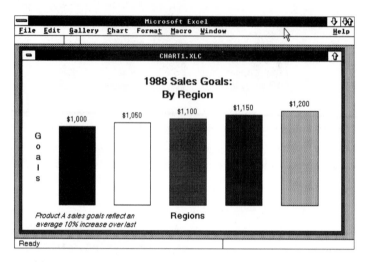

FIGURE 10-20. *We cancelled the Axes options to remove the axis lines and tick-mark labels from the chart.*

The Scale command

The Scale command on the Format menu gives you several more formatting options. The options available to you depend on which axis you select from the chart before you choose the command.

Formatting the category axis
If you select the category axis and then choose Scale from the Format menu, you'll see a dialog box like the one in Figure 10-21.

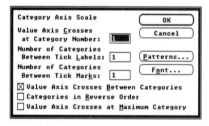

FIGURE 10-21. *This dialog box appears if you select the category axis before issuing the Scale command.*

The first setting in the Category Axis Scale dialog box, Value Axis Crosses at Category Number, lets you specify where the value axis will intersect the category axis. The default value (the one you'll use most often) is 1, meaning that the value axis will be placed in front of the first data-point marker (or the first cluster of markers), as it has been in our sample charts thus far. If you change the value to 3, Microsoft Excel will place the value axis in front of the third data-point marker or cluster, as shown in Figure 10-22. (Notice that the value labels along the axis overlap the second data column. To overcome this problem, you can change the tick-mark label position in the Patterns dialog box.)

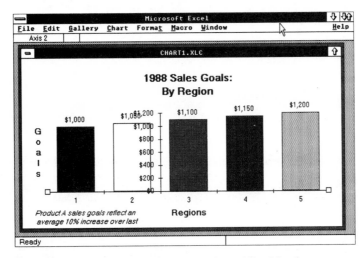

FIGURE 10-22. *To move the value axis to the middle of the chart, we changed the Value Axis Crosses at Category Number setting to 3.*

The Number of Categories Between Tick Labels setting controls the number of category labels that appear on the chart. You can use any whole number from 1 through 127 for this setting, but keep in mind that too many gaps between tick-mark labels will make your chart hard to interpret. The default value is 1, which means that every tick mark at the bottom of the chart will be accompanied by a tick-mark label. Normally, this is the value you'll want to use.

However, if a chart contains a large number of data points or if the category-axis tick-mark labels are too long to fit across the chart, Microsoft Excel may break the tick-mark labels into two lines. For example, Figure 10-23 shows a column chart with 12 data points. Microsoft Excel has broken several tick-mark labels into two lines in order to fit all the labels along the axis. To avoid this problem, you can enter a 2 in the Number of Categories Between Tick Labels edit bar. Microsoft Excel will then omit every other tick-mark label, as shown in Figure 10-24.

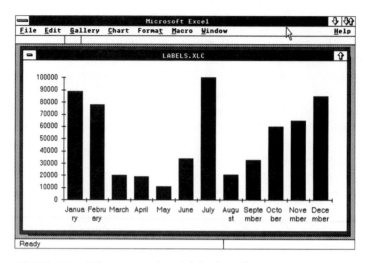

FIGURE 10-23. *When you use long labels along the category axis or when your chart contains a large number of data points, the tick-mark labels may become difficult to read.*

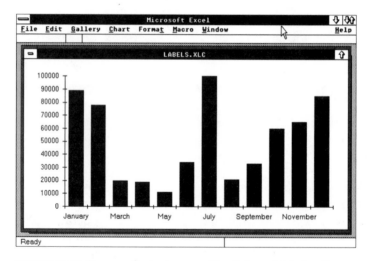

FIGURE 10-24. *You can eliminate every other tick-mark label on the category axis to make the text more readable.*

The third setting in the Category Axis Scale dialog box, Number of Categories Between Tick Marks, controls the number of data points (or clusters, if you're working with a multiseries column or bar chart) that appear between tick marks. Microsoft Excel accepts any whole number from 1 through 127 for this option. The default value is 1, which means that one data point or cluster will be displayed between each pair of tick marks. Normally, you'll want to use this value.

Just as you can tell Microsoft Excel to omit some of the tick-mark labels, you can omit some of the tick marks. To do this, enter a number that indicates the tick marks you want to omit in the Number of Categories Between Tick Marks edit box. For example, if you want to omit every other tick mark, enter a 2 in the Number of Categories Between Tick Marks edit box. Microsoft Excel will then eliminate every other tick mark along the axis.

The Value Axis Crosses Between Categories option is the default, as indicated by its preset selection. If you deselect this option, Microsoft Excel will shift the columns on the chart, as shown in Figure 10-25. Notice that the value axis and its labels now fall in the middle of the first column rather than to its left. Notice also that each column appears centered on a tick mark along the category axis rather than between tick marks. In addition, half of the first and fifth columns in the chart seem to have been erased. For this reason, you'll want to be sure that the Value Axis Crosses Between Categories option is selected for column and bar charts. However, you'll find that deselecting this option works well with line charts, causing the first data point for each series to appear next to the value axis and the last data point to appear flush with the last category on the category axis.

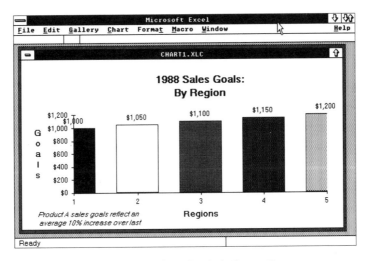

FIGURE 10-25. *We deselected the Value Axis Crosses Between Categories option in this chart.*

The Value Axis Crosses at Maximum Category option tells Microsoft Excel to move the value axis from the left edge to the right edge of the chart. You may want to use this option when you create overlay charts that use different scales (more about this in Chapter 12). Figure 10-26 shows the sample chart after we selected the Value Axis Crosses at Maximum Category option.

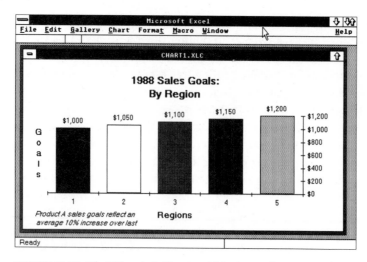

FIGURE 10-26. *The Value Axis Crosses at Maximum Category option moves the value axis to the right edge of the chart.*

You can reverse the order in which the categories are displayed by selecting the Categories in Reverse Order option. If you select this option with our sample chart, the Region 5 column will appear first, the Region 4 column second, and so on. The value axis will move to the right side of the chart; however, you can select the Value Axis Crosses at Maximum Category option to move the value axis back to the left side of the chart.

Formatting the value axis

If you select the value axis before you choose the Scale command from the Format menu, you'll see a dialog box like the one in Figure 10-27.

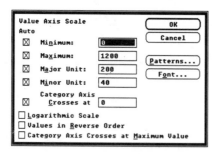

FIGURE 10-27. *Use the Value Axis Scale dialog box to format the value axis.*

The Minimum and Maximum values determine the scaling along the value axis. Microsoft Excel automatically creates an equal distribution of values between

Maximum and Minimum. The value in the Minimum edit bar determines the origin of the value axis—typically, zero. The Maximum edit bar contains the highest value on the axis; it will be equal to or slightly higher than the highest value in the data series you're plotting. In our sample chart, Microsoft Excel has set the maximum value to 1200, which is the highest value of our data series.

You can override Microsoft Excel's automatic scaling by typing your own values. For example, if you select the Minimum edit bar and type *800*, Microsoft Excel will automatically adjust the Maximum, Major Unit, Minor Unit, and Category Axis Crosses at values as needed to create an evenly spaced series of values along the value axis. The resulting chart will look like Figure 10-28.

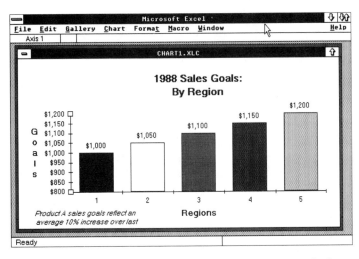

FIGURE 10-28. *We changed the Minimum setting for our sample chart to 800.*

The Minimum and Maximum settings are particularly important if you need to compare data in two or more charts. To make it easier to compare various trends, you may want to change the Minimum and Maximum values so that all your charts use the same scales.

In the Value Axis Scale dialog box, you'll notice check boxes to the left of the first five settings, under the word *Auto*. When you change one of these settings, the X in the Auto box for that setting will disappear. To return to the original value, simply select the Auto box for that setting so that the X reappears. For example, to change the minimum value along our axis back to zero, we could simply select the Auto box next to the Minimum setting.

When we changed the Minimum value to create the chart in Figure 10-27, we let Microsoft Excel adjust the Major Unit, Minor Unit, and Category Axis Crosses at settings automatically. You'll generally want Microsoft Excel to determine the Major Unit and Minor Unit settings. If you enter your own numbers, however, remember that Microsoft Excel may change your Maximum setting slightly so that the values between Minimum and Maximum can be evenly distributed.

In all the charts we've shown so far, the category axis crosses the value axis at the lowest point on that axis. When 0 is the minimum on the value-axis scale, the category axis crosses at 0. But in Figure 10-28, the category axis crosses the value axis at 800, the minimum value on that axis scale. As you might expect, you can change the position of the category axis by typing a number in the Category Axis Crosses at edit bar. Figure 10-29 shows the chart from Figure 10-28 after we changed the Category Axis Crosses at value to 900.

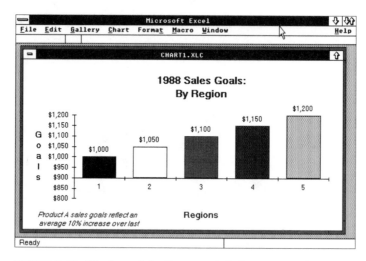

FIGURE 10-29. *We changed the Category Axis Crosses at setting to 900.*

As with the category axis, you can reverse the order of the values on the value axis by selecting the Values in Reverse Order option. Microsoft Excel will automatically move the category axis to the top of the chart and "flip" each column. The labels along the category axis will appear above the columns, and the data-point labels you created with the Attach Text command will be moved below the columns, as shown in Figure 10-30. (We reverted to the automatic Maximum and Category Axis Crosses at settings in this chart.) You can move the category labels back to the bottom of the chart by selecting the axis and then choosing the High option in the Patterns dialog box; however, you can't change the position of the data-point labels.

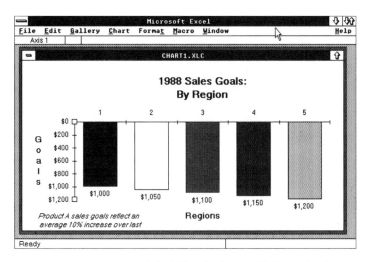

FIGURE 10-30. *We activated the Values in Reverse Order option for our sample chart.*

All the charts we've shown so far in this chapter have used arithmetic scales. Arithmetic scales are divided into segments of equal size and value. In Microsoft Excel, you can change the value-axis scale from an arithmetic scale to a logarithmic scale. Logarithmic scaling means that the value-axis scale is divided into tiers. Each tier represents a power of 10, so the value axis displays the numbers 10, 100, 1000, and so on. If your chart contains values less than 10, Microsoft Excel uses the number 1 as its Minimum value.

You'll seldom use this scaling technique unless you're charting scientific or engineering data. However, you may want to consider using a log scale if the values in your chart are widely distributed. For example, Figure 10-31 shows a chart with data-point values ranging from 7 to 1000. Notice that some of the data markers nearly disappear in this chart. Because the scale is so large, the smaller values are overpowered by the larger ones. Now look at the chart in Figure 10-32, which plots the same data on a logarithmic scale. As you can see, the tiered scaling of the logarithmic values creates columns more equal in size.

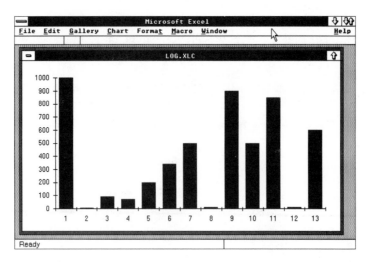

FIGURE 10-31. *We created this chart by plotting a series of values from 7 to 1000 on an arithmetic scale.*

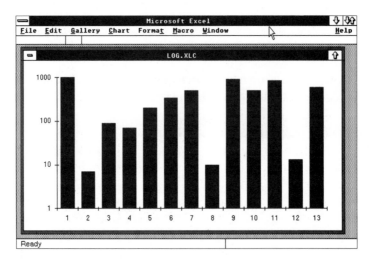

FIGURE 10-32. *We changed to a logarithmic scale on the value axis.*

Formatting gridlines

The Gridlines command on the Chart menu lets you add horizontal and vertical gridlines to your charts. When you choose the Gridlines command, Microsoft Excel displays the dialog box shown in Figure 10-33.

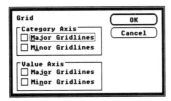

FIGURE 10-33. *Use the Gridlines dialog box to add gridlines to your chart.*

As you can see, both the Category Axis and Value Axis sections of this dialog box include Major Gridlines and Minor Gridlines options. If you select Major Gridlines for either axis, Microsoft Excel will display a gridline for each tick mark along that axis. For example, Figure 10-34 shows how our sample chart will look if you select Major Gridlines for both axes. If you select Minor Gridlines, Microsoft Excel will display the intermediate gridlines as well, as shown in Figure 10-35. If you select Minor Gridlines without selecting Major Gridlines, Microsoft Excel will include both in the chart.

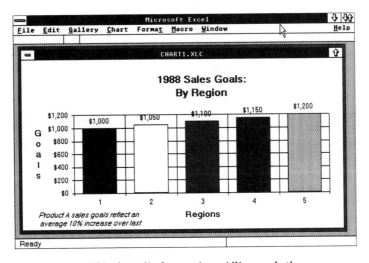

FIGURE 10-34. *This chart displays major gridlines on both axes.*

Notice in Figure 10-35 that our gridlines make some of the data-point labels in the chart difficult to read. To avoid this problem, select one of the data-point labels, choose the White Out option in the Font dialog box, and activate Apply to All. This procedure will block out an area behind each of the labels so that they are easier to read.

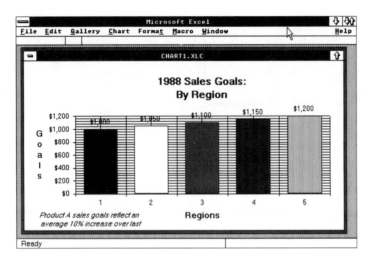

FIGURE 10-35. *We added minor gridlines to both axes.*

Using arrows for emphasis

Although arrows should be used with moderation because they tend to clutter your charts, they can be an effective way to point out key information. When you choose Add Arrow from the Chart menu, Microsoft Excel places a black arrow on the screen, as shown in Figure 10-36.

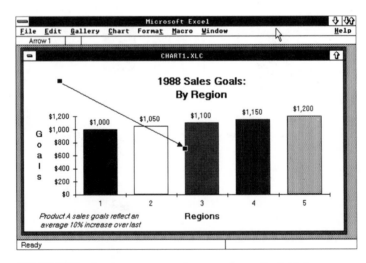

FIGURE 10-36. *An arrow appears when you choose the Add Arrow command on the Chart menu.*

Notice the black squares that appear at either end of the arrow. By moving these squares, you can change the length or angle of the arrow. When you drag the square at one end of the arrow with the mouse, the square at the other end remains anchored, making it easy to drag the arrowhead to the desired point on the chart. After the arrowhead is in place, you can use the opposite square to pivot the arrow to the desired angle and drag it to the desired length. You also can change the length or angle of the arrow with the keyboard. Simply select the arrow and choose the Size command from the Format menu. Then use the arrow keys to move the arrowhead. Press the Ctrl key along with the arrow keys to fine-tune your changes. When the arrow reaches the desired length and angle, press Enter to lock in your changes.

To move the entire arrow with the mouse, point to the shaft and drag the arrow to the desired position. With the keyboard, choose the Move command from the Format menu and then use the arrow keys to move the arrow around on the screen. Again, you can use the Ctrl key in conjunction with the arrow keys to fine-tune the position of the arrow. Press Enter to lock in the new arrow position. You can also use the Patterns command to format your chart arrows.

To delete an arrow you've placed on a chart, first select that arrow. Microsoft Excel will replace the Add Arrow command on the Chart menu with the Delete Arrow command. Simply choose the Delete Arrow command to get rid of the selected arrow. (If an arrow is not selected, Microsoft Excel will again display the Add Arrow command on the Chart menu, allowing you to place additional arrows on the chart.)

The Patterns command

The Patterns command on the Format menu allows you to change the patterns and borders that Microsoft Excel uses to display chart objects. To use this command, you must first select the item you want to format; then choose Patterns from the Format menu. The contents of the Patterns dialog box vary according to the type of chart and the chart object you're working with. For example, if you select one of the column markers in our sample sales chart, you'll see a dialog box like the one shown in Figure 10-37.

You can use the Patterns command, in conjunction with the Select Chart and Select Plot Area commands, to specify patterns and to create and format borders around the plot area or around the entire chart. For example, in the sample charts we've seen so far, the background pattern has been plain and no border has appeared around the chart area. Suppose you want to change the background to a shaded pattern and add a shadow border. First choose the Select Chart command from the Chart menu and then select Patterns from the Format menu.

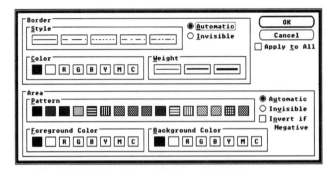

FIGURE 10-37. *The contents of the Patterns dialog box vary, depending on the chart type and the chart object you select.*

The default area pattern and the default border setting are both Invisible when the entire chart is selected. To change these settings, simply select the options you want to use. For instance, if you select the fourth option in the Area Pattern portion of the dialog box, Microsoft Excel places a light screen behind the chart. (You can also choose the color in which you want this pattern to appear, although we can't show the effects of color options in our sample charts.) After specifying the Area Pattern option, choose the solid Style option in the Border section of the dialog box. Also select the first Weight option (the lightest weight) and activate the Shadow option. Figure 10-38 shows the results of these selections.

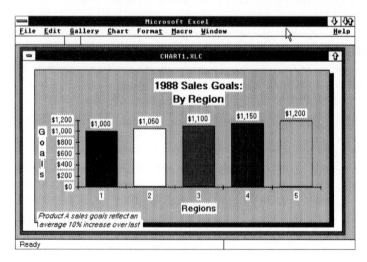

FIGURE 10-38. *We changed the Area Pattern and Border settings for our sample chart.*

Notice that our area pattern fills the background of the plot area as well as the surrounding chart area. This occurs because the default area pattern for the plot area is Invisible. To separate the plot area from the rest of the chart with a thin border and use a white area pattern in the plot area so that the screen pattern from the chart area doesn't show through, issue the Select Plot Area command from the Chart menu and then choose the Patterns command. In the Patterns dialog box, select the first Border Style option (a plain line). Notice that when you choose this option, Microsoft Excel selects the black Border Color and the first Border Weight option. Now choose the white Foreground Color option in the Area portion of the dialog box. When you click OK or press Enter, your chart will look like the one in Figure 10-39.

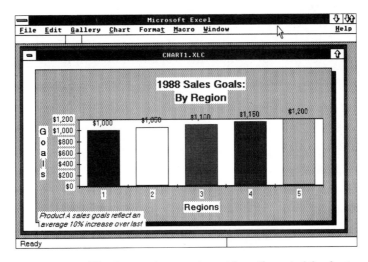

FIGURE 10-39. *The plot area is now set apart from the rest of the chart with a thin border and a plain white background.*

Notice that some of the data-point labels—the ones that fall outside the plot area—are now difficult to read because of the background chart pattern. To fix this problem, choose one of the data-point labels and then choose Font from the Format menu. In the Font dialog box, select the White Out Background option and then choose Apply to All. When you choose OK or press Enter, each data-point label will once again appear against a blocked-out solid background.

Saving charts

If you've used other integrated spreadsheet programs, you may be accustomed to thinking of a chart as a specialized extension of a worksheet. In programs like

Symphony and Lotus 1-2-3, for example, charts are a part of the worksheet file. They are stored with the worksheet and cannot be edited independently of the worksheet file. In Microsoft Excel, however, each chart is a file unto itself. Thus, you create new charts from the File menu, not from the Window menu. In addition, you must save each chart—and reopen it—as a separate file. Your charts will not be saved automatically when you save the worksheet from which they were created.

In most cases, your charts are linked to one or more supporting worksheet files. Thus, you should follow the same rules when working with chart files that you follow when working with any other type of dependent file. For more on working with linked files, see Chapter 8.

There are several advantages to Microsoft Excel's method of storing chart files. For example, it is simple to combine data from several worksheets in one chart file. In addition, you can copy data and formats from one chart to another and open chart files without opening the worksheet files on which they depend.

11

Plotting More Than One Series

*S*o far, we've been working with charts that plot only one data series. In this chapter, we'll show you how to create and format charts that contain more than one data series.

Adding a data series to a chart

To add a data series to the chart we created in Chapter 10, you must return to the worksheet window and select the cells that contain the second data series you want to plot. We'll use cells C3:C8 in the worksheet shown in Figure 11-1. After selecting the cells, choose Copy from the Edit menu. Now move back to the chart window and choose Paste from the chart Edit menu. Figure 11-2 shows the chart with the new data series added.

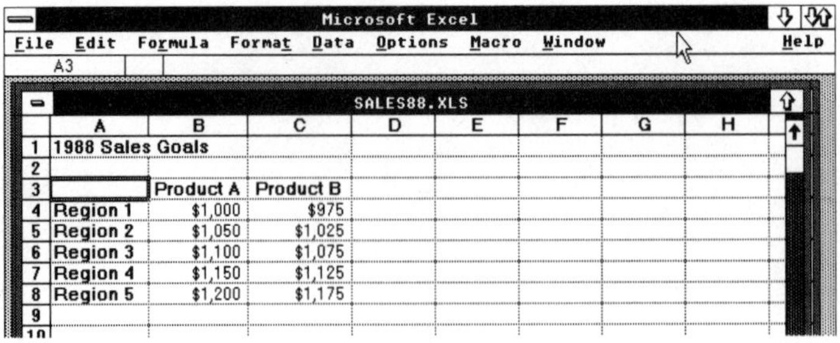

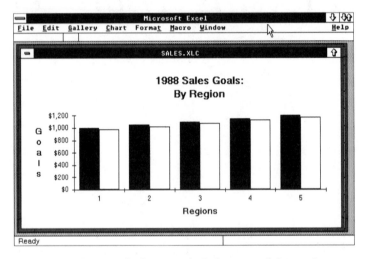

FIGURE 11-1. *We'll continue with this Sales worksheet from Chapter 10 as we demonstrate how to plot more than one series on a chart.*

FIGURE 11-2. *Our sample chart now includes a second data series.*

The sales goals for Product B are now included in the chart. Notice that Microsoft Excel grouped each of the values in cells C4:C8 into the appropriate category—Region 1, Region 2, and so on. Whenever you create a chart with more than one data series, each series should contain an equal number of data points. Otherwise, Microsoft Excel won't be able to group the data points correctly.

Although it's not apparent on the chart, the label *Product B* from cell C3 has become the series name for the new set of data points. The importance of this name will become clear in a few pages.

An alternative approach

Of course, you can also create this chart from scratch instead of adding a second data series to an existing chart. Simply activate the worksheet and select the range

A3:C8. Then choose New from the File menu, select Chart, and choose OK or press Enter. Figure 11-3 shows the result. Although this chart lacks the text and formatting enhancements that had already been added to the previous version, it's identical in every other way. (You can't use this technique as long as Microsoft Excel is displaying a marquee around a selection you've chosen to copy or cut. In that case, the program apparently expects you to issue the Paste command when you open a new chart window. Thus, when you issue the New command, you see a blank chart.)

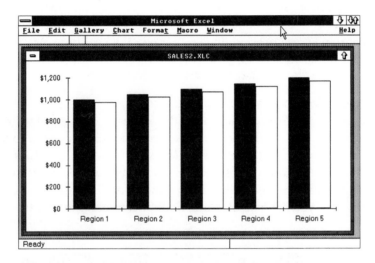

FIGURE 11-3. *We created this two-series chart from scratch.*

Notice that the chart in Figure 11-3 doesn't have a title, even though we included the entry in cell B3, Product A, in the selection. As we saw in Chapter 10, Microsoft Excel uses the series name as a chart title if the chart is created with only one data series. In charts with two or more series, however, Microsoft Excel does not provide a default title. When you choose the Attach Text command from the Chart menu, only the word *Title* appears in the formula bar. Of course, after you have created the chart, you can use any of the techniques we've explained so far to enhance it.

To create data-point labels for the second series, use the Attach Text command, select the Series or Data Point option, and then type 2 in the Series Number edit bar and the data-point number in the Point Number edit bar.

How Microsoft Excel distinguishes data series from categories

When you chart the range A3:C8, how does Microsoft Excel know which cells fall into which data series and which data points fall into which category? It refers to the shape of the range you selected and the kinds of entries contained in each cell of the selection. If you select a horizontal range (that is, a range that is wider than it is tall), the values are plotted by row. If you select a vertical range (one that is taller than it is wide), the values are plotted by column. If your selection contains an equal number of rows and columns, it is treated as a vertical range—that is, each row becomes a data series and each column becomes a category.

Perhaps this rule will be easier to remember if you keep in mind that Microsoft Excel always assumes you want fewer data series than data points. Thus, if your selection has more rows than columns, each column becomes a data series. Each row, in turn, becomes a category. Because the range we selected to create the chart in Figure 11-3 contained more rows than columns, Microsoft Excel organized the values in each column into a data series and each row became a category.

Overriding Microsoft Excel's default organization

Suppose you want to create a chart using the values in cells A3:D10 of the worksheet in Figure 11-4. You would like the exam scores for each name in column A to be a separate data series, with the categories Exam 1, Exam 2, and Exam 3. When you select the range A3:D10, Microsoft Excel would typically organize the chart by rows, plotting the categories as Allen, Burns, and so on. To override Microsoft Excel's organization, you can use the Paste Special command to plot the values by columns.

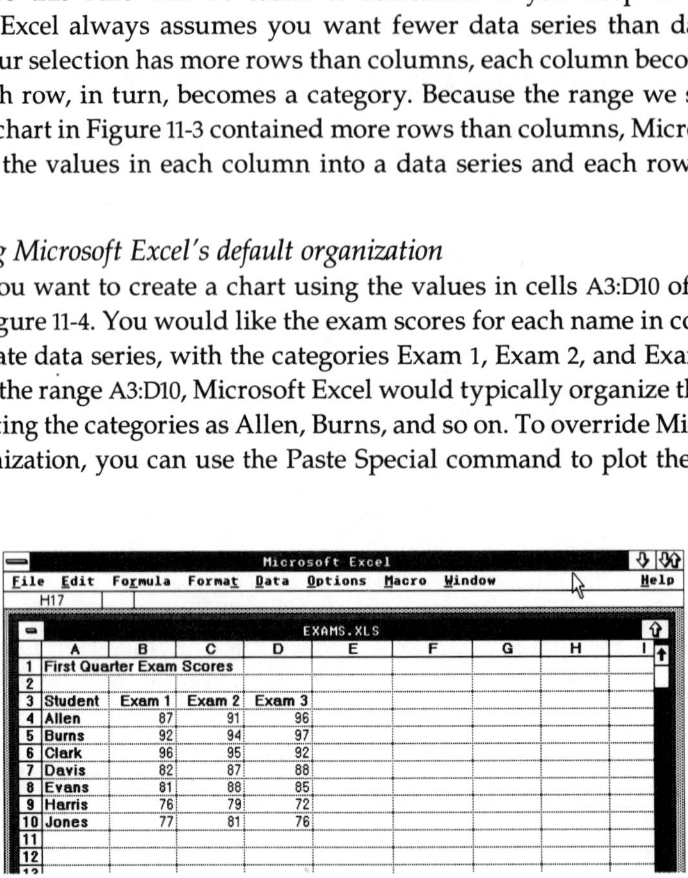

FIGURE 11-4. *We want to plot the exam scores in this worksheet by rows instead of by columns.*

Begin by selecting the range A3:D10; then choose Copy from the Edit menu. Now choose New from the File menu and select the Chart option. When Microsoft Excel displays an empty chart window, choose Paste Special from the chart Edit menu. You'll see a dialog box like the one in Figure 11-5.

FIGURE 11-5. *Use the Paste Special dialog box to override Microsoft Excel's default organization.*

As you can see, Microsoft Excel assumes you want to organize the chart data by columns, using the labels in row 3 (Exam 1, Exam 2, Exam 3) as series names and the labels in column A (Allen, Burns, and so forth) as category names. If you select the Rows option, however, Microsoft Excel changes the bottom two options in the dialog box to Series Names in First Column and Categories in First Row. Assuming you want to accept these settings, choose OK or press Enter in the Paste Special dialog box to create a chart like the one shown in Figure 11-6. When you use Paste Special to organize the data in rows, Microsoft Excel uses the labels in row 3 as category names and the labels in column A as series names.

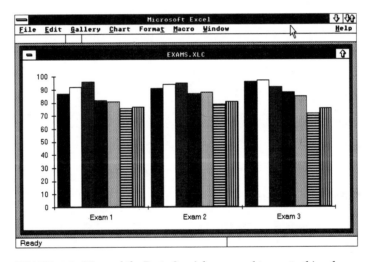

FIGURE 11-6. *We used the Paste Special command to create this column chart from a vertical range of data.*

The Paste Special dialog box also offers a Replace Existing Categories option. Select this option if you want to use the categories in the current copy range as your data-series names, thus overwriting any existing series names. Before the categories are replaced, Microsoft Excel will ask you to confirm your decision.

For example, suppose you've created a chart that uses the default category labels *1, 2, 3,* and *4* below the category axis. Now suppose you decide to add a new data series to this chart. Cells A1:A4 of your worksheet contain the labels *1st Qtr, 2nd Qtr, 3rd Qtr,* and *4th Qtr.* Cells B1:B4 contain four numeric values. To add the labels as well as the four new values to your chart, select the range A1:B4 and issue the Copy command. Then activate the chart window, issue the Paste Special command, and choose the Replace Existing Categories option. Microsoft Excel will add the new data series to the chart and use the labels from cells A1:A4 as the new category labels.

Overriding Microsoft Excel's choice of labels

As we mentioned earlier, if Microsoft Excel doesn't find labels in the first row or first column of the range you select to plot, it assumes that you don't want to use category labels or series names in your chart. But suppose you want to use numeric labels in your chart? For example, suppose you want to use the values in column A of Figure 11-7 as category labels in a chart. Begin by selecting cells A3:B13 and choosing the Copy command. Then create a new chart and choose the Paste Special command. The Paste Special dialog box will look like the one in Figure 11-8.

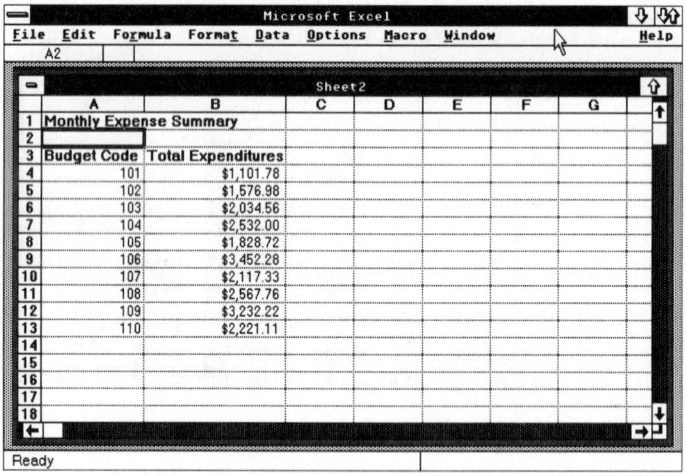

	Budget Code	Total Expenditures
1	Monthly Expense Summary	
2		
3	Budget Code	Total Expenditures
4	101	$1,101.78
5	102	$1,576.98
6	103	$2,034.56
7	104	$2,532.00
8	105	$1,828.72
9	106	$3,452.28
10	107	$2,117.33
11	108	$2,567.76
12	109	$3,232.22
13	110	$2,221.11

FIGURE 11-7. *You can create a chart that uses the values in column A of this worksheet as category labels.*

FIGURE 11-8. *The Paste Special dialog box looks like this when you select cells A3:B13 of the worksheet shown in Figure 11-7.*

Notice that the Categories in First Column option is not selected. Because column A contains numeric values, Microsoft Excel assumes these cells are to be used as data points. If you select the Categories in First Column option, however, Microsoft Excel will use the values in column A as category labels. Figure 11-9 shows the result.

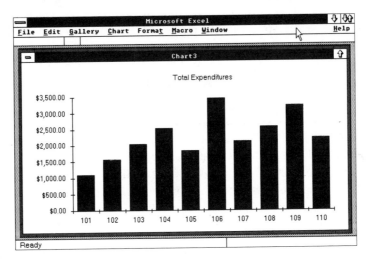

FIGURE 11-9. *This chart uses numeric category labels.*

By the way, although dates are stored as numeric values in your worksheet, Microsoft Excel assumes you want to use dates in the first row or first column of your copy area as labels. If you've assigned one of Microsoft Excel's date formats to the values in the first row or first column of your chart range, those dates will be treated as series names or category labels. If you want Microsoft Excel to plot your date values instead of using them as labels, you can choose the Paste Special command and turn off the Series Names or Categories option.

Deleting a data series from a chart

To eliminate a data series from a chart, simply select the series by clicking on one of the data-point markers in the series or by using the arrow keys. Then press the Backspace key and press Enter or click on the Enter box in the formula bar.

After you've eliminated a data series from a chart, you can't use the Undo command to replace it. If you want to add the series back to your chart, you must use the Copy and Paste commands, just as if you were creating a new data series.

Enhancing the chart

In the previous chapter, we explained many of Microsoft Excel's chart-formatting options. Some options, however, apply only to charts with more than one data series. In addition, a few options behave a bit differently when you add more than one series to a chart. We'll cover those options next.

The Main Chart command

As you know, the Main Chart command on the Format menu lets you control the way your chart is displayed. You've already seen how the Vary by Categories and the % Cluster Spacing options work. We'll address those options here only to show how they differ when you add more than one series to the chart. The 100%, Stacked, and Overlapped options apply only to charts that contain two or more data series.

The Vary by Categories option
As you saw in the previous chapter, when you create a chart with only one data series and select the Vary by Categories option in the Main Chart dialog box, Microsoft Excel displays each column in a different pattern or color. As you've seen in this chapter, when a chart contains more than one data series, each data series appears in a different pattern or color. Thus, selecting Vary by Categories in a chart with more than one data series has no effect on the chart.

The % Cluster Spacing option
The % Cluster Spacing option lets you control the spacing between the columns (or clusters of columns) in a chart. The default cluster spacing, 50 percent, means that the distance between each column or cluster of columns in the chart will be half the width of one column. Of course, you can change the spacing between

each column or cluster by typing a new number in the % Cluster Spacing edit bar. For example, Figure 11-10 shows the chart from Figure 11-2 after the % Cluster Spacing setting has been changed to 100 percent.

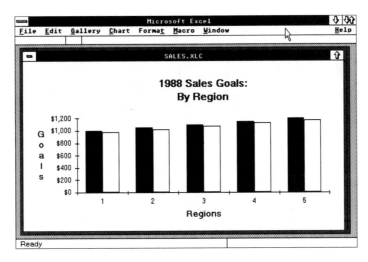

FIGURE 11-10. *We changed the % Cluster Spacing setting from 50 percent to 100 percent to increase the amount of space between the clusters of columns in this chart.*

The Overlapped option

The Overlapped option lets you control how the columns in each cluster are positioned relative to one another. Overlapping is controlled by two settings in the Main Chart dialog box: Overlapped and % Overlap. Initially, the Overlapped option is unselected and the default setting for % Overlap is 0. This means that the columns in each cluster do not overlap but appear side by side.

In order to create overlapped columns, you must activate the Overlapped option and enter a number in the % Overlap edit bar. For example, in our sample chart, if you select the Overlapped option and enter 25 in the % Overlap edit bar, the result will look like Figure 11-11. (We returned to 50-percent cluster spacing in this chart as well.) Notice that each column overlaps the column to its left by one quarter of a column width. You can use any percentage from 0 through 100 as your overlap in a column chart.

The Overlapped format works best when the heights of the columns within each cluster differ noticeably. If all the columns in a cluster are about the same height, using Overlapped simply makes the column that is plotted last look wider than the other columns. In addition, if your chart contains data-point labels, these may overlap the columns slightly when you use the Overlapped option.

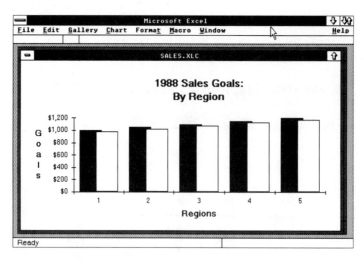

FIGURE 11-11. *We selected the Overlapped option and specified 25-percent overlap and 50-percent cluster spacing.*

Although you'll usually use the % Overlap setting only when the Overlapped option is selected, you can enter a percentage other than 0 in the % Overlap edit bar when the Overlapped option is not selected. When you do this, Microsoft Excel separates the columns in each cluster by the amount of space indicated by the percentage. For example, if you choose the Main Chart command, deselect the

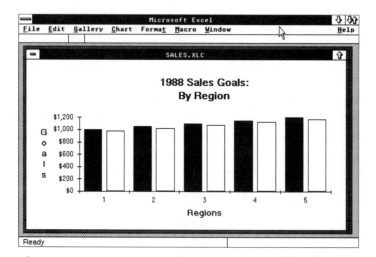

FIGURE 11-12. *To create the space between the columns in each cluster, we deselected the Overlapped option without changing the 25-percent overlap setting.*

Overlapped option, enter 25 in the % Overlap edit bar, and choose OK or press Enter, your chart will change to look like Figure 11-12. Notice that the columns in each cluster are now separated by 25 percent of a column width.

The Stacked option

The Stacked option allows you to convert clustered columns into sets of stacked columns. For example, Figure 11-13 shows what would happen to the chart in Figure 11-2 if you chose the Main Chart command and selected the Stacked option.

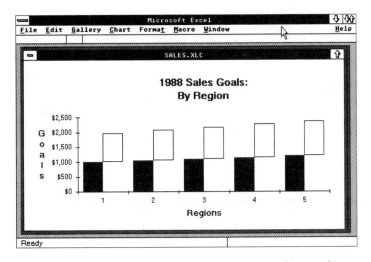

FIGURE 11-13. *You can use the Stacked option to create this step chart.*

Notice that, although the bottom of the second column in each cluster of this chart appears where the first column ends, the columns in each cluster are still side by side instead of being stacked one above the next. This type of chart is called a step chart. If you want to convert the chart into a true stacked column chart, you must select the Overlapped option and enter *100* in the % Overlap edit bar. Until you do this, the columns in the chart will not align properly. Figure 11-14 shows our chart with 100-percent overlap.

Notice that Microsoft Excel adjusts the scale along the value axis to accommodate the new format, reflecting the sum of the two series. Thus, if you decide to use the Stacked option, be sure that the Auto box is activated for your value-axis Minimum and Maximum settings or else enter values large enough to accommodate the stacked chart format. Otherwise, Microsoft Excel will not be able to adjust the value scale and your columns will be truncated.

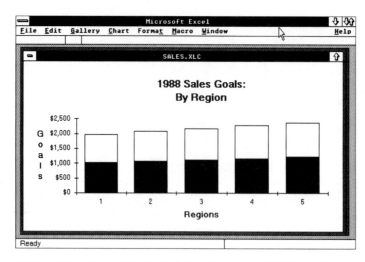

FIGURE 11-14. *We used the Stacked, Overlapped, and 100% Overlap settings to create this stacked column chart.*

If you do find that some of your columns are truncated, select the value axis and choose Scale from the Format menu. Then select the Auto box for the Minimum and Maximum options or enter larger values to accommodate your stacked columns.

The 100% option

The 100% option, which is effective only when you've selected the Stacked and Overlapped options and have entered *100* in the % Overlap edit bar, changes the value-axis scale in the chart from actual values to a percentage scale. For example, Figure 11-15 shows the chart from Figure 11-14 after we selected the 100% option in the Main Chart dialog box.

Notice that the value axis now has a minimum value of 0 and a maximum value of 100. Thus, each of the data-point markers reflects the relative value of that data point on a 100-percent scale. However, the value-axis labels still carry dollar signs. Unfortunately, you can't change the format of the value-axis labels without also changing the format of your worksheet values. Of course, if you assign the 0% or 0.00% format to the cells in your worksheet, Microsoft Excel will display the values 10% and 1000%, which is probably not the effect you intended. If you don't want your value-axis labels to appear in currency format, your best bet is to format the values in your worksheet to appear in the default General format or in the 0 or 0.00 format.

You might think of the chart in Figure 11-15 as a series of pie charts in column format, with each column representing the entire pie for that category and each

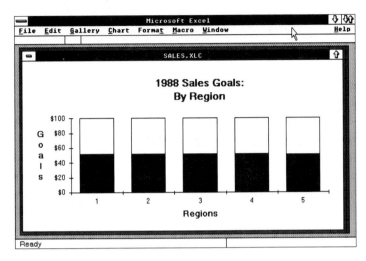

FIGURE 11-15. *We converted the value axis to a percentage scale.*

data-point value representing a proportional slice of the column. For example, the column for Region 1 represents 100 percent of the sales forecast for that region. The stacked sections in the Region 1 column show what percentages of the forecast sales are accounted for individually by Product A and Product B.

Selecting patterns for multiseries charts

You can use the Format menu's Patterns command to change the pattern Microsoft Excel uses to display the columns or stacked portions of columns in a multiseries chart. When you select a pattern in the Patterns dialog box, it applies to all the columns in a series, not to an individual column.

To use patterns in a multiseries chart, you must first select the data series you want to format. When you do this, Microsoft Excel places squares in some of the markers in that series to indicate your selection. After you've selected the series, choose Patterns from the Format menu.

The default Area Pattern setting is Automatic. With this setting, if you've created a multiseries chart and you're viewing that chart on a monochrome screen, Microsoft Excel assigns the first pattern option to the first series in the chart, the second pattern to the second series, and so on. When you're viewing a multiseries chart in color, Microsoft Excel uses a solid pattern but assigns a different color to each series. The colors are assigned in the order in which they appear in the Patterns dialog box—red, then green, then blue, and so forth.

To alter the default patterns and colors in a chart, select one of the data series and then choose one of the 16 pattern options, one of the 8 color options, or one of each. For example, Figure 11-16 shows the result of selecting the first series in our sample chart, choosing Patterns, and selecting a diagonal area pattern. (We moved back to a nonstacked, nonoverlapped format to make our pattern selection clearer.) Notice that the new pattern has been assigned to every column in the first data series.

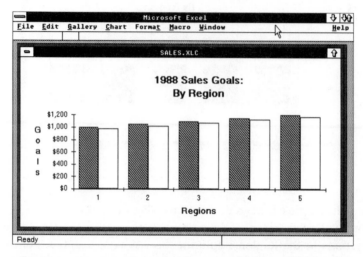

FIGURE 11-16. *You can change the pattern or color of any data series in a chart.*

If you apply the Invisible option to a data series, Microsoft Excel displays only the column borders. When you use the Invisible option on an overlapping column, the overlapped column "shows through" the top column. To avoid this problem, select a solid white pattern for the overlapping column instead of using the Invisible option.

The last option in the Patterns dialog box is Apply to All. If you activate this option, Microsoft Excel uses the Area Pattern, Border Pattern, and Border Weight options that you define in the dialog box for all the data series in your chart. If this option is not selected, the settings you define are applied only to the selected data series (but to every column in that series).

Using legends

Legends are special labels that identify the data series in your charts. You can use legends in single-series or multiseries charts. For most chart types, however, you'll find that legends add little information to a single-series chart, because Microsoft Excel simply repeats the tick-mark labels that already appear below the category axis. However, if you've assigned a different pattern to each category in a single-series chart, a legend might be helpful. Pie charts, which we'll discuss in the next chapter, are probably the only single-series charts that frequently need legends.

If your chart includes more than one data series, you'll probably want to add a legend to help the reader distinguish each series. To add a legend to the chart we created in Figure 11-16, choose Add Legend from the Chart menu. As you can see in Figure 11-17, the series names Product A and Product B now appear in the legend. Microsoft Excel used these names in the legend because we included them in the range we selected in building the chart.

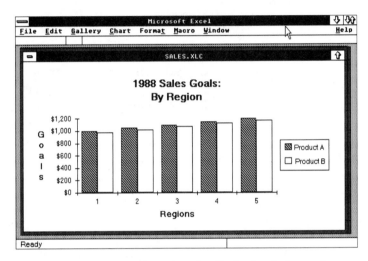

FIGURE 11-17. *We added a legend to identify the chart's data series.*

Changing the legend text

Microsoft Excel does not allow you to edit the contents of the legend box. To alter the text in the legend box, you must edit the cells of the worksheet that contain the category labels. You also can change the legend text by editing the SERIES functions used to create the chart. We'll cover the SERIES function fully in Chapter 13.

If your chart doesn't include series names (that is, if you didn't include cells containing labels in the columns or rows you selected for your data series), Microsoft Excel doesn't display any text in the legend box. Only the data-point-marker keys will appear. In order to create the legend text, you must alter the SERIES functions that form the basis for the chart.

Moving the legend

Microsoft Excel automatically centers the legend along the right side of the chart area and adjusts the size of the plot area to accommodate the addition. If you want to reposition the legend on the screen, you must select the legend box and then choose Legend from the Format menu. When you choose this command, Microsoft Excel displays the dialog box shown in Figure 11-18. This dialog box offers four options: Bottom, Corner, Top, and Vertical. Vertical is the default.

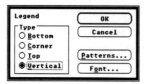

FIGURE 11-18. *Use the Legend dialog box to position your chart's legend.*

If you select Corner, Microsoft Excel moves the legend to the upper right corner of the chart. If you select Top, Microsoft Excel changes the legend to a horizontal format and centers it under the chart title. If you select Bottom, Microsoft Excel moves the legend to one line at the bottom of the chart, where it will be less conspicuous and take up less room. The Vertical option, of course, positions the legend on the right side of the chart, as shown in Figure 11-17.

Formatting legend text

You can use the Font command to change the appearance of text in the legend box. To do this, select the Font button in the Legend dialog box. (If the Legend dialog box is not open, you can select the legend and then choose Font from the Format menu.) Microsoft Excel will display a Font dialog box, like the one shown in Figure 10-11, that allows you to specify the typeface, size, and style of the legend text.

As you might expect, if you select a larger type size, Microsoft Excel expands the size of the legend box; if you reduce the type size, Microsoft Excel makes the legend box smaller.

In addition to formatting the legend text, you can also format the area in which the text appears—not the entire area inside the legend box, but the area immediately under the text itself. You can change this area by using the options in the Background section of the Font dialog box. If you choose the Automatic option, Microsoft Excel selects the background color and pattern. If you choose the Transparent option, the area under the legend text allows anything under it to show through. The White Out option blocks out an area under the legend text. With the White Out Background option selected, the area blocked out under the text always appears in white.

You can also select the color—black, white, red, green, blue, yellow, magenta, cyan—in which the legend text appears. Selecting the Automatic color option tells Microsoft Excel to choose the color.

Selecting legend patterns

You can control the pattern that Microsoft Excel uses to display the legend area and the legend border. To do this, select the Patterns button in the Legend dialog box. (If the Legend dialog box is not open, you can select the legend and then choose Patterns from the Format menu.) When the Patterns dialog box appears, you'll notice that the default background and foreground colors are white, the default border style is a plain line, and the default border weight is light.

The white Background Color setting ensures that any chart objects that might be under the legend will not be visible through it. The white background also means that your legend box will always appear with a white background, even if you use a background pattern in the chart area.

You can fill the legend box with a different pattern by selecting any pattern in the Area Pattern box. If you change the legend background pattern, you must be sure to choose a pattern different from those you're using for the series in the chart; otherwise, the key box for that series will fade into the background.

Besides changing the pattern in the legend box, you can change the color by selecting a new foreground color in the Patterns dialog box. Of course, if you're displaying each chart series in a different color, you should choose a color for the legend box that is different from any of the colors assigned to the data series.

You can use the Invisible option to eliminate the background pattern altogether. If you set the Area Pattern to Invisible, however, any background pattern you assign to the chart will also appear in the legend box. In addition, any chart options that may be under the legend will show through.

As with the plot and chart areas, you can also change the pattern, weight, and color of the border box that appears around the legend. If you don't want a border, you can use Invisible as the Border option.

To add a black drop-shadow border to your legend box, select the Shadow option. The shadow always appears in black, no matter what border pattern or color you select.

More about legends

Deleting a legend is as easy as adding one. Add Legend is a toggle command, so as soon as you choose it from the Chart menu, its name changes to Delete Legend. To delete a legend you've created, simply choose the Delete Legend command. When you delete the legend, Microsoft Excel expands the size of the plot area again, to use the space that was occupied by the legend.

As you would expect, Microsoft Excel changes your legend keys whenever you alter the patterns or colors assigned to the series in the chart. It also changes the text in the legend box when you edit the contents of the worksheet cells that contain that text.

E X C E L

Using the Show Key option

If you're short on space, use the Show Key option in the Text dialog box instead of a chart legend. First, select one of the data-point markers on the chart. Then choose Attach Text from the Chart menu. In the Attach Text dialog box, Microsoft Excel will already have indicated the current series number and data-point number, so simply choose OK. You'll then see a value just above the data-point marker you selected. Now choose the Text command from the Format menu. In the Text dialog box, activate the Show Key option and then deactivate the Show Value option. When you choose OK, you'll see a small pattern box or marker symbol above your selected data point. Next to this box or symbol, you'll see the series name. (By deactivating the Show Value option, you tell Microsoft Excel to replace the value that formerly appeared as your data-point marker with the series name.) In a multiseries chart, you can keep your markers and labels from crowding into one another by placing each one over a different category.

12

Other Types of Charts

Microsoft Excel has six major chart types: Area, Bar, Column, Line, Pie, and Scatter. In addition, you can create combination charts using the Chart menu's Add Overlay or the Gallery menu's Combination command.

So far, we've looked mainly at column charts. In this chapter, we'll consider these other chart types.

Changing the type of a chart

As you've already seen, the default chart type in Microsoft Excel is the column chart. Every chart you create will appear as a column chart unless you tell Microsoft Excel that you prefer another initial chart format. You can change the default chart type to any of Microsoft Excel's other types. We'll show you how to do that in this section.

Of course, even if you leave the default chart type as it is, you're not limited to working with column charts. You can use the Gallery menu commands or the Main Chart command on the Format menu to change the chart type. We'll also show you how those commands work.

The Main Chart command

In the last chapter, you learned how to use the Main Chart command on the Format menu to format column charts like the one in Figure 12-1. As you may have noticed, you can also use the Main Chart dialog box to select a new chart type. For example, to convert the column chart in Figure 12-1 into a bar chart, simply select the Main Chart command from the Format menu and then choose the Bar option. Your chart will be redrawn to look like Figure 12-2.

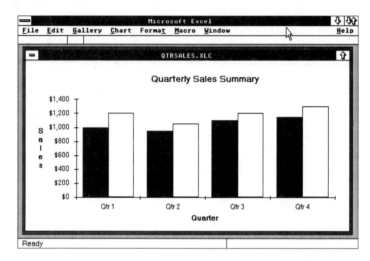

FIGURE 12-1. *This is a basic column chart like the ones we've worked with in earlier chapters.*

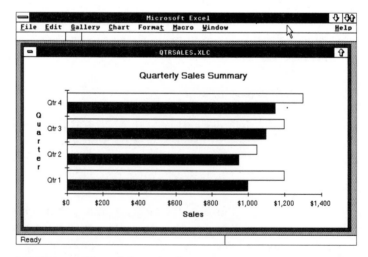

FIGURE 12-2. *We used the Main Chart command to convert our column chart to a bar chart.*

Notice that we changed the orientation of our category-axis and value-axis titles when we converted our column chart to a bar chart. Because the category axis now appears on the left side of the chart, running vertically, we used the Text command to assign the Vertical Text format to that title. We deselected the Vertical Text option for the value-axis title because that axis is now oriented horizontally.

Microsoft Excel activates different formatting options in the lower half of the Main Chart dialog box, depending on the chart type you select in the upper portion of the dialog box or the type of chart you're working with before you open the dialog box. For example, if you choose the Main Chart command from the Format menu while you're working with a line chart, the Stacked, Vary By Categories, Drop Lines, 100%, and Hi-Lo Lines options are available. The Overlapped, % Overlap, % Cluster Spacing, and Angle of First Pie Slice options appear dimmed, indicating that they don't apply to a line chart.

Browsing through the chart gallery

You've already seen all the hard ways to format a Microsoft Excel chart. Now that you've learned the basics of how charts are created and formatted, let's take a quick look at some shortcuts you can use.

The easiest way to format your chart in Microsoft Excel is to select the chart type and format you want from the Gallery menu. When you pull down this menu, you'll notice that the current chart format is marked in this list with a check mark. When you select a chart type, Microsoft Excel displays a "gallery" of common formats for that chart. For example, Figure 12-3 shows the gallery that appears when you choose the default chart type, Column, from the Gallery menu. Notice that this gallery offers eight common column-chart formats.

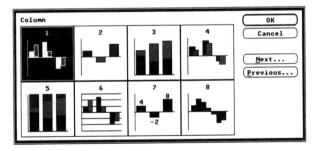

FIGURE 12-3. *Use the column-chart gallery to quickly select a column-chart format.*

To choose a format, simply select the picture of the chart you want. Microsoft Excel will select all the appropriate axis, main chart, and pattern options for you.

For example, if you select the fifth column-chart option, the program will convert the chart into a stacked column chart with a 100% format on the value-axis scale.

Often, you'll find it much easier to use a Gallery menu command to do the basic formatting on a chart than to issue all the required formatting commands separately. However, it's best to use the Gallery menu to select a chart type and format only when you first create a new chart. Otherwise, Microsoft Excel may override some of the formatting changes you've made to your existing chart so that the new chart will conform to the chosen type and format. For example, if you've used the Scale command on the Format menu to change the position of your value or category axis, Microsoft Excel may move the axis again to fit the chart type and format you select using the Gallery menu.

If you've already made changes to the format of your chart, you can use the Main Chart command on the Format menu to change the chart type. That way, you needn't be concerned with the automatic changes that can occur when you use the Gallery menu. When you use the Main Chart command to change the type of a chart, Microsoft Excel converts the current chart into the selected type without disturbing the other format options you've selected. (Of course, any formats that aren't applicable for the chart type you select will be ignored. For example, your axis settings will have no effect on a pie chart.)

Even if none of the Gallery options exactly meet your needs, you can still benefit by using this command. Simply choose the format closest to the one you want and then use the manual formatting commands to tailor the chart further.

If you're not sure what type of chart you want to build, you can use the Next and Previous buttons in the Gallery dialog box to browse through each of the chart galleries and see the available options for each chart type. For example, if you choose Previous from the Column gallery shown in Figure 12-3, you'll see the Bar gallery dialog box; if you choose Next, you'll see the Line gallery dialog box.

Changing the default chart type

Every chart you create initially appears in the Preferred format—a simple column chart. This initial format is equivalent to the first chart format in the Column gallery. If you modify the format of your chart and then decide you don't like the changes, you can always choose Preferred from the Gallery menu to return to the initial format.

If you use another type of chart more often than the column type, you can change the Preferred (default) chart type. Simply select the format you prefer and then choose Set Preferred from the Gallery menu. Until you issue another Set Preferred command, every new chart you create during the session will initially appear in the new Preferred format, which will have every characteristic (even such details as line thickness, position of tick marks, and text formats) of the chart that was active when you chose Set Preferred. Of course, the formats of existing charts will not be changed. To retain a Preferred format after a Microsoft Excel session, you must save your charts and worksheets with the Save Workspace command. Then, when you want to begin a session using charts with that Preferred format, simply open the workspace file you saved. Otherwise, Microsoft Excel will not retain or recognize your Preferred format.

Usually, you'll want to set the Preferred format to match one of the basic options in Microsoft Excel's gallery. If none of Microsoft Excel's chart formats meet your needs, however, you can tailor your own Preferred format. Simply format a chart with all the features you want and then select Set Preferred from the Gallery menu. Of course, you can always return to the default Preferred format by choosing Column from the Gallery menu, selecting the first column-chart option, and then choosing Set Preferred.

Bar charts

The bar chart we created in Figure 12-2 is quite similar to the column charts we've been using until now, except that the data series are organized vertically rather than horizontally. Seven standard bar-chart formats are available in Microsoft Excel, as shown in Figure 12-4. You can use these options to modify the basic format of your bar charts.

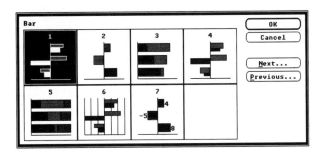

FIGURE 12-4. *Use the Bar gallery to choose a bar-chart format.*

If none of these formats is exactly right, you can use the Chart and Format menu commands to tailor the chart to your own needs. You can add titles, a legend, attached text, unattached text, and many other enhancements to a bar chart, using the same techniques you applied in enhancing the column charts in Chapters 10 and 11. (Keep in mind as you format your bar chart that the category axis is now vertical and the value axis is now horizontal.)

Column and bar charts are well suited to illustrating data trends over a period of time. The specific format you use for these charts will depend on the type of trend you're plotting. For example, stacked bar charts work best when you need to illustrate the relationship between two or more data series across time. The length of the stacked bar gives the reader an idea of the general trend and the stacked sections illustrate the relative contribution of each item to the whole. Clustered bar charts, on the other hand, make it easy to compare the relative value of a set of data points over time.

Line charts

Line charts offer another excellent tool for illustrating trends over time. Generally, you will find that line charts are preferable for plotting continuous data, where subtle variations are important. Bar and column charts are more useful for plotting discrete data, where the emphasis falls on comparative analysis of two or more sets of values.

To convert a chart into the line format, choose Line from the Gallery menu and select one of the options shown in Figure 12-5. Figure 12-6 shows the chart that results if you select the fifth option. (Of course, you can also create this chart by selecting the Line option from the Main Chart dialog box and then using the Gridlines and Patterns commands to enhance the chart.)

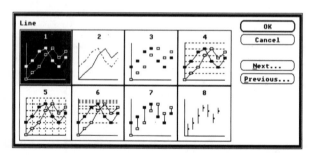

FIGURE 12-5. *Use the Line gallery to choose a line-chart format.*

As you can see, Microsoft Excel plots each data series as a line and uses symbols to mark the data points. By selecting the fifth option in the Line gallery, you tell Microsoft Excel to include major category-axis and value-axis gridlines in the new chart.

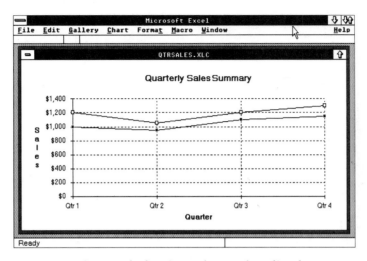

FIGURE 12-6. *Our sample chart is now formatted as a line chart.*

Formatting the line chart

You can enhance a line chart in almost every way you can enhance bar and column charts. There are a few differences, however, worth covering in more detail.

The Stacked and 100% options

When you're working with a line chart, the first Format option in the Main Chart dialog box is Stacked. (Obviously, this option applies only to multiseries charts.) If you select this option, Microsoft Excel creates a "stacked" line chart. For example, consider the two line charts in Figures 12-6 and 12-7. Figure 12-6 shows a standard line chart; Figure 12-7 shows a stacked line chart. In the stacked chart, the top line represents the sum of Product A and Product B sales; the bottom line represents only Product B sales. The distance between the top line and the bottom line represents Product A sales.

Stacked line charts are a rather odd format that you'll want to use with care. When you create stacked bar and column charts, the reader can easily see that the values of the different data series are additive. Each stacked column or bar shows both the value of the individual data points and the total of the parts. In a line chart, however, readers are accustomed to interpreting each data series as a separate entity, and they may not realize that the values in a stacked line chart are additive.

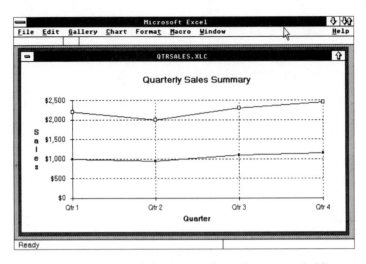

FIGURE 12-7. *We converted the chart in Figure 12-6 to a stacked line chart.*

Stacked line charts become even more confusing when you select the 100% option. As with column and bar charts, the 100% option converts the value axis in a line chart from an absolute scale to a percentage scale. The result, if you select this option, will look like Figure 12-8. In this chart, the top line represents 100% of the combined Product A and Product B sales. The bottom line represents Product B sales as a percentage of the combined sales.

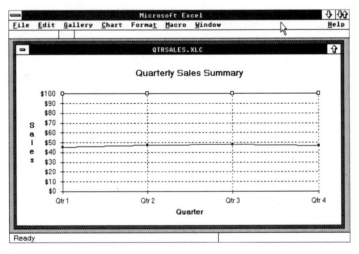

FIGURE 12-8. *Choosing the 100% option converts the value axis from an absolute scale to a percentage scale.*

You'll probably agree that this chart is difficult to understand. One of the major problems with it—and with most Microsoft Excel charts that use a percentage scale on the value axis—is that the numbers along the axis are still formatted as dollar values.

If you want to use the 100% option or the Stacked option, we recommend that you use an area chart rather than a line chart, so that the additive values are clearly illustrated. We'll show you how to create an area chart in a few pages. If you do use these options in a line chart, be sure the chart is clearly labeled.

The Hi-Lo Lines option

If you use Microsoft Excel to track stock market trends, you'll be happy to know that a hi-lo format is available for line charts. Hi-lo charts use vertical lines to connect the data points in each *category*, rather than horizontal lines to connect the data points in each series. For example, the worksheet in Figure 12-9 tracks daily stock prices for Soft Wares, Inc. To plot the daily high and low stock prices for this company, select cells A3:C8 and open a new chart file. Next, choose Line from the Gallery menu and select the seventh line-chart option. As you can see in Figure 12-10, the marker symbols that appear for each data series make it easy to find the high and low values at a glance. You can also add the stock's opening and closing prices.

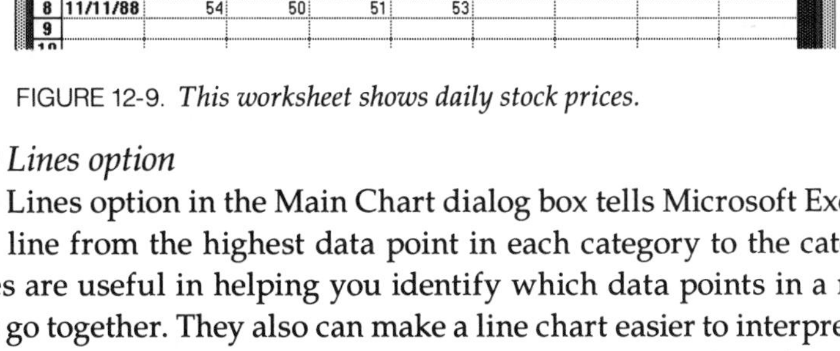

	A	B	C	D	E
1	Daily Stock Prices: Soft Wares, Inc.				
2					
3	Date	High	Low	Open	Close
4	11/7/88	58	54	56	58
5	11/8/88	57	52	55	56
6	11/9/88	56	53	54	55
7	11/10/88	55	49	52	53
8	11/11/88	54	50	51	53
9					

FIGURE 12-9. *This worksheet shows daily stock prices.*

The Drop Lines option

The Drop Lines option in the Main Chart dialog box tells Microsoft Excel to draw a vertical line from the highest data point in each category to the category axis. Drop lines are useful in helping you identify which data points in a multiseries line chart go together. They also can make a line chart easier to interpret when the lines crisscross each other. Figure 12-11 shows a two-series line chart with drop lines added. Notice that, unlike hi-lo lines, the drop lines extend all the way to the category axis.

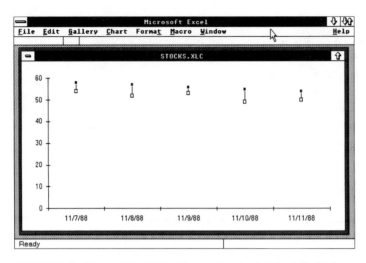

FIGURE 12-10. *We used the Hi-Lo Lines option to plot the daily high and low stock prices.*

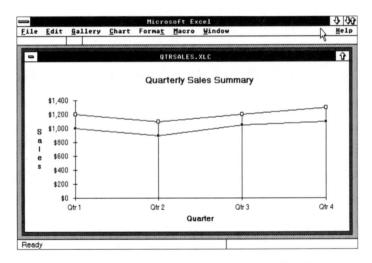

FIGURE 12-11. *We used the Drop Lines option to create this chart.*

Selecting patterns and colors for a line chart

Just as Microsoft Excel allows you to change the area pattern, area colors, border style, border color, and border weight in column and bar charts, it also allows you to change the line style, line weight, line color, marker symbols, and marker colors used for each line in a line chart. Simply select the line you want to format and choose Patterns from the Format menu. Microsoft Excel will display a dialog box like the one in Figure 12-12. As you can see, the default Line Style setting is Automatic. When Automatic is in effect, Microsoft Excel uses the lightest of the three Line Weight options.

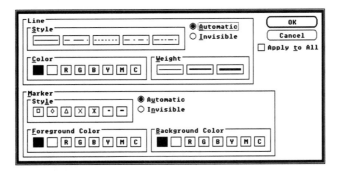

FIGURE 12-12. *This Patterns dialog box appears when you work with a line chart.*

The default Line Style setting usually displays all lines in the chart in solid black, with a different type of data-point marker on each series. If you decide to eliminate the data-point markers, however, the Automatic setting tells Microsoft Excel to use a different line pattern or color for each line in the chart.

In general, you're better off staying with the lightest of the three Line Weight options. If you use the heavier options, you'll find that the resulting lines clutter the plot area considerably, especially if the chart displays three or more series.

You may find occasions to set Line Style to Invisible. When you do this, Microsoft Excel does not connect the points in the selected data series with a line; instead, it displays only the markers that identify the data points. To suppress the display of lines on all your data series, choose Apply to All after you select the Invisible option.

The default Marker Style option is also Automatic. When the Marker Style is set to Automatic and you're viewing a chart on a monochrome monitor, Microsoft Excel assigns the first symbol in the Marker Style box to the first data series, the second symbol to the second data series, and so on. If you're viewing a line chart on a color monitor, Microsoft Excel uses the same marker symbol for each data series but assigns a different color to each series—red for the markers in the first series, green for the second data series, and so forth. After plotting the first eight data series, Microsoft Excel assigns a new marker symbol to the ninth data series and recycles the color assignments, beginning again with red.

To change the marker symbol for the currently selected data series, simply choose the symbol or color you want to use in the Patterns dialog box. If you don't want any markers to appear, select the Invisible option. To suppress the display of the markers for all the data series in the chart, choose Apply to All after selecting Invisible. When you choose not to display marker symbols, Microsoft Excel displays each line in your chart in a different color or pattern to help distinguish the data series. Keep in mind that it is more difficult to distinguish between line patterns or colors than between marker patterns, particularly if you're using a thin line weight.

Area charts

Area charts, sometimes referred to as surface charts, are similar to stacked line charts. Unlike regular stacked line charts, however, in area charts the area under each line is shaded or colored. Area charts allow you to illustrate subtle trends in an easy-to-interpret format, and they don't force you to trace dozens of lines as they crisscross the screen. In addition, the area between lines is filled in so that the reader can easily compare the relative values of each data point in the chart. Area charts are generally used only to graph more than one data series; if you're graphing only one data series, you're probably better off using a line chart.

To create an area chart, choose Area from the Gallery menu and then select one of the area-chart options shown in Figure 12-13. Figure 12-14 shows the result of converting the chart in Figure 12-7 to an area chart, using the first option in the Area gallery.

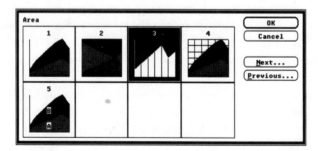

FIGURE 12-13. *This dialog box shows the gallery of area-chart formats.*

The area chart in Figure 12-14 looks similar to the stacked line chart in Figure 12-7, except that Microsoft Excel has shaded the areas between lines to emphasize relationships. As we mentioned in our discussion of stacked line charts, the area format is a good way to show the relative proportions of two or more data series, because it is easier for the reader to interpret.

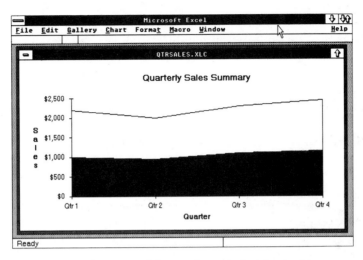

FIGURE 12-14. *We converted the sample quarterly sales chart to an area chart.*

Formatting an area chart

If you choose the Main Chart command from the Format menu while you're working with an area chart, you'll see that only three Format options are available: Stacked, 100%, and Drop Lines. When you create an area chart using any of the formats in the Area gallery, the Stacked option is automatically selected. You can turn off this option if you prefer, but part or all of one or more of your data series will be hidden.

As with line, bar, and column charts, the 100% option changes the value axis on an area chart from an absolute scale to a percentage scale. The Drop Lines option creates a vertical line from the highest point in each category to the category axis. Drop lines can be helpful for marking the categories of an area chart. When you select Drop Lines, Microsoft Excel may change the area patterns or colors to make the drop lines more visible.

Selecting patterns and colors for an area chart

You can use the Format menu's Patterns command to change the area patterns and colors, the border style and colors, and the border weight for each of the data series in an area chart. The Patterns dialog box for an area chart is the same as the one we used earlier for our column and bar charts. For example, suppose you want to change the color of a data series. First select that series; then choose Patterns from the Format menu. In the Patterns dialog box, select the color you want to use

and choose OK or press Enter. You can also use the Patterns dialog box to remove
the thin lines that appear between the different series of an area chart. Simply
select the Invisible Border option and choose Apply to All.

Pie charts

The fifth choice on the Gallery menu is Pie. Pie charts make it easy to illustrate the
relationships between components of a total. To change a chart to the pie format,
choose Pie from the Gallery menu and select one of the pie-chart options shown in
Figure 12-15.

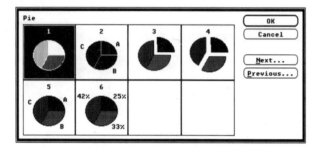

FIGURE 12-15. *This dialog box shows the gallery of pie-chart formats.*

One major difference between pie charts and the other charts we've discussed
is that pie charts can graph only a single data series at a time. You can't use a pie
chart to compare two or more data series. If you convert a multiseries chart into a
pie chart, only the first data series appears in the pie chart. Your other data series
will reappear if you change the chart type again, but they remain in limbo while
you're using the pie-chart format.

Notice in the pie gallery that, if you choose pie-chart format 6, Microsoft Excel
assigns data-point labels to your chart, reflecting the proportion of each slice of the
pie. Because pie charts plot only one data series at a time, each data point in your
pie chart becomes a category. If you use the Add Legend command from the Chart
menu to create a legend for your pie chart, Microsoft Excel uses the category
names, instead of series names, in the legend box. For example, Figure 12-16 shows
a simple pie chart with data-point labels and a legend.

Some of the options available for other types of charts are not available when
you're working with pie charts. For example, because pie charts have no axes, you
can't use the Axes command on the Chart menu when working with a pie chart.
However, you can still do a lot to format a pie chart.

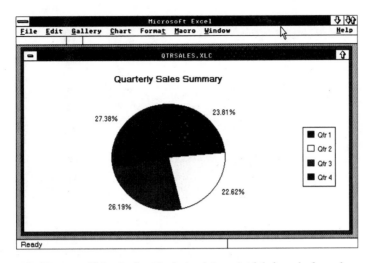

FIGURE 12-16. *This pie chart includes data-point labels and a legend.*

Formatting a pie chart

If you choose the Main Chart command from the Format menu while working with a pie chart, only two options will be available: Vary by Categories and Angle of First Pie Slice.

When you create a pie chart using any of the Pie gallery options except the second one, the Vary by Categories option is selected as the default so that Microsoft Excel will assign a different pattern or color to each slice in the pie. (If you create a pie chart using the Pie option in the Main Chart dialog box, you must select Vary by Categories manually.)

You can use the Angle of First Pie Slice option to rotate your pie charts. The default setting is 0, which means that the line that forms the left edge of the first slice in the pie (the first data point in the series) points straight up. You can use any whole number through 360 (degrees) to change the position of the first slice of the pie. For example, to convert the chart in Figure 12-16 to the chart in Figure 12-17, we typed 90 in the Angle of First Pie Slice edit bar. This caused the first slice in our pie to move from the upper right quadrant of the chart to the lower right quadrant, or 90 degrees.

Selecting patterns and colors for a pie chart

Using the Patterns command, you can assign specific patterns and colors to individual slices of a pie chart. When you're working with a pie chart, the Patterns dialog box is identical to the one used for column, bar, and area charts. As with those

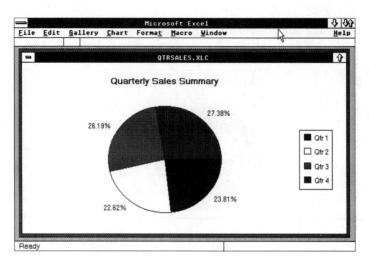

FIGURE 12-17. *We used the Angle of First Pie Slice option to rotate the pie chart 90 degrees.*

types of charts, this command allows you to change the area patterns and colors, the border style and color, and the border weight of each section of the pie.

Exploding sections of a pie chart

You can create exploded pie sections by selecting the segment you want and moving it away from the main chart. To move a pie slice with a mouse, simply point to the slice and drag it to the desired position. To move a pie segment with the keyboard, first select the segment; then choose the Move command from the Format menu. Use the arrow keys to move the slice where you want it and press Enter to lock in the new location. Figure 12-18 shows the pie chart from Figure 12-17 with the Qtr 1 segment exploded.

When you create an exploded section, you won't want to move the section far. As you can see in Figure 12-18, Microsoft Excel reduces the size of the pie chart when you create one or more exploded sections. You'll usually find that the exploded section stands out well even if you move it only a small distance from the rest of the pie sections. If necessary, you can move the legend to another part of the chart to give the exploded section more room.

Microsoft Excel doesn't allow you to move a pie section in any direction other than straight out from the center of the pie. You can, however, "slide" the section across the pie by moving it toward the pie's center. In fact, you can even move it to the other side of the chart, but the resulting chart will be very small.

To put exploded sections back in place, you can move them individually or you can choose Pie again from the Gallery menu and select any option that doesn't offer exploded sections. Microsoft Excel will put the pieces back together for you.

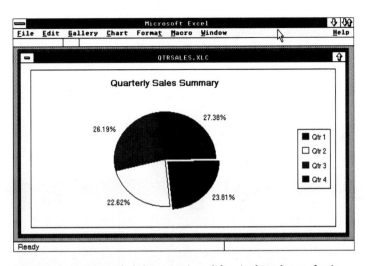

FIGURE 12-18. *We exploded one section of the pie chart for emphasis.*

Scatter diagrams

Scatter diagrams are used to illustrate the relationship between two characteristics of a population. For example, you've probably seen scatter diagrams that illustrate the relationship between things like age and income, or height and weight, or net income and stock prices of a company. In Microsoft Excel, scatter diagrams are much like line charts, with one important difference: The categories in a scatter diagram are more than simply labels; they are coordinates that help to determine the locations of the data points in the chart. Thus, in a scatter diagram two or more data points can share the same category; in a line chart, two or more points in the same series cannot share a category.

Creating a scatter diagram in Microsoft Excel is different from creating a line, bar, column, or area chart. In scatter diagrams, the cells you select for your category axis must contain values. In effect, therefore, every scatter diagram has two value axes.

For example, the worksheet in Figure 12-19 lists the annual income and education levels of several individuals. To compare income and education levels in a scatter diagram, select cells A6:B17 and choose the Copy command. Then choose New from the File menu and select the Chart option. Microsoft Excel will display an empty chart window. Next, choose Paste Special from the Edit menu.

Microsoft Excel will assume you don't want to use category names in your chart, because both columns in the worksheet contain values. (You may remember from our discussion of the Paste Special command in Chapter 11 that Microsoft Excel looks for labels in the first row and first column of the selected area of your

☐			Microsoft Excel						⬇ ⬇⬇
File	**Edit**	**Formula**	**Format**	**Data**	**Options**	**Macro**	**Window**	☝	**Help**
I18									

☐				EDUSIN.XLS				⬆
	A	B	C	D	E	F	G	H	I
1	Income vs Education								
2									
3									
4	Education	Annual							
5	Level	Income							
6	12	$12,104							
7	10	$11,270							
8	11	$11,437							
9	15	$17,205							
10	14	$14,138							
11	16	$17,373							
12	14	$14,839							
13	11	$12,187							
14	12	$13,464							
15	16	$16,972							
16	19	$21,173							
17	9	$8,903							
18									

Ready

FIGURE 12-19. *We'll use this income* vs *education worksheet to create a scatter diagram.*

worksheet. If it finds no labels, it assumes you want to use all the selected cells as data-point values.) In order to create a scatter diagram, you must select the Categories in First Column option to let Microsoft Excel know that the values in column A of your worksheet are to be used as category-axis values.

After you choose OK to execute the Paste Special command, Microsoft Excel will display the new chart in the default format. To change this chart into a scatter diagram, choose Scatter from the Gallery menu and select one of the options shown in Figure 12-20. We used the first chart format to create the chart in Figure 12-21. As you can see, this chart shows a positive correlation between education and annual income.

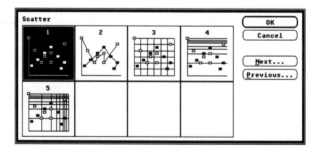

FIGURE 12-20. *This dialog box shows the gallery of scatter-diagram formats.*

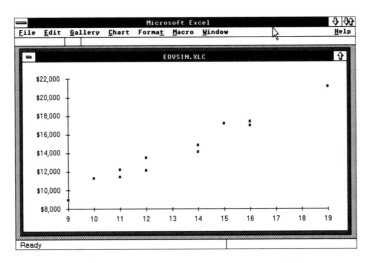

FIGURE 12-21. *This scatter diagram shows the relationship between income and education.*

Most of the time you'll want to use the first or third scatter-diagram options. If you use the second option, you'll generally find that the lines connecting your data points create confusion, especially when you're charting two or more data series. The logarithmic options, 4 and 5, are typically used only for scientific and engineering data. The fourth format uses a semilogarithmic scale; that is, only one axis is logarithmic. The fifth format uses a log-log scale; that is, both axes are logarithmic.

Formatting a scatter diagram

Microsoft Excel offers fewer formatting options for scatter diagrams than for other chart types. In fact, when you choose Main Chart from the Format menu with a scatter diagram, you'll find only one option in the Main Chart dialog box: Vary by Categories. If you're working with a single-series scatter diagram, you can use the Vary by Categories option to assign a different marker symbol or color to each data point in the chart.

You can use the Patterns command to change the marker styles, marker colors, line styles, line colors, and line weights in a scatter diagram. Be sure to choose the Apply to All option if you want all the markers and lines in the scatter diagram to be displayed in the same style and color.

Of course, you can add attached and unattached text to scatter diagrams; change the typeface, style, and size of the text; and control the display and format of your axes, just as you can with a line chart.

Combination charts

To add an overlay chart to an existing chart, choose Combination from the Gallery menu. Microsoft Excel offers five types of combination charts, as shown in Figure 12-22. Each type really includes two charts: a main chart and an overlay chart.

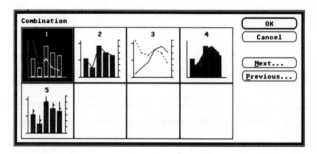

FIGURE 12-22. *This dialog box shows the gallery of combination-chart formats.*

To create a combination chart, first select the range you want to chart; then use the New command from the File menu to open a new chart window. Next, select Combination from the Gallery menu and choose one of the four combination-chart options.

For example, the chart in Figure 12-23 contains quarterly sales statistics for two products for 1987, as well as sales totals for the year. Suppose you want to chart the sales for the two products as a column chart and display the quarterly totals as an overlaid line chart. To do this, choose Combination from the Gallery menu and select the second combination-chart option. Figure 12-24 shows the result.

When you create a combination chart, Microsoft Excel divides the data series evenly between the main chart and the overlay chart. For example, if your chart has four data series, the first two will appear in the main chart and the second two will appear in the overlay chart. If your chart has an odd number of data series, the main chart will contain one more data series than the overlay chart. As you can see in Figure 12-24, the first two data series appear in the main column chart and the last data series appears in the overlay line chart. In other words, Microsoft Excel has drawn the first two ranges as columns and the last range as an overlaid line. (You can specify how many data series you want to appear in the overlay chart by using the First Series in Overlay Chart edit bar in the dialog box that appears when you choose Overlay from the Format menu. We'll show you how to do this in a few pages.)

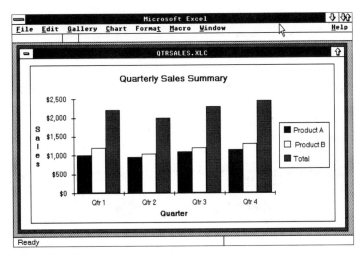

FIGURE 12-23. *This chart shows quarterly sales for two products, as well as total sales.*

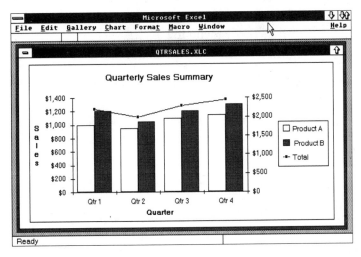

FIGURE 12-24. *We plotted the sample quarterly sales chart as a combination chart.*

Because we chose the second option in the Combination dialog box to create the chart in Figure 12-24, Microsoft Excel included two value axes in the sample chart. The value axis on the right is for the totals in the overlay chart. Both the second and third options in the combination-chart gallery cause Microsoft Excel to include two value axes. Two value axes are particularly useful when you're plotting data series with widely disparate scales. For example, if we had used a single value axis to plot the product sales and quarterly totals in Figure 12-24, the columns representing the product sales figures would have seemed quite small in comparison to the height of the line representing the totals.

Not only can you add a second value axis to an overlay chart, you can also add a second category axis, for a total of four axes. To do this, select the Axes command from the Chart menu and then select the Category Axis option in the Overlay box. When you select OK or press Enter, Microsoft Excel will display a chart like the one in Figure 12-25.

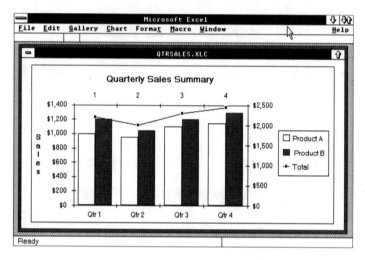

FIGURE 12-25. *This combination chart contains four axes.*

Formatting the overlay chart

After you select the combination you want, you can use the Overlay command on the Format menu to tailor the overlay chart to your needs. When you choose this command, Microsoft Excel displays the dialog box shown in Figure 12-26. Notice that this dialog box is nearly identical to the Main Chart dialog boxes you've seen when working with Microsoft Excel's other chart types. In fact, the main difference between the Main Chart dialog box and the Format Overlay Chart dialog box is that the second box includes a First Series in Overlay Chart option that lets you control the distribution of data series between the main and overlay charts. When you enter a number in the First Series in Overlay Chart edit bar, you tell Microsoft Excel to chart that data series and all higher data series in the overlay chart. For example, if your chart contains five data series, entering a 3 in the First Series in Overlay Chart edit bar tells Microsoft Excel to include the third, fourth, and fifth data series in the overlay chart. In our sample chart, you could type a 2 in the Overlay Chart dialog box to display the Product B data series as well as the Total data series in the overlay chart, while leaving the Product A data series in the main chart.

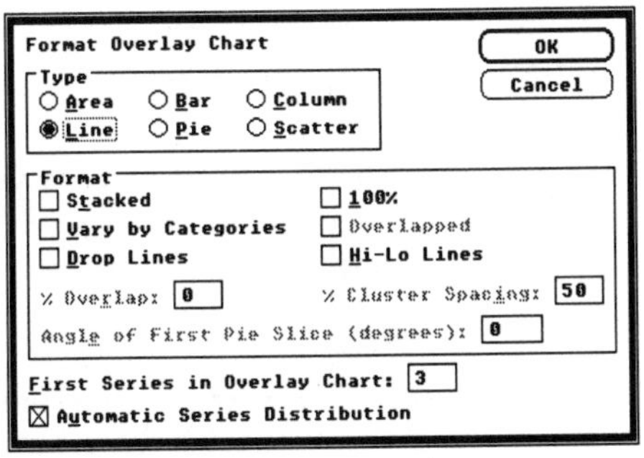

FIGURE 12-26. *The Format Overlay Chart dialog box is similar to the Format Main Chart dialog box.*

When you enter a number in the First Series in Overlay Chart bar, Microsoft Excel deselects the Automatic Series Distribution option at the bottom of the dialog box. To return to Microsoft Excel's default series distribution scheme, simply select the Automatic Series Distribution option again.

Suppose you want to plot data series 1 and 3 on your main chart and data series 2 and 4 on your overlay chart. You can control which data series appear in which chart by changing the number assigned to the data series. We'll explain this technique in the next chapter, when we discuss the SERIES command.

All the other options in the Format Overlay Chart dialog box have exactly the same effect on the overlay chart that the corresponding options in the Main Chart dialog box have on the main chart.

Creating your own combination charts

You can also create your own combination charts from an existing chart by selecting Add Overlay from the Chart menu. When you choose this command, Microsoft Excel divides the data series in the chart evenly between the main chart and the overlay chart. For example, if your chart has four data series, the first two will appear in the main chart and the second two will appear in the overlay chart.

After the combination chart has been created, you can change the type of either the main chart or the overlay chart. To change the type of the overlay chart, select one of the data series in the overlay chart and then choose Overlay from the Format menu. In the dialog box, choose the type of chart you want to use and then choose OK or press Enter. Microsoft Excel will display all the data series in the overlay chart in the format you specified. Similarly, to change the type of chart used for the main chart, simply select a data series in the main chart and then choose Main Chart from the Format menu. In the Main Chart dialog box, select the chart type and then choose OK or press Enter.

After you've created a combination chart and selected your chart types, you'll probably need to use the Main Chart and Overlay commands to format the result. If you want to use independent axes for the main and overlay charts, choose Axes from the Chart menu and select the appropriate options from the Overlay portion of the dialog box. To format the overlay-chart axes, select the axis you want to work with and then choose Scale from the Format menu. Then you can use the techniques we described in Chapter 10 to format the selected axis.

Deleting overlay charts

If you decide you no longer want to use the overlay chart format, simply choose Delete Overlay from the Chart menu. Microsoft Excel will merge the data series in the overlay chart back into the main chart. Alternatively, you can choose a new chart format from one of the chart galleries to convert the combination chart to another chart type.

13

Other Chart Topics

*I*n the first three chapters of this section, we've shown you how to create and format charts in Microsoft Excel. In this chapter, we'll take a look behind the scenes to see how the program plots your worksheet data. We'll also show you how to use the Edit menu commands with charts as well as how to print the charts you create.

The SERIES function

As you've worked through the examples in the last three chapters, you may have noticed the long formula that appeared in the formula bar whenever you selected a data-point marker on a chart. This long formula is a SERIES function, which tells Microsoft Excel how to interpret your worksheet data. The SERIES function takes the form

=SERIES("*series name*",*categories reference,values reference,plot order number*)

The *series name* argument is the name of the data series being charted. The *categories reference* argument indicates where your category labels are located in the worksheet. The *values reference* argument indicates where the data-point values are located in the worksheet. The *plot order number* argument determines the order in which your data series appear on the chart.

Whenever you create a chart in Microsoft Excel, one SERIES formula is created for each data series in that chart. Let's use the chart shown in Figure 13-1 to illustrate the mechanics of the SERIES function. This chart was drawn from cells A3:D7 of the worksheet shown in Figure 13-2. As you can see in the formula bar in Figure 13-1, the SERIES formula for the first data series is

=SERIES(SHEET1.XLS!$B$3,SHEET1.XLS!$A$4:$A$7,SHEET1.XLS!$B$4:$B$7,1)

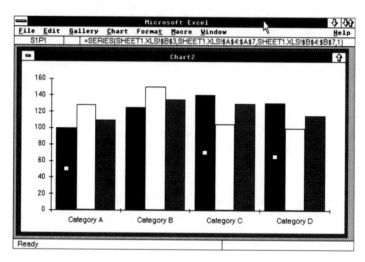

FIGURE 13-1. *This sample chart shows the SERIES function in the formula bar.*

	A	B	C	D	E	F	G	H	I
1									
2									
3		Series 1	Series 2	Series 3					
4	Category A	100	128	110					
5	Category B	125	150	135					
6	Category C	140	105	130					
7	Category D	131	100	115					
8									
9									

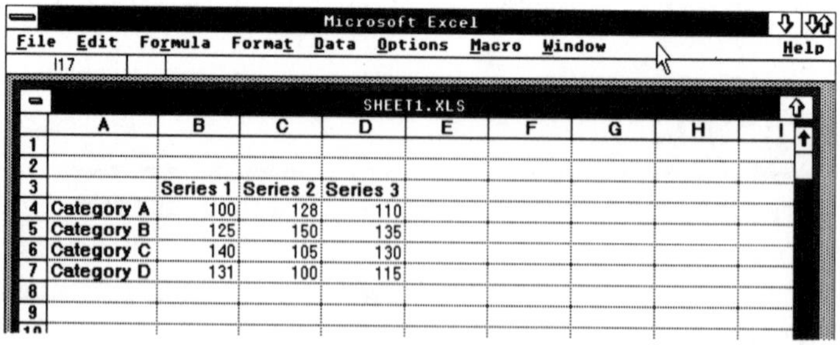

FIGURE 13-2. *The sample chart in Figure 13-1 was plotted from this worksheet.*

The *series name* argument in this formula is SHEET1.XLS!$B$3. The *categories reference* and *values reference* arguments are SHEET1.XLS!$A$4:$A$7 and

SHEET1.XLS!$B$4:$B$7. You may remember from our discussion of linked work-sheets in Chapter 8 that Microsoft Excel always uses the worksheet name followed by an exclamation point to indicate a reference to an external worksheet. As you would expect, this same convention is used in defining the arguments of a SERIES function. Also notice that Microsoft Excel uses absolute cell references in its external references.

The *plot order number* argument in the example SERIES formula, 1, tells Microsoft Excel to plot this data series before any of the others in this chart. As you'll soon see, you can change the order in which data series are plotted simply by changing the *plot order number* argument at the end of the formula.

The *series name* and *categories reference* arguments won't always appear in the SERIES formula. Microsoft Excel uses these arguments only if you select cells in your worksheet that contain category and series labels. For example, if you were to select only cells B4:B7 in the worksheet shown in Figure 13-2, Microsoft Excel would create a single-series chart like the one in Figure 13-3.

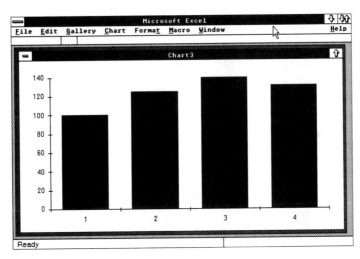

FIGURE 13-3. *This column chart contains only one data series with no series name or category labels.*

The SERIES formula for this single-series chart is

=SERIES(,,SHEET1.XLS!$B$4:$B$7,1)

Notice that the first two arguments—*series name* and *categories reference*—are missing from this formula. Also notice that Microsoft Excel automatically assigns the plot order number 1 to this data series, even though no other data series exist at this point. If we were to paste another data series into this chart, Microsoft Excel would assign that data series the plot order number 2.

Editing the SERIES function

In general, the SERIES function works much like the worksheet functions you learned about in Chapter 6. To edit a SERIES formula, you must first select the series you want to work with by selecting any of its data-point markers. When the SERIES function appears in the formula bar, you can then edit it to change the contents of the chart window, using the same techniques you would use to edit a worksheet function.

Changing the plot order

To change the order in which data series are charted, you simply change the *plot order number* argument at the end of the SERIES formula. For example, the chart shown in Figure 13-1 contains three data series. Suppose you want the first data series to be plotted last. Simply select that data series by first selecting one of its markers and then select the number 1 at the end of the SERIES formula in the formula bar. To replace the existing plot order number, type a 3 and select the Enter box or press Enter. Microsoft Excel will move the first data series behind the other two. Series 2 will then become series 1, and series 3 will become series 2. Notice that single quotation marks now appear around each reference to the worksheet. These marks will disappear when you move to another part of the chart and then return to the formula. Figure 13-4 shows the result of this change.

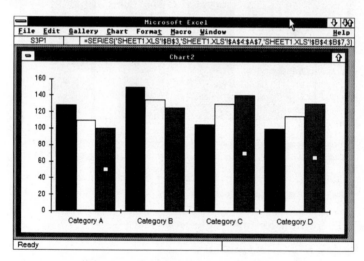

FIGURE 13-4. *By changing the plot order number of one data series, you can alter the order in which data series are presented.*

As you know, when you use the Combination command from the Gallery menu or the Add Overlay command from the Chart menu, Microsoft Excel distributes your data series evenly between the main chart and the overlay chart. However, you can control which data series appear in which chart by changing the plot order numbers of the SERIES formulas that make up your chart.

For example, suppose you choose the Add Overlay command to create an overlay line chart for the column chart shown in Figure 13-1. Microsoft Excel will automatically use data series 3 in the overlay chart, as shown in Figure 13-5.

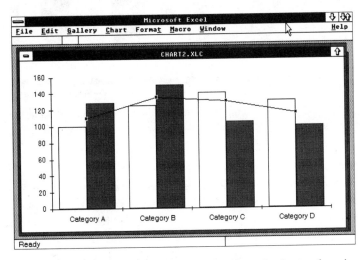

FIGURE 13-5. *Two of the series are plotted in the main chart and one in the overlay chart.*

Now suppose you want the first data series to appear in the overlay chart, instead of series 3. If you selected the Overlay command from the Format menu and entered a 1 in the First Series in Overlay Chart edit bar, all three data series would appear as lines in the overlay chart and the main chart would be empty. To get around this problem, you need to change the series number of the first data series. First select the data series you want to include in the overlay chart—in this case, series 1. Then change its plot order number in the SERIES formula to 3, as we just described. Finally, choose the Overlay command from the Format menu and make sure that the First Series in Overlay Chart is set to 3. Microsoft Excel will change data series 2 to 1, 3 to 2, and so on. The resulting chart will look like Figure 13-6.

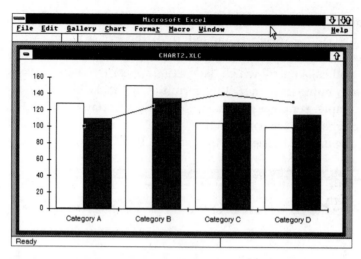

FIGURE 13-6. *By changing the plot order number in a SERIES function, you can change the distribution of the data series between the
main chart and the overlay chart.*

Adding series names and category labels

If your worksheet doesn't include suitable series names or category labels, you
can insert your own labels in the SERIES formula. For example, suppose you want
to add a series name to the chart in Figure 13-3. Select the column for the first data
series and then place the insertion point in front of the first comma in the formula
bar. Now type *"New Series 1"* (be sure to include the quotation marks around your
literal text string) and then select the Enter box or press Enter. If you compare the
formula for the data series in Figure 13-3 with the formula for the same data series
in Figure 13-7, you'll see that they're identical except for the addition of the series
name. Also notice that Microsoft Excel has used the series name to create a title for
the chart in Figure 13-7. If this were a multiseries chart, Microsoft Excel would not
display the new series name as the chart title but would include it in the chart
legend.

Now suppose you want to change the rather cryptic default category labels—
1, 2, 3, and 4—in the chart in Figure 13-7. To add more meaningful category labels,
you can edit the SERIES formula to include a *categories reference* argument that indicates the location of category labels in your worksheet. For example, you might
edit the formula

    =SERIES("New Series 1",,SHEET1.XLS!$B$4:$B$7,1)

in Figure 13-7 by placing your insertion point between the first and second
commas in the formula and typing

    SHEET1.XLS!$A$4:$A$7

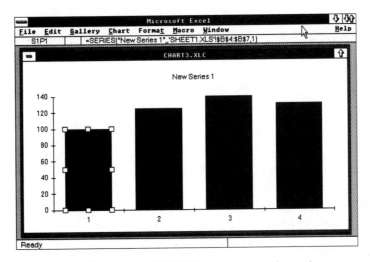

FIGURE 13-7. *We edited the SERIES formula to provide a series name.*

Microsoft Excel would then use the labels in cells A4:A7 as labels along the chart's category axis.

If your worksheet doesn't contain appropriate category labels, you can use a text-string array to create your own labels. For example, you might place the insertion point between the first and second commas of the formula and type

{"First Quarter","Second Quarter","Third Quarter","Fourth Quarter"}

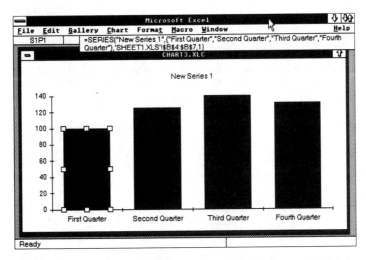

FIGURE 13-8. *We edited the SERIES formula to provide category labels.*

You must enclose the entire array in braces, enclose each of the text strings in double quotation marks, and use a comma to separate each text string from the next. The results of these two techniques are identical—Microsoft Excel uses the labels from the worksheet or the labels you insert in the SERIES formula to identify the categories in your chart. Figure 13-8 shows the sample chart after the quarter labels have been added.

Pasting references into the SERIES function

Another way to add category labels to an existing chart is to paste the cell references into the SERIES formula. For example, to create the single-series chart in Figure 13-3, you selected cells B4:B7. To add the labels in cells A4:A7 as category labels to the chart, begin by selecting a column in the first data series. Microsoft Excel will display the formula

=SERIES(,,SHEET1.XLS!$B$4:$B$7,1)

in the formula bar. Place the insertion point after the first comma in the SERIES formula. Now move back to the worksheet window by choosing the worksheet name from the Windows menu. When you're in the worksheet, you'll notice that the SERIES function remains active in the formula bar. Select cells A4:A7. Microsoft Excel will paste the cell references in the formula bar and use the selected cells as its *categories reference* argument. When you press Enter, Microsoft Excel will return to your chart window and convert the labels in cells A4:A7 into category labels, as shown in Figure 13-9. The SERIES formula will now read

=SERIES("New Series 1",SHEET1.XLS!$A$4:$A$7,SHEET1.XLS!$B$4:$B$7,1)

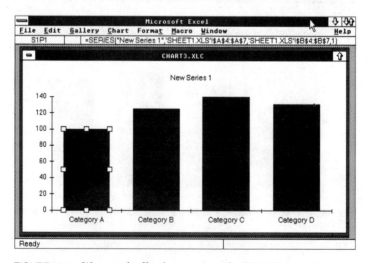

FIGURE 13-9. *We pasted cell references into the SERIES formula to create category labels.*

If you're working with a multiseries chart, you must select one of the data-point markers for the first data series to add your category labels. Microsoft Excel always looks to the first series formula in a chart for its category labels.

Building a SERIES formula from scratch

The easiest way to add a data series to your chart is to copy the cells you want to plot into a chart window. However, you can also build a data series by creating the SERIES formula from scratch. For example, you could have created the data series in the chart in Figure 13-9 by typing its SERIES formula into an empty chart document.

To open an empty chart document, select a blank cell in your worksheet. (If you select a cell or range that contains data, Microsoft Excel will attempt to plot that data when you open the new chart file.) Then choose New from the File menu and choose the Chart option. When the new chart document appears, type the beginning of the SERIES function

=SERIES(,

Then use the pasting technique described above to enter the appropriate *categories reference* and *values reference* arguments so that the final formula looks like this:

=SERIES(,SHEET1.XLS!$A$4:$A$7,SHEET1.XLS!$B$4:$B$7,1)

The resulting chart will look exactly like the one in Figure 13-9. (If you like, you can also type a series name in front of the first comma to use in your chart title or legend.)

You can also create a SERIES formula that is not dependent on a worksheet. For example, to create the chart shown in Figure 13-9 you could type this SERIES formula in a new chart document:

=SERIES(,{"Category A","Category B","Category C","Category D"},{100,125,140,131},1)

The *values reference* argument is actually the only required argument in this function. As you've already seen, the *series name* and *categories reference* arguments are optional. If you decide not to include these arguments, however, you must enter the commas that separate the arguments from the rest of the formula. The *plot order number* argument is also optional. As long as you enter the comma that separates the plot order number from the *values reference* argument, Microsoft Excel will fill in the plot order number for you.

Deleting a data series

To delete a data series from a chart, simply bring the SERIES formula for that series into the formula bar by selecting one of the markers in the series. Without placing the insertion point in the formula bar, press the Backspace key. Microsoft Excel

will immediately erase the SERIES function from the formula bar. When you select
the Enter box or press Enter, the SERIES function will be deleted and Microsoft Excel will remove the data series from the chart.

    If you decide not to remove the series from the chart after all, select the Cancel
box or press Esc before you lock in your change.

Copying information between chart files

Microsoft Excel allows you to copy the contents or format of one chart file into
another chart file. Copying chart information is much like copying data between
cells in a worksheet.

    For example, suppose you want to copy the chart in one chart window into
another chart window. Choose the Select Chart command from the Chart menu
and then choose Copy from the Edit menu. When you choose this command,
Microsoft Excel places a marquee around the chart area, just as it does when
you're copying worksheet cells. Now activate the chart window into which you
want to paste the information or use the New command to create a new chart window; then select Paste Special from the Edit menu. Microsoft Excel will display the
Paste Special dialog box shown in Figure 13-10.

FIGURE 13-10. *Use this Paste Special dialog box to paste in a chart*
window.

    If you select All, Microsoft Excel duplicates both the contents and the formats
of the copied chart in the new chart window. If the chart window into which
you're pasting already contains data, Microsoft Excel adds the copied data series
to any existing data series. If the chart window is empty, Microsoft Excel simply
creates a replica of the existing chart.

    If you select Formats, Microsoft Excel applies to the chart in the current win-
dow any special formats you've assigned to the copied chart. This is a convenient
method of assigning consistent formats to several charts when you don't want to
change the Preferred format (discussed in Chapter 12). If you select Formats when
you're pasting into a new, blank chart window, you won't see any results until you
build a chart in that window.

    Finally, if you select Formulas, Microsoft Excel pastes the SERIES formulas
from the copied chart into the selected chart window. If you're pasting information into a new chart window, the data series you have copied will appear in the

current Preferred format. If you're adding the data series to an existing chart, the copied data series will appear in the same format as the existing data series. Similarly, if you've used Microsoft Excel's chart commands to change the destination chart's type or format, the copied data series will display the formatting features you've assigned in the destination chart window.

Copying SERIES formulas

You can also copy an individual SERIES formula from one chart to another. For example, suppose you want to copy the data series in Figure 13-9 into another chart window. Further, suppose you created this data series from scratch and you don't want to retype the long formula. Instead of retyping, you can simply select one of the markers for the data series you want to copy, select the entire formula in the formula bar, and choose Copy from the Edit menu. Choose the Enter box or press Enter to leave the formula bar; then activate another chart window or choose the New command to create a new chart window. Be sure no data points are selected and activate the formula bar. Then choose Paste from the Edit menu and select the Enter box or press Enter. Microsoft Excel will immediately display the copied data series in the chart window.

Of course, you can copy any part of a SERIES function. Suppose you've typed a set of special category labels in a SERIES formula, like the ones in Figure 13-8. If you want to use these labels in another chart, simply select one of the markers for the data series and then select the *categories reference* argument in the formula bar. In our example, you would select

    {"First Quarter","Second Quarter","Third Quarter","Fourth Quarter"}

Next, choose the Copy command and select the Enter box or press Enter. Now move to the chart window into which you want to paste the category labels. If this window contains more than one series, select one of the markers for the first series, to display its SERIES formula in the formula bar. (Remember that Microsoft Excel always applies the category labels in the first data series to the entire chart.) Place the insertion point between the first and second commas, choose Paste from the Edit menu, and then select the Enter box or press Enter. Microsoft Excel will display the pasted labels below the category axis.

If you want to copy the *categories reference* argument into a SERIES formula you're creating from scratch, activate the formula bar and type

    =SERIES(,

Then choose Paste from the Edit menu. After Microsoft Excel pastes the category labels into your SERIES formula, type another comma and then enter the *values reference* argument, a third comma, and the *plot order number* argument. Finally, type the closing parenthesis and choose the Enter box or press Enter.

The Clear command

You can use the Clear command on the Edit menu to erase the contents of a chart window, the formats assigned to that window, or both. To delete all the data series in your chart without affecting the chart's format settings, begin by choosing the Select Chart command on the Chart menu; then choose Clear from the Edit menu. Microsoft Excel will display the dialog box shown in Figure 13-11.

FIGURE 13-11. *This Clear dialog box appears when a chart window is active.*

If you select All from this dialog box, Microsoft Excel erases all your SERIES formulas, as well as any special formats you've assigned to the chart. The chart window will be completely empty—even the chart axes will have disappeared. Any new data series you subsequently create for this window will appear in the Preferred format.

As you might expect, if you select Formulas, Microsoft Excel erases all the data series from the chart, but it does not erase the formats you've assigned to the chart window.

Finally, if you select Formats, Microsoft Excel leaves your SERIES formulas unchanged but changes the chart formats back to the Preferred format.

The Calculation command

If you're working with a complex chart or if you have several charts on the Microsoft Excel desktop at once, you may notice that the worksheet calculation time increases considerably. This is because Microsoft Excel must redraw each of the visible charts every time it recalculates your worksheet.

If you don't want to wait for Microsoft Excel to redraw your charts every time you change a worksheet entry, you can save time by choosing the Calculation command from the Options menu in the worksheet window and selecting Manual from the Calculation dialog box. This setting instructs Microsoft Excel not to recalculate your worksheet—or any linked chart documents—until you choose the Calculate Now command from the Options menu. But be careful! If you select Calculate Now from the Options menu while the formula bar is active, Microsoft Excel won't calculate the worksheet; instead, it will erase the formula and insert its calculated value.

Microsoft Excel also includes a Calculate Now command on the Chart menu so that you don't have to switch back to the worksheet window each time you want Microsoft Excel to update your chart.

Building a chart from two or more worksheets

Often, you'll want to combine data from two or more worksheet files to create a single chart. For example, the worksheet in Figure 13-12 contains 1986 summary budget statistics. The worksheet in Figure 13-13 contains a similar set of historical data for 1987.

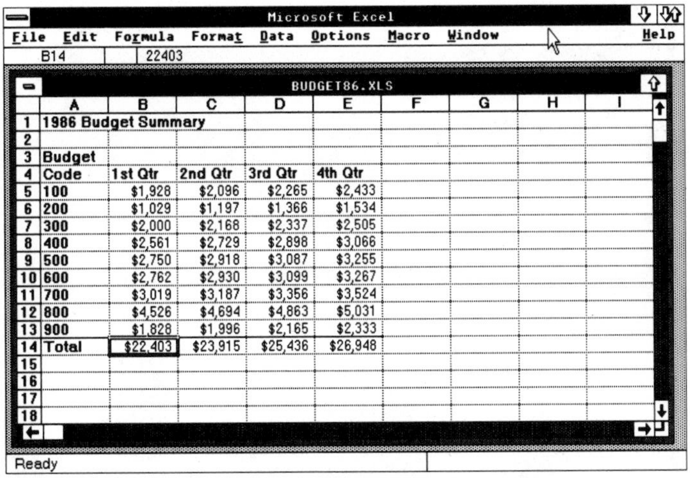

	A	B	C	D	E
1	1986 Budget Summary				
2					
3	Budget				
4	Code	1st Qtr	2nd Qtr	3rd Qtr	4th Qtr
5	100	$1,928	$2,096	$2,265	$2,433
6	200	$1,029	$1,197	$1,366	$1,534
7	300	$2,000	$2,168	$2,337	$2,505
8	400	$2,561	$2,729	$2,898	$3,066
9	500	$2,750	$2,918	$3,087	$3,255
10	600	$2,762	$2,930	$3,099	$3,267
11	700	$3,019	$3,187	$3,356	$3,524
12	800	$4,526	$4,694	$4,863	$5,031
13	900	$1,828	$1,996	$2,165	$2,333
14	Total	$22,403	$23,915	$25,436	$26,948

FIGURE 13-12. *This worksheet contains our 1986 budget summary.*

Suppose you want to compare the 1986 and 1987 budget totals in a single chart. Begin by opening both worksheet files. Then select cells B4:E4 and B14:E14 in the Budget86 worksheet. Next, use the New command to plot this data in a chart window. Microsoft Excel will create a single-series chart, using the labels from row 4 as your category labels. The SERIES formula for this data series is

=SERIES(,BUDGET86.XLS!$B$4:$E$4,BUDGET86.XLS!$B$14:$E$14,1)

Now select the Budget87 worksheet, select cells B14:E14, and choose Copy. Then return to the chart window and use the Paste command to add this data series to your chart. Finally, save the combined chart under the name Budget.XLC. The results of all this maneuvering appear in Figure 13-14.

Microsoft Excel
File Edit Formula Format Data Options Macro Window Help
B14 =SUM(B5:B13)
BUDGET87.XLS

	A	B	C	D	E
1	1987 Budget Summary				
2					
3	Budget				
4	Code	1st Qtr	2nd Qtr	3rd Qtr	4th Qtr
5	100	$1,928	$2,096	$2,265	$2,433
6	200	$1,029	$1,197	$1,366	$1,534
7	300	$2,000	$1,880	$2,337	$2,505
8	400	$2,561	$2,729	$2,898	$3,144
9	500	$2,750	$2,478	$3,087	$3,255
10	600	$2,762	$2,930	$3,099	$3,267
11	700	$3,019	$3,187	$2,455	$3,524
12	800	$4,526	$4,694	$4,863	$5,031
13	900	$2,879	$1,996	$2,165	$2,333
14	Total	$23,454	$23,187	$24,535	$27,026

Ready

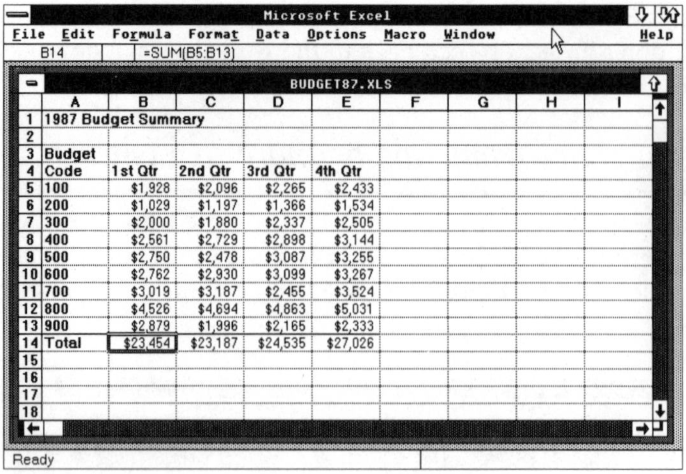

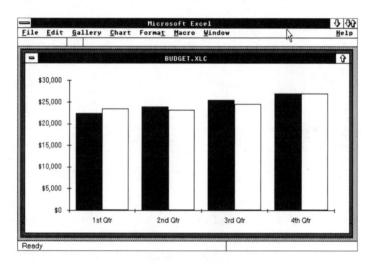

FIGURE 13-13. *This worksheet contains our 1987 budget summary.*

FIGURE 13-14. *This two-series column chart draws data from two worksheets.*

Notice that, even though you don't include a set of category cells in your second data series, Microsoft Excel applies the category labels from the first data series to all subsequent data series. As long as the second data series contains the same number of cells as the first, both sets of data points will be evenly distributed along the category axis.

Protecting a chart

If you've created a chart and don't want anyone else who views it to be able to change the chart's data series or formats, you can use the Protect Document command on the Chart menu to lock the chart. This command works the same way as the Protect Document command on the worksheet Options menu, explained in Chapter 4.

You can also use the Password option in the Save As dialog box to prevent others from opening the chart file without the correct password.

Printing charts

You're already familiar with the basic techniques for printing Microsoft Excel documents, discussed in Chapter 9. For the most part, printing charts is the same as printing worksheets. However, you'll need to know about a few minor differences.

The Page Setup command

The first step in printing a chart is to choose the Page Setup command from the chart window's File menu. This command allows you to define the layout of the page on which you will be printing. Although your margin options are the same in both the chart and worksheet environments, the Row & Column Headings and Gridlines options you saw in the worksheet Page Setup dialog box are replaced in the chart dialog box by three new options: Screen Size, Fit to Page, and Full Page. Fit to Page, the default setting, tells Microsoft Excel to print the chart as large as possible without losing the height-width dimension shown on the screen. If you want to control the dimensions of the printed chart manually, select the Screen Size option. This option tells Microsoft Excel to print your chart exactly as it is shown on the screen. To vary the size of the screen image, you can resize the window just as you would resize a worksheet or macro sheet window. The Full Page option tells Microsoft Excel to fill the entire page, regardless of the height:width ratio of the chart.

The Print command

When you choose the Print command in the Microsoft Excel chart environment, you'll see a dialog box identical to the one you see when you choose the Print command in the worksheet environment, except that it does not contain options for printing the worksheet and notes.

Of course, the Pages option does not apply when you're in the chart environment, because all your charts will be one page in length. However, you can use the Copies edit bar to indicate the number of charts you want to print.

If you want to see what your chart will look like before you print it, select the Preview option. As in the worksheet environment, Microsoft Excel will display the chart as it will appear on the printed page. Your pointer will be shaped like a magnifying glass so that you can select parts of the chart to get a full-scale view of the finished product. (If you're not using a mouse, you can use the Zoom button, described in Chapter 9, to get a closer view of the preview of the printed chart.)

DATABASES

14

Database Management

*S*o far, we've seen how Microsoft Excel can be used as an electronic spreadsheet and as a graphics program. As you probably know, Microsoft Excel is also a database manager. In this chapter, we'll explore the fundamentals of databases. We'll begin by discussing the structure of a database. Then we'll show you how to create, define, and format a database. Next, we'll show you how to add, delete, and move records and fields, and then we'll look at calculated fields. We'll end the chapter with a discussion of data forms—special dialog boxes through which you can enter and edit database records.

What is a database?

A database is a structured collection of information. By structured, we mean that the information is arranged in some convenient, logical, consistent order. This structure makes it easy to locate and retrieve individual pieces of information quickly.

The information in a database can be anything from telephone numbers and names to part numbers and prices. You probably use simple databases every day, perhaps without even realizing that they are databases. For example, a dictionary is a database of words and their definitions. Another commonly used database is the telephone book.

A telephone book contains thousands of listings, each of which generally includes four pieces of information: a last name, a first name, a street address, and a telephone number. If you think about it for a moment, you'll see that the information in a telephone book is arranged in a rough tabular form. Each listing occupies one line, or row, in the book, and each piece of information (last name, first name, and so on) occupies a single column. As you'll see, Microsoft Excel databases use this same row-and-column structure. In database terminology, each of the listings in the telephone book is called a record. The individual pieces of information within a listing are called fields.

The usefulness of a database depends on how well the information it contains is organized and how easily it can be reorganized. For example, the alphabetic order of the listings in a telephone book is the key to its usefulness. Because the listings are arranged in alphabetic order based on the last-name entry of each listing, you can easily find the name (and thus the phone number) of any person you want to call.

However, the usefulness of a telephone book is limited. Because a telephone book is printed, the order of the information in it is fixed—the records in a telephone book can't be reordered so that they're sorted by street or by number. For this reason, it would be nearly impossible to locate all the listings for people who live on a certain street or who have the same first name. Furthermore, computing statistics for groups of the listings in a telephone book (such as the number of people called Williams) would have to be done manually and would be very difficult.

Unlike the printed telephone book, Microsoft Excel stores information electronically. For this reason, the database is dynamic and can be easily manipulated. For example, if you entered the listings (records) from a telephone book into a Microsoft Excel database, you could sort the records in that database into ascending or descending order based on any of the pieces of information (fields) in the listings. As you'll see in the next chapter, you could also locate, extract, and delete any information in the database that shared a common characteristic—for example, all the records for people who live on Elm Street, or all the records for people named Jones.

As you might expect, Microsoft Excel can do more than just sort a database and locate information in that database. It can also print hard-copy reports of the information in your databases. It can even perform statistical calculations on records that meet certain criteria.

The structure of a database

Figure 14-1 shows a sample database that contains 10 records, each of which has six fields. As you can see, this database is really nothing more than a rectangular range of worksheet cells. Within this range, each row contains a single record and each column is a separate field. For example, row 3 contains the record for John Johnson and column D contains the Date of Birth field.

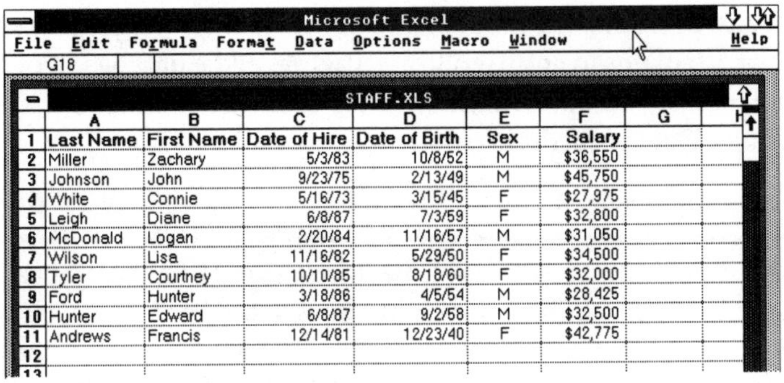

	A	B	C	D	E	F	G	
1	Last Name	First Name	Date of Hire	Date of Birth	Sex	Salary		
2	Miller	Zachary	5/3/83	10/8/52	M	$36,550		
3	Johnson	John	9/23/75	2/13/49	M	$45,750		
4	White	Connie	5/16/73	3/15/45	F	$27,975		
5	Leigh	Diane	6/8/87	7/3/59	F	$32,800		
6	McDonald	Logan	2/20/84	11/16/57	M	$31,050		
7	Wilson	Lisa	11/16/82	5/29/50	F	$34,500		
8	Tyler	Courtney	10/10/85	8/18/60	F	$32,000		
9	Ford	Hunter	3/18/86	4/5/54	M	$28,425		
10	Hunter	Edward	6/8/87	9/2/58	M	$32,500		
11	Andrews	Francis	12/14/81	12/23/40	F	$42,775		
12								

FIGURE 14-1. *A database is simply a specially organized group of worksheet cells.*

Notice that the top row of this database contains a series of field names. These names, which must always be entered in the top row of the database, identify the information that is stored in each field. For example, the entries in the First Name field are all first names, the entries in the Salary field are annual salary values, and so forth. These field names are the key to using selection criteria.

Creating a database

Creating a database is as easy as creating a worksheet. For example, to create the database shown in Figure 14-1, begin by entering the field names *Last Name, First Name, Date of Hire, Date of Birth, Sex,* and *Salary* into any six adjacent cells on a single row of a worksheet. These field names are simple text entries. They can go in any row, but for this example we've entered them in row 1.

You'll usually want to keep the field names in your databases fairly short so that they're easy to remember and use. However, like all text entries in Microsoft Excel, field names can be as many as 255 characters and can contain any character, including blank spaces. Although field names are usually simple labels, they can also be the results of text-producing functions. You should not use numbers or value-producing formulas or functions as field names.

Now that you've defined how you want to organize the fields in your database, you're ready to start entering records. You can make the same kinds of entries in a database that you can make in a worksheet: text, numbers, formulas, and functions.

After you've created a database, you'll usually want to change the format and alignment of the cells in selected fields and alter the width of certain fields. You can format and align the entries in a database in the same way you format and align the cells in any other worksheet. Because all the entries in each field of most databases are of a similar type, you'll typically want to assign the same formats and alignment attributes to entire columns (fields) of the database. For example, in our sample database, we applied the m/d/yy format to all the date entries in the Date of Hire and Date of Birth fields.

Defining the database

Although you may recognize the worksheet in Figure 14-1 as a database, Microsoft Excel does not know it is a database until you use the Set Database command on the Data menu. To define a block of cells as a database, first select the entire rectangle that contains the database, including the field names. (In this case, you would select the range A1:F11.) Then choose the Set Database command.

The Set Database command does nothing more than assign the range name *Database* to the selected block of cells. You could achieve the same effect by selecting the block of cells, choosing the Define Name command from the Formula menu, typing the name *Database*, and pressing Enter. However, you'll find the Set Database method much faster and easier in most cases.

When you choose a database command, Microsoft Excel looks for the name *Database* in order to know which area of the worksheet to operate on. For this reason, each worksheet can have only one defined database at a time. (You can have any number of databases set up in a worksheet, but only the one you're actively working with can be defined with the name *Database*.) To switch between databases, you must redefine the database range.

Changing records and fields

After you've created a database, you might find that you need to add, delete, or move one or more of its records or fields. Because records are worksheet rows and fields are worksheet columns, the process of adding, deleting, and moving records and fields is no different than that of adding and deleting rows and columns in the worksheet.

Adding records and fields

To add a record to the end of a database, simply enter each field of the new record in the first blank row below the last existing record. Then select the entire range that contains the database (including the new record) and choose Set Database from the Data menu to expand the database range to include this new record. Whenever you add one or more new records to the end of a database, you must use the Set Database or Define Name command to redefine the range so that it includes the new records. If you omit this step, Microsoft Excel will not include the new records in the database.

To avoid this problem, you can add new records in the middle of the database rather than at the end. Alternatively, you can include an extra blank row at the bottom of the database so that you can select that row whenever you want to add a new record.

To add a record in the middle of a database, select the row where you want to add the record and choose the Insert command from the Edit menu. When you choose this command, Microsoft Excel adds a blank row to the database above the selected row and pushes the existing rows down one row. Because the database range is a named range, Microsoft Excel will expand this range automatically when you add a new record in the middle of the database.

If you want to keep your database records in their order of entry, you may prefer to include an extra blank row at the bottom of the database. For example, if your database records currently occupy cells A1 through G50, you could define the database range as A1:G51. Then, whenever you want to add a new record, you can select the last row of the database, which is blank, and use the Insert command. As in the example above, Microsoft Excel adds a blank row to the database above the selected row and pushes the existing "dummy record" down one row.

You can also add new fields to existing Microsoft Excel databases. To add a new field at the right edge of a database, select the cell in the field-names row (the first row of the database range) immediately to the right of the last existing field name and type the new field name. Then make entries in the new field for the existing records in the database. Because the new field is outside the original database range, you'll have to use the Set Database or Define Name command to include the new field.

Of course, you can also add a new field within an existing database range. To do this, select the column where you want to add the new field and choose the Insert command. Microsoft Excel will insert a blank column in the worksheet to the left of the selected column and push the existing columns one column to the right.

Deleting records and fields

To delete a record, select the row that contains the record and choose the Delete command from the Edit menu. Microsoft Excel will remove that record from the database, shift all the rows below the removed record up one row to fill in the "empty" space, and contract the database range to reflect the deletion.

Deleting a field is just as simple. Select the column that contains the field and then choose the Delete command. Microsoft Excel will remove that column from the database and contract the database range to reflect the deletion, whether the field is at the end or in the middle of the range.

Reordering records and fields

You can reorder records and fields within a Microsoft Excel database by moving the rows and columns of the worksheet. To move a field to a new location within the database range, first insert a new column at the destination of the move. Then select the column containing the field you want to move, choose Cut, select the newly inserted column, and choose Paste. To move a record within the database range, insert a new row at the destination of the move, select the row containing the record that you want to move, and choose Cut. Then select the newly inserted row and choose Paste. Microsoft Excel adjusts the database range to properly reflect the movement of records and fields.

Calculated fields

Most of the entries you'll make into the fields of a Microsoft Excel database will be text, numbers, and dates. However, you can also make formula entries. Fields whose entries are the result of formulas or functions are called calculated fields.

The database shown in Figure 14-2 contains an example of a calculated field. This database is almost identical to the one in Figure 14-1, except for the addition of the Age field. To add this field to the database, we entered the text *Age* into cell G1 and then expanded the database range by selecting cells A1:G11 and choosing Set Database from the Data menu. Then we entered the formula

    =YEAR(NOW())–YEAR(D2)

into cell G2. This formula tells Microsoft Excel to subtract the serial date value in cell D2 (the Date of Birth entry for the first record) from the current date (the result of the NOW function). To calculate the Age field for the remaining records, use the Copy and Paste commands or the Fill Down command to copy this formula to the range G3:G11.

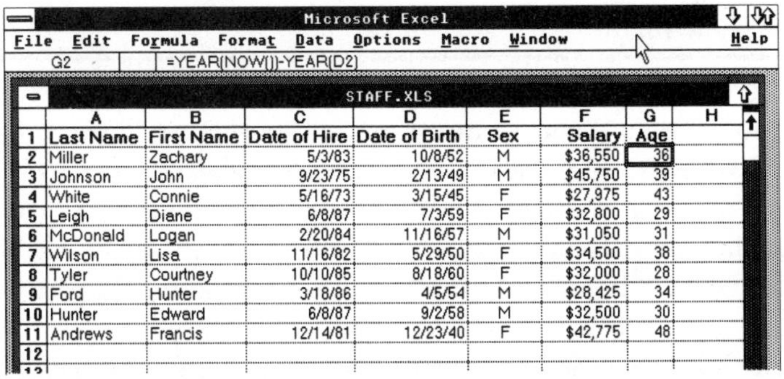

Microsoft Excel

File Edit Formula Format Data Options Macro Window Help

G2 =YEAR(NOW())-YEAR(D2)

STAFF.XLS

	A	B	C	D	E	F	G	H
1	Last Name	First Name	Date of Hire	Date of Birth	Sex	Salary	Age	
2	Miller	Zachary	5/3/83	10/8/52	M	$36,550	36	
3	Johnson	John	9/23/75	2/13/49	M	$45,750	39	
4	White	Connie	5/16/73	3/15/45	F	$27,975	43	
5	Leigh	Diane	6/8/87	7/3/59	F	$32,800	29	
6	McDonald	Logan	2/20/84	11/16/57	M	$31,050	31	
7	Wilson	Lisa	11/16/82	5/29/50	F	$34,500	38	
8	Tyler	Courtney	10/10/85	8/18/60	F	$32,000	28	
9	Ford	Hunter	3/18/86	4/5/54	M	$28,425	34	
10	Hunter	Edward	6/8/87	9/2/58	M	$32,500	30	
11	Andrews	Francis	12/14/81	12/23/40	F	$42,775	48	
12								

FIGURE 14-2. *We added the calculated field Age to the employee database.*

As you can see, the entries in calculated fields result from individual formulas in the cells of that field. Whenever you add a new record to a database, you can Copy and Paste the formula into the new record so that Microsoft Excel can calculate a value for it. If you're entering a group of records, you can save time by entering all the records first, selecting the cells where the calculated field is to appear, and then using the Copy and Paste commands or Fill Down to enter the formula into the calculated field of every new record in one step.

Data forms

As you've learned, a database is a listing of information in the cells of a Microsoft Excel worksheet. In many cases, you'll find it convenient to view your databases as lists. However, Microsoft Excel also allows you to view the contents of a database through a simple one-page form. Using data forms, you can add records to a database, delete records from a database, and edit existing records. You can even specify criteria in the form window and use those criteria to help you locate database records. (We'll talk more about that in Chapter 16.)

The primary advantage of data forms is that they allow you to view all the fields of a record at once. When you view a database in list form, only a few fields are visible at a time and you see several records at once on the screen. (The number of fields that are visible depends on the width of the columns displayed on your screen.) Data forms let you view one complete record at a time.

Let's take a look at Microsoft Excel's default data form. Then we'll show you how to put forms to work.

Creating a data form

Before you can create a data form, you must use the Set Database command on the Data menu to define a database range in your worksheet. Be certain to include the cells that contain the database's field names in the database range—Microsoft Excel uses these labels to identify each of the fields in your data form. After you define your database range, choose the Form command from the Data menu. Microsoft Excel will tailor a data form for your database and display it in a special dialog box.

For example, to create a data form for the database shown in Figure 14-2, select the range A1:G12 and choose the Set Database command from the Data menu to define the database range. Next, choose the Form command from the Data menu to create a data form like the one in Figure 14-3.

FIGURE 14-3. *This Form dialog box appears when you select Form from the Data menu.*

As you can see in Figure 14-3, at the top of the data form Microsoft Excel displays the name of the worksheet that contains the database on which the data form is based. Immediately under this title bar are all the field names from the first row of the database. If you've already entered some records into your database, you'll see the field entries for your first record to the right of the field names. At the top right corner of the dialog box is a notation in the form *x of y* that tells you which record is currently displayed and how many records are currently located in the database range. For example, the *1 of 10* that appears in the dialog box in Figure 14-3 indicates that the first record of 10 total records is being displayed. If you haven't yet entered any records, the entry boxes to the right of the field names will be blank and you'll see the notation *New Record* at the top right corner of the dialog box. Down the right side of the data form are several command buttons that allow you to work with the database records. We'll discuss these options in the next section, when we talk about selecting records, and in Chapter 16.

Fields whose entries are displayed in boxes—in our example, Last Name, First Name, Date of Hire, Date of Birth, Sex, and Salary—are called editable fields and can, as their name implies, be edited. Fields whose entries do not appear in a box—Age, in our example—are called calculated fields. Calculated fields display the result of a function or formula and cannot be edited. (We'll show you how to define calculated fields in a form in a few pages.) If you've used the Cell Protection and Protect Document commands to lock and protect any of the cells in the database, your data form may contain protected fields. Again, Microsoft Excel will display the contents of a locked field on the data form, but the field won't appear inside a box, thus indicating that you can't edit it.

To close a data-form dialog box, you can choose the Close command from the dialog-box Control menu (or press Alt-F4), choose the Exit button at the bottom right corner of the dialog box, or simply press the Escape key. The data form will disappear from view. If you want to reopen the form, you'll have to choose the Form command from the Data menu again.

If you need to peek at the worksheet while you're working in the data form, you can move the form aside by dragging the title bar with the mouse. Alternatively, you can reposition the form by choosing Move from the Control menu (or pressing Alt-F7) and using the arrow keys to move the box.

Microsoft Excel will not allow you to activate another window or issue any commands while the data-form dialog box is open. If you want to issue a command or activate a window, you'll have to close the form.

Navigation techniques

The scroll bar in the center of the data-form dialog box allows you to scroll through the records in your database. You can move backward or forward through the database one record at a time by clicking on the up or down scroll arrow. You can move through the database 10 records at a time by clicking in the gray area of the scroll bar above or below the scroll box. You can also drag the scroll box to the approximate position of a record. For example, if your database contains 10 records and you drag the scroll box to the middle of the scroll bar, the fifth record will appear in the form. If you drag the scroll box to the bottom of the scroll bar, Microsoft Excel will display a set of empty entry fields, ready for a new database record.

You can also use Microsoft Excel's navigation keys to move through the database. To move from one record to the next record or the previous record, press the Up arrow key or the Down arrow key. To move to the first record in the database, press Ctrl-Up arrow; to move to the end of the database so that you can enter a new record, press Ctrl-Down arrow. To move through the database 10 records at a time, press PgUp or PgDn.

There are also several techniques you can use to move from field to field in a record in a data form. With the mouse, you can move to a new field simply by clicking on that field. If you prefer to use the keyboard, you can use Tab to move forward to the next field or Shift-Tab to move backward to the previous field.

Alternatively, you can move to a field in the current record by pressing Alt and typing the underlined letter in the name of that field. (Because Microsoft Excel tailors each data form to reflect the underlying worksheet, you may find that two or more fields contain the same underlined letter. If this happens, simply continue to press Alt and the letter until Microsoft Excel highlights the correct field.)

Table 14-1 summarizes the selection and navigation techniques you'll use to move around in a data form.

Table 14-1. Selection and navigation techniques for Microsoft Excel data forms.

Action	Technique
Select an option	Click on the desired option button.
	Press Alt in conjunction with the underlined letter.
Move to same field, next record	Click on the down arrow icon on the scroll bar.
	Press the Down arrow key.
Move to same field, previous record	Click on the up arrow icon on the scroll bar.
	Press the Up arrow key.
Move to next field	Click on the field.
	Press Tab.
Move to previous field	Click on the field.
	Press Shift-Tab.
Move to first field, next record	Click on the first field, then click on the down arrow icon on the scroll bar.
	Press Enter.
Move to same field, 10 records forward	Click below the scroll box in the scroll bar.
	Press PgDn.
Move to same field, 10 records back	Click above the scroll box in the scroll bar.
	Press PgUp.
Move to last record	Drag the scroll box to the bottom of the scroll bar.
	Press Ctrl-PgDn.
Move to first record	Drag the scroll box to the top of the scroll bar.
	Press Ctrl-PgUp.
Move/edit within field	Click for the insertion point.
	Use the Home, End, and Left and Right arrow keys to position the insertion point.

Editing records

To edit a record in a form, simply bring that record into view in the form, move to the field that contains the entry you want to change, and then edit the information in that field using the usual Microsoft Excel editing techniques. Use the navigation keys or the scroll bars to bring the record you want to edit into view and then use the Tab key or the mouse to move to the field you want to edit. To add characters to an entry in a field, position the insertion point in that field and type the additional characters. To delete characters, highlight the characters you want to erase and press Del. To replace characters with new characters, highlight the characters you want to replace and type the new characters. To lock in your change, press Enter, move to another record or another field, or choose the Exit button.

For example, suppose you want to edit the record for employee McDonald. You want to raise his salary from $31,050 to $50,000. To begin, you have to bring this record (number 5) into view in the form, as shown in Figure 14-4. To display the record, press the Down arrow key five times or drag or click on the scroll bar. When the record is in view, select the Salary field by using the Tab key, clicking on the field, or pressing Alt-y. (Notice that the letter *y* is underlined in the field name *Salary* on the left side of the dialog box.) Then type *50000* and press Enter to lock in your change. Figure 14-5 shows the result.

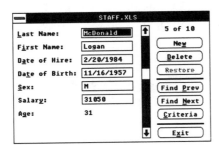

FIGURE 14-4. *You can use data forms to edit records.*

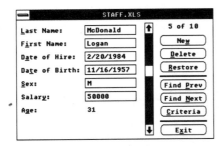

FIGURE 14-5. *We changed the entry in the Salary field from 31050 to 50000.*

As soon as you make a change to a record, the Restore button on the right side of the dialog box becomes available. If you make a change to an existing record and then discover a mistake before you move to another record, you can choose Restore to return the record to its original condition.

Remember, you can edit only those fields that are displayed in boxes. You cannot edit calculated or protected fields. In fact, you can't even move to a calculated or protected field in a form.

Adding records

It's easy to add a record to a database using the data form. First, select the New option or drag the scroll box to the bottom of the scroll bar. Microsoft Excel will scroll to the first blank record at the end of the database and display *New Record* at the upper right corner of the data form. You can now add a new record by entering the information for that record into the fields of the form. If you make an error while you're entering a record through a form, you can edit the field entries in the data form just as you would edit an existing entry. When you're finished, lock in the new record by moving to another record, selecting the New or Exit button, or pressing the Enter key. Microsoft Excel will add the new record to the database.

For example, suppose you want to add a new record to the example database. To begin, use the New button, the Ctrl-Down arrow key combination, or the scroll box to move to the first blank record at the end of the database. Then add the new record by making entries in the fields of the form. Figure 14-6 shows a new record in the form and on the worksheet. When we entered the record, Microsoft Excel

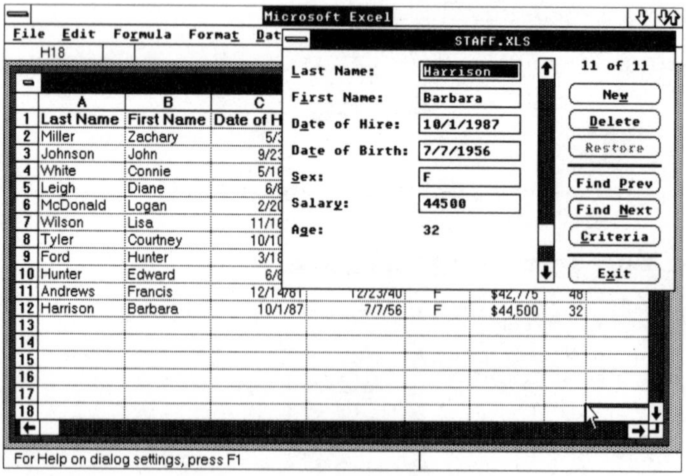

FIGURE 14-6. *We added a new record for Barbara Harrison.*

added the record to the end of the database range, filled in the calculated Age field, and formatted the numeric entries in columns C, D, and F. (We moved the form dialog box to the upper right corner of the screen so that we could view the added record for Barbara Harrison.)

When you use the data form to add new records to your database, Microsoft Excel adds those new records to the bottom of the database and extends the database range to include your additions. In addition, if the last record in the database includes calculated fields, Microsoft Excel "copies" the formulas from those fields into the new record. Always be sure that plenty of extra room for new records is available below the database range. If Microsoft Excel can't find room to expand the database, you'll see the alert message *Can't extend database range* when you try to create a new record.

Deleting records

To delete a record through a data form, simply bring that record into view in the form and select the Delete button. Microsoft Excel will present an alert box reminding you that the current record will be permanently deleted from the database. If you select OK in the alert box, the record will vanish from both the data form and the worksheet. Any records below that record in the worksheet will be shifted upward to fill in the resulting gap. If you choose Cancel, the record will not be deleted.

Defining criteria and selecting records

You can also use a form to define selection conditions (called criteria) and to find records in the database based on the criteria you've defined. This capability comes in handy when you need to move from one record to another that contains a particular entry. We'll explain criteria and show how you can define and use criteria in forms in Chapter 16.

Custom data forms

The data forms you've seen thus far can help to speed your database entry and editing tremendously. However, these simple default forms represent only the beginning of Microsoft Excel's forms capabilities. You can also develop your own custom form dialog boxes to collect input from the user and display information in any format and arrangement you choose. We'll show you how to create custom forms in Chapter 20.

15

Sorting

The Sort command on the Data menu allows you to rearrange the records in a database based on the entries in one, two, or three fields, making particular records easier to locate as you scan through the database. The Sort command is one of Microsoft Excel's most important database-management tools.

Sorting basics

To sort a database, first select the range that contains the database. The range you select should include all the records and all the fields in the database, but it should not include the field names at the top of the database. After you've selected the database you want to rearrange, choose Sort from the Data menu. Microsoft Excel will present the Sort dialog box shown in Figure 15-1. The entries you make in this dialog box tell Microsoft Excel which fields to use to sort the database.

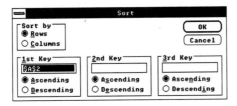

FIGURE 15-1. *Use the Sort dialog box to rearrange your database.*

When the Sort dialog box appears, use the 1st Key, 2nd Key, and 3rd Key edit bars to define the fields on which you want to sort and the order of the sort. When you issue the Sort command, Microsoft Excel always displays the reference of the cell in the upper left corner of the selected range in the 1st Key edit bar. To redefine the first sort field, simply enter a reference to any cell in the column that contains the field on which you want to sort. (The chosen cell doesn't have to be within the group of cells you're sorting; it can be anywhere in that column.)

After you've specified the sort field, specify the order of the sort. The default order, Ascending, instructs Microsoft Excel to arrange the records so that the record with the lowest value in the sort field appears at the top of the database and the one with the highest value appears at the bottom. The Descending option tells Microsoft Excel to arrange the records so that the one with the highest value in the sort field appears first and the one with the lowest value appears last.

If you want to sort on more than one field, enter a cell reference into the 2nd Key (and 3rd Key) edit bar and again choose the appropriate sort order. When all the sort fields have been defined, select OK or press Enter. Microsoft Excel will then sort the database so that the entries in the specified fields are arranged in the selected order.

An example

Let's use the Sort command to rearrange the records in the database in Figure 15-2. As you can see, this database includes two fields: Student and GPA (grade-point average). The records are in an apparently random order. To make this information more useful, we can sort the database so that the record with the highest GPA is at the top of the database and the record with the lowest GPA is at the bottom.

To sort this database, first select the range A2:B18, which includes every record in the database. (Notice that the sort range does not include the two field names at the top of the database.) Next, choose Sort from the Data menu. When the Sort dialog box appears, define the sort fields. Because you want Microsoft Excel to sort the database on the values in the GPA field, which is located in column B of the worksheet, type a reference to any cell from column B (such as B1) into the 1st Key edit bar. If you're using a mouse, you can enter a cell reference simply by activating the edit bar and clicking on any cell in column B.

Next, specify the order of the sort. In this case, select Descending, so that Microsoft Excel will place the record with the highest GPA at the top of the database.

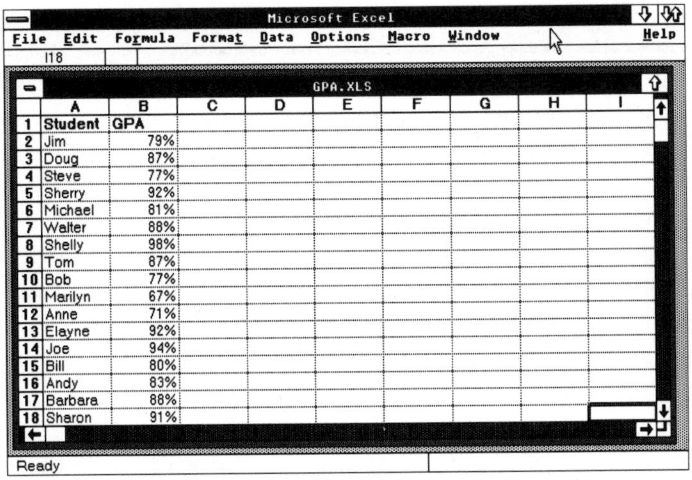

FIGURE 15-2. *This database contains two fields: Student and GPA.*

When you're satisfied with the sort settings, select the OK button or press Enter. Microsoft Excel will immediately rearrange the database into the order you specified in the Sort dialog box. In this case, Microsoft Excel places the record with the highest GPA at the top of the database, the record with the second highest GPA next, and so forth. Figure 15-3 shows the result of the sort.

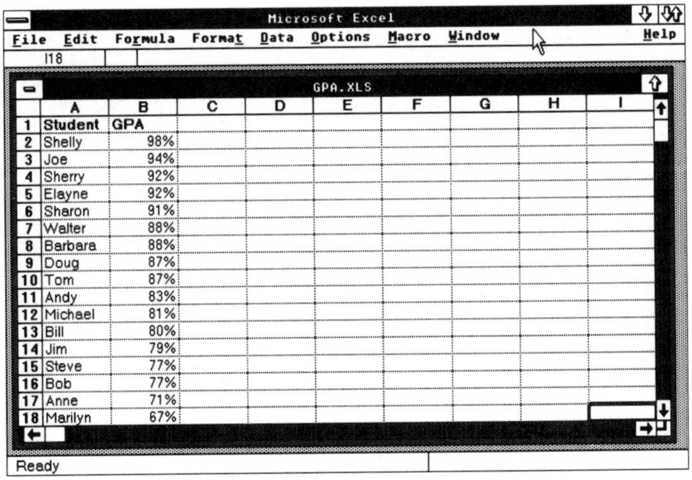

FIGURE 15-3. *We sorted the database into descending order by GPA.*

Sort order

As we've already pointed out, Microsoft Excel sorts the entries in a database field based on the "value" of those entries. If a field contains any numbers or number-producing formulas or functions, an ascending sort puts the smallest numbers at the top of the database and the largest numbers at the bottom. A descending sort on a numeric field places the largest numbers first and the smallest numbers last.

When Microsoft Excel performs an ascending sort on the entries in a text field, it arranges those entries in ascending alphabetic order; that is, entries that begin with A come first and entries that begin with Z come last. For purposes of sorting, Microsoft Excel does not differentiate between the uppercase and lowercase letters; that is, *a* is the same as *A* and *Z* is the same as *z*.

When two entries begin with the same letter, Microsoft Excel uses the second letter in the word as a tiebreaker. If both the first and second letters are the same, Microsoft Excel then uses the third letter, and so forth. For example, in an ascending sort, AAA would come before AAB, which would come before AAC.

Occasionally, text fields will contain characters other than letters of the alphabet. The sort order that governs sorts on this kind of entry is

(space) ! " # $ % & ' ( ) * + , - . / 0 1 2 3 4 5 6 7 8 9 : ; < = > ? A B C D E F G H I J K L M N O P Q R S T U V W X Y Z @ [\ ] ^ _ ` { ¦ } ~ ¢ ¥ ±

(The uppercase version of each letter in this list represents both the uppercase and lowercase forms of that letter.)

In most cases, the entries in any field of a database are either numbers or text. In some databases, however, one field might contain both number and text entries. If a field contains both text and number entries, Microsoft Excel places all number

E X C E L

Sorting worksheets

Although you'll usually use the Sort command to sort the records in a database, you can also use this command to sort any range in any worksheet. All you have to do to sort a range in a worksheet is select the range you want to sort, define the sort keys for that range, and choose OK. You need not define the range you want to sort as a database before you sort it. Of course, the range you choose to sort should be arranged so that the sort makes sense.

entries before text entries in an ascending sort. If a field contains other entries, such as logical results (TRUE or FALSE) and error messages, Microsoft Excel performs an ascending sort in this order:

    Numbers
    Text
    Logical values
    Error values
    Blank cells

Descending sorts arrange the field's entries in the opposite order.

Undoing a sort

After you've sorted a database, it is usually difficult, if not impossible, to get that database back into its original order.

Of course, you can always use the Undo Sort command on the Edit menu to put the records back into their previous order, but the Undo command is of no use unless you catch your error before you issue another command or make an entry in your worksheet. However, you can take some precautions to make the task of restoring your database to its original order easier.

The easiest way to ensure that you can return a database to its original order is to save it before you sort it. To do this, simply use the Save or Save As command immediately before sorting the database. You can then return the database to its presort order by using the Open command to bring the saved database to the desktop. Unfortunately, this technique is really only useful for restoring a database to its original order immediately after you use the Sort command. If you make other changes to the database after you sort it, the presort version will not reflect them.

An alternative technique allows you to restore a database to its original order at any time. Simply add to the unsorted database a new field that contains ascending numbers or text. Then you can restore the database to its original order whenever you wish by performing an ascending sort on this new field.

Multiple-field sorts

In most circumstances, you'll sort a database on only a single field, as we did in the previous example. However, when a database contains many fields and some contain duplicate entries, you'll want to sort on more than one field. As we explained earlier, Microsoft Excel lets you sort on as many as three fields at a time.

The database in Figure 15-4 includes three fields: Product, Size, and Color. The records in this database are arranged in a random order. To make this information more meaningful, you might want to sort the database on the basis of the entries in the Product field. To do this, select cells A2:C17, choose Sort, specify any cell in column A as the sort key, select Ascending, and then press Enter. Figure 15-5 shows the result of this single-field sort.

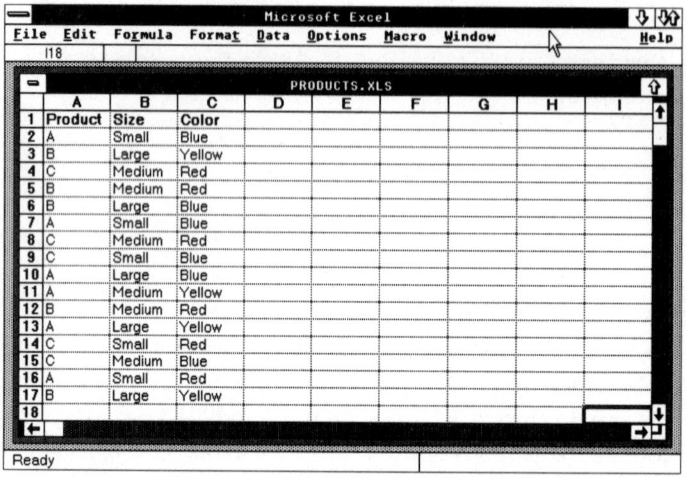

FIGURE 15-4. *The records in this database are arranged in random order.*

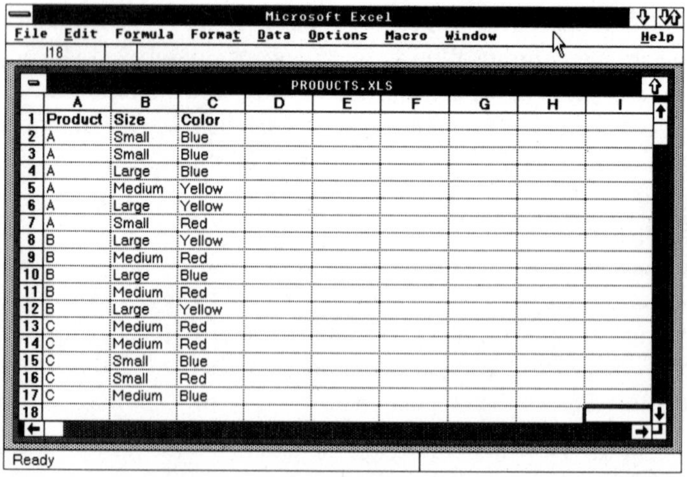

FIGURE 15-5. *We sorted the database into ascending order by product.*

As you can see, Microsoft Excel has rearranged the database in ascending order based on the entries in the Product field. Because this field contains duplicate entries, the sort has grouped the records according to the entries in that column.

Even though the database in Figure 15-5 is better organized than the database in Figure 15-4, the records within each group still appear too randomly arranged. In fact, the records *within* each group are in the same relative order as they were in the original database. You can use a secondary sort to add some order to the records within the groups produced by a primary sort.

For example, to arrange the records in the Products database into ascending order based on the entries in the Product field and arrange the records within each product group in ascending order based on the entries in the Size field, select cells A2:C17 and choose Sort from the Data menu to display the Sort dialog box. Then type the reference of any cell in column A into the 1st Key edit bar and select Ascending. Next, type the reference of any cell in column B (the Size field) into the 2nd Key edit bar and again select Ascending. Finally, select OK or press Enter to initiate the sort. Figure 15-6 shows the result of this two-key sort.

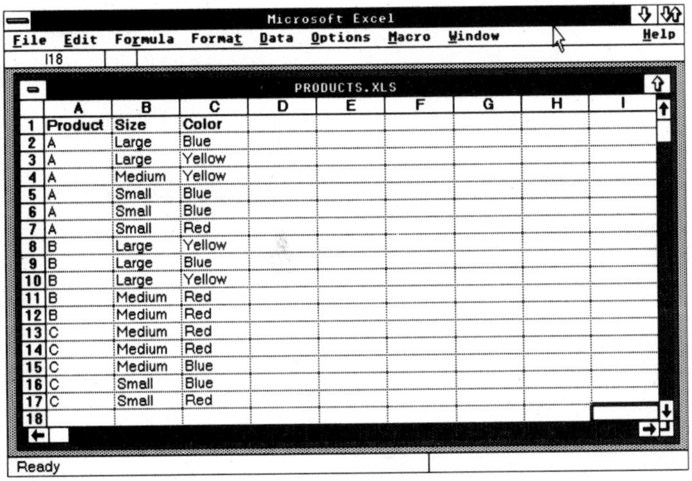

	A	B	C	D	E	F	G	H	I
1	Product	Size	Color						
2	A	Large	Blue						
3	A	Large	Yellow						
4	A	Medium	Yellow						
5	A	Small	Blue						
6	A	Small	Blue						
7	A	Small	Red						
8	B	Large	Yellow						
9	B	Large	Blue						
10	B	Large	Yellow						
11	B	Medium	Red						
12	B	Medium	Red						
13	C	Medium	Red						
14	C	Medium	Red						
15	C	Medium	Blue						
16	C	Small	Blue						
17	C	Small	Red						
18									

FIGURE 15-6. *The database is now arranged in ascending order by product and by size.*

As you can see, Microsoft Excel has grouped all the Product A records at the top of the database, followed by the Product B records and then the Product C records. In this respect, this sort is like the original one-key sort. A look at column B (the Size field), however, reveals the difference. Instead of being arranged in their original order, the records within each group are now arranged in order of size. All the Large records come first within each group, then the Mediums, then the Smalls. Microsoft Excel is able to arrange the records this way not because it knows that Large is bigger than Medium, which is in turn bigger than Small, but because L, the first letter in Large, comes before M, the first letter in Medium, in the alphabet. Similarly, the Medium records come before the Small records because M comes before S in the alphabet.

Obviously, specifying a secondary sort field adds additional organization to the database. You can use a three-key sort to further organize the data. For example, if you look at the Color field, you'll see that the records within each size group still appear to be arranged randomly. To organize the records within each secondary sort group, you can perform a three-field sort.

In this case, let's sort the database so that the records within each secondary sort group are arranged in descending order based on the entries in the Color field. To perform this sort, again select cells A2:C17 and choose Sort from the Data menu. Next, type the reference of any cell in column A in the 1st Key edit bar and select Ascending. Then type the reference of any cell in column B in the 2nd Key edit bar and select Ascending. Finally, type the reference of any cell in column C in the 3rd Key edit bar and this time choose Descending. After you've entered these settings, press Enter to start the sort. Figure 15-7 shows the results of this three-field sort.

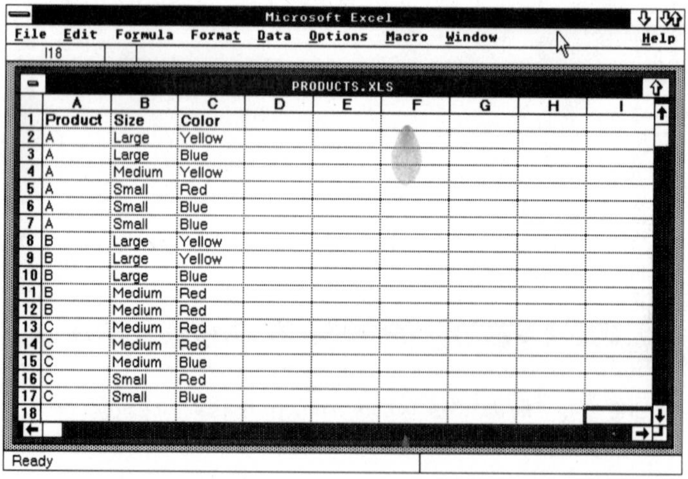

FIGURE 15-7. *The database is now sorted by product, by size, and by color.*

As you can see, Microsoft Excel has arranged the records so that all the Product A entries appear at the top of the database, all the Product B entries next, and all the Product C entries last. Within each product group, Microsoft Excel presents the records in descending order by size (or ascending order alphabetically). Within each size group, Microsoft Excel has arranged the records into descending alphabetic order on the basis of the entries in the Color field.

Column sorts

The Sort by field of the Sort dialog box offers two options—Rows and Columns—that let you determine whether Microsoft Excel will sort the selected range by rows or by columns. You'll usually use the Rows option when you choose the Sort command. The Rows option tells Microsoft Excel to treat each row of the selected sort range as an unbreakable unit and, therefore, to sort the database by switching the positions of entire rows.

The Columns option changes the way Microsoft Excel looks at the sort range by "tilting" it 90 degrees. This option tells Microsoft Excel to consider the cells in each *column* in that range to be inseparable. Therefore, Microsoft Excel sorts the

EXCEL

Sorting on more than three fields

Microsoft Excel allows you to sort a database on only three fields at a time and, in most cases, you won't need more than three fields. However, on those occasions when you want to sort a large database on more than three fields, you can do so by performing successive single-field or multiple-field sorts.

When you perform a three-field sort, you specify the sort fields in order of their importance. You use the least important field as the third key and the most important field as the first key. Follow this same rule when you sort a database on more than three fields.

For example, suppose you want to sort a database on the basis of five fields. To do this, first decide which field is the primary (first) field and which are the second, third, fourth, and fifth. Then perform a two-key sort of the entire range of the database with the fifth most important field as the second key and the fourth most important field as the first key. Next, perform a three-field sort on the rearranged database, with the third field as the third key, the second as the second key, and the most important field as the first key. You can use this technique to sort a database on any number of fields.

selected range by switching the positions of entire columns, not rows, within the database range.

Although the Columns option is seldom used for sorting the fields in a database, it can be useful in other worksheet applications. For example, suppose you've created the simple financial worksheet shown in Figure 15-8. As you can see, this model consists of five columns of financial information, each of which contains Revenues, Expenses, and Profit entries. Currently, columns B, C, D, E, and F contain the information for 1985, 1984, 1983, 1982, and 1981, respectively. To rearrange this worksheet so that the information for 1981 is in column B, the information for 1982 is in column C, and so on, you can perform a "by-column" sort.

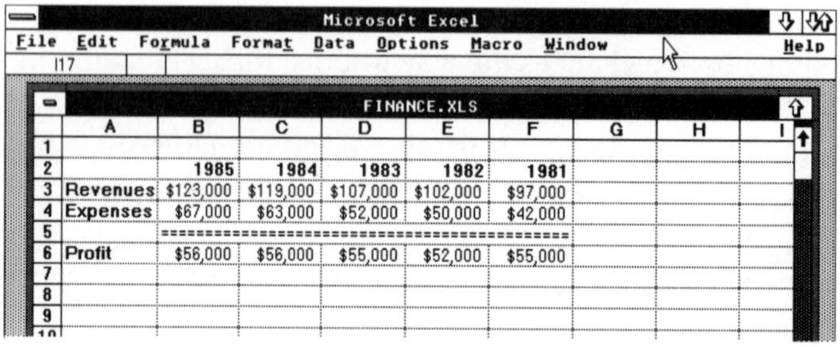

FIGURE 15-8. *We want to reorganize this simple financial worksheet.*

Begin by selecting the sort range—in this case, B2:F6. Then choose Sort from the Data menu to display the Sort dialog box. Because you want Microsoft Excel to sort this range on the basis of the entries in row 2 (the year headers), type the reference of any cell in that row (such as cell B2) into the 1st Key edit bar. You want Microsoft Excel to place 1981's information in column B and 1985's in column F, so select the Ascending option. Before you sort this range, select the Columns option in the Sort by box. When you select OK or press Enter, Microsoft Excel will sort the range into the order shown in Figure 15-9.

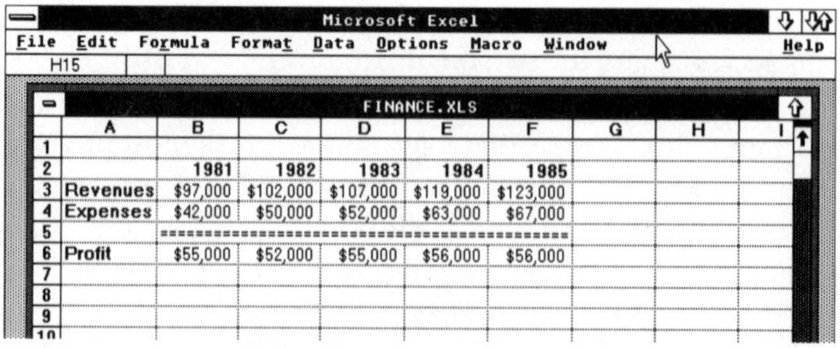

FIGURE 15-9. *We used the Columns option of the Sort command to reverse the years on the financial worksheet.*

16

Working with a Database

So far, we've been concerned with how Microsoft Excel stores information in a database, but, of course, Microsoft Excel can do much more than simply store your data. After you've created a database range, you can locate and manipulate the information stored in that range. In the previous chapter, you learned how to sort database entries. In this chapter, you'll learn about three other Data menu commands that operate on the records in a database: Find, Extract, and Delete. The Find command instructs Microsoft Excel to locate, one at a time, those records in the database that match the criteria in the criteria range. The Extract command allows you to copy the entries from those records that match the criteria to another location in the worksheet. The Delete command allows you to delete from the worksheet all the records that match the criteria.

Microsoft Excel also offers eleven special database statistical functions: DSUM, DAVERAGE, DCOUNT, DCOUNTA, DMAX, DMIN, DPRODUCT, DSTDEV, DSTDEVP, DVAR, and DVARP. These functions calculate statistics about the records that match the criteria you've defined.

Before you can use these commands and functions, however, you must know how to specify selection criteria. We'll discuss that topic first.

Selection criteria

Selection criteria are the tests Microsoft Excel uses to determine which database records it should act upon when you use a database command or function. For example, you might use a criterion such as "all the people who live on Main Street" to extract information from a telephone book database.

Like the records in a Microsoft Excel database, selection criteria are simply entries in a worksheet. Also like Microsoft Excel databases, selection criteria must be stored in a specially defined range of cells known as the criteria range.

Creating and defining a criteria range is a three-step process: First, you enter one or more field names across one row of a worksheet; second, you enter selection criteria into the cells below the field names; third, you select the cells that contain the field names and the criteria and choose Set Criteria from the Data menu. The Set Criteria command assigns the range name *Criteria* to the selected cells and thereby tells Microsoft Excel that those cells are the criteria range. Each worksheet can have only one range at a time with the name *Criteria.* Although you can have a number of different criteria ranges in a worksheet, only one can be active when you're using criteria commands and functions.

Cells A15:G16 in Figure 16-1 contain a sample criteria range that could be used to select records from the employee database above it. As you can see, the structure of a criteria range is much like that of a database range. The first row of a criteria range must contain one or more of the field names from the database with which the criteria range is associated. The first row of the criteria range in Figure 16-1 contains all the field names from the database. The entries in the row or rows

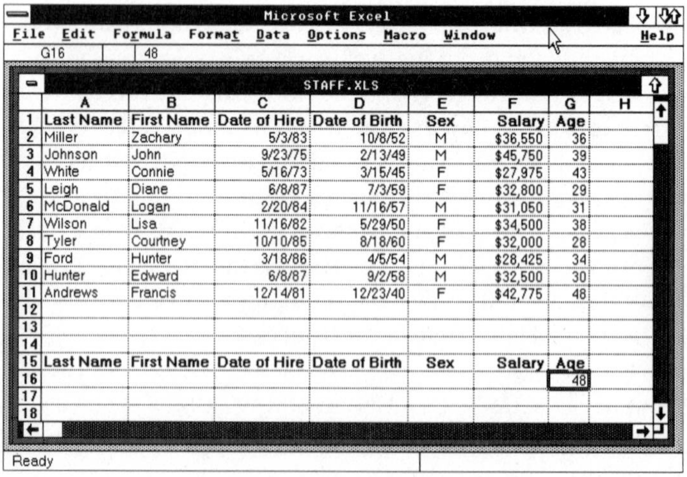

	A	B	C	D	E	F	G	H
1	Last Name	First Name	Date of Hire	Date of Birth	Sex	Salary	Age	
2	Miller	Zachary	5/3/83	10/8/52	M	$36,550	36	
3	Johnson	John	9/23/75	2/13/49	M	$45,750	39	
4	White	Connie	5/16/73	3/15/45	F	$27,975	43	
5	Leigh	Diane	6/8/87	7/3/59	F	$32,800	29	
6	McDonald	Logan	2/20/84	11/16/57	M	$31,050	31	
7	Wilson	Lisa	11/16/82	5/29/50	F	$34,500	38	
8	Tyler	Courtney	10/10/85	8/18/60	F	$32,000	28	
9	Ford	Hunter	3/18/86	4/5/54	M	$28,425	34	
10	Hunter	Edward	6/8/87	9/2/58	M	$32,500	30	
11	Andrews	Francis	12/14/81	12/23/40	F	$42,775	48	
12								
13								
14								
15	Last Name	First Name	Date of Hire	Date of Birth	Sex	Salary	Age	
16							48	
17								
18								

FIGURE 16-1. *Cells A15:G16 contain our criteria range.*

immediately below these field names are the criteria themselves. You might want to think of each row as a "criteria record."

The field names in the criteria range must be identical to the corresponding field names in the database. If a field name in the criteria range does not exactly match one in the database (except for capitalization differences), Microsoft Excel will be unable to use the criteria you enter into that field.

To construct the criteria range in Figure 16-1, select cells A1:G1 (the cells of the database range that contain the field names) and choose the Copy command. Then select cell A15 and choose the Paste command to place a copy of those entries in cells A15:G15. Next, select cells A15:G16 and choose the Set Criteria command from the Data menu to define that block of cells as the criteria range. Finally, enter the selection criteria into the cells in row 16. (You could construct this criteria range by typing the field names directly into cells A15:G15 instead of copying them from cells A1:G1, but by copying the field names, you eliminate the risk of misspellings.)

Although the example criteria range includes every field name from the database, your criteria ranges don't have to include every field name. In fact, you need only include the name of one field in the criteria range—the field you want to use to select records. For instance, if you want to select records only on the basis of the entries in the Age field, the criteria range could include only the name of that one field. If you want to make selections based on the entries in more than one field, you must include all those field names in your criteria range. In general, we recommend that you include the names of all the fields from your database in a criteria range to make it easy to specify criteria for any field.

Database criteria can be divided into two broad categories: comparison criteria and computed criteria. Comparison criteria compare the entries in one field to a numeric or text value (is the entry in the Salary field greater than $50,000?). Computed criteria are more complex because they use the values in two or more fields (is Salary divided by Age greater than 1000?) or they use Microsoft Excel functions to act upon field entries. We'll explore comparison criteria first.

Comparison criteria

Comparison criteria compare the entries in a field of a Microsoft Excel database to text, numbers, or the results of formulas. The comparison can be an equality (=) or one of Microsoft Excel's five relational operators (>, <, >=, <=, or <>).

In Figure 16-1, the criteria range encompasses cells A15:G16. The top row of the criteria range contains the field names to which the criteria relate. The entries below the field names tell Microsoft Excel which entries to look for in each field when it selects records from the database. In this example, the number 48 below the field name *Age* in the criteria range (an exact-match number criterion) will cause Microsoft Excel to operate on only those records that contain the number 48 in the Age field when you use one of the criterion-dependent commands or functions.

Instead of simply entering the value you want Microsoft Excel to match, you can preface that value with an equal sign. For example, you could enter

=48

in cell G16 and achieve the same result as when you entered only the number 48.

You can also use the >, <, >=, <=, and <> signs in numeric comparison criteria. For example, if you enter the criterion

>35

into cell G16, Microsoft Excel will operate on only those records with an Age entry greater than 35.

Text criteria

You can also use comparison criteria in text fields. For example, suppose you want Microsoft Excel to select each record in the database shown in Figure 16-1 that has a Sex entry of M. To do this, you can enter the single letter M into cell E16 (the cell immediately below the field name *Sex* in the criteria range).

When you enter a simple number into a cell of the criteria range, Microsoft Excel selects only those records that have that exact number in the specified field. However, when you use a simple text entry as a criterion, Microsoft Excel selects each record that has an entry in the specified field that begins with the text string you've specified. For example, the criterion M will match not only records that have the entry M in the Sex field, but all records that have Sex entries that begin with M, such as Male or man. (Notice that Microsoft Excel doesn't differentiate between uppercase and lowercase letters in evaluating text criteria.)

Similarly, suppose you want to select all the records that have a Last Name entry that begins with M. To do this, you can erase the current contents of the criteria range and enter the letter *M* in cell A16 (below the field name *Last Name* in the criteria range). This criterion will cause Microsoft Excel to select each record with a Last Name entry that begins with M. In this case, the program will select two records: the one in row 2, Miller, and the one in row 5, McDonald.

If you want to make the criterion more selective, you can replace the single letter *M* in cell A16 with the letters *Mc*. This criterion will cause Microsoft Excel to select each record that has a Last Name entry that begins with Mc—in this case, only the record in row 5, which contains the Last Name entry McDonald.

You can also use the >, <, >=, <=, and <> signs in a text criterion. These operators act upon the "value" of the text entry, where A is less than B, B is less than C, and so on. Uppercase and lowercase forms of the same letter are equal; that is, Z and z have the same value. For example, you could enter

    <N

in cell A16 of our example criteria range to select all records whose Last Name entry begins with a letter before N (the first half of the alphabet). Or you could enter

    <>M

in cell E16 to select all records whose Sex entry does *not* start with M (or m).

Exact-match criteria

If you wish, you can force Microsoft Excel to select only those records with an entry that exactly matches your criterion in the specified text field. To do this, you have to enter the criterion in the form

    ="=*text*"

where *text* is the string you want to match. You should always use this alternate form when you want Microsoft Excel to match a text criterion exactly. For example, if you enter the criterion

    ="=White"

in cell A16 (under the Last Name header in the criteria range), Microsoft Excel will select only those records that have a Last Name entry of White—not records that have a Last Name entry like Whiteman, Whitehall, and so on.

Wildcards

Microsoft Excel allows you to use the wildcard characters ? and * as part of any text criterion. The ? symbol takes the place of any single character. For example, the criterion

    ="=Sm?th"

will match the names *Smith* and *Smyth*. You can also use multiple question marks within the same criterion. For example, the entry

    ="=H??t "

will match the names *Hart, Hurt, Heit*, and so forth.

The * symbol can replace any number of characters. For example, the exact-match criterion

    ="=S*n"

will match, among others, the names *Stevenson, Svenson,* and *Smithson*. You can also use the * wildcard at the beginning of an exact-match text criterion. When you do this, Microsoft Excel selects every entry that ends with the letters that follow the *. For example, the criterion

="=*th"

will match the names *North, Smith, Roth,* and any others that end with the letters *th.*

Similarly, you can use the * wildcard at the end of an exact-match text criterion to make Microsoft Excel select all entries that begin with the specified text but end with any characters. For example, the criterion

="=St*"

will match the names *Stevenson, Stack,* and any others that begin with the letters *St.* (However, you could accomplish the same thing with the simple text criterion St, which will also select any entries that begin with the letters *St.*)

You can use wildcards in text criteria that are not exact-match criteria. However, the results you get may not be what you expect. For example, the criterion

Sm?th

will match the names *Smith* and *Smyth,* but it will also match the names *Smythe, Smithson,* and *Smithsonian.* Similarly, the criterion

*th

will match not only the names *Smith* and *Roth* but also the name *Smithson.*

(To find an actual asterisk or question mark in your data field, precede the character in the criteria range with a tilde [~]. For example, ~? will match any entry beginning with a question mark.)

Combining criteria

In many cases, you'll want Microsoft Excel to select records that meet several different criteria or that meet at least one of several criteria. For example, you might want to select every record in a database that has a Salary value greater than $30,000 and a date of hire before January 1, 1980. Or you might want to select every record that has a Salary value less than $20,000 and a date of hire after December 31, 1983. In these cases, you have to make entries into more than one cell below the criteria field names.

Logical AND. When you make two or more entries on the same row of a criteria range, Microsoft Excel selects only those records that meet both (or all) of those criteria. This condition is called a logical AND. For example, suppose you want to select only the males who are over 36 years of age from the database shown in Figure 16-2. To do this, enter >36 in cell G16 and enter M in cell E16. Because both of these criteria are on the same line of the criteria range (which we defined as cells A15:G16), Microsoft Excel will operate on only those records that meet both criteria. In our example database, it will operate only on the record for

Johnson when you use a criterion-dependent command or function. The record for Miller in row 2 would not meet these criteria unless you changed the entry in cell G16 of the criteria range to >=36.

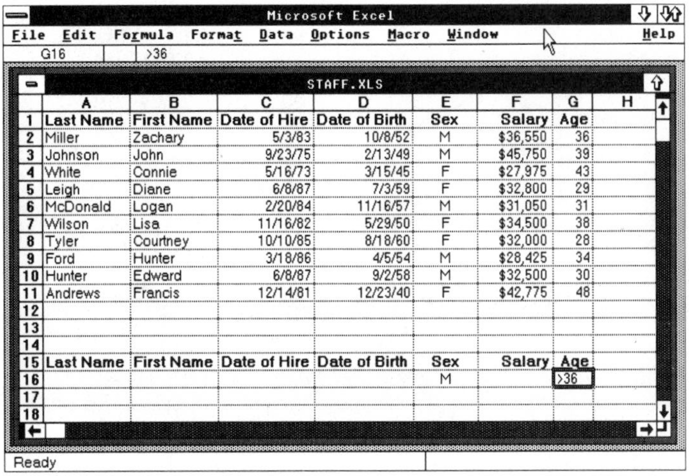

FIGURE 16-2. *We combined two criteria with a logical AND to select only the males who are over 36 years of age.*

You'll sometimes want to match records that have an entry that falls between two values in a particular field. In this case, you'll need to combine two criteria that relate to the same field into a logical AND form. For example, suppose you want Microsoft Excel to select those records from the database shown in Figure 16-2 that have an Age entry between 40 and 50, inclusive. To do this, you need to specify two criteria that relate to the Age field: >=40 and <=50. Because both of these criteria relate to the Age field but you have only one cell to put them in, you must add another Age column to the criteria range to accommodate the extra Age entry. To do this, select cell H15 and type *Age* (or copy that entry from cell G1 or G15). Next, type >=40 in cell G15 and <=50 in cell H15 (or vice versa). Finally, include column H in the criteria range by selecting cells A15:H16 and choosing Set Criteria. When you finish, your criteria range will look like the one in Figure 16-3.

Because these two entries are on the same row of the criteria range and both are beneath an Age header, Microsoft Excel combines them with a logical AND and therefore selects only those records with Age entries that are both greater than or equal to 40 and less than or equal to 50. In this example, Microsoft Excel will select the records in rows 4 and 11 when you use any criterion-dependent command or function.

	Microsoft Excel								
File	Edit	Formula	Format	Data	Options	Macro	Window		Help
H16		<=50							

STAFF.XLS

	A	B	C	D	E	F	G	H
1	Last Name	First Name	Date of Hire	Date of Birth	Sex	Salary	Age	
2	Miller	Zachary	5/3/83	10/8/52	M	$36,550	36	
3	Johnson	John	9/23/75	2/13/49	M	$45,750	39	
4	White	Connie	5/16/73	3/15/45	F	$27,975	43	
5	Leigh	Diane	6/8/87	7/3/59	F	$32,800	29	
6	McDonald	Logan	2/20/84	11/16/57	M	$31,050	31	
7	Wilson	Lisa	11/16/82	5/29/50	F	$34,500	38	
8	Tyler	Courtney	10/10/85	8/18/60	F	$32,000	28	
9	Ford	Hunter	3/18/86	4/5/54	M	$28,425	34	
10	Hunter	Edward	6/8/87	9/2/58	M	$32,500	30	
11	Andrews	Francis	12/14/81	12/23/40	F	$42,775	48	
12								
13								
14								
15	Last Name	First Name	Date of Hire	Date of Birth	Sex	Salary	Age	Age
16							>=40	<=50
17								
18								

Ready

FIGURE 16-3. *We added an extra Age entry to the criteria range in order to select those records whose Age entries fall between two criteria.*

Logical OR. In some cases, you'll want Microsoft Excel to select records that meet either of two (or more) criteria. This condition is called a logical OR. Whenever you make entries into more than one row below the criteria field names and then include those rows in the criteria range, Microsoft Excel selects records that match the specified criteria in any one or more of the rows.

	Microsoft Excel								
File	Edit	Formula	Format	Data	Options	Macro	Window		Help
H17		>=40							

STAFF.XLS

	A	B	C	D	E	F	G	H
1	Last Name	First Name	Date of Hire	Date of Birth	Sex	Salary	Age	
2	Miller	Zachary	5/3/83	10/8/52	M	$36,550	36	
3	Johnson	John	9/23/75	2/13/49	M	$45,750	39	
4	White	Connie	5/16/73	3/15/45	F	$27,975	43	
5	Leigh	Diane	6/8/87	7/3/59	F	$32,800	29	
6	McDonald	Logan	2/20/84	11/16/57	M	$31,050	31	
7	Wilson	Lisa	11/16/82	5/29/50	F	$34,500	38	
8	Tyler	Courtney	10/10/85	8/18/60	F	$32,000	28	
9	Ford	Hunter	3/18/86	4/5/54	M	$28,425	34	
10	Hunter	Edward	6/8/87	9/2/58	M	$32,500	30	
11	Andrews	Francis	12/14/81	12/23/40	F	$42,775	48	
12								
13								
14								
15	Last Name	First Name	Date of Hire	Date of Birth	Sex	Salary	Age	Age
16							<=30	
17								>=40
18								

Ready

FIGURE 16-4. *We combined two criteria with a logical OR to select those records with Age entries that are 30 or less or 40 or more.*

For example, suppose you want to select from the employee database all records with an Age entry less than or equal to 30, as well as all records with an Age entry greater than or equal to 40. To do this, type *<=30* in cell G16 and *>=40* in cell H17 (or vice versa), as shown in Figure 16-4. Then expand the criteria range to include row 17. Because these entries are on two separate rows of the worksheet and both rows are within the criteria range, Microsoft Excel will select any record that meets either condition. In this example, it will select rows 4, 5, 8, 10, and 11.

Combining logical AND and OR. You can also combine logical ANDs and ORs by making more than one entry in one or more rows of a multirow criteria range. For example, suppose you want to select the females over 40 years old and the males over 35 years old from the employee database. To do this, you have to create the criteria range shown in Figure 16-5.

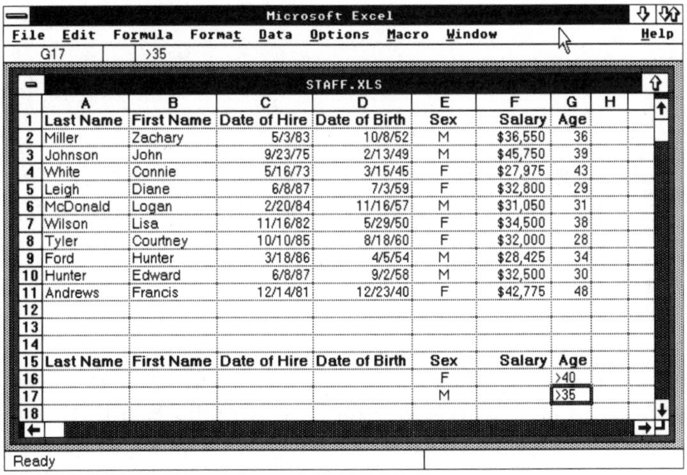

	Microsoft Excel									
File	**Edit**	**Formula**	**Format**	**Data**	**Options**	**Macro**	**Window**			**Help**

G17		>35						

STAFF.XLS

	A	B	C	D	E	F	G	H
1	Last Name	First Name	Date of Hire	Date of Birth	Sex	Salary	Age	
2	Miller	Zachary	5/3/83	10/8/52	M	$36,550	36	
3	Johnson	John	9/23/75	2/13/49	M	$45,750	39	
4	White	Connie	5/16/73	3/15/45	F	$27,975	43	
5	Leigh	Diane	6/8/87	7/3/59	F	$32,800	29	
6	McDonald	Logan	2/20/84	11/16/57	M	$31,050	31	
7	Wilson	Lisa	11/16/82	5/29/50	F	$34,500	38	
8	Tyler	Courtney	10/10/85	8/18/60	F	$32,000	28	
9	Ford	Hunter	3/18/86	4/5/54	M	$28,425	34	
10	Hunter	Edward	6/8/87	9/2/58	M	$32,500	30	
11	Andrews	Francis	12/14/81	12/23/40	F	$42,775	48	
12								
13								
14								
15	Last Name	First Name	Date of Hire	Date of Birth	Sex	Salary	Age	
16					F		>40	
17					M		>35	
18								

Ready

FIGURE 16-5. *You can combine logical ANDs and ORs to select females over 40 years old and males over 35 years old.*

In this criteria range, the entries in row 16 tell Microsoft Excel to select only those females whose age is greater than 40. The entries in row 17 instruct Microsoft Excel to select only those males whose age is greater than 35. Because the logical AND pairs are on separate rows of the criteria range, Microsoft Excel combines them with a logical OR. As a result, Microsoft Excel will select each record that meets both of the criteria on either line—that is, each record that has an Age entry over 35 AND a Sex entry of M (rows 2 and 3), OR that has an Age entry over 40 AND a Sex entry of F (rows 4 and 11).

Blank rows. In each of the previous examples, we left some blank cells in each row of the criteria range. When Microsoft Excel encounters a blank cell underneath any field name in a criteria range, it selects whatever entry is in that field. For example, the criterion shown in Figure 16-6 can be interpreted like this: *Select all records that have any entry in the Last Name, First Name, Date of Hire, Date of Birth, Salary, or Age field and an M in the Sex field.*

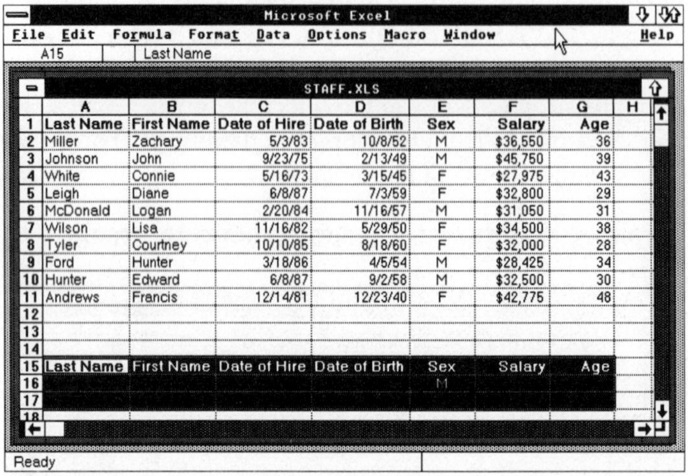

FIGURE 16-6. *The blank cells in the criteria range will match any entry in that field.*

As long as at least one of the cells in each row of a criteria range contains an entry, blank cells do no harm. If you include a totally blank row in the criteria range, however, the criteria will match every record in the database instead of the subset of records you intended. To see why, suppose you've made the entry

    =M

in cell E16, as shown in Figure 16-6, intending to select only the males from the database in cells A1:G11. Instead of specifying cells A15:G16 as the criteria range, however, you specify cells A15:G17. Because a totally blank row causes Microsoft Excel to select any entries in any fields and a multirow criteria range causes Microsoft Excel to select records that meet the criteria in any row, this criteria range tells Microsoft Excel to select all records that have the text M in the Sex field, as well as all records that have any entry in any field! As a result, Microsoft Excel selects every record in the database. This mistake can be particularly disastrous when you use the Delete command from the Data menu to delete from the database all records that match the current criteria.

Formulas and functions in comparison criteria

Most of your comparison criteria will compare the entries in a field of a database to a simple text or numeric entry. However, these criteria can also compare the entries in a field to the result of a formula or function.

For example, suppose you want to locate in the sample database any employee who was hired on May 16, 1973. To do this, enter the criterion

=DATE(73,5,16)

in cell C16, as shown in Figure 16-7. This criterion causes Microsoft Excel to select each record with a Date of Hire entry equal to 26800 (the serial date equivalent of May 16, 1973). In this example, the only employee with this date of hire is Connie White.

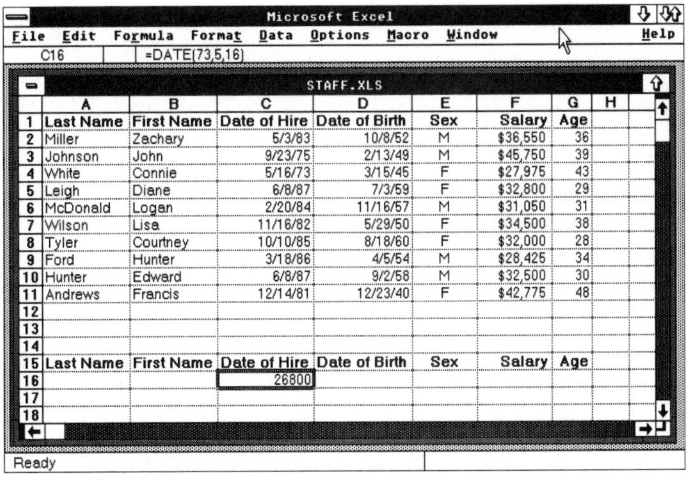

	A	B	C	D	E	F	G	H
1	Last Name	First Name	Date of Hire	Date of Birth	Sex	Salary	Age	
2	Miller	Zachary	5/3/83	10/8/52	M	$36,550	36	
3	Johnson	John	9/23/75	2/13/49	M	$45,750	39	
4	White	Connie	5/16/73	3/15/45	F	$27,975	43	
5	Leigh	Diane	6/8/87	7/3/59	F	$32,800	29	
6	McDonald	Logan	2/20/84	11/16/57	M	$31,050	31	
7	Wilson	Lisa	11/16/82	5/29/50	F	$34,500	38	
8	Tyler	Courtney	10/10/85	8/18/60	F	$32,000	28	
9	Ford	Hunter	3/18/86	4/5/54	M	$28,425	34	
10	Hunter	Edward	6/8/87	9/2/58	M	$32,500	30	
11	Andrews	Francis	12/14/81	12/23/40	F	$42,775	48	
12								
13								
14								
15	Last Name	First Name	Date of Hire	Date of Birth	Sex	Salary	Age	
16			26800					
17								
18								

FIGURE 16-7. *We used the DATE function in our comparison criterion.*

Cell references in comparison criteria

In some cases, you might want to operate on records that have an entry in a certain field that matches the contents of a cell located outside the database and criteria ranges. For example, suppose you want to operate on the records that have an Age entry equal to the number in cell G18. To do this, enter

=G18

into cell G16. (Be sure your criteria range includes only rows 15 and 16.) Now when you use a criterion-dependent command or function, Microsoft Excel will check the current value in cell G18 and then act upon any records with Age entries that equal that value. For example, if cell G18 contains the number 29, Microsoft Excel will operate on only the record in row 5.

Comparison criteria determined by cells outside the database range can also be in the form of formulas. For example, you can enter the criterion

=G18*G19

into cell G16 to select those records with Age entries equal to the product of the numbers in these two cells. You can also use the formula

=G18+25

in that cell to select records that have Age entries equal to the number in cell G18 plus 25.

Computed criteria

Suppose you want to select from a database every record with an Age entry less than the value in cell G18. You might attempt to do this by entering the criterion

<G18

in cell G16 of the criteria range. Unfortunately, this would not work. Instead of selecting those records that have an Age entry less than the number in cell G18, Microsoft Excel would select those records that have the text *<G18* in that cell. Whenever you begin comparison criteria with the symbols >, <, >=, <=, or <>, Microsoft Excel treats the entry as text.

To instruct Microsoft Excel to select the records with Age entries less than the value in cell G18, you must use a computed criterion. To create the criterion for this example, enter the formula

=G2<$G$18

in cell G16 and then select the range G15:G16 and choose the Set Criteria command from the Data menu to define the criteria range. Figure 16-8 shows the worksheet at this point. (Notice that cell G18 contains the value 40.)

You should notice several things about this simple computed criterion. First, we've placed the computed criterion in a cell under a blank cell. (Recall that a comparison criterion is always entered beneath a cell that contains a field name.) You must enter a computed criterion beneath a blank cell or beneath a cell that contains a label other than a field name. If you try to use a computed criterion beneath a cell that contains a field name, the computed criterion will not work as you intended it to. For the sake of convenience, you'll usually want to enter the computed criterion in the same row as your other criteria but in the column to the right of the last field in the existing criteria range. If you do make a text entry above the computed criterion, you'll probably want it to be a description of the purpose of the criterion. For example, you might want to enter the label *Age Test* into cell G15.

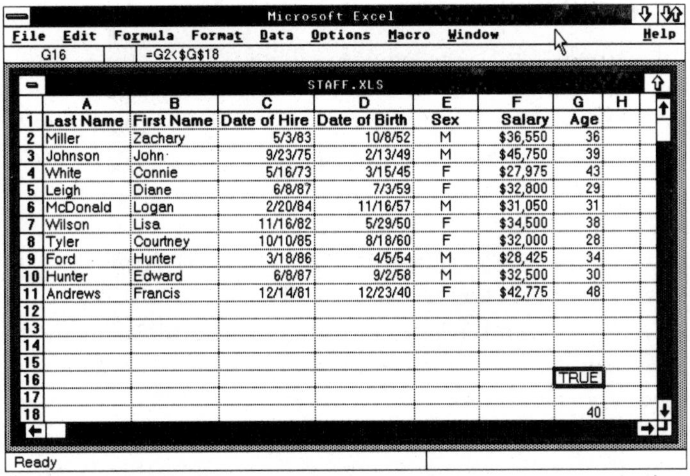

FIGURE 16-8. *This computed criterion will cause Microsoft Excel to select those records with an Age entry less than the value in cell G18.*

Also notice that the computed criterion in our example includes a reference to cell G2, the first cell in the database under the field name *Age*. This reference tells Microsoft Excel that the criterion applies to the Age field. Every computed criterion must include a reference to the cell immediately below a field name in the database. This reference tells Microsoft Excel which field the criterion applies to. In our example database, any computed criteria that apply to the Age field must refer to cell G2. In a like manner, any computed criteria that apply to the Salary field must refer to cell F2.

Computed criteria generally must refer to the cells in the second row of the database; they should not refer to the fields of a database by name. For example, the criterion

=Age<$G$18

causes Microsoft Excel to return the error message #NAME?. (Oddly, this type of formula selects the desired records as long as the field-name entry does not contain any spaces.)

As you can see in Figure 16-8, Microsoft Excel displays TRUE as the result of the computed criterion in cell G16. This criterion refers directly to the entry in cell G2, so Microsoft Excel uses the number in that cell when it evaluates the criterion's formula. Because cell G2 contains the number 36, and 36 is less than 40 (the value in cell G18), the test is true for that record and Microsoft Excel displays the logical constant TRUE. If the entry in cell G2 had been 41, or the entry in cell G18 had been 35, Microsoft Excel would have displayed the result FALSE in cell G16.

The result of any computed criterion is generally either TRUE or FALSE. However, the result that Microsoft Excel displays in the criteria range has absolutely no meaning, other than telling you whether or not the criterion matches the first record in the database. When Microsoft Excel evaluates a computed criterion, it calculates the criterion's function or formula once for every record in the database, using the entries in the referenced fields of the current record. If the result of the evaluation is TRUE, Microsoft Excel selects the record; if the result is FALSE or zero or is a text or error value, Microsoft Excel ignores the record. In this example, Microsoft Excel will select all records except those in rows 4 and 11.

Notice also that the reference to cell G18 in this formula is an absolute reference. Whenever you create a computed criterion that refers to a cell outside the database range, you must make the reference to that cell absolute (or at least mixed, with the row reference absolute). Unless the reference is fixed in terms of rows, Microsoft Excel will move down one cell each time it tests a new record.

Let's consider another example of a computed criterion. Suppose you want to act on those records for which the result of dividing the Salary entry by the Age entry is a value greater than 1000. To do this, you would use the criterion formula

=F2/G2>1000

Notice that this criterion refers to more than one cell in the database, demonstrating another property of computed criteria: They allow you to compare the contents of one field with the contents of another field in the same record. Whenever you create a criterion that applies to more than one field in a database, the criterion must refer to the first cell under the field name of each of those fields. In this case, the criterion applies to the Age and Salary fields, so it must refer to both cells G2 and F2. (This formula selects rows 2, 3, 5, 6, 8, and 10.)

Using functions in computed criteria

You can use computed criteria to test the result of a function operating on the entries in a database field. For example, suppose you want Microsoft Excel to select only those records from our sample database with a Last Name entry five characters long. To do this, enter the function

=LEN(A2)=5

in cell G16 (or any other blank cell that has another blank cell above it) and define the criteria range to include that cell. In this case, Microsoft Excel will select only the records in rows 4, 5, and 8.

Logical AND and OR in computed criteria. Functions in computed criteria also provide an alternative way to create logical ANDs and ORs, all within a single cell. For example, the criterion

=AND(F2>40000,F2<50000)

will match every record that has a Salary entry between $40,000 and $50,000. This is equivalent to entering >40000 and <50000 in separate cells with the field name *Salary* in the same criteria row. In a similar way, the criterion

=OR(F2<20000,F2>60000)

will match every record whose Salary entry is less than $20,000 or greater than $60,000. This is equivalent to entering <20000 and >60000 in the same column as under the field name *Salary*.

Comparing entries in different records

You can also use a computed criterion to compare the entry in a field of one record with the entry in the same field of the record above it. For example, suppose you want to select every record in the employee database with an Age entry at least five years greater than the record above it. (This sort of criterion is most useful after you've sorted the database.) The criterion

=G2>G1+5

will do the trick. This criterion explicitly compares the entry in cell G2 with the entry in cell G1. However, as with all other computed criteria, Microsoft Excel evaluates this criterion formula once for every record in the database, comparing each entry in the Age field to the entry immediately above it in that field.

You can extend this technique to compare an entry in any record to the record that is two, three, four, or more records above it. Just be sure that enough blank rows exist above the database to set up comparison criteria for the first few records. In this database, for example, you could use the criterion

=G3>G1

to compare each entry in the Age field to the entry two records above it.

Creating linked references to a database

Although you can have only one active database and criteria range per worksheet, Microsoft Excel does allow you to create criteria that act on a database located in another worksheet by using a linked external reference to that database range. This technique is particularly useful when you've created a very large database. Calculation time can be slowed considerably when you're working with very large files. You can alleviate this problem by storing your database records in one worksheet and maintaining your database calculations and reports in one or more separate linked worksheets. The worksheet that contains your database serves as the supporting worksheet and the worksheets that contain your reports and other calculations are the dependent worksheets. That way, you need open the linked worksheets only when you want to update your calculations.

For example, suppose you're preparing a report and you want to create a separate worksheet that contains a subset of the data in your main database. You can set up a criteria range in another worksheet and then use the Extract command, discussed in a few pages, to draw the needed data from the main database. Similarly, suppose you want to create a summary worksheet that lists statistical information about the records in a database. Rather than clutter your database with these statistics, you can set up your criteria range in a second worksheet and then use the database statistical functions discussed at the end of this chapter to perform the needed calculations.

As we explained in Chapter 14, the Set Database command on the Data menu does nothing more than define a named range called Database. The cells that are highlighted in the active worksheet when you issue that command are the cells that Microsoft Excel looks to when you perform database operations. However, if you want to refer to a database located in another worksheet, you must define the named range Database manually instead of using the Set Database command.

To create a linked reference to a database stored in another worksheet, begin by issuing the Define Name command. Then type the name *Database* in the Name edit bar. Now activate the Refers to edit bar and enter an external reference to the worksheet and range that contain the database. For example, if the database range is stored in cells A1:G11 of the worksheet named STAFF.XLS, you would type the reference

=STAFF.XLS!$A$1:$G$11

When you use cell references to define the database range in a remote worksheet, keep in mind that Microsoft Excel does not update those cell references when you add or delete records from the database. However, you can work around this updating problem by using the range name *Database* in the Refers to edit bar instead of cell references. For example, suppose you've applied the name *Database* to cells A1:G11 in the worksheet STAFF.XLS. You can then use the remote reference

=STAFF.XLS!Database

to create a linked database definition. Microsoft Excel will update the definition of the Database range in your dependent worksheet whenever you change the definition of the Database range in the main (supporting) worksheet.

After creating this linked name reference, you can proceed as usual in setting up your criteria range. Of course, the criteria range you define should include one or more field names from the database in the remote worksheet. Then you can use the Extract command or any of Microsoft Excel's database functions to create your database report.

For example, in Figure 16-9 we've created a criteria range in a new worksheet, Sheet1, that refers to the database stored in STAFF.XLS. This criteria range instructs Microsoft Excel to act on all the records in the STAFF.XLS database that have entries greater than $35,000 in the Salary field and entries greater than 30 in the Age field.

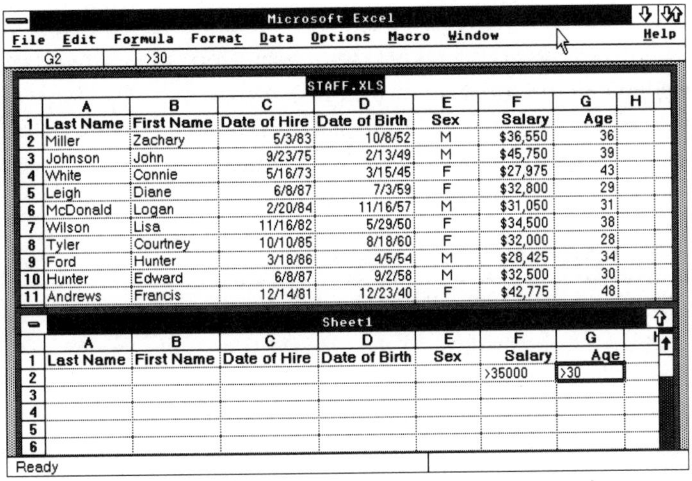

	Microsoft Excel							
File	Edit	Fo**r**mula	Forma**t**	**D**ata	**O**ptions	**M**acro	**W**indow	Help

G2   >30

STAFF.XLS

	A	B	C	D	E	F	G	H
1	Last Name	First Name	Date of Hire	Date of Birth	Sex	Salary	Age	
2	Miller	Zachary	5/3/83	10/8/52	M	$36,550	36	
3	Johnson	John	9/23/75	2/13/49	M	$45,750	39	
4	White	Connie	5/16/73	3/15/45	F	$27,975	43	
5	Leigh	Diane	6/8/87	7/3/59	F	$32,800	29	
6	McDonald	Logan	2/20/84	11/16/57	M	$31,050	31	
7	Wilson	Lisa	11/16/82	5/29/50	F	$34,500	38	
8	Tyler	Courtney	10/10/85	8/18/60	F	$32,000	28	
9	Ford	Hunter	3/18/86	4/5/54	M	$28,425	34	
10	Hunter	Edward	6/8/87	9/2/58	M	$32,500	30	
11	Andrews	Francis	12/14/81	12/23/40	F	$42,775	48	

Sheet1

	A	B	C	D	E	F	G	
1	Last Name	First Name	Date of Hire	Date of Birth	Sex	Salary	Age	
2						>35000	>30	
3								
4								
5								
6								

Ready

FIGURE 16-9. *We entered our database criteria in a separate linked worksheet.*

To create this criteria range, we opened a new worksheet and used the Move and Size commands to create nonoverlapping windows. Then we selected cells A1:G1 in the STAFF.XLS worksheet, selected the Copy command, activated cell A1

EXCEL

Using different windows for database and criteria ranges

In this chapter, we've intentionally kept our sample database small so that we can display both the database and the criteria range at the same time on the screen, within the same window. When you work with larger databases, it's a good idea to use two windows: one for the database itself and one for the criteria range. That way, you can easily switch back and forth between the database and criteria range by activating a window, instead of scrolling to distant parts of the worksheet within a single window.

in the Sheet1 worksheet, and issued the Paste command. After entering our criteria in row 2 of Sheet1, we selected cells A1:G2 and issued the Set Criteria command. Finally, we issued the Define Name command and created a linked reference to STAFF.XLS to define our linked database range.

Using selection criteria

Now that you know how criteria work, let's take a look at what you can use them for. We'll begin with a discussion of Microsoft Excel's three criterion-dependent commands: Find, Extract, and Delete. These commands, which are located on the Data menu, instruct Microsoft Excel to locate, copy, and erase criteria-matching records from a database range.

The Find command

The Find command instructs Microsoft Excel to select, one at a time, the records in a database that match the criteria in the criteria range. For example, suppose you want Microsoft Excel to find in the database in Figure 16-10 every record that has the entry M in its Sex field. To begin, highlight the range A1:G11 and use the Set Database command on the Data menu to define the database range. Then enter the field name *Sex* in cell E15 and the letter *M* in cell E16, select both cells, and choose the Set Criteria command. Now you're ready to use the Find command. When you choose this command from the Data menu, Microsoft Excel selects the first record

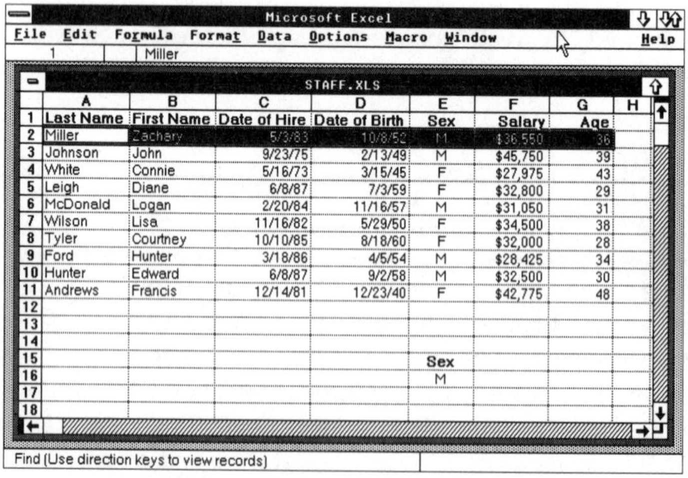

FIGURE 16-10. *We used the Find command to locate the first record in the database with M in its Sex field.*

in the database that matches the current criterion. In our example, Microsoft Excel has selected the record in row 2, the first record in the database.

The record Microsoft Excel finds first when you use the Find command depends on which cell of the worksheet is active when you choose the command. If a cell outside the database range is the active cell, Microsoft Excel finds the criteria-matching record closest to the top of the database, as in our example. This will often be the case in your work with Microsoft Excel. If, on the other hand, a cell within the database is active when you choose the Find command, the program locates the first criteria-matching record below the record that contains the active cell. If no records in the database meet the stated criteria, Microsoft Excel beeps and displays the alert message *No match*.

As soon as you choose the Find command, Microsoft Excel changes the name of that command to Exit Find. When you want to move freely between database records again, choose this command from the Data menu. Alternatively, you can exit from Find mode by selecting any worksheet cell outside the database range, issuing another command, or editing a cell entry.

If your database does contain criteria-matching records, the scroll bars at the right side and bottom of the window change to a striped pattern. These stripes indicate that the actions of these tools are restricted. While in Find mode, you can use the scroll arrows only to move up and down through the database, locating those records that meet the stated criteria. To move to the next criteria-matching record in the database, click on the down arrow icon. Microsoft Excel will select the record in row 3. If you click on the down arrow icon again, Microsoft Excel will skip to row 6, then to row 9, and finally to row 10. If you click on the down arrow icon when the last record that matches the criteria is selected, Microsoft Excel will beep at you and will not move the highlight.

Similarly, to move backward through the database, click on the up arrow icon in the vertical scroll bar. Microsoft Excel will move to the next criteria-matching record that appears above the current active record.

To search the database in reverse order, hold down Shift as you choose Find. For example, suppose a cell in row 8 of our sample database is active. If you press the Shift key as you issue the Find command, Microsoft Excel will select the record in row 6 instead of moving down to row 9.

In addition to the scroll arrows, you may want to use the scroll bars to move more quickly between records when you're using Find in a large database. When you move the scroll box while Microsoft Excel is in Find mode, the program selects the criteria-matching record whose position in the database is proportional to the position of the scroll box in the scroll bar. By clicking in the gray area of the scroll bar above or below the scroll box, you can move to the next criteria-matching record that is at least one screen up or down from the current selection.

Although the horizontal scroll bar remains active while you're in Find mode, Microsoft Excel will not allow you to scroll the last column in the database out of view; the scrolling action locks when the last column of the database reaches the left edge of the screen. To scroll further, you must leave Find mode by choosing Exit Find from the Data menu or by selecting a cell outside the database range.

You can also use the keyboard to move from one criteria-matching record to the next. Use the Up and Down arrow keys to move forward or backward one record at a time. Use the Left and Right arrow keys to bring additional columns of the database into view. (As with the horizontal scroll bar, however, you can't scroll past the boundaries of the database range with the Left and Right arrow keys.) You can also use the PgUp and PgDn keys to move to the next criteria-matching record that is at least one screen above or below the current selection.

Editing in Find mode

While Microsoft Excel is in Find mode, you can use the Cut, Copy, and Clear commands to move, copy, and delete any criteria-matching record. First choose the Find command and use the selection techniques described above to locate the record you want to cut, copy, or clear. When this record is highlighted, choose the Cut, Copy, or Clear command from the Edit menu.

If you choose Cut, Microsoft Excel removes that record from the database the next time you use the Paste command. If you choose Copy, Microsoft Excel saves the cell references of that record on the Clipboard but doesn't remove the record from the database. If you choose Clear, Microsoft Excel removes the record from the database immediately.

As soon as you choose any of these commands, Microsoft Excel leaves Find mode, so you have to repeat the process to locate each record you want to edit.

The Extract command

Unlike the Find command, which finds criteria-matching records in their original location within the database, the Extract command allows you to copy the criteria-matching records, as a group, to another location in the worksheet. Extracting records is a three-step process: First, you use the Set Criteria command to define a criteria range; second, you define the area where you want Microsoft Excel to place the records it extracts; and third, you choose Extract from the Data menu.

Specifying criteria

Suppose you want Microsoft Excel to extract the entries from the Last Name and Salary fields in the employee database for only those records with a Salary entry between $30,000 and $40,000, inclusive. First, enter the criterion

=AND(F2>=30000,F2<=40000)

into your worksheet, as shown in Figure 16-11. Then select the criteria range (we'll use cells F13 and F14) and issue the Set Criteria command.

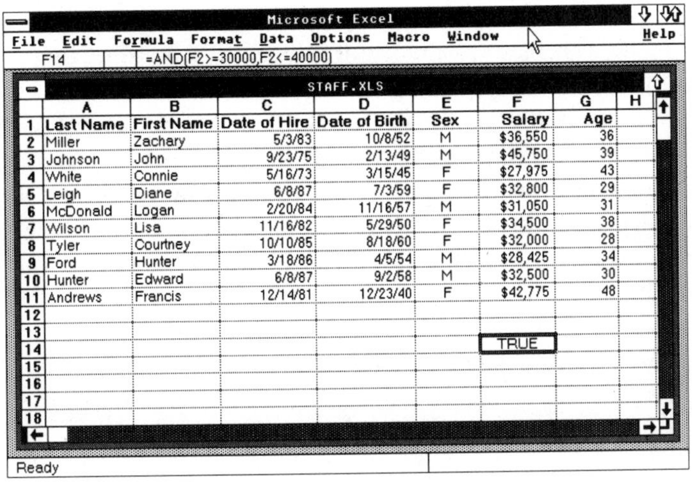

FIGURE 16-11. *We want to extract the Last Name and Salary entries for employees with incomes between $30,000 and $40,000.*

Defining the extract range

Now you must define the area where you want Microsoft Excel to copy the selected records. We'll call this area the extract range. The first step in defining the extract range is to enter the names of the fields you want Microsoft Excel to extract into a row of cells in a blank portion of the worksheet. In this example, we want Microsoft Excel to extract only entries from the Last Name and Salary fields, so we need include only those two field names at the top of the extract range. Although we could place these field names anywhere in the Microsoft Excel worksheet, we'll put them in cells A16 and B16.

The field names in the extract range must be in a single row. When you choose the Extract command, Microsoft Excel places the extracted information into the cells below these names.

If you type the field names into the top row of the extract range, be sure to enter them exactly as they appear in the database range. If a field name in the extract range doesn't exactly match its counterpart in the database (except for capitalization differences, which Microsoft Excel ignores), Microsoft Excel will not recognize the field name in the extract range. You can avoid this problem by using the Copy and Paste commands to copy the field names from the top row of the database into the extract range.

Although *you* recognize the entries you made in cells A16 and B16 as headers for the extract range, Microsoft Excel doesn't know where you want it to place the extracted field entries until you tell it. To define the extract range, simply select it.

You can define the extract range as only the cells that contain the field names (in this case, cells A16:B16) or as a block of cells headed by those field names (such as the range A16:B30). Your choice affects the number of records Microsoft Excel can extract. If you define only the field-name entries as the extract range, Microsoft Excel extracts the specified fields of every record in the database that matches the current criteria. If you select a multirow block of cells, however, Microsoft Excel extracts only as many matching records as will fit into the selected area. For example, if you select cells A16:B18 as the extract range, Microsoft Excel will extract a maximum of two records, because the range has only two blank rows. If Microsoft Excel fills up the extract range before it can copy every criteria-matching record from the database, it beeps at that point and displays the message *Extract range is full.*

Extracting information

When you've specified the criteria, decided which fields you want to extract, and selected the extract range, you're ready to extract the records that match your criteria. With the extract range still selected, choose the Extract command from the Data menu. Microsoft Excel will display the dialog box shown in Figure 16-12. This dialog box controls whether Microsoft Excel extracts the selected fields from all the records that match the criteria or only from those records with entries in the extracted fields that are not duplicates of the entries in another record.

FIGURE 16-12. *Use the Extract dialog box to indicate whether you want to extract all records or unique records only.*

In most cases, you'll want Microsoft Excel to extract every criteria-matching record to the extract range. To do this, simply select the OK button or press Enter. Microsoft Excel will first erase the contents of every cell in the extract range and then copy the entries in the selected fields of the records that match the criteria to the cells of the extract range, beginning from the top of the database. Figure 16-13 shows the result of our example extraction.

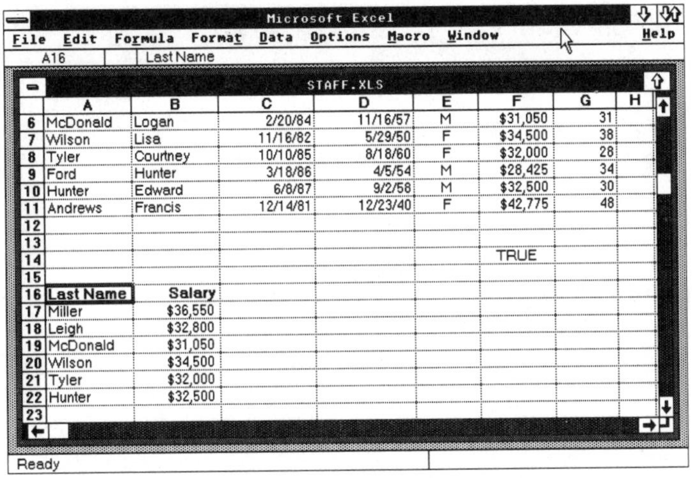

FIGURE 16-13. *Microsoft Excel extracted the criteria-matching records.*

The Unique Records Only option

Microsoft Excel can also copy to the extract range only the set of unique entries in the database. Perhaps your database contains several duplicate records and you want only one record from each set of duplicates to be extracted. If you select the Unique Records Only option in the Extract dialog box, Microsoft Excel will copy only one record from each set of duplicates to the extract range.

A record does not have to be identical in all fields to be omitted from the extraction. Only the entries in the extracted fields need match the entries of a previously extracted record.

For example, suppose we add a record for Robert McDonald to our sample database. Let's assume that, like Logan McDonald, whose record appears in row 6, Robert McDonald earns $31,050. Figure 16-14 shows the result of performing a unique extraction on the employee database. As you can see, Microsoft Excel has excluded the new record in row 12 from the extraction (even though many of the entries in the nonextracted fields of the excluded record differ from those in the record in row 6), because the entries in the two extracted fields, Last Name and Salary, are identical to the entries in the record in row 6.

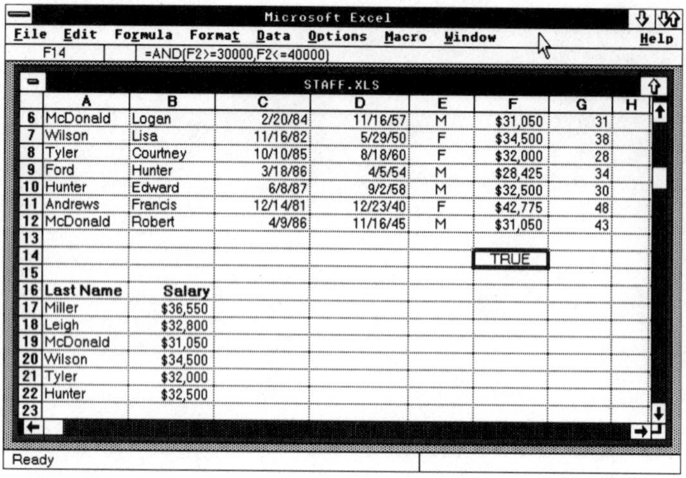

⊟				Microsoft Excel				⇩ ⇪⇩
File	**Edit**	**Formula**	**Format**	**Data**	**Options**	**Macro**	**Window**	**Help**

F14   =AND(F2>=30000,F2<=40000)

⊟			STAFF.XLS					⇧
	A	**B**	**C**	**D**	**E**	**F**	**G**	**H**
6	McDonald	Logan	2/20/84	11/16/57	M	$31,050	31	
7	Wilson	Lisa	11/16/82	5/29/50	F	$34,500	38	
8	Tyler	Courtney	10/10/85	8/18/60	F	$32,000	28	
9	Ford	Hunter	3/18/86	4/5/54	M	$28,425	34	
10	Hunter	Edward	6/8/87	9/2/58	M	$32,500	30	
11	Andrews	Francis	12/14/81	12/23/40	F	$42,775	48	
12	McDonald	Robert	4/9/86	11/16/45	M	$31,050	43	
13								
14						TRUE		
15								
16	**Last Name**	**Salary**						
17	Miller	$36,550						
18	Leigh	$32,800						
19	McDonald	$31,050						
20	Wilson	$34,500						
21	Tyler	$32,000						
22	Hunter	$32,500						
23								

Ready

FIGURE 16-14. *When we used the Unique Records Only option,*
Microsoft Excel didn't extract the record in row 12.

EXCEL

Erasing the extract range

As we mentioned, when you use the Extract command, Microsoft Excel erases the contents of the extract range before it begins extracting records. This can lead to problems if you've designed a one-row extract range. If you define only the row of field names as the extract range, Microsoft Excel considers the extract range to extend from that row to the bottom of the worksheet. The program therefore erases any entries in the cells below the field names, all the way to the bottom of the worksheet, whenever you issue the Extract command. Any information in those cells is permanently erased.

When you define a multirow extract range, however, Microsoft Excel considers the extract range to be only that block of selected cells. Microsoft Excel still erases the contents of the entire extract range when you choose the Extract command, but because the range is limited, you don't risk erasing valuable information unintentionally.

The Delete command

The Data menu's Delete command allows you to delete all the records that match the current criteria. For example, suppose you want to delete from the employee database every record that has the entry M in the Sex field. First enter the criterion *M* in cell E16 and the field name *Sex* in cell E15. Then define the criteria range by selecting cells E15:E16 and choosing the Set Criteria command. Finally, choose the Delete command from the Data menu. When you choose this command, you'll see the warning message *Matching records will be deleted permanently*. If you don't want to delete the records that match the current criterion, select Cancel to terminate the command. If you really do want to delete those records, select OK or press Enter. When you do this, Microsoft Excel deletes the entries in every field of every criteria-matching record and then shifts the remaining records up underneath the field-name row.

Figure 16-15 shows the result of using the Delete command with the criteria in our previous example. As you can see, Microsoft Excel has removed the records from rows 2, 3, 6, 9, and 10 of the original database and contracted the database so that the remaining records fill rows 2 through 6.

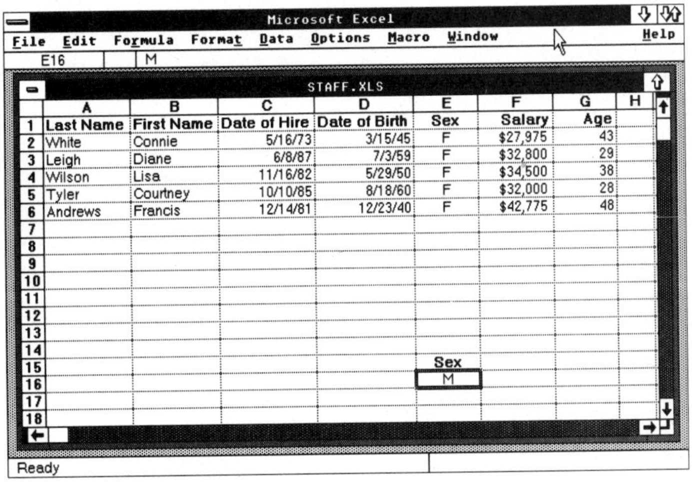

FIGURE 16-15. *We used the Delete command to delete all the records in the database with M in their Sex field.*

Because the effects of the Delete command are potentially disastrous, you should use it with extreme caution. You can't use Undo on a Data menu Delete command. When you delete records, you can't get them back. You can minimize the disastrous effects of unintentionally deleting records from a database in two ways. First, you can use the Save or Save As command immediately before you choose the Delete command. That way, you'll have an exact copy of the database as it existed before the deletion and you can recover the lost information by opening the same worksheet again. When you choose the Open command from the File menu and select the worksheet name from the list box, a dialog box will appear, asking if you wish to revert to your last saved version. (You'll lose any other changes you've made to the database since you last saved it.)

Alternatively, you can use the Extract command to make a copy, just before you choose the Delete command, of every field of each record that matches the current criteria. This technique allows you to view the records that Microsoft Excel will delete before it deletes them; it also stores a backup copy of the deleted entries within the worksheet. We strongly recommend that you always use Save or Extract before you use Delete.

Using criteria in forms

You can also use criteria to select database records from within the Form dialog box. The Form dialog box includes three options that let you define and use criteria: Criteria, Find Next, and Find Prev. The Criteria option allows you to define criteria in a form. The Find Next and Find Prev options let you use those criteria to find matching records—Find Next searches down through the database for the next matching record; Find Prev searches up through the database for the previous match.

To define criteria from within a form, select the Criteria option in the Form dialog box. Microsoft Excel will blank out all edit bars in the data form to allow you to establish the criteria. As you can see in Figure 16-16, the word *Criteria*

E X C E L *Tip*

Watch out for blank rows in the criteria range!

Using the Delete command when your criteria range contains a totally blank row is a common mistake that you'll want to avoid. As we've pointed out, a criteria range that contains a blank row matches every record in the database. Therefore, if you choose the Delete command when the criteria range contains a blank row, Microsoft Excel will erase the entire database.

appears in the upper right corner of the form and the Criteria button changes to read *Form*. When you finish entering the record-selection criteria, you can select the Form option to return to the data form.

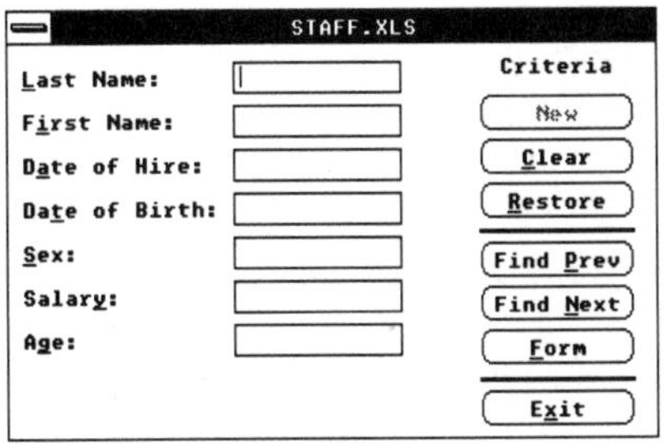

FIGURE 16-16. *Use the Criteria option to enter selection criteria in the Form dialog box.*

For example, let's create a criterion that will find the record for employee McDonald in the database in Figure 16-11. Open the worksheet and use the Set Database command to define the database range as A1:G11. Next, select the Form command from the Data menu to create the data form. When the data form appears, it will display the first record in the database. To define the criterion, select the Criteria option. Microsoft Excel will blank out the fields on the data form and change the Criteria option to Form, as shown in Figure 16-16. Now select the Last Name field and then enter the criterion *McDonald*, as shown in Figure 16-17. Finally, select the Find Next option. Microsoft Excel will display the record for employee McDonald in the data form, as shown in Figure 16-18.

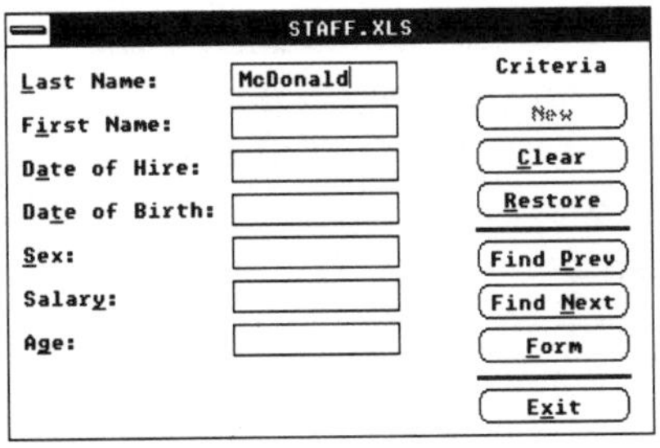

FIGURE 16-17. *To define a criterion, we simply made an entry in one of the fields of the form.*

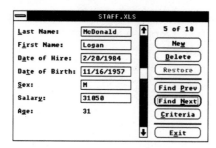

FIGURE 16-18. *We chose Find Next to display the matching record.*

You can use most of the selection criteria we've discussed in data-form criteria. You can ask Microsoft Excel to match a series of characters by entering text, numbers, or logical values. If you want to compare a quantity, you can enter =, >=, >, <=, <, or <>. You can also use the wildcard characters ? and * in your selection criteria. (Remember, if you're searching for a literal ? or *, you must precede the character with a tilde [~].) However, you can't use computed criteria to search in the data form. For example, you can't enter a criterion that uses the values in two or more fields.

If you have several records that share one or more characteristics, you can combine criteria to narrow your search. As an example, suppose that our database contained several employees named McDonald. To search for a specific record, then, we would enter McDonald in the Last Name field and a name in the First Name field, or an F or M in the Sex field, to further restrict the search for employee McDonald.

Database statistical functions

Microsoft Excel offers eleven statistical functions—DSUM, DAVERAGE, DCOUNT, DCOUNTA, DMAX, DMIN, DPRODUCT, DSTDEV, DSTDEVP, DVAR, and DVARP— that operate on the records in a database. These database functions, which are closely related to the worksheet statistical functions you learned about in Chapter 6, calculate the sum, average, total of numeric cells, total of non-blank cells, maximum value, minimum value, product, standard deviation, and variance of the values in a specified field of the records in a database that match the criteria you've defined. Except for DCOUNTA, these functions can be used only on fields that contain numeric entries.

Although each database function calculates a different statistic, they all have the same form:

=DFUNCTION(*database range,field,criteria range*)

The first argument of every database function specifies the database range upon which it should act. This argument can be either a range name or the coordinates of a range. If you've used the Set Database command to name your database range, you can use the range name *Database* as the first argument of these functions. In all cases, the range you specify must be in the form of a Microsoft Excel database.

The second argument of any database function tells Microsoft Excel which field of the database contains the entries it should use to calculate the statistic. This argument can be in either of two forms. You can enter the name of the field, enclosed in double quotation marks. For example, if you want a function to work on the Salary field of a database, you can enter the second argument as

"Salary"

Except for capitalization, *field* must be identical to the field name in the database range. If the name you use in the function is not identical to the name of one of the fields in the database, the function will return the error value #VALUE!. Alternatively, you can specify *field* as the position of the field within the database. To use the entries in the leftmost column of the database, enter the field index number 1 as the second argument of the function; to use the entries in the second column of the database, enter the number 2; and so on. When you specify *field* in this manner, you need not enclose the number in quotation marks.

The third argument of any database function identifies the criteria range the function should use to select the records on which it will operate. You can use either a range name or cell coordinates to specify this range. If you've used the Set Criteria command to define your criteria range, you can use the name *Criteria* as the third argument of the database function. The range you specify must be in the form of a Microsoft Excel criteria range.

Let's use a database function to calculate the average value in the Age field for the females in our example employee database. As a first step, create a criterion in cell E16 that will select only records with the entry F in the Sex field. Then use the Set Criteria command to define cells E15:E16 as the criteria range. Next, be sure the proper block of cells (in this case, A1:G11) is defined as the database range. Now enter the formula

=DAVERAGE(Database,"Age",Criteria)

into any empty cell of the worksheet outside the database and criteria ranges. In this case, enter the function into cell G16, as shown in Figure 16-19. Microsoft Excel will calculate its result by summing the entries in the Age field for those records that meet the selection criterion and dividing the sum by the total number of records that meet the criterion. In this case, Microsoft Excel adds the Age values of the records in rows 4, 5, 7, 8, and 11 (total 186), divides by the number of criteria-matching records (5), and returns the value 37.2.

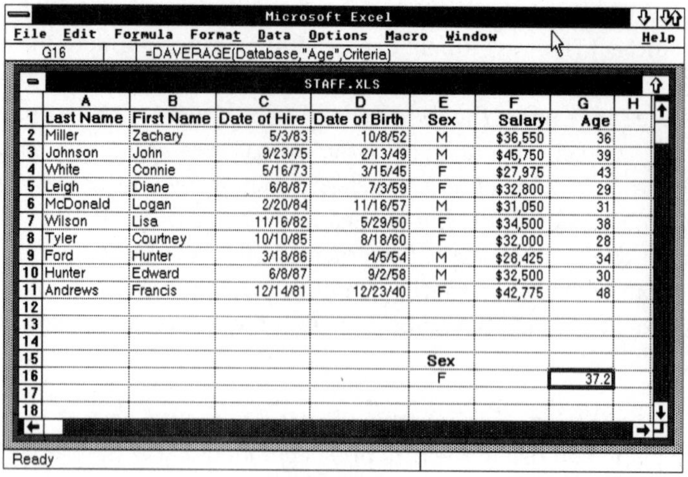

	A	B	C	D	E	F	G	H
1	Last Name	First Name	Date of Hire	Date of Birth	Sex	Salary	Age	
2	Miller	Zachary	5/3/83	10/8/52	M	$36,550	36	
3	Johnson	John	9/23/75	2/13/49	M	$45,750	39	
4	White	Connie	5/16/73	3/15/45	F	$27,975	43	
5	Leigh	Diane	6/8/87	7/3/59	F	$32,800	29	
6	McDonald	Logan	2/20/84	11/16/57	M	$31,050	31	
7	Wilson	Lisa	11/16/82	5/29/50	F	$34,500	38	
8	Tyler	Courtney	10/10/85	8/18/60	F	$32,000	28	
9	Ford	Hunter	3/18/86	4/5/54	M	$28,425	34	
10	Hunter	Edward	6/8/87	9/2/58	M	$32,500	30	
11	Andrews	Francis	12/14/81	12/23/40	F	$42,775	48	
12								
13								
14								
15					Sex			
16					F		37.2	
17								
18								

FIGURE 16-19. *We used the DAVERAGE function to calculate the average age of the females in the employee database.*

You can state this formula in other ways. For instance, you could replace the second argument, "Age", with a field index number that indicates the position of the Age field within the database:

=DAVERAGE (Database,7,Criteria)

You could also replace the range names *Database* and *Criteria* with the coordinates of the database range and the criteria range:

=DAVERAGE (A1:G11,7,E15:E16)

After you enter this formula, you can use it to calculate the average age for other groups of records simply by changing the entries in the criteria range. For example, the function will calculate the average age of the males in the database if you replace the F in cell E16 with an M. Or, if you want to calculate the average income of the females in the database, you can replace the second argument, "Age", with "Salary".

The remaining ten database functions work the same way as DAVERAGE. Table 16-1 describes the results of each function.

Table 16-1. The results of Microsoft Excel's database functions.

Function	Action
=DSUM	Computes the total of the values in the specified field of the criteria-matching records.
=DCOUNT	Returns the number of numeric entries in the specified field of the criteria-matching records.
=DCOUNTA	Returns the number of non-blank cells in the specified field of the criteria-matching records.
=DMAX	Returns the greatest value from the specified field of the criteria-matching records.
=DMIN	Returns the smallest value from the specified field of the criteria-matching records.
=PRODUCT	Returns the product of the values from the specified field of the criteria-matching records.
=DSTDEV	Returns the sample standard deviation of the values in the specified field of the criteria-matching records.
=DSTDEVP	Returns the population standard deviation of the values in the specified field of the criteria-matching records.
=DVAR	Returns the sample variance of the values in the specified field of the criteria-matching records.
=DVARP	Returns the population variance of the values in the specified field of the criteria-matching records.

MACROS

17

Macro
Basics

A macro is a series of formulas and statements that instruct Microsoft Excel to take an action or perform a calculation for you. Macros are like computer programs that run completely within Microsoft Excel. You can use them to automate tedious or frequently repeated tasks.

Macros can be divided into two broad categories: command macros and function macros. Command macros carry out sequences of actions for you much more quickly than you could carry them out manually. For example, you can create a command macro that enters a series of dates across a row of the worksheet and then centers those dates in the cells. Or you can create a command macro that chooses the Page Setup command from the File menu, defines your print settings, and then chooses the Print command. Command macros can be very simple or extremely complex. They can even be interactive; that is, you can write macros that request information from the user and then act upon that information.

Function macros perform calculations and return values. For example, you can create a function macro that computes the interest paid to date on a loan, or one that computes the weighted average of a range of numbers. Often, function macros let you condense to one cell calculations that would otherwise occupy a large amount of space in your worksheet.

We'll cover command macros in this chapter. After reviewing Microsoft Excel's many macro functions in Chapter 18, we'll look at function macros in Chapter 19. In Chapter 20, we'll discuss advanced macro techniques, including the use of interactive command macros.

Macro sheets

In Microsoft Excel, macros are created and stored on macro sheets, which are very similar to worksheets. In many spreadsheet programs, macros are stored in the cells of the related worksheet. Because Microsoft Excel macros are created and stored independently, you can create one macro and use it with many worksheets. In fact, you can store several macros in one macro sheet and use that sheet as a macro library. Storing the macro in a separate file also helps to prevent accidental deletions or other errors that might damage the macro or the worksheet data.

Creating a macro sheet

To create a Microsoft Excel macro, you must first open a macro sheet by choosing the New command from the File menu and selecting the Macro Sheet option. A blank macro sheet like the one in Figure 17-1 will appear. As you can see, a macro sheet looks very much like a worksheet. A macro sheet is divided into rows and columns, with numbers and letters as headings, and the menu bar above a macro sheet is identical to the one above a worksheet.

Macro sheets do differ from worksheets, however. For instance, the columns in the macro sheet appear wider than those in the worksheet environment. (Actually, the difference is that the Formulas option of the Display command on the Options menu is selected by default. Thus, you'll see the formulas in the cells in the macro sheet instead of the results of those formulas.) In addition, macro formulas are calculated only when you execute the macro and then always in a strict linear order. For this reason, Microsoft Excel doesn't give you any control over recalculation or iteration in a macro sheet. Finally, as you'll see, the Define Name command works differently in macro sheets.

Other than these differences, macro sheets are nearly identical to worksheets. The processes of making and editing entries, copying and moving entries, inserting and deleting rows, and so forth in a macro sheet are all identical to the same processes in a worksheet. Similarly, you use the same commands and techniques to save and open macro files as you use to save and open worksheets and charts.

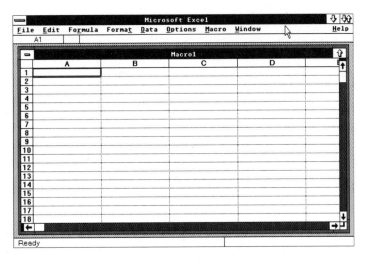

FIGURE 17-1. *A macro sheet looks very much like a worksheet.*

The Microsoft Excel macro language

If you choose the Paste Function command from the Formula menu in a macro sheet, you'll immediately see the most important difference between a worksheet and your macro sheet: Macro sheets offer many more functions than worksheets do. These functions are the building blocks you'll use to construct your command and function macros. Collectively, these functions make up the Microsoft Excel macro language.

Macro functions fall into four groups. The first group includes functions that exist in both worksheets and macro sheets and have the same purpose in both. These functions return values to the macro, much as worksheet functions, which you learned about in Chapter 6, return values to the worksheet. You can use these functions in your macros in the same way you use them in the worksheet.

Macro sheets offer a second class of functions that take the place of the commands on Microsoft Excel menus. We call them command-equivalent and action-equivalent functions because they are the macro equivalents of Microsoft Excel's menu commands. For example, the CLEAR function is the macro equivalent of the Clear command on the Edit menu. This function allows you to create macros that erase cells. Similarly, the ACTIVATE function is the equivalent of selecting a window name from the Window menu. Some of these functions allow you to make entries in cells, select ranges, and perform other similar tasks from within a macro.

The third set of functions is unique to macro sheets. The functions in this group perform a variety of programming tasks. For example, you can use these functions to create loops and branches in your macro programs and to collect information about certain conditions in the workspace.

The final set of functions consists of the customizing functions you use to create your own menus, commands, and dialog boxes. When you create a command macro, you can use these specialized functions to automate the macro process even further. For example, you may want to add your macro to a menu so that the user can select it like a standard command. Often, you'll want your macros to take different actions depending on certain conditions. Or you may want to combine two or more macro routines into one routine for efficiency. Using Microsoft Excel's customizing functions, you can create your own dialog boxes to collect information from the user and then use that information to vary the effects of the macro.

We'll show you examples of many of these functions in this chapter as we show you how to create and use macros. We will not, however, cover each function in detail here. We'll save that discussion for Chapter 18.

Creating a simple command macro

Creating a command macro is a three-step process: First, you create a new macro sheet or open an existing sheet; second, you enter the functions that make up the macro, one function per cell, generally into a single column in the macro sheet; third, you use the macro-sheet Define Name command to assign a name to the macro and identify it as a command macro. To run the macro you've created, you use the Run command on the Macro menu (or the assigned Ctrl-key combination).

Let's create a simple command macro to illustrate each step. If you haven't already done so, begin by creating a new macro sheet. In cell A1, type the text entry *First*. Although this name is not technically a part of the macro, it serves an important purpose, as you'll see in a moment. Next, move to cell A2 and enter the statement

=FORMULA("This is my first Microsoft Excel macro.")

Then select cell A3 and enter the function

=RETURN()

Your screen should now look like Figure 17-2. (We widened column A so that you could view the entire FORMULA statement.)

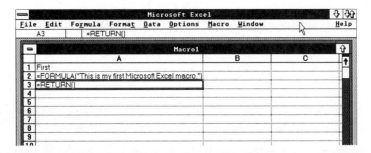

FIGURE 17-2. *We entered a label and two functions to create a simple command macro.*

FORMULA and RETURN are two of the functions from Microsoft Excel's macro language. FORMULA allows you to enter text, numbers, or formulas into the cells of the worksheet. In this case, the FORMULA function in cell A2 will enter the label

This is my first Microsoft Excel macro.

into the cell that is selected when you run the macro. The information described by the argument of FORMULA can also be a formula or a value. For example,

=FORMULA(100)

will enter 100 in the selected cell.

The RETURN function signals the end of the macro. All Microsoft Excel macros must end with a RETURN function or a HALT function. (We'll talk about HALT in the next chapter.) If you don't end your macro with one of these functions, when you try to run it Microsoft Excel will display the alert message *Did not encounter RETURN() or HALT() on macro sheet.*

Now that the macro is in place, you should give it a name. The name of a macro is simply a range name assigned to the first cell in the macro. You name macros the same way you name cells in the worksheet—by selecting the cell you want to name and choosing Define Name from the Formula menu.

For example, to name this sample macro, select cell A2 and choose Define Name from the Formula menu. You'll see a dialog box like the one in Figure 17-3. Notice that Microsoft Excel has entered the reference of the selected cell, A2, in the Refers to edit bar, and has entered the text from cell A1, First, in the Name edit bar. (You'll recall from Chapter 2 that, when you use the Define Name command, Microsoft Excel always looks for a possible name in the cells above or to the left of the cell you select.)

FIGURE 17-3. *Use the Define Name dialog box to identify your macros.*

Before you select OK or press Enter to accept the suggested name, you should tell Microsoft Excel that the macro you've created is a command macro. To do this, simply select the Command option at the bottom of the dialog box. If you forget to select this option, Microsoft Excel will still assign the name *First* to cell A2, but it won't know that cell A2 is the first cell in a command macro.

When you select the Command option, the Key: Ctrl+ option becomes available. This option allows you to assign an alternate name to the macro so that you can run it by simply pressing the Ctrl key along with the specified key. (We'll come back to this option later in this chapter.)

After you've selected Command, select the OK button or press Enter to lock in the name. Although you don't have to enter the name of your macro in the macro sheet, you'll find that doing so makes your life a great deal easier.

Now let's run the macro. To do this, move back to your worksheet window and select any empty cell. Now select Run from the Macro menu. You'll see a dialog box like the one in Figure 17-4.

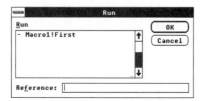

FIGURE 17-4. *You can use the Run dialog box to invoke macros.*

The scroll box at the top of the Run dialog box shows you the names of all the command macros that reside in open macro sheets. Because you've created only one macro, only one name appears in the list. Notice that the name has two parts: the name of the macro sheet that contains the macro, and the name of the actual macro. As with all external references in Microsoft Excel, the two names are separated by an exclamation point.

To run the macro, select its name in the Run dialog box, choose OK or press Enter, and watch what happens!

In effect, this simple command macro is a storehouse for a series of keystrokes. After you've created this macro, you need never type these keystrokes again. Instead, to enter these characters in a cell, you simply select that cell and run the macro.

Although this macro is trivial, it illustrates all the basic concepts of macros: It is stored in a macro sheet; it is made up of functions; it has a name, which is simply a range name assigned to its first cell; and it is executed by selecting its name from the list in the Run dialog box. Every command macro we create will follow these same basic rules.

Now suppose you're creating a monthly report and you want to enter abbreviations for the names of the months (Jan, Feb, Mar, and so on) into the range B4:M4. Because you create reports like this fairly often, you decide to write a macro that will perform this task for you. You can use a macro like the one in Figure 17-5 to create these headers. Let's walk through this macro one line at a time.

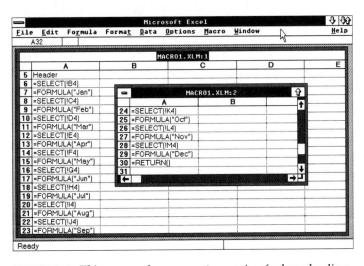

FIGURE 17-5. *This command macro creates a series of column headings.*

The label in cell A5, *Header*, serves as the name of the macro. The statement in cell A6 is

=SELECT(!B4)

The SELECT function, one of the most commonly used functions in the Microsoft Excel macro language, is action-equivalent; it corresponds to the action of selecting a cell. For example, the result of this function in our example is identical to selecting cell B4. Notice that the reference to cell B4 is preceded by an exclamation point, marking it as an external reference. Because the exclamation point is not preceded by a document name, Microsoft Excel assumes you're referring to cell B4 in the active worksheet. By not linking the action to a specific worksheet, you can perform this macro on any active worksheet.

The FORMULA statement in the next line of the macro tells Microsoft Excel to enter the text *Jan* into the selected cell. Then the statement in cell A8

=SELECT(!C4)

selects cell C4 and the FORMULA statement in cell A9 enters the text *Feb* into that cell. The macro continues in this way to cell A30, which marks the end of the macro with a RETURN function.

Before you can use this macro, of course, you must give it a name. Select cell A6 and choose the Define Name command. Microsoft Excel will suggest the label from cell A5, *Header*, as the name for the macro. After you name the macro, select the Command button to define this as a command macro and then select OK or press Enter.

To run the Header macro, activate an open worksheet and select any cell. Then pull down the Macro menu and choose the Run command. When Microsoft Excel presents the list of available macro names, select the name *Macro1!Header* and select OK or press Enter. Figure 17-6 shows the result. (We narrowed the columns so that you could see all the label entries in columns B through M.)

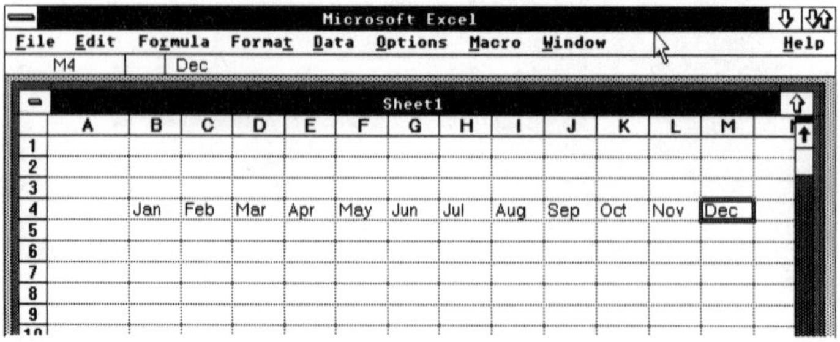

FIGURE 17-6. *This worksheet shows the results of the column-heading macro.*

A closer look

Let's take a closer look at how macros work. When you run a macro, Microsoft Excel begins by calculating the formula or function in the first cell in the macro. Then it moves down one row and calculates the formula or function in the next cell in that column, and then the next, and the next, and so on. Macro calculation continues in this linear fashion until Microsoft Excel comes across a RETURN or a

HALT function (which stops the macro), a GOTO or a REF function (which causes the macro to branch to another macro routine), or an error.

Macros can include formulas that return values, functions that take actions, and constant values. If a cell contains a function that takes an action, the macro takes that action immediately when the cell is calculated. If a cell contains a formula that produces a value, Microsoft Excel calculates the value of the formula, which can then be used by other formulas later in the macro. If a cell contains a constant value—a text entry or number—or is blank, Microsoft Excel simply skips over that cell and proceeds to the next cell.

Macro-sheet rules

Although the macros we've built so far have been in column A, you can put a macro anywhere in a macro sheet. We could easily have entered our first macro in cells AZ100:AZ102. But convention—and sound practice—calls for macros to be entered only in the first few columns of your macro sheets. If you stick macros in faraway corners of your macro sheets, you'll have a very difficult time figuring out where they are when you need to edit them. In addition, if you include lots of blank space between your macros or if you store macros in remote locations, you'll waste memory.

You can run any macro from within any worksheet. The only rule to keep in mind is that you can run only macros that are stored in open macro sheets. The number of macro sheets that can be open at any time is limited only by your computer's memory. As soon as you open a macro sheet, Microsoft Excel adds the names of the macros in that sheet to the list in the Run dialog box. When you close a macro sheet, Microsoft Excel removes the names of the macros in that sheet from the list. As you've seen, the name of every macro in the Run list includes the name of the sheet in which the macro is stored, making it easy to locate a given macro.

Microsoft Excel assigns the name *Macro1* to the first macro sheet you create in a given work session, the name *Macro2* to the second sheet you create, and so on. Of course, you can always use the Save As command to save any macro sheet under any name you desire.

One macro sheet can hold many macros. To enter a new macro in an existing sheet, simply select a blank portion of the sheet and enter the macro. As soon as you name a new macro in an existing macro sheet, Microsoft Excel adds the name of that macro to the Run list.

As you might expect, each macro in a macro sheet must have a different name. If you attempt to assign a name that already exists in the macro sheet, Microsoft Excel will remove the name from its old location as it assigns it to the new one.

Another example

Let's look at another simple macro, shown in Figure 17-7. The Dater macro enters the label *Last Revision* into cell A2 of a worksheet and the NOW function into cell B2 and then formats the result of the function in cell B2 to be displayed in the m/d/yy date format.

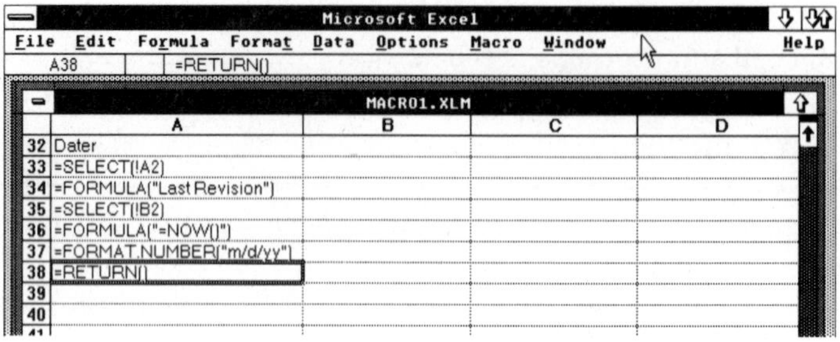

FIGURE 17-7. *The Dater macro enters the revision date of a worksheet.*

As before, we've entered the name of the macro, *Dater*, into the cell above the first cell of the macro. The first cell of the macro, A33, contains the statement

=SELECT(!A2)

which selects cell A2 in the active worksheet. The FORMULA statement in cell A34 tells Microsoft Excel to enter the text *Last Revision* into the selected cell. The statement in cell A35

=SELECT(!B2)

selects cell B2 in the active worksheet, and the statement

=FORMULA("=NOW()")

in cell A36 enters the formula =NOW() into that cell. Notice that the NOW function in this statement is enclosed in quotation marks. As we'll explain in Chapter 18, these quotation marks are required.

The statement in cell A37

=FORMAT.NUMBER("m/d/yy")

is a command-equivalent function that instructs Microsoft Excel to assign the m/d/yy date format to the selected cell, B2. Finally, the RETURN function in cell A38 tells Microsoft Excel that this is the end of the macro.

After naming the macro, we can invoke it with the Run command. Figure 17-8 shows the result. Notice that Microsoft Excel has entered the text *Last Revision* in cell A2 and the current date in cell B2 with the format m/d/yy.

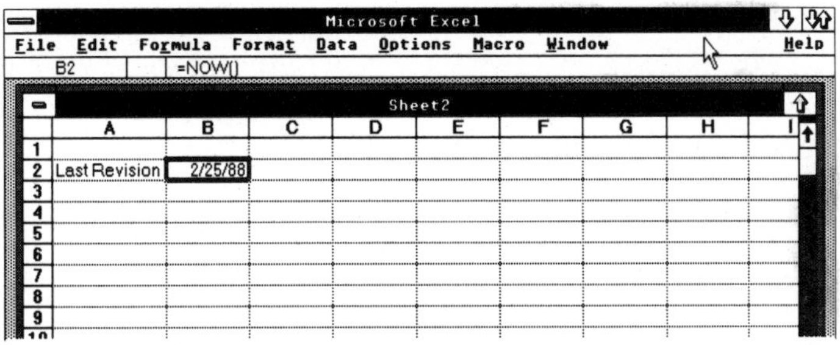

FIGURE 17-8. *This worksheet shows the results of the Dater macro.*

This simple but useful macro illustrates a couple of important concepts. First, it shows how you can use the FORMULA function to enter formulas into cells. In addition, it shows how you can use a command-equivalent function to choose a menu command from within a macro.

Using the recorder

Now that you're familiar with the structure and syntax of Microsoft Excel macros, we'll show you a shortcut for creating command macros. Instead of typing macros character by character into the cells of a macro sheet, you can instruct Microsoft Excel to create macros by simply recording the keystrokes you type and the commands you issue.

After you've recorded a set of commands, you can ask Microsoft Excel to "play back" those commands. When Microsoft Excel plays back the recorded macro, it will duplicate exactly the actions you performed when you created it. As you might expect, this playback capability is most useful for writing scripts that automate long or repetitive processes such as entering month headers in the worksheet or printing a certain section of the worksheet.

Creating a macro with the recorder is usually a four-step process. First, you define your Recorder range—the macro-sheet cells in which your macro will be stored. Next, you select the Record command on the Macro menu to turn the recorder on. After the recorder is on, you choose the commands and type the keystrokes you want Microsoft Excel to record. When you're finished, you use the Stop Recorder command on the Macro menu to turn the recorder off.

Let's create a simple macro that inserts your company name and address into a worksheet. Begin by activating a worksheet. If you haven't defined a recorder range (more on this in a moment), select Record from the Macro menu. Microsoft Excel will display a dialog box like the one shown in Figure 17-9. Here, you can assign a name and Ctrl-key short name to your new macro. You can either accept Microsoft Excel's suggested name (*Record1*, *Record2*, *Record3*, and so on) or enter a name of your own in the Name edit bar. If no macro sheet is currently open in the workspace, Microsoft Excel will open a new macro sheet to hold your recorder entries. (The new macro sheet will appear behind the active document window so that it won't interfere with your recording actions.)

FIGURE 17-9. *The Record Macro dialog box appears when you issue the Record command without first defining a recorder range.*

If you've just used the recorder to create a macro, Microsoft Excel will start recording in the first empty column of that open macro sheet. As you enter keystrokes and issue commands in the worksheet, Microsoft Excel will be recording your actions in the macro sheet. You can watch this process, if you like, by choosing the Arrange All command from the Window menu so that both the worksheet and the macro sheet are visible on your screen. You'll notice that Microsoft Excel displays the message *Recording* in the status bar.

After you name the macro, select any cell in an unused part of the worksheet. We'll select cell A6 for this example. In cell A6, enter

Consolidated Manufacturing Company

Move to cell A7 and enter

3012 West First Street

Then move to cell A8 and enter

Louisville, KY 40202

Then turn off the recorder by selecting the Stop Recorder command from the Macro menu. This step is very important. When the recorder is on, Microsoft Excel records every keystroke you type and every command you use. If you leave the recorder on accidentally, Microsoft Excel will record keystrokes that you don't want in the macro.

Now switch back to the macro sheet. As you were entering your company's name in the worksheet, Microsoft Excel was recording your keystrokes in the macro sheet. The sheet should now look like Figure 17-10.

The entries that appear in cells B2 to B8 are the recorder versions of the keystrokes you typed when you entered the address into the worksheet. For example, the statement in cell B3

=FORMULA("Consolidated Manufacturing Company")

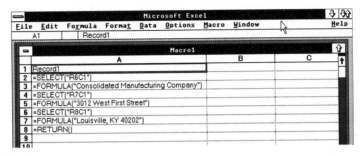

FIGURE 17-10. *Microsoft Excel recorded our keystrokes as we made our worksheet entries.*

is the macro equivalent of typing the company name in worksheet cell A6. The statement in cell B4

=SELECT("R7C1")

is the macro equivalent of selecting worksheet cell A7. Notice that Microsoft Excel has recorded this cell as an absolute reference in the R1C1 format.

Microsoft Excel now holds the instructions for inserting your company's name and address into a worksheet whenever you run this macro. For a demonstration, activate the worksheet and clear cells A6:A9. Select any cell and then select the Run command from the Macro menu. When you select Record1 in the Run dialog box, Microsoft Excel will insert your company name and address into the worksheet.

Setting the recorder range

As you just saw, Microsoft Excel automatically recorded the macro you created beginning in the first cell of the first blank column. But what if you want to position a macro elsewhere in a macro sheet or want to add to an existing macro? For example, suppose you want your macro statements to begin in cell C20 of an existing macro sheet. All you need do is define the recorder range by selecting cell C20 of the macro sheet and then selecting Set Recorder from the Macro menu. Then use the Start Recorder command and proceed as usual. (You'll probably want to activate the window you'll be working with before you choose Start Recorder. Otherwise, your window selection will be recorded too.)

Let's recreate the simple date-header macro from Figure 17-5 using the Recorder. To begin, define the recorder range in the macro sheet being used. Microsoft Excel offers two options for selecting the recorder range. If you select one cell in the macro sheet and choose the Set Recorder command from the Macro menu, Microsoft Excel uses the entire column below that cell as the recorder range. If, on the other hand, you select a range of cells, Microsoft Excel uses only that range. It is very difficult to predict in advance how long a macro will be when you create it with the recorder. Because the one-cell option allows your macros to be as long as necessary, we greatly prefer it.

To set the recorder range in our example, select cell A50 in Macro1 and choose the Set Recorder command from the Macro menu. Next, open a new worksheet and select Start Recorder. Now select cell B4 and type *Jan*, press Tab, type *Feb*, press Tab, type *Mar*, press Tab, and so on. As you type, Microsoft Excel will record your keystrokes.

When you've finished entering the header labels, choose the Stop Recorder command on the Macro menu. Now switch back to the macro sheet. It should look like Figure 17-11. The entries that now appear in cells A50 through A74 are the recorded versions of the keystrokes you typed when you entered the date labels across row 4.

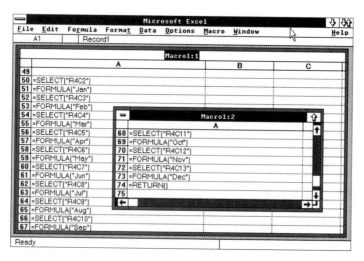

FIGURE 17-11. *The macro sheet should look like this after you've recorded commands and entries in the worksheet.*

Before you use this macro, you must give it a name, if you haven't done so already. Select cell A50 and choose Define Name from the Formula menu. Type the name (let's call it Header2) in the Name field, select the Command button, and select OK or press Enter.

Now use the New command to create a new worksheet. When the new worksheet is ready, select any cell, choose the Run command from the Macro menu, and select the name *Header2*. As soon as you do this, Microsoft Excel will select cell B4 in the new worksheet and enter the labels *Jan*, *Feb*, and so on in cells B4:M4.

Adding to the macro

Now suppose you want to change the Header macro so that it not only enters the headers into row 4 but also centers them. To make this change, select the worksheet in which you just used the macro, choose the Start Recorder command from the Macro menu, and choose the cells you want to format. Next, choose Alignment from the Format menu, select Center, and choose OK or press Enter. Then select the Stop Recorder option from the Macro menu to stop recording. Figure 17-12 shows the result of this action in the macro sheet.

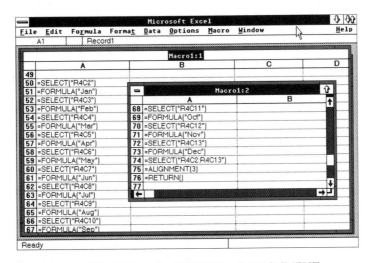

FIGURE 17-12. *We added a pair of SELECT and ALIGNMENT functions with the recorder.*

Notice that the entries in cells A74 and A75 are now

=SELECT("R4C2:R4C13")

and

=ALIGNMENT(3)

and that the RETURN function that was in cell A74 is now in cell A76. Here's what happens. When you turn on the recorder without having reset the recorder range, Microsoft Excel writes over the RETURN statement, adding the new commands to the bottom of the macro. As long as you haven't reset your recorder range and space remains in the range, you can stop and restart the recorder as often as you like. This allows you to make changes to the worksheet or execute commands and then restart the recorder again without resetting it.

If you've reset the recorder range but want to add to a previously created macro, activate the cell that contains the RETURN statement and use the Set Recorder command. You can now begin adding to your macro.

Using absolute and relative references

When you opened the Macro menu, you may have noticed the Relative Record command. Relative Record and Absolute Record are toggle commands that allow you to tell Microsoft Excel whether you want the cell references to be recorded as relative references or absolute references. If you choose Relative Record, its name on the menu will change to Absolute Record, allowing you to switch back to absolute references later. No matter which option you choose, Microsoft Excel records any cell references in the R1C1 format. For this example, we accepted the default, Absolute Record.

Let's recreate the macro we just created, this time using Relative Record instead of Absolute Record. Select cell B51 in Macro1 and choose the Set Recorder command. Now, create a new worksheet and select cell B4 in that worksheet. Next, use the Start Recorder command to turn on the recorder and the Relative Record command to change the recording method to relative. Type *Jan*, press Tab, type *Feb*, press Tab, type *Mar*, press Tab, and so on until you've entered labels for the entire year. When you're finished, use the Stop Recorder command to turn off the recorder.

Figure 17-13 shows the macro sheet as it should look after you create this macro. Because we started the new macro in cell B51, it appears side by side with the equivalent commands in the absolute-reference version. As you can see, the

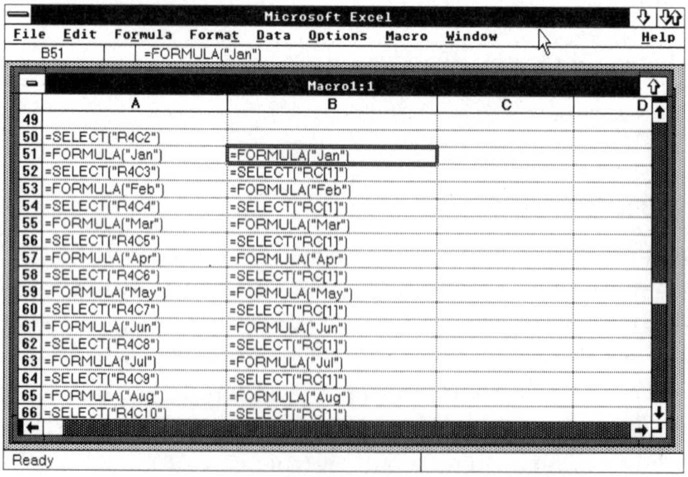

FIGURE 17-13. *We created this macro using relative references.*

new version of the macro in column B uses only relative references. For example, the statement in cell A52 is

=SELECT("R4C3")

but the entry in cell B52 is

=SELECT("RC[1]")

The first macro will always create the column headings in the range B4:M4, no matter which cell is active when the macro is run. The second macro, on the other hand, will create the column headings in the current row, beginning with the active cell. The advantage of this version is that it allows you to enter these headings anywhere in any worksheet.

Obviously, the position of the active cell makes a great deal of difference when you use a macro that was recorded with relative references. Before you run the macro, always select the specific cell in which you want to start the series. Otherwise, the series will be created beginning wherever the active cell happens to be.

You can switch back and forth between Relative Record and Absolute Record at any time—even in the middle of recording a macro. This allows you to make some of the references in a recorded macro absolute and others relative.

Which form is better? Neither, and both. Absolute cell references are useful when you want to perform the same action in exactly the same spot in several worksheets or when you want to perform the same action repeatedly in the same part of one worksheet. Relative cell references are useful when you want the freedom to perform an action anywhere in a worksheet.

More about recording

Microsoft Excel's macro recorder runs much more smoothly than others we've used. In some programs, if you type a word incorrectly or select the wrong command, the mistake and your efforts to correct it are recorded in the macro. Fortunately, Microsoft Excel will not record an action until you complete it. For example, Microsoft Excel will not record a cell as being selected until you take some action on it, such as choosing a formatting or an editing command. Similarly, Microsoft Excel will not record a command until you fully complete it. If you select Cancel to abandon the command, Microsoft Excel will not include the command in the macro.

Suppose you select the range B1:D1 while the recorder is on. As you would expect, Microsoft Excel enters the coordinates of the selected cells into your macro sheet in a SELECT statement as soon as you make the selection. This record is not permanent, however, until you take an action on the selected cells. If you change the selection to B2:D2 before acting on the previously selected cells, Microsoft Excel will change the SELECT statement to reflect the change. As soon as you take an action on the selected range, however, the selection becomes permanent. For example, if, after selecting B2:D2, you choose the Number command from the Format menu, select #,##0, and select OK or press Enter, Microsoft Excel will make the SELECT statement permanent and will add the new statement

=FORMAT.NUMBER("#,##0")

in the cell below. However, if you select Cancel in the Format Number dialog box instead of OK, Microsoft Excel will not add this new line to the macro and will not make the SELECT statement permanent.

You'll find this feature of the recorder very helpful. Because Microsoft Excel waits until you're sure you want to do something before it records your actions, you'll end up with fewer errors in your recorded macros. Even so, realize that Microsoft Excel records your commands literally while the recorder is on, so be careful to only choose commands, select cells, and make entries that you want to be recorded. Also, remember to turn the recorder off when you're finished recording or when you need to correct a mistake.

If you choose to use a range instead of a single cell as the recorder range, the recorder range may become full before you're finished recording your macro. If that occurs, Microsoft Excel will display an alert box with the message *Recorder range is full.* and stop recording. If you see this error and want to continue recording, you can activate the macro sheet and select a new and larger recorder range that includes the incomplete macro. If no blank cells are available below the recorder range, you will have to define a new recorder range in a different part of the macro sheet and use a GOTO function to join the two macros together.

For example, suppose you define the recorder range to be A1:A10 in the macro sheet and then fill that range with a macro. When the range becomes full, Microsoft Excel displays the error message, stops recording, and places a RETURN function in cell A10. Now suppose that you redefine the recorder range to be cells B1:B10 and continue recording. Before you can use the macro, you must replace the RETURN function in cell A10 with the statement

=GOTO(B1)

This statement lets Microsoft Excel know that the next instruction in this macro is in cell B1. In programming terms, it tells Microsoft Excel to branch to cell B1. We'll explain the GOTO function in more detail in Chapter 18.

Debugging macros

Macros don't always work correctly. They can fail because of syntax errors or because of function arguments that don't make sense. For example, the statement

=COLUMN.WIDTH(−1)

will cause an error because the argument –1 is not acceptable. Similarly, the statement

=GALLERY.PIE(10)

will cause an error because its argument is invalid.

One thing is certain: If you create macros, you'll create macros that contain errors. Like all programmers, you'll spend a good part of your time correcting, or debugging, your macros. Fortunately, Microsoft Excel makes it relatively easy to debug macros. When you're running a macro and the program encounters an error, it stops calculating the macro and displays an alert box like the one in Figure 17-14. This alert box tells you that an error has occurred, shows you the location of the error, and gives you three options: Halt, Continue, or Step.

FIGURE 17-14. *This alert box tells you where in your macro an error has occurred.*

Most of the time, you'll select Halt to stop the macro and then select the macro sheet and try to discover the source of the error. Because Microsoft Excel tells you where the error occurred, it's usually fairly easy to identify and correct the error.

The Continue option causes Microsoft Excel to ignore the error and continue to the next statement in the macro. You won't usually select this option, because an error in one line of a macro often results in errors in other parts of the macro as well. If you select the Continue option, you'll likely encounter more errors before the macro is finished.

The Step option causes Microsoft Excel to continue processing the macro one step at a time, beginning with the line after the line that caused the error. As Microsoft Excel calculates each line of the macro, it stops, displays a dialog box like the one shown in Figure 17-15, and waits for your instructions. Because the macro proceeds step by step, you can easily locate errors.

FIGURE 17-15. *Use the Single Step dialog box to walk through a macro one line at a time.*

Selecting Step *after* an error has occurred is usually not very helpful, because Microsoft Excel begins stepping with the cell following the cell that contains the error. You're better off selecting the Halt option and then rerunning the macro from the beginning using Step mode.

Microsoft Excel provides two ways to invoke the Step mode before an error occurs. First, you can interrupt a running macro at any time by pressing Esc. When you do this, Microsoft Excel displays an alert box similar to the one shown in Figure 17-14. Again, you can stop the macro, use Step mode, or continue. If you use Esc to halt a macro just after it has begun and then select Step, you can step through all but the first few lines of the macro.

Alternatively, you can insert one or more STEP functions in the form

=STEP()

into your macro at the spot(s) where you want to begin using Step mode. When it runs into a STEP function, Microsoft Excel will present the dialog box shown in Figure 17-15 and allow you to walk through the macro statements one at a time. The Single Step dialog box displays the reference of the cell that will be executed next, not the reference of the cell that was just executed. If your macro contains more than one STEP function, you can use the Continue button in the Single Step dialog box to tell Microsoft Excel to run the macro as usual until it locates another STEP function, whereupon the program will enter Step mode again.

E X C E L *Tip*

Keep an eye on the macro sheet!

If you want to see what's going on in the macro sheet as the macro runs, try using the Display command on the Options menu to display values rather than formulas. Then use the Arrange All command to resize and reposition the macro sheet and other documents in your workspace so that you can see all the action. (It's a good idea to close any documents that aren't "part of the action" before you test a macro; that way, you can avoid accidental destruction of data.) Activate the document on which you want the macro to operate and then run the macro. (If the macro operates on more than one document, activate the first document in the sequence.) Now when you run the macro, you'll be able to see the results of the macro formulas as they are calculated. At the same time, you'll be able to see the effects of those calculations on the active document(s).

A different kind of error

So far, we've considered only errors that make it impossible for Microsoft Excel to compute the macro. However, another type of macro error can be even more troublesome. This type of error occurs when a macro runs properly but doesn't do what you expect it to. The error can occur when you're running a macro for the first time or when you use a macro in the wrong situation. Because Microsoft Excel doesn't recognize this type of error, it won't stop the macro when such an error occurs. As a result, the error can be very destructive. If the macro includes such functions as CLEAR or EDIT.DELETE, your worksheet may be ruined before you know it.

To avoid this type of error, build your macro in stages and test each stage before you add more functions. This allows you to debug the macro a few lines at a time, which is much easier than debugging the entire macro at once. We also suggest that you use a "dummy" worksheet, whenever possible, to test macros. You can either use a blank sheet or create a copy of the worksheet in which you plan to run the macro, so that your original worksheet is safe from damage.

The Ctrl-key option

Earlier in this chapter, we mentioned that Microsoft Excel lets you assign a Ctrl-key-combination "name" to a macro. If you assign this special kind of name, you can run the macro by simply pressing Ctrl and the key you've assigned to it.

For example, let's give a Ctrl-key name to the relative-reference date-header macro, which begins in cell B51 of Macro1 (Figure 17-13). First, select cell B51 and choose the Define Name command. When the Define Name dialog box comes into view, type *Header3* in the Name box (or select the name if you've already defined it) and select Command. The Key: Ctrl+ option will become available. To assign a Ctrl-key name, simply select this edit bar and type a letter (we'll use the letter *a*). Now select OK or press Enter to lock in the name.

To run the macro using this new name, simply select any cell in a worksheet and press Ctrl and *a* at the same time. The macro should run immediately, entering the date headers across the row you selected.

Of course, you could still run the macro by choosing the Run command and selecting its name from the list. The Ctrl-key name is simply an alternative that allows you to run the macro more quickly.

You can assign only single-letter Ctrl-key names to macros. If you attempt to use two or more letters, Microsoft Excel will beep. In addition, Microsoft Excel distinguishes between uppercase and lowercase letters in Ctrl-key names. For example, the name *A* is different from the name *a*. You can't use a number or the letter *e*, *i*, *n*, or *u* as a Ctrl-key name. When you use the Record Macro command to create a macro, the dialog box automatically assigns a Ctrl-key name. If you like, you can edit this name to choose a more appropriate letter.

Documenting your macros

As you're probably beginning to realize, even relatively simple macros can be difficult to read. After all, you're used to reading English and Microsoft Excel macros are written in Microsoft Excel's own special macro language. You can do a lot to make your macros easier to understand, however.

First, you can enter explanatory text in the cells next to a macro in the macro sheet. For example, Figure 17-16 shows the modified Dater macro. Notice the text in cells B33:B38. As you can see, it explains the purpose of each line in the macro.

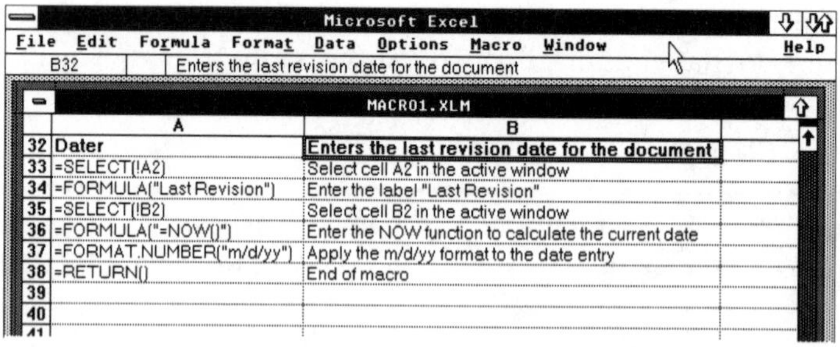

FIGURE 17-16. *We added comments to the Dater macro.*

Because Microsoft Excel ignores any text values it encounters in the process of calculating a macro, you can even include documentation between the statements in your macros. For example, in Figure 17-16 you could also insert some identifying phrases between the lines of the macro to flag named cells or subroutines.

How you document your macros is a matter of personal preference. It doesn't matter which method you select, as long as you do include documentation. Documentation is most important for long and complex macros, for macros that you'll look at only once in a long while, and for macros you must explain to others. We suggest that you document *all* your macros.

Another way to "document" your macros is to give them descriptive names. The more descriptive the name, the better. For example, instead of naming a macro Header, you could name it Rel_Months_Header, where Rel indicates that the macro uses relative references and Months_Header describes the type of header the macro creates. Because you don't have to type the names of your command macros to run them, you need not keep the names of these macros short (although, if the name is too long, it won't be completely visible in the Run scroll box). Using descriptive names for your macros becomes more important as you create more and more macros and particularly as you create macros that have similar, but not identical, purposes.

Interestingly, you don't have to name command macros in Microsoft Excel (although you must name function macros). If you don't give a command macro a name, you can still run it by choosing the Run command from the Macro menu. Of course, the macro you want to use will not appear in the list of macros in the Run dialog box. You'll have to type its location in the Reference field at the bottom of the dialog box. For example, suppose you've created a macro that begins at cell G40 of the macro sheet named HEADERS and you haven't given it a name. To run that macro, you can choose the Run command, type

=HEADERS!G40

and select OK or press Enter.

Similarly, if you don't tell Microsoft Excel that a macro you've created is a command macro, it won't include the name of that macro in the Run list. Therefore, we suggest you always tell Microsoft Excel the type of each macro you create.

Subroutines

Microsoft Excel allows you to run one macro from within another by including the name of the second macro as a function in the first macro. For example, if you include the statement

=TEST()

in a macro, that statement will immediately activate and run the macro that begins at the cell named TEST. Alternatively, you can use a cell reference to direct Microsoft Excel to the appropriate starting cell:

=B50()

When Microsoft Excel encounters the RETURN function at the end of the second macro, it will return to the cell below the one that contains the calling statement and resume executing the original macro.

This feature of Microsoft Excel allows you to create subroutines in your macros. A subroutine is a nested program that contains instructions that are used in a larger macro. Subroutines simplify macros because they allow you to write a set of frequently used instructions once, instead of including those instructions in full everywhere they're needed in the macro.

The header macro in Figure 17-13 can be simplified considerably by using a subroutine. Instead of repeating the statement

=SELECT("RC[1]")

11 times in this function, you can enter that statement in a cell named GORIGHT and then call GORIGHT as a subroutine when you need to use it.

Let's look at how this works. To begin, select cell C50 in Macro1 and enter the name GORIGHT. Then select cell C51 and enter the statement

=SELECT("RC[1]")

While C51 is selected, use the Define Name command to name it GORIGHT and identify the macro as a command macro. Then enter

=RETURN()

in cell C52. Next, select cell B52 and replace the statement in that cell with the statement

=GORIGHT()

E X C E L *tip*

Protecting the macro sheet

After you've finished entering one or more macros into a macro sheet, you'll probably want to protect the macro sheet to prevent any accidental changes or destruction of data. Fortunately, you can apply all the same protection techniques to your macro sheets that are available for worksheets. For example, you can protect the document by entering a password in the Save As dialog box.

You can also easily lock the cells in the macro sheet by applying the Locked setting in the Cell Protection dialog box and then using the Protect Document command on the Options menu. You may also want to use the Windows option in the Protect Document dialog box to prevent the user from activating the macro sheet. You can even hide the macro sheet from view by using the Hide command on the Window menu.

If your macro is designed to work with a worksheet template, you may want to apply many of the same protection measures to the template as well. For example, you may want to lock all the cells in the template except for the specific input cells in which you want the user to enter data.

Now when you run the macro, Microsoft Excel will first enter the text *Jan* in the active cell. Then, the GORIGHT() function in cell B52 will "call" the subroutine in cell C51, which will move the active cell one cell to the right. When Microsoft Excel encounters the RETURN function in cell C52, it will jump back to cell B53 and calculate the function in that cell. (Of course, if you were actually going to use this function, you would want to replace all the SELECT functions in column B with GORIGHT functions.)

18

Macro
Functions

*I*n Chapter 17, we introduced you to the concept of macro functions and gave you a few examples of how these functions could be used in macros. In this chapter, we'll explain the form and purpose of Microsoft Excel's many macro functions. We'll save a few specialized functions for Chapters 19 and 20. For example, in Chapter 19 we'll look at the ARGUMENT and RESULT functions, which appear only in user-defined functions. In Chapter 20, we'll look at a group of advanced functions you can use to customize your Microsoft Excel applications.

Most of the commands available on Microsoft Excel's menus can also be duplicated from within a macro. For example, to issue the Paste Special command from within a macro, you use the PASTE.SPECIAL function. Most of those commands that use dialog boxes (that is, commands that are followed by an ellipsis on the menus) can be entered in two forms: You can select the desired dialog-box options yourself by entering the appropriate arguments in the function, or you can add a question-mark (?) character after the function name to instruct Microsoft Excel to display the dialog box and allow the user to manually select the desired options. When you use the question-mark form of a command-equivalent function, you can enter the function arguments or omit them. If you omit them, you'll see the default entries in the dialog box when it is displayed on the screen. If you include them, Microsoft Excel will select the specified options in the dialog box but leave the dialog box open so that you can change or confirm the selections. Enter the following macro functions in question-mark form:

=ALIGNMENT?()	=FORMAT.NUMBER?()	=SCALE?()
=APP.MOVE?()	=FORMAT.SIZE?()	=SELECT.SPECIAL?()
=APP.SIZE?()	=FORMULA.FIND?()	=SIZE?()
=APPLY.NAMES?()	=FORMULA.GOTO?()	=SORT?()
=ATTACH.TEXT?()	=FORMULA.REPLACE?()	=STYLE?()
=AXES?()	=GALLERY.*xxx*?()	=TABLE?()
=BORDER?()	=GRIDLINES?()	=UNHIDE?()
=CALCULATION?()	=INSERT?()	=WORKSPACE?()
=CELL.PROTECTION?()	=MAIN.CHART?()	
=CHANGE.LINK?()	=MOVE?()	
=CLEAR?()	=NEW?()	
=COLUMN.WIDTH?()	=OPEN?()	
=COMBINATION?()	=OPEN.LINKS?()	
=COPY.CHART?()	=OVERLAY?()	
=CREATE.NAMES?()	=PAGE.SETUP?()	
=DATA.DELETE?()	=PASTE.SPECIAL?()	
=DATA.SERIES?()	=PATTERNS?()	
=DEFINE.NAME?()	=PRINT?()	
=DISPLAY?()	=PRINTER.SETUP?()	
=EDIT.DELETE?()	=PROTECT.DOCUMENT?()	
=EXTRACT?()	=ROW.HEIGHT?()	
=FILE.DELETE?()	=RUN?()	
=FORMAT.FONT?()	=SAVE.AS?()	
=FORMAT.MOVE?()	=SAVE.WORKSPACE?()	

Notice that a few of these functions, such as SIZE and MOVE, do not represent commands that display dialog boxes. Instead, they are action-equivalent functions that require instructions.

A few reminders before we begin the individual function descriptions. First, many macro functions don't require arguments. However, as with standard worksheet functions such as PI and RAND, when you enter these functions into your macro sheet you must include the parentheses. For example, to issue the Copy command from within a macro, enter the statement

=COPY()

In addition, many macro functions contain optional arguments. If you omit these arguments from your formulas, be sure to include the comma that separates the omitted argument from the next argument. The commas serve as placeholders to preserve the order in which the arguments are presented. If no additional arguments follow the omitted argument or if you're using the question-mark form of a function and include no arguments at all, you need not enter the commas.

Finally, you'll notice that many of the function arguments described in this chapter are enclosed in quotation marks, indicating that these arguments must be presented as literal text strings. If the quotation marks are omitted, the macro will not function properly.

File-management functions

The following 12 functions let you carry out file-management commands from within a macro. The first 11 functions are command-equivalent functions that correspond to commands on the File menu. The last function, DIRECTORY, lets you change the current drive and directory.

The NEW function

The NEW function lets you create a new Microsoft Excel document. It is equivalent to the New command on the File menu.

The NEW function takes the form

=NEW(*type*)

The *type* argument is a numeric code that describes the kind of document you want to create. The available *type* arguments are

Code	Document
1	Worksheet
2	Chart
3	Macro sheet

The OPEN function

The OPEN function lets you open an existing document. It is equivalent to the Open command on the File menu.

The form of the OPEN function is

=OPEN("*name*",*update*,*read only*)

The *name* argument represents the name of the document you want to open. This argument, which can include a drive and pathname, must be a text string enclosed in quotation marks. If you use the question-mark form of this function, you can include the * and ? wildcard characters in the *name* argument. For example, if you want to open a macro sheet, you might use a statement like

=OPEN?("*.XLM")

This procedure is equivalent to typing *.XLM in the File Name edit bar of the Open dialog box to display those files in the current directory that carry the XLM filename extension.

When you open a linked worksheet file, Microsoft Excel asks if you want to update references to supporting documents. To respond to this message, you can choose from the following *update* arguments:

Code	Meaning
0	Update neither external nor remote references
1	Update external references only
2	Update remote references only
3	Update both remote and external references

The *read only* argument is a logical value. A TRUE argument selects the Read Only check box in the Open dialog box. If the *read only* argument is omitted, it is assumed to be FALSE.

If the document is not in the specified directory, Microsoft Excel displays an alert message and gives you a choice of Retry or Cancel. If you choose Cancel, Microsoft Excel returns a macro error message, because subsequent commands in the same macro will undoubtedly assume the file has been opened. If the document name is not specified, as when you use the question-mark form of this function, you can select Cancel without receiving the error message.

If the document you want to open is not located in the current directory, use the full pathname, like this:

=OPEN("C:\MYDIR\MYSUBDIR\TEST",1)

Alternatively, if you want to change the default directory, use a DIRECTORY function to change the directory before you use the OPEN function.

The FILE.CLOSE and CLOSE.ALL functions

The FILE.CLOSE function closes the active document. It is equivalent to the Close command on the File menu. The FILE.CLOSE function takes an optional *logical* argument of TRUE to save the document or FALSE to close the document without saving. When the argument is omitted, Microsoft Excel asks whether you want to save the document.

The CLOSE.ALL function is equivalent to the Close All command on the File menu. (To choose Close All, press the Shift key as you open the File menu.) This function, which takes no arguments, closes all unprotected windows currently open in the workspace.

If you've made any changes to the document or documents to be closed, Microsoft Excel asks whether you want to save your changes before it executes a FILE.CLOSE or CLOSE.ALL command.

The SAVE and SAVE.AS functions

The SAVE function saves the active document to disk. It is equivalent to the Save command on the File menu. The SAVE function takes no arguments.

The SAVE.AS function is equivalent to the Save As command on the File menu. This function takes the form

=SAVE.AS("*name*",*type*,"*password*",*backup*)

where *name* is a text string, enclosed in quotation marks, that specifies the name under which you want to save the document. If you're saving the document in the current directory, you need enter only the document name. To save the document in another directory, you must enter the full pathname. If a document of the same name is already stored on the disk, Microsoft Excel asks if you want to overwrite the version on disk.

The *type* argument is a numeric code from the following list that identifies the type of file in which you want to save the document:

Code	File type	Use
0	Marks file as saved but does not save it to disk	To close a document without saving changes and without returning a message asking to save changes
1	Normal	
2	SYLK	To transfer data to another Microsoft spreadsheet
3	Text	To transfer data to or from a word processor
4	WKS	To transfer data to Lotus 1-2-3 version 1A or Symphony
5	WK1	To transfer data to Lotus 1-2-3 version 2
6	CSV	To transfer data with comma-separated values to or from a word processor
7	DBF2	To transfer database range to dBASE II
8	DBF3	To transfer database range to dBASE III
9	DIF	To transfer and save values, not formulas

If you're saving a chart, the *type* argument doesn't apply. If you're saving a macro sheet, only options 1, 2, 3, 6, and 9 apply. If the *type* argument is omitted, it is assumed to be 1.

To protect the document with a password, you must include the *password* argument as a text string in quotation marks. The *backup* argument, which is equivalent to the Create Backup File check box in the Options portion of the Save As dialog box, is a logical value that tells Microsoft Excel whether to create a backup file. If the *backup* argument is omitted, it is assumed to be FALSE.

For example, the statement

=SAVE.AS("Test",1,"Secret",TRUE)

saves the active document into a file named Test. This file will be protected by the password *Secret* and will be automatically backed up.

If you want Microsoft Excel to use a file extension other than the default .XLS, .XLM, or .XLC, include your own file extension in the *name* argument.

The SAVE.WORKSPACE function

The SAVE.WORKSPACE function saves a list of all the windows and documents you have open in Microsoft Excel. You can also use this function to save all open documents that you've changed since they were last saved. This function is equivalent to the Save Workspace command on the File menu.

The form of the SAVE.WORKSPACE function is

=SAVE.WORKSPACE ("*name*")

where *name* is the name of the workspace document you want to save. The *name* argument, which can include a drive and pathname, must be a text string enclosed in quotation marks. If you omit *name*, it is assumed to be either RESUME.XLW or the name of the last workspace document, if any, opened during the current session.

The FILE.DELETE function

The FILE.DELETE function deletes a file from disk. It is equivalent to the Delete command on the File menu.

The form of the FILE.DELETE function is

=FILE.DELETE("*name*")

where *name* represents the name of the document you want to delete. This argument must be a text string enclosed in quotation marks.

Before Microsoft Excel deletes the selected file, it displays an alert box that gives you a chance to change your mind. If you select Yes, Microsoft Excel deletes the selected file and moves on to the next line in the macro. For example, the statement

=FILE.DELETE("Test")

deletes the file Test from the current directory. If you select No, Microsoft Excel does not delete the file but simply moves on to calculate the next statement in the macro. If the specified document is not in the current directory, Microsoft Excel displays an error message.

As with the other file-management functions, you can include the entire document pathname in your *name* argument. When you use the question-mark form of this function, you can also use the * and ? wildcard characters in your *name* argument to control which files are included in the list box.

The OPEN.LINKS function

The OPEN.LINKS function opens the documents linked to the active document. It is equivalent to the Links command on the File menu.

The form of the OPEN.LINKS function is

=OPEN.LINKS("*name1*","*name2*",...,*read only*)

The *name* arguments are text strings, enclosed in quotation marks, that identify the linked documents you want to open. You can specify up to 14 document names in one OPEN.LINKS function. The *read only* argument is a logical value that represents the Read Only check box; if *read only* is TRUE, the check box is selected. If *read only* is omitted, it is assumed to be TRUE.

For example, the statement

=OPEN.LINKS("Sheet1","Sheet2","Sheet3")

opens three worksheets. If any of the linked documents contain external references to a supporting file, Microsoft Excel updates both the external and remote references.

You can make the OPEN.LINKS function more flexible by using the LINKS function as its argument. LINKS returns a vertical array of the names of all the documents linked to the active document. Thus, the statement

=OPEN.LINKS(LINKS())

opens all the documents linked to the active document. If you often work with multiple-document models, you'll probably want to include this simple but useful macro in your library. We'll talk more about LINKS later in this chapter.

The CHANGE.LINK function

The CHANGE.LINK function changes the supporting documents that serve as external references for the active document. Its action is equivalent to choosing the Links command on the File menu, selecting from the Links list box the document whose link you want to change, selecting the Change button, and choosing from the Files list box the name of the document you want to include in the link.

The form of the CHANGE.LINK function is

=CHANGE.LINK("*old link*","*new link*")

The *old link* argument represents the supporting document you want to change. The *new link* argument represents the document you want to link to the active document. Both arguments must be text strings enclosed in quotation marks.

When you use the question-mark form of this function, the *new link* argument is optional. If you include only the *old link* argument, Microsoft Excel displays a list of files from which to select your new link. (With this technique, only the second Links dialog box is displayed.)

The QUIT function

The QUIT function terminates the Microsoft Excel session. It is equivalent to the Quit command on the File menu. The QUIT function takes no arguments.

If you have any unsaved files, Microsoft Excel asks if you want to save them before quitting.

The DIRECTORY function

The DIRECTORY function changes the current drive and directory and returns the name of the new current directory to the macro sheet. Its action is equivalent to choosing a new directory from the Directory list box in the Open or Delete command dialog boxes.

The DIRECTORY function takes the form

=DIRECTORY("*path*")

where *path* is the drive and directory you want to make current. The *path* argument must be a text string enclosed in quotation marks.

If you omit the drive name from the *path* argument, Microsoft Excel assumes you want to use the current drive. If you omit the *path* argument, Microsoft Excel makes no change but simply returns the name of the current directory.

For example, the statement

=DIRECTORY("A:\1986\PROFITS")

changes the current directory and returns the text value *A:\1986\PROFITS*. If you omit the drive specifier, Microsoft Excel assumes you're using the current drive and includes that specifier in the path text it returns to the worksheet. For example, if the current drive is C, the statement

=DIRECTORY("\1986\PROFITS")

sets the current drive to C, sets the directory to \1986\PROFITS, and returns the text value *C:\1986\PROFITS* to the macro sheet.

Windowing functions

The following command-equivalent and action-equivalent functions take the place of the scroll bars, document-window Control menu commands, and other tools that let you navigate through worksheets and macro sheets and move and resize document windows.

The SIZE function

The SIZE function changes the size of a document window. Its action is equivalent to dragging the size box at the lower right corner of a document window or choosing Size from the document-window Control menu.

The SIZE function takes the form

=SIZE(*width,height,"window"*)

The *width* and *height* arguments are numeric values that represent the desired width and height of the specified window. Both arguments are expressed in points, a unit of measurement equal to $1/72$ of an inch. SIZE moves the lower right corner of the window as necessary to achieve the desired width and height but does not move the upper left corner.

The *window* argument is a text string, in quotation marks, that specifies the name of the window you want to resize. If *window* is omitted, it is assumed to be the current active window. If the *window* argument designates a window other than the active window, SIZE changes its size but does not activate the window.

If you use the question-mark form of the function, Microsoft Excel changes the pointer to an arrow shape so that you can manually resize the window.

The MOVE function

The MOVE function changes the position of a document window on the screen. Its action is equivalent to dragging the title bar of a document window or choosing the Move command from the document-window Control menu.

The MOVE function takes the form

=MOVE(*x,y,"window"*)

where the *x* and *y* arguments are numeric values that identify the desired horizontal and vertical positions of the upper left corner of the window. Both arguments are expressed in points, a unit of measurement equal to $1/72$ of an inch. The *x* argument is measured from the left edge of the workspace to the left edge of the window; the *y* argument is measured from the top edge of the workspace to the top edge of the window. MOVE repositions the upper left corner of the window but does not change the size of the window.

If you use the question-mark form of the function, Microsoft Excel changes the pointer to an arrow so that you can manually reposition the window.

The *window* argument is a text string, in quotation marks, that specifies the window you want to reposition. If *window* designates a window other than the active window, MOVE changes its position but does not activate the window. If you omit the *window* argument, Microsoft Excel moves the active window.

The FULL function

The FULL function expands the active document window to fill the workspace. Its action is equivalent to choosing the Maximize icon, choosing the Maximize command from the Control menu of the active document window, or pressing Ctrl-F10.

The FULL function takes the form

=FULL(*logical*)

If *logical* is TRUE, Microsoft Excel expands the active window to fill the screen. If *logical* is FALSE, Microsoft Excel returns the active window to its original size, exactly as it does when you choose the Restore icon, choose the Restore command, or press Ctrl-F5.

The NEW.WINDOW function

The NEW.WINDOW function opens a new window to a worksheet or macro sheet. It is equivalent to the New Window command on the Window menu. The NEW.WINDOW function takes no arguments.

The NEW.WINDOW function applies to worksheets and macro sheets only. If you run a macro that contains this function when the active window is a chart window, Microsoft Excel returns an error message.

The HIDE and UNHIDE functions

The HIDE and UNHIDE functions conceal or redisplay document windows. They are equivalent to the Hide and Unhide commands on the Window menu.

The HIDE function takes no arguments and acts on the active window. The UNHIDE function takes the form

=UNHIDE("*window*")

where *window* is the name of the window you want to redisplay. If you omit this argument in the UNHIDE function, Microsoft Excel returns an error message.

Microsoft Excel does allow you to use the ACTIVATE command and perform other actions on hidden windows from within a macro. Thus, you can use HIDE to suppress the display of windows while a macro is running, eliminating the need for screen updating and thereby speeding macro processing.

The ACTIVATE.NEXT and ACTIVATE.PREV functions

The ACTIVATE.NEXT and ACTIVATE.PREV functions activate either the next window in the stack or the previously active window. Their actions are equivalent to pressing the Ctrl-F6 and Ctrl-Shift-F6 key combinations. Neither of these functions takes an argument.

Suppose three windows are currently open: Sheet1, Sheet2, and Sheet3. Sheet1 is the active window and Sheet3 is the previously active window. The statement

=ACTIVATE.NEXT()

activates Sheet2. The statement

=ACTIVATE.PREV()

activates Sheet3.

The CLOSE function

The CLOSE function closes the active document window. It is equivalent to the Close command from the document-window Control menu.

The CLOSE function takes the form

=CLOSE(*save*)

where *save* is a logical value that indicates whether you want to save your changes to the document. (TRUE saves the changes; FALSE leaves the document unchanged.) This argument goes into effect only when you close the last window displaying the document. If you omit the *save* argument and you've made changes to the document since it was last saved, Microsoft Excel presents an alert message asking whether you want to save your changes.

The SPLIT function

The SPLIT function divides a worksheet window vertically, horizontally, or both. Its action is equivalent to dragging the split bars or choosing the Split command on the document window's Control menu.

The SPLIT function takes the form

=SPLIT(*column,row*)

The *column* argument tells Microsoft Excel where to split the document window vertically, with the leftmost column numbered 1. The *row* argument tells Microsoft Excel where to split the window horizontally, with the topmost row numbered 1.

To remove a split window, enter 0 for the appropriate argument. (If you simply omit an argument, Microsoft Excel won't change the related split.) When you enter the SPLIT function for a window with frozen panes, Microsoft Excel returns a macro error.

For example, the statement

=SPLIT(,4)

produces a horizontal split below the fourth row of the document window. If you've already split the window vertically, the vertical split remains unchanged. The statement

=SPLIT(2,0)

creates a vertical split to the right of the second column in the active window and removes any horizontal split.

The FREEZE.PANES function

The FREEZE.PANES function freezes the top pane, the left pane, or both in the active document window. It is equivalent to the Freeze Panes and Unfreeze Panes commands on the Options menu.

The FREEZE.PANES function takes the form

=FREEZE.PANES(*logical*)

If *logical* is TRUE, Microsoft Excel freezes the panes. If *logical* is FALSE, Microsoft Excel unfreezes the panes.

The ACTIVATE function

The ACTIVATE function activates document windows and individual panes in a split document window. Its action is equivalent to pressing F6 or Shift-F6 to move between windows or panes.

The ACTIVATE function takes the form

=ACTIVATE("*window*",*pane*)

where *window* is the name of the window you want to work with. The name must be a text string enclosed in quotation marks. If you've split the window into panes, you can use the *pane* argument to specify the pane you want to work with. This argument is a numeric code that describes the pane you want to activate:

Code	Pane activated
1	Top left (the only pane if the window is unsplit; the top pane if the window is split horizontally; the left pane if the window is split vertically)
2	Top right (the right pane if the window is split only vertically)
3	Bottom left (the bottom pane if the window is split only horizontally)
4	Bottom right

If you've opened more than one window in a document and the *window* argument doesn't specify which window you want to work with, Microsoft Excel activates the first window that displays that document. For example, suppose a document has two windows: Sheet1:1 and Sheet1:2. The statement

=ACTIVATE("Sheet1")

activates the Sheet1:1 window, the first window that displays the document. If you want to work with the second window, you must use the complete argument Sheet1:2.

If you omit the *window* argument, Microsoft Excel activates the requested pane on the current document. If you omit the *pane* argument, Microsoft Excel doesn't change the active pane.

The ARRANGE.ALL function

The ARRANGE.ALL function arranges all open document windows to make the most efficient use of your workspace. It is equivalent to the Arrange All command on the Window menu. The ARRANGE.ALL function takes no arguments.

The SHOW.INFO function

The SHOW.INFO function displays the information window. It is equivalent to the Show Info command on the Window menu.

The SHOW.INFO function takes the form

=SHOW.INFO(*enable*)

The *enable* argument is a logical value. If *enable* is TRUE, the SHOW.INFO function activates the Info window. If *enable* is FALSE and the Info window is the active window, Microsoft Excel activates the document linked to the Info window.

Application-window functions

All the windowing functions we've discussed so far apply to document windows. The action-equivalent and command-equivalent functions we'll discuss here let you manipulate the Microsoft Excel application window from within a macro.

The APP.SIZE function

The APP.SIZE function is similar to the SIZE function; it changes the size of the application window. The action of the APP.SIZE function is equivalent to dragging the application-window border or choosing the Size command from the application-window Control menu.

The APP.SIZE function takes the form

=APP.SIZE(*width,height*)

where the *width* and *height* arguments are the desired width and height of the window. As with the SIZE function, these arguments are expressed in points, a unit of measurement equivalent to $1/72$ of an inch.

If you use the question-mark form of the APP.SIZE function, Microsoft Excel changes the mouse pointer to an arrow shape so that you can manually resize the application window.

The APP.MOVE function

The APP.MOVE function is similar to the MOVE function; it changes the position of the application window. The action of this function is equivalent to dragging the application window's title bar or choosing Move from the application-window Control menu.

The APP.MOVE function takes the form

=APP.MOVE(*x,y*)

where the *x* and *y* arguments represent the desired horizontal and vertical positions of the upper left corner of the window relative to the top and left edges of the screen. These arguments are expressed in points, a unit of measurement equivalent to $1/72$ of an inch.

The APP.MINIMIZE, APP.MAXIMIZE, and APP.RESTORE functions

The APP.MINIMIZE function reduces an application window to an icon. Its action is equivalent to choosing the Minimize command from the application-window

Control menu or clicking on the Minimize icon. The APP.MINIMIZE function takes no arguments.

The APP.MAXIMIZE function maximizes the size of an application window. Its action is equivalent to choosing the Maximize command from the application-window Control menu or clicking on the Maximize icon. The APP.MAXIMIZE function takes no arguments.

The APP.RESTORE function restores the size of the application window to it previous size after using the Maximize or Minimize command. Its action is equivalent to choosing the Restore command from the application-window Control menu or pressing Alt-F5. The APP.RESTORE function takes no arguments.

The SHOW.CLIPBOARD function

The SHOW.CLIPBOARD function displays the Microsoft Windows Clipboard. Its action is equivalent to choosing the Run command on the Microsoft Excel application's Control menu and selecting Clipboard from the Run Application dialog box. To close the Clipboard, use the macro function CLOSE.

You can also activate the Clipboard window by using the APP.ACTIVATE function or the EXEC function. Microsoft Excel included SHOW.CLIPBOARD to make Microsoft Excel macros written for the PC compatible with Microsoft Excel macros written for the Macintosh.

Navigational functions

The following functions help you move around in the worksheet, scroll windows, and make selections.

The VLINE, VPAGE, and VSCROLL functions

VLINE, VPAGE, and VSCROLL scroll vertically through a worksheet. They change your view of the worksheet but do not change the active cell. These functions take the forms

=VLINE(*rows*)

and

=VPAGE(*screens*)

and

=VSCROLL(*position,logical*)

The action of VLINE is equivalent to clicking the scroll arrows in the vertical scroll bar or pressing the Scroll key and then using the Up and Down arrow keys. The *rows* argument is a numeric value that controls how many rows you scroll. To scroll toward the bottom of the worksheet, use a positive *rows* value; to scroll toward the top of the worksheet, use a negative *rows* value.

For example, if cells A1:F19 are currently in view, the statement

=VLINE(5)

scrolls the window down five lines so that cells A6:F24 are in view. If rows A20:F38 are currently in view, the statement

=VLINE(–5)

scrolls the window to bring cells A15:F33 into view.

The action of VPAGE is equivalent to clicking in the gray area of the scroll bar or pressing the Scroll key and then PgUp or PgDn to bring a new screenful of information into view. As with VLINE, the *screens* argument tells Microsoft Excel how many pages to scroll and whether to scroll toward the top or the bottom of the worksheet. To scroll toward the bottom of the worksheet, use a positive *screens* value; to scroll toward the top of the worksheet, use a negative *screens* value.

For example, the statement

=VPAGE(1)

scrolls one page down through the worksheet and the statement

=VPAGE(–1)

brings the previous screenful of information into view.

As when you click in the scroll bar or press PgUp or PgDn, the actual distance you move depends on the size of the active window. If the current window is 20 rows deep, then the statement

=VPAGE(1)

scrolls the next 20 rows into view. If the window is only 10 rows deep, however, the same statement scrolls only the next 10 rows into view.

The action of VSCROLL is equivalent to dragging the vertical scroll box to position the window over the desired cells in the worksheet. You can type a row number as the *position* argument to this function or you can use a percentage or formula to represent the relative position of the rows you want to view.

The *logical* argument is a logical value that determines what type of *position* argument you're using. If *logical* is TRUE, Microsoft Excel scrolls to the row specified in the function. If *logical* is FALSE or omitted, Microsoft Excel scrolls to the row represented by the percentage in the *position* argument. When *logical* is FALSE, the *position* argument 0 represents row 1, or 0% of the entire worksheet; the *position* argument 1 represents row 16384, or 100% of the worksheet.

For example, the following statements all tell Microsoft Excel to scroll to row 4096 of the 16384-row worksheet (one quarter of the way down the worksheet):

```
=VSCROLL(4096,TRUE)
=VSCROLL(.25,FALSE)
=VSCROLL(25%,FALSE)
=VSCROLL(4096/16384)
```

The HLINE, HPAGE, and HSCROLL functions

The HLINE, HPAGE, and HSCROLL functions scroll horizontally through a worksheet. They are similar to VLINE, VPAGE, and VSCROLL. These functions change your view of the worksheet but do not change the active cell. They take the forms

=HLINE(*columns*)

and

=HPAGE(*screens*)

and

=HSCROLL(*position,logical*)

As with VLINE and VPAGE, the arguments of the HLINE and HPAGE functions are numbers that tell Microsoft Excel how many columns or screens to scroll and in which direction. For example, if columns A through F are currently visible on your screen, the statement

=HLINE(3)

scrolls the window three columns to the right so that columns D through I are in view. Similarly, the statement

=HPAGE(2)

brings columns M through R into view.

Like VSCROLL, the HSCROLL function can take a column value, a percentage, or a formula. For example, the statements

```
=HSCROLL(64,TRUE)
=HSCROLL(.25,FALSE)
=HSCROLL(25%,FALSE)
=HSCROLL(64/256)
```

all scroll column BL of the worksheet into view. The *position* argument must be a number. Microsoft Excel does not accept column letters as arguments to the HSCROLL function.

The SELECT function

The SELECT function has two forms, one for a worksheet or macro sheet and another for a chart. We'll discuss the form for a chart later in this chapter; here, we'll discuss the form that applies to worksheets and macro sheets.

The SELECT function for a worksheet or macro sheet selects a cell or range. It takes the form

=SELECT(*selection,active cell*)

The *selection* argument represents the cell or range you want to select. If you're selecting a range, you can use the *active cell* argument to determine which cell is active within that range.

You can enter the *selection* and *active cell* arguments in two ways: as absolute references to the active worksheet, such as !A4:A7 or !Total, or as R1C1-style relative references in the form of text, such as "R[1]C[1]:R[–1]C[–1]". Use the R1C1 style when you need to make a selection relative to the current active cell in the worksheet or macro sheet. In the R1C1 style, the *active cell* argument determines the active cell's position relative to the selected range.

For example, if you want to select the range B5:B10 from within a macro, you can use the statement

=SELECT(!B5:B10,!B10)

No matter where the active cell is located when this instruction is executed, the function selects cells B5:B10 in the active worksheet and activates cell B10.

Now suppose cell A1 is the active cell and you want to select the range one column to the right that begins four rows below the active cell and ends nine rows below the active cell. If cell A1 is the current active cell and you want the last cell in that range to become the active cell, you would use the statement

=SELECT("R[4]C[1]:R[9]C[1]","R[5]C[0]")

Like the statement above, this instruction selects cells B5:B10 and activates cell B10. However, if cell C5 is the active cell when this instruction is executed, Microsoft Excel will select cells D9:D14 and activate cell D14.

If you omit the *selection* argument, SELECT won't change the current range selection but will activate the cell you specify in the *active cell* argument. (Be sure the *active cell* value lies within *selection*.) If you omit the *active cell* argument, SELECT activates the cell in the upper left corner of the *selection* range.

The SELECT.LAST.CELL function

The SELECT.LAST.CELL function selects the last cell in the active area of the worksheet. Its action is equivalent to pressing Ctrl-End. The SELECT.LAST.CELL function takes no arguments.

For example, if your worksheet is 26 columns wide and 100 rows deep, the SELECT.LAST.CELL function selects the cell at the intersection of column Z and row 100: cell Z100.

The SELECT.END function

The SELECT.END function moves the active cell to the edge of the next block of entries in your worksheet or macro sheet. Its action is equivalent to pressing the Ctrl key in conjunction with one of the arrow keys.

The SELECT.END function takes the form

=SELECT.END(*direction*)

The *direction* argument is a numeric code that specifies the direction in which to move the active cell:

Code	Direction	Keyboard equivalent
1	Left	Ctrl-Left arrow
2	Right	Ctrl-Right arrow
3	Up	Ctrl-Up arrow
4	Down	Ctrl-Down arrow

The SHOW.ACTIVE.CELL function

The SHOW.ACTIVE.CELL function brings the active cell into view. Its action is equivalent to pressing Ctrl-Backspace. When you're using a macro to work in a remote area of your worksheet, this function offers a handy way to bring the active cell back into view in the current window. The SHOW.ACTIVE.CELL function takes no arguments.

The UNLOCKED.NEXT and UNLOCKED.PREV functions

The UNLOCKED.NEXT and UNLOCKED.PREV functions select either the next or the previous unlocked cell in a protected worksheet. Their actions are equivalent to pressing Tab or Shift-Tab. The UNLOCKED.NEXT and UNLOCKED.PREV functions take no arguments.

Printing functions

The next seven Microsoft Excel functions carry out printing commands without opening a menu.

The PAGE.SETUP function

The PAGE.SETUP function defines print parameters such as header, footer, margins, and so on. It is equivalent to the Page Setup command on the File menu.

   If you're printing a worksheet or macro sheet, the PAGE.SETUP function takes the form

   =PAGE.SETUP("*header*","*footer*",*left,right,top,bottom,headings,gridlines*)

The *header* and *footer* arguments are optional text values that define the header and footer you want to include in the report, if any. Both arguments must be enclosed in quotation marks. You can include the special header and footer symbols you learned about in Chapter 9 in these strings. The *left*, *right*, *top*, and *bottom* arguments are numbers that describe, in inches, the left, right, top, and bottom margins you want to use for the document. The *headings* and *gridlines* arguments are logical values that determine whether headings and gridlines are included in the printed report. If these arguments are TRUE, headings and gridlines are included.

   If you're printing a chart, the PAGE.SETUP function takes the form

   =PAGE.SETUP("*header*","*footer*",*left,right,top,bottom,size*)

The first six arguments in this function are identical to the arguments described above. The *size* argument is a number that indicates whether the chart is to be printed screen size (1), fit to page (2), or full page (3).

The PRINTER.SETUP function

The PRINTER.SETUP function selects a printer. It is equivalent to the Printer Setup command on the File menu.

   The PRINTER.SETUP function takes the form

   =PRINTER.SETUP("*printer*")

Because the name of the printer is entered as text, it must be enclosed in quotation marks. For example, the statement

   =PRINTER.SETUP("Epson FX-80 on LPT1:")

changes the printer to an Epson FX-80 on LPT1. To ensure that the printer name is entered correctly, it's easiest to use the recorder to enter this function into your macro sheet.

The PRINT function

The PRINT function sends your document to the printer. It is equivalent to the Print command on the File menu.

The PRINT function takes the form

=PRINT(*range,from,to,copies,draft,preview,parts*)

where *range* is a code: 1 for all pages, 2 for a subset of pages. The *from* and *to* arguments specify the starting and ending pages to print. These arguments are ignored unless *range* is 2.

The *copies* argument tells Microsoft Excel how many copies of the selected pages you want printed. The *draft* argument is a logical value which, if TRUE, tells Microsoft Excel to print in draft quality. The *preview* argument is a logical value that, if TRUE, lets you preview the material before printing. Finally, the *parts* argument tells Microsoft Excel which elements to print in a worksheet or macro sheet: 1 for a sheet, 2 for notes, and 3 for both sheet and notes.

The SET.PRINT.AREA and SET.PRINT.TITLES functions

The SET.PRINT.AREA function defines the range of cells to print. It is equivalent to the Set Print Area command on the Options menu. The SET.PRINT.TITLES function creates print titles in your documents. It is equivalent to the Set Print Titles command on the Options menu.

Neither of these functions takes an argument. You'll usually use a SELECT statement to select the range you want to work with before you use the SET.PRINT.AREA or SET.PRINT.TITLES function.

The SET.PAGE.BREAK and REMOVE.PAGE.BREAK functions

The SET.PAGE.BREAK and REMOVE.PAGE.BREAK functions create and delete page breaks in your documents. They are the equivalents of the Set Page Break and Remove Page Break commands on the Options menu.

Neither SET.PAGE.BREAK nor REMOVE.PAGE.BREAK takes an argument. You'll usually use a SELECT statement to select the place where you want the page break inserted or removed before you use these functions. For example, the statements

```
=SELECT(!F10)
=SET.PAGE.BREAK()
```

create page breaks between columns E and F and between rows 9 and 10. The statements

```
=SELECT(!F10)
=REMOVE.PAGE.BREAK()
```

remove that page break.

Edit menu functions

The 12 command-equivalent functions in this section allow you to automate the commands on Microsoft Excel's Edit menu.

The UNDO function

The UNDO function reverses the effects of the previous command. It is equivalent to the Undo command on the Edit menu. The UNDO function takes no arguments.

The CUT function

The CUT function lets you move the contents of a cell or range to another location via the Clipboard. It is equivalent to the Cut command on the Edit menu.

The CUT function takes no arguments. You'll use CUT in conjunction with a SELECT statement or some other cell-selection function, such as FORMULA.GOTO. For example, to cut the range A1:A5 you might use the statements

```
=SELECT(!A1:A5)
=CUT()
```

If you had previously used the Define Name command to assign the name *Totals* to cells A1:A5, you could also use the statements

```
=FORMULA.GOTO("Totals")
=CUT()
```

to accomplish the same purpose. After you've used the CUT function, you'll need to use the PASTE or PASTE.SPECIAL function to paste the contents of the cut range elsewhere in the document.

As with the Cut command, the range you select for the CUT function must be a single rectangular range. You can't use multiple discontinuous cell ranges with this function.

The COPY function

The COPY function lets you copy the contents of a cell or range to other locations via the Clipboard. It is equivalent to the Copy command on the Edit menu.

Like the CUT function, the COPY function takes no arguments. You'll use COPY in conjunction with a SELECT statement or some other cell-selection function, such as FORMULA.GOTO. For example, you might use the statements

```
=SELECT(!A1:A5)
=COPY()
```

to copy the contents of cells A1:A5.

After you've used the COPY function, you'll need to use the PASTE or PASTE.SPECIAL function to paste the contents of the copy range elsewhere in the document.

The CANCEL.COPY function

The CANCEL.COPY function clears the marquee after you copy or cut a cell or range. Its action is equivalent to pressing the Esc key. The CANCEL.COPY function takes no arguments.

The COPY.PICTURE function

The COPY.PICTURE function copies the selected range onto the Clipboard as a picture. Its action is equivalent to holding down the Shift key while you choose the Copy command from the Edit menu.

The COPY.PICTURE function takes the form

=COPY.PICTURE(*appearance,size*)

The *appearance* argument indicates whether you want to copy the picture as it appears on the screen (1) or as it will appear when printed (2).

The *size* argument applies only to charts. If you want to copy the picture in the size it appears on the screen, use 1. If you want to copy the picture in the size it will appear when printed, use 2.

The PASTE function

The PASTE function places the contents of the Clipboard in another location. It is equivalent to the Paste command on the Edit menu.

Like CUT and COPY, the PASTE function takes no arguments. You'll use PASTE in conjunction with a CUT or COPY statement and a SELECT statement or some other cell-selection function, such as FORMULA.GOTO. For example, you could use the statements

```
=SELECT(!A1:A5)
=CUT()
=SELECT(!B1)
=PASTE()
```

to cut the contents of cells A1:A5 and paste them into the range B1:B5.

The PASTE.LINK function

The PASTE.LINK function pastes data from a supporting document into the active document and creates a link between the two documents. It is equivalent to the Paste Link command on the Edit menu.

The PASTE.LINK function takes no arguments. You'll use it in conjunction with the COPY function. For example, the statements

```
=ACTIVATE("Sheet1")
=SELECT(!A1)
=COPY()
=ACTIVATE("Sheet2")
=SELECT(!B1)
=PASTE.LINK()
```

instruct Microsoft Excel to select cell A1 in the worksheet Sheet1, issue the Copy command, activate Sheet2, select cell B1, and enter the linked reference

```
=Sheet1!A1
```

The PASTE.SPECIAL function

The PASTE.SPECIAL function is equivalent to the Paste Special command on the Edit menu. It has three different forms, depending on whether you're using it in a worksheet or a chart. We'll cover only the first form here and look at the other two when we examine the charting functions later in this chapter.

If you're working in a worksheet, the PASTE.SPECIAL function pastes the contents of the cut or copied cells into the selected paste range using certain special parameters. This PASTE.SPECIAL function takes the form

```
=PASTE.SPECIAL(parts,operation,skip,transpose)
```

The *parts* argument is a numeric code that tells Microsoft Excel what you want to paste into the selected range:

Code	Part pasted
1	All
2	Formulas only
3	Values only
4	Formats only
5	Notes only

The *operation* argument describes how you want the contents of the copied cells to interact with any existing contents of the selected paste range:

Code	Operation
1	None
2	Add
3	Subtract
4	Multiply
5	Divide

The *skip* argument is a logical value that indicates whether you want to skip blank cells when you paste. The *transpose* argument, also a logical value, lets you switch the orientation of the data when you paste.

These two arguments correspond to the check boxes in the PASTE.SPECIAL dialog box. To select the option, use a logical value of TRUE.

The CLEAR function

The CLEAR function erases the contents, the formats, the notes, or all three from the selected cells in the worksheet. It is equivalent to the Clear command on the Edit menu.

The CLEAR function takes the form

=CLEAR(*parts*)

where *parts* is a numeric code representing the part of the selected entries you want to delete:

Code	Part deleted
1	All
2	Formats only
3	Formulas only
4	Notes only

For example, the statements

=SELECT(!A1:C10)
=CLEAR(1)

clear all parts of the entries in cells A1:C10 in the active worksheet. If you omit the *parts* argument, it is assumed to be 3.

The EDIT.DELETE function

The EDIT.DELETE function deletes the current selection from the worksheet. It is equivalent to the Delete command on the worksheet Edit menu.

The EDIT.DELETE function takes the form

=EDIT.DELETE(*direction*)

where *direction* is a number that tells in which direction you want to shift the cells in the worksheet to fill the space left by the deletion. If *direction* is 1, Microsoft Excel shifts cells left; if *direction* is 2, Microsoft Excel shifts cells up. For example, the statements

=SELECT(!1:3)
=EDIT.DELETE(2)

delete rows 1, 2, and 3 from the worksheet and shift the remaining rows up to fill in the space.

If you omit *direction*, Microsoft Excel guesses at the direction in which it should shift the cells, based on the range you select. For instance, the statements

```
=SELECT(!A1:E1)
=EDIT.DELETE ()
```

select the range A1:E1 for deletion and, because this range is wider than it is tall, shift the remaining cells up.

The INSERT function

The INSERT function inserts cells into a worksheet. It is equivalent to the Insert command on the worksheet Edit menu.

The INSERT function takes the form

```
=INSERT(direction)
```

where *direction* is a number that tells in which direction you want Microsoft Excel to shift the cells in the worksheet when it inserts new cells. If *direction* is 1, Microsoft Excel shifts cells right; if *direction* is 2, Microsoft Excel shifts cells down.

For example, the statements

```
=SELECT("R3")
=INSERT(2)
```

insert a blank row above row 3 of the worksheet and shift the old row 3 and the rows below it down.

If you omit *direction*, Microsoft Excel guesses at the direction in which it should shift the cells, based on the range you select. For instance, the statements

```
=SELECT(!A1:A10)
=INSERT()
```

select the range A1:A10 and, because this range is taller than it is wide, insert new cells to the left of the range, shifting the original cells to the right.

The FILL.RIGHT, FILL.LEFT, FILL.DOWN, and FILL.UP functions

The FILL.RIGHT, FILL.LEFT, FILL.DOWN, and FILL.UP functions copy an entry across, down, or up several adjacent cells. They are the equivalents of the Fill Right, Fill Left, Fill Down, and Fill Up commands on the Edit menu.

None of these functions takes an argument. You'll usually use them in conjunction with a SELECT statement. For example, the statements

```
=SELECT(!F3:F6)
=FILL.DOWN()
```

copy the entry from F3 (the first cell in the selected range) into cells F4, F5, and F6.

Formula menu functions

The 12 functions in this section allow you to automate the commands on Microsoft Excel's Formula menu.

The DEFINE.NAME function

The DEFINE.NAME function lets you name cells, ranges, formulas, and values in your worksheets and macro sheets. It is equivalent to the Define Name command on the Formula menu.

The DEFINE.NAME function takes the form

=DEFINE.NAME("*name*",*refers to,type,key*)

The *name* argument represents the name you want to define and must be a text string enclosed in quotation marks. The *refers to* argument is the cell or range reference, formula, or value to which you want to assign the name. If *refers to* is an external reference to the active worksheet, such as !A1:C10, Microsoft Excel assigns the specified name to the cells identified by that reference. If *refers to* defines a formula, that formula must be in text form and, if the formula contains references, those references must be in R1C1 form. (When you're recording a macro and you refer to a formula that contains A1-style references, Microsoft Excel converts the references to R1C1 style.)

The *type* and *key* arguments apply only in a macro sheet. The *type* argument is a numeric code defining the item being named: 1 for function, 2 for command, and 3 for none (if *name* doesn't refer to a macro). If *type* is omitted, Microsoft Excel assumes it to be 3. The *key* argument is a single letter that defines the Ctrl-key equivalent you want to assign to the name, if any.

For example, the statement

=DEFINE.NAME("Test",100)

creates the name *Test* in the active worksheet and assigns that name to the value 100. The statement

=DEFINE.NAME("Test",!A1:A10)

creates the name *Test* in the active worksheet and applies that name to cells A1:A10. The statement

    =DEFINE.NAME("Test","=R1C1+100")

assigns the name *Test* to the formula

    =R1C1+100

If you omit the *refers to* argument, Microsoft Excel assigns the indicated name to the currently selected cells. For example, the statements

    =SELECT(!A1:A10)
    =DEFINE.NAME("Test")

assign the name *Test* to the range A1:A10 in the active worksheet.

The DEFINE.NAME function creates the specified name in the active worksheet or macro sheet. You can't create a name in a sheet other than the active sheet. However, you can use a statement like

    =DEFINE.NAME("Test",Sheet2!A1)

to create a remote reference to a cell in another worksheet. This formula creates the name *Test* in the active worksheet, not in Sheet2, and assigns that name to the formula

    =Sheet2!A1

The LIST.NAMES function

The LIST.NAMES function creates a list of all the named cells, ranges, values, and formulas in your worksheet or macro sheet. Its action is equivalent to choosing the Paste List option in the Paste Name dialog box. The LIST.NAMES function takes no arguments.

Before you use this function, be sure to select an empty region of your document large enough to accommodate the list. Otherwise, Microsoft Excel will overwrite any existing data in that region. When you use the LIST.NAMES function in a worksheet, the list will occupy a range two columns wide; when you use the function in a macro sheet, the list will occupy a range four columns wide. (The worksheet listing contains each name and its definition. The macro listing contains each name, its definition, 1 for a function macro or 2 for a command macro, and the short-cut key, if any.) Of course, the depth of the range varies, depending on the number of names defined in the active worksheet.

The DELETE.NAME function

The DELETE.NAME function removes the specified name from the list of names defined for the active worksheet or macro sheet. Its action is equivalent to selecting the Delete button in the Define Name dialog box.

The DELETE.NAME function takes the form

=DELETE.NAME("*name*")

where *name* is the name you want to delete and must be a text string enclosed in quotation marks. Microsoft Excel assumes *name* is defined in the active worksheet or macro sheet.

The CREATE.NAMES function

The CREATE.NAMES function uses the labels in the top or bottom row or left or right column of a selected range as names for the cells in adjacent rows or columns. This function is equivalent to the Create Names command on the worksheet Formula menu.

The CREATE.NAMES function takes the form

=CREATE.NAMES(*top,left,bottom,right*)

where *top*, *left*, *bottom*, and *right* are logical values. If *top* is TRUE, Microsoft Excel uses the labels in the top row of the selected range as names for the other cells in the range. If *left* is TRUE, Microsoft Excel uses the labels in the left column of the selected range. If *bottom* is TRUE, Microsoft Excel uses the labels in the bottom row of the selected range. Finally, if right is TRUE, Microsoft Excel uses the labels in the right column of the selected range.

If you omit all four arguments and you've selected more than one column, Microsoft Excel assumes the *left* argument is TRUE and uses the labels in the left column. If you omit all four arguments and you've selected more than one row, Microsoft Excel assumes the *top* argument is TRUE and uses the labels in the top row of the selected range.

The APPLY.NAMES function

The APPLY.NAMES function tells Microsoft Excel to search for a name definition in a formula array and replace the definition with the name. It is equivalent to the Apply Names command on the Formula menu.

The APPLY.NAMES function takes the form

=APPLY.NAMES(*name array,ignore,use row/col,omit col,omit row,order,append*)

The *name array* argument represents the names you want to apply. You must enter these names as text strings in array form; each string within the array must be enclosed in quotation marks. The *ignore* argument is a logical value that tells Microsoft Excel whether to ignore relative and absolute references. If this argument is TRUE, the program ignores reference type in the formula. The *use row/col* argument is a logical value that tells Microsoft Excel whether to use row and column names. If this argument is FALSE, Microsoft Excel ignores the next two arguments. The *omit col* and *omit row* arguments are logical values that correspond to the Omit Column Name if Same Column and Omit Row Name if Same Row check boxes. The *order* argument tells Microsoft Excel which name to list first: 1 for the Row Column option, 2 for the Column Row option. Finally, the *append* argument is a logical value which, if TRUE, replaces the name definitions in the name array and also replaces the definition most recently created by the Define Name or Create Names command. If *append* is FALSE, Microsoft Excel replaces the name definitions in the name array only.

For example, the statement

=APPLY.NAMES({"Sum", "Test", "Total"}, TRUE, TRUE, TRUE, TRUE, 1, FALSE)

searches for all occurrences of the formulas that define Sum, Test, and Total and applies those names to them.

The NOTE function

The NOTE function adds or edits notes attached to cells. It is equivalent to the Note command on the Formula menu.

The NOTE function takes the form

=NOTE(*text,reference,start,count*)

The *text* argument, which can be as many as 255 characters, must be enclosed in quotation marks. The *reference* argument tells Microsoft Excel which cell you want to work with. If you omit this argument, Microsoft Excel assumes you want to work with the current active cell. The *start* argument determines at which character the change begins. If you omit *start*, Microsoft Excel assumes you want to start at the beginning of the note. The *count* argument determines how many characters to replace. If you omit *count*, Microsoft Excel assumes you want to replace the remainder of the note—that is, all the characters from *start* to the end of the existing note. If you omit both *start* and *count*, the entire note will be replaced.

For example, to add a note saying *Call about car insurance in June* to cell G477 in a worksheet, use the statement

=NOTE("Call about car insurance in June",G477,1)

Later, after the note has expired, delete it with the statement

=NOTE(,G477,1)

The FORMULA.GOTO function

The FORMULA.GOTO function moves directly to the specified cell in your worksheet or macro sheet. Its action is equivalent to choosing the Goto command from the Formula menu or pressing F5.

The FORMULA.GOTO function takes the form

=FORMULA.GOTO(*reference*)

The *reference* argument is the destination cell. This argument can be an external reference to a worksheet or another macro sheet. To select a cell in the current worksheet, you must precede the name or reference of the cell with an exclamation point. To select a cell in another worksheet, *reference* must include the name of that worksheet, followed by an exclamation point, and then the name or reference of the destination cell.

For example, the statement

=FORMULA.GOTO(!$A$1)

selects cell A1 in the current worksheet and the statement

=FORMULA.GOTO(SHEET2.XLS!$A$10)

selects cell A10 in Sheet2.

The *reference* argument can also be stated in R1C1 form in quotation marks, even if you're using the A1 cell-referencing convention. For example, the statement

=FORMULA.GOTO("SHEET2.XLS!R2C2")

selects cell B2 in Sheet2.

To return to the cell or range that was active before Microsoft Excel carried out your last FORMULA.GOTO instruction, simply enter a second FORMULA.GOTO statement with no reference argument.

The FORMULA.FIND, FORMULA.FIND.NEXT, and FORMULA.FIND.PREV functions

The FORMULA.FIND function searches for a specified text string throughout the worksheet or macro sheet. It is equivalent to the Find command on the worksheet Formula menu.

The FORMULA.FIND function takes the form

=FORMULA.FIND("*find text*",*look in*,*look at*,*look by*,*direction*) where *find text* is the string you want to search for and must be enclosed in quotation marks. You can use wildcard characters in the *find text* argument to find strings that may vary in content. For example, if the names *Jensen* and *Jansen* appear in your worksheet, you can use the *find text* argument *J?nsen* to find both entries. The ? wildcard represents a single character; the * character represents any sequence of characters. To enter literal * and ? characters, type ~* and ~?.

The *look in, look at,* and *look by* arguments are numeric codes that specify the parameters for the search. Use the *look in* argument to indicate whether you want Microsoft Excel to locate the text string in the worksheet formulas, displayed values, or cell notes:

Code	Search area
1	Formulas
2	Values
3	Notes

The *look at* argument indicates whether you want to use the Whole option or the Part option. If *look at* is 1, Microsoft Excel looks for exact matches between *find text* and the contents of the worksheet cells; if *look at* is 2, Microsoft Excel looks for any entry that contains *find text*. The *look by* argument controls the direction of the search: 1 to search by rows, 2 to search by columns.

The *direction* argument tells Microsoft Excel in which direction to search: 1 for Next, 2 for Previous. If *direction* is omitted, it is assumed to be 1.

For example, the statement

=FORMULA.FIND("=A1",1,2,1)

looks for the *find text* argument *=A1* in the contents of the cells of the active worksheet. Microsoft Excel finds any formula that includes *=A1*. The search is conducted by rows. If Microsoft Excel finds the string, it selects the cell that contains the string and moves on to the next line in the macro. If it can't find the string, it displays an alert box telling you so and doesn't proceed with the next line in the macro until you select OK.

When you use the FORMULA.FIND.NEXT and FORMULA.FIND.PREV functions after you've used the FORMULA.FIND function, Microsoft Excel searches for the next occurrence, or the previous occurrence, of *find text*. These functions are the macro equivalents of the F7 and Shift-F7 keyboard commands. They take no arguments.

For example, the statements

=FORMULA.FIND("=A1",1,2,1)
=FORMULA.FIND.NEXT()

cause Microsoft Excel to look for the *find text* argument =*A1* in the contents of the cells of the active worksheet. When Microsoft Excel has found the first occurrence, it selects the cell containing the value and moves on to the second line of the macro, which causes the program to search for the next occurrence.

The FORMULA.REPLACE function

The FORMULA.REPLACE function finds text in a formula or a cell and replaces it. This function is equivalent to the Replace command on the Formula menu.

The form of the FORMULA.REPLACE function is

=FORMULA.REPLACE(*"find text","replace text",look at,look by,current cell*)

where *find text* is the string you want to search for and *replace text* is the string you want to substitute. Both of these arguments must be enclosed in quotation marks. As with FORMULA.FIND, you can use the wildcard characters ? and * in the *find text* argument.

The *look at* and *look by* arguments are numeric codes that specify the parameters for the search. If *look at* is 1, Microsoft Excel looks for exact matches between *find text* and the contents of the worksheet cells; if *look at* is 2, Microsoft Excel looks for any entry that contains *find text*. The *look by* argument controls the direction of the search: 1 to search by rows, 2 to search by columns.

The *current cell* argument is a logical value that tells Microsoft Excel where to put the replacement text. If *current cell* is TRUE, Microsoft Excel puts *replace text* in the current cell only. If *current cell* is FALSE or omitted, Microsoft Excel puts *replace text* in every matching cell in the range you've selected. If you've selected a single cell, a FALSE or omitted *current cell* argument causes Microsoft Excel to put *replace text* in every matching cell in the worksheet.

For example, the statement

=FORMULA.REPLACE("Sales","Gross Sales")

replaces the string *Sales* with *Gross Sales* throughout a worksheet if you've selected a single cell, or throughout a selection if you've selected a range.

The SELECT.SPECIAL function

The SELECT.SPECIAL function selects cells that have specific characteristics. It is equivalent to the Select Special command on the Formula menu.

The SELECT.SPECIAL function takes the form

=SELECT.SPECIAL(*type,value,levels*)

where *type* is a numeric code describing what you want to select, as shown in the table at the top of page 548.

Code	Selection
1	Notes
2	Constants
3	Formulas
4	Blanks
5	Current region
6	Current array
7	Row differences
8	Column differences
9	Precedents
10	Dependents

The *value* argument, which is optional, applies only to *type* arguments 2 and 3. This argument tells Microsoft Excel what type of value to select:

Code	Value type
1	Numbers
2	Text
4	Logicals
16	Error

These codes can be added to specify more than one data type; that is, the code 3 will cause Microsoft Excel to select both numbers and text.

The *levels* argument, which is also optional, applies only to *type* arguments 9 and 10. A *level* argument of 1 selects the Direct Only option; 2 selects the All Levels option.

For example, the statement

=SELECT.SPECIAL(2,1)

selects all cells in the worksheet that contain constant numeric values.

Worksheet and cell formatting functions

These Microsoft Excel functions let you format worksheets and cells without opening a menu.

The FORMAT.NUMBER function

The FORMAT.NUMBER function lets you assign a numeric format to any cell in the worksheet. It is equivalent to the Number command on the Format menu.

The FORMAT.NUMBER function takes the form

=FORMAT.NUMBER("*format*")

where *format* is a text string representing the format you want to assign to the selected range. The *format* argument can be any one of Microsoft Excel's 21 built-in formats or it can be a user-defined format. The argument must be enclosed in quotation marks.

For example, the statements

=SELECT(A1:C10)
=FORMAT.NUMBER("0%")

assign the built-in 0% format to cells A1:C10 and the statements

=SELECT(A1:C10)
=FORMAT.NUMBER("0.000%")

create a new format, 0.000%, and assign it to the range A1:C10.

The DELETE.FORMAT function

The DELETE.FORMAT function lets you delete your own custom formats. Its action is equivalent to choosing the Delete button in the Number dialog box. (You can't delete Microsoft Excel's 21 built-in formats.)

The DELETE.FORMAT function takes the form

=DELETE.FORMAT("*format name*")

where *format name* is the exact name of your custom format. For example, if you created the custom format $#,##0.000, you can use the statement

=DELETE.FORMAT("$#,##0.000")

to delete that format.

The ALIGNMENT function

The ALIGNMENT function lets you change the alignment of the entries in the selected range in the worksheet. It is equivalent to the Alignment command on the worksheet Format menu.

The ALIGNMENT function takes the form

=ALIGNMENT(*type*)

where *type* is a numeric code that defines the alignment you want to assign to the selected range, as shown in the table at the top of page 550.

Code	Alignment
1	General
2	Left
3	Center
4	Right
5	Fill

For example, the statements

=SELECT(A1:C10)
=ALIGNMENT(2)

left-align all the entries in the range A1:C10.

The STYLE function

The STYLE function is included for compatibility with Microsoft Excel macros written for the Macintosh. STYLE controls the use of bold and italic type in the worksheet. To change a font to bold or italic with Microsoft Excel for the PC, use FORMAT.FONT or REPLACE.FONT.

The STYLE function takes the form

=STYLE(*bold,italic*)

where *bold* and *italic* are logical values that tell Microsoft Excel which style options you want to turn on or off. If the argument is TRUE, the specified option is activated; if the argument is FALSE, the option is deactivated.

The BORDER function

The BORDER function adds borders or shading to the selected cell or range. It is equivalent to the Border command on the Format menu.

The BORDER function takes the form

=BORDER(*outline,left,right,top,bottom,shade*)

All the arguments are logical values that tell Microsoft Excel which Border options you want to use. If an argument is TRUE, that option is selected. If an argument is FALSE or omitted, that option is deselected.

For example, the statement

=BORDER(,TRUE)

draws a border line at the left edge of every cell in the selected range and the statement

=BORDER(TRUE)

outlines the selected range.

The COLUMN.WIDTH function

The COLUMN.WIDTH function lets you change the widths of selected columns in your worksheet or macro sheet. It is equivalent to the Column Width command on the Format menu.

The COLUMN.WIDTH function takes the form

=COLUMN.WIDTH(*width,reference*)

where *width* is the new width you want to assign to the columns specified by *reference*. The *reference* argument must be either an external reference to the active worksheet, such as !A:C, or a string in R1C1 form. If you omit *reference*, Microsoft Excel adjusts the columns in the current selection.

For example, the statement

=COLUMN.WIDTH(15,!A:C)

changes the widths of columns A, B, and C in the active worksheet to 15. If A1 is the active cell, the statement

=COLUMN.WIDTH(25,"C:C[+3]")

changes the widths of columns A, B, C, and D to 25.

When you're recording a macro and use the mouse to drag across the column border, Microsoft Excel records the *reference* argument as text in R1C1 style.

The ROW.HEIGHT function

The ROW.HEIGHT function changes the height of selected rows in your worksheet or macro sheet. It is equivalent to the Row Height command on the Format menu.

The ROW.HEIGHT function takes the form

=ROW.HEIGHT(*height,reference,default height*)

where the *height* argument tells Microsoft Excel how high you want the rows to be. If you omit *height*, Microsoft Excel sets the rows to the standard height. The *reference* argument identifies the rows to be changed and must be either an external reference to the active worksheet or an R1C1-style text reference. If you omit *reference*, Microsoft Excel changes the row height in the current selection. The *default height* argument is a logical value. If TRUE, *default height* causes Microsoft Excel to set the row height according to the height of the fonts used in those rows.

When you're recording a macro and use the mouse to drag across the row border, Microsoft Excel records the reference in R1C1 style.

The JUSTIFY function

The JUSTIFY function arranges the text in each cell of the selected range so that it is approximately the same width. This function is equivalent to the Justify command on the Format menu. The JUSTIFY function takes no arguments.

For example, suppose cell A1 in your worksheet contains the label *The rain in Spain falls mainly on the plain, except when it falls elsewhere.* The statements

```
=SELECT(!A1:A4)
=COLUMN.WIDTH(20)
=JUSTIFY()
```

select cells A1:A4, set the width of column A to 20 characters, and distribute the label in cell A1 into cells A1:A4, like this:

```
The rain in Spain falls
mainly on the plain,
except when it falls
elsewhere.
```

The A1.R1C1 function

The A1.R1C1 function changes Microsoft Excel's method of referencing cells from the A1 method to the R1C1 method or vice versa. The action of this function is equivalent to choosing the Workspace command from the Options menu and selecting the R1C1 check box.

The A1.R1C1 function takes the form

=A1.R1C1(*logical*)

If *logical* is TRUE, the function activates the R1C1 option. If *logical* is FALSE, the function deactivates the R1C1 option.

The PRECISION function

The PRECISION function controls what form of a value is used in calculations. Its action is equivalent to choosing the Calculation command from the Options menu and selecting the Precision as Displayed check box.

The PRECISION function takes the form

=PRECISION(*logical*)

If *logical* is TRUE, Microsoft Excel uses worksheet values with full precision in calculations. If *logical* is FALSE, Microsoft Excel uses worksheet values with the displayed precision only.

The FORMAT.FONT function

The FORMAT.FONT function lets you select, from the four current fonts, the font and type size that Microsoft Excel uses to display the contents of a worksheet or chart. It is equivalent to the Font command on the Format menu.

The FORMAT.FONT function has two forms: one for worksheets and another for charts. We'll discuss the form for charts later in this chapter. The worksheet and macro-sheet version of the FORMAT.FONT function takes the form

=FONT("*name*",*size*,*bold*,*italic*,*underline*,*strike*)

where *name* is the name of the font you want to use and must be a text string enclosed in quotation marks. The *name* argument must match one of the names in the font set that is listed when you first choose the Font command. The *size* argument represents the font size, in points, and should be a size available in the Size dialog box for the corresponding name. The *bold*, *italic*, *underline*, and *strike* arguments are logical values that correspond to the choices presented in the Style section of the Fonts dialog box. For these arguments to work properly, they must be represented among the four fonts available in the Fonts dialog box. Otherwise, Microsoft Excel makes the closest match possible from the available fonts.

For example, when Microsoft Excel encounters the statement

=FONT("Helv",10,TRUE,TRUE)

it changes the worksheet font to Helv 10-point bold italic.

The REPLACE.FONT function

The REPLACE.FONT function changes the current font set. Its action is equivalent to choosing the Font command from the Format menu, selecting the Fonts button, choosing a new font, and selecting the Replace option.

The REPLACE.FONT function takes the form

=REPLACE.FONT(*font*,"*name*",*size*,*bold*,*italic*,*underline*,*strike*)

where *font* is a numeric code from 1 to 4 that indicates which font in the current set of four you want to replace, *name* is the name of the new font you want to use, and *size* is the point size you want to use. The *name* argument, which must be a text string enclosed in quotation marks, must match one of the names in the font list that appears when you choose the Fonts button. The *size* argument can be any value from 4 through 127. The *bold*, *italic*, *underline*, and *strike* arguments are logical values that correspond to the choices presented in the Style section of the Fonts dialog box.

The DISPLAY function

The DISPLAY function has two forms. The first form lets you control the screen display. This form is equivalent to the Display command on the Options menu.

This version of the DISPLAY function takes the form

=DISPLAY(*formula,gridlines,heading,zero,color*)

where the *formula, gridlines, heading,* and *zero* arguments are logical values that tell Microsoft Excel which display options you want to turn on or off. If the argument is TRUE, the specified option is activated; if the argument is FALSE, the option is deactivated. If the argument is omitted, the status of the option remains unchanged. The *color* argument is a numeric code that tells Microsoft Excel which color to apply to the gridlines and headers:

Code	Color
0	Automatic
1	Black
2	White
3	Red
4	Green
5	Blue
6	Yellow
7	Magenta
8	Cyan

This form of the function lets you bypass the Display dialog box and directly specify display parameters. For example, the formula

=DISPLAY(,FALSE)

turns off the display of gridlines in the worksheet and the formula

=DISPLAY(TRUE)

turns on the display of formulas.

The second form of the DISPLAY function lets you control what will be displayed in the Info window. This version of DISPLAY is equivalent to the commands on the Info menu when Show Info is activated. It takes the form

=DISPLAY(*cell,formula,value,format,protect,names,precedents,dependents,note*)

All these arguments except *precedents* and *dependents* are logical values that tell Microsoft Excel which options you want to turn on or off. If the argument is TRUE, the specified option is activated; if the argument is FALSE, the option is deactivated. If the argument is omitted, the option status remains unchanged. The *precedents* and *dependents* arguments tell Microsoft Excel what level of precedents and dependents you want to list:

Code	Level
0	None
1	Direct only
2	All levels

The SHORT.MENUS function

The SHORT.MENUS function displays the short or full versions of Microsoft Excel menus. It is equivalent to the Short Menus and Full Menus commands on the Options menu in an active worksheet or macro sheet and on the Chart menu in the chart environment.

The SHORT.MENUS function takes the form

=SHORT.MENUS(*logical*)

If *logical* is TRUE, Microsoft Excel displays short menus. If *logical* is FALSE, Microsoft Excel displays full menus.

The WORKSPACE function

The WORKSPACE function tells Microsoft Excel how to set up your workspace. It is equivalent to the Workspace command on the Options menu.

The WORKSPACE function takes the form

=WORKSPACE(*fixed,decimals,r1c1,scroll,formula,status,menu,remote*)

where all but the *decimals* and *menu* arguments are logical values. The *fixed* argument tells Microsoft Excel whether to fix the decimal places. When this argument is TRUE, the numeric *decimals* argument fixes the number of automatic decimal places. The *r1c1* argument tells Microsoft Excel whether to use the R1C1 style. The *scroll, formula,* and *status* arguments are logical values that determine whether the scroll, formula, and status bars are displayed. The *menu* argument is a text value that tells Microsoft Excel which key you're using as an alternate menu key, and the *remote* argument is a logical value that determines whether Microsoft Excel ignores remote requests.

Other command-equivalent and action-equivalent functions

The following functions allow you to control access to the data in your documents and to control recalculation of your worksheets.

The CELL.PROTECTION function

The CELL.PROTECTION function controls access to and viewing of the cells in your worksheet by activating or deactivating the locked and hidden formats. It is equivalent to the Cell Protection command on the Format menu.

The CELL.PROTECTION function takes the form

=CELL.PROTECTION(*locked,hidden*)

where *locked* and *hidden* are logical values that tell Microsoft Excel which protection attributes you want to use. If an argument is TRUE, Microsoft Excel activates that attribute; if an argument is FALSE, Microsoft Excel deactivates that attribute. If you omit either argument, Microsoft Excel leaves the setting unchanged.

The PROTECT.DOCUMENT function

The PROTECT.DOCUMENT function controls whether cell protection takes effect and whether windows can be sized or moved. It is equivalent to the Protect Document command on the Options menu or the Chart menu.

The PROTECT.DOCUMENT function takes the form

=PROTECT.DOCUMENT(*contents,windows*)

where *contents* and *windows* are logical values that determine whether these types of protection are on or off. If the argument is TRUE, that category is protected; if the argument is FALSE, protection is turned off. If *contents* is omitted, it is assumed to be TRUE. If *windows* is omitted, it is assumed to be FALSE. Setting both arguments to FALSE is equivalent to selecting the Unprotect Document command.

The CALCULATION function

The CALCULATION function lets you control the method of recalculation of your worksheets, as well as the number of iterations. It is equivalent to the Calculation command on the Options menu.

The form of the CALCULATION function is

=CALCULATION(*type,iteration,max number,max change,update,precision,1904*)

The *type* argument is a numeric code representing the type of calculation you want to specify: 1 for automatic, 2 for automatic except tables, 3 for manual. The *iteration* argument is a logical value. If this argument is TRUE, iteration is turned on; if it is FALSE, iteration is turned off. The *max number* argument defines the maximum number of iterations you want Microsoft Excel to perform each time the worksheet is calculated. It can be any value from 1 through 32767. The *max change* argument is the maximum change that can occur from one iteration to the next without stopping the calculation. The *update* argument is a logical value. If TRUE, Microsoft Excel updates remote references. The *precision* argument is also a logical value. If TRUE, Microsoft Excel calculates using the displayed values; if FALSE,

Microsoft Excel calculates using the underlying values stored in the worksheet. The *1904* argument, also a logical value, tells Microsoft Excel to accept the 1904 date system used by Microsoft Excel for the Macintosh.

The CALCULATE.DOCUMENT function

The CALCULATE.DOCUMENT function causes Microsoft Excel to immediately calculate the active document. It is equivalent to the Calculate Document command displayed when you hold down the Shift key while selecting the Options menu. The CALCULATE.DOCUMENT function takes no arguments.

The CALCULATE.NOW function

The CALCULATE.NOW function causes Microsoft Excel to immediately recalculate all open documents. It is equivalent to the Calculate Now command on the worksheet Options menu and the Chart menu. This function takes no arguments.

Data menu functions

These Microsoft Excel functions let you use commands from the Data menu without opening it.

The SET.DATABASE function

The SET.DATABASE function defines the current database. It is equivalent to the Set Database command on the Data menu. This function takes no arguments.

To define a database from within a macro with SET.DATABASE, you must first use the SELECT function to select a range of cells. For example, the statements

```
=SELECT(!A10:E275,!A10)
=SET.DATABASE()
```

define the range A10:E275 in the active worksheet as the database range.

The SET.CRITERIA function

The SET.CRITERIA function defines a database criteria range. It is equivalent to the Set Criteria command on the Data menu. The SET.CRITERIA function takes no arguments.

To define a criteria range from within a macro with SET.CRITERIA, you must first use the SELECT function to select a range of cells. For example, the statements

```
=SELECT(!A1:E3,!A1)
=SET.CRITERIA()
```

define the range A1:E3 in the active worksheet as the criteria range.

The SORT function

The SORT function arranges the records of a database in order within a specified field. It is equivalent to the Sort command on the Data menu.

The SORT function takes the form

=SORT(*sort by,key1,order1,key2,order2,key3,order3*)

where *sort by* is a number that indicates whether you want to sort by rows or by columns: 1 for rows, 2 for columns. The *key1*, *key2*, and *key3* arguments tell Microsoft Excel which columns to use as sort keys. These arguments can be external references to the active worksheet, such as !$A:$A and !$A$3; range names that refer to the active worksheet; or R1C1-style references in text form, such as "C1." The *order* arguments are numbers that tell Microsoft Excel the order of the sort: 1 for ascending, 2 for descending. Only *sort by*, *key1*, and the first *order* argument are required.

The DATA.FIND, DATA.FIND.NEXT, and DATA.FIND.PREV functions

The DATA.FIND function locates records in your database that match specified criteria. It is equivalent to the Find command on the Data menu.

The DATA.FIND function takes the form

EQDATA.FIND(*logical*)

If *logical* is TRUE, Microsoft Excel carries out the Find command; if *logical* is FALSE, Microsoft Excel carries out the Exit Find command.

After you've used the DATA.FIND function in a macro to select the first record that matches the selection criteria you've defined, you can use the DATA.FIND.NEXT and DATA.FIND.PREV functions to select the next and previous matching records. These functions are the macro equivalents of pressing the Up or Down arrow key after choosing the Find command from the Data menu.

The EXTRACT function

The EXTRACT function copies records from a database into an extraction range. It is equivalent to the Extract command on the Data menu.

The EXTRACT function takes the form

=EXTRACT(*unique*)

where *unique* is a logical value. If *unique* is TRUE, Microsoft Excel extracts only the unique records from the database. If *unique* is FALSE or is omitted, Microsoft Excel extracts all records that match the specified criteria.

The DATA.DELETE function

The DATA.DELETE function deletes records from a database. It is equivalent to the Delete command on the Data menu.

The DATA.DELETE function takes no arguments. However, if you use the question-mark form of the function, Microsoft Excel will present an alert box warning you that the records will be permanently deleted from the database. If you don't want the alert message to appear, use the standard form of the function.

The DATA.SERIES function

The DATA.SERIES function creates series of evenly spaced numbers in your worksheets. It is equivalent to the Series command on the Data menu.

The DATA.SERIES function takes the form

=DATA.SERIES(*series in,type,date unit,step,stop*)

The *series in* argument defines the orientation of the series: 1 for Row, 2 for Column. The *type* argument describes the type of the series: 1 for Linear, 2 for Growth, 3 for Date. The *date unit* argument describes the date unit you're working with: 1 for Day, 2 for Weekday, 3 for Month, 4 for Year. (This option comes into play only if you're creating a date series.) The *step* argument is a number that describes the interval you want between each number in the series, and *stop* is the maximum value in the series.

The DATA.FORM function

The DATA.FORM function displays a dialog box arranged as a database form. It is equivalent to the Form command on the Data menu. The DATA.FORM function takes no arguments.

The TABLE function

The TABLE function lets you create a what-if table. It is equivalent to the Table command on the Data menu.

The TABLE function takes the form

=TABLE(*row input,column input*)

where *row input* is the reference of the row input cell and *column input* is the reference of the column input cell. The *row input* and *column input* arguments should be either external references to a cell in the active worksheet, such as !A1 or !Test, or R1C1-style references in text form.

Charting functions

The functions described in this section let you automate the process of creating, editing, and formatting Microsoft Excel charts.

The SELECT function

The SELECT function lets you select a chart area. It is equivalent to the Select Chart command on the Chart menu.

The SELECT function takes the form

=SELECT(*item*)

The *item* argument is text, enclosed in quotation marks, that identifies the object you want to select:

Argument	Area selected
"Chart"	Entire chart
"Plot"	Plot area
"Legend"	Legend
"Axis 1"	Main-chart value axis
"Axis 2"	Main-chart category axis
"Axis 3"	Overlay-chart value axis
"Axis 4"	Overlay-chart category axis
"Title"	Chart title
"Text Axis 1"	Label for main-chart value axis
"Text Axis 2"	Label for main-chart category axis
"Text n"	Nth floating text item
"Arrow n"	Nth arrow
"Gridline 1"	Major gridlines of value axis
"Gridline 2"	Minor gridlines of value axis
"Gridline 3"	Major gridlines of category axis
"Gridline 4"	Minor gridlines of category axis
"Dropline 1"	Major-chart drop lines
"Dropline 2"	Overlay-chart drop lines
"Hiloline 1"	Main-chart hi-lo lines
"Hiloline 2"	Overlay-chart hi-lo lines
"$SnPm$"	Data for point m in series n
"Text $SnPm$"	Text for point m in series n
"Text Sn"	Series title text for series n of area chart

For example, the statement

=SELECT("Text Axis 1")

causes Microsoft Excel to select the label for the main-chart value axis.

The SELECT.CHART function

The SELECT.CHART function is provided for compatibility with Microsoft Excel macros written for the Macintosh. It selects the entire chart. The SELECT.CHART function is equivalent to the Select Chart command on the Chart menu. It takes no arguments.

This function has the same effect as the statement

=SELECT("Chart")

The SELECT.PLOT.AREA function

The SELECT.PLOT.AREA function is provided for compatibility with Microsoft Excel macros written for the Macintosh. It selects the plot area of the active chart. The SELECT.PLOT.AREA function is equivalent to the Select Plot Area command on the Chart menu. This function takes no arguments.

The COPY.CHART function

The COPY.CHART function is provided for compatibility with Microsoft Excel macros written for the Macintosh. This function lets you copy an entire chart onto the Clipboard.

The COPY.CHART function is the same as the COPY.PICTURE function without the *copy* argument. It takes the form

=COPY.CHART(*as shown*)

where *as shown* determines how Microsoft Excel copies the chart. If *as shown* is 1, Microsoft Excel copies the chart to the Clipboard as it appears on the screen; if *as shown* is 2, Microsoft Excel copies the chart to the Clipboard as it will appear when it is printed.

The PASTE.SPECIAL function

When used with a chart, PASTE.SPECIAL has two forms. The first form lets you paste from a worksheet or macro sheet to a chart. The second form lets you paste from one chart to another.

To copy data from a worksheet or macro sheet into a chart, use the form

=PASTE.SPECIAL(*values in,series names,categories,apply*)

In this form, *values in* is a number that tells Microsoft Excel whether the values are in rows (1) or columns (2). The *series names* argument is a logical value that tells Microsoft Excel whether to use the entries in the first row of the selection as series names. Similarly, *categories* is a logical value that tells Microsoft Excel whether to use the entries in the first column of the selection as category labels. The *apply* argument is a logical value that tells Microsoft Excel whether to apply the category names to all series in the chart.

To copy data between chart windows, use the second form of the PASTE.SPECIAL function:

=PASTE.SPECIAL(*parts*)

The *parts* argument is a numeric code that indicates which parts of the copied chart to paste into the active chart window:

Code	Part pasted
1	All
2	Formats only
3	Formulas only

The MAIN.CHART and MAIN.CHART.TYPE functions

The MAIN.CHART function defines the current chart type and format. It is equivalent to the Main Chart command on the Format menu.

The MAIN.CHART function takes the form

=MAIN.CHART(*type,stack,100,vary,overlap,drop,hilo,overlap%,cluster,angle*)

where *type* is a numeric code that specifies the type of chart to use:

Code	Chart type
1	Area
2	Bar
3	Column
4	Line
5	Pie
6	Scatter

The *stack, 100, vary, overlap, drop,* and *hilo* arguments are logical values that define chart format. If the argument is TRUE, that option is selected. The *overlap%, cluster*, and *angle* arguments are numeric values that define the percentage of overlap and the cluster spacing for column and bar charts and the angle of the first "slice" of a pie chart. Not all of these arguments apply to every chart. If you include an argument that doesn't apply to the type entered, Microsoft Excel ignores the argument.

The MAIN.CHART.TYPE function is included for compatibility with Microsoft Excel macros written for the Macintosh. This function takes the form

=MAIN.CHART.TYPE(*type*)

and is equivalent to the MAIN.CHART function described above.

The ADD.OVERLAY and DELETE.OVERLAY functions

The ADD.OVERLAY and DELETE.OVERLAY functions divide the current chart into a main chart and an overlay chart or delete an existing overlay chart. They are the equivalents of the Add Overlay and Delete Overlay commands on the Chart menu. Neither function takes an argument.

The OVERLAY and OVERLAY.CHART.TYPE functions

The OVERLAY function tells Microsoft Excel how to format an overlay chart. It is equivalent to the Overlay command on the Format menu.

The OVERLAY function takes the form

=OVERLAY(*type,stack,100,vary,overlap,drop,hilo,overlap%,cluster,angle,series,auto*)

These arguments are identical to those described for the MAIN.CHART function.

The OVERLAY.CHART.TYPE function is included for compatibility with Microsoft Excel macros written for the Macintosh. This function takes the form

=OVERLAY.CHART.TYPE(*type*)

and is equivalent to the OVERLAY.CHART function described above. Entering a type of 0 is the same as using the DELETE.OVERLAY function.

The LEGEND and FORMAT.LEGEND functions

The LEGEND function adds or deletes a legend from a chart. It is equivalent to the Add Legend and Delete Legend commands on the Chart menu.

The LEGEND function takes the form

=LEGEND(*logical*)

If *logical* is TRUE, the function carries out the Add Legend command; if *logical* is FALSE, the function carries out the Delete Legend command.

The FORMAT.LEGEND function changes the position of the legend on a chart. It is equivalent to the Legend command on the Format menu.

The FORMAT.LEGEND function takes the form

=FORMAT.LEGEND(*position*)

where *position* is a numeric code that tells Microsoft Excel where to display the legend:

Code	Legend position
1	Bottom
2	Corner
3	Top
4	Vertical

The GALLERY functions

Microsoft Excel offers a group of functions—one function for each of Microsoft Excel's six chart types—that are the macro equivalents of the various Gallery menu options. For example, the GALLERY.PIE function is equivalent to the Pie option on the Gallery menu and the GALLERY.COLUMN function is equivalent to the Column option on the Gallery menu. Other possible functions in this group are GALLERY.AREA, GALLERY.BAR, GALLERY.LINE, and GALLERY.SCATTER.

The GALLERY functions take the form

=GALLERY.*xxx*(*format,delete overlay*)

where *format* is a numeric code representing one of the options available in the chart's gallery.

For example, the formula

=GALLERY.PIE(1)

changes the type of the chart in the active window to the first pie-chart format in the gallery—a basic pie chart.

The *delete overlay* argument is a logical value. If this argument is TRUE, Microsoft Excel deletes any overlays on the current chart and formats the main chart. If the argument is FALSE or omitted, Microsoft Excel applies the new format to the chart that contains the currently selected chart item.

The COMBINATION function

The COMBINATION function sets the type of the active chart to one of Microsoft Excel's five combination chart types. It is equivalent to the Combination command on the Gallery menu.

The COMBINATION function takes the form

=COMBINATION(*type*)

where *type* is a numeric code representing one of the five combination chart types in the Combination dialog box.

The PREFERRED and SET.PREFERRED functions

The PREFERRED function changes the current chart format to the format that you've defined with the Set Preferred command. It is equivalent to the Preferred command on the Gallery menu. If you haven't changed the preferred chart type, Microsoft Excel uses the default chart type—a simple column chart.

The SET.PREFERRED function sets Microsoft Excel's Preferred chart format to the type of the current chart. This function is equivalent to the Set Preferred command on the Gallery menu.

Neither of these functions takes an argument.

The ATTACH.TEXT function

The ATTACH.TEXT function adds text to various parts of a chart. It is equivalent to the Attach Text command on the Chart menu.

The ATTACH.TEXT function takes the form

=ATTACH.TEXT(*attach to,series,point*)

where *attach to* is a numeric code telling Microsoft Excel what to attach the text to:

Code	Location
1	Chart title
2	Value axis
3	Category axis
4	Series or data point

If the *attach to* argument is 4, you can use the *series* and *point* arguments to tell Microsoft Excel the numbers of the series and the data point within the series to work with.

The AXES function

The AXES function tells Microsoft Excel which axes to display in the current chart. It is equivalent to the Axes command on the Chart menu.

The AXES function takes the form

=AXES(*main category,main value,overlay category,overlay value*)

These arguments are logical values that represent the four choices inside the Axes dialog box. The first two arguments apply to the main chart; the third and fourth arguments apply to an overlay chart. Use a TRUE argument to display an axis; use a FALSE argument to suppress the display of an axis.

The ADD.ARROW and DELETE.ARROW functions

The ADD.ARROW and DELETE.ARROW functions add and remove arrows from a chart. They are equivalent to the Add Arrow and Delete Arrow commands on the Chart menu. Neither function accepts an argument.

The GRIDLINES function

The GRIDLINES function tells Microsoft Excel which gridlines to display in the current chart. It is equivalent to the Gridlines command on the Chart menu.

The GRIDLINES function takes the form

=GRIDLINES(*category major,category minor,value major,value minor*)

These arguments are logical values that represent the four choices inside the Gridlines dialog box. The first two arguments apply to the category axis; the third and fourth arguments apply to the value axis. Use TRUE arguments to display the gridlines; use FALSE arguments to suppress the gridline display.

The PATTERNS function

The PATTERNS function changes the patterns and colors of the selected object. It is equivalent to the Patterns command on the Format menu.

As you can see in the following table, the PATTERNS function has five forms, depending on the object you select:

Object	Function form
Chart, plot area, legend, text label, area, or bar	PATTERNS(*BAuto,BStyle,BColor,BWeight,* *shadow,AAuto,APattern,AFore,ABack,apply*)
Axis	PATTERNS(*LAuto,LStyle,LColor,LWeight,* *TMajor,TMinor,TLabel*)
Gridline, hi-lo line, or drop line	PATTERNS(*LAuto,LStyle,LColor,LWeight*)
Arrow	PATTERNS(*LAuto,LStyle,LColor,LWeight,* *HWidth,HLength,HType*)
Data line	PATTERNS(*LAuto,LStyle,LColor,LWeight,* *MAuto,MStyle,MFore,MBack,apply*)

Table 18-1 describes each of the available PATTERNS arguments.

Table 18-1. Effects of the PATTERNS options.

Argument	Controls	Code	Action
apply	Apply to All check box	TRUE	Turns check box on
		FALSE	Turns check box off
LAuto	Automatic line settings	0	Set by user
		1	Automatic
		2	Invisible
LStyle	Line style options	1–5	Selects one of the 5 line styles
LColor	Line color options	1–8	Selects one of the 8 color options
LWeight	Line weight options	1–3	Selects one of the 3 weight options
BAuto	Automatic border settings	0	Set by user
		1	Automatic
		2	Invisible
BStyle	Border style options	1–5	Selects one of the 5 line styles
BColor	Border color options	1–8	Selects one of the 8 color options
BWeight	Border weight options	1–3	Selects one of the 3 weight options
shadow	Shadow check box	TRUE	Turns check box on
		FALSE	Turns check box off
AAuto	Automatic area settings	0	Set by user
		1	Automatic
		2	Invisible
APattern	Area patterns	1–16	Selects one of the 16 area patterns
AFore	Area foreground color	1–8	Selects one of the 8 foreground colors
ABack	Area background color	1–8	Selects one of the 8 background colors
TMajor	Major tick-mark position	1	Invisible
		2	Inside
		3	Outside
		4	Cross
TMinor	Minor tick-mark position	1	Invisible
		2	Inside
		3	Outside
		4	Cross

(continued)

Table 18-1. *continued*

Argument	Controls	Code	Action
TLabel	Tick label position	1	None
		2	Low
		3	High
		4	Next to axis
MAuto	Automatic marker settings	0	Set by user
		1	Automatic
		2	Invisible
MStyle	Marker style	1–7	Selects one of the 7 style options
MFore	Marker foreground color	1–8	Selects one of the 8 foreground colors
MBack	Marker background color	1–8	Selects one of the 8 background colors
HWidth	Arrowhead width	1	Narrow
		2	Medium
		3	Wide
HLength	Arrowhead length	1	Short
		2	Medium
		3	Long
HType	Arrowhead type	1	No head
		2	Open head
		3	Closed head

The FORMAT.FONT function

The FORMAT.FONT function for charts changes the font in which the selected chart object is displayed. It is equivalent to the Font command on the chart environment's Format menu.

The FORMAT.FONT function takes the form

=FORMAT.FONT(*color,background,apply,"name",size,bold,italic,underline,strike*)

The *color* argument is a number from 0 through 8; 0 tells Microsoft Excel to choose the color automatically and 1 through 8 correspond to the eight colors in the Font dialog box. The *background* argument is a numeric code that tells Microsoft Excel what type of background to use, as shown on the following page.

Code	Background
1	Automatic
2	Transparent
3	White out

The *apply* argument is a logical value that corresponds to the Apply to All check box. This argument applies only when you're formatting data labels. The *name* argument specifies the name of the font to use and must be entered as text enclosed in quotation marks. The *size* argument tells Microsoft Excel the type size to use, in points. The *bold, italic, underline,* and *strike* arguments are logical values that correspond to the Style check boxes in the Font dialog box.

The FORMAT.TEXT function

The FORMAT.TEXT function changes the text settings of a selected chart object. It is equivalent to the Text command on the Format menu.

The FORMAT.TEXT function takes the form

=FORMAT.TEXT(*x,y,vertical,text,size,key,value*)

The *x* argument tells Microsoft Excel how to align the text horizontally: 1 for left; 2 for center; 3 for right. The *y* argument tells Microsoft Excel how to align the text vertically: 1 for top; 2 for center; 3 for bottom.

The *vertical, text,* and *size* arguments are logical values. If the argument is TRUE, Microsoft Excel formats the selected text with vertical text, automatic text, or automatic sizing. Similarly, the *key* and *value* arguments are logical values that correspond to the Show Key and Show Value check boxes and apply only when the selected text is an attached data label.

The FORMAT.SIZE function

The FORMAT.SIZE function tells Microsoft Excel how to size the selected chart object. It is equivalent to the Size command on the Format menu.

The FORMAT.SIZE function takes the form

=FORMAT.SIZE(*width,height*)

The *width* argument specifies the horizontal size of the selected chart object and the *height* argument specifies the vertical size. Both arguments are expressed in points. You can't size portions of a pie chart. If Microsoft Excel can't size a chart object, the FORMAT.SIZE function returns FALSE.

The FORMAT.MOVE function

The FORMAT.MOVE function moves the selected chart object. It is equivalent to the Move command on the Format menu.

The FORMAT.MOVE function takes the form

=FORMAT.MOVE(*x position,y position*)

where *x position* specifies the horizontal position (the bottom) of the selected chart object and *y position* specifies the vertical position (the left edge). The position arguments are measured in points from the lower left corner of the screen. The base of a text label is the lower left corner of the text rectangle. The base of an arrow is the end without the arrowhead. The base of a pie slice is its point. If Microsoft Excel can't move a chart object, FORMAT.MOVE returns FALSE.

The SCALE function

The SCALE function controls the appearance of the axes. It is equivalent to the Scale command on the Format menu.

The SCALE function has two forms: the first for category axes and the second for value axes. (Both axes in a scatter diagram are treated as value axes.) If you've selected a category axis, the SCALE function takes the form

=SCALE(*cross,labels,marks,between,max,reverse*)

where *cross* is a numeric argument that specifies the category at which you want the value axis to cross. The *labels* argument tells Microsoft Excel how many categories to put between tick-mark labels, and the *marks* argument tells Microsoft Excel how many categories to put between tick marks. The last three arguments are logical values. If *between* is TRUE, the value axis crosses the category axis between categories. If *reverse* is TRUE, Microsoft Excel displays the categories in reverse order. If *max* is TRUE, the value axis crosses the category axis at the maximum category.

If you've selected a value axis, the SCALE function takes the form

=SCALE(*min,max,major,minor,cross,log,reverse,maximum*)

The first five arguments are the same as the five variables in the Scale dialog box. Each can be either TRUE or a number. If you enter TRUE, Microsoft Excel uses the automatic scale for that variable. The *min* argument specifies the minimum point on the value-axis scale and the *max* argument specifies the maximum point. The *major* and *minor* arguments define the distances between the major and minor tick marks. The *cross* argument tells Microsoft Excel where the category axis crosses the value axis. The last three arguments are logical values. If *log* is TRUE, Microsoft Excel uses the logarithmic scale. If *reverse* is TRUE, Microsoft Excel lists the values in reverse order. If *maximum* is TRUE, the value axis crosses the category axis at the maximum category.

Information functions

Often, the actions you want to perform in your macros depend on certain conditions. For example, you may want to branch to one of several subroutines, depending on the type of information contained in the current active cell. The macro functions described in this section let you obtain information about such conditions and analyze it from within a macro. You'll frequently use these functions in conjunction with Microsoft Excel's logical functions IF, AND, and OR.

The DOCUMENTS function

The DOCUMENTS function returns an alphabetic list of all open documents. This function takes no arguments.

For example, suppose four windows appear on the screen: Sheet1:1, Sheet1:2, Sheet2, and Chart1. The statement

=DOCUMENTS()

returns the horizontal array {"Chart1","Sheet1","Sheet2"}. Notice that the second Sheet1 window is not included in the list, because it is not a separate document.

Typically, you'll use DOCUMENTS with the SET.NAME or SET.VALUE function. For example, the statement

=SET.NAME("Documents",DOCUMENTS())

stores the list of document names as a horizontal array under the name *Documents*. The statement

=SET.VALUE(C1:Z1,DOCUMENTS())

enters the list into cells C1:Z1 in the macro sheet.

After you've created an array of document names, you can select the name of the document you want to use with the INDEX function. For example, the statements

=SET.NAME("Documents",DOCUMENTS())
=SET.NAME("DocName",INDEX(Documents,2))

store the array of document names under the name *Documents* and then store the name of the second document in the array under the name *DocName*.

The WINDOWS function

The WINDOWS function returns a list of all open windows. This function takes no arguments.

The first name in the list returned by WINDOWS is the name of the active window. The names of the remaining windows appear in the same order in which the windows are stacked on the screen. For example, suppose there are three windows stacked on the screen in the following order: Sheet1:2, Sheet1:1, and Sheet2. The statement

    =WINDOWS()

returns the horizontal array {"Sheet1:2","Sheet1:1","Sheet2"}.

Typically, you'll use WINDOWS with the SET.NAME or SET.VALUE function. For example, the statement

    =SET.NAME("Windows",WINDOWS())

stores the list of window names as a horizontal array under the name *Windows*, and the statement

    =SET.VALUE(C1:Z1,WINDOWS())

enters the array into cells C1:Z1 in the macro sheet.

After you've created a list of window names, you can select the name of the window you want to use with the INDEX function. For example, the statements

    =SET.NAME("Windows",WINDOWS())
    =ACTIVATE(INDEX(Windows,2))

store the array of window names under the name *Windows* and then activate the second window listed in the array.

The FILES function

The FILES function returns the names of all files in a directory. It takes the form

    =FILES(*directory*)

where *directory* is a text argument that represents the directory name. The *directory* argument can include the ? and * wildcard characters. If you omit *directory*, it is assumed to be *.*. If you don't specify the drive name in the *directory* argument, Microsoft Excel assumes you mean the current drive. This function returns the filenames as a horizontal array of text values.

The SELECTION function

The SELECTION function returns the reference of the selected cells in the worksheet as an external reference. This function takes no arguments.

For example, if the active window is named Sheet1 and cells A1:A10 in that document are selected, the statement

    =SELECTION()

returns Sheet1!A1:A10.

The SELECTION function is handy when you need to refer to the current worksheet range from within a macro. For example, suppose you want to assign the name *TestRange* to the selected range of cells in your worksheet. You could embed the SELECTION function within a DEFINE.NAME function, like this:

    =DEFINE.NAME("TestRange",SELECTION())

The ACTIVE.CELL function

The ACTIVE.CELL function returns the reference of the active cell in the worksheet as an external reference. This function takes no arguments.

For example, if Sheet1 is the active worksheet and B2 is the active cell, then the ACTIVE.CELL function returns the reference Sheet1!B2.

ACTIVE.CELL is frequently used in combination with the DEFINE.NAME function. For example, if cell B2 in Sheet1 is the active cell, the statement

    =DEFINE.NAME("Active",ACTIVE.CELL())

assigns the name *Active* to cell B2.

Generally, when you use ACTIVE.CELL in another function, Microsoft Excel returns the value in the active cell instead of its reference; in effect, the reference is translated into the contents of the reference. To be sure of working with the actual reference, use REFTEXT to convert the cell reference to text.

The NAMES function

The NAMES function returns, as a horizontal array, all names defined in a document. It takes the form

    =NAMES(*document*)

where *document*, a text argument enclosed in quotation marks, is the name of the document you want to refer to. If you omit *document*, Microsoft Excel returns the names defined in the active document.

The LINKS function

The LINKS function returns a list of all worksheets that serve as external references for a specified document. It takes the form

=LINKS(*document*)

where *document*, a text argument enclosed in quotation marks, is the name of the document for which the links are sought. If you omit *document*, Microsoft Excel assumes you mean the active document. If Microsoft Excel can't find any worksheets serving as external references for a document, it returns #N/A!.

For example, suppose the current document is a chart named CHART1, developed from data in worksheets named PROFITS.XLS and LOSSES.XLS. The statement

=LINKS(CHART1)

returns the array {"PROFITS.XLS","LOSSES.XLS"}.

Typically, you'll use LINKS with the SET.NAME or SET.VALUE function. For example, the statement

=SET.NAME("Profits",LINKS())

stores the list of worksheets with external references as an array under the name *Profits*, and the statement

=SET.VALUE(F1:J1,LINKS())

enters the array into cells F1:J1 in the macro sheet.

After you've created an array of linked names, you can select the name of the document you want to use with the INDEX function.

The GET.FORMULA function

The GET.FORMULA function returns the contents of a cell. It takes the form

=GET.FORMULA(*reference*)

where *reference* is a cell or range reference. The function returns, as a text string, the contents of the cell in the upper left corner of *reference*. If *reference* contains a formula with cell references, that formula is presented in R1C1 notation.

For example, if cell A1 in the current worksheet contains the value 100, the statement

=GET.FORMULA(!A1)

returns 100.

If cell B3 contains the formula =B2, the statement

=GET.FORMULA(!B3)

returns the string

=R[–1]C

The GET.NAME function

The GET.NAME function returns the definition of the name of a cell, range, value, or formula. This function takes the form

=GET.NAME("*name*")

where the *name* argument is a name in the macro sheet (*"name"*), in the active worksheet (*"!name"*), or in a specific worksheet (*"worksheet name!name"*). In all cases, *name* must be a text string enclosed in quotation marks.

The definition returned is the same as that in the Refers to edit bar of the DEFINE NAME dialog box. If *name* describes a cell or range, Microsoft Excel returns the reference of that cell or range. If *name* describes a value or formula, Microsoft Excel returns a string containing that value or formula. When *name* describes a formula or a range, the result is presented in R1C1 notation.

For example, if the name *Test* has been assigned to cell A1 in the active worksheet, the statement

=GET.NAME("!Test")

returns R1C1. If the name *Number* describes the value 100 in the macro sheet, the statement

=GET.NAME("Number")

returns 100.

The GET.DEF function

The GET.DEF function returns the name for a defined cell, range, value, or formula. This function takes the form

=GET.DEF("*definition*","*document*")

where *definition* is the description of the location or value for which the name is sought and *document* is the name of the document in which *definition* occurs. Both arguments must be entered in text form with quotation marks. References for the *definition* argument must be in R1C1 style. If Microsoft Excel finds more than one name for a definition, it returns the first name it finds.

For example, if cell A1 in SHEET1.XLS is defined as Test, the statement

=GET.DEF("R1C1","SHEET1.XLS")

returns Test.

The GET.CELL function

The GET.CELL function returns information about a cell's formatting, location, or contents. This function takes the form

=GET.CELL(*type,reference*)

where *type* is a numeric code that defines the information you seek and *reference* is the cell about which information is sought. Table 18-2 lists the possible *type* values. If *reference* refers to a range, Microsoft Excel returns information about the upper left cell of the range. If you omit *reference*, it refers to the current selection.

Table 18-2. Codes for the GET.CELL function's *type* argument.

Code	Information returned
1	Reference of first cell in *reference*, as text
2	Row of top cell in *reference*
3	Column of leftmost cell in *reference*
4	TYPE(*reference*)
5	Contents of *reference*
6	Formula in *reference*, as text
7	Cell format, as text
8	Cell alignment (1 = General, 2 = Left, 3 = Center, 4 = Right, 5 = Fill)
9	TRUE if cell has left border, FALSE if not
10	TRUE if cell has right border, FALSE if not
11	TRUE if cell has top border, FALSE if not
12	TRUE if cell has bottom border, FALSE if not
13	TRUE if cell shaded, FALSE if not
14	TRUE if cell locked, FALSE if not
15	TRUE if cell hidden, FALSE if not
16	Column width of cell
17	Row height of cell
18	Font name, as text
19	Font size, in points
20	TRUE if cell bold, FALSE if not
21	TRUE if cell italic, FALSE if not
22	TRUE if cell underlined, FALSE if not
23	TRUE if cell struck through, FALSE if not

The GET.CHART.ITEM function

The GET.CHART.ITEM function returns the horizontal or vertical position of a selected object in a chart. It takes the form

=GET.CHART.ITEM(*x-y,point,item*)

The *x-y* argument is a numeric code that tells Microsoft Excel which coordinate to select: 1 for the horizontal coordinate, 2 for the vertical coordinate. The *point* argument identifies the position on the chart object. If you've selected a rectangle or an area in an area chart, use these values for the *point* argument:

Code	Position on object
1	Upper left
2	Upper middle
3	Upper right
4	Right middle
5	Lower right
6	Lower middle
7	Lower left
8	Left middle

If you've selected an arrow, use these values for the *point* argument: 1 for the base; 2 for the head. If you've selected a slice of a pie chart, use the following values for the point argument:

Code	Position
1	Counterclockwise point furthest outside
2	Outer center point
3	Clockwise point furthest outside
4	Midpoint of most clockwise radius
5	Center point
6	Midpoint of most counterclockwise radius

If the object you've selected is a point, the *point* argument must be 1. If you've selected any line except a data line, the *point* argument must be 1 for lower left or 2 for upper right.

The *item* argument is text, enclosed in quotation marks, that identifies the object you want to select. Table 18-3 shows the possible values for *item*.

**Table 18-3. Values for the GET.CHART.ITEM
function's *item* argument.**

Argument	Selection
"Chart"	Entire chart
"Plot"	Plot area
"Legend"	Legend
"Axis 1"	Main-chart value axis
"Axis 2"	Main-chart category axis
"Axis 3"	Overlay-chart value axis
"Axis 4"	Overlay-chart category axis
"Title"	Chart title
"Text Axis 1"	Label for main-chart value axis
"Text Axis 2"	Label for main-chart category axis
"Text n"	Nth floating text item
"Arrow n"	Nth arrow
"Gridline 1"	Major gridlines of value axis
"Gridline 2"	Minor gridlines of value axis
"Gridline 3"	Major gridlines of category axis
"Gridline 4"	Minor gridlines of category axis
"Dropline 1"	Major-chart droplines
"Dropline 2"	Overlay-chart droplines
"Hiloline 1"	Main-chart hi-lo lines
"Hiloline 2"	Overlay-chart hi-lo lines
"SnPm"	Data for point m in series n
"Text SnPm"	Text for point m in series n
"Text Sn"	Series title text for series n of area chart

The GET.DOCUMENT function

The GET.DOCUMENT function returns information about a document. This function takes the form

=GET.DOCUMENT(*type*,"*name*")

where *type* is a numeric code that defines the information you seek. Table 18-4 lists the available *type* arguments and their results. The *name* argument is the name of a document that is currently open. The name must be entered as a text string enclosed in quotation marks. If you omit *name*, Microsoft Excel assumes you want to refer to the active document.

Table 18-4. Codes for the GET.DOCUMENT function's *type* argument.

Code	Information returned
1	Filename without extension
2	Directory pathname of *name* as text; #N/A! if *name* hasn't been saved
3	Document type: 1 = worksheet, 2 = chart, 3 = macro sheet, 4 = Info window active
4	TRUE if document has been changed since it was saved, FALSE if not
5	TRUE if file read-only, FALSE if not
6	TRUE if file protected, FALSE if not
7	TRUE if document contents protected, FALSE if not
8	TRUE if document windows protected, FALSE if not
For charts:	
9	Type of main chart: 1 = area, 2 = bar, 3 = column, 4 = line, 5 = pie, 6 = scatter
10	Type of overlay chart; same numbers as for main chart, above; #N/A! if no overlay chart
11	Number of series in main chart
12	Number of series in overlay chart
For worksheets and macro sheets:	
9	Number of first row used, 0 if document empty
10	Number of last row used, 0 if document empty
11	Number of first column used, 0 if document empty
12	Number of last column used, 0 if document empty
13	Number of windows
14	Calculation mode: 1 = automatic, 2 = automatic except tables, 3 = manual
15	TRUE if Iteration on, FALSE if not
16	Maximum iterations
17	Maximum change between iterations
18	TRUE if Update Remote References on, FALSE if not
19	TRUE If Precision as Displayed on, FALSE if not
20	TRUE if 1904 Date System on, FALSE if not
21	4-item horizontal text array of four font names
22	4-item horizontal number array of four font sizes
23	4-item horizontal logical array indicating which of four fonts are bold
24	4-item horizontal logical array indicating which of four fonts are italic
25	4-item horizontal logical array indicating which of four fonts are underlined
26	4-item horizontal logical array indicating which of four fonts are struck through

The GET.NOTE function

The GET.NOTE function returns the text from a note attached to a cell. This function takes the form

=GET.NOTE(*reference,start,count*)

where *reference* is a reference to the cell whose note you want to work with. The *start* argument tells Microsoft Excel where in the text string of the note to start reading. The *count* argument, which must be less than or equal to 255, tells the program how many characters to return. If you omit the *start* argument, Microsoft Excel begins with the first character in the note. If you omit the *count* argument, the program returns the remainder of the note—that is, all the characters from *start* to the end of the note.

The GET.WINDOW function

The GET.WINDOW function returns information about a window. This function takes the form

=GET.WINDOW(*type,name*)

where *type* is a numeric code from Table 18-5 that defines the information you seek and *window* is the name of the window you want to work with, enclosed in quotation marks. If you omit the name of the window, Microsoft Excel assumes you mean the active document.

Table 18-5. Codes for the GET.WINDOW function's *type* argument.

Code	Information returned
1	Name of document contained in *name*, as text
2	Number of window
3	x position (from left edge of screen to left edge of window, in points)
4	y position (from screen top to window top, in points)
5	Width in points
6	Height in points
7	TRUE if window is hidden, FALSE if not
For worksheets and macro sheets:	
8	TRUE if formulas displayed, FALSE if not
9	TRUE if gridlines displayed, FALSE if not
10	TRUE if row and column headings displayed, FALSE if not
11	TRUE if zeros displayed, FALSE if not
12	A number indicating header and gridline color: 0 = automatic, 1–8 = colors corresponding to those in Display dialog box from Options menu

(continued)

Table 18-5. *continued*

Code	Information returned
For window's panes (horizontal numeric arrays indicating which rows or columns appear at the edges):	
13	Leftmost column of each pane
14	Top row of each pane
15	Rightmost column of each pane
16	Bottom row of each pane

The GET.WORKSPACE function

The GET.WORKSPACE function returns information about the workspace. This function takes the form

=GET.WORKSPACE(*type*)

where the *type* argument is a numeric code from Table 18-6 that defines the information you seek.

Table 18-6. Codes for the GET.WORKSPACE function's *type* argument.

Code	Information returned
1	Name of environment and version number, as text
2	Microsoft Excel version number, as text
3	Number of decimals if auto-decimal on, 0 if not
4	TRUE if R1C1 mode on, FALSE if A1 mode on
5	TRUE if scroll bars displayed, FALSE if not
6	TRUE if status bar displayed, FALSE If not
7	TRUE if formula bar displayed, FALSE if not
8	TRUE if remote requests on, FALSE if not
9	Alternate menu key, as text; #N/A! if no key set
10	Special modes: 0 = no special mode set, 1 = data find, 2 = copy, 3 = cut
11	x position of window (from left edge of screen to left edge of window, in points)
12	y position of window (from top of screen to top of window, in points)
13	Width of usable workspace, in points
14	Height of usable workspace, in points
15	Application workspace: 1 = Microsoft Excel not minimized or maximized, 2 = minimized, 3 = maximized
16	Memory free, in kilobytes
17	Total memory, in kilobytes
18	TRUE if math coprocessor used, FALSE if not
19	TRUE if mouse used, FALSE if not

The ABSREF function

The ABSREF function returns the address of the cell or range at the position described by the relationship to the reference cell or range. This function takes the form

=ABSREF("*relationship*",*reference*)

where *relationship* is a relative reference in R1C1 form, enclosed in quotation marks, and *reference* is the cell on which the relationship is based.

For example, the statement

=ABSREF("R[–1]C[–1]",B2)

returns the reference A1. If C3 is the active cell, the formula

=ABSREF(R[2]C[1],ACTIVE.CELL())

returns the reference D5.

The RELREF function

The RELREF function returns a relative reference, in R1C1 form, that describes the relationship between two cells. This function takes the form

=RELREF(*ref1*,*ref2*)

where the *ref1* and *ref2* arguments are cell references. The direction of evaluation is from *ref2* to *ref1*.

For example, the statement

=RELREF(A1,B2)

returns the relative reference R[–1]C[–1] and the statement

=RELREF(D5,C3)

returns the relative reference R[2]C[1].

The OFFSET function

The OFFSET function returns the address of the cell or range that has the specified offset relationship to the reference cell. This function takes the form

=OFFSET(*reference*,*rows*,*columns*,*height*,*width*)

where *reference* represents a cell or a single continuous range. If *reference* refers to a range, Microsoft Excel uses the cell at the top left corner of the range. The *row* and *column* arguments are numeric values that represent how far you want to move. The *height* and *width* arguments represent the number of rows and columns in the offset range. If you omit *height* and *width*, Microsoft Excel assumes the offset range is the same height and width as the reference range.

For example, the statement

=OFFSET(A1,2,2)

returns the reference C3 and the statement

=OFFSET(A1:C5,2,3,2,4)

returns the reference D3:F7.

The *row* and *column* arguments can be negative numbers as well. For example, the statement

=OFFSET(B2,–1,–1)

return the reference A1.

If *row* or *column* refers to a range outside the addressable area of the worksheet, Microsoft Excel returns #REF!.

The REFTEXT and TEXTREF functions

The REFTEXT function changes a reference to an absolute reference in text form. This function takes the form

=REFTEXT(*reference,a1*)

where *reference* is the reference you want to convert. The *a1* argument is a logical value that specifies the type of reference you want to create. If TRUE, Microsoft Excel returns the address in A1 form. If FALSE or omitted, Microsoft Excel returns the address in R1C1 form.

Generally, you'll embed the REFTEXT function inside other functions that require that cell and range reference arguments be presented in text form.

The TEXTREF function converts references in text format to standard references. This function takes the form

=(*text,a1*)

where *text* is the text reference you want to convert to standard reference form. The *a1* argument is a logical value that specifies the type of reference you're converting. If TRUE, Microsoft Excel assumes *text* to be an A1-style reference. If FALSE or omitted, Microsoft Excel assumes *text* to be an R1C1-style reference. When the arguments don't correspond, Microsoft Excel returns #REF!.

The DEREF function

The DEREF function returns the value of a specified cell or range. This function takes the form

=DEREF(*reference*)

where *reference* is a reference to a cell or range.

For example, if cell A1 contains the value 100, the statement

=DEREF(A1)

returns 100. If *reference* refers to a range, the DEREF function results in an array of values. For example, if cells A1:A3 contain the values 10, 20, and 30, the statement

=DEREF(A1:A3)

returns the array {10;20;30}.

You must use an absolute reference if *reference* refers to the active sheet. Relative references will be converted to absolute references.

In most Microsoft Excel formulas, you can use either a value or a reference to a cell that contains that value. For example, if A1 contains the value –100, the statements

=ABS(A1)

and

=ABS(–100)

return the same result. However, in some cases there is a big difference between using the reference and using the value. For example, the statement

=SET.NAME("Test",C13)

stores the formula =$C$13 under the name *Test*. If you want to store the *value* from cell C13 under the name *Test*, you must use the statement

=SET.NAME("Test",DEREF(C13))

Other macro functions

In this section, we'll cover the functions unique to Microsoft Excel's macro environment. This group includes functions that take actions, repeat actions, run macros, make entries, assign values, and test macros.

The HALT and RETURN functions

The HALT and RETURN functions can be used to stop the execution of a macro.

The HALT function stops all macros from running. It takes no arguments. For example, the statement

=IF(Test>100,HALT())

stops the macro immediately if the value of the name *Test* is greater than 100. If the macro containing this statement is embedded in another macro, the calling macro also stops.

The RETURN function stops the execution of a specific macro or subroutine. This function takes the form

=RETURN(*value*)

The *value* argument in a function macro tells Microsoft Excel to return the value of the macro to the calling cell. You can't use *value* in a command macro.

If the macro was started with the Run command from the Macro menu or with a shortcut key, the macro ends with the RETURN function. If the RETURN function is embedded in a subroutine, Microsoft Excel returns to the cell immediately after the calling cell that branched processing to the subroutine.

The FORMULA, FORMULA.FILL, and FORMULA.ARRAY functions

The FORMULA and FORMULA.FILL functions make entries in cells from within macros. The FORMULA function takes the form

=FORMULA(*entry,reference*)

The *entry* argument can be a logical value, a number, a formula, or a text string. Formulas and text strings must be enclosed in quotation marks. If *entry* is a formula, all references in the formula must be in R1C1 form. The *reference* argument tells Microsoft Excel where to make the entry. If you omit this argument, the entry is made in the active cell.

For example, the statement

=FORMULA(100)

enters the number 100 in the active cell and the statement

=FORMULA("This is a string")

enters the label *This is a string* in the active cell. For more examples of this function, see Chapter 17.

If you're working in the chart environment, you can use the FORMULA function to add and edit text labels and SERIES formulas. The effects of the FORMULA function depend on what type of chart object you've selected. For example, if you select a SERIES function in a chart and use FORMULA to create a SERIES function, Microsoft Excel overwrites the existing SERIES function. If, however, you select some other chart object and use FORMULA to create a SERIES function, Microsoft Excel adds the new SERIES formula to the chart. Similarly, if you select a text label and use FORMULA to enter a text label, Microsoft Excel overwrites the existing label. If, however, you select some other chart object and use FORMULA to create a text label, Microsoft Excel adds the new label to the chart.

The FORMULA.FILL function fills a range with an entry. Its action is equivalent to pressing the Shift key while locking in a formula. Like the FORMULA function, FORMULA.FILL takes the form

=FORMULA.FILL(*entry,reference*)

The FORMULA.ARRAY function lets you enter an array formula into a range of cells. Its action is equivalent to entering an array formula into the worksheet by pressing Control-Shift-Enter. The FORMULA.ARRAY function also takes the form

=FORMULA.ARRAY(*entry,reference*)

The SET.NAME function

The SET.NAME function creates a name in the macro sheet from within a macro and assigns a value to that name. It takes the form

=SET.NAME("*name*",*value*)

where the *name* argument is the name you want to create and the *value* argument is the value you want to store under that name. The *name* argument must be a string enclosed in quotation marks.

For example, the statement

=SET.NAME("Test",100)

stores the value 100 under the name *Test*. If, after running the macro that contains this line, you pull down the macro-sheet Formula menu and choose Define Name, you'll see the name *Test* in the list. If you select this name, you'll see that it refers to the value 100.

The *value* argument is usually a number; however, it can also be a formula, a text string enclosed in quotation marks, an array, or a cell reference. For example, if you've already created the name *Test* and assigned it to the value 100, the statement

=SET.NAME("Test",Test+1)

increases the value of Test by 1. Because Test is currently assigned to the value 100, this function stores the number 101 under the name *Test*.

The statement

=SET.NAME("Test",{1;2;3;4;5})

stores the vertical array {1;2;3;4;5} under the name *Test*. Finally, the *value* argument can also be a cell reference.

If you want to assign a name to a value that currently resides in a cell in the macro sheet, you must use the DEREF function within the SET.NAME function. For example, if cell C1 contains the value 100, the statement

=SET.NAME("Test",DEREF(C1))

stores the value 100 under the name *Test*.

The SET.NAME function is very similar to the DEFINE.NAME function; however, DEFINE.NAME creates a name only in the active worksheet. The SET.NAME function is best used for storing temporary values during macro execution.

The SET.VALUE function

The SET.VALUE function assigns a value to a cell in the macro sheet. This function takes the form

=SET.VALUE(*cell reference,value*)

where *cell reference* is the reference of the cell or range into which you want to enter *value*. For example, the statement

=SET.VALUE(C1,100)

enters the number 100 in cell C1 on the macro sheet.

The *value* argument is usually a number, but it can also be a text string enclosed in quotation marks, a formula, or an array. For example, the statement

=SET.VALUE(C2,"Test")

enters the text value *Test* in cell C2. The statement

=SET.VALUE(C1,C1+1)

increases the value in cell C1 by 1. If C1 contains the value 100, this function enters the number 101 in cell C1.

The statement

=SET.VALUE(C1:C5,{1;2;3;4;5})

enters the value 1 into cell C1, the value 2 into cell C2, and so on. If the *value* argument specifies an array that doesn't fit in the selected range, the function fills the specified range with as much of *value* as will fit.

One of the most important applications for SET.VALUE is incrementing coun-
ters in looping macros. We'll explain the concept of loops in the next chapter.

The GOTO function

The GOTO function lets you redirect the calculation of a macro. GOTO can be used
to branch from one macro to another or to create a loop within a macro. This function takes the form

    =GOTO(*reference*)

where *reference* is the reference or name of the cell that contains the next macro
function you want Microsoft Excel to execute. After it branches to *reference*,
Microsoft Excel continues to process the functions in the cells below *reference* until
it encounters a RETURN function, a HALT function, or another GOTO function.

For example, suppose you've created one macro in the range A2:A10 and
another in the range C2:C5 of the same macro sheet. You want Microsoft Excel to
run the second macro as soon as it completes the first one. To link these macros,
enter the statement

    =GOTO(C2)

in cell A10, the last cell in the first macro.

GOTO is also used frequently to create loops. A loop is a section of a macro
that is computed over and over a specified number of times. In Chapter 19, we'll
show you several examples of looping macros.

It is a good idea to name the cells referred to by GOTO functions and to include
those names as labels in the macro sheet. For example, suppose you've written a
macro that includes the statement

    =GOTO(C2)

This statement is easier to understand if you assign a name to cell C2 and then enter
that name as a label in cell C1.

The ref function

The *ref* function tells Microsoft Excel where to go to perform a subroutine macro.
This function takes no arguments; instead, you enter the cell reference, followed
by a pair of parentheses. For example, to route macro processing to cell B20, you
would enter the statement

    =B20()

If *ref* is a range, Microsoft Excel moves to the upper left corner of the reference. If
you want to run a macro on another macro sheet, *ref* can be an external reference.
In addition, *ref* can be a formula that returns a reference.

The RUN function

The RUN function lets you start one macro from within another macro. It is equivalent to the Run command on the Macro menu.

The form of the RUN function is

=RUN(*reference*)

where *reference* is either an external reference to the macro sheet that contains the macro you want to run or an R1C1 external reference in the form of text.

For example, the statement

=RUN(Macro1!A15)

runs the macro at cell A15 in the macro sheet Macro1, as does the statement

=RUN("Macro1!R15C1")

If cell A1 in Macro1 is named Test, the statement

=RUN(Macro1!Test)

also runs the macro.

The CALLER function

The CALLER function returns the reference of the cell containing the formula that started the currently running macro. This function takes no arguments.

For example, suppose you have two macros in a macro sheet: TEST and TEST1. Cell A10, which is part of the macro TEST, contains the statement

=TEST1()

If TEST1 contains the statement

=CALLER()

that function returns the address R10C1.

If the macro that contains the CALLER function is a command macro, the function returns the error #REF!.

The WAIT function

The WAIT function suspends the execution of a macro until a specified time. This function takes the form

=WAIT(*time*)

where *time* is the serial-number time to resume execution. For example, to pause execution until 2:00 PM, you could use the statement

=WAIT(0.583)

To pause execution for a specified amount of time, you can include an embedded NOW function in your *time* argument. Keeping in mind that one second is equal to about 0.00001, one minute to about 0.0007, and one hour to about 0.042, you could use the statement

=WAIT(NOW()+.00005)

to suspend a macro for about five seconds.

(You can also resume execution by pressing Esc, unless you've disabled the Esc key with a CANCEL.KEY function.)

The RESTART function

The RESTART function terminates a branch (nested) macro and forgets the location of the command that called it, enabling you to return control to whatever macro level you want. This function takes the form

=RESTART(*level*)

When you include this function without a *level* argument in a subroutine macro and Microsoft Excel subsequently encounters a RETURN statement, the macro simply stops and does not return control to the parent macro. The *level* argument, when included, tells Microsoft Excel to what level in the calling hierarchy to return control. The *level* argument is an integer that specifies how many preceding macros to jump over before returning control. For example,

=RESTART(1)

returns control not to the macro that initiated the current macro, but to the macro preceding the initiating macro.

The RESTART function does not take the place of a HALT or RETURN function.

The BEEP function

The BEEP function sounds the computer's bell. It takes the form

=BEEP(*number*)

where *number* represents a tone, 1 through 4. The tone your computer delivers for each number depends on your system. On some computers, such as the IBM PC, the tone for all four numbers is the same. If you omit *number*, Microsoft Excel assumes it to be 1.

BEEP is used most often to signal the user that some important event has occurred in the processing of a macro. For example, you might use BEEP to alert the user that some input is required or to signal the end of the macro.

The ECHO function

The ECHO function controls the updating of the screen during execution of a macro. It takes the form

=ECHO(*logical*)

If *logical* is FALSE, Microsoft Excel turns off screen updating. If *logical* is TRUE or omitted, the screen is updated as the macro runs. By turning off updating of the screen, you can increase the speed of your macros. You need not include an ECHO (TRUE) statement at the end of your macro. When the macro stops running, Microsoft Excel automatically sets ECHO back on. The same thing occurs when the macro is interrupted by an error message.

Turning ECHO off does not prevent Microsoft Excel from displaying dialog boxes on the screen.

The STEP function

The STEP function invokes Microsoft Excel's step mode and begins executing the current macro one step at a time. This function takes no arguments. For more on the STEP function, see Chapter 17.

The DISABLE.INPUT function

The DISABLE.INPUT function stops all keyboard and mouse input. This function takes the form

=DISABLE.INPUT(*logical*)

If *logical* is TRUE, Microsoft Excel accepts no input except from dialog boxes. If *logical* is FALSE, the user's input ability is restored.

The looping functions

Macro loops let you repeat a set of calculations. Loops come in handy for two reasons: First, they save space in the macro sheet because you can "recycle" a set of instructions instead of repeating them several times; second, the number of times a set of calculations should be repeated may vary from one situation to the next. By creating conditional tests, you can vary the number of times a macro subroutine is repeated.

You can use the next four functions—FOR, WHILE, NEXT, and BREAK—in a macro to repeat a calculation or action. To do this, you create FOR-NEXT and WHILE-NEXT loops. First, we're going to look at the functions. Then we'll discuss looping techniques.

The FOR function

The FOR function repeats a set of calculations a specific number of times. It takes the form

=FOR("*counter*",*start,stop,step*)

The *counter* argument identifies the named value that Microsoft Excel will use to keep track of how many times it has executed the loop. This argument must be a text string enclosed in quotation marks. The *start* argument is the value you want to begin with; the *stop* argument tells Microsoft Excel when to stop repeating the calculation or action. The *step* argument determines the increment Microsoft Excel uses each time it executes the loop. If you omit *step*, Microsoft Excel assumes it is 1.

You need not use the Define Name command to define your named counter value before running the macro. Microsoft Excel will create this named value automatically and reset it to its initial *start* value each time you run the macro.

The WHILE function

The WHILE function lets you repeat a set of calculations until a specified condition is met. This function takes the form

=WHILE(*logical*)

where *logical* is a logical value that determines whether Microsoft Excel executes the macro again. Generally, this argument is an embedded logical test that results in a TRUE or FALSE value. When *logical* is TRUE, Microsoft Excel continues to execute all statements up to the NEXT statement until *logical* becomes FALSE. If *logical* is FALSE the first time the macro reaches WHILE, Microsoft Excel skips the loop entirely and continues with the macro.

The NEXT function

The NEXT function ends FOR-NEXT loops and WHILE-NEXT loops and continues with the function following NEXT. This function takes no arguments.

The BREAK function

The BREAK function allows Microsoft Excel to escape from FOR-NEXT loops or WHILE-NEXT loops and continue with the function immediately after the NEXT function. The BREAK function takes no arguments.

Using Loops

Now that you're familiar with the building blocks of loops, let's look at how loops work within macros.

The FOR-NEXT loop tells Microsoft Excel to repeat a calculation or action for a specified number of times before continuing with the next macro function. You designate a counter name, a start value, a stop value, and, if desired, a step value to increment the counter. After each pass through the loop, Microsoft Excel adds the value in the *step* argument to the current value of *counter*. If *counter* is not greater than *stop*, Microsoft Excel goes through the loop again. When the counter value is greater than the stop value, Microsoft Excel stops the loop and continues with the macro function following NEXT.

For example, the series of statements

```
=FOR("Test",1,10,1)
=SET.VALUE(B1,B1*2)
=NEXT()
```

doubles the value in cell B1 of the macro sheet 10 times. Suppose cell B1 initially contains the value 2. On the first loop through this subroutine, Microsoft Excel will set that cell equal to 4 and add 1 to the counter value, which we've named Test. Then the program will double the value in the active cell again, setting that cell equal to 8, and increase the counter value to 3. This process will continue until the counter value, *Test*, is greater than 10. In fact, if you issue the Define Name command after this loop is completed, you'll see that Test equals 11. (At this point, A1 equals 2048.) The next time you run the macro, *Test* will automatically be reset to its start value, 1.

A WHILE-NEXT loop tells Microsoft Excel to repeat a calculation or action while a specified logical test is TRUE. Microsoft Excel continues its repetition until the logical test is FALSE and then continues with the next macro statement.

For example, consider this simple macro loop:

```
=WHILE(B1<2048)
=SET.VALUE(B1,B1*2)
=NEXT()
```

This looping routine works much like the FOR-NEXT loop you saw above. It doubles the value in cell B1 of the macro sheet. This time, however, the macro continues until cell B1 is greater than or equal to the test value 2048.

The BREAK function stops either a FOR-NEXT loop or a WHILE-NEXT loop before completion. Often, you'll want to embed the BREAK function in your loops to help you avoid error conditions. For example, in the series of statements

```
=WHILE(B1<2048)
=IF(TYPE(B1)<>1,BREAK())
=SET.VALUE(B1,B1*2)
=NEXT()
```

we used a logical function to ensure that cell B1 contains a numeric value. If cell B1 contains a text value, an error value, or any other type of entry, then Microsoft Excel will break the loop and continue with the macro formula immediately after the NEXT statement.

19

User-defined Functions

*U*ser-defined functions are one of the most innovative and exciting features of Microsoft Excel. The types of tasks that can be simplified, generalized, or streamlined with user-defined functions are nearly unlimited. These functions accept information from the worksheet, perform calculations, and then return the result to the worksheet.

Although Microsoft Excel includes a multitude of built-in functions, you probably still have sets of calculations that you perform regularly that could easily be condensed into functions. For example, suppose your company uses a complex mathematical formula for computing sales commissions. Wouldn't it be convenient if you had a function called COMMIS that would perform this calculation for you? Or suppose your company has a stepped discount schedule. Wouldn't it be helpful if you had a function called DISC that could compute the discount on any order for you automatically? In this chapter, we'll show you how to create such functions.

Function macro basics

User-defined functions are a special type of macro. However, to create a user-defined function, you need use only two macro commands: ARGUMENT and RETURN. The ARGUMENT function allows you to define the arguments your user-defined function will use. (We'll discuss the ARGUMENT function in detail later in this chapter.) The RETURN function returns the result of the user-defined function to the worksheet.

To see how these functions work, we'll build a simple example. Suppose your company pays a commission of 10 percent on all sales. Each week, the payroll department has to compute the commission on each salesperson's sales for that week. The worksheet in Figure 19-1 shows the weekly sales of four salespeople. Let's create a user-defined function to compute their commission for this week.

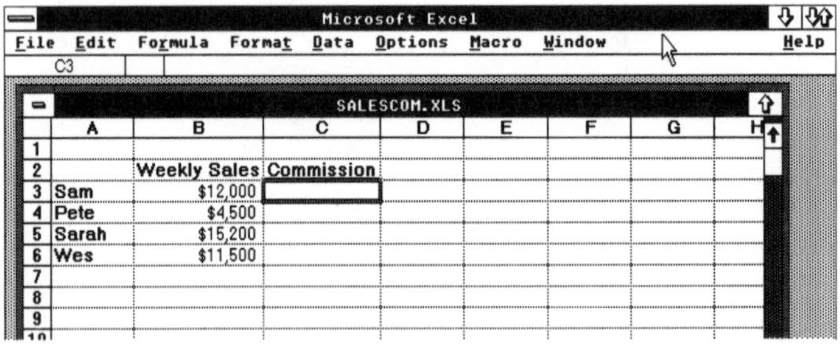

FIGURE 19-1. *We want to calculate each salesperson's commission.*

To begin, choose the New command from the File menu and select the Macro Sheet option. When the new macro sheet appears, type *COMMIS* in cell A1. (This first step is not required, but it's a good idea. You'll see why in a moment.) Next, select cell A2 and enter the statement

=ARGUMENT("Sales")

Now select cell A3 and enter the formula

=Sales*0.1

Finally, enter the statement

=RETURN(A3)

in cell A4. Figure 19-2 shows the macro sheet at this point.

Next, you must give this function macro a name. As with all other macros, this name is simply a label you assign to the first cell in the macro. In this case, the first cell in the macro is cell A2. (The name in cell A1 isn't technically a part of the macro.) To name this cell, select the cell and choose the Define Name command

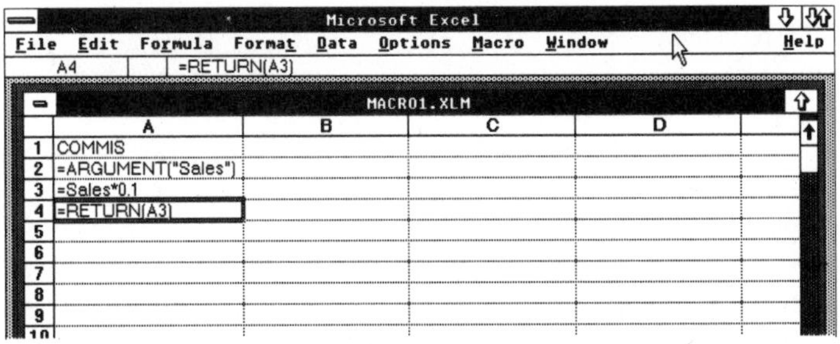

FIGURE 19-2. *This function macro calculates salespeople's commissions.*

from the Formula menu. You'll notice that the Refers to edit bar contains the coordinates of the selected cell, $A$2, and the Name edit bar contains the label from cell A1, COMMIS. First, tell Microsoft Excel that the macro you're naming is a function macro by selecting the Function button. Then, to accept the default name, COMMIS, simply select the OK button or press Enter.

Now you're ready to use the function you've defined. To do this, activate the worksheet and then select cell C3. Now enter

=MACRO1.XLM!COMMIS(B3)

in that cell. Notice that the name of this user-defined function includes two parts: The first part, MACRO1.XLM!, identifies the macro sheet that contains the function; the second part is simply the macro name, COMMIS. The function's argument, B3, identifies the cell you want the function to operate on. When you press Enter to lock in this function, it will calculate and return the correct commission for the sales amount in cell B3: $1,200. Of course, you'll want to copy this formula into cells C4:C6 as well, as shown in Figure 19-3. To do this, you can use the Fill Down command from the Edit menu. Because the reference to cell B3 in the original formula

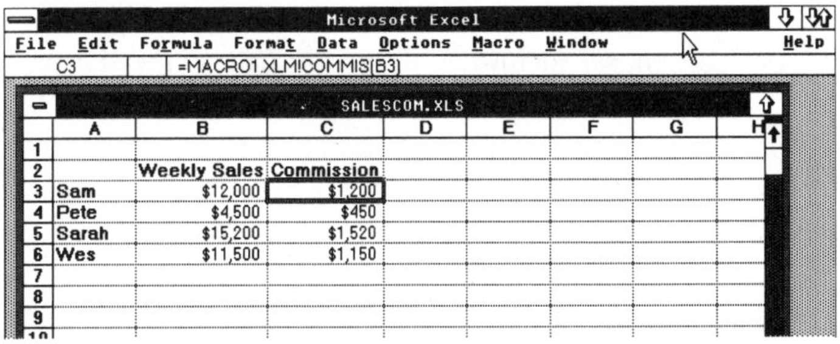

FIGURE 19-3. *The worksheet shows the result of the user-defined function COMMIS.*

is a relative reference, it will change as this formula is copied into the new cells, so that the formula in cell C4 is

=MACRO1.XLM!COMMIS(B4)

and so forth.

Let's consider what happens when you enter this function in the worksheet. When you press Enter, Microsoft Excel immediately looks on macro sheet MACRO1 for the cell named COMMIS (cell A2). Then it processes the statements in cells A2, A3, and A4 of the macro sheet, one at a time. The ARGUMENT statement in cell A2 assigns the name *Sales* to the value in cell B3, $12,000. (Remember that B3 is the cell we used as the argument for the function in cell C3.) In effect, Microsoft Excel "passes" the value from cell B3 to the sheet MACRO1, where it is stored under the name *Sales*. If you now select the macro sheet and choose the Define Name command from the Formula menu, you'll see the name *Sales* in the list of names. If you select this name, you'll see the value 11500 (the last value in the Weekly Sales column of the worksheet) in the Refers to edit bar.

Next, the formula in cell A3 multiplies the value of Sales by 0.1. Finally, the RETURN statement in cell A4 passes the value of the formula in cell A3, $1,200, back to C3, the worksheet cell that contains the COMMIS function.

Now suppose you need to change the values in cells B3:B6. As you might expect, Microsoft Excel will update the commission calculations in cells C3:C6 as you enter the new sales figures.

This first example is trivial, but when the computations become more complex, user-defined functions can be real time-savers. In a page or two, we'll expand on this example to make the advantages of user-defined functions clear.

Function macro rules

Although the example we've just looked at is very simple, it illustrates many of the characteristics of function macros. First, every function macro must include at least one ARGUMENT function and a RESULT function. Most function macros will also include one or more formulas that perform computations using the arguments.

The order of the functions in a user-defined function macro is important. The macro must begin with one or more ARGUMENT functions and must end with the RETURN function. The formulas that actually do the work of the function must be between the ARGUMENT functions and the RETURN function.

Often, you'll begin your function macro in cell A2 in a blank macro sheet, as we did in the example. The location of the macro in the macro sheet is not restricted, however. You could as easily enter this macro in cells Z101 to Z103 and assign the name *COMMIS* to cell Z100.

You can use only function macros that are located in open macro sheets. If you close a macro sheet that contains a function macro referred to by user-defined functions in open worksheets, the values of those functions will change to #REF!. To recompute the functions, you must reopen the macro sheet.

Names for user-defined functions

As a general rule, you should give a user-defined function the shortest name that sufficiently describes the function's purpose and yet sets it apart from other functions. For example, you might call a function that computes federal income taxes FEDERAL_INCOME_TAX, but you would be better off shortening that long name to FEDINCTAX, FEDTAX, or FEDTX. Be sure you don't make the names of your user-defined functions so short that they aren't descriptive. For example, you probably wouldn't want to call your federal income tax function TAX, because this name doesn't tell you what kind of tax the function computes. You also should not give your functions names that conflict with the names of Microsoft Excel's built-in functions, such as PV, SUM, LINEST, or IF.

Similarly, you must specify the name of a macro sheet every time you use a user-defined function, so we suggest you get in the habit of using very short, descriptive names for your macro sheets. For example, you might want to use a name like UD1 (for User-defined 1) for the first macro sheet in which you create user-defined functions, UD2 for the second such sheet, and so on. Alternatively, you can use short macro-sheet names that describe the user-defined functions in the sheet. For example, you might name a macro sheet that contains depreciation functions DEP or name a sheet that contains tax functions TAX. Then you can assign names to the individual functions that describe the particular purpose of that function within the general group. For example, you might have a federal income tax function named FED stored in a macro sheet named TAX. To use the function, you would type

=TAX.XLM!FED()

To change the name of a macro sheet, use the Save As command on the File menu. When you choose this command, Microsoft Excel offers you an opportunity to supply a new name for the sheet. To save the sheet with a new name, simply type the name and select the OK button.

If you've used in a worksheet any of the user-defined functions on the macro sheet you're saving and the worksheet is still open, the names of those functions will change automatically when you save the macro sheet. For example, suppose a cell contains the formula

=MACRO1.XLM!COMMIS(C5)

If you use Save As to change the name of MACRO1 to SALES, the formula will change to

=SALES.XLM!COMMIS(C5)

The Paste Function command

After you've created a user-defined function, Microsoft Excel adds the name of that function to the list you see when you choose the Paste Function command from the Formula menu. User-defined functions always appear in alphabetic order at the end of the list.

Instead of typing the macro-sheet name and function name, you can now select the user-defined function you want to use from the list. When you do this, Microsoft Excel enters the macro-sheet name and the function name into the formula bar. All you need do is supply the arguments (by typing or pasting) and choose the Enter box or press Enter to lock in the function.

The Paste Function list always includes the names of all the user-defined functions contained in any *open* macro sheets. When you open a macro sheet, Microsoft Excel adds the names of any user-defined functions in that sheet to the Paste Function list; when you close a macro sheet, all the names in that sheet are removed from the list.

Making a change

Let's expand our simple commission calculation to see how function macros can be edited. Suppose your company uses a more complex commission formula: Salespeople receive a 10-percent commission if they sell less than $5,000 worth of goods, an 11-percent commission if they sell more than $5,000 worth of goods but less than $15,000 worth, and a 12-percent commission if they sell more than $15,000 worth of goods.

To modify our simple function to perform this new calculation, select the macro sheet MACRO1.XLM, select cell A3 (the cell that contains the commission calculation), and enter the formula

=IF(Sales>15000,Sales*0.12,IF(Sales>5000,Sales*0.11,Sales*0.1))

That's all there is to it: The user-defined function will now compute commissions using the new formula.

If you switch back to the worksheet, however, you'll see that the values in cells C3 to C6 haven't changed. Microsoft Excel doesn't update the user-defined functions in your worksheet when you make a change to the macro that defines the function. To update the results in the worksheet, it is necessary to re-enter the user-defined functions in cells C3:C6. You can do this manually by selecting each of the cells and retyping the function. Fortunately, however, the mouse provides an easier method: You can select each of the cells in the range, one by one, and, while the cell is selected, click on the formula bar and then immediately choose the Enter box. "Editing" each cell in this way updates the functions. Figure 19-4 shows the worksheet after the functions have been updated.

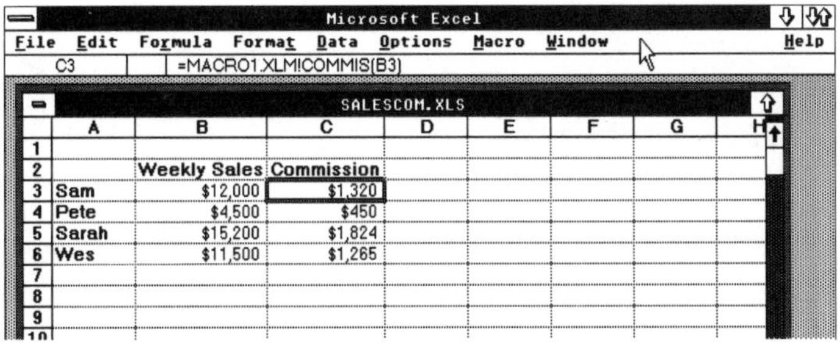

FIGURE 19-4. *We recalculated the commissions using the revised function macro.*

Notice that cell A3 in the revised function macro contains a complicated IF statement. Microsoft Excel allows you to use all the functions you learned about in Chapter 6 in macro sheets. These functions behave exactly the same way in a macro sheet as they do in a worksheet. In a few pages, we'll look at a complex user-defined function that uses the VLOOKUP function.

Functions with more than one argument

Now let's consider a more complex example. Suppose your company sells three products and each product carries a different discount schedule. Salespeople earn a 10-percent commission on all sales of Product 1 and an 8-percent commission on sales of Product 2. They earn a commission on Product 3 of 10 percent on sales to $5,000 and 12 percent on sales of $5,000 or more. Any salesperson who sells at least $25,000 total for all three products in a period earns an additional 1-percent bonus commission.

Let's create a new function macro to make this computation. Move to cell A6 in the MACRO1.XLM sheet and enter the name *COMMIS2*. Then enter the macro shown in Figure 19-5 into cells A7:A16. When you've finished, select cell A7 and choose the Define Name command from the Formula menu. Microsoft Excel suggests the name *COMMIS2* for the selected cell. To accept this name, first select the Function button and then select OK or press Enter.

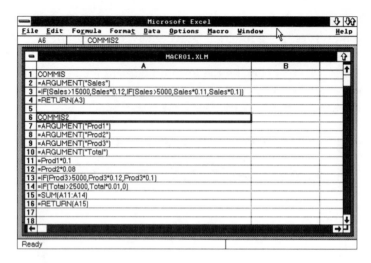

FIGURE 19-5. *We created a more complex commission function macro.*

This new function macro is considerably more complex than the other two we've built. First, notice that it includes four ARGUMENT functions. When we use this user-defined function in the worksheet, it will have the form

=MACRO1.XLM!COMMIS2(*Prod1,Prod2,Prod3,Total*)

where *Prod1* is the sales of Product 1, *Prod2* is the sales of Product 2, *Prod3* is the sales of Product 3, and *Total* is the total sales for the period. The four ARGUMENT functions will store the values you specify for these four arguments under the names *Prod1*, *Prod2*, *Prod3*, and *Total*.

Notice that the order of the arguments in the user-defined function matches that of the ARGUMENT statements in the macro. This is critical; if you enter the arguments in the function in a different order, the function will not compute the correct result. Of course, you're free to define the order of the arguments in any way you wish by changing the order in which the ARGUMENT statements are presented in the macro sheet.

Also notice that the COMMIS2 function macro includes five formulas, in cells A11 through A15, whereas the earlier examples included only one formula. The first three formulas compute the commissions on sales of Product 1, Product 2, and Product 3. The formula in cell A14 computes the bonus commission on sales over $25,000, and the formula in cell A15 computes the total commission by summing the results of the first four formulas.

The RETURN statement in cell A16 returns the result of the formula in cell A15 in the macro sheet to the cell in the worksheet that contains the user-defined function.

Notice that this macro follows the rules outlined earlier regarding the order of the terms in a function macro: ARGUMENT functions first, followed by the computing formulas, followed by the RETURN function. This order is absolutely required.

Also notice that we've called this function COMMIS2 instead of COMMIS, because there can't be two user-defined functions with the same name in the same macro sheet. Microsoft Excel would have allowed you to name this new macro COMMIS, but it would then have removed the name from cell A2 and, hence, from the simpler macro.

Now let's put this user-defined function to work. Create the new commissions worksheet shown in Figure 19-6, select cell F3, and enter

=MACRO1.XLM!COMMIS2(B3,C3,D3,E3)

When you press Enter to lock in the function, Microsoft Excel will compute the macro COMMIS2 and display the correct commission for Sam in cell F3. To complete the job, use the Fill Down command to copy the formula from cell F3 into cells F4:F6.

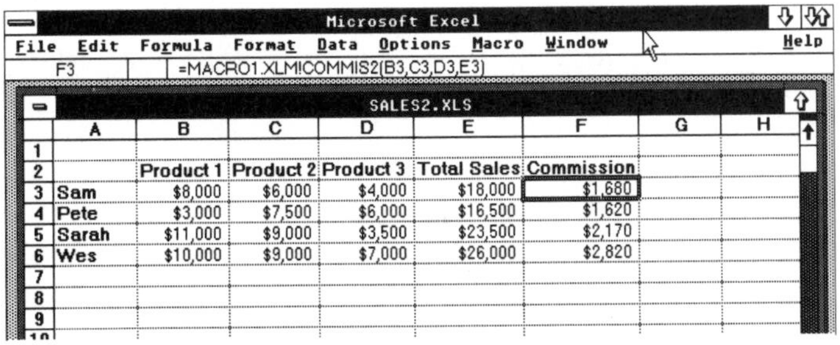

FIGURE 19-6. *We entered the user-defined function COMMIS2 in cells F3:F6.*

Here's how the function works. As soon as you lock the function in the worksheet cell, Microsoft Excel calculates the macro. The four ARGUMENT statements store the values from cells B3, C3, D3, and E3 under the names *Prod1*, *Prod2*, *Prod3*, and *Total*. (Now you see why the order of the arguments in the function must match the order of the ARGUMENT functions in the macro.) The formulas in cells A11:A14 in the macro sheet then compute the commissions on all three products and the bonus commission (if any). Next, the formula in cell A15 computes the total commission. Finally, the RETURN function in cell A16 returns the value from cell A15 in the macro sheet to cell F3 in the worksheet.

A compound-interest function

Suppose you're contemplating investing $100,000 in an account that will pay an-
nual interest of 10 percent—guaranteed—for as long as you hold the investment.
You want to know what the value of the investment will be at any given time in the
future. Let's build a user-defined function that will make this computation.

To begin, set up a worksheet like the one shown in Figure 19-7. Cell C2 in this
worksheet contains the guaranteed rate of interest, cell C3 contains the amount
you want to invest, and cell C4 contains the term of the investment. We'll use these
three variables as the arguments in our function.

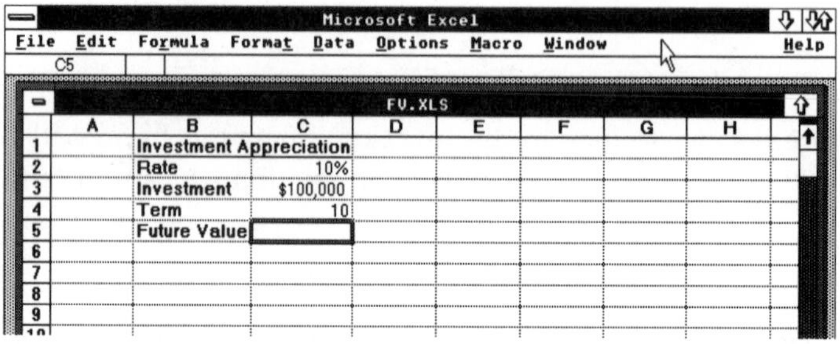

FIGURE 19-7. *This worksheet is designed to calculate the future value of
an investment.*

Now let's create a new macro sheet named COMPFV to hold our macro and enter the label COMPOUND in cell A1. This text entry will become the name of the
function. Next, enter the function macro shown in Figure 19-8 into cells A2:A6 in
the macro sheet.

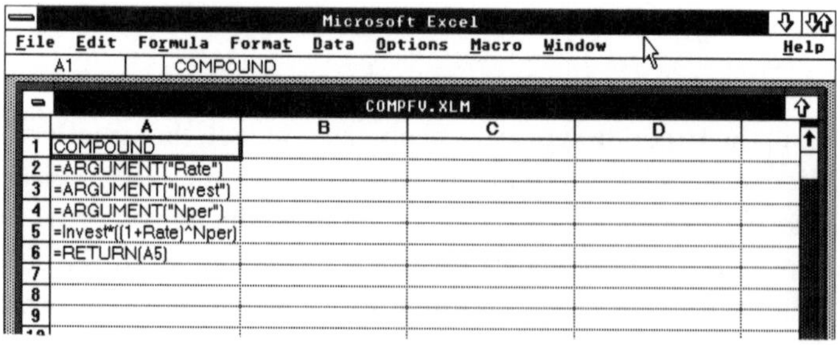

FIGURE 19-8. *This function macro returns the future value of an
investment.*

When you've finished entering the macro, select cell A2, choose the Define Name command from the Formula menu, select Function to tell Microsoft Excel this is a function macro, and select OK or press Enter to accept the default name, COMPOUND.

Now select your worksheet again, select cell C5, and type

=COMPFV.XLM!COMPOUND(

As with Microsoft Excel's built-in functions, you can paste arguments into user-defined functions, so instead of typing the references to cells C2, C3, and C4, select cell C2, type a comma, select cell C3, type another comma, and select cell C4. Finally, type a closing parenthesis to finish the function and press Enter. Figure 19-9 shows the result.

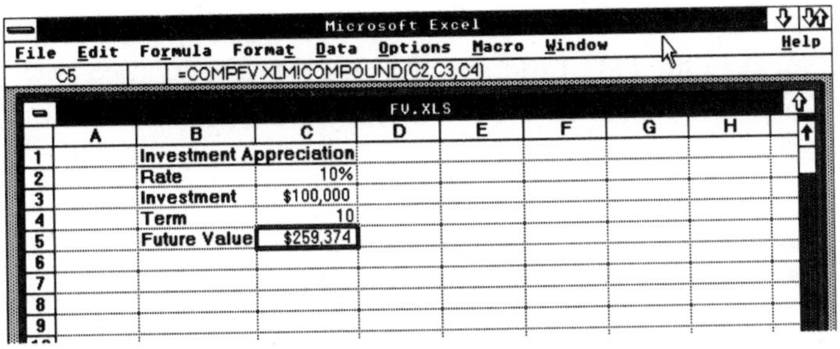

FIGURE 19-9. *We used the COMPOUND function to compute the future value of our investment.*

Here's how the function works. The three ARGUMENT functions in cells A2, A3, and A4 of the macro sheet store the values from cells C2, C3, and C4 of the worksheet under the names *Rate*, *Invest*, and *Nper*. Then the formula in cell A5

=Invest*((1+Rate)^Nper)

computes the future value of the investment Nper periods into the future. Finally, the RETURN function in cell A6 returns the result of the computation from cell A5 to cell C5 in the worksheet.

As with the other user-defined functions we've created, if you change the values of the arguments in cells C2, C3, and C4 of the worksheet, the value of the function in cell C5 will also change.

Like the COMMIS function, this user-defined function is fairly simple. In fact, you could perform the same computation using Microsoft Excel's built-in FV function. Our purpose in presenting this example is simply to demonstrate the form and operation of user-defined functions. Later in this chapter, we'll show some examples of user-defined functions that are considerably more complex.

Interest and principal paid-to-date functions

As you learned in Chapter 6, Microsoft Excel offers several financial functions, such as PV, FV, and IRR, that allow you to make complex financial computations simply and easily. Among the most useful of these functions is PMT, which computes the periodic payment required to amortize a loan. However, although PMT is a very helpful tool, several other loan repayment calculations are often needed.

Figure 19-10 shows a worksheet that includes all the data you need to compute the periodic payment on a loan. Cell B3 in this worksheet contains the amount you've borrowed, $10,000. Cell B4 contains the periodic interest rate, 1.00% (we're assuming that this loan requires monthly payments). The term of the loan in months, 60, appears in cell B5. Finally, cell B6 contains the formula

    =PMT(B4,B5,−B3)

which computes the monthly payment on the loan: $222.44. (Notice that we made the last argument in the PMT function negative. Normally, the result of the PMT function is a negative number because it represents a cash outflow. We find the use of negative numbers for payments confusing, however. By changing the sign of the last argument, we make the result of PMT positive instead of negative.)

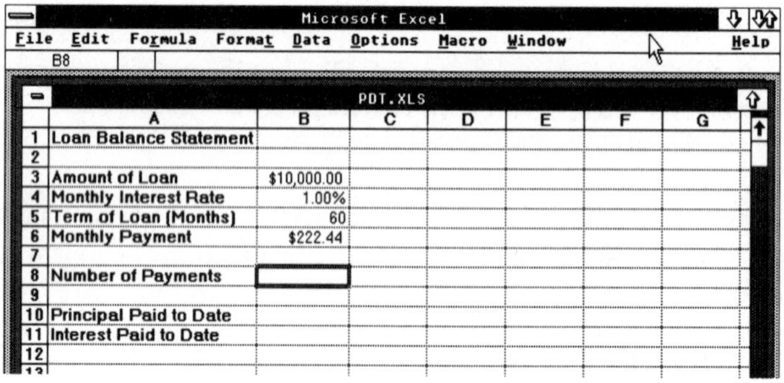

FIGURE 19-10. *This worksheet is designed to display principal and interest paid to date.*

Now suppose you want to know how much principal and interest you will have paid after you've made five payments. To make these calculations, you can create two function macros like the ones shown in Figure 19-11. Let's look at these macros in detail.

The first function macro, PPTD (for Principal Paid To Date), begins with five ARGUMENT statements that define the arguments Rate, Term, Prin, Payment, and PayNum. The formula in cell A7

    =Prin+PV(Rate,(Term−PayNum),Payment)

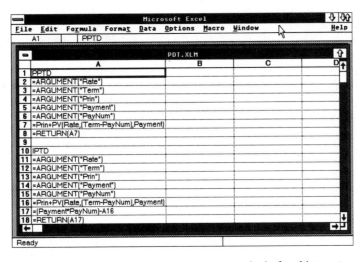

FIGURE 19-11. *These function macros compute principal and interest paid to date.*

determines the principal paid to date by computing the present value of the remaining payments and then adding that value (which is a negative number) to the beginning principal balance. The RETURN statement in cell A8 of the macro sheet then returns this value to the worksheet.

The second function macro, IPTD (for Interest Paid To Date), begins in cell A11. Like the PPTD macro, IPTD begins with five ARGUMENT functions that define the arguments Rate, Term, Prin, Payment, and PayNum. The formula in cell A16, which is identical to the one in cell A7 in the PPTD function macro, computes the principal paid to date. Then the formula in cell A17

=(Payment*PayNum)–A16

computes the interest paid to date by subtracting the principal paid to date in cell A16 from the total amount paid to date. The total amount paid to date is computed by multiplying Payment (the monthly payment) by PayNum (the number of payments that have been made). After this computation is made, the RETURN statement in cell A18 returns this value to the worksheet.

Of course, before you can use these functions, you must assign the name *PPTD* to cell A2 and the name *IPTD* to cell A11.

Let's see how these functions work. Return to the worksheet and enter the number 5 in cell B8. Now enter

=PDT.XLM!PPTD(B4,B5,B3,B6,B8)

in cell B10 and

=PDT.XLM!IPTD(B4,B5,B3,B6,B8)

in cell B11. Figure 19-12 shows the result. The number in cell B10, $624.59, is the amount of principal paid in the first five monthly payments; the number in cell B11, $487.63, is the amount of interest paid during the same period.

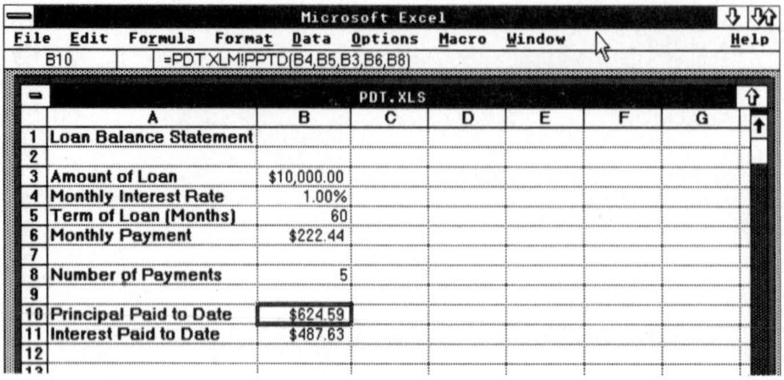

FIGURE 19-12. *We entered the user-defined functions PPTD and IPTD in cells B10 and B11 of the worksheet.*

Omitting arguments

Some of Microsoft Excel's built-in functions allow you to omit certain arguments. For example, you can omit the *type* and *future value* arguments from a PV function and Microsoft Excel will still compute the result of the function. If you omit an argument from a user-defined function, however, Microsoft Excel assigns the value #N/A to that argument. As you learned in Chapter 2, any formula that refers to a cell or a name that contains the value #N/A generally assumes the value #N/A as well. Thus, if you omit an argument, the function will probably return the value #N/A. You can avoid this problem by using the IF function to test the value of each of the arguments you might omit from the user-defined function to see if they have the value #N/A.

For example, suppose you want to create a simple function, called Triangle, that uses the Pythagorean theorem to compute the length of any side of a right triangle, given the lengths of the other two sides. The function macro shown in Figure 19-13 performs this task.

The first three lines in this macro, which is stored in the macro sheet TRI.XLM, include three ARGUMENT statements that define Long, Short1, and Short2. The next three lines all contain IF statements that test the values of these arguments for possible #N/A errors. The statement in cell A5

=IF(ISNA(Long),RETURN(SQRT((Short1^2)+(Short2^2))))

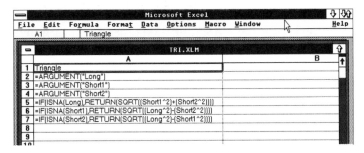

FIGURE 19-13. *This function macro computes the length of any side of a right triangle, given the lengths of the other two sides.*

tests the value of Long. If Long contains #N/A, Microsoft Excel computes the square root of the sums of the squares of the lengths of the two short sides and returns that value to the worksheet. If not, Microsoft Excel processes the statement in cell A6

=IF(ISNA(Short1),RETURN(SQRT((Long^2)−(Short2^2))))

which tests the value of Short1. If Short1 contains #N/A, Microsoft Excel computes the square root of the difference of the square of the length of the long side and the square of the length of the other short side and returns that value to the worksheet. If not, Microsoft Excel processes the statement in cell A7

=IF(ISNA(Short2),RETURN(SQRT((Long^2)−(Short1^2))))

which tests the value of Short2. If Short2 equals #N/A, then Microsoft Excel computes the square root of the difference of the square of the length of the long side and the square of the length of the other short side and returns that value to the worksheet.

To name this function, select cell A2, choose the Define Name command from the Formula menu, select the Function button, and select OK or press Enter to accept the default name, Triangle.

Now let's see how the function works. The formula

=TRI.XLM!Triangle(5,4,)

returns the value 3, the length of the missing short side. Similarly, the formula

=TRI.XLM!Triangle(5,,3)

returns 4, the length of the other missing short side. And finally, the formula

=TRI.XLM!Triangle(,4,3)

returns 5, the length of the long side.

In this macro, we were able to avoid using the omitted argument in any calculations. For this reason, we didn't have to worry about a #N/A value being passed from formula to formula in the macro. If you must use an omitted argument in a calculation, you can use the SET.NAME function to assign that argument the value 0 or 1, so that it has no effect on the calculation.

A lookup function

Suppose your company uses the following discount schedule for the products it sells to wholesalers and retailers:

Quantity purchased	Wholesale discount (%)	Retail discount (%)
0–5	0	0
6–10	0	40
11–20	50	41
21–50	51	43
51 or more	52	45

You want to create a user-defined function that will return the correct discount, given the type of customer you're selling to and the quantity purchased.

Figure 19-14 shows a simple invoice worksheet. Cell B4 contains a code that describes the type of customer: W for wholesale, R for retail. Cell C13 contains the total quantities ordered by the customer. The values in these cells will be the arguments for the function we're going to define.

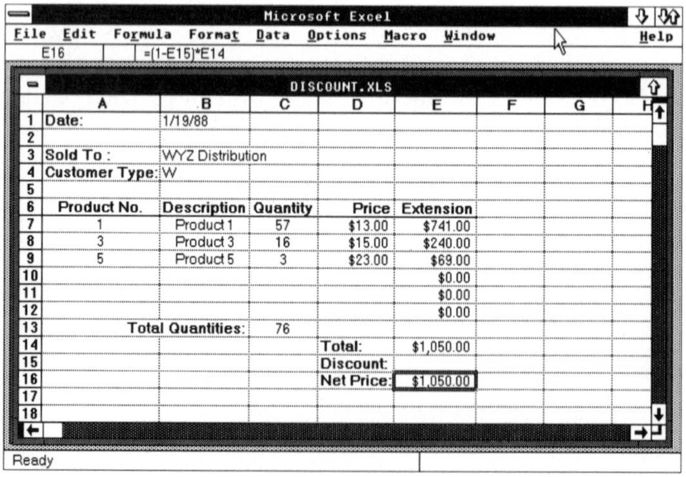

FIGURE 19-14. *This worksheet is set up to calculate the correct discount for the type of customer and the quantity ordered.*

To define the function, create a new macro sheet (we'll call it DISCOUNT.XLM) and enter the macro shown in Figure 19-15. Let's walk through this macro so that you can see how it works.

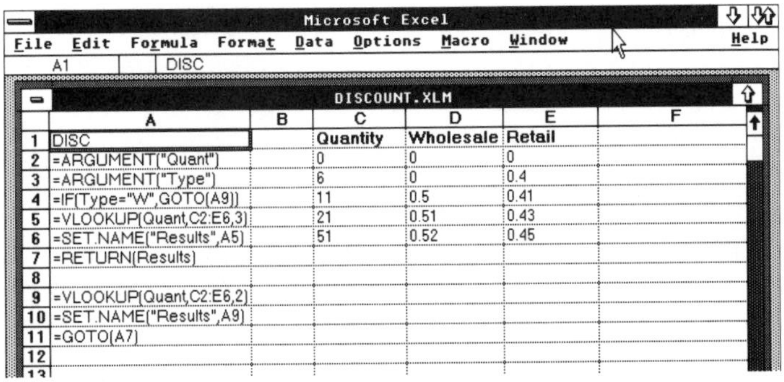

	A	B	C	D	E	F
1	DISC		Quantity	Wholesale	Retail	
2	=ARGUMENT("Quant")		0	0	0	
3	=ARGUMENT("Type")		6	0	0.4	
4	=IF(Type="W",GOTO(A9))		11	0.5	0.41	
5	=VLOOKUP(Quant,C2:E6,3)		21	0.51	0.43	
6	=SET.NAME("Results",A5)		51	0.52	0.45	
7	=RETURN(Results)					
8						
9	=VLOOKUP(Quant,C2:E6,2)					
10	=SET.NAME("Results",A9)					
11	=GOTO(A7)					
12						

FIGURE 19-15. *The DISC function macro calculates customer discounts.*

Cell A1 of the macro sheet contains the text entry DISC, which will become the name of the macro. Cells A2 and A3 contain ARGUMENT statements that define the arguments Quant and Type. Notice that we don't have to do anything special to define Type as a text argument. The ARGUMENT function can accept either numeric or text arguments. The statement in cell A4

=IF(Type="W",GOTO(A9))

tests the value of Type. If Type is W, the GOTO statement tells Microsoft Excel to jump to cell A9 and execute the instruction it finds there. The statement in cell A9

=VLOOKUP(Quant,C2:E6,2)

uses the value of Quant to look up the appropriate discount from the second column of the lookup table in the range C2:E6. The SET.NAME statement in cell A10 then stores the result of the lookup under the name *Results*. Next, the GOTO statement in cell A11 sends the macro back to cell A7. The RETURN function in cell A7 then returns the value of Results to the worksheet.

If Type is not W, the macro continues with the statement in cell A5

=VLOOKUP(Quant,C2:E6,3)

instead of branching to cell A9. This statement uses the value of Quant to look up the appropriate discount from the third column of the lookup table in the range C2:E6. The statement in cell A6 then stores the result instruction of the lookup under the name *Results* and the RETURN statement in cell A7 returns the value of Results to the worksheet.

After you've created this function, select cell A2 and choose the Define Name command from the Formula menu. Microsoft Excel will suggest the name DISC for the selected cell. To accept this name, simply select Function and then select OK or press Enter.

Now let's use the DISC function. Activate your worksheet, select cell E15, and then enter

=DISCOUNT.XLM!DISC(C13,B4)

Figure 19-16 shows the result. As you can see, Microsoft Excel has looked up the correct discount from the table in the macro sheet and returned that value to cell E15 of the worksheet. The formula in cell E16

=(1–E15)*E14

uses this result to compute the net price of the order. Of course, if you change either the entry in cell B4 or the total in cell C13, the result of the function will change.

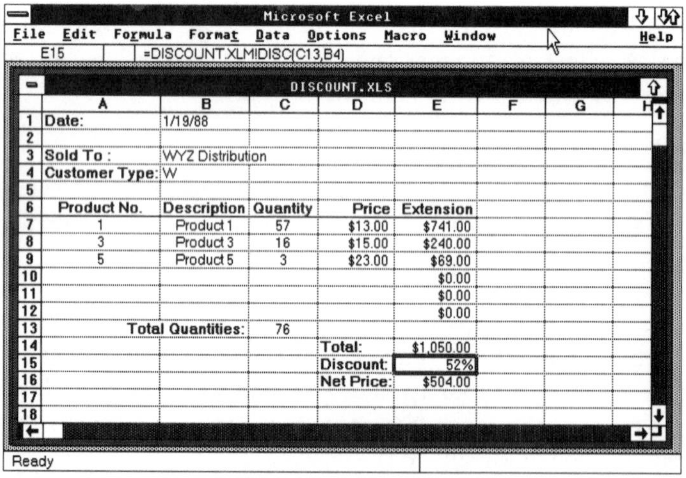

FIGURE 19-16. *We used the DISC function to calculate the discount.*

A modification

What if the user makes an entry other than W or R in cell B4? The way the macro is presently structured, the function will return the retail discount no matter what else is entered in cell B4. The IF function in cell A4 tests to see if Type is W. If Type is not W, the macro assumes it is R and uses the first VLOOKUP function to compute the discount.

To overcome this problem, you can modify the macro as shown in Figure 19-17. To make this change, select row 7, choose the Insert command from the Edit menu to insert a new row, and then enter the statement

=IF(AND(Type<>"R",Type<>"W"),SET.NAME("Results","#VALUE!"),)

in the new cell A7. The SET.NAME function lets you create a name on the macro sheet from within a macro and then assign a value to that name. Here we've used the SET.NAME function to create the name *Results* and assign #VALUE! to it.

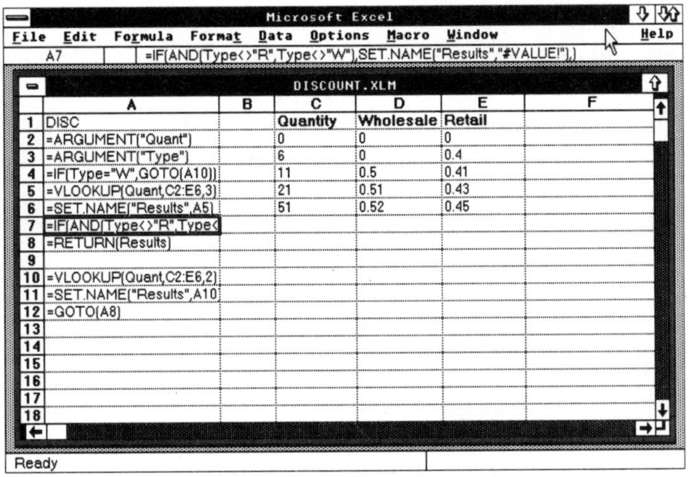

FIGURE 19-17. *We modified the DISC function macro to trap erroneous entries.*

This change prevents the kind of error we described. The new macro tests the value of Type just before it returns Results to the worksheet. If Type is not R or W, the statement in cell A7 changes the value of Results to the error value #VALUE! so that the function no longer returns an erroneous value. (Notice that user-defined functions can return error values as well as numbers and text.)

By the way, notice that, after we inserted a new row in the macro, we had to change a couple of cell references. The SET.NAME function in cell A11 now refers to cell A10, and the GOTO function in cell A12 now refers to cell A8. Whenever you insert or delete rows in a macro, be sure to check all cell references for possible modifications.

The basic concept presented in this macro—storing a lookup table on a macro sheet and using a function macro to look up values from that table—can be applied to many different types of user-defined functions. For example, you can use this technique to create functions that perform complicated tax computations based on tax tables you store in a macro sheet.

The ARGUMENT function

The full form of the ARGUMENT function is

=ARGUMENT("*name*",*type*,*cell reference*)

where *name* is the name of the argument, *type* is a number that specifies the type of the argument, and *cell reference* is the cell where you want Microsoft Excel to store the value of the argument (more about this later). The *type* and *cell reference* arguments are optional.

Each argument in a function macro must have a unique name. If you use the same name for two arguments in a function macro, Microsoft Excel will replace the first definition of the name with the second definition.

For instance, suppose you've written a macro named QUIZ that begins with the statements

=ARGUMENT("Test")

and

=ARGUMENT("Test")

When you enter the formula

=QUIZ(A1,A2)

into the worksheet, the first ARGUMENT statement will store the value from cell A1 in the worksheet under the name *Test*. Then the second statement will store the value from cell A2 under the same name and remove the name from the value in cell A1.

For the same reason, be sure not to use the SET.NAME function to define range names that conflict with your argument names. If you do, the value of the argument will be replaced with the value defined by SET.NAME.

You can, however, have two function macros in one macro sheet that have arguments with the same names. Because Microsoft Excel calculates each function separately, the names will not conflict.

The type *argument*

The *type* argument allows you to use different types of entries as arguments in your user-defined functions. The possible values of the *type* argument and their meanings are shown on the following page.

Value	Expected data type
1	Number
2	Text
4	Logical
8	Reference
16	Error
64	Array

You can also use the sum of any two or more of these codes as the *type* argument. If you do this, Microsoft Excel will accept any of those data types in the argument being defined. For example, if you use the number 3, which is the sum of codes 1 and 2, Microsoft Excel will allow the argument being defined to be of either type 1 (number) or type 2 (text). In fact, the default *type* argument is 7, which is the sum of codes 1 (number), 2 (text), and 4 (logical).

You'll rarely, if ever, need to specify any type but the default, 7. In fact, about the only time you'll use the *type* argument is when you want to use an array as an argument in one of your user-defined functions. Let's look at an example of a function that uses array arguments.

Array arguments

Many of Microsoft Excel's built-in functions operate on ranges of cells. For example, the SUM function totals the values in a range. At times, you'll want to use ranges as arguments in your user-defined functions. To do this, you must set the *type* argument in the ARGUMENT function to 64.

For example, the worksheet in Figure 19-18 includes the semester grades in Business 101 for Joe Jones. Column B in this worksheet shows Joe's scores for the semester, and column C shows the weights the professor has assigned to each of those scores. You need to compute Joe's weighted average score for the semester.

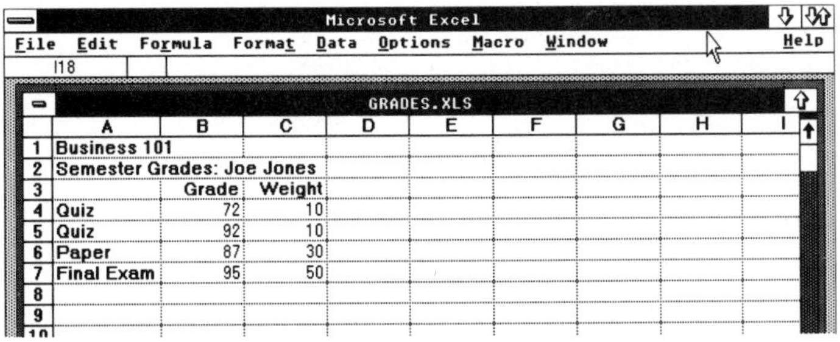

FIGURE 19-18. *This worksheet is designed to compute weighted average scores.*

You can compute the weighted average in one of three ways. First, you could enter the formula

=B4*C4

in cell D4 and then copy that formula into cells D5, D6, and D7. Then you could enter the formula

=SUM(C4:C7)

in cell C8 and copy that formula into cell D8. Finally, you could enter the formula

=D8/C8

in cell D9 to obtain the weighted average: 90.

Alternatively, you could enter the array formula

=SUM(B4:B7*C4:C7)/SUM(C4:C7)

in cell D9. (Remember, to make this function an array formula, you have to press Ctrl-Shift-Enter to lock it in.) This formula tells Microsoft Excel to compute the sum of the products of the values in cells B4:B7 and C4:C7 and then divide that result by the sum of the values in the range C4:C7.

Instead of using either of these methods, you can create a user-defined function, called WAVG, that will compute the weighted average of any list of values. To do this, first create a macro sheet (or open an existing sheet) and then enter the macro shown in Figure 19-19.

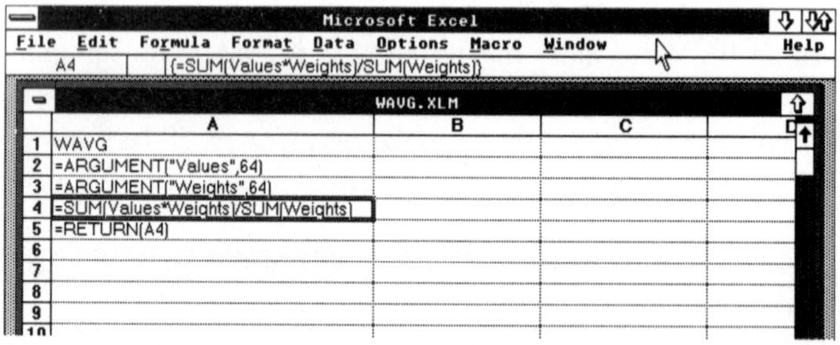

FIGURE 19-19. *This function macro calculates weighted averages.*

The entry in cell A1 of this macro sheet, WAVG, is the name of the new function. The statement in cell A2

=ARGUMENT("Values",64)

defines the Values argument and informs Microsoft Excel that Values will be an array. Similarly, the statement in cell A3

=ARGUMENT("Weights",64)

defines the Weights array argument. The formula in cell A4

=SUM(Values*Weights)/SUM(Weights)

is similar to the array formula we would have created had we used the second method above. This formula tells Microsoft Excel to compute the sum of the products of the values in the Values array and the Weights array and to divide that result by the sum of the values in the Weights array. To make this formula an array formula, we pressed Ctrl-Shift-Enter to lock it in.

The last line in the macro

=RETURN(A4)

returns the result of the calculation in cell A4 to the cell in the worksheet that contains the user-defined function.

After you've entered the macro, select cell A2 and choose the Define Name command from the Formula menu. A Define Name dialog box will appear, proposing WAVG as the name for cell A2. Select Function to define the macro as a function macro and select OK or press Enter to accept the default name.

Now go back to the worksheet, select cell D9, and enter

=WAVG.XLM!WAVG(B4:B7,C4:C7)

Microsoft Excel will calculate the macro named WAVG in the macro sheet called WAVG, beginning with cell A2 and continuing through cell A5. The two ARGUMENT statements store the arrays B4:B7 and C4:C7 (the argument ranges you specified) under the names *Values* and *Weights*. The array formula in cell A4 then uses these arrays to compute the weighted average. The RETURN statement returns the result from cell A4 to D9, the cell in the worksheet that contains the function. Figure 19-20 shows the result.

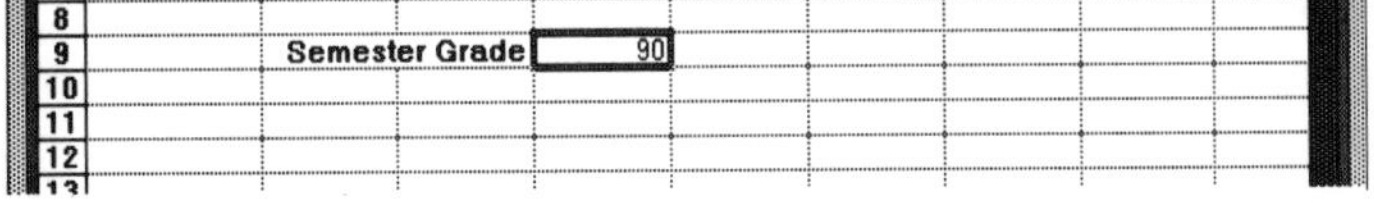

FIGURE 19-20. *We computed a weighted average score with the user-defined WAVG function.*

This function is much more flexible than either of the two formulas it replaces. Both of the first two methods were limited to computing the weighted average of four values in cells B4:B7. The WAVG function, however, can be used to compute the weighted average of a virtually unlimited list of values stored anywhere in the worksheet. For instance, you could enter

=WAVG.XLM!WAVG(D1:D15,E1:E15)

in any blank cell in any worksheet to compute the weighted averages of the values you've entered in cells D1:D15.

The cell reference *argument*

The *cell reference* argument allows you to tell Microsoft Excel which cell it should use to store the value that will be passed to the macro sheet. For example, the statement

=ARGUMENT("Test",7,C1)

will store the value that is passed to the argument Test in cell C1 in the macro sheet and then assign the name *Test* to that cell.

To see how this works, let's go back to the weighted-average macro in Figure 19-19 and make a few changes. Change the first ARGUMENT statement to

=ARGUMENT("Values",64,B1:B4)

and change the second ARGUMENT statement to

=ARGUMENT("Weights",64,C1:C4)

When you enter the formula

=WAVG.XLM!WAVG(B4:B7,C4:C7)

in cell D9 of the worksheet, this function will still return the result 90. But now switch back to the macro sheet. Figure 19-21 shows the sheet after the macro has

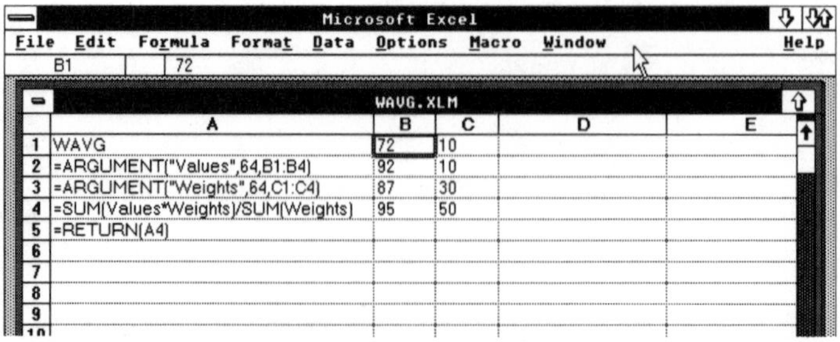

FIGURE 19-21. *You can store argument values in the cells of a macro sheet.*

run. As you can see, Microsoft Excel has entered the values from cells B4:B7 in the worksheet into cells B1:B4 in the macro sheet as well as the values from cells C4:C7 in the worksheet into cells C1:C4 in the macro sheet. In addition, it has assigned the name *Values* to the range B1:B4 and the name *Weights* to the range C1:C4.

If you use the *cell reference* argument to enter an array into the macro sheet, be sure that *cell reference* defines a range large enough to accommodate the array. Otherwise, only as many elements of the array as will fit in the defined space will be passed to the macro sheet. To be safe, use a *cell reference* argument that defines a range you know is larger than the array. Microsoft Excel will assign the designated name to only those cells in the range that are used, not to the entire range.

Most of the time, you won't want to store the values you pass to a macro sheet in the cells of that sheet. However, this capability comes in handy when you're debugging your function macros. If you enter each value that is passed to the function macro into one of the cells in the macro sheet, you'll be able to tell at a glance if all the values have been received correctly.

The RESULT function

Just as a function macro can accept different types of arguments, it can also return different types of results. The type of result a function macro will return is determined by the RESULT function. This function has the form

    =RESULT(*type*)

where *type* is a numeric code that specifies the type of the function's result. The numeric codes for RESULT are the same as those for ARGUMENT, and as with the ARGUMENT function, the *type* argument of the RESULT function can be the sum of two or more codes. Also as with ARGUMENT, the default type is 7, which allows for number, text, and logical results.

You don't have to include the RESULT function in your function macros unless you want the function to return a result that is not text, a number, or a logical value. Because most of your functions will return numbers or text, you probably won't use RESULT very often, but if you want to create a function that returns an array, you'll need to use this function at the beginning of your function macro.

Array results

Just as some of Microsoft Excel's built-in functions return arrays, you can also create user-defined functions that return arrays. Creating a user-defined function that returns an array is quite a bit more complex than any of the examples we have considered so far. Let's look at a relatively simple example of a user-defined function that returns an array.

Suppose you have $100,000 to invest in an interest-bearing account. You want to know what the value of that investment will be, including interest, at the end of each of the next five years. You've set up a worksheet to solve this problem. Cell C2 contains the rate of interest, 10 percent, that you expect to earn across the next few years; cell C3 contains the amount you plan to invest, $100,000; and cell C4 contains the term of the investment, 5 years. Now you want to create a user-defined function that will compute the value of the investment at the end of year 1, year 2, year 3, and so on and enter those values in cells C7 through C11.

Because the result of this function will occupy several cells, it must be an array function. Figure 19-22 shows a function macro called PFV (for Periodic Future Value) that performs the task.

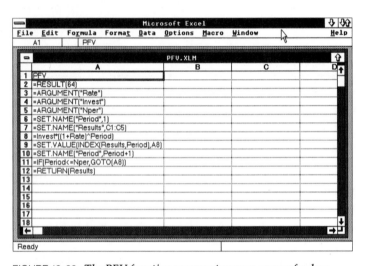

FIGURE 19-22. *The PFV function macro returns an array of values.*

The first statement in the macro, RESULT(64), tells Microsoft Excel that this function returns an array. As we've said, any function macro that you expect to return an array must begin with a RESULT(64) statement.

The next three lines in the macro contain the ARGUMENT statements that define the three arguments the function will pass to the macro: Rate (the interest rate), Invest (the amount invested), and Nper (the term of the investment).

The next two statements use the SET.NAME function to define two names, Period and Results. The first of these

=SET.NAME("Period",1)

stores the value 1 under the name *Period*. This name will be used as a counter by the macro. The second statement

=SET.NAME("Results",C1:C5)

assigns the name *Results* to the range C1:C5. The macro will store the results of each calculation in the cells of this range. (Notice that the name in the SET.NAME function is, as always, enclosed in quotes.)

The next statement

=Invest*((1+Rate)^Period)

actually performs the future-value calculation, using the Invest and Rate arguments and the named value Period.

The instruction in cell A9

=SET.VALUE(INDEX(Results,Period),A8)

is a bit tricky. This statement says: *Store the result of the calculation in cell A8 in the cell at location Period in the range Results*. The INDEX function uses the variable Period to select a cell reference from the range Results and the SET.VALUE function stores the value from cell A8 in that cell.

The statement in cell A10

=SET.NAME("Period",Period+1)

increases the value stored under the name *Period* by 1.

The next statement

=IF((Period<=Nper),GOTO(A8))

creates a loop in the function macro. This statement says: *If the value of Period (which was just increased by 1 in the previous line of the macro) is less than or equal to the value of Nper (which is passed to the macro by the user-defined function), then begin executing the function in cell A8.* This statement causes Microsoft Excel to repeat the functions in cells A8, A9, and A10 for all values of Period from 1 to the number of periods specified by Nper.

After you've entered these functions in the macro sheet, select cell A2 and choose the Define Name command. Then select the Function button and select the OK button or press Enter to accept the default name, PFV. (PFV is also the name of our macro sheet.)

Here's how this function works. When you run the macro, Microsoft Excel processes the statements in cells A2:A7 as you would expect. The statement in cell A6 sets the value of Period to 1. When Microsoft Excel calculates the formula in cell A8, it uses 1, the current value of Period, to compute the future value of the investment at the end of one period. Then the statement in cell A9 stores that result in the first cell of the range Results. Next, the statement in cell A10 increases the value of Period from 1 to 2. Because the value of Period, 2, is less than the value of Nper, 5, when Microsoft Excel computes cell A11, the macro branches to cell A8.

Now, because Period is 2, the statement in A8 computes the future value of the investment at the end of the second period and the statement in cell A9 stores the computed result in the second cell in the range Results. Next, the statement in cell A10 increases the value of Period to 3, which is still less than 5, so the statement in cell A11 loops the macro back to cell A8.

This process will repeat five times. When the value of Period is 6, the statement in cell A11 will break the loop and allow the RETURN statement in cell A12 to return the results from the range Results to the cells of the worksheet that contain the function.

Now let's go to the worksheet and watch this macro work. To begin, select the range C7:C11 and type the formula

    =PFV.XLM!PFV(C2,C3,C4)

To lock in this function as an array function, press Ctrl-Shift-Enter. Figure 19-23 shows the result. As you can see, Microsoft Excel has entered the PFV function as an array formula in cells C7:C11 and has returned the values from the range Results to those cells.

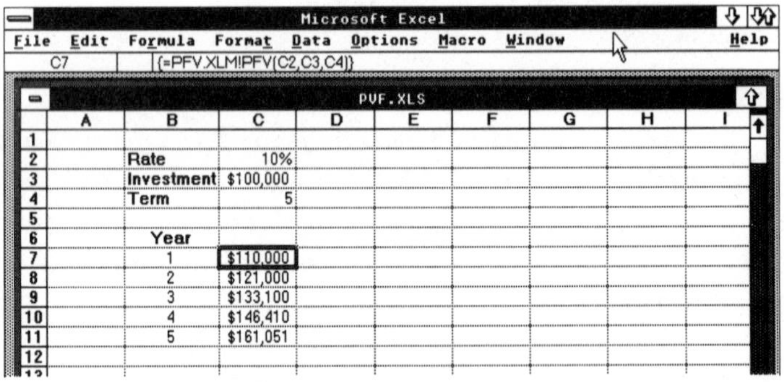

FIGURE 19-23. *We used the PFV function to calculate the value of an investment at the end of each of the next five years.*

If you switch back to the PFV macro sheet after using this function macro, you'll see that cells C1:C5 in the macro sheet, to which the macro assigned the name Results, contain the results of each computation. The RETURN statement in cell A12 returns these values from the macro sheet to the worksheet.

A modification

The macro shown in Figure 19-22 is a useful tool, but it is not very flexible. As it stands, it can compute the future value of an investment only five years into the future because cell A7 contains an explicit reference to a cell range. To make the function open-ended so that it could compute the future value for any number of periods, you could change the statement in cell A7, which defines the range Results, to

=SET.NAME("Results",C1:INDEX(C:C,Nper))

The embedded INDEX function reserves all of column C for the Result array. Microsoft Excel will assign the name *Results* to the range from cell C1 to the cell in column C determined by Nper. If Nper is 10, the name *Results* will be assigned to the range C1:C10; if Nper is 100, the name will be assigned to the range C1:C100.

20

Customizing Microsoft Excel

*I*n the previous chapters in this section we showed you how to create command macros and function macros. We also introduced you to most of the functions you'll need to build your own macros. In this final chapter we'll explore some advanced techniques you can use to customize your Microsoft Excel program.

We'll start with the INPUT function, which lets you create a simple one-field dialog box to prompt the user for information during the execution of a macro. Then we'll look at the MESSAGE and ALERT functions, two more built-in macro functions that help you communicate with the user. Next, we'll show you how to create more complex custom dialog boxes by defining a dialog-box descriptor range on your macro sheet. Then we'll move on to customizing Microsoft Excel's built-in menus and creating your own commands and menus. Finally, we'll look at several techniques for running your macros automatically.

The INPUT function

The INPUT function displays a simple dialog box that prompts the user for information. This macro function takes the form

=INPUT("*prompt*",*type*,"*title*","*default*",*x*,*y*)

The *prompt*, *title*, and *default* arguments must be text enclosed in quotation marks. The *type*, *x*, and *y* arguments must be numbers.

The *prompt* argument represents the text you want to appear in the dialog box. For example, you might use a prompt like *Select the records to include in your report.* The *title* argument lets you add an identifying title to your dialog box. If you omit *title*, Microsoft Excel displays the word *Input* in the dialog-box title bar.

The *default* argument lets you define a default value for the dialog box. The default appears in the dialog-box edit bar. To accept this default, the user can simply choose OK or press Enter. If you omit the default argument, the dialog-box edit bar will be empty.

The *type* argument identifies the data to be entered. The possible values for this argument are

Value	Data type
0	Formula
1	Number
2	Text
4	Logical
8	Reference
16	Error
64	Array

By adding these values together, you can create an INPUT function that accepts two or more kinds of entries. For example, if you enter 3 as the *type* argument, Microsoft Excel will accept both numbers and text.

If you enter 8 for the *type* argument, the INPUT function returns an absolute reference to the cell or range indicated by the user. If you enter 0, the function returns the formula that the user enters in the dialog-box edit bar as text. If the formula includes references, Microsoft Excel converts those references to R1C1 style. For example, if the user enters the formula

=SUM($A$1:$A$10)

Microsoft Excel converts that formula to "=SUM(R1C1:R10C1)".

The *x* and *y* arguments, which are optional, tell Microsoft Excel where to position the dialog box horizontally (*x* argument) and vertically (*y* argument) on the screen. These arguments are expressed in points (a point is $^1/_{72}$ of an inch) and are measured from the upper left corner of the screen. For example, to position the dialog box near the right edge of the application window, use an *x* argument of 200. To position the dialog box near the top of the application window, just below the formula bar, use a *y* argument of 1. If you omit either the *x* or *y* argument or enter one of them as 0, Microsoft Excel centers the dialog box in that direction.

Suppose you're creating a report-generator macro and you want the user to select a group of records to include in the report. You might use an INPUT statement like

=INPUT("Select the records to include in the report.",8,"Custom
    Report","=Database",,,)

to create a dialog box like the one in Figure 20-1. This input dialog box is designed to accept cell references. Notice, however, that we used the range name *Database* as our default argument. If the user doesn't select another range, the INPUT function will return the address of the range named Database. For example, if the worksheet named Clients is active when the user runs the macro and the Clients database is defined as cells A1:F100, then this INPUT function will result in the reference Clients!$A$1:$F$100.

FIGURE 20-1. *This dialog box prompts the user for a range reference.*

Instead of typing references in the dialog box, the user can select cells with the mouse or the keyboard. This technique is equivalent to pasting cell references into the worksheet formula bar.

When the user selects OK or presses Enter, Microsoft Excel returns the contents of the dialog-box edit bar to the macro sheet. Thus, you can refer to the results of the INPUT function in later formulas to select, format, or otherwise manipulate the specified range. If, however, the user selects Cancel, the INPUT function simply returns FALSE.

When the information a user enters in the dialog box is not of the correct data type, Microsoft Excel tries to translate it. If the attempt is unsuccessful, the INPUT function returns an error value. For example, if you use a *type* argument of 1 and the user enters a formula in the dialog box, Microsoft Excel will attempt to resolve that formula and return the resulting numeric value.

The ALERT function

With the ALERT function, you can create your own alert boxes. This function takes the form

=ALERT("*text*",*type*)

where *text* is the message you want to display in the alert box and must be a text string enclosed in quotation marks.

The *type* argument represents the type of alert box you want to create. A type argument of 1 displays an alert box with OK and Cancel buttons. For example, the statement

=ALERT("You have selected an invalid range. Choose OK to try again or Cancel to
    halt macro.",1)

displays the alert box shown in Figure 20-2. You might use this kind of ALERT function to give users a "second chance" to correct an error condition. If the user chooses OK in this alert box, the ALERT function returns a TRUE value. If he or she selects Cancel, the function returns a FALSE value. Often, you can use these logical results to set up different macro branches. For example, if we entered the ALERT statement described above in cell A10 of a macro sheet, we might then use a logical text such as

=IF(A10=TRUE,GOTO(A1),HALT())

in cell A11. This statement tells Microsoft Excel to branch back to the beginning of the macro (cell A1, in our example) if the user chooses OK or to end the macro if the user chooses Cancel.

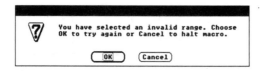

FIGURE 20-2. *A* type *argument of 1 in the ALERT function displays a caution alert box.*

The *type* arguments 2 and 3 create alert boxes with OK buttons only. The user must choose OK to acknowledge the message before the macro will resume processing. Type 2 alert boxes display an asterisk rather than a question-mark symbol; type 3 alert boxes display an exclamation point. Although type 2 and type 3 alert boxes differ only in these symbols, you'll generally reserve type 2 boxes for informational messages and type 3 boxes for stop alerts. As a rule, when you use type 3 alert boxes, you'll follow the ALERT function with a HALT or RETURN function or you'll branch to another macro subroutine that corrects the error condition.

The MESSAGE function

The MESSAGE function lets you display messages in the status box at the lower left corner of the application window while your macros are running. The MESSAGE function takes the form

=MESSAGE(*logical*,"*text*")

where *logical* tells Microsoft Excel whether it should display the message specified by *text*. If *logical* is TRUE, Microsoft Excel displays the message; if *logical* is FALSE, Microsoft Excel erases the message. The *text* argument must be a text string enclosed in double quotation marks. If you omit the *text* argument but the *logical* argument is TRUE, Microsoft Excel displays a blank message line. As a result, the command help messages that usually appear in this area will be hidden. Because only one message can be displayed at a time, you need not enter a *text* argument to identify the message you want to remove when you use a FALSE *logical* argument to turn off the message display.

The MESSAGE function is useful for displaying reminder information and for informing the user when one of your macros is about to perform a protracted calculation. For example, the statement

=MESSAGE(TRUE,"Please wait. Report being generated.")

creates a message like the one shown in Figure 20-3 to let the user know there will be a delay while the macro is processing information.

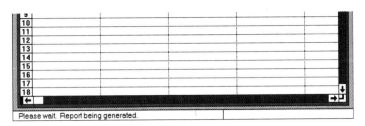

FIGURE 20-3. *Use the MESSAGE function to display status messages while a macro is running.*

When you use a MESSAGE function in a macro, be sure to include the statement

=MESSAGE(FALSE)

in the macro. Otherwise, when you halt the macro, the last message you created will be displayed until you end the current session.

Building your own dialog boxes

At times you may need to create complex dialog boxes that prompt the user for several pieces of information or that offer more than one option. For example, you may want to create a dialog box that contains two or more edit bars, a list box, a group of option buttons, or a series of check boxes from which to choose. With Microsoft Excel's DIALOG.BOX function, you can create your own custom dialog boxes to meet these specifications.

To create a dialog box, you must first build a descriptor range in your macro sheet. Then, to display the dialog box, you must include a DIALOG.BOX statement in your macro that tells Microsoft Excel where the descriptor range is located. The DIALOG.BOX function takes only one argument:

=DIALOG.BOX(*ref*)

The *ref* argument is simply a reference to the descriptor range. If *ref* is invalid, the DIALOG.BOX statement results in a #VALUE! error.

Let's look at an example. Then we'll show you in more detail how to define your own custom dialog boxes. Cells C2:J40 in Figure 20-4 contain a descriptor range that produces a dialog box like the one in Figure 20-5.

	B	C	D	E	F	G	H	I	J
1	Description	Item	X	Y	Width	Height	Text	Default/Result	Major:
2	Dialog box size								Biology
3	First Name field	5	5	7	88		&First Name:		Education
4	First Name edit bar	6	95	5	150				English
5	MI field	5	250	7	20		M&I:		History
6	MI edit bar	6	276	5	22				Journalism
7	Last Name field	5	310	7	80		&Last Name:		Literature
8	Last Name edit bar	6	392	5	150				Math
9	ID field name	5	5	31	90		SID &Number:		Pre-Law
10	ID edit bar 1	6	95	29	35				Pre-Med
11	ID field divider	5	133	29	6		-		Undeclared
12	ID edit bar 2	6	147	29	26				
13	ID field divider	5	176	29	6		-		
14	ID edit bar 3	6	190	29	40				
15	Year group box	14	270	27	110	143	&Year		
16	Year group	11	280	27	36			3	
17	Freshman radio	12	280	48	90	18	F&reshman		
18	Sophomore radio	12	280	68	90	18	Sop&homore		
19	Junior radio	12	280	88	90	18	&Junior		
20	Senior radio	12	280	108	90	18	&Senior		
21	Graduate radio	12	280	128	90	18	&Graduate		
22	Post-Graduate radio	12	280	148	90	18	&Post-Graduate		
23	Major list-box title	5	392	29	40		&Major		
24	Major list box	15	392	50	150	107	J2:J11	2	
25	Scores group box	14	5	50	110	120	&Test Scores		
26	Exam 1 field	5	10	75	60		Exam &1		
27	Exam 1 edit bar	8	72	73	32				
28	Exam 2 field	5	10	100	60		Exam &2		
29	Exam 2 edit bar	8	72	98	32				
30	Exam 3 field	5	10	125	60		Exam &3		
31	Exam 3 edit bar	8	72	123	32				
32	Exam 4 field	5	10	150	60		Exam &4		
33	Exam 4 edit bar	8	72	148	32				
34	Extra Credit check	13	125	55	130		E&xtra Credit	FALSE	
35	Attendance check	13	125	80	130		&Attendance	FALSE	
36	Participation check	13	125	105	130		Parti&cipation	FALSE	
37	Preparation check	13	125	130	130		P&reparation	FALSE	
38	Progress check	13	125	155	130		Pr&ogress	FALSE	
39	OK button	1	390	150			&OK		
40	Cancel button	2	475	150			&Cancel		

FIGURE 20-4. *This descriptor range creates a dialog box like the one shown in Figure 20-5.*

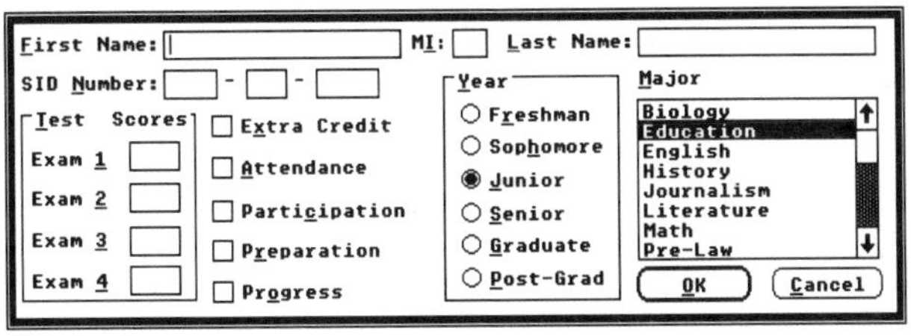

FIGURE 20-5. *This custom dialog box collects information about students.*

The descriptor range must contain seven columns (columns C through I in Figure 20-4) and at least two rows. Any columns in your descriptor range beyond the first seven essential ones can be used to store entries for list boxes within the dialog box. (We've used column J in Figure 20-4 for this purpose.) The field names included in row 1 of the sample macro sheet shown in Figure 20-4 are not required. We entered them only to help identify the columns. Similarly, we added the labels in column B only to help identify the many entries in the descriptor range.

The first row of the descriptor range describes the height and width of the entire dialog box, as well as its position on the screen. If you don't make any entries in this row, Microsoft Excel centers the dialog box and adjusts the size as necessary to accommodate the contents of the box. If you've created a help file to explain the dialog-box options, you can include that help-file name in the first cell of the descriptor range (cell C2 in the sample); otherwise, leave this cell blank. (We'll talk more about developing custom help files later in this chapter.) Subsequent rows of the descriptor range describe each item you want to display in the dialog box.

It is important to keep the sequence of the first seven columns in the descriptor range in the order Item, X, Y, Width, Height, Text, and Default/Result. Table 20-1 offers a brief description of each of the seven columns and Table 20-2 defines the numeric codes used in the Item descriptions.

Table 20-1. Contents of the descriptor range used to create a custom dialog box.

Column	Description
Item	A numeric code that defines each object in the dialog box. (See Table 20-2.)
X	A numeric value that defines the horizontal position of the dialog box on the screen and of each item within the dialog box. Although the descriptor range must contain an X column, the X *values* are optional. If you omit the X value in the first line of the descriptor range or enter a zero in this line, Microsoft Excel centers the dialog box between the left

(continued)

Table 20-1. *continued*

Column	Description
	and right edges of the screen. If you omit the X value from your item descriptions, the program positions the items in the dialog box for you.
	When defining the position of the dialog box, the X value is expressed in points ($\frac{1}{72}$ of an inch) from the left edge of the screen to the left edge of the dialog box. When defining the position of items within the dialog box, the X value is expressed in horizontal screen units (approximately $\frac{1}{8}$ the width of a character in the System font) from the left edge of the dialog box to the left edge of the item.
Y	A numeric value that defines the vertical position of the dialog box on the screen and of each item within the dialog box. Although the descriptor range must contain a Y column, the Y *values* are optional. If you omit the Y value in the first line of the descriptor range or enter a zero in this line, Microsoft Excel centers the dialog box between the top and bottom edges of the screen. If you omit the Y value from your item descriptions, the program positions the items in the dialog box for you.
	When defining the position of the dialog box, the Y value is expressed in points ($\frac{1}{72}$ of an inch) from the top edge of the screen to the top of the dialog box. When defining the position of items within the dialog box, the Y value is expressed in vertical screen units (approximately $\frac{1}{12}$ the height of a character in the System font) from the top of the dialog box to the top of the item.
Width	A numeric value that defines the width of the dialog box (when entered in the first row of the descriptor range) and of items in the dialog box. Width is expressed in horizontal screen units. Although the descriptor range must contain a Width column, the width *values* are optional. If you omit this value, Microsoft Excel sizes the dialog box and the items in the dialog box for you.
Height	A numeric value that defines the height of the dialog box (when entered in the first row of the descriptor range) and of items in the dialog box. Height is expressed in vertical screen units. Although the descriptor range must contain a Height column, the height *values* are optional. If you omit these values, Microsoft Excel sizes the dialog box and the items in the dialog box for you.
Text	The text to be displayed in the dialog box. Microsoft Excel ignores the contents of the Text column in the first line of the descriptor range. In Microsoft Excel's built-in dialog boxes, one character is underlined in most option and button names, check-box names, option-group names, list-box names, and edit-bar names. You can quickly move to that item by pressing the Alt key in conjunction with the underlined character. You can achieve the same effect in a custom dialog box by typing an ampersand character (&) in front of the desired access character in the Text column.

(continued)

Table 20-1. *continued*

Column	Description
Default/ Result	The default selections and edit-bar entries you want to appear when the dialog box is first displayed. In the first line of the descriptor range, you can include a numeric value in this column to specify which item is to be highlighted when the dialog box is initially displayed. Items are numbered sequentially, starting with the second row of the descriptor range. When the user chooses the OK button, the current selection and entries overwrite the default entries. The next time the dialog box is displayed, the user's most recent entries and selections will appear. These new settings will remain in effect until you edit them directly in the macro sheet or until you make new dialog-box selections. You can reset all or some of the default values in the Default/Result column by including a series of SET.VALUE functions in your dialog-box macro, just before the DIALOG.BOX function.

Table 20-2. Numeric codes for the objects in the dialog box.

Item Code	Description
1	Default OK button. When you use this item code, the OK button appears with a thick black border and is chosen when the user presses Enter. This button closes the dialog box, enters the data from the dialog box into the Default/Result column of the descriptor range, and continues processing the macro sheet with the next cell after the DIALOG.BOX statement used to display the dialog box. You must define the text that appears in the button by typing an entry in the Text column of the descriptor range. You can use the standard text, OK, or your own text, such as Enter Record.
2	Cancel button. This button closes the dialog box without entering the data from the dialog box into the Default/Result column of the descriptor range. Macro-sheet processing continues with the next cell after the DIALOG.BOX statement used to display the dialog box. You must define the text that appears in the button by typing an entry in the Text column of the descriptor range. You can use the standard text, Cancel, or your own text, such as Halt or Escape.
3	OK button. Same as item 1, except that the OK button is not automatically selected when the user presses Enter.
4	Default Cancel button. Same as item 2, except that the Cancel button appears with a thick black border and is automatically chosen when the user presses Enter.
5	Fixed text. You can use this item code to enter descriptive labels or other instructions into the dialog box. Text items do not have to be attached to dialog-box items; you can enter descriptive labels, explanatory text, or any other message or symbols you want to display in the dialog box. Often, however, your text items will describe an edit

(continued)

Table 20-2. *continued*

Item Code	Description
	bar, list box, or other item in the dialog box. When this is the case, Microsoft Excel associates the text item with the item immediately following it in the next line of the descriptor range. For example, the text item that we defined in row 3 of our sample descriptor range in Figure 20-4 applies to the edit bar defined in row 4.
6	Text edit bar. This code displays an edit bar in which the user can make entries. Unlike the case with codes 7 through 10, Microsoft Excel accepts any kind of entry in this type of edit bar. Microsoft Excel ignores the contents of the Text column for this item type. If you want to label the edit bar, you must include a text item in the row of the descriptor range immediately above the row that defines the text edit bar, as described under item code 5. To define an initial value for the edit bar, enter the desired text in the Default/Result column.
7	Integer edit bar. Same as item 6, except that the user can enter only integer values between –32765 and +32767. If the user makes an invalid entry, Microsoft Excel beeps, displays an alert message, and highlights the contents of the edit bar. To define an initial value for the edit bar, enter the desired text in the Default/Result column.
8	Number edit bar. Same as item 6, except that the user can enter only numeric values. Number edit bars accept decimal as well as integer values. If the user makes an invalid entry, Microsoft Excel beeps, displays an alert message, and highlights the contents of the edit bar. To define an initial value for the edit bar, enter the desired text in the Default/Result column.
9	Formula edit bar. Same as item 6, except that the user can enter only formulas. Any references in the formula are converted to R1C1 style when the formula is transferred to the Default/Result column on the macro sheet; however, when the dialog box is reopened, Microsoft Excel converts these references back to the reference style that has been selected in the Workspace dialog box. If the user makes an invalid entry in a formula edit bar, Microsoft Excel beeps, displays an alert message, and highlights the contents of the edit bar. To define an initial value for the edit bar, enter the desired text in the Default/Result column.
10	Reference edit bar. Same as item 6, except that the user can enter only cell and range references. References entered in A1 style notation are converted to R1C1 style when they are transferred to the Default/Result column of the descriptor range. Microsoft Excel also accepts range names in reference edit bars. These too are converted to an R1C1-style reference. If the user makes an invalid entry, Microsoft Excel beeps, displays an alert message, and highlights the contents of the edit bar. To define an initial value for the edit bar, enter the desired text in the Default/Result column.
11	Radio-button group. Before you include a group of radio buttons (described below) in your dialog box, you must define that group with

(continued)

Table 20-2. *continued*

Item Code	Description
	a radio-button group description, which appears in the descriptor-range row immediately above the rows that describe the individual buttons. You can designate the default radio-button selection by entering the option number in the Default/Result field. Options are numbered sequentially, beginning with the row immediately below the radio-button group definition. For example, in our sample descriptor range, row 16 contains a description of the radio-button group in rows 17 through 22. We entered a 3 in cell I16 to select the Junior option as the default. If you don't make an entry in the Default/Result column, the first button is initially selected. Only one button in a group can be selected at a time. If you enter #N/A, no button is selected. After the user makes a dialog-box selection, the number of the button selected appears in the Default/Result column.
	Microsoft Excel ignores the contents of the Text column for this item. If you want to place a box around the radio-button group and label the buttons, you'll need to include a group-box definition (item 14) in the row immediately above the radio-button group definition.
12	Radio-button option. This code displays a radio button and descriptive label in the dialog box. Unlike the case with edit bars, you can label radio-button options by entering the desired text in the text column of the descriptor range; you need not create a separate text item to display the name of the option. The contents of the Default/Result field are ignored for this item type. To activate a radio button, you must make an entry in the Default/Result column of the preceding radio-button group definition.
13	Check box. This code displays a check box and descriptive label in the dialog box. As with radio-button options, you can display the check-box option name in the dialog box simply by entering that name in the Text column of the descriptor range. A TRUE value in the Default/Result field indicates that the check box is selected; a FALSE value or a blank cell indicates that it is deselected; an #N/A value indicates that the check box is grayed.
14	Group box. This code allows you to draw a box around a group of related items in the dialog box. You can label the group by entering a descriptive phrase in the Text column. You enter the group-box item definition in the descriptor-range row immediately above the items you want to group.
15	List box. This code displays a list box that contains a list of items defined in a range on the macro sheet. To define the items to be listed in the box, you must enter the items in a separate range and then enter a reference to that range or a range name in the Text column of the descriptor range. For example, in our sample dialog-box descriptor range, we entered our Major list in cells J2:J11 of the macro sheet. To refer to this list, we entered the reference J2:J11 in the Text column of row 24. To label the list box, include a Text definition (item 5) in the descriptor-range row immediately above the list-box definition.

(continued)

Table 20-2. *continued*

Item Code	Description
	You can designate the default list-box selection by entering the option number in the Default/Result field. The options in the list are numbered sequentially, beginning with the first row of the list range. Only one item in a list box can be selected at a time. If you don't make an entry in the Default/Result column, the first list item is initially selected; if you enter #N/A, no list item is selected. After the user makes a selection, the number of the list item selected appears in the Default/Result column.
16	Linked list box. Same as item 15, except that the selected list-box item is displayed in a text edit bar. The text edit bar (item 6) must be defined in the descriptor-range row immediately above the linked list-box definition.
17	Icon. This code displays one of three icons in the dialog box. These icons are identical to the ones that appear when you use the ALERT function, discussed earlier in this chapter. A 1 in the Text column displays a question mark (?), a 2 displays an asterisk (∗), and a 3 displays an exclamation point (!).
18	Linked file list box. Similar to item 16, except that this option displays a list of files in a directory. Unlike the case with a linked list box (item 16), you don't need to refer to a separate list of items in the macro sheet in order to generate the contents of the linked file list box. Microsoft Excel automatically reads the filenames from disk and displays them in the list box. You must follow item 18 with a linked drive-and-directory list box (item 19) and precede it with a text edit bar (item 6), which will display the name of the file that's currently selected in the file list box. The user can also use this text edit bar to restrict the filenames that appear in the list box. For example, to see a list of all Microsoft Excel chart files in the current directory, the user can type ∗.XLC in the edit bar. (To get a clearer picture of how a linked file list box works, look at the Open dialog box.)
19	Linked drive-and-directory list box. Similar to item 18, except that this option lists available drives and directories. Again, Microsoft Excel automatically supplies the drive and directory names in the list box. You must precede this item with a linked file list-box definition (item 18). To change directories, enter the desired pathname in the text edit bar preceding that linked file list-box definition. If a fixed text item (item 5) appears immediately after the linked drive-and-directory definition, Microsoft Excel displays the name of the current drive and directory. This name is updated if the drive or directory is changed.
20	Directory text. This code displays the name of the current directory. This item does not change when the user chooses a new drive or directory. To update the drive-and-directory text, you must place a fixed-text item (item 5) in the descriptor-range row immediately below the linked drive-and-directory list-box definition (item 19).

Building custom data forms

As we mentioned in Chapter 14, you can replace Microsoft Excel's built-in data form with a custom data form. To create your own data form, first create a descriptor range in the same worksheet that contains your database. This descriptor range should be set up like the one we created in Figure 20-4. A custom data form should use item 5 for static text and items 6, 7, 8, 9, and 10 for the edit bars where the user types field entries when entering information into the database. You need not include items to create the standard buttons that appear in a data form (New, Delete, Restore, Find Prev, Find Next, Criteria, and Exit); Microsoft Excel creates these buttons automatically. In addition, Microsoft Excel creates the record-number designation in the upper right corner of the data form (such as *1 of 10*) and the data-form scroll bar you use to move among records.

After setting up your descriptor range, select that range and issue the Define Name command. The range reference will appear in the Refers to edit bar. Type the name *Data_Form* in the Name edit bar and choose OK. Your custom data form will now appear whenever you choose Form from the Data menu.

The custom data form will not be linked to your database range, however. To link each field in the data form to a database field, you must enter the database-field name in the Default/Result column of the descriptor range, in the same row as the item that defines the edit bar where the field data will be input. This field name must exactly match the name that appears in the field header row of the database; otherwise, Microsoft Excel will not transfer the contents of the form window to your database correctly.

Although the field names in the Default/Result column must exactly match the field names in the field header row of the database, the field names in the text you use to label each field or edit bar of the form need not match the database-field names. For example, your database might contain a field named FName, but in your custom data form the edit bar where this field's data is input might be labeled First Name. In addition, the fields in your custom data form need not appear in the same order as the fields in your database; however, every field you create in the data form must correspond to one of the fields in the database range.

You aren't required to include all the database fields in the data form. If you include locked or calculated fields, they will appear in the form window without boxes and will not be available for editing.

Customizing menus

In addition to allowing you to create your own dialog boxes and data forms, Microsoft Excel allows you to create your own commands and menus. You can add new commands to Microsoft Excel's built-in menus or you can rename existing commands. You can even create your own menus to be added to a built-in menu bar or to appear on a new menu bar of your own design.

Many of Microsoft Excel's custom-menu functions require a *bar id* argument that identifies the menu bar you want to work with. The program's six built-in menu bars are numbered from 1 to 6:

Bar ID	Menu bar
1	Macro and worksheet (full menus)
2	Chart (full menus)
3	Nil (contains File menu only; appears when no documents are open in the workspace)
4	Info
5	Macro and worksheet (short menus)
6	Chart (short menus)

Many custom-menu functions also require that you identify the specific menu you want to work with. You can identify menus either by number or by name. If you use the menu name, you must enclose the argument in quotation marks. The menus are numbered from left to right. Thus, in the worksheet environment, a *menu id* argument of 3 refers to the Formula menu, the third menu in a worksheet document. Alternatively, you could use the *menu id* argument "Formula" to specify the menu you want to alter.

Finally, some functions require a *command id* argument. This argument can be a number that reflects the position of the command on the menu or it can be the command name enclosed in quotation marks. When specifying *command id*, you must include the dividing lines that appear between commands. For example, the Save command on the File menu has a *command id* value of 6 because it is preceded by four commands (New, Open, Close, and Links) and one dividing line.

Renaming commands

Let's start with the simplest of Microsoft Excel's custom-menu functions, the RENAME.COMMAND function. The RENAME.COMMAND function assigns a different name to a specified command on a menu. You can rename both built-in and custom commands. This function has the form

=RENAME.COMMAND(*bar id,menu id,command id,*"*name*")

We've already described the *bar id*, *menu id*, and *command id* arguments. The *name* argument represents the new name you want to assign to the command and must be enclosed in quotation marks.

For example, suppose you want to change the Open command on the File menu to Retrieve. You can use the statement

=RENAME.COMMAND(1,1,2,"Retrieve")

Disabling and enabling commands

On occasion, you may want to disable a command. The ENABLE.COMMAND function lets you enable and disable both built-in and custom commands. The ENABLE.COMMAND function takes the form

=ENABLE.COMMAND(*bar id,menu id,command id,logical*)

You are already familiar with the *bar id*, *menu id*, and *command id* arguments. Using 0 as your *command id* argument, you can enable or disable the entire menu.

If *logical* is TRUE, Microsoft Excel makes the command you specify available; if *logical* is FALSE, Microsoft Excel dims or grays the command, making it unavailable for selection. For example, suppose you've developed your own macro routine to replace the Delete command on the Data menu. If you don't want the user to select the built-in Delete command, you could use the statement

=ENABLE.COMMAND(1,5,5,FALSE)

to disable that command.

Note that we used a *command id* value of 5, even though Delete is the fourth command on the Data menu. Remember, in your *command id* argument you must account for the dividing line that appears between the Form and Find commands.

Deleting commands

As you might expect, the DELETE.COMMAND function removes a command from a specified menu. You can delete both built-in and custom commands. This function has the form

=DELETE.COMMAND(*bar id,menu id,command id*)

We described all these arguments at the beginning of this section.

Again, suppose you want to prevent the user from using the Delete command on the Data menu. Rather than simply disabling the command, you could use the statement

=DELETE.COMMAND(1,5,5)

to remove the command altogether.

Creating new commands

The ADD.COMMAND function lets you place a new command on a menu. If ADD.COMMAND succeeds, Microsoft Excel adds the command to the appropriate menu and returns the new command's position number.

This function has the form

=ADD.COMMAND(*bar id,menu id,ref*)

You've already seen how the *bar id* and *menu id* arguments work. Like custom dialog boxes, new menus and commands are defined in a descriptor range. The *ref* argument locates this descriptor range for Microsoft Excel.

The descriptor range

The descriptor range you use to define a new command consists of five columns: Name, Reference, Option, Description, and Help. The Name column contains the name of the command. The Reference column contains an external reference to the first cell of the macro that will be invoked when the command is selected. (This macro must be located on a separate macro sheet.) The Option column is ignored but serves as a placeholder. The Description column, which is optional, contains a label that describes the menu or command. When the user selects the command, this label appears in the status area at the lower left corner of the application window. For example, when you select the Cut command from the Edit menu, you see the description *Remove contents of selected cells in the status bar.*

The last column in the descriptor range, Help, which is also optional, may contain a help reference. If you've created a custom help file to explain a menu or command, you can identify that help file in this column.

An example

Suppose you've created a formatting macro that displays total values in bold type, centered, with an outline border. The macro also assigns the currency format to the totals range. Let's create a command called Totals that will invoke the Totals macro from the Format menu. We'll assume that the Totals formatting macro is located in a macro sheet named FORMATS.XLM.

We can use the statement

=ADD.COMMAND(1,4,C1:F2)

to add the Totals command to the Format menu. This statement refers to a descriptor range located in cells C1:F2 of the macro sheet. Figure 20-6 shows that range.

As you can see, the first row in this sample descriptor range contains only a single hyphen character in cell C1. This hyphen indicates that you want a divider line to appear between the new command and the previous command on the menu. The second line of the descriptor range defines the Total command. In cell

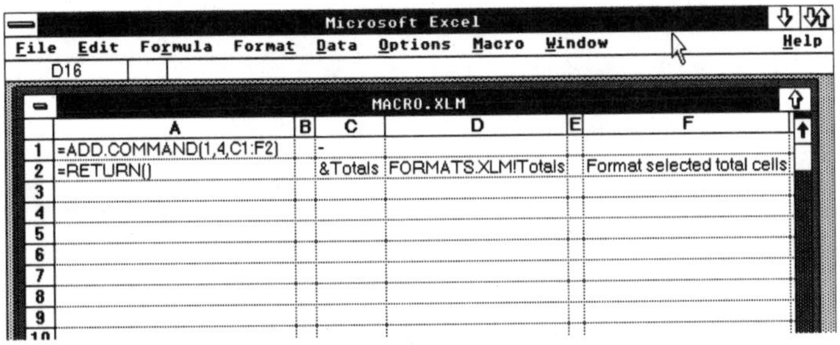

FIGURE 20-6. *This is the macro and descriptor range to create a new command named Totals.*

C2, we entered the command name. Notice that we included an & character in front of the letter *T*. The ampersand lets us underline the T so that the user can select the command by simply typing a T.

In cell D2, we entered the external reference text *FORMATS.XLM!Totals*. This entry tells Microsoft Excel that the command macro associated with this command is located on the FORMATS.XLM macro sheet and that the macro starts in the cell named Totals. (Of course, you could alternatively use a simple cell reference in your Reference column, such as A20.) When the user issues the Totals command, Microsoft Excel will run the macro specified in cell D2.

The third column, column E, acts as a placeholder and is ignored. The fourth column of our descriptor range contains the message we want to appear in the status bar. As you can see in Figure 20-7, this message appears at the lower left corner of the application window when the command is selected.

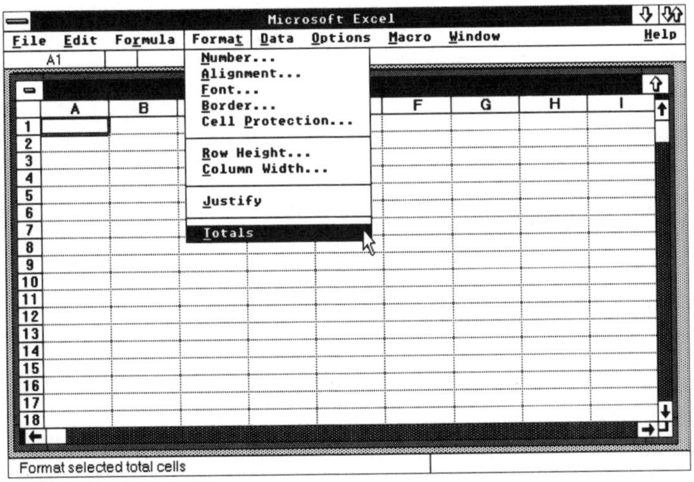

FIGURE 20-7. *The divider line and Totals command now appear on the Format menu.*

We've omitted the fifth column from our descriptor range in this example. If you've created a custom help file to guide the user, however, you can use this column to include a reference to that help file.

Creating new menus

You've seen how to add a command to an existing menu. Now let's see how you can create your own custom menu to display your custom commands.

To add a custom menu to an existing menu bar or to a custom menu bar, use the ADD.MENU function. This function has the form

=ADD.MENU(*bar id,ref*)

You're already familiar with the *bar id* argument. The *ref* argument locates the descriptor range of the new menu. If ADD.MENU succeeds, Microsoft Excel adds the menu to the right of the existing menus and returns the new menu's position number to the macro sheet.

The descriptor range you use to define a new menu is similar to the one you use to create a new command. Figure 20-8 shows a sample descriptor range we developed to create a menu called Students.

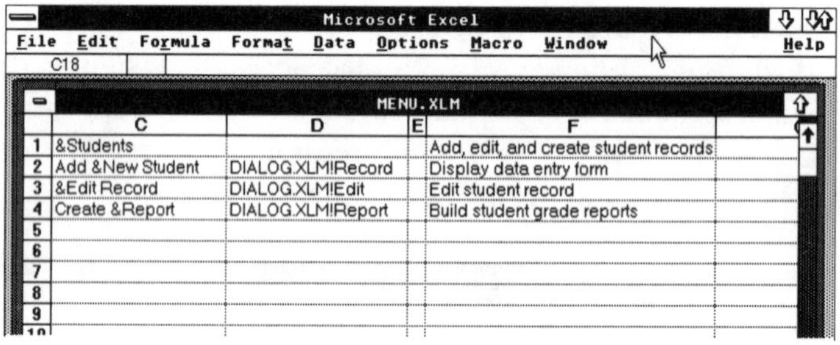

FIGURE 20-8. *This sample descriptor range creates a custom Students menu containing three commands.*

In the first cell of the descriptor range, we entered the name of the menu. This name will be displayed on the menu bar. Again, notice that we included an & before the S; this letter will be underlined and the user can select the menu by pressing Alt-S. In cell F1, we entered the descriptive text that will appear in the status bar at the lower left corner of the screen when the user selects the menu name from the edit bar.

In rows 2 through 4 of the descriptor range, we defined the commands for our new menu: Add New Student, Edit Record, and Create Report. Column D contains references to the command macro that will be invoked when the user selects each of these commands. Column F contains our command descriptions. We omitted the fifth column from our descriptor range, but you can use this column to identify a custom help topic for each command. Figure 20-9 shows our new menu.

FIGURE 20-9. *This custom menu was generated by the descriptor range in Figure 20-8.*

Deleting a menu

The DELETE.MENU function can remove a built-in or custom menu. This function has the form

=DELETE.MENU(*bar id,menu id*)

The *bar id* argument and the *menu id* argument specify the location of the menu on the menu bar.

After the menu is removed, Microsoft Excel decreases the menu position numbers by one for all menus to the right of the deleted menu. If you try to delete a nonexistent menu, DELETE.MENU returns a #VALUE! error.

Creating new menu bars

If you want to develop an entire application within Microsoft Excel, you may decide to develop your own custom menu bar to display your menus and commands. You can create as many as 15 custom menu bars with the ADD.BAR, ADD.MENU, and SHOW.BAR functions.

The ADD.BAR function lets you create a menu bar. This function has the form

=ADD.BAR

and takes no arguments. ADD.BAR returns the bar number of the new menu bar. If more than 15 custom menu bars have been defined at one time, it returns #VALUE!.

ADD.BAR does not display the menu bar. To make the bar appear, you must use the SHOW.BAR function. First, however, you need to use one or more ADD.MENU functions to fill in your new menu bar. You can use the result of the ADD.BAR function as the *bar id* argument in your ADD.MENU functions.

To display your menu bar and new menus, use the SHOW.BAR function. This function takes the form

=SHOW.BAR(*bar id*)

Again, to enter the *bar id* argument, you can refer directly to the cell that contains your ADD.BAR function. (To redisplay a built-in menu, use a *bar id* argument of 1 through 6.) If you omit the *bar id* argument, the default menu bar for the current window type will be displayed.

Figure 20-10 shows a sample macro and descriptor range that create a custom menu bar like the one in Figure 20-11.

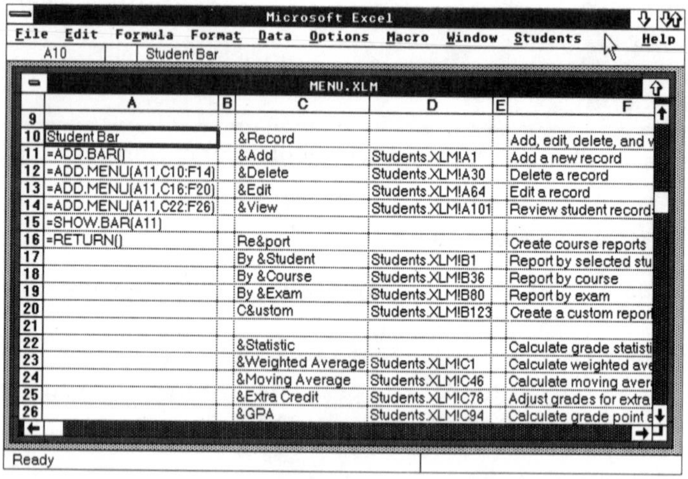

FIGURE 20-10. *The macro in cells A10:A16 and the descriptor ranges in columns C through F create the custom menu bar shown in Figure 20-11.*

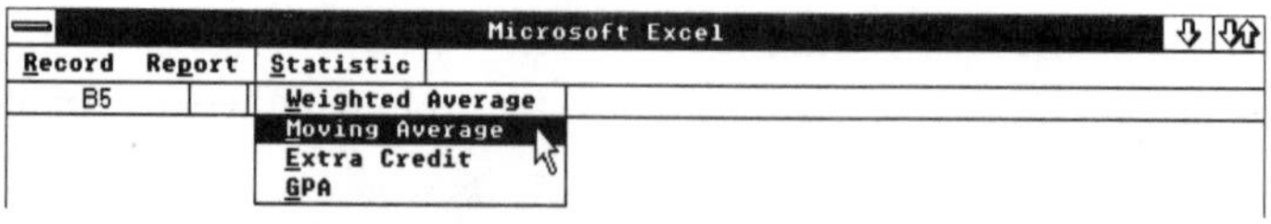

FIGURE 20-11. *We developed a custom menu bar to process student records.*

As you can see in Figure 20-10, after entering the ADD.BAR function in cell A11, we entered three ADD.MENU functions that use the reference A11 as their *bar id* arguments. Our ADD.MENU functions refer to the descriptor ranges in cells C10:F14, C16:F20, and C22:F26. These descriptor ranges are set up exactly like the ones you saw in Figure 20-8. Finally, we used the SHOW.BAR function in cell A15 to display the menu bar on the screen.

Deleting a menu bar

To eliminate a custom menu bar, use the DELETE.BAR function. This function has the form

=DELETE.BAR(*bar id*)

The *bar id* argument must be the number of a menu bar returned by the ADD.BAR function. You cannot delete a built-in menu bar (bars 1 through 6), nor can you use the bar number of a currently displayed menu bar as the argument of a DELETE.BAR function. Before deleting a bar, you must use the SHOW.BAR command to display another menu bar.

The GET.BAR function

The GET.BAR function returns the bar number of the active menu bar. This function has the form

=GET.BAR()

and takes no arguments. You'll find this function handy when you're creating a custom menu bar and need to include the bar number as an argument in a function. For example, the ADD.COMMAND function requires a *bar id* argument. To add a command to the current menu bar, you can embed a GET.BAR function as your *bar id* argument.

The CHECK.COMMAND function

The CHECK.COMMAND function places or removes a check mark next to a command on a menu. This function has the form

=CHECK.COMMAND(*bar id,menu id,command id,logical*)

If *logical* is TRUE, CHECK.COMMAND places a check mark next to the specified command; if logical is FALSE, the check mark is removed.

Creating a custom help facility

After you've created your custom menus and dialog boxes, you may need to add some instructions to help the user put these tools to work. Microsoft Excel allows you to add custom text to its built-in Help facility. As you'll see in a moment, you can display this help information with the HELP macro function or by adding help references to your dialog-box and menu descriptor ranges.

The first step in using the custom help facility is to create a text file containing your help text. To do this, enter your text in a Microsoft Excel worksheet and then use the Text option of the Save As command to save the document.

The information in the text file should be divided into topics. You can include as many topics as you like in each file. To identify each topic, you must define it with an asterisk and an ID number. You can also include a comment after the ID number to help document the topic. Thus, the ID line takes the form

number comment

The ID number must be an integer. The comment is optional, but if you include a comment, you must precede it with a blank space. The topics can appear in any order in the text file. All the text from the line below the specified ID line to the next ID line will appear when you display the help topic in the Help window. The comment text will not appear.

For example, Figure 20-12 shows a sample help file we created to document the Student Record dialog box shown in Figure 20-5. Notice that the first line of text in the help file contains our help topic ID:

*1 Student Record dialog-box description

Following the ID number, we entered a blank space and a descriptive comment to document the help topic. As you can see in Figure 20-13, all the text below this ID line and as far as the next ID line (near the bottom of the worksheet shown in Figure 20-12) appears in the Help window when we access this help topic. (If your help text is too long to be displayed on one screen, you can use the vertical scroll bar on the right side of the Help window to bring additional information into view or you can resize the window.)

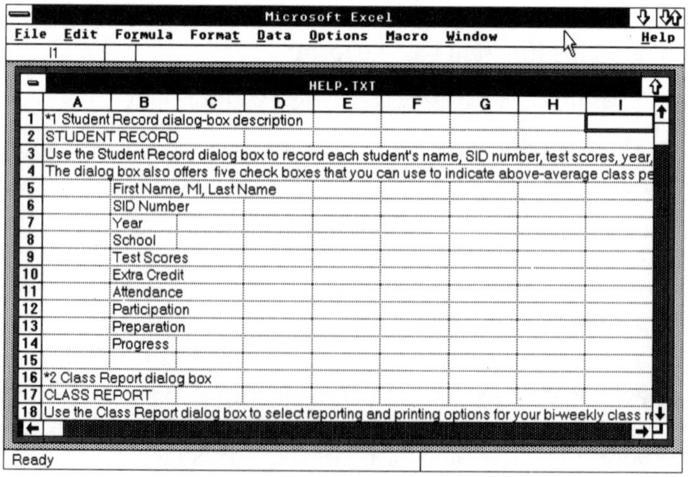

FIGURE 20-12. *This file contains the text for our custom help screen.*

FIGURE 20-13. *This custom help screen describes our Student Record dialog box.*

Notice that we entered each paragraph of text in one cell in the help text file. In the Help window, Microsoft Excel uses a wordwrap feature much like that in a word processor to display these long labels in the Help window. If you change the width of the window, Microsoft Excel automatically rejustifies the text display. Also notice that we included an extra blank line after each paragraph of text.

By placing your text in different columns of the text file, you can indent selected paragraphs. For example, to indent the list in the sample help screen shown in Figure 20-13, we entered the list in column B of the HELP.TXT file.

When you save your help file as a text file, Microsoft Excel may change the text to make it more compatible with other applications. Quotation marks are added around the entries with commas in order to preserve these lines. Otherwise, a program like Microsoft Word would separate the text at the comma when it read the file. When you access the Help window in Microsoft Excel, these additional quotation marks appear. To prevent this, open your text file in Windows and use the Notepad word processor to make any changes; then save the file and return to Microsoft Excel. When you subsequently access the Help window, your text file will appear as you saved it in Notepad.

One way to access the help file is to create a macro that contains a HELP function. This function takes the form

    =HELP("*id*")

The *id* argument is similar to a remote reference; it includes the name of the text file that contains your help text, followed by an exclamation point and the help topic ID number. (If the text file is not located in the default directory, include the full pathname in your *id* argument.) The help reference must be a literal text string entered in quotation marks. For example, to access the help topic we defined in Figure 20-12, we would use a HELP function like this:

    =HELP("HELP.TXT!1")

When Microsoft Excel executes this macro formula, it will display the Help window shown in Figure 20-13. If you omit the *id* argument, Microsoft Excel will display the standard help topic listing you see when you press F1 or choose Index from the Help menu.

As we hinted earlier, you can also make your custom help facility context-sensitive by giving the user access to related help topics while your custom Microsoft Excel menus and dialog boxes are active. To attach a help topic to a dialog box, simply enter the appropriate help ID reference in the first cell of your dialog-box descriptor range. This help ID takes the same form as the *id* argument in the HELP function: *file!topic.*

For example, to give the user access to the custom help screen shown in Figure 20-13, we could enter the help reference

HELP.TXT!1

in cell C2 of the dialog-box descriptor range shown in Figure 20-4. When you use this technique, the user can access the custom help screen simply by pressing F1 while the Student Record dialog box is displayed on the screen.

Similarly, to attach a help topic to a command you've added to a custom menu, simply enter the help reference ID in the last column of the menu descriptor range. For example, in Figure 20-8 we created a custom menu and several commands. To instruct the user how to use these commands, you could create a text file similar to the one shown in Figure 20-12, with a separate numbered topic for each command. Then you would enter references to the topics in that file in column G of the descriptor range shown in Figure 20-8.

After you've defined the context-sensitive help topic, you can display information about your custom commands in the same manner you display context-sensitive information about Microsoft Excel's built-in commands. Simply press Shift-F1 to turn the pointer into a question-mark shape and then select the name of the command you want to read about.

Creating autoexec macros

If you want Microsoft Excel to run a macro every time a document is opened or closed, you can identify that macro as an autoexec macro—a special type of macro that is executed automatically, without a Run command or a Ctrl-key command from the user.

To run a macro automatically when a document is opened, begin by activating the document with which you want the macro to be associated. Next, choose the Define Name command from the Formula menu. When the Define Name dialog box appears, enter the name *Auto_Open* in the Name edit bar. In the Refers to edit bar, enter the reference of the first cell of the macro you want to run. If you enter an external reference, Microsoft Excel will open the macro sheet and then execute the macro. Finally, select OK or press Enter.

That's all there is to it. From now on, whenever that document is opened, Microsoft Excel will automatically run the specified macro. If you want to open the document and bypass the autoexec macro, select the Open command from the File menu, select the filename from the list box, and hold down the Shift key while you select Open or press Enter.

If you use the *Auto_Open* autoexec macro to open a macro sheet that has an autoexec of its own, Microsoft Excel won't run the second macro. To avoid this problem, you can include a RUN statement in the first autoexec macro.

To run a macro automatically whenever a document is closed, you follow the same process, except that you enter *Auto_Close* in the Name edit bar of the Define Name dialog box. Microsoft Excel will execute the macro whenever the document is closed, providing its macro sheet is open. To close the document without executing the macro, press the Shift key as you issue the Close command.

For example, earlier we created a macro that displays the new menu in Figure 20-9. Suppose we want this macro to run every time we open the worksheet that contains our student records. All we need do is open the worksheet that contains the student records, issue the Define Name command, enter the external reference MENU.XLM!A10 in the Refers to edit bar, and enter the name *Auto_Open* in the Name edit bar. Now, whenever we open the records worksheet, Microsoft Excel will look to the macro sheet named MENU.XLM and execute the macro that begins in cell A10.

Let's look at another example. Suppose you've created a macro, called Setup, that opens a new worksheet and enters a series of headers, dates, and category labels for you. You may want to specify that macro as an autoexec macro that runs each time you open the macro sheet in which it is contained. To do this, simply activate the macro sheet that contains Setup, assign the name *Auto_Open* to the first cell in the macro, and then define the macro name using the Define Name command. (By the way, when you're assigning the name Auto_Open, you can use the macro name, rather than its reference, in the Refers to edit bar.) Now, whenever you open the macro sheet, the Setup routine will be invoked automatically.

Other autoexec techniques

Microsoft Excel offers several additional functions that allow you to invoke macros automatically: ON.DATA, ON.KEY, ON.TIME, ON.WINDOW, CANCEL.KEY, and ERROR. You can include these functions in your Microsoft Excel macros to invoke other macros when a specified condition arises.

The ON.DATA function

The ON.DATA function runs a macro when Microsoft Excel receives data from another application. This function takes the form

=ON.DATA("*document*","*macro*")

The *document* argument tells Microsoft Excel which document is receiving the data. Obviously, the receiving document must have at least one external reference. The *macro* argument, which must be an R1C1-style reference entered as a text string enclosed in quotation marks, identifies which macro you want Microsoft Excel to run. If the data requires recalculation, Microsoft Excel performs the recalculation before executing the macro. Be sure the macro sheet that contains *macro* is open. If the macro sheet is closed, Microsoft Excel returns an error when the data is transferred.

ON.DATA continues to function until you turn it off or quit Microsoft Excel. To turn off ON.DATA, simply use the function again without the *macro* argument.

The ON.KEY function

The ON.KEY function runs a macro when you press a specific key. This function takes the form

=ON.KEY("*key*","*macro*")

The *key* argument identifies the key the user must press to run the macro specified by the *macro* argument. The *key* argument can be any single key or any key combined with Shift and/or Ctrl and/or Alt. The Appendix of the *Microsoft Excel Functions and Macros* manual contains the code numbers for keys.

If you use a reference in text form for the *macro* argument, Microsoft Excel executes the specified macro whenever a user presses the designated key. If you use empty text—that is, ""—for the *macro* argument, Microsoft Excel does nothing when a user presses the specified key. If you omit the *macro* argument, the key specified in this function returns to its normal use. Be sure the macro sheet that contains *macro* is open. If the macro sheet is closed, Microsoft Excel returns an error when the user presses the specified key.

ON.KEY continues to function until you turn it off or quit Microsoft Excel. To turn off ON.KEY, simply use the function again without the *macro* argument.

The ON.TIME function

The ON.TIME function runs a macro at a specified time. The ON.TIME function takes the form

=ON.TIME(*time*,"*macro*",*tolerance*,*insert*)

The *time* argument is a serial time value that represents the time at which you want the macro to run. The *macro* argument is an R1C1-style text reference to a macro. The *tolerance* argument, another serial time value, tells Microsoft Excel how long you're willing to wait for the *insert* argument to be TRUE. If you omit *tolerance*, its value is assumed to be infinite. If *insert* is TRUE or omitted, Microsoft Excel runs the macro at the specified time; if *insert* is FALSE, Microsoft Excel ignores all prior instructions to execute the macro.

Under some circumstances, Microsoft Excel may not respond to the ON.TIME function as expected. If the macro sheet containing the macro isn't in memory when the correct time is reached, Microsoft Excel ignores the request. Similarly, if Microsoft Excel isn't in Ready mode at the specified time or during the tolerance period, it waits until the tolerance period has elapsed and then cancels the macro's run. If you create two ON.TIME functions, Microsoft Excel executes the first and ignores the second, returning #N/A!.

The ON.WINDOW function

The ON.WINDOW function runs a macro when a user activates a specified window. This function takes the form

    =ON.WINDOW("*window*","*macro*")

The *window* argument specifies the name of the window that activates the execution. The *macro* argument refers to the macro to be run. Both of these arguments must be in text form. If you omit the *window* argument, Microsoft Excel executes the specified macro when a user activates *any* window, except for those included in other ON.WINDOW statements. If you omit the *macro* argument, Microsoft Excel doesn't run a macro when the window is activated.

The CANCEL.KEY function

The CANCEL.KEY function continues a disrupted macro or tells Microsoft Excel which macro to run when a macro is disrupted. This function takes the form

    =CANCEL.KEY(*enable,ref*)

where *enable* is a logical value. If *enable* is FALSE or omitted, Microsoft Excel doesn't allow the interruption of a macro by the Esc key. If enable is TRUE, Microsoft Excel allows the Esc key to function. If the *ref* argument is omitted, the current macro simply halts when interrrupted; if *ref* is included, the macro located at *ref* runs when the current macro is interrupted.

The ERROR function

As you learned in Chapter 17, Microsoft Excel usually displays an alert box when it encounters an error during the calculation of a macro. The ERROR function lets you use a more advanced form of error checking in your macros.

This function takes the form

=ERROR(*logical,ref*)

If *logical* is TRUE, the macro branches to the cell indicated by *ref*, where you should have stored a macro subroutine that can deal with the error. If you omit the *ref* argument, Microsoft Excel simply displays the standard error-alert box and doesn't branch to any cell.

If *logical* is FALSE, Microsoft Excel doesn't display an error message. If the program encounters an error in this situation, it ignores the error and continues with the macro. Needless to say, you don't want to turn off error checking until your macro is completely and thoroughly debugged.

Microsoft Excel will not display any messages with ERROR(TRUE,*ref*) and ERROR(FALSE). In addition, Microsoft Excel won't display the message you usually see when you save an unsaved document. Before you use either of these forms, be certain you won't need any of these messages when the macro runs.

BEYOND MICROSOFT EXCEL

APPENDIX

Sharing Data with Other Programs

*A*s you work with Microsoft Excel, you may sometimes need to transfer information to another program or receive information into Microsoft Excel from another program. For example, you might want to exchange worksheets with Lotus 1-2-3 or Symphony. You might import a macro from the Macintosh version of Microsoft Excel or transfer a chart picture or a table of data from Microsoft Excel to a report you're writing in Microsoft Word or Write.

Microsoft Excel offers several methods to exchange data with other programs. You can convert a file by using the Save As command to save it in a format other programs can read. Or you can share data via the Clipboard with other programs that run under Microsoft Windows. Alternatively, you can create "live" links between documents created in different programs with the Dynamic Data Exchange (DDE) facility.

In this appendix, we'll show you how to exchange information between Microsoft Excel and other programs, including Microsoft Excel for the Macintosh, Lotus 1-2-3, Multiplan, dBASE, and Write. We'll discuss the Macro Translation Assistant and the Parse command on the Data menu. Finally, we'll show you some macro functions you can use to communicate with other programs.

The Save As command

You can share data with other programs by saving the file in a format other programs can read. To save files in another format, use the Save As command on the File menu. If you choose the Options button in the Save As dialog box, the dialog box expands to show nine file-format choices: Normal, Text, CSV, SYLK, WKS, WK1, DIF, DBF 2, and DBF 3. As you already know, the default choice in the Save As dialog box is Normal. This is the standard format you use to save your Microsoft Excel worksheets, macro sheets, and charts. When you use this format, Microsoft Excel automatically adds the appropriate filename extension to the document: .XLS, .XLM, or .XLC.

In addition, all Microsoft programs can produce SYLK (symbolic link format) files. The SYLK option is Microsoft's "generic" file format. You'll want to save Microsoft Excel worksheets in the SYLK file format when you plan to share data with other Microsoft products, such as Multiplan or Microsoft Excel for the Macintosh. Microsoft Excel saves the file with the .SLK filename extension.

Some programs, such as Visicalc, require that files be saved in the DIF (data interchange) format. This file-format option saves only values, not the formulas that produce them. When you use this option to save a worksheet, Microsoft Excel saves the file with the .DIF filename extension.

As you'll see later in this chapter, the WKS and WK1 file formats let you share data with Lotus 1-2-3 and Symphony. The DBF 2 and DBF 3 formats let you exchange information with dBASE, and the Text and CSV formats let you convert documents to ASCII text format, for exchange with a variety of programs.

When you use the Save As command to save your worksheet in a format another program can read, compatible attributes such as text and numbers, functions and formulas, formats, and calculation options are converted to the other program. However, window attributes such as size, position, panes, and the position of the active cell are not converted. In addition, none of your print settings are converted.

As you might guess, other programs won't be able to read some data in your Microsoft Excel worksheet. For example, the program to which you're exporting may not have an equivalent for one of Microsoft Excel's built-in functions. In that case, the Microsoft Excel formula or function will generally be converted to a constant value. For example, suppose a worksheet you're exporting to 1-2-3 contains a formula that returns the number 100. If 1-2-3 can't interpret this formula, it will instead use the current value of the formula, 100. (Of course, when you save a file in Text format, only the current values are stored; all underlying formulas are lost.)

Similarly, when you're importing data from another program, you may run into a formula or function that Microsoft Excel doesn't recognize. When Microsoft

Excel can't translate a formula either into or out of a different file format, it pauses and displays an alert box, like the one in Figure A-1, that shows the location of the cell that contains the error. The alert box also asks if you want Microsoft Excel to tell you each time it can't convert a formula. If you select Yes, Microsoft Excel will display this dialog box each time it can't convert a formula. If you select No, Microsoft Excel will not pause until it has completed conversion of the whole worksheet; then it will display an alert box that shows the total number of formulas that could not be converted.

FIGURE A-1. *If Microsoft Excel can't convert a formula, it displays an alert message like this one.*

Your choice of Yes or No depends on the worksheet you're converting. If the worksheet contains many similar formulas and Microsoft Excel can't convert the first one, you might want to select No to avoid seeing the dialog box over and over and to speed the conversion process. If, on the other hand, you think the worksheet contains only a few formulas that can't be converted, you'll want to choose Yes so that you can note the location of each problem.

Sharing with Microsoft Excel for the Macintosh

The PC and Apple Macintosh versions of Microsoft Excel can share data very easily. All numbers and text values and most formulas and cell formats are converted without problems. A document's protection status, calculation and iteration settings, and display settings are also converted.

To exchange data between the two Microsoft Excel programs, you begin by saving the documents in the SYLK file format. Then you must transfer those files from one computer to the other. You can accomplish this with a special cable that has the proper configuration to connect the two computers, or with a modem. If your PC uses a disk drive that accepts 3¼-inch disks, you can also use a utility program such as Matchmaker to transfer data between the PC and Macintosh. If you're connected to a network that supports both the IBM PC (and compatibles) and the Macintosh, you're in luck. You'll probably be able to transfer files from one computer to another without any extra equipment or software. Your hardware dealer can help you choose the best transfer method for your needs.

Although we'll discuss transferring worksheets in this section, the same instructions apply to transferring macro sheets. Unfortunately, you can't transfer charts between the two programs, because Microsoft Excel doesn't allow you to save charts in the SYLK format.

Importing Macintosh files

As we've already mentioned, the first step in importing a Macintosh file is to save the document in the SYLK format. To do this, load Microsoft Excel for the Macintosh and then open the document you want to transfer. Choose the Save As command from the File menu and choose the SYLK file-format option in the Save As dialog box. Then communicate the file so that it can be used by the PC.

Next, start the PC version of Microsoft Excel, choose the Open command from the File menu, and type the name of the document you want to open. Because the Macintosh does not automatically add filename extensions when you save a file, you won't be able to zero in on your Macintosh files by typing a wildcard and filename extension, such as *.SLK. However, to see a list of all available files, you can type *.* in the File Name edit bar. (If the worksheet isn't in the default directory, simply precede *.* with the full pathname.) When you select OK or press Enter, Microsoft Excel will display all available files in the list box. When you select the appropriate worksheet from the Open dialog box, Microsoft Excel will automatically identify the selected file as a SYLK file and will convert the file as it loads it.

Exporting PC files

Transferring data from the MS-DOS version of Microsoft Excel to the Macintosh is just as easy. Simply open the worksheet you want to transfer, issue the Save As command, and specify the name under which you want to save the file. Then select the Options button, choose the SYLK file format, and select OK or press Enter. After communicating the file so that it can be used by the Macintosh, start Microsoft Excel and use the Open command to load the SYLK file.

Adjusting date values

Although the PC and Macintosh versions of Microsoft Excel share many characteristics and abilities, they do not share the same date system. In Microsoft Excel for the PC, the base date is January 1, 1900. In Microsoft Excel for the Macintosh, the base date is January 2, 1904. When you transfer a Macintosh worksheet to the PC, the date will be adjusted automatically. However, this is not the case when you transfer a file from the PC to the Mac. Instead, when you're creating a worksheet on the PC for later use on the Mac, you must choose the Calculation command from the Options menu and select the 1904 Date System option *before* you enter any data on the worksheet. If you've already created a worksheet using the 1900 date system, you must open a new worksheet, change the date system to 1904, and then copy the contents of the original worksheet onto the new worksheet.

Other differences

The PC version of Microsoft Excel offers several worksheet and macro-sheet functions, such as ADD.ARROW and ATTACH.TEXT, that are not found in versions 1.04 and earlier of Microsoft Excel for the Macintosh. If your worksheet or macro sheet contains functions that have no Mac equivalents, the formulas are simply ignored, or they return error values.

A few other attributes, such as cell notes and shading, are not transferred to the Macintosh version of the worksheet because these options are not yet supported on the Mac. We are confident that future versions of Microsoft Excel for the Macintosh will close this gap substantially, however.

Sharing with Microsoft Multiplan

In many respects, the Microsoft Excel worksheet and the Microsoft Multiplan worksheet are similar. There are a few important differences, however. This discussion applies primarily to transferring data to and from Multiplan version 2.0 and later. Although you can share data with earlier versions, the exchange will not be as complete.

Importing Multiplan files

To prepare a Multiplan file for transfer to Microsoft Excel, load Multiplan and then open the document you want to transfer. Choose the Transfer Options command and select the Symbolic option. To save the document, choose Transfer Save.

To import a Multiplan file saved in the SYLK format, simply start Microsoft Excel, choose the Open command from the File menu, and type the filename. To see a list of all available SYLK files, type *.SLK in the File Name edit bar and select OK or press Enter. (If the worksheet isn't in the default directory, precede *.SLK with the full pathname.) When you select OK or press Enter, Microsoft Excel will display the names of all your SYLK worksheets in the list box. When you select the appropriate worksheet from this list, Microsoft Excel will automatically identify the selected file as a SYLK file and will convert the file as it loads it.

Microsoft Excel does a good job of importing Multiplan worksheets. Most of the basic data in the Multiplan worksheet, including all numeric and text entries, names, formats, and protection status, are converted correctly. Multiplan formulas are converted to Microsoft Excel formulas.

Cell formats

Multiplan offers seven numeric formats: General, Dollar, Percent, No Decimal, Decimal, Scientific, and Bar Graph. Microsoft Excel offers a format that corresponds to each of these options except for Bar Graph. The Bar Graph format is converted to Microsoft Excel's General format. If the Microsoft Multiplan worksheet contains formats with other than zero or two decimals, Microsoft Excel creates a custom format with the number of decimals used in the Multiplan format. In addition, if a Multiplan worksheet was created with the Commas command turned on, all Microsoft Excel formats will have commas.

Alignment and column-width formats from the Multiplan file also transfer to Microsoft Excel.

Operators

Both Microsoft Excel and Multiplan accept references to single cells, ranges, and multiple areas. Both also use the range (:), intersection (space), and union (,) reference operators. Although the Microsoft Excel and Multiplan range operators are identical, the precedence of the intersection operator (space) and the range operator (:) is reversed: In Multiplan, intersection references are resolved before range references.

In addition, with Microsoft Excel's comparison operators you can compare any type of argument—logical, numeric, or text. In Multiplan, you can't use comparison operators with logical arguments.

Linking worksheets

In both Microsoft Excel and Multiplan, you can link one worksheet to another. The method of linking worksheets in Microsoft Excel, however, is vastly different from the method in Multiplan. When you import a Multiplan worksheet that includes linking formulas, those formulas are converted into external array formulas. For instance, suppose cells C1:C5 in a Multiplan worksheet are linked to cells A1:A5 in another worksheet named Subsidiary. If you import the first worksheet into Microsoft Excel, cells C1:C5 in the Microsoft Excel worksheet will contain the array formula

    =Subsidiary!$A$1:$A$5

Calculation differences

In Multiplan, worksheets are calculated in strict linear order: column 1 first, then column 2, then column 3, and so on. Microsoft Excel uses natural-order calculation instead.

In most cases, this difference will not cause a problem. In a very few instances, however, the worksheet may not calculate properly after being imported. In that event, you might want to move the converted worksheet into a macro sheet.

Because macro sheets use linear (column-by-column) calculation, chances are good that the converted worksheet will compute properly on a macro sheet.

Both Microsoft Excel and Multiplan allow you to use iterative calculation. The method for controlling iterative calculation in the two programs is different, however. In Multiplan, iterative calculation is controlled by two functions: DELTA and ITERCNT. DELTA measures the change in a given value in the worksheet from one iteration to another; ITERCNT counts the number of iterations. These functions are used in a completion-test formula that you enter into a cell of the worksheet and define with the Set Completion Test command. Iteration continues until the value of the completion-test formula changes from TRUE to FALSE.

Microsoft Excel supports every Multiplan function except DELTA and ITERCNT. The program will not convert a formula that contains either of these functions. In Microsoft Excel, the DELTA and ITERCNT functions are replaced with two settings in the Calculation dialog box: Maximum Change and Maximum Iterations. These settings determine the number of iterations that will occur when you calculate the sheet. If you import a Multiplan worksheet that uses iterative calculation into Microsoft Excel, you'll need to replace the completion-test formula with the proper Maximum Change and Maximum Iterations settings. Usually, Microsoft Excel will calculate the worksheet properly after this change.

Exporting Microsoft Excel files to Multiplan

To export a Microsoft Excel file to Multiplan, you must first save the file in the SYLK format. To save a worksheet as a SYLK file, choose the Save As command and specify the name under which you want to save the file. Then, select the Options button, choose the SYLK file format, and select OK or press Enter.

When you open the SYLK file in Multiplan, all text entries and most numbers in your Microsoft Excel worksheet will be converted correctly. However, Microsoft Excel does support a larger range of numbers than Multiplan does, and Microsoft Excel macros can't be converted to Multiplan.

Cell formats

As we mentioned earlier, most Microsoft Excel numeric formats are supported by Multiplan. However, some of your custom formats may not transfer. If a Microsoft Excel format doesn't have a corresponding Multiplan format, it will appear in Multiplan's General format.

Microsoft Excel also allows you to use formatted date, currency, and percentage values enclosed in quotation marks as arguments in your formulas. Multiplan doesn't support this type of formatted string value. For example, a formula like

="$1,000.00"*12

is invalid in Multiplan.

The Column Width and Alignment options that you applied in Microsoft Excel will carry over in Multiplan.

Formulas

When you convert Microsoft Excel files to Multiplan files, the formulas are transferred to the SYLK file just as they appear in Microsoft Excel; no conversion occurs. Because the formulas don't convert, you may run into trouble when Multiplan tries to read some of the Microsoft Excel formulas. If Multiplan cannot read the imported data, it will either ignore the data or return an error value.

Although Multiplan supports many of the same functions as Microsoft Excel, Microsoft Excel supports as many as 14 arguments per function, whereas Multiplan allows only 5. Microsoft Excel also offers a larger range of functions.

Both Multiplan and Microsoft Excel support seven error values: #NOVALUE!, #NOREF!, #NODIV/0!, #NONAME?, #N/A, #NULL!, and #NUM!. Multiplan, however, can return these error values only as the result of a formula. It will not accept them as constant values in cells and formulas. Unlike Microsoft Excel, Multiplan does not support array formulas or array arguments.

References

Microsoft Excel's worksheet is 16,394 rows by 256 columns. Multiplan's worksheet covers only 4095 rows and 255 columns. Any formula that refers to a cell beyond column 255 or in a row below 4095 in the Microsoft Excel worksheet will not be calculated in Multiplan.

Like Microsoft Excel, Multiplan does allow linked references to other worksheets. However, Multiplan allows a range in one worksheet to refer only to a range of the same size and shape in a second worksheet. In addition, Multiplan does not allow you to use external references as part of larger formulas. For example, the external reference

    =Sheet1!A1*12

will work in Microsoft Excel but not in Multiplan.

Using names

In Multiplan, as in Microsoft Excel, you can assign a name to a cell, a range, or a multiple range. But in Microsoft Excel, you can also assign a name to a constant value or to a formula. Multiplan cannot interpret named values and formulas.

Sharing with Lotus 1-2-3

Microsoft Excel can read and write Lotus 1-2-3 worksheets. Thus, you can easily exchange worksheets with friends and coworkers who use 1-2-3. If you're a 1-2-3 user, this capability also means that you can upgrade to Microsoft Excel with little difficulty. The instructions below also apply to Lotus Symphony.

Importing 1-2-3 files

Importing a 1-2-3 file to Microsoft Excel is easy. All you have to do is start Microsoft Excel, choose the Open command from the File menu, type *.WK* in the File Name edit bar, and press Enter. (If the worksheet isn't in the default directory, precede the *.WK* with the full pathname.) Microsoft Excel will display the names of all your 1-2-3 worksheets in the Files list box. When you select a worksheet from this list and choose OK, Microsoft Excel will automatically identify the selected file as a 1-2-3 file and will convert the file as it loads it.

Microsoft Excel does a good job of importing 1-2-3 worksheets. All the values and labels in the 1-2-3 worksheet are converted properly into numeric and text values. Most of the formulas in the 1-2-3 worksheet are also converted into Microsoft Excel formulas, as are most cell formats and cell and range name definitions.

Format conversion

Most 1-2-3 formats have counterparts in Microsoft Excel. When you load 1-2-3 worksheets into Microsoft Excel, all formats are converted as shown in Table A-1. If your 1-2-3 worksheet contains a format other than the ones listed (for example, currency with three decimal places), Microsoft Excel creates a custom format that matches the incoming one.

Table A-1. Format conversions from Lotus 1-2-3 to Microsoft Excel.

1-2-3 format	Microsoft Excel format
Fixed, 0 decimals	0
Fixed, 2 decimals	0.00
Scientific, 0 decimals	0E+00
Scientific, 2 decimals	0.00E+00
Currency, 0 decimals	$#,##0 ;($#,##0)
Currency, 2 decimals	$#,##0.00 ;($#,##0.00)
Percent, 0 decimals	0%
Percent, 2 decimals	0.00%
Comma, 0 decimals	#,##0 ;(#,##0)
Comma, 2 decimals	#,##00.00 ;(#,##0.00)
General	General
+/−	General
D1 (DD-Mmm-YY)	d-mmm-yy
D2 (DD-Mmm)	d-mmm
D3 (Mmm-YY)	mmm-yy
Text	General
Hidden (version 2.0 or higher)	;;(numbers) or ;;; (text)

Microsoft Excel and 1-2-3 both support cell protection. In Microsoft Excel, however, a cell can be both locked (protected from accidental changes) and hidden. In 1-2-3, cells can only be protected. When you import a 1-2-3 worksheet to Microsoft Excel, all protected cells in the 1-2-3 worksheet are locked in Microsoft Excel. In addition, you can assign a number format in both Microsoft Excel and 1-2-3 version 2.0 or higher to hide cell values.

Formula conversion

The Microsoft Excel range operator (:) is different from the 1-2-3 range operator (..). When Microsoft Excel encounters the .. range operator in a formula, it converts that operator to Microsoft Excel form.

There is also a slight difference in the precedence of Microsoft Excel and 1-2-3 mathematical operators. In Microsoft Excel, the negation operator takes precedence over the exponentiation operator. In 1-2-3, the exponentiation operator takes precedence. Thus, the formula =–2^2 will return 4 in Microsoft Excel but –4 in 1-2-3. You can overcome this difference by careful use of parentheses.

Microsoft Excel supports only natural-order calculation. In addition to natural-order calculation, 1-2-3 also supports by-row and by-column calculation. When you import a 1-2-3 worksheet to Microsoft Excel, recalculation is set to Natural.

All 1-2-3 functions have counterparts in Microsoft Excel. Some functions have slightly different names, but they are otherwise identical. For example, the function that computes the average of a set of values is =AVERAGE in Microsoft Excel and @AVG in 1-2-3. When you convert one of these functions, Microsoft Excel automatically changes the name of the function.

In a few cases, a Microsoft Excel function and its 1-2-3 equivalent don't work in exactly the same way. Usually, Microsoft Excel overcomes the differences during translation. Some of these transformations are quite sophisticated. For example, both 1-2-3 and Microsoft Excel have CHOOSE functions. In Microsoft Excel, the function has the form

=CHOOSE(*index,value1,value2,…*)

In 1-2-3, this function has the form

@CHOOSE(*offset,value0,value1,…*)

The difference between these functions is that the first value in the Microsoft Excel function has an index value of 1, whereas the first value in the 1-2-3 list has an offset (index) of 0. In other words, the function

=CHOOSE(1,100,200,300)

will return 100 in Microsoft Excel, but the function

@ CHOOSE(1,100,200,300)

will return 200 in 1-2-3.

Microsoft Excel overcomes this difference by subtracting 1 from the index when it converts a Microsoft Excel CHOOSE function to 1-2-3 or by adding 1 to the offset when it loads a 1-2-3 worksheet into Microsoft Excel. The same technique is used with the VLOOKUP and HLOOKUP functions and with all database statistical functions (DSUM, DAVERAGE, and so on).

Another example of this kind of difference relates to the PV, FV, and PMT functions. In Microsoft Excel, the *payment* and *principal* arguments of these functions are negative. In 1-2-3, the same arguments are positive. For this reason, when Microsoft Excel translates one of these functions from Microsoft Excel to 1-2-3, or from 1-2-3 to Microsoft Excel, it changes the sign of the *payment* and *principal* arguments.

The 1-2-3 @IRR function has the form

@IRR(*guess,values*)

whereas the Microsoft Excel IRR function has the form

=IRR(*values,guess*)

To account for this difference, Microsoft Excel always transposes the *values* and *guess* arguments when it translates an IRR or @IRR function.

Microsoft Excel statistical functions (AVERAGE, COUNT, and so on) handle cells that contain nonnumeric values differently than do 1-2-3 statistical functions. If you include a cell that contains a label in the argument of a 1-2-3 statistical function, the function assigns a value of 0 to that label. The Microsoft Excel version of the function, however, ignores the label. This small difference can make a big difference in the result of the function. You'll have to watch for this quirk when you translate statistical functions.

Microsoft Excel's INT function is also different from the 1-2-3 @INT function. In 1-2-3, @INT always rounds toward zero. In Microsoft Excel, INT always rounds down. As a result, the formula

@INT(−3.65)

returns −3 in 1-2-3, but the formula

=INT(−3.65)

returns −4 in Microsoft Excel. This difference can also cause the MOD and @MOD functions to return different answers if both of the function's arguments are negative.

Dates

Microsoft Excel and 1-2-3 use the same serial date system for calculating date and time values. However, the Microsoft Excel DATE function accepts *year* arguments from 0 through 178, whereas the 1-2-3 @DATE function accepts *year* arguments from 0 through 199. As long as the *year* argument of a 1-2-3 @DATE function you're importing is less than 179 and greater than –1, the function will be converted correctly. If the *year* argument of a 1-2-3 @DATE function is outside this range, Microsoft Excel will not recognize it as a date value.

Data tables

If your 1-2-3 worksheet contains a data table, the input values, table formula(s), and results of the table are imported into Microsoft Excel. However, the definition of the table is lost. You'll have to use the Table command on the Data menu to redefine the table in Microsoft Excel.

Microsoft Excel data tables are slightly different from those in 1-2-3. First, the results of a Microsoft Excel data table are defined by an array formula; arrays are not supported in 1-2-3. In addition, Microsoft Excel data tables are calculated automatically whenever you calculate the worksheet, just like other formulas. In 1-2-3, data tables have to be calculated by issuing a command or by pressing a function key. Finally, Microsoft Excel allows more flexibility with the input values in a one-input table: They may be in either the first column or the first row of the table. In 1-2-3, the input values in a one-input table must be in the first column of the table.

Databases

Microsoft Excel database commands are also similar to 1-2-3 commands. When you load a 1-2-3 database into Microsoft Excel, the database input-range (database-range) and the criterion-range (criteria-range) definitions are preserved but the output-range (extract-range) definition is lost. Microsoft Excel does not use a permanent output or extract range; instead, you must highlight the extract range each time you use the Extract command.

Graphs

When Microsoft Excel opens a 1-2-3 worksheet that contains one or more graphs, it displays an alert box like the one in Figure A-2. If you choose the Yes option to convert all your 1-2-3 graphs into Microsoft Excel charts, Microsoft Excel opens a new chart file for each graph it converts. These files are linked to the converted worksheet. If you choose the No option, Microsoft Excel simply ignores any graphs that exist in the 1-2-3 worksheet. You might want to choose this option if you no longer have any need for the graphs or if you intend to create your Microsoft Excel charts from scratch.

FIGURE A-2. *This dialog box allows you to convert 1-2-3 graphs to Microsoft Excel charts.*

For example, if you convert the graph shown in Figure A-3 to Excel, the resulting chart will look like the one in Figure A-4.

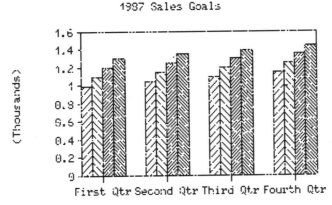

FIGURE A-3. *We want to convert this 1-2-3 graph to a Microsoft Excel chart.*

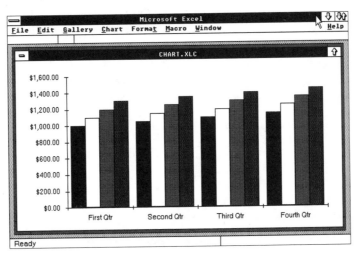

FIGURE A-4. *The graph has been successfully converted to a Microsoft Excel .XLC file.*

The Macro Translation Assistant

As you probably know, the procedures you use to create and run macros in Microsoft Excel are completely different from those you use in 1-2-3. In Microsoft Excel, you create your macro in a macro sheet instead of in a worksheet, and after you've created a macro sheet, you can run the macros on that sheet from within *any* worksheet, as long as both the macro sheet and the worksheet are open in the workspace. Because of these differences, you'll have to expend a little effort to convert your 1-2-3 macros into Microsoft Excel macros.

You can convert most 1-2-3 macros into functioning Microsoft Excel macros with the Microsoft Excel Macro Translation Assistant.

To use the Macro Translation Assistant, begin by opening the 1-2-3 file that contains the macro(s) you want to convert. The macro will be displayed in its original form in a standard Microsoft Excel worksheet. Next, choose the Run command on the Control menu (or press Alt-Spacebar-U). When the Run Application dialog box appears, choose Macro Translator and then select OK or press Enter. Microsoft Excel will display the Macro Translation Assistant dialog box shown in Figure A-5.

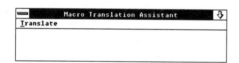

FIGURE A-5. *The Macro Translation Assistant dialog box allows you to convert macros from other applications into Microsoft Excel macros.*

Next, select the Lotus 123 command from the Translate menu. Microsoft Excel will list the names of all open 1-2-3 documents. Select the name of the worksheet(s) you want to convert and then select OK or press Enter. Now Microsoft Excel will display a dialog box like the one shown in Figure A-6, so that you can specify which macros you want to translate. (You can select more than one macro by holding down Shift and then using either the arrow keys or the mouse.)

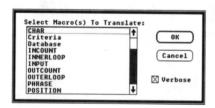

FIGURE A-6. *Use this dialog box to choose the macros you want to translate.*

The Verbose option lets you place the 1-2-3 macro statements next to the corresponding Microsoft Excel statements in the macro sheet. If you don't want to see the 1-2-3 commands on the macro sheet, turn off the Verbose check box.

The Macro Translation Assistant will now open a new Microsoft Excel macro sheet and begin to convert the 1-2-3 macros to Microsoft Excel macros. The Assistant will display its progress inside the dialog box. If it encounters any problems translating the 1-2-3 macros, you'll see an alert message in the Macro Translation Assistant window and a translation comment in bold characters above or below the problem on the new macro sheet. To continue the translation, select OK. To stop the conversion process, press the Esc key. When the translation process is complete, your Microsoft Excel macro sheet will look like the one in Figure A-7.

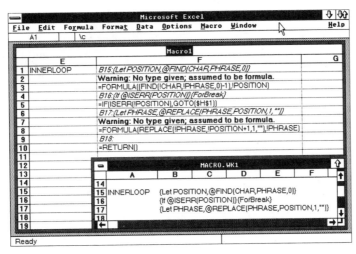

FIGURE A-7. *The original macro code, at the bottom of the screen, has been translated into the Microsoft Excel macro language.*

Exporting Microsoft Excel files to 1-2-3

Microsoft Excel can save worksheets as 1-2-3 files. Simply choose the Save As command, specify the name under which you want to save the file, select Options and the appropriate file format (WKS or WK1), and select OK or press Enter. When you save the file with either the WKS or WK1 option, Microsoft Excel converts the worksheet into a 1-2-3 file.

Unfortunately, you can't convert Microsoft Excel charts into 1-2-3 graphs, nor can you convert Microsoft Excel macro sheets into 1-2-3 worksheets.

Formula conversion

Translating Microsoft Excel formulas to 1-2-3 formulas is more difficult than moving in the other direction. For example, because 1-2-3 doesn't support arrays, any Microsoft Excel formula that involves arrays is not converted, nor are multiple selections. Similarly, because 1-2-3 version 1A doesn't accept formulas that refer to text, any Microsoft Excel formula that involves text is not converted. In addition, because 1-2-3 doesn't support references to cells in other worksheets, any Microsoft Excel formula that contains an external reference is not converted.

Although all numbers and text entries are converted correctly, as are most of the formulas, Microsoft Excel offers a number of functions that 1-2-3 doesn't support.

In addition, in a few cases a Microsoft Excel function and its 1-2-3 equivalent don't work in exactly the same way. In most of these cases, Microsoft Excel overcomes the differences during translation. In a few cases, however, the conversion may not always work. For example, the Microsoft Excel PV, FV, and PMT functions can take as many as five arguments, but 1-2-3 doesn't support the fourth (*future value*) and fifth (*type*) arguments. If you translate a Microsoft Excel worksheet that contains these functions, they will be converted properly as long as they have only three arguments. However, if you translate a PV, FV, or PMT function that has more than three arguments, Microsoft Excel will change that function to a constant value during translation.

The Microsoft Excel NPV function is similar to the 1-2-3 @NPV function, except that the Microsoft Excel function will accept as many as 13 *cash flow* arguments, whereas the 1-2-3 function will accept only one. As long as your Microsoft Excel NPV function has only one *cash flow* argument, it will convert properly, but if the function has more than one *cash flow* argument, it will be changed to a constant value during conversion.

As we mentioned, some functions in Microsoft Excel do not have 1-2-3 counterparts. For example, there is no 1-2-3 equivalent to the Microsoft Excel GROWTH function. Table A-2 lists these functions, all of which are changed to constant values when they're converted to 1-2-3.

Lotus 1-2-3 offers three logical operators that are only indirectly supported by Microsoft Excel: #AND#, #OR#, and #NOT#. The Microsoft Excel equivalents of these operators are the functions AND, OR, and NOT. When you transfer a Microsoft Excel worksheet to 1-2-3, all AND, OR, and NOT functions are changed to the operators #AND#, #OR#, and #NOT#. When you transfer a 1-2-3 worksheet to

Table A-2. Microsoft Excel functions without Lotus 1-2-3 equivalents.

AND	ISERROR	OR
AREAS	ISLOGICAL	PPMT
COLUMN	ISNUMBER	PRODUCT
COUNT	ISREF	ROW
DCOUNT	LINEST	SEARCH
DOLLAR	LOG	STDEV
DPRODUCT	LOGEST	SUBSTITUTE
DSTDEV	LOOKUP	TEXT
DVAR	MATCH	TRANSPOSE
FACT	MDETERM	TREND
GROWTH	MINVERSE	TYPE
INT	MIRR	VAR
IPMT	MMULT	WEEKDAY
ISBLANK	NOT	

Microsoft Excel, the reverse occurs: The operators are changed into the functions. For example, the Microsoft Excel function

=AND(A1>100,A1<200)

would be converted into the 1-2-3 operator

(A1>100#AND#A1<200)

Microsoft Excel supports seven error values: #VALUE!, #REF!, #DIV/0!, #NAME?, #N/A, #NULL!, and #NUM!. These values can appear as constants in cells and formulas and also as the result of formulas. 1-2-3 supports only two error values—ERR and NA—both of which appear only as the result of formulas. When you export a Microsoft Excel worksheet to 1-2-3, the error value #N/A is converted to the error value NA. Any other error value is translated to ERR. When you import a 1-2-3 worksheet to Microsoft Excel, any NA value is translated to the #N/A error constant. Any ERR value is translated to the error constant #VALUE!.

Microsoft Excel offers two other reference operators that 1-2-3 does not support: union (,) and intersection (space). Any formula that contains a union or intersection operator will not be converted. Versions 2.0 and higher of 1-2-3 support the concatenation operator (&). With earlier versions, concatenated text strings are converted to simple labels in the 1-2-3 worksheet.

Format conversion

In 1-2-3, all numeric entries are right-aligned in cells, whereas label entries can be right-aligned, left-aligned, or centered. In Microsoft Excel, you can control the alignment of both numeric and text entries. When you export a Microsoft Excel worksheet to 1-2-3, only cells that contain text entries retain their alignment attributes. All numbers become right-aligned.

Because 1-2-3 does not support bold and italic type styles, these style attributes are removed when you export a Microsoft Excel worksheet to 1-2-3.

All standard Microsoft Excel numeric formats have 1-2-3 counterparts and are converted properly, according to the relationships shown in Table A-1. If you've defined your own formats in your Microsoft Excel worksheet, Microsoft Excel will attempt to convert those formats to 1-2-3 formats. For example, the custom format $#,##0.000 ;($#,##0.000) will be converted to currency with two decimal places in 1-2-3. However, if Microsoft Excel can't convert the format, the cell will be unformatted in the 1-2-3 worksheet. For example, the custom format dddd, mmmm d, yyyy displays Microsoft Excel dates in the following form: Tuesday, January 1, 1904. This format has no counterpart in 1-2-3, however, so the resulting cell in the 1-2-3 worksheet will be unformatted.

Other differences

Although the Microsoft Excel worksheet includes 16,384 rows, the 1-2-3 version 1A worksheet includes only 2048 rows and version 2.0 (and higher) worksheets include only 8192 rows. Any formula that refers to a cell in a row below row 2048 or 8192 in the Microsoft Excel worksheet is not converted when you save a file in the WKS or WK1 format. Instead, Microsoft Excel changes the formula to a constant value. Of course, the entries below row 2048 or 8192 are lost in the transfer.

In Microsoft Excel, you can assign names to cells or ranges in the worksheet or to constant values and formulas that aren't entered in cells. 1-2-3, on the other hand, allows you to assign names only to cells or ranges, not to multiple areas, constant values, or formulas. Any formula that contains a reference to a named cell or range converts properly from Microsoft Excel to 1-2-3. If you convert a worksheet containing formulas that use named constants or formulas, however, those named constants and formulas are converted into constant values. For example, suppose you've assigned the name *Test* to the constant 100 in a Microsoft Excel worksheet and then used that name in the formula

=Test*A1

When this formula is converted, the name *Test* will be changed to the value 100.

When Microsoft Excel can't translate a formula, it displays an alert box that shows the location of the cell containing the error. The alert box also asks if you want Microsoft Excel to tell you each time it can't convert a formula. If you select

Yes, Microsoft Excel displays this dialog box each time it can't convert a formula. If you select No, Microsoft Excel doesn't pause until it has completed conversion of the whole worksheet; then it displays one alert box that shows the total number of formulas that could not be converted. Microsoft Excel changes the untranslatable formulas to constant values, if possible.

Lotus 1-2-3 and Microsoft Excel both support Manual and Automatic calculation. However, 1-2-3's Automatic calculation is the same as Microsoft Excel's Automatic Except Tables. When you transfer worksheets from Microsoft Excel to 1-2-3, Automatic remains Automatic, Manual remains Manual, and Automatic Except Tables becomes Automatic. Although it accepts your Maximum Iterations setting, 1-2-3 ignores your Maximum Change setting when the file is converted.

Most other attributes of your Microsoft Excel worksheet are lost when you save the worksheet as a 1-2-3 file. For example, even if you've created several windows on a single Microsoft Excel worksheet, the resulting 1-2-3 worksheet will have only one window. In addition, none of the print settings you've defined in Microsoft Excel will be transferred.

When the Microsoft Excel worksheet contains a data table, the table formula and the input values (variables) are usually converted properly for 1-2-3. Keep in mind that 1-2-3 requires that your input values appear in the first column of the table range, however. The results in a Microsoft Excel data table are array formulas; these formulas are changed to constant values during the conversion. In addition, you'll have to redefine the table range and the input cell(s) before you can use the table in 1-2-3.

As we mentioned earlier, Microsoft Excel and 1-2-3 both support cell protection. In Microsoft Excel, however, a cell can be both locked (protected from accidental change) and hidden. In 1-2-3, cells can only be protected. Thus, when you export a Microsoft Excel worksheet to 1-2-3, all locked cells will be protected in the 1-2-3 worksheet; however, cells that are hidden in Microsoft Excel will not be hidden in 1-2-3 unless you've used the Hidden number format.

Sharing with dBASE

Microsoft Excel can also exchange database ranges with dBASE II or dBASE III.

Importing dBASE files

To import a dBASE file into Microsoft Excel, simply choose the Open command from the File menu and type the name of the file you want to open. To see a list of available dBASE files, type *.DBF in the File Name edit bar and select OK or press Enter. (If the database is not in the default directory, precede the *.DBF with the full pathname.) When you select the appropriate database from this list, Microsoft

Excel will automatically identify the selected file as a DBF file and will convert the file as it loads it.

Microsoft Excel places the dBASE field names in the first row of a new Microsoft Excel worksheet and then uses them as field names in the Microsoft Excel database. Each dBASE field appears in a different Microsoft Excel column. The dBASE records appear in rows immediately under the field-names row. Microsoft Excel sets the worksheet column width to match the width of the dBASE fields. Columns that contain data from dBASE character and numeric fields will be the same width as their corresponding fields in dBASE.

Exporting Microsoft Excel files to dBASE

Before you save a Microsoft Excel document in the DBF format, be sure you've defined the database. Then, to convert the file, choose the Save As command on the File menu, select the Options button, and choose the appropriate file format: DBF 2 if you're transferring a Microsoft Excel database range to dBASE II; DBF 3 if you're transferring a Microsoft Excel database range to dBASE III. Microsoft Excel will save the file with the .DBF filename extension. After you leave Microsoft Excel, you can load dBASE III and load the .DBF file.

Working with text files

The Text option in the Save As dialog box saves your worksheet and macro-sheet files as ASCII text files. When you save a document as ASCII text, Microsoft Excel saves the text and values as they appear in the worksheet cells; the underlying formulas in the worksheet or macro sheet aren't saved. The Text option is commonly used to convert a Microsoft Excel worksheet into a form that is usable by a word-processing program such as Microsoft Write or Microsoft Word. Many other programs can also read and write ASCII files.

To save a worksheet in the Text file format, first choose the Save As command. When the Save As dialog box appears, choose Options and then select Text. Microsoft Excel will save the file as ASCII text with the .TXT filename extension.

For example, suppose you want to use the Microsoft Excel worksheet called SALES.XLS, shown in Figure A-8, in a Microsoft Word document. To do this, first issue the Save As command. When Microsoft Excel displays the Save As dialog box, select Options and then Text to save the worksheet in the Text file format. Then select OK or press Enter.

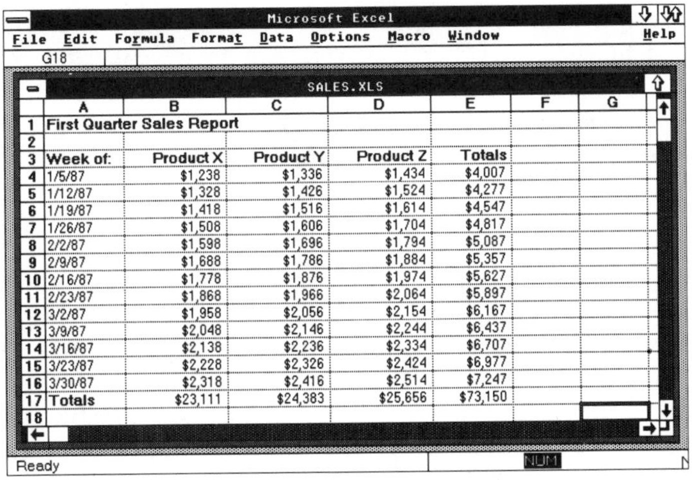

FIGURE A-8. *We'll save this worksheet in Text format.*

To use this ASCII file in Microsoft Word, load Word and then use the Open command to load the ASCII file. As you can see in Figure A-9, only the text and values have been transferred to the Word document. Each column of data is separated by a tab, and each row is separated by a carriage return. You can now use Word's character and paragraph formatting commands to format this data, just as you would format any other Word document.

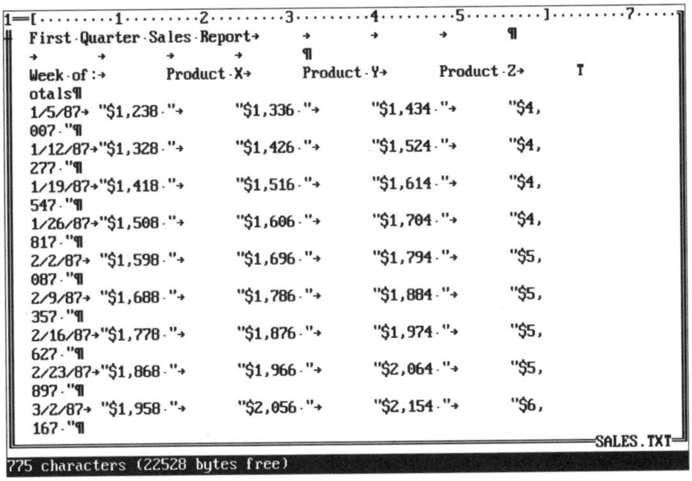

FIGURE A-9. *When you transfer a worksheet saved in the Text format, tabs separate the columns and carriage returns separate the rows.*

Notice that quotation marks appear around each piece of numeric text in the Word document. This occurs because Word can accept either tab-separated or comma-separated values. The quotation marks prevent Word from treating the number as two separate entries. Unless you plan to use the transferred text as a data document for a form letter, you can use the Replace command to eliminate the quotation marks.

The CSV file format

The CSV (Comma-Separated Values) file format is similar to the Text file format. Instead of tabs, however, the CSV format uses commas to separate columns or fields. Microsoft Excel saves the file with the .CSV filename extension.

Whether you use the Text or the CSV file format depends on the program with which you're sharing data. Some programs can accept files saved in either file format; others can use only one of these formats.

If you open a CSV file into Microsoft Excel, the program begins a new column whenever it reads a comma. The contents of any cell containing a literal comma character will be enclosed in double quotation marks.

Transferring data with the Clipboard

As you already know, when you cut or copy data in Microsoft Excel, you place the data on the Clipboard to store it. Any program that runs under Microsoft Windows can use the Clipboard to exchange data with other programs that run under Microsoft Windows. You can use the Clipboard to transfer either values or pictures. Cell values are transferred as text (numbers and letters). The underlying formulas are not transferred; only the displayed values are copied. Images of charts are transferred as graphics. In addition, you can take a "picture" of your worksheet and use the Clipboard to transfer it into another document as a graphic.

Transferring values and formulas

The first step in transferring worksheet data from Microsoft Excel to another application with the Clipboard is to select the cells whose contents you want to transfer and issue the Copy command. After you've copied the information to the Clipboard, choose Exit from the File menu to leave Microsoft Excel. Then load the application into which you want to copy the data. Alternatively, if you have enough memory available to run two or more applications concurrently, start the other program and load the document without leaving Microsoft Excel. This technique is handy when you need to transfer several individual pieces of information.

To start a second application while in Microsoft Excel, press Alt-Esc to activate the MS-DOS Executive screen. Then run the second application as usual. You can resize and reposition the two application windows so that both are accessible with the mouse, or you can use the Alt and Esc keys to move between them.

After starting or activating the second application, create a new document, if necessary, or open the document into which you want to paste the copied information. Because you haven't turned off your computer, the Clipboard to which you copied the information from Microsoft Excel is still active, so simply use the target program's equivalent of the Paste command to paste the data in its new location.

To illustrate, let's use the Clipboard to transfer some data from Microsoft Excel to Microsoft Write. Because both of these programs run under Windows, the transfer is easy. Suppose you want to copy the values from cells A3:E17 of the worksheet named SALES.XLS, shown in Figure A-8. Begin by selecting cells A3:E17 in the Microsoft Excel worksheet and then choose the Copy command from the Edit menu to place the selection on the Clipboard. Now load or activate the Write program and open the document into which you want to paste the data. Move the insertion point to the position where you want the Microsoft Excel data to appear and then choose the Paste command from the Edit menu. The selected worksheet entries will appear in the Write document, via the Clipboard. Your Write document will be similar to the report in Figure A-10.

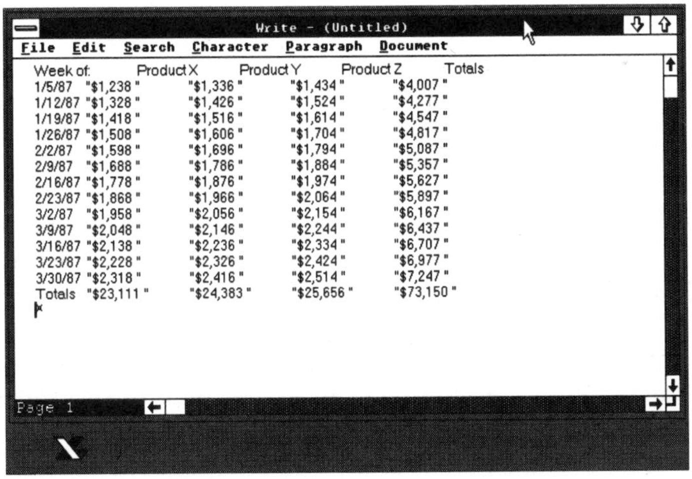
Write - (Untitled)
File Edit Search Character Paragraph Document
Week of: ProductX ProductY Product Z Totals
1/5/87 "$1,238 " "$1,336 " "$1,434 " "$4,007 "
1/12/87 "$1,328 " "$1,426 " "$1,524 " "$4,277 "
1/19/87 "$1,418 " "$1,516 " "$1,614 " "$4,547 "
1/26/87 "$1,508 " "$1,606 " "$1,704 " "$4,817 "
2/2/87 "$1,598 " "$1,696 " "$1,794 " "$5,087 "
2/9/87 "$1,688 " "$1,786 " "$1,884 " "$5,357 "
2/16/87 "$1,778 " "$1,876 " "$1,974 " "$5,627 "
2/23/87 "$1,868 " "$1,966 " "$2,064 " "$5,897 "
3/2/87 "$1,958 " "$2,056 " "$2,154 " "$6,167 "
3/9/87 "$2,048 " "$2,146 " "$2,244 " "$6,437 "
3/16/87 "$2,138 " "$2,236 " "$2,334 " "$6,707 "
3/23/87 "$2,228 " "$2,326 " "$2,424 " "$6,977 "
3/30/87 "$2,318 " "$2,416 " "$2,514 " "$7,247 "
Totals "$23,111 " "$24,383 " "$25,656 " "$73,150 "
Page 1

FIGURE A-10. *We pasted the Microsoft Excel data into our Write document.*

Notice that the bold formatting we applied in the Microsoft Excel worksheet has been lost, as has the alignment for cell entries. In general, when you transfer information via the Clipboard, any character formatting won't survive the exchange. However, as you can see, the currency format we applied to the Microsoft Excel cells with the Number command from the Format menu has been carried over into the Write document. After transferring the data to Write, you can format it like any other text in a Write document.

When you copy a multirow range to Write, each row of data occupies one paragraph. For example, the data in cells A3:E17 of our sample worksheet occupies 15 paragraphs in the Write document. When you copy a multicolumn range, a tab separates the data in each column. You can take advantage of this fact by using Write's Tabs command to position the columnar data in your document.

Copying worksheet and macro-sheet pictures

Rather than copy worksheet or macro-sheet entries as text, you can transfer a "snapshot" of selected cells with the Copy Picture command. As with any other copy-and-paste procedure, you begin by selecting the range you want to copy. Then press the Shift key and choose Copy Picture from the Edit menu. (The Copy Picture command appears on the Edit menu only when you press the Shift key before pulling down the menu.) When you issue the Copy Picture command, you'll see a dialog box like the one in Figure A-11.

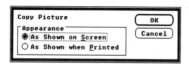

FIGURE A-11. *Use the Copy Picture dialog box to control the appearance of a "snapshot" of selected cells.*

The As Shown on Screen and As Shown when Printed options let you control the appearance of the snapshot. If you want your worksheet or macro-sheet picture to look exactly as it is displayed on the screen, choose the As Shown on Screen option. If you want your snapshot to more closely resemble the way your document will look when printed, choose As Shown when Printed.

For example, let's use the As Shown on Screen option to copy the data in cells A3:E17 of Figure A-8 and then activate a Write document and issue the Paste command. As you can see in Figure A-12, a snapshot of the selected range, complete with cells borders and row and column headers, appears in our report. (To eliminate the cell borders and row and column headers, deselect the Gridlines and Row and Column Headers options in the Options menu Display dialog box before copying the worksheet.)

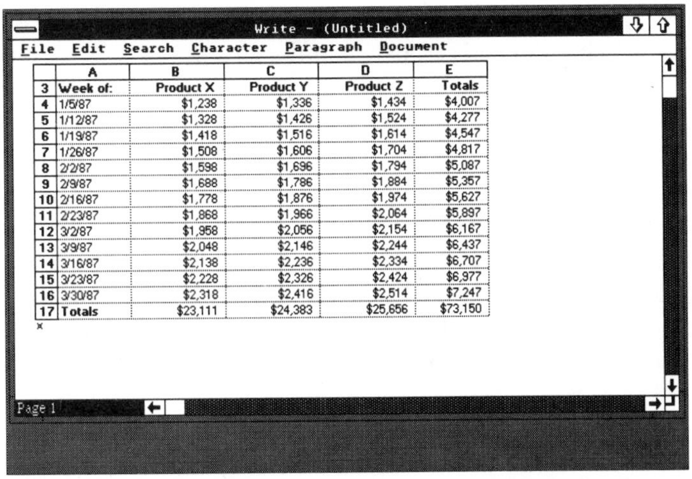

	A	B	C	D	E
3	Week of:	Product X	Product Y	Product Z	Totals
4	1/5/87	$1,238	$1,336	$1,434	$4,007
5	1/12/87	$1,328	$1,426	$1,524	$4,277
6	1/19/87	$1,418	$1,516	$1,614	$4,547
7	1/26/87	$1,508	$1,606	$1,704	$4,817
8	2/2/87	$1,598	$1,696	$1,794	$5,087
9	2/9/87	$1,688	$1,786	$1,884	$5,357
10	2/16/87	$1,778	$1,876	$1,974	$5,627
11	2/23/87	$1,868	$1,966	$2,064	$5,897
12	3/2/87	$1,958	$2,056	$2,154	$6,167
13	3/9/87	$2,048	$2,146	$2,244	$6,437
14	3/16/87	$2,138	$2,236	$2,334	$6,707
15	3/23/87	$2,228	$2,326	$2,424	$6,977
16	3/30/87	$2,318	$2,416	$2,514	$7,247
17	Totals	$23,111	$24,383	$25,656	$73,150

FIGURE A-12. *A snapshot of cells A3:E17 appears in our Write document.*

Copying chart pictures

Transferring a Microsoft Excel chart is a lot like transferring a picture of a worksheet range. For example, suppose you want to copy the Microsoft Excel chart shown in Figure A-13 to a Microsoft Write document.

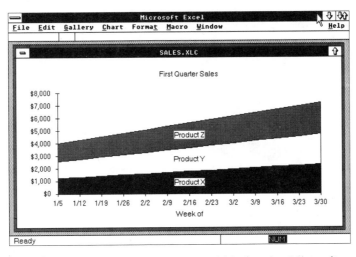

FIGURE A-13. *We want to place a picture of this chart in a Microsoft Write document.*

Begin by placing the Microsoft Excel chart on the Clipboard. To do this, select the chart by choosing the Select Chart command on the Chart menu. Next, hold down Shift while you pull down the Edit menu and then choose the Copy Picture command. Microsoft Excel will display the Copy Picture dialog box shown in Figure A-14. The appearance options work like those that appear when you copy a worksheet picture. You can also control the size of the chart that Microsoft Excel copies to the Clipboard. If you select As Shown on Screen, the chart on the Clipboard will be exactly the same size as the one on the Microsoft Excel screen. If you select As Shown when Printed, Microsoft Excel will make the chart on the Clipboard as big as it would appear if you printed it. When you select OK or press Enter, Microsoft Excel will copy the chart to the Clipboard.

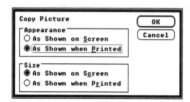

FIGURE A-14. *Use the Copy Picture dialog box to control the appearance and size of a chart picture.*

Now load or activate the program to which you want to transfer the picture and open the document into which you plan to paste the picture. After moving the insertion point to the position where you want to paste the graphic, issue the Paste

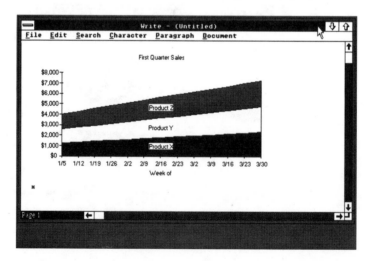

FIGURE A-15. *Our chart picture now appears in a Write document.*

command. Figure A-15 shows the results of pasting this Microsoft Excel chart into a Write document. Because we selected the As Shown on Screen option, the chart is the same size as the one we copied from Microsoft Excel.

The Clipboard window

To see the Clipboard, choose the Run command from the Control menu or press Alt-Spacebar-U. Inside the Run Application dialog box, Clipboard is the default choice. To choose Clipboard, simply select OK or press Enter. You'll see a window like the one in Figure A-16.

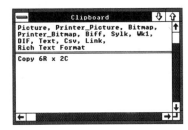

FIGURE A-16. *The Clipboard window reflects the contents of your copy range.*

As you can see, at the top of the Clipboard Microsoft Excel lists terms such as Text and Bitmap. These are the formats in which Microsoft Excel can trade the Clipboard data with other applications. This information is helpful because some applications require that incoming data be presented in a specific format.

Notice also that the Clipboard doesn't display the contents of your copy range. Instead, it describes the shape of the copied area—in our example, the notation 6R x 2C represents a range 6 rows deep and 2 columns wide. Because Microsoft Excel doesn't display the actual contents on the Clipboard, exchanging data within Microsoft Excel documents takes less time.

The Parse command

Occasionally, when you transfer information from another program into Microsoft Excel, several columns of the incoming data are crammed together in a single cell. This problem is particularly common with database programs that don't use a compatible method of separating field entries. Of course, before the data can be used effectively in your Microsoft Excel worksheet, you must divide it into more manageable portions. The Parse command on the Data menu lets you separate the data so that each field is contained in a separate cell.

For example, Figure A-17 shows an imported file that contains five fields. Currently, all these field entries are strung together in column A. The first step in breaking this data into a usable form is to select the entries you want Microsoft Excel to parse. Microsoft Excel places no limit on the number of rows it can parse, but your selection must be only one column wide. In our example, we want to parse all the records in column A, so we'll select the entire column. (Of course, if additional data appears below the range to be parsed, you can select only the cells you want to parse—cells A3:A8 in our example.)

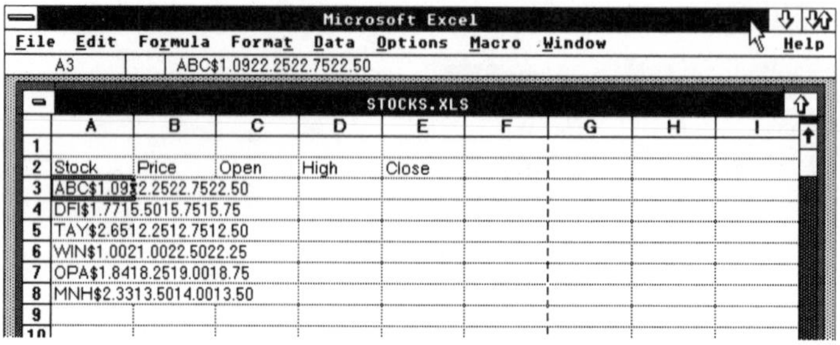

File	Edit	Formula	Format	Data	Options	Macro	Window				Help
A3			ABC$1.0922.2522.7522.50								

STOCKS.XLS

	A	B	C	D	E	F	G	H	I
1									
2	Stock	Price	Open	High	Close				
3	ABC$1.09	22.2522.7522.50							
4	DFI$1.7715.5015.7515.75								
5	TAY$2.6512.2512.7512.50								
6	WIN$1.0021.0022.5022.25								
7	OPA$1.8418.2519.0018.75								
8	MNH$2.3313.5014.0013.50								
9									
10									

FIGURE A-17. *All five data fields in this sample worksheet are lumped together in column A.*

A word of warning: When Microsoft Excel parses the records, it places each piece of information in a separate cell to the right of the selected column. Before you begin, be sure your worksheet has room to expand the records. In our example, the data will be redistributed into columns A through E.

When you've highlighted the entries to be parsed, select the Parse command from the Data menu. You'll see the dialog box shown in Figure A-18. As you can see, the contents of the first selected cell that contains an entry (A3) appear in the Parse Line edit bar at the top of the dialog box. You use this parse line to indicate how the field entries should be divided.

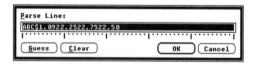

Parse Line:
ABC$1.0922.2522.7522.50

Guess   Clear   OK   Cancel

FIGURE A-18. *Use the Parse dialog box to break entries into separate fields.*

You use brackets to indicate the number of fields you want to create and the number of characters in each field. The [character marks the beginning of a field and the] character marks the end. You can insert as many pairs of brackets as you like. (If you omit an opening or closing bracket, Microsoft Excel will warn you with an *Error in parse line* message.) If you want to exclude some of the data from your worksheet when you parse, don't include those characters in brackets.

The Guess button at the bottom of the dialog box tells Microsoft Excel to make a guess as to how the selected entries should be divided. Microsoft Excel bases its guess on the type of data it finds in the parse line—text or numbers, for example—and on the position of blank characters. If necessary, you can adjust the position of the brackets that Microsoft Excel inserts.

To specify the length of each field manually, position the insertion point at the spot where you want to type a bracket, or use the Left and Right arrow keys to move through the parse line. Then insert the [and] characters into the parse line.

If you want to remove all the brackets from the parse line and make a fresh start, choose the Clear button to remove these characters. To remove individual brackets, use the Left and Right arrow keys to position the insertion point; then press the Backspace or Del key.

Figure A-19 shows the position of the brackets in our sample parse line. When you select OK or press Enter, Microsoft Excel will separate all the selected entries into the five fields you delineated with the brackets. Figure A-20 shows the results.

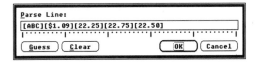

FIGURE A-19. *We have separated the parse line into five fields.*

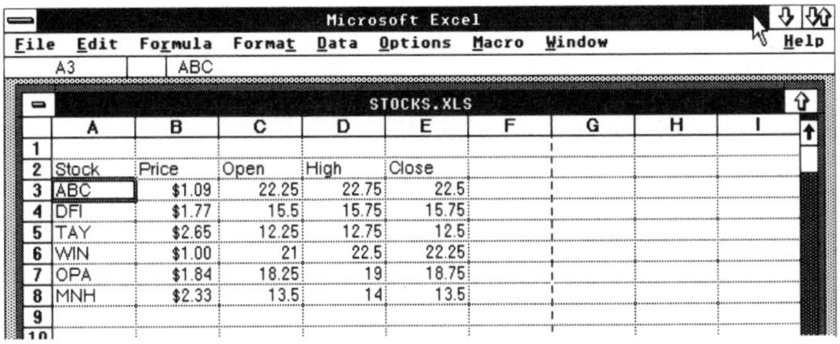

	A	B	C	D	E	F	G	H	I
1									
2	Stock	Price	Open	High	Close				
3	ABC	$1.09	22.25	22.75	22.5				
4	DFI	$1.77	15.5	15.75	15.75				
5	TAY	$2.65	12.25	12.75	12.5				
6	WIN	$1.00	21	22.5	22.25				
7	OPA	$1.84	18.25	19	18.75				
8	MNH	$2.33	13.5	14	13.5				
9									

FIGURE A-20. *Using the brackets as its guide, Microsoft Excel split the entries in column A into five fields.*

Obviously, the Parse command is most useful for fixed-length entries. If the fields in the parse selection vary in length, they will not be divided correctly. In that case, you must edit each record individually.

Dynamic Data Exchange (DDE)

In Chapter 8, you learned how to build dynamic links between two or more Microsoft Excel documents with external references. With the Dynamic Data Exchange (DDE) facility, you can establish similar "hot links" between Microsoft Excel and documents in other applications. That is, changes made to the document in the other application are immediately reflected in your linked Microsoft Excel document. To use this technique, both applications must run under Microsoft Windows version 2.0 or higher and must support DDE.

To link a worksheet to a document created in another application, you create a remote reference formula. This formula includes three parts: the name of the application, the name of the document, and the item you want to refer to. The application and document names must be separated by a vertical bar character (|) and the document name and item name must be separated by an exclamation point (!), like this:

=*Application* | *Document!Item*

Depending on the application you're linking to, the *Item* reference can be a cell or range reference, a value, or a data field. The form in which this argument is presented depends on the application to which you're creating the link. For more information, see the user's manual for the linking application.

Instead of trying to remember the exact format of the linking formula, use the Paste Link command on the Edit menu to establish a remote link. Begin by starting Microsoft Excel and the program with which you want to establish your link. After opening the dependent worksheet and the supporting document, activate the supporting-document window and select the data you want to refer to. Choose Copy from the Edit menu and then move back to the Microsoft Excel window and activate the worksheet into which you want to paste the reference. Finally, select the cell at the top left corner of the range into which you want to paste the data and choose Paste Link from the Edit menu to create a link between the two files. (If the data you're pasting occupies more than one cell, it will be entered in the worksheet as an array.)

When you open a worksheet or macro sheet that contains a remote reference to a document in another application, Microsoft Excel asks whether you want to reestablish the link and update references to the supporting document. If you choose OK, Microsoft Excel attempts to reestablish the link; if you choose Cancel, Microsoft Excel freezes the linked references and displays the values shown when you last saved the file.

If you choose to update the remote references, Microsoft Excel checks to see if the supporting application is open. If it is not, Microsoft Excel asks whether you want to start that application. If you choose OK, Microsoft Excel loads the application and updates your remote reference. If you choose Cancel or if Microsoft Excel can't start the supporting application, the cells containing your remote references display error values.

You can suspend your dynamic link *temporarily* by choosing the Calculations command from the Options menu and deselecting the Update Remote References check box. Microsoft Excel will then use the last set of values received from the supporting document.

In addition to initiating remote requests to other applications, Microsoft Excel can also receive DDE requests. For procedures on creating external references to Microsoft Excel from within another application, see the user's manual for that application. Microsoft Excel automatically responds to any DDE request it receives. If you want to close Microsoft Excel to DDE requests, choose the Workspace command from the Options menu and select the Ignore Remote Requests check box.

Using macros to communicate with other programs

If you're running Microsoft Excel under Microsoft Windows version 2.0 or higher, you can create a Microsoft Excel macro that loads another application, activates it, and even enters data and issues commands. You begin by starting the application with the EXEC function; then you use the APP.ACTIVATE function to activate the application window. After the application is active, you use the SEND.KEYS function to perform actions by "remote control."

The EXEC function

To start another Windows program from within a macro, use the EXEC function. This function takes the form

=EXEC(*program,window*)

The *program* argument is a text argument, enclosed in quotation marks, that identifies the application you want to load. You must use the exact filename that appears on the MS-DOS Executive screen. For example, to manually load the Write program, you would choose WRITE.EXE from the MS-DOS Executive screen and choose the Run command. To load Write from within a macro, you would use the formula

=EXEC("WRITE.EXE",1)

The *window* argument is a numeric code that determines the size of the application window:

Code	Description
1	Normal
2	Minimized
3	Maximized

If you omit the *window* argument, it is assumed to be 2; thus, the newly opened application will appear as an icon at the bottom of the screen.

The EXEC function returns a task ID number to the macro sheet. You can use this number in later macro functions, such as INITIATE, to identify the application you want to work with.

The APP.ACTIVATE function

The APP.ACTIVATE function lets you activate a document window in an open application. This function is available only when you're running Microsoft Excel from within Microsoft Windows.

The APP.ACTIVATE function takes the form

=ACTIVATE("*title*",*wait*)

The *title* argument represents the name of the application window you want to activate. This argument, which must appear in quotation marks, should be the exact text that appears in the title bar of the window you want to activate. If you omit the *title* argument, the macro activates Microsoft Excel.

The *wait* argument is a logical value that determines whether Microsoft Excel should suspend macro processing until Microsoft Excel is activated. If *wait* is TRUE (the default), Microsoft Excel waits to be activated before activating the specified application. If *wait* is FALSE, Microsoft Excel activates the specified window immediately.

The SEND.KEYS function

After activating an application, you can use the SEND.KEYS function to issue commands, navigate, and make entries in a document created in another application. As its name implies, this function actually lets you send a series of keystrokes to the active application.

The SEND.KEYS function takes the form

=SEND.KEY("*keys*",*wait*)

The *wait* argument is a logical value that determines whether Microsoft Excel should suspend macro processing until the keystrokes you've sent are processed.

The default value, FALSE, indicates that the macro should continue processing without waiting for the keystrokes to be processed.

The *keys* argument represents the keys you want to "press." This argument, which must be a text string enclosed in quotation marks, can include any keyboard characters—letters, numbers, and symbols—as well as special function keys. To enter a standard keyboard character, simply type the character you want to use. To enter special function keys such as Backspace and Enter, use one of the codes listed in Table A-3.

Table A-3. Key codes for the SEND.KEYS function.

Key	Code
Backspace	{BACKSPACE} or {BS}
Break	{BREAK}
Caps Lock	{CAPSLOCK}
Clear	{CLEAR}
Delete	{DELETE} or {DEL}
Down arrow	{DOWN}
End	{END}
Enter	{ENTER} or ~ (tilde)
Esc	{ESCAPE} or {ESC}
Help	{HELP}
Home	{HOME}
Ins	{INSERT}
Left arrow	{LEFT}
Num Lock	{NUMLOCK}
PgDn	{PGDN}
PgUp	{PGUP}
PrtSc	{PRTSC}
Right arrow	{RIGHT}
Tab	{TAB}
Up arrow	{UP}
F1, F2,...F16	{F1}, {F2},...{F16}
Shift	+
Ctrl	^
Alt	%

As you know, some keyboard commands and actions require that you press the Shift, Ctrl, or Alt key while pressing another key. To indicate that a key should be held down while another key is pressed, enclose the second set of key codes in parentheses. For example, you might hold down the Alt key while pressing the W and A keys to issue the Arrange All command on the Windows menu. This sequence would be written as %(WA).

Because the +, ^, and % characters serve special functions, you'll have to use braces whenever you want to enter these characters as literal text, For example, if you want to type a plus sign, you'll need to enter that character as {+}.

Often, you'll want to repeat the same key sequence several times. For example, to move down 10 lines in a document, you would press the Down arrow key 10 times. Fortunately, you don't have to repeat the {DOWN} code 10 times in your macro. To repeat a key sequence, simply specify the number of repetitions inside the brackets, like this:

{*code number*}

You must include one blank space between the *code* and *number* arguments. For example, to move down 10 lines in a document you would use {DOWN 10}.

Let's look at a practical example. The macro

```
=SELECT(!Results)
=COPY()
=EXEC("WRITE.EXE",1)
=APP.ACTIVATE("Write - (Untitled)",FALSE)
```

copies a range of cells named Results in your Microsoft Excel worksheet, issues the Copy command, and then activates the Write word-processing program. You might then use a SEND.KEYS function such as

```
=SEND.KEYS("The results of our survey are summarized in the table
    below.~%(EP)",TRUE)
```

to type the characters *The results of our survey are summarized in the table below*, press the Enter key (represented by the ~ character) to start a new paragraph, and then issue the Paste command. (The %(EP) is equivalent to choosing the Paste command from the Edit menu.)

Working with ASCII files

Microsoft Excel also offers a set of macro functions you can use to work with ASCII text files. These functions let you open, read, and write ASCII files, as well as letting you determine the size of the file and control your position in the file.

The FOPEN and FCLOSE functions

The FOPEN function lets you open an existing ASCII file or create a new ASCII file. This function takes the form

=("*file*",*access*)

The *file* argument, which is the name of the ASCII file you want to open, must be a text value enclosed in quotation marks. Microsoft Excel assumes the ASCII file you're opening or creating is located in the current directory. If you want to open or store a file in another directory, include the full pathname in your *file* argument.

The *access* argument is a numeric code that specifies the type of access you want to allow to the document:

Code	Type of access
1	Read file and write to it
2	Read file but not write to it
3	Create a new file with read and write access

If the file you specify doesn't exist and you've specified an *access* argument of 1 or 2, the FOPEN function will return a #NA! error value.

When Microsoft Excel executes the FOPEN function, it returns a document ID value that you use to refer to the ASCII file in subsequent macro functions.

When you're finished working with a file, you should use the FCLOSE function to close it. This function takes the form

=FCLOSE(*id*)

The *id* argument is the document identification number that Microsoft Excel returned when you used the FOPEN function to open or create the ASCII file. This argument can be a constant value or a reference to the cell that contains the FOPEN function.

The FPOS function

The FPOS function lets you specify a character position in an ASCII file. For example, before you use the FWRITE function to write a series of characters to an ASCII file, you can use FPOS to specify the location at which you want those characters to be inserted.

The FPOS function takes the form

=FPOS(*id,position*)

where *id* is the file identification number Microsoft Excel returned when you opened the file with the FOPEN function. If the *id* argument is not valid, Microsoft Excel returns #VALUE!.

The *position* argument is a numeric value that specifies your character position in a file. The first character in a file is numbered 1, the second is numbered 2, and so forth. If you omit *position*, Microsoft Excel uses the current position.

The FSIZE function

The FSIZE function returns the number of characters in an ASCII file. This function takes the form

   =FSIZE(*id*)

where *id* is the file identification number Microsoft Excel returned when you opened the file with the FOPEN function. If the *id* argument is not valid, Microsoft Excel returns #VALUE!.

The FREAD and FREADLN functions

The FREAD and FREADLN functions let you retrieve data from an ASCII file. The FREAD function lets you read a specified number of characters. This function takes the form

   =FREAD(*id,number of characters*)

where *id* is the file identification number Microsoft Excel returned when you opened the file with the FOPEN function. If the *id* argument is not valid, Microsoft Excel returns #VALUE!.

   Microsoft Excel begins reading the file at the current position and returns the specified number of characters to the macro sheet. (You can use the FPOS function, described above, to specify your starting position.) If Microsoft Excel reaches the end of the file before reading the specified number of characters or for some reason can't read the file, it returns the #NA! error value.

   The FREADLN function is similar to FREAD, except that it reads an entire line of text rather than a specified number of characters. This function returns to the macro sheet all the characters from the current position up to but not including the linefeed or carriage return at the end of the line.

   The FREADLN function takes the form

   =FREADLN(*id*)

The FWRITE and FWRITELN functions

The FWRITE function lets you write text to an ASCII file. The FWRITE function takes the form

   =FWRITE(*id,text*)

where *id* is the file identification number Microsoft Excel returned when you opened the file with the FOPEN function. If the *id* argument is not valid, Microsoft Excel returns #VALUE!.

Microsoft Excel begins writing the text at the current position. (You can use the FPOS function, described above, to specify your starting position.) If Microsoft Excel can't write to the file, it returns the #NA! error value.

The FWRITELN function is similar to FWRITE. This function also writes text to an ASCII file, beginning at the current position. However, FWRITELN also adds a carriage return or linefeed character at the end of the text string.

The FWRITELN function takes the form

=FWRITELN(*id,text*)

If executed successfully, the FWRITE and FWRITELN functions return to the macro sheet the number of characters written to the ASCII file.

Index

K

keyboard 36–38
Keyboard command (Help
    facility) 26
keyboard-indicator area 9
keyboard shortcuts 12
key fields 446–47

L

LEFT function 206–7
LEGEND macro function 563–64
LEN function 201
line charts 394–400
Line command 394–400
LINEST function 260–61
linking worksheets
    calculating linked worksheets
        278–80
    copying, cutting, and pasting in
        282–84
    creating links 275–77
    dependent formulas 278–82
    multiple links 276–77
    opening dependent worksheets 280
    redirecting links 282
    saving linked worksheets 277–78
    severing links 285
    updating dependent formulas
        278–80
Links command 281–82
LINKS macro function 574
list boxes 15
LIST.NAMES macro function 542
literal strings 44
LN function 183
loading Microsoft Excel 6–7
locating and replacing strings 285–90
locked attribute 296–97
locking in entries 40–41

LOG10 function 183
logarithmic functions. *See* functions,
    logarithmic *and individual*
    function names
LOGEST function 263–64
LOG function 183
logical functions. *See* functions,
    logical *and individual function*
    names
LOOKUP function 222–24
lookup functions. *See* functions,
    lookup *and individual function*
    names
Lotus 1-2-3 662–73
Lotus 1-2-3 command (Help
    facility) 26
LOWER function 207

M

macro functions
    charting 560–71
    Data menu 557–59
    defined 515–16
    Edit menu 536–41
    file-management 517–23
    Formula menu 541–48
    information 571–84
    looping 591–93
    macro environment 584–91
    navigational 529–34
    printing 534–35
    using loops 592–93
    windowing 523–29
    worksheet and cell formatting
        548–57
macro functions by name
    A1.R1C1 552
    ABSREF 582
    ACTIVATE 526–27
    ACTIVATE.NEXT 525

S

Douglas Cobb is president of The Cobb Group, Inc., a company that specializes in writing and publishing high-quality books, journals, and workbooks that support business software products. He is coauthor of *Using 1-2-3*, perhaps the most successful computer book ever published. His most recent books published by Microsoft Press include the bestselling **EXCEL IN BUSINESS; DOUG COBB'S TIPS FOR MICROSOFT EXCEL**, written for the Apple Macintosh; and **PUTTING MICROSOFT WORKS TO WORK**, written for the IBM PC. In addition, Doug Cobb is a columnist for *PC Magazine*.

Judy Mynhier is an author with The Cobb Group and is the editor of *Excellence: The Microsoft Excel User's Journal*. She is also coauthor of **EXCEL IN BUSINESS** and *Hands-on Excel*, a workbook. She is the editor of *Inside Word*, a journal on Microsoft Word for the Apple Macintosh, and the editor of *Word For Word*, a journal on Word 4.0 for the IBM PC.

OTHER TITLES FROM MICROSOFT PRESS

RUNNING MS-DOS, 3rd ed.
The Classic, Definitive Work on DOS—Now Completely Expanded to Include All Versions of PC/MS-DOS—Including Hard-Disk Management Tips and Techniques
Van Wolverton

"This book is simply the definitive handbook of PC-/MS-DOS."   **BYTE**

Join the more than one million PC and PS/2 Users—from novice to expert—who use RUNNING MS-DOS, a richly informative overview of the PC-DOS and MS-DOS operating systems. If you have a PC- or MS-DOS machine, RUNNING MS-DOS is a must-have reference. Author Van Wolverton guides you through hands-on examples of PC- and MS-DOS commands and capabilities. You'll learn how to take control of your computer: how to effectively manage files and directories on a floppy- or hard-disk system; how to work with printers, monitors, and modems; how to automate frequently performed tasks with batch files; and much more. RUNNING MS-DOS is packed with straightforward information and scores of examples. Now updated for version 3.3 with a new chapter on hard-disk management and an expanded command reference section. RUNNING MS-DOS—accept no substitutes.

496 pages   softcover $22.95   Order Code: 86-96262
**   hardcover $35.00   Order Code: 86-96270**

SUPERCHARGING MS-DOS
The Microsoft Guide to High Performance Computing for the Experienced PC User
Van Wolverton

When you're ready for more, this sequel to RUNNING MS-DOS provides tips for intermediate to advanced business users on maximizing the power of MS-DOS. Control your screen and keyboard with ANSI.SYS; create, examine, or change any file; personalize your CONFIG.SYS file; and construct your own menu system. Includes programs and dozens of valuable batch files.

320 pages   softcover $18.95   Order Code: 86-95595

SUPERCHARGING MS-DOS is also available with a handy 5.25-inch companion disk that contains all the batch files, script files, and programs in the book, and will save you the time of having to type them in. Used in conjunction with the book, the companion disk is a valuable, timesaving tool.
SUPERCHARGING MS-DOS Book/Disk Package, by Van Wolverton
320 pages   softcover with one 5.25-inch disk $34.95   Order Code: 86-96304

WORD PROCESSING POWER WITH MICROSOFT WORD, 2nd ed.
Peter Rinearson

"Word owners should not be without Rinearson's book, even if they read no more than a tenth of it."   **The New York Times**

Here, from a Pulitzer Prize-winning author, is the most comprehensive, authoritative book on Microsoft Word. You will learn about style sheets, windows, how to create personalized form letters, how to outline with the glossary feature, and much more. The dozens of tested tips will save you time and frustration. Covers every feature of version 3.1 of Microsoft Word for PC- and MS-DOS computers!

432 pages   softcover $19.95   Order Code: 86-95546

MICROSOFT WORD STYLE SHEETS (Software Version)

Peter Rinearson and JoAnne Woodcock

MICROSOFT WORD STYLE SHEETS (Software Version) is a solid, timesaving value for all Microsoft Word users. Style sheets are just a few keystrokes away with the help of this package. The accompanying 5.25-inch disk features more than one hundred ready-to-use style sheet templates, including models for correspondence, memos, newsletters, press releases, and résumés. You'll save yourself hours of typing, and that endless struggle of those inevitable typing errors, all with this one disk! This book/disk package is updated for version 4, but you can use it with all versions of Word since 2.0.

352 pages   softcover with one 5.25-inch disk $29.95   Order Code: 86-96320

QUICK REFERENCE GUIDE TO MS-DOS COMMANDS

Van Wolverton

Forgotten how to remove a directory? Sort a file? Compare two disks? Or use EDLIN, the DOS text editor? Here's a conveniently organized, handy alphabetic guide to 80 of the most commonly used MS-DOS system service calls. Perfect for quick lookups. Portable computer users will find it indispensable.

48 pages, 4¼ x 11   softcover $4.95   Order Code: 86-95876

Microsoft Press books are available wherever fine books are sold, or credit card orders can be placed by calling 1-800-638-3030 (in Maryland call collect 824-7300).

The manuscript for this book was prepared and submitted to Microsoft Press in electronic form. Text files were processed and formatted using Microsoft Word.

Cover design by Ted Mader and Associates
Interior text design adapted from original design by Craig Bergquist
Principal typography by Jean Trenary
Principal production art by Becky Geisler-Johnson

Text composition by Microsoft Press in Palatino with display in Palatino Bold, using the Magna composition system and the Linotronic 300 laser imagesetter.